INDEX

TO THE

DICTIONARY OF

ENGLISH FURNITURE MAKERS

1660–1840

Due to a computer sorting error surnames beginning with 'C' or 'F' were omitted from the entries arranged alphabetically under English cities and towns. A supplement is given at p. 169.

INDEX

TO THE
DICTIONARY OF
ENGLISH FURNITURE
MAKERS
1660–1840

EDITED BY

ANGELA EVANS

THE
FURNITURE HISTORY SOCIETY
1990

PUBLISHED IN 1990

ISBN 0 903335 07 7

PRINTED IN GREAT BRITAIN
BY W S MANEY AND SON LIMITED
HUDSON ROAD LEEDS LS9 7DL

EXPLANATION

This is an Index to the *Dictionary of English Furniture Makers, 1660–1840*, published in 1986 by The Furniture History Society and W. S. Maney & Son, of Leeds, who have been the Society's printers since its founding in 1964. The *Dictionary* was edited by Geoffrey Beard and Christopher Gilbert, respectively the first and second editors of the Society's annual *Journal*, with the assistance of three sub-editors, Brian Austen, the late Arthur Bond, CBE, and Angela Evans. When the *Dictionary* was well advanced in its five-year programme of compilation, it became apparent that it would be difficult to provide it with a full index at the time of publication. Such an index was estimated to need 160 pages, necessitating publication of the *Dictionary* in two volumes. Despite the generosity of many donors, the Society did not have the financial resources to do that. It was resolved to give the *Dictionary* an index of those tradesmen and craftsmen who were not included in the main alphabetical sequence of surnames, and to work over a longer period towards publishing a fuller index. The present volume is the result of that additional endeavour, some 30,000 names contained within 166 pages.

The Council of the Society is indebted to the late C. F. Davies, who bequeathed £2,000 to the Society to be used towards the cost of publications, and to the Trustees of the Marc Fitch Fund who gave us a grant of £2,000 specifically for the Index. The compilation of the Index has received the editorial attention of Geoffrey Beard and Angela Evans.

The Index (which incorporates the one in the *Dictionary* already referred to) is arranged in one alphabetical sequence of Names (surname followed by Christian name), and Places. London is subdivided into its respective areas, such as Clerkenwell. The Index does NOT give a page reference to the main (alphabetically arranged) entry in the *Dictionary* for a craftsman. It includes details of craftsmen working at a particular house, or within a town or suburb, for example 'Croome Court, Worcs., Vile, William', or 'Exeter, Devon, Alden, Anne'. It is thus possible to discover the craftsmen used by a particular patron, or to gauge the strength of the industry in a town over the 180 years of activity which the *Dictionary* attempted to record, 1660–1840.

INDEX

A

Abb, Stephen, 832
Abbat, 728
Abberley (Worcs.): Thorp, S., 891
Abbey, Thomas, 607
Abbis, Thomas, 175–6, 894
Abbot, Hannah Heath, 934
Abbot Hall (Cumbria): Gillow, 341
Abbots Bromley (Staffs.): Hill,
    James, 430
Abbotsford (Roxburghshire):
    Bullock, George, 128
Abbott, 205
Abbott, James, 909
Abbott, Philip, 656
Abbott, Samuel, 556, 917
Abbott, William, 1, 728
Abel, Sarah, 1
Aberford (Yorks.): Wood,
    Sampson, 997
Abingdon (Berks.):
    Bayley, C., 52
    Beckensall, W., 56
    Gennings, William, 335
    Goldby, Henry, 348
    Grainge, John, 363
    Grange, Susanna, 363
    Hobbs, James, 435
    Jennings, William, 485
    Lewis, Samuel, 540
    Saunders, Thomas, 785
    Staniland, William, 849
    Tagg, Charles, 870
    Yates, Simon, 1012
Ackermann & Co., 20
Ackers, James, 213
Ackworth (Yorks.):
    Roberts, William, 754
    Simpson, John, 816
    Topham, William, 899
    Ward, Thomas, 944
Acres, John, 220
Acton, John, 59
Adams, 580
Adams, Benjamin, 763
Adams, David, 859
Adams, G., 3
Adams, George, 603

Adams, J., 3
Adams, Job, 202
Adams, John, 959
Adams, Robert, 3, 422, 713
Adams, Thomas, 3
Adams, William, 347, 911
Adderbury (Oxon.): Williams,
    George, 979
Adderbury House (Glos.): Mayhew,
    John & Ince, William, 594
Addicott, John, 266
Addison, J., 406, 759
Adwalton (Yorks.):
    Barraclough, Thomas, 44
    Rhodes, John, 740
Agar, Edward, 605
Agnew, Thomas, 1015
Ailesbeer (Devon): Toby, James,
    896
Airey, Edward, 371
Albrook, William, 59
Alcester (Warks.): Scrambler,
    Edmund, 791
Alcock, William Roscoe, 716
Aldborough (Suffolk):
    Block, R., 81
    Everitt, Thomas, 285
    Somerton, William, 839
    Topham, George, 899
Aldby Park (Yorks.): Reynoldson,
    George, 740
Alden, Anne, 973
Alder, Caleb, 833
Aldermanbury (London):
    Bayley, Daniel, 52
    Darby, William, 226
    Dunbar, Robert, 259
    Granger, Hugh, 363
    Gray, William, 366
    Kirkman, Thomas, 517
    Lycett, Sampson, 562
    Meader, John, 599
    Palleday, William, 671
    Phillips, Somerset, 696
    Prankard, John, 712
    Pritchard, William, 718
    Re(y)nolds, William, 738
    Salisbury, Thomas, 776
    Sibthorpe, Christopher, 814

Spender, Samuel, 844
Whitehead, Thomas, 968
Woodward, John, 1000
Alderney, William, 6
Aldersgate (London):
    Bailey, Thomas, 31
    Binns, Edward, 73
    Brook, Joseph, 111
    Bruce, David, 121
    Evans, John, 284
    Emmitt, William, 280
    Goodcheap, William, 351
    Goodman, Fraser & Speare, 354
    Gurney, Thomas, 380
    Hadnutt, William, 382
    Harris, Josiah, 401
    Hatt, John, 410
    Holmes, Jon Joseph & Robert,
    445
    Jay, Thomas, 481
    Nicholl, Charles, 645
    Pallison, Joseph, 671
    Pattison, Joseph, 680
    Potter, Richard, 708
    Potter, Stephen, 708
    Richardson, Samuel, 744
    Seddon, George, 793
    Sommers, Thomas, 839
    Tarn, William, 872
    Webb, Charles, 953
Aldgate (London):
    Ball, Thomas, 35
    Hall, Robert, 386
    Hankin, Thomas, 394
    Hicks, William, 428
    Hinchcliff, James, 432
    Jones, Isaac, 495
    Kent, John, 508
    Kerrington, Richard & Robert,
    510
    Lamb, William, 522
    Markham, George, 574
    Markham, John le George, 574
    Markham, Lawrence, 574
    Nicholls, Thomas, 646
    Richardson, William, 745
    Sadler, Francis, 775
    Stafford, William, 847
    Tibbs, Percival snr, 893

Waight, John, 932
Walker, Samuel, 937
Wannerton, John, 942
Watson, Sarah, 950
Watton, James, 951
Wilkinson, W., 977
Aldred, John, 777
Aldridge, 20
Aldridge, John, 322
Alexander, John, 557, 855
Alford (Lincs.):
 Ashton, William, 21
 Johnson, Jeremiah, 490
 Makin, John, 570
 Wood, Cary, 996
Alfreton (Derbs.): Bacon, Samuel, 28
Alken, Samuel, 8
Alken, Sefferin, 96, 183, 435, 531, 924
Allanson, Thomas, 740
Allchin, 915
Alldridge, 20
Allen, 408
Allen, Anthony, 10
Allen, John, 300, 408, 650, 800
Allendale (Northumb.):
 Lee, Isaac, 534
 Potts, Joseph, 709
 Robinson, William, 761
 Robson, William, 762
 Short, Nicholas, 812
 Spark, John, 841
Allsop, Thomas, 365
Allured, John, 792
Almond, Joseph, 18
Almond, William, 652
Alnwick (Northumb.):
 Athey, Joseph & William, 23
 Hunter, Henry, 465
 Jackson, —, 475
 Jackson, Peter, 476
 Jeffrey, John, 483
 Jobson, Robert, 488
 Kearney, James, 501
 Leathead, William, 534
 Leithhead, William, 537
 Lough, William, 555
 Marvin, Robert & Thomas, 582
 Mavin, Robert, 588
 Mavin, Thomas, 588
 Mavin, William, 588
 Purvis, Edward Hutchinson, 722
 Richardson, George, 743
 Roberts, William, 754
 Robertson, Thomas, 755
 Russell, James, 772
 Sanderson, John, 779
 Sewell, —, 801
 Shepherd, Vincent, 808
 Swinton, Edward, 868
 Tranent, William, 902
 Tranent & Davi(d)son, 902
 Turner, Ralph, 911

Turner, Thomas, 912
Wilson, Charles G., 986
Alnwick Castle (Northumb.):
 Deeker, James, 238
 Fuhrlohg, Christopher, 324
 Langlois, Pierre 526
 Linnell, John, 545
 Morel, Nicholas and Morel & Hughes, Robert, 624
 Walle, Henry & Reilly, Peter, 939
Alresford (Hants.):
 Dancaster, Henry, 225
 Waight, Robert, 932
 White, Thomas, 967
Alresford House (Hants.): Webb, Henry, 953
Alscot Park (Warks.):
 Bradshaw, William, 100
 Cauty, William, 152
 Chippendale, Thomas snr, 166
 Cobb, John, 182, 184
 Collett, Jonathan, 188
 Dobyn(s), Thomas, 248
 Dunning, James, 261
 Hallett, William snr and William jnr, 389
 Linnell, William, 547
 Mayhew, John & Ince, William, 594
 Samber, Samuel, 778
 Stanton, William, 849
 Thornton, Osborn, 891
 Wells, Gervase, 957
 West, John, 959
Alsop, 632
Alston (Cumb.):
 Halden, William, 383
 Pattinson, Hugh, 680
 Walton, Jonathon, 942
Althorp (Northants.):
 Ashlin, William, 21
 Daguerre, Dominique, 223
 Dalrymple, Hugh, 224
 Edwards, Richard, 270
 Goodison, Benjamin, 352, 354
 Gordon, John & Taitt, John & Richard, 356, 357
 Herve, Francois, 424
 King, John, 514
 Nelson, Sefferin, 641
 Vardy, Thomas, 919
 West, John, 960
Altofts (Yorks.): Robinson, Thomas, 760
Alton (Hants.):
 Binsted, John, 73
 Gard(e)ner, Thomas, 330
 Hayes, Henry, 414
 Jordan, Joseph, 499
 Wright, John, 1006
Altrincham (Cheshire):
 Ardean, John, 17
 Arstall, Joseph, 19

Boardman, Thoephicks, 82
Goulden, Michael, 360
Knight, John, 519
Massey, William, 585
Partington, Joseph, 678
Starkey, John, 850
Worsley, John, 1003
Worsley, Micaiah, 1003
Ambleside (Westmld):
 Jackson, John L., 476
 Jackson, L., 476
 Wilcock, Samuel, 973
 Woodburn, Christopher, 998
 Woodburn, John, 998
Amersham (Bucks.):
 Line, William, 543
 Potter, William, 708
 Redding, Arthur, 733
 Reed, John, 734
 Statham, Charles, 850
 Stone, Edward, 858
 Toovey, Sampson, 899
 Tucker, William, 907
Ammerdown House (Som.):
 Andrews, Thomas, 14
 Linnell, John, 546
Amphlett, Thomas, 854
Ampthill (Beds.):
 Battison, George, 50
 Battison, William, 50
 Handscombe, Isaac, 394
 Ramsay, T.G., 726
Ampthill Union Workhouse (Beds.):
 Battison, George, 50
Amry, 675
Ancoats Hall (Manchester, Lancs.):
 Becket(t), William, 56
Anderson & Perry, 472
Anderson, Christopher, 364
Anderson, Edward, 500
Anderson, Henry, 398
Anderson, John, 135
Anderson, Robert, 12
Andover (Hants.):
 Ayling, Thomas, 28
 Bear & Drew, 55
 Bunny, Jacob, 129
 Burt, John, 134
 Dale, Charles, 223
 Drew, Robert, 256
 Mason, Christopher, 583
 New, Thomas, 641
Andrews, William, 584
Angus, 38
Annapolis (USA): Hepbourne, Francis, 422
Ansell, William, 58
Ansford (Som.), for Rev. James Woodforde: Hoddinet, —, 436
Apley Park (Salop):
 Hanson, Samuel, 395
 Hutchinson & Co., 468
Appleby, Christopher, 45

Appleby (Westmld):
  Birkett, Thomas, 75
  Errington, Thomas, 282
  Groves, Thomas & Robert, 376
  Hart, Thomas, 406
  Robinson, John, 759
  Steadman, John, 851
  Storrow, John, 860
  Thompson, James snr, 886
  Wilkinson, George snr, jnr, 976
  Wilson, William, 990
Appletree, 250
Applewhite, George, 422
Appuldurcombe House (Isle of
  Wight):
  Chippendale, Thomas snr, 168
  Chippendale, Thomas jnr, 168
  Mayhew, John & Ince, William,
  596
Arbunot, James, 16
Arbury Hall (Warks.): King,
  Benjamin, 514
Arbuthnot, 79
Archer, 31
Ardleigh (Essex):
  Cross, Edmund, 213
  Holland, Robert, 442
  Lodge, Henry, 553
Argles, Edward, 138, 267
Armadale Castle (Isle of Skye):
  Bullock, George, 127
Armitage, John, 1007
Armitage, William, 104
Armley (Yorks.): Ellis, Joseph, 275
Armley House, Leeds (Yorks.):
  Planta, John, 702
Armstrong, 71
Armstrong, John, 11, 564, 599, 955
Armstrong, Thomas, 460
Armthwaite: Milbourn, William,
  605
Arne, Thomas, 439, 800, 959
Arniston House (Midlothian):
  Chippendale, Thomas snr, 166
  Livingstone, James, 550
Arnold (Notts.): Skellington,
  William, 818
Arnold, George, 580, 762
Arnold, Joseph, 891
Arnold, Samuel, 264
Arnolde, Samuel, 556
Arnott, Robert, 19
Arnott, William P., 853
Arnott, William Prince, 19
Arrowsmith, John, 62, 410
Arundale, W., 1002
Arundel, C., 109
Arundel (Sussex):
  Bone, Charles, 85
  Brewer, John, 106
  Hatcher, Charles, 410
  Hunt, George, 464
  Langrich, John, 527
  Lear, Henry, 533

Lear, James, 533
  Nutcher, John, 657
  Ward, James, 943
  White, Edward, 965
  White & Son, 968
Arundel Castle (Sussex):
  Bayley, Blew & Chapman, 52
  Cuenot, John Antoine, 217
  Edlin, Edward C., 267
  Gillow, 341
  Jensen, Gerrit, 487
  Taprell, Stephen & Holland,
  William, 871, 872
  White, Edward, 965
Ashbourne (Derbs.): Swinton,
  Thomas, 868
Ashburner, 259
Ashburnham Place (Sussex):
  Dowbiggin(g), Thomas, 253
Ashburton (Devon):
  Halls, Richard, 390
  Husson, Edward, 467
  Maddock, John, 569
  Metherill, Thomas, 604
  Mogridge, Thomas, 615
  Monday, William, 616
  Quint, William, 724
  Saunders, John, 782
Ashby, Miles, 20
Ashby-de-la-Zouch (Leics.):
  Buckley, Samuel, 124
  Davenport, William, 227
  Gilbert, Thomas, 338
  Gilbert, William, 339
  Hammond, Richard, 392
  Higgins, Charles, 428
  Lovatt, Robert, 555
  Orchard, Robert, 664
  Sampson, Thomas, 778
  Shaw, Richard, 805
  Stroud, Joseph, 862
  Widdowson, Benjamin, 972
  Winks, Henry, 991
  Winterbotham, George, 993
Ashcroft, Joshua, 70
Ashford (Kent):
  Ayerst, —, 27
  Barns, James, 43
  Bayley, John, 52
  Hammon(d), Richard, 392
  Nye, Robert, 658
  Polhill, John, 704
  Reeve, Ann, 735
  Reeve(s), Lewis Ambrose, 735
  Richardson, Henry, 743
  Sampson, Thomas, 778
  Tunbridge, John, 908
  Varham, Vincent, 920
Ashley, Thomas, 970
Ashlin, 393
Ashridge (Herts.): Wyatt, Edward,
  1010
Ashton, James, 732
Ashton, John, 371

Ashton, William, 216
Ashton Clinton : Nelson, Sefferin,
  641
Ashton-under-Lyne (Lancs.):
  Ainsworth, John, 5
  Ashforth, George, 20
  Bagshaw, Joseph, 29
  Bamford, John, 36
  Beckwith, Samuel, 57
  Bennett, William, 65
  Bintliff, George, 73
  Booth, William, 87
  Briscoe, William, 108
  Buckley, Ann, 124
  Gee, John, 334
  Gill, Joseph, 340
  Goldthorp, Benjamin, 348
  Haselden, William, 408
  Heap, William, 417
  Hughes, Edward, 460
  Hughes, John, 461
  Hutchinson, Peter, 468
  Mellor, James, John, 601
  Miller, James, 608
  Miller, John, 608
  Mitchell, George, 613
  Moss, Samuel, 632
  Oldham, Thomas, 662
  Ousey, H., 667
  Ratcliffe, John, 728
  Smith, James, 827
  Stephenson, Thomas, 854
  Stones, James, 859
  Swift, William, 868
  Walker, William, 938
  Wright, Edmund, 1004
Ashworth, T., 494, 859
Aske Hall (Yorks.):
  Chippendale, Thomas snr, 166
  Fell, Lawrence, 294
  Lawson, James, 531
  Norman, Matthew, 651
  Norman, Samuel, 652, 653
  Vile, William, 927
Askey, 789
Askrigg (Yorks.):
  Bell, Clement, 60
  Bell, George, 61
Asling, William, 534
Aspatria (Cumb.): Robinson, John,
  759
Astle, Thomas, 110, 358, 394, 477
Aston (Warks.): Yates, James &
  Whitworth, John, 1012
Aston Clinton House (Bucks.):
  Nelson, Sefferin, 641
Aston Hall, Birmingham: Bullock,
  George, 127
Astwood Court (Worcs.): Bettridge,
  Josh., 69
Athelhampton (Dorset): Coade,
  Eleanor and her successors, 181
Atherstone (Warks.):
  Brabant, Rob., 94

Brown, J., 114
Brown, Robert, 118
Goode, Basil, 351
Lloyd, John & William, 550
Pullin, William, 722
Ray, J., 730
Sketchley, Power, 819
Swinehat, Mrs, 868
Taylor, T., 879
Trentham, Timothy, 903
Wiln, Richard, 984
Atherton, James, 732
Athertone (Warks.): Bingham,
    William, 72
Atkins, 336, 817
Atkins, Robert, 341
Atkins, Samuel, 23
Atkins, Thomas, 844
Atkinson, 463, 851
Atkinson, George, 839, 859
Atkinson, John, 496
Atkinson, Thomas, 59, 551
Atkinson, William, 24, 403, 410,
    557
Attenborough, 892
Attfield, 902
Attfield, Richard, 712
Attingham Park (Salop):
    Donaldson, Thomas, 250
Attleborough (Warks.):
    Hackett, Joshua, 381
    Lake, Cockell, 521
Attwaters, Joseph, 59
Audley, John, 26
Audley End (Essex):
    Adair, John, 2
    Adair, William Robert, 2
    Alken, Sefferin, 8
    Ansell, Robert, 15
    Aycliffe, Thomas jnr, 27
    Balls, John & Co., 36
    Beckwith, Samuel, 57
    Belcher, Cathern, 59
    Belcher, Thomas, 59
    Benwell, —, 67
    Beyer, James, 70
    Boulnois, —, 91
    Bradshaw, Thomas, 99
    Brown, J., 114
    Burnett, Thomas, 132
    Burrows, Richard, 134
    Bush, Richard, 136
    Butler & Co., 138
    Carter, Adcock, 147
    Chambers, —, 157
    Chipchase, Robert & Lambert,
        Robert, 163
    Chippendale, Thomas snr, 167
    Chippendale, Thomas jnr, 169
    Chowles, Charles, 170
    Coade, Eleanor and her
        successors, 181
    Cobb, John, 182, 183
    Columbani, Placido, 190

Cooper, George, 196
Cross, Edward, 213
Cutter, Charles, 223
Dalrymple, Hugh, 224
Davis, —, 230
Dawes, Richard, 234
Dowbiggin(g), Thomas, 253
Dunn, –, 260
Durham, Robert, 262
Dury, Andrew, 262
Elward, George & Marsh,
    William, 279
Eyre(s), James & Large, James,
    287
Farmb(o)rough, William, 289
Fox, Solomon, 314
French, –, 321
Fuhrlohg, Christopher, 324–5
Gantry, —, 329
Gibson, George, 337
Gilding, Francis, 339
Gordon, John & Taitt, John &
    Richard, 356, 357
Gough, James, 359
Gravel, Robert, 364
Gray, Stephen, 365
Hankinson, V.J., 394
Harris, —, 400
Harris & King, 403
Higgs & Ford, 429
Hobcraft, John, 435
Hoby, —, 436
Hughes, —, 460
Hutchinson, John, 468
Impey, William, 471
Ivory, William, 474
Jackson, John, 476
Jacob, John, 477
Jean, Peter Dominique, 482
Jones, Richard, 496
Joseph, B., 499
Kennett, Robert & Kidd,
    William, 506, 507
King, John, 514
Lambert, Robert, 523
Like, Thomas & Turner, Henry,
    542
McDouall, James, 564
Mason, Jos., 584
Mayhew, John & Ince, William,
    592, 594
Merlin, John Joseph, 603
Miles, Henry & Edwards, John,
    606
Nash, Robert, 638
Nelson, Sefferin, 641
Paul, Robert, 682
Pecquer, Louis & Son, 686
Pritts, Joseph, 701
Prussurot, John, 720
Pyner, George, 723
Robinson, William, 760
Romsey, —, 765
Ross, David, 766

Rumsey, William, 771
Saggers, John, 775
Sandys, Charles, 780
Saunders, Paul, 785
Searle, John, 792
Seddon, George, 796
Seneschal, J., 800
Shennan, William, 807
Smallbone, Thomas, 822
Smart, Jonathan, 823
Smith, Charles, 824
Stephens, Samuel, 853
Stovell, George, 860
Tayler (or Taylor), —, 874
Town & Emanuel, 901
Tratt & Attfield, 902
Turner, J., 910
Webb, Henry, 953
Whitmore, Thomas, 969
Wilcke, Friedrich, 973
Wilson, Thomas, 989
Wilson & Son, A., 990
Wyatt, Edward, 1010
Auckland Castle (Co. Durham):
    Hall, James, 385
Auster, John, 944
Austin, Cornelius, 72, 828
Austin, Cornelius jnr, 366
Austin, John, 696
Aven, Charles, 283, 517, 667
Aveyard & Buck, 210
Axbridge (Som.):
    Jenkins, James, 483
    Swearse, James, 867
Axminster (Devon):
    Bowdige, Samuel, 92
    Pere8m, Andrew, 690
    Pitcher, Amos, 700
    Seymour, John, 801
    Spence, John, 843
    Wills, James, 984
Ayles, Benjamin, 444
Aylesbury (Bucks.):
    Berry, Thomas, 68
    Eustace, Harrington, 283
    Eustace, William, 283
    Gibbs, Samuel, 336
    Jackson, Frances, 475
    Jackson, George, 475
    Jackson, Jasper, 475
    Jackson, Joseph, 476
    Mayne, Goldsworth, 598
    Willison, Jno, 984
Aylsham (Norfolk):
    Armes, John, 17
    Bowers, Robert, 92
    Deeker, James, 238
    Gimson, John, 344
    Grimson, John, 375
    Harvey, Robert, 408
    Phillips, Benjamin, 695
    Porrett, Thomas, 706
Aynho Park (Northants.):
    Chippendale, Thomas jnr, 169

Ayre, James, 286
Ayre, Samuel, 814

B

Bacon, Daniel, 122
Bacon, J., 269
Bacup (Lancs.): Hudson, William,
459
Badminton House (Glos.):
Boson, John, 89
Chippendale, Thomas snr, 167
Cleer(e), William, 177
Duffour, William, 258
Fenton, William, 296
Gosset, Isaac, 359
Hallett, William snr and William
jnr, 388
Kennett, Robert & Kidd,
William, 507
Linnell, William, 546, 547
Mayhew, John & Ince, William,
595
Medcalfe, —, 600
Oldham, —, 662
Phillips, John, 695
Seddon, George, 796, 797
Vile, William, 925
Bagley, James, 339
Bagnall & Sanderson, 779
Bagnigge Wells (London):
Evans, David, 283
Hill, I., 430
Mansford, David, 573
Bagot, Thomas, 402
Bagshot Park (Surrey):
Peacock, Robert, 683
Saunders, Paul, 785
Tilbury, Mr or Mrs, 894
Baildon, Thomas, 261
Baildon (Yorks.):
Bolton, Joseph, 84
Brierley, John, 107
Robinson, John, 758
Bailey, 544, 635, 1001
Bailey, Edmund, 489
Bailey, Edward, 103, 947
Bailey, John jnr, 510
Bailey, Thomas, 288, 399, 923
Bailey & Saunders, 30
Baines, A., 989
Baines, H., 244, 438, 687, 940, 970
Baines, Henry, 41, 77, 82
Baines, John, 32
Baines, T., 31
Baines, William, 859
Baker, 82
Baker, Barnard, 369
Baker, Benjamin, 431
Baker, Bernard, 697
Baker, John, 489
Baker, W., 32
Baker & Spencer, 843

Baker & Webb, 32, 953
Bakewell, William, 460
Bakewell (Derbs.): Senea, William,
800
Balch, Hannah, 34
Baldock (Herts.):
Humberston, J., 462
Rickerby, John, 746
Seymour, George, 801
Ball, 717
Ball, Henry, 911, 932
Ball, John, 263, 954
Ball, Joseph William, 575
Ball, W., 804
Balscot (Oxon.): Aris, John, 17
Balson, J., 36
Bamber, 92
Bamber, Richard, 36
Bampton (Devon): Gale, George,
327
Banbury (Oxon.):
Blaby, Richard, 76
Blofeld, Thomas, 81
Bosfield, Thomas, 88
Devonshire, Abraham, 242
Dods, Archibald, 249
Golsby, James, 349
Holloway, —, 443
Hollowell, Charles, 444
Hollowell, Mrs, 444
Humphris, Mrs, & Richard, 463
Jarvis, Robert, 481
Mallam, C.R., 571
Oxley, Thomas, 669
Pain, John, 670
Partridge, William, 678
Penny, Philip, 689
Quartermaine, Abraham, 723
Sansbury, Amos, 781
Stanley, Richard, 849
Tasker, William, 873
Thompson, William, 888
Webster, William, 956
Banham, Sarah, 199
Banister, Zachariah, 192
Bankes & Fletcher, 37
Banks, Henry, 132
Banks, Thomas, 249
Banks, William, 234, 792
Banner, Francis, 339
Banner & Bruce, 37
Banting, 674
Bantleman, Robert, 304
Barber, James, 135
Barber, John, 40, 292, 293, 789, 943
Barber, Richard, 958
Barber, Thomas, 351
Barclay, Jacob, 465
Bardin, Samuel, 602
Barelli, 900
Barfe, Mark, 79
Barfoot, 386
Barkas, 671
Barker, 498, 962

Barker, John, 38, 218, 667
Barker, Matthew, 94
Barker, Robert, 739, 775, 1007
Barker, Robert jnr, 29
Barker, Thomas, 40
Barking (Essex): Gunnel, Ralph,
380
Barking Hall (Suffolk): Singleton,
Thomas, 818
Barlow, J., 533
Barlow, William, 298
Barn Elms (Surrey):
Coxed, John & G., and Woster,
Thomas, 205
Gilding, Edmund, 339
Gomm, Tom, 349
Gomm, William & Richard, 349
Grendy, Giles, 371, 372
Hilker, Anthony, 430
Holland, Thomas, 442
How, John, 453
Kelsey, John, 503
Linnell, William, 546, 547
North, Robert snr, 655
Pardoe, John, 672
Rackstrow, Benjamin, 725
Savage, John, 786
Barnaby, Edward Alden, 264
Barnard, 381, 1010
Barnard Castle (Co. Durham):
Atkinson, Christopher, 23
Bayles, William, 52
Bell, Anthony, 60
Bell, John, 62
Bell, William, 63
Dalkin, Joseph, 224
Ewbank, James, 286
Hodgson, Leonard, 438
Howson, Robert, 456
Hutchinson, John, 468
Ladderdale, John, 521
Stobbs, Robert, 857
Thompson, William C., 888
Weldon, George, 957
White, William, 967
Wouldhave, Michael, 1003
Barnes, Elizabeth, 191
Barnes, John, 74
Barnes, Richard, 73
Barnes, William, 274
Barnes (Surrey):
Gray, John, 365
Mitchell, John, 613
Simmons, William, 815
Barnet (Herts.): Beatty, William, 55
Barnett, 686
Barnoldswick (Yorks.): Robinson,
R. snr & jnr, 759
Barnsley (Yorks.):
Allat, Richard, 9
Allott, David, 11
Allott, Richard, 11
Bullas, Thomas, 125
Bullough, John, 128

Green, John, 367
Green, William, 368
Holde, Thomas, 441
King, William, 515
Mirfin, Thomas, 613
Norman, Albert, 651
Oxerby, Geo., 669
Senior, George, 800
Tomlin, William, 898
Barnstaple (Devon):
Hancock, John, 392
Harding, J.M., 396
Harding, John, 396
Harris, William, 403
Hearson, Charles, 418
Hearson, George, 418
Hewell, William, 425
Hunt, William, 465
Hutton, William, 469
Jerritt, James, 487
Jewell, William, 488
Jones, Nicholas, 496
Jones, Thomas, 497
Langdon, John, 525
Manley, Samuel, 572
Marks Harding, John, 575
Quick, James, 724
Skinner, Catherine, 819
Spry, Messrs, 846
Stribling, William, 861
Symonds, Philip, 869
Westacott, Samuel, 960
Whittle, R., 971
Baron, Benjamin, 473, 666
Baron, Francis, 997
Baron, John, 554
Baron, Randolph, 474, 997
Baron, Robert, 160
Barras, William, 160
Barrell, Beniah, 44
Barret, William, 216
Barrett, 375, 639
Barrett, James, 630
Barrett, John, 923
Barron, James, 847
Barron, Robert, 43
Barroth, James, 646
Barrow, 219
Barrow, John, 172
Barrowby Hall (Yorks.): George, Remy, 335
Barrsbridge (Northumb.): Burnup, Cuthbert, 132
Bartleman, Robert, 304
Bartlett, 232
Bartlett, Philip, 46
Barton, James, 616, 817
Barton, Thomas, 657
Barton, William, 873
Barton (Bristol): Board, W. & H., 82
Barton (Lancs.): Newton, James, 644

Barton (Westmld): Jackson, John, 476
Barton-upon-Humber (Lincs.):
Barkworth, John, 41
Beck, George, 56
Bell, John, 62
Brown, Absalom, 113
Graburn, William, 361
Hall, John, 385
Johnson, Edward & Sons, 489
Jonstones, —, 498
Newton, John, 645
Reed, John, 734
Saunderson, William, 786
Stephenson, Thomas, 854
Watson, John, 950
Willingham, John, 983
Wilson, William, 990
Young, Mathew, 1014
Barwick, James, 613
Barwick, William, 268, 293
Basildon Park (Berks.): Murray, Alexander, 636
Basin, 53
Basingstoke (Hants.):
Joyce, George, 499
Lane, Edward, 524
Mason, John, 584
Moody, John & James, 616
Moth, William, 632
Paice, George & William, 670
Paice, William, 670
Rice, John, 741
Ring, John, 750
Spencer, John snr, 843
Tolfree, James & Son, 897
Baskerville, John, 176
Baskett, Joseph, 79
Basnett, Thomas, 557
Bass, Samuel, 764
Bassana, 719
Basset, Stephen, 48
Bastable, 130
Bastallas, Richard, 430
Bastard, William, 48
Baston (Cumb.): Bowman, Edmund, 93
Batchelor, 500
Batchelor, Thomas, 48
Bateman, 369, 773
Bateman, R., 210, 573
Bateman, Redman, 310
Bateman & Forrest, 438
Bates, James, 359, 608
Batey, William, 49
Batger, Anthony, 696, 840
Bath (Som.):
Albin, Joseph, 6
Bailey, Benjamin, 29
Bailey, James, 30
Bain, William, 31
Baker, Nicholas, 33
Baldwin, Thomas, 34
Bally, —, 36

Banbury, James, 36
Banks, William, 37
Barnard, J., 42
Bartrum, William, 47
Batt, John, 49
Becks, Andrew Berkley, 57
Beer, Samuel, 58
Birchall, William, 74
Bird, John Soale, 74
Bird, Thomas, 74
Blacklock, J., 77
Blatchley, William, 80
Block, W., 81
Bond, T., 85
Boyce, J., 94
Bradbeer, A., 95
Briscoe, W., 108
Britten, James, 109
Broad, Robert, 109
Bryant, John, 122
Bryer, John, 123
Bryer, Robert, 123
Davis, George, 231
Davis, John, 231
Davis, Marks, 232
Dawson, A., 235
Deare, F. & Son, 238
Dixon, T., 246
Dowsing, William, 255
Eades, James, 263
East, T., 265
Edwards, John, 270
Ellis, G., 275
Elliston, A., 276
English, Edmund, 281
English & Son, 281
Evatt, James, 285
Evatt, Richard, 285
Evill, Mark, William, 286
Eyles, T.G., 286
Gale, R., 327
Giles, F., 339
Giles, John, 339
Goddard, —, 346
Greenwood, E., 368
Gutteridge, John, 380
Gwynn, —, 381
Halladay, —, 386
Hammersley, G., 391
Handcock, James, 393
Hanne, J., 395
Harman, James, 399
Harris, J., 400
Harris, William, 403
Hartery, George, 406
Hawkins, George, 412
Hawkins, John, 412
Heath, E., 418
Hills, Henry, 432
Hockey, Thos., 436
Hodges, William, 437
Holbrook, James, 440
Holding, W., 441
Hooper, —, 447

Hopkins, J., 448
Horton, Henry, 451
Howard, Joseph, 454
Hubberts, Messrs, 457
Hughes, John, 461
Hulbert, Messrs, 461
Hyde, Thomas, 470
Hyde, W., 470
Jafferis, Richard, 482
Jenkins, Richard, 484
Jones, Benjamin, 494
Jones, S., 496
Jones & Son, 498
Kelson, Chas., 503
Knight, Thomas, 519
Langdon, William, 525
Lasbury, F., 528
Lawless, J., 530
Lewis, Adam, 539
Llewellyn, William, 550
Lucas, —, 559
Lyons, John, 563
Maddox, John, 569
Maggs, G., J., John, 570
Mais, Henry, 570
Mallet, William, 571
Manley, R., 572
Mansfield, H., 573
Mattocks, R., 587
Maynard, James, 598
Mead, J., 598
Mear, John, 599
Mendall, J., 601
Mendinhall, G., 601
Miller, David, 608
Moody, Edmund, 616
Mumford, F. jnr, 635
Mumford, Francis, 635
Mumford & Bailey, 635
Newton, Nathaniel, 645
Orchard & Sons, 664
Osborne, —, 666
Palmer, J., 671
Palmer, William, 672
Parker & Harris, 675
Parsons, —, 678
Paul, William, 682
Peacock, Thomas, 683
Perry, Charles, 691
Perry, T., 692
Pizzie, Thomas, 702
Pluva, John, 703
Porter, & Radford, 707
Potters, John, 708
Potter, William, 708
Preece, James, 713
Pritchard, C., 718
Purnell, John, 722
Rainey, J., 725
Richards, H., 741
Riddout, J., 746
Rivers, Wm, 750
Robinson, James, 758
Ross, Joshua, 766

Roswell, Samuel, 767
Russell, G., 771
Sanderson, James, 779
Self, John, 799
Semper, William, 799
Shuttleworth, T., 813
Simms, G., 815
Smart, Abraham Chubb, 823
Smith, G., 826
Smith, J., 827
Smith & Theweneti, 836
Spragg, T., 845
Stafford, John & successors, 847
Symes, Charles, 869
Tar, George, 872
Thurston, Horatio, 892
Thurston, John Noel, 893
Tidmarsh, Thos., 894
Trimmell, C., 904
Trimnell, Anthony, 904
Trimnell, Charles, 904
Trimmell & Cross, 904
Tucker, George, 907
Veal, Edwin, 921
Veal, J., 921
Viel, John, Matthew, 923
Viels, Messrs F., 923
Wakefield, Thomas, 933
Walter, J., 941
Walter, Joseph, 941
Walter, Mathias, Matthew, 941
Webb, Charles, 953
Wheeler, William, 963
Wilcocks, 973
Willcox & Son, 978
Williams, James, 981
Williams, Job, 981
Wood, J., 996
Woodman, D., 999
Young, Thomas, 1015
Young, W., 1015
Bath Assembly Rooms (Som.):
  Eyles, T.G., 286
  Walter, Joseph, 941
Bath Corporation (Som.):
  Coxhead, Robert, 206
  Cross, William, 214
Bath Town Hall (Som.): Cooke, Isaac, 193
Bather, Thomas, 576
Batho, Nathaniel, 49
Bathurst, 161
Batleman, Robert, 304
Batley, 325
Batt, 749
Battersby, John, 99, 438, 553, 780
Battersby, Robert, 438, 553
Battersby, Thomas, 198
Battistessa, 1016
Battle, 565
Battle (Sussex):
  Mankelow, Edmund, 572
  Rand, William, 726
  Sargent, George, 781

Battle Abbey (Sussex): Bullock, George, 128
Battle Barrow (Westmld): Robinson, George, 757
Batty, E., 246, 272
Baty, 517
Baudovin (Paudevin), Nicholas, 681
Baughan, 574
Bawtry, Barnaby, 290, 604, 916
Bawtry (Yorks.):
  Bedford, John, 58
  Drew, William, 256
  Hackford, John, 381
  Hind, Richard, 433
  Howard, Charles, 453
  Lambert, William Henry, 523
  Lightfoot, Robert, 542
  Parker, Jonathon, 674
  Smith, William, 834
  Stubbs, Daniel, 863
  Swift, Joseph, 868
  Travis, Thomas, 902
  Wilson & Bedford, 990
  Winter, Richard, 993
Baxendale, Joseph, 760
Baxendale, Josiah, 408, 557, 708, 866, 892, 943
Baxendale, Lloyd, 162, 213, 302, 767
Baxfield, John, 70
Baxfield, Richard, 104
Baxfield, William, 70
Baxter, John, 52, 387
The Bayle, Bridlington (Yorks.): Taylor, John, 877
Bayley, William, 362
Baylies (Bucks.): Boson, John, 88, 89
Bayne, 132
Bayne, George, 240
Baynes, John, 53, 258
Baynes, Richard, 63, 114, 859
Beaker, Nicholas, 895
Beal, George, 116, 604, 740, 955
Beale, Joseph, 388
Beaminster (Dorset):
  Gerrard, John, 335
  Slade, Henry, 820
  Warr, John & Son, 945
Beamish, 232
Bean, George, 377
Beard, David, 866
Beardsley, Joseph, 256
Beasley, John, 956
Beaumont, 835
Beaumont, P., 527
Beaumont, Thomas, 55
Beaumont, William, 55, 559, 925
Beccles (Norfolk):
  Aldous, John, 7
  Brooks, John Bobbett, 112
  Buck, William, 123
  Elleys, Thomas, 272
  Lane, James, 525

Love, John Alger, 556
Maplestone, Charles jnr, 574
Maskill, Boyce, 583
Mayfieldstone, Charles jnr, 589
Syder, George, 869
Woolnough, George, 1002
Beck, Frederick, 324
Beck, William, 934
Beckenham Manor House (Kent):
 Chippendale, Thomas snr, 167
Beckerstaffe, Edward, 20
Beckerstaffe, William, 340
Beckett, 27
Becks, Andrew Berkley, 281
Beckwith, Samuel, 95, 315, 317
Beckwith, William, 317
Bedale (Yorks.):
 Alton, John, 11
 Ballon, John, 35
 Bowman, Thomas, 93
 Breckin, Ralph, 105
 Gill, William, 340
 Hogson, Charles, 437
 Mace, John, 565
 Peacock, William, 683
 Place, Mary, 702
 Santon, Vincent, 781
 Stanton, Vincent, 849
 Storey, Henry, 859
 Thwaites, Robert, 893
 Wake, Anthony, 933
 Webster, Christopher, 955
Bedells, John, 604
Bedford, 990
Bedford (Beds.):
 Abbot(t), David, 1
 Barker, James, 40
 Bowers, William, 92
 Burr, James, 132
 Day, Samuel, 236
 Eagle(s), Thomas, 264
 Jackson, William, 477
 Kilpin, Joseph, 513
 Kilpin, William, 513
 Pickering, Joseph, 697
 Randall, Edward, 726
 Reynolds, Thomas, 738
 Russell, John, 772
 Sear, Henry, 792
 Shelton, Robert, 807
 Snook, James, 837
 Tacchi, Anthony, 870
 Trapp, Bejamin, 902
 Ward, Samuel, 943
 Warden, William, 944
 Wells, George, 957
Bedlington (Northumb.):
 Langlands, Robert, 526
Bedminster (Bristol): Ward, John, 943
Beecock, John, 53
Beeks, Frederick, 57
Beesley, Thomas, 58

Beeston (Notts.): Ward, Edward, 942
Begbie, James, 2, 25, 120, 511
Beilby, John Alexander, 63
Beilby, Matthew, 71
Beilby, William, 71
Belchier, John, 24, 468, 618
Bele, Robert, 463
Belford (Northumb.):
 Bennet(t), Thomas, 64
 Burns, Thomas, 132
 Hat(t)ley, William, 410
Belhus (Essex): Cox, John, 204
Bell, 333, 962
Bell, A., 990
Bell, Daniel, 620, 621
Bell, Elizabeth, 62
Bell, Henry, 62, 205
Bell, James, 688
Bell, John, 121
Bell, Philip, 61, 510
Bell, Phillip, 515
Bell, R., 49
Bell, William, 933
Bellerby, John, 53, 59, 79, 148, 258, 588, 946
Bellingham, 6
Bellingham, William, 497
Belmont Castle (Essex): Kent, William, 509
Belper (Derbs.):
 Harrison, James, 403
 Harrison, John, 404
 Holmes, James, 445
 Johnson, Thomas, 492
 Pym, Joseph, 723
 Ride, Thomas, 746
 Summers, Thomas, 865
 Sumner, Thomas, 865
 Watson, William, 950
 Weston, Joseph, 961
 Wigley, Benjamin, 973
Belshaw, Edward, 804
Belshaw, William, 64, 171
Belton House (Lincs.): Bradshaw, William, 99
Belvoir Castle (Lincs.): Hume, —, 462
Bencroft, John, 356
Bendall, Mathew, 811
Benham Park (Berks.):
 Mayhew, John & Ince, William, 595
 Wood, Henry, 996
Bennet, Edward, 56
Bennet, John, 915
Bennet, Joseph, 726
Bennet, Thomas, 914
Bennett, 582
Bennett, John, 786
Bennett, Joseph, 804
Bennett, Thomas, 75, 504, 543
Bennifold, John, 64

Benniworth (Lincs.): Moakes, J.K., 614
Benson, James, 764
Benson, John, 453
Benson, William, 997
Benson (Oxon.): Powell, Peter, 710
Bentley, James, 110
Benton, 806
Bere Regis (Dorset): Gaulton, Henry, 333
Berew, Peter, 486
Berkeley (Glos.):
 Hallett, J.B., 387
 Smith, Thomas, 832
 Webb, John, 953
Berkenn, 604
Berkhampstead (Herts.):
 Hawkins, William, 413
 Johnson, Richard, 490
 Webb, William, 954
Bermondsey (London):
 Aston, Andrew, 22
 Davies, T., 230
 Drummond, Robert, 257
 Dunnings, George W., 261
 Jeanes, Charles, 482
 Jones, M., 496
 Joseph, William, 499
 King, William, 515
 Knight, George, 519
 Littell, Thomas, 549
 Menday, James, 601
 Munday, James, 635
 Nobbs, William, 650
 Parrott, Nathan, 677
 Price, Philip, 716
 Shorey, Ebenezer, 812
 Stainer, John, 847
 Story, James, 860
 Taylor, Samuel, 879
 Towler, William, 900
 Trilley, William, 904
 Verall, David, 922
 Walter, William, 941
Berrow, John, 921
Berry, Edward, 957
Berselaer, John, 774
Berwick-upon-Tweed (Northumb.):
 Bowhill, John, 92
 Brown, R., 117
 Burn, John, 131
 Davidson, William, 228
 Hamilton, William, 391
 Hatley & Purves, 410
 Hetley & Purvis, 425
 Hindmarsh, Thomas, 433
 Jackson, George, 475
 Jackson, John, 476
 Mace, Charles, 565
 Menzie(r)s, John, 601
 Nesbitt, Cornelius, 641
 Patterson, Alexander, 680
 Pearson, Thomas, 685
 Purves, James, 722

Richardson, Richard, 744
Robinson, George, 757
Sanderson, George, 779
Scott, John, 790
Smith, Jane, 827
Smith, John, 829
Thompkins, George, 885
Todd, Richard, 897
Turvin, Samuel, 914
Bethnal Green (London):
  Banter, Isaac, 37
  Burdett, James, 130
  Buttery, Robert, 139
  Dent, Joseph, 241
  Drake, Thomas, 255
  Guidot, William, 378
  Grimes, Christopher, 375
  Harris, Benjamin, 400
  Hewett, Mary, 425
  Hewett, Richard, 425
  Hewett, William, 425
  Hucks, William, 457
  Hughes, Benjamin, 460
  Jarvis, William, 481
  Kidston, James, 512
  McAndrew, James, 563
  Mann, W.R., 573
  Marchant, William, 574
  Marshall, John, 579
  Martin, Minton, 581
  Mecham, Joseph, 600
  Mitcham, Joseph, 613
  Mitchell, George, 613
  Norris, Elizabeth, 653
  Perkins, Thomas, 691
  Proctor, John, 719
  Read, Thomas, 732
  Reeve, Thomas, 735
  Smith, Isaac, 827
  Stone, T., 858
  Thompson, John, 887
  Upton, John, 918
  Winter, David, 992
Bettridge, 176, 484–5
Bevan, Edward, 452
Beverley (Yorks.):
  Aldridge, John, 7
  Anderson, Edwards, 12
  Andre, Percy James, 14
  Andrew, Joseph, 14
  Arnott, George, 19
  Arnott, George & Robert, 15
  Atkinson, George, 24
  Atkinson, Thomas, 24
  Barton, William, 47
  Bell, Wallis, 63
  Bishoprick, Xerxes, 76
  Bradford, John, 97
  Bradley, John, 98
  Brigham, George, 107
  Brown, Robert, 117
  Button, William, 139
  Dales, John, 224
  Dennison, William, 240

Dossor, R., 251
Doyle, William, 255
Ellrington, William, 276
Gelder, Robert, 335
Heensley, Peter, 419
Hide, John, 428
Hunsley, Peter, 464
Hunter, William, 465
Issott, Joseph, 474
Jakeman, John, 478
Jameson, Richard, 480
Kirby, Robert, 516
Kirkby, Robert, 517
Loft, William, 553
Lumley, John, 560
Lundie, William, 561
Mason, Henry, 583
May, John, 589
May & Loftus, 589
Meadley, Richard, 599
Milner, Francis jnr, 611
Mitchell, Robert, 614
Mitchel, William, 613
Padget, William, 669
Rawley, Charles, 729
Rawling, Charles, 729
Rayley, Joseph, 730
Riccall, William, 741
Robinson, Robert, 760
Sever, Matthew, 800
Shaw, James, 804
Stephenson, John, 853
Stephenson, Robert, 854
Stephenson, William, 854
Sugdon, James, 864
Swaby, Robert, 866
Thompson, William, 888
Thompson, William snr & jnr, 888
Watson, Henry, 949
Watson, John, 950
Watson, Robert, 950
White, James, 965
Whitelock, Robert, 968
Wilson, John, 987
Wilson, Nathaniel, 988
Wrightson, William, 1009
Beverley Guildhall (Yorks.):
  Foster, Edmund, 311
  Thompson, William snr and jnr, 888
Beverley Minster (Yorks.): Foster, Edmund, 311
Beverley Sessions House (Yorks.):
  Jameson, Richard, 480
Beves, 888
Bewdley (Worcs.):
  Allen, Charles, 9
  Bennett, Thomas, 65
  Bevan, James, 69
  Biddell, Thomas, 71
  Griffin, Richard, 373
  Griffin, William, 373
  Maulin, Hurmee, 587

Maullin, Shernice, 587
Moullin, Sternec, 633
Mountford, Joseph, 633
Mumford, Joseph, 635
Payton, Nathaniel, 683
Piper, James, 700
Weyman & Smith, 962
Worroll, Thomas, 1003
Bewerley (Yorks.): Horner, Jonathon, 450
Bexfield, Joseph, 511
Bexleyheath (Kent): Moneyment, Matthew, 616
Bicester (Oxon.):
  King, —, 513
  Maynard, John E., 598
  Wright, William Hollands, 1009
Biass, 470
Bibby, George, 637
Bickerstaff, William, 217, 307, 414, 424, 955
Bideford (Devon):
  Barratt, Richard, 44
  Brown, Christopher, 113
  Ellis, James, 275
  Ellis, William, 276
  Heard, Richard, 417
  Lee, John, 535
  Lee, Samuel, 535
  Lock, George, 551
  Reid, Joseph, 736
  Smale, James, 822
  Wheeler, Richard, 963
Biel (East Lothian): Bullock, George, 127
Biffin, Charles, 71
Biffin, John, 71
Biggins, Samuel, 866
Biggleswade (Beds.):
  Robarts, Martha, 751
  Robarts, Martin, 751
  Stewart, —, 855
Bigham, William, 71
Bilbie, William, 847
Bilby, George, 266
Bilby, William Bonner, 469
Bildeston (Suffolk): Johnson, William, 493
Billericay (Essex): Thompson, William, 888
Billing, 525
Billingbear (Berks.):
  Coldicott, —, 186
  Davis, —, 230
  Dawes, —, 233
  Dowbiggin(g), Thomas, 253
  Elward, George & Marsh, William, 279
  French, —, 321
  Harris, —, 400
  Higgs & Ford, 429
  Hoby, —, 436
  Lambden, Edward, 522

Miles, Henry & Edwards, John, 606
Pequer, Louis & Son, 686
Romsey, —, 765
Tayler (or Taylor), —, 874
Town & Emanuel, 901
Tratt & Attfield, 902
Billups, Thomas, 26
Billups, William, 692
Bilston (Staffs.):
 Bennett, Joseph, 65
 Dolman, Frederick & Son, 250
 Gettings, —, 336
 Green, William, 368
 Harden, John, 396
 Harding, George, 396
 Harding, John, 396
 Hardy, George, 397
 Harrison, Joseph, 404
 Hickman, Richard, 427
 Ireland, John, 473
 Kimberley, Joseph, 513
 Leech, James, 535
 Lindon, Joseph, 542
 Meredith, William, 602
 Pearson, Samuel, 685
 Price, William, 717
 Riley, Edward, 748
 Sansom, Henry, 781
 Shale, William, 802
 Stone, John, 858
 Thompson, James, 886
 Wright, John, 1006
Bines, William, 950
Bingham, Christopher, 388
Bingham (Notts.):
 Stone, Richard, 858
 Whitworth, George, 971
 Widdowson, Thomas, 972
Bingley, Ralph, 107, 109, 248, 276
Bingley, Randall, 674
Bingley, Randle, 789
Bingley (Yorks.):
 Bales, Joshua, 34
 Balme, Joshua, 36
 Barnes, Joshua, 42
 Dean, John, 237
 Hanson, Christopher, 395
Binney, John, 502
Binnington, James, 850
Binnington, Richard, 157
Binns, 614
Binns, Edward, 442, 933
Binns, Joshua, 73
Birch, 646
Birchall, Daniel, 664
Birchall, William, 995
Bird, 811
Bird, John, 859
Bird, Robert, 42
Bird, Samuel, 383
Bird, William, 453
Birdseye, John, 541
Birkby (Yorks.): Dyson, John, 263

Birkenhead (Cheshire):
 Bell, George, 61
 Belshaw, William, 64
 Brattan, James, 103
 Burland, Thomas, 130
 Danson, Thomas, 226
 Davies, Catherine, 228
 Davies, Thomas, 230
 Drinkwater, James, 256
 Houston, James, 453
 Moran, James, 622
 Pickering, Joseph, 697
 Platts, Luke, 702
 Warlow, William, 945
 Young, Robert, 1015
Birkett, H., 650
Birkett, Henry, 933
Birmingham, Robert, 75
Birmingham:
 Adcock, William, 4
 Adderley, Samuel, 4
 Aldridge, Charles, 7
 Alebon, John, 7
 Alford, James, 7
 Allen, Charles, 9
 Allen, John, 10
 Allen, William, 10
 Allridge, Charles, 9
 Allridge, Edwin, 9
 Anderson, William, 13
 Anderton, William, 14
 Andrew, John, 14
 Andrew, Thomas, 14
 Andrew(s), Christopher, 14
 Andrews, George, 14
 Andrews, John, 14
 Andrews, William, 14
 Ansell, Samuel, 15
 Ansley, Thomas, 15
 Apletree, Frederick, 16
 Appletree, M., 16
 Ashford, Charles, 20
 Ashford, Thomas, 20
 Ashford & Al(l)dridge, 20
 Asplen, John, 22
 Astley, Thomas, 22
 Aston, John, 22
 Aston, Joseph, 22
 Aston, Thomas, 22
 Atkins, John, 23
 Auster, Roger, 26
 Aylett, G., 27
 Bailey, William, 31
 Baker, Thomas, 33
 Baker, William, 33
 Bakewell, Mathew, 33
 Ball, William, 35
 Banks, Thomas, 37
 Barlow, George, 41
 Barlow, J., 41
 Barlow, William, 42
 Barnard, J., 42
 Barrow, John, 45
 Barrs, Thomas, 45

 Baskerville, John, 47
 Beach, George, 53
 Beach & Maschwitz, 53
 Bean, William, 55
 Beesley, Thomas, 59
 Bell, Elizabeth, 61
 Bell, Joseph, 62
 Bellion, James, 63
 Bennett, Robert, 65
 Benson, Joseph, 66
 Bent, William, 66
 Best, Joseph, 68
 Best, Read & Co., 68
 Bettridge, Josh., 69
 Beven, William, 69
 Bevins, —, 69
 Bianchi, Peter, 70
 Biggs, Joseph, 71
 Bill, Richard & George, 71
 Birch, George, 73
 Birch, Joseph, 74
 Bird, George, 74
 Bird, Thomas, 74
 Birks, Joseph, 75
 Bishop, John, 76
 Bishop, William Henry, 76
 Bland, John, 80
 Bloore, Samuel, 81
 Bodenham, George, 83
 Borini, Peter, 87
 Bosworth, Joseph, 90
 Boyce, John, 94
 Brace, Henry, 94
 Bradbury, Thomas, 97
 Bradley, Francis, 97
 Brammich, Thomas, 102
 Bratt, William, 103
 Briggs & Brown, 107
 Brisband, Roger, 108
 Broadfield, Benjamin, 109
 Bromwich, Thomas, 110
 Brown, Charles, 113
 Brown, John, 116
 Brown, Thomas, 118
 Brown, William, 119
 Browne, John, 120
 Buckerfield, John, 123
 Buckerfield, Thomas, 123
 Buckler, Elizabeth, 124
 Burt, Richard, 134
 Buswell & Scarott, 137
 Butler Brothers, 138
 Butler, John, 137
 Davis, Thomas, 232
 Davis, William, 233
 Davis & Griffin, 233
 Deakin, Thomas, 237
 Decker, Henry, 238
 Dewerson, John, 242
 Dewson, James, 243
 Docker, Henry, 248
 Dore, Samuel, 251
 Drakeford, John, 255

Drakeford, John & Price, Richard F., 255
Draper, John, 255
Dudley, John, 258
Dudley, Nathaniel, 258
Dukes, John, 259
Eagles, William, 264
Edmonds, Joseph, 267
Edwards, Anthony, 269
Edwards, David, 269
Edwards, Edward, 269
Edwards, Sarah, 270
Edwards, William, 271
Eginton, Francis, 271
Ellis, Thomas, 275
Emuss, Thomas, 281
England, John Frederick, 281
England, Robert, 281
Ethell, Mary, 282
Ethell, Stephen, 282
Ethell, Stephen & Ann, 282
Ethell, Thomas, 282
Ethell, William, 282
Evans, John, 284
Evans, William, 285
Everitt, Allen, 285
Gabriel, William, 326
Gamerson, John, 328
Gardner, John, 330
Gazy, Thomas, 333
Gibson, Thomas, 338
Glasgow, Abraham, 345
Glasgow, Robert, 345
Glover, Charles, 345
Goffe, Thomas, 348
Goodsall, John, 354
Grainger, John, 363
Green, Henry, 367
Green, Thomas, 368
Green, William, 368
Griffith, Samuel, 374
Griffiths, Charles, 374
Griffiths, Henry, 374
Griffiths, Samuel, 375
Grubb, Edward, 376
Grubb, Samuel, 376
Haden, William, 382
Hadley, Thomas, 382
Haiden, William, 382
Hales, Samuel, 383
Hall, George, 385
Hall, Samuel, 386
Hall & Rostill, 386
Hammond, Mary, 392
Hammond, William, 392
Hancock, John, 393
Hancox, James, 393
Hands & Jenkins, 394
Harper, Anthony, 399
Harriot, James, 400
Harris, John, 401
Harris, Thomas, 402
Hart, Joseph, 406
Hart & Son, 406

Hawkesford, William, 412
Heath, Richard, 418
Helm, Robert, 420
Henderson, Alexander, 420
Hensman, Thomas, 422
Heptinstall, Joseph, 422
Hickin, James, 427
Hickin, William, 427
Hicklin, William, 427
Hill, James, 430
Hill, John, 431
Hill, Samuel, 431
Hilton, William, 432
Hindes, William, 433
Hinds, William, 433
Hodges, Thomas, 437
Hodgkins, Charles, 437
Hodgkins, William, 437
Hodskins, William, 439
Hollis, John, 443
Hollyoak, Roach, 444
Homer, William, 446
Honor, George, 447
Hope, Samuel, 448
Hopkin, William, 448
Horner, George, 450
Hors(e)ley, John, 451
Horton, John, 451
Horton, Joseph, 451
Howe, Joseph, 455
Howell, Edward, 455
Howell, George, 455
Hughes, Edward, 460
Hughes, James, 460
Hughes, Thomas, 461
Hulse, Henry, 462
Hulston, John, 462
Humphreys, Leonard, 463
Ibbe(r)tson, James Mortimer, 470
Izon, John, George & Thomas, 474
Izon, John Parnell & Sons, 474
Jee, Edward, 482
Jeffries, Edward, 483
Jenkinson, John, 484
Jennens & Bettridge, 484
Johnson, —, 489
Johnson, Isaac, 489
Johnson, W., 492
Jones, Edward, 494
Jones, Francis, 494
Jones, Thomas, 497
Jones, William, 496
Jones & Barker, 498
Jordan, William Jones, 499
Joseph, Sarah, 499
Kendall & Sons, 505
Kenworthy, Joseph Brook, 509
Kimberley, Jesse, 513
Knight, Thomas, 519
Lambley, Abraham, 523
Lambley, James, 523
Lambley, James William, 523
Lambley, William, 523

Lander, Francis, 524
Langford, John, 525
Lates, John, 529
Latham, Edmund, 529
Lee, Abraham, 534
Lee, James, 534
Lees, John, 536
Ley, George, 541
Ley, Sarah, 541
Linwood, Matthew, 548
Lloyd, Thomas, 551
Lomax, William, 554
Longmore, Thomas, 555
Lowe, Charles, 557
Lucas, William, 559
Macefield, Robert, 565
Machin, Edward, 565
Machin, Thomas, 565
Mal(l)ins, William Hill, 571
Mansell, Joseph, 573
Manton, George, 573
March, Edward, 574
Mares, John, 574
Markland, Ralph, 574
Marlow, Thomas, 575
Marsh, Edward, 576
Martin, William, 582
Mason, Robert Crump, 584
Masters, Joseph, 585
Mears, John, 600
Miles, Thomas, 607
Mills, Thomas, 611
Minshull, George, 612
Molesworth, Thomas, 615
Mortimer, William, 630
Moseley, Charles, 631
Nation, Robert, 639
Natt, Thomas, 639
Needle, Thomas, 640
Newbrook, John, 642
Newey, E. & R., 642
Newey, Richard, 642
Newman, John, 643
Newton, Gabriel, 644
Nicholas, William, 645
Nixon, William, 650
Norman, John, 651
Norton, George, 656
Ogden, Samuel, 661
Onions, George, James, 664
Orton, Joseph, 665
Overton, James, 667
Paine, Joseph, 670
Paine, Thomas, 670
Pare, John, 672
Parker, James, 674
Parkes, Edwin, 675
Patterson, Edmund, Edward, 680
Payne, Joseph, 682
Payne, Thomas, 683
Pearson, Benjamin, 684
Pearson, Samuel, 685
Perks, John, Thomas, 691
Phillips, James, 694

Potter, David J., 708
Powell, James, 710
Powell, Thomas, 711
Preston, John, 714
Price, James, 715
Price, John, 716
Price, William, 717
Pritchitt, John, 719
Purcell, Thomas, 722
Purser, William, 722
Radford, Joseph, 725
Read, James, 732
Remington, Thomas, 737
Rice, James & Richard, 741
Richardson, Elizabeth, 743
Richardson, James, 743, 744
Ricketts, John, 746
Roberts, John, 752
Roberts, Josiah, 752
Roberts, Thomas, 754
Robinson, —, 756
Robinson, I.B., 757
Robinson, Ralph, 759
Robinson, Richard, 760
Robinson, Thomas Baker, 760
Rock, Edward, 762
Rodway, John, 762
Rogers, William, 764
Rollas(t)on, William, 764
Rostill, William, 767
Rowley, Francis, 769
Ryley, William, 774
Scarrott, Thomas, 788
Scarrott & Busswell, 788
Sharp, John, 803
Sharpe, John, 803
Shaw, W.B., 805
Sheldon & Benton, 806
Shelton, William, 807
Shenstone, William, 807
Shenton, William, 807
Sherratt, Charles, 809
Shuttleworth, Charles, 813
Sidebotham, Thomas, 814
Simcox, Jane, William, 815
Skidmore, Thomas, 819
Smalls & Hipkiss, 822
Smallwood, Edward, 822
Smallwood, Thomas, William & Co., 823
Smallwoods & Appletree, 823
Smith, James, 827
Smith, John, 829, 830
Smith, William, 834, 835
Snape, Thomas, 836
Soloman, Samuel, 838
Solomon, Moses, 838
Spreadborough, Richard, 846
Starling, James, 850
Steeple(s), John, Thomas, 851
Steevens, John, 852
Stock, George, 857
Stone, John, 858
Storer, Joseph, 859

Stow, Jonathon, 860
Summerland, Thomas, 864
Tanner, —, 871
Tanner, Jane, 871
Tanner, Richard, 871
Tanner, Thomas, 871
Tanner, Thomas Alexander, 871
Tarplee, William, 872
Taylor, Joseph, 878
Thomas, John, 884
Thompson, William, 888
Thowless, William, 891
Throwless, William, 892
Tibbatts, John, 893
Tieldsley, Thomas, 894
Tipping, Isaac, 895
Toakley, John, 896
Towell, Thomas, 900
Truman, George, 906
Turner, Anthony, 909
Turner, William, 913
Underwood, John, 917
Underwood, Joseph, 917
Vaughan, Thomas, 921
Vowles, Elizabeth, 930
Wagner & Cottrell, 931
Wakefield, Thomas, 933
Wallis, James, 940
Walton, Edward, 942
Ward, George, 942
Watts, Thomas, 951
Wellings, Richard, 957
Westbury, Daniel, 960
Westwood, James & John, 961
Westwood, Obadiah, 961
Wheeler, Charles, 963
Wheeler, James, 963
Whitbread, W.E., 964
Whitehead, Jos, 968
Whitehead, William, 968
White, James, 965
White, Richard, 966
White, William, 967
White, William jnr, 967
White, William & Sons, 968
Whittall, Joseph, Thomas, 970
Williams, John, 981
Williams, Joseph, 981
Williams, Thomas, 982
Wilson, John, 988
Wilson, Mary, 988
Wilson, Thomas, 989
Winfield, R.W., 991
Winn, Robert, 992
Winskell, William, 992
Winwood, J., 993
Woodfield, Henry, 998
Woodfield, Samuel, 999
Woodhouse, Hubbard, 999
Woodhouse, Hubert, 999
Woodhouse, Humphrey, 999
Woolfield, Henry, Samuel, 1001
Wright, George, 1005
Wright, Jeremiah, 1005

Wright, John, 1005, 1006
Yates, Sarah, 1012
Yates & Co., 1012
Yates, Son & Harper, 1012
Birstall (Yorks.):
Brook, Charles, 110
Gill, Jonas, 340
Hall, William, 386
Hichcliffe, John, 433
Hopkinson, Henry, 449
Keighley, John, 502
Lord, Isaac, 555
Saville, Benjamin, 786
Saville, Benoni, 786
Shepley, William, 808
Thorpe, William, 891
Ward, Samuel, 943
Birstwith (Yorks.): Snow, Thomas, 837
Birset, John, 76
Birt, James, 65, 240
Birthwaite Hall (Yorks.): Boulnois, —, 91
Bisett, Thomas, 864
Bishop, Thomas, 232
Bishop Auckland (Co. Durham):
Atkinson, John, 24
Braithwaite, Matthew, 101
Brown, Matthew, 117
Gilmore, William, 344
Gray, William, 366
Hall, James, 385
Nelson, Robert, 640
Newton, John, 645
Pearson, Oswald, 685
Proud, William, 719
Ramshaw, William, 726
Taylor, Joseph, 878
Taylor, William, 880
Thompson, Thomas, 887
Bishop Wearmouth (Co. Durham):
Barnes, George, 42
Burn, William, 131
Ditchburn, Richard Nightingale, 245
Hallowell, Edw., 390
Hugall, Thomas, 460
Mackenzie & Son, 566
Maddison, Philip, 569
Marshall, John, 579
Martin, John, 581
Nesbit, John, 641
Preston, George, 714
Robinson, John, 758
Sampson, Nicholas, 778
Scott, Thomas, 790
Bishoprick, Xerxes, 853
Bishops Castle (Salop):
Green, Richard, 367
Medlicott, Thomas, 600
Richards, Thomas, 743
Bishops Hull (Som.): White, David, 965

Bishop's Stortford (Herts.):
 Barber, William, 39
 Jones, Francis, 494
 King, Joseph, 514
 Ramsey, Peter, 726
 Scarfe, James, 788
 Slater, John, 820
 Summers, J.H., 864
 Summers, James, 864
 Sumners & Sworder, 865
 Thurgood, Thomas, 892
 Tyler, Frederick, 915
 Worpell, Henry, 1003
Bishops Waltham (Hants.):
 Horner, Malachi, 450
 Limpus, John, 542
 Vernon, Thomas, 922
 Weston, William, 961
Bishopsgate (London):
 Boulter, William, 91
 Browning, John, 120
 Brown, William, 119
 Bull, Sarah, 125
 Davies, Horatio David, 228
 Davis, George, 231
 Davis, Henry David, 231
 Duchesne, John & Thomas, 257
 Dunn, Joseph, 260
 Entwisle, Thomas, 281
 Goodman, Richard, 354
 Hall, Robert, 386
 Harvey, Henry, 407
 Issard, John, 474
 James, Jordan, 479
 Joel, George, 488
 Johnson, Rob., 491
 Johnson, Samuel, 491
 Jordan, William James, 499
 Kiberd, George, 511
 Kincey, T., 513
 King, —, 514
 Le Nain, Ivon, 538
 Metcalf(e), —, 603
 Morgan, James, 625
 Raybold, Richard, 730
 Royboult, Richard, 769
 Whitaker, Samuel, 964
Bispham, Edward, 213
Bispham, John, 75
Bittlestone, 553
Bitton (Bristol): Bayly, Richard, 52
Bitton (Glos.): Brain, John, 101
Black, 488
Black Burton (Yorks.): Barker,
 William, 41
Blackburn, Christopher, 827
Blackburn, G., 369
Blackburn, Thomas, 161
Blackburn, W., 210, 475, 824, 900,
 960
Blackburn, William, 24, 49, 56, 310,
 385, 532, 611, 639, 880
Blackburn, Bateman & Forrest, 773

Blackburn (Lancs.):
 Alderson, Robert, 7
 Bamber, George, 36
 Banister, Robert, 36
 Bannister, Ann, 37
 Baron, Robert, 43
 Barton, James, 47
 Baxendale, William, 51
 Beesley, Joshua, 59
 Beesley, William, 59
 Boardman, Thomas, 82
 Boustead, James, 91
 Bradshaw, James, 99
 Brockband, George, 109
 Brookbank, Joseph, 111
 Brown, Thomas, 118
 Bulcock, Thomas, 125
 Dean, Henry, 237
 Dewhurst, John, 242
 Dixon, Ger(r)ard, 246
 Dixon, Jarat, 246
 Duckworth, Thomas, 257
 Edge, Joseph, 266
 Graham & Boardman, 363
 Hall, Thomas, 386
 Holt, James, 446
 Houlker, William, 452
 Jones, James, 495
 Kay, A. & Co., 500
 Langley, James, 526
 Moon, William, 617
 Nicholson, John, 646
 Parkinson, John, 676
 Pickup, Thomas, 697
 Pilkington, Richard, 699
 Sawer, William, 786
 Sawyer, Thomas, 787
 Sharp, John, 803
 Sharples, John, 804
 Slater, Luke, 821
 Slater, Samuel, 821
 Stones, James & Thomas, 859
 Thompson, John, 886
 Tomlinson, Thomas, 898
 Towers, Thomas, 900
 Vickers, —, 923
 Walsh, Thomas, 941
 Wigglesworth, Robert &
 William, 973
 Wilkinson, Richard, 977
 Winder, Robert, 991
 Wolstenholme, Lawrence, 995
 Wolstenholme, William, 995
 Wolstenholme & Vickard, 995
 Woods, William, 1000
 Woolfall, Robert, 1001
Blackfriars (London):
 Booth, Henry, 87
 Bowman, John, 93
 Bradford, James, 97
 Butler, John, 137
 Dixon, Charles, 246
 Evans, Tempest, 285
 Gardner, John, 330

 Gardner, William, 330
 Gee, Martha, 334
 Goldsping, John, 348
 Gosby, Edward, 358
 Grant, Robert, 364
 Griffin & Row, 373
 Harris, William, 403
 Jenks, Robert, 484
 Kay, Quintin, 500
 Laycock, Thomas, 532
 McLauchlan, David, 567
 Matthews, John, 587
 Mitchell, George, 613
 Morgan, William, 626
 Nordon, Jacob, 651
 Purdom, Thomas, 722
 Quintus, Martin, 724
 Rodbart, Thomas, 762
 Row, Charles John, 768
 Waddilove, James, 930
 Warner, Joshua, 945
 Wells, Stephen, 958
 Westwood & Smith, 961
 Wright, Thomas, 1008
Blackheath (London):
 Bagnall, Walter, 29
 Bone, William, 85
 Hawkins, J.D., 412
 Kirkham, John, 517
 Ponder, Charles, 705
Blackley, John, 673
Blackmore, Sarah, 77
Blackpool (Lancs.):
 Banks & Topping, 37
 Parr, William, 677
Blackwall (London):
 Dunn, John, 260
 Sweetman, Arthur, 868
Blackwell, Henry, 78
Blackwell, John, 432, 587
Blaiklock, Musgrave, 77
Blain, A., 160
Blain, A.T., 79
Blain, Thomas, 78
Blair Castle (Perthshire):
 Bullock, George, 127
 Caitcheon, John, 140
 Chipchase, Robert & Lambert,
 Robert, 163
 Chipchase, Robert & Henry, 163
 Chippendale, Thomas snr, 166
 Cole, George, 187
 Cullen, James, 218
 Gianinetty, Joseph, 336
 Gordon, John & Taitt, John &
 Richard, 355, 356
 Henderson, William, 421
 Hodson, John, 439
 Innes, John, 472
 Johnson, Thomas, 492
 Masters, William, 585
 Trotter, John, 906
 Willerton & Roberts, 978
Blakeburn, Thomas, 77

Blakesley, Robert, 48, 464, 898
Blakey, John, 63
Blakley, Joseph, 814
Blamer, Thomas, 562
Blanchard, Richard, 477
Bland, William, 376
Blandford, 979
Blandford (Dorset):
  Bastard, John, 48
  Biles & Co., 71
  Brown, John Cossons, 116
  Doe, Cornelius, 249
  Dugdale, Richard, 258
  Hibberd, William, 427
  Kendall, O., 505
  Marsh, Samuel, 577
  Newman, John, 643
  Norris, George, 653
  Park, Mark, 673
  Penning, J., 688
  Percy, E., 690
  Pope, John, 706
  Portus, John, 707
  Powell, Rees, 710
  Rayns, Robert, 731
  Robins, William, 756
  Saunders, Thomas, 785
  Spearing, Perrias, 842
  Stayner, Robert snr & jnr, 850
  Thompson, John, 886
  Thompson, Samuel, 887
  Zanfrini & Gugeri, 1016
Blankinsop, Peter, 81
Blarchard, Samuel, 80
Blaxlan, 727
Blaxland, Henry, 210, 238, 274, 504, 717
Blaydon (Co. Durham):
  Lawson, John, 532
  Mitford, James, 614
Blayney, Thomas, 80, 916
Blease, John, 75, 795
Blease & Seddon, 795, 798
Blenheim Palace (Oxon.):
  Alken, Sefferin, 8
  Ansell, Robert, 15
  Bradshaw, —, 98
  Gibbons, Grinling, 336
  Goodison, Benjamin, 354
  Mayhew, John & Ince, William, 592, 593, 595
  Moore, James snr, 618, 619
  Stephens, Edward, 852
Blew, 52
Blickling Hall (Norfolk):
  Freeman, Jeremiah, 321
  Hodson, —, 439
  Hudson, Solomon, 459
  Perrin, Henry, 691
  Trotter, John, 906
  Vile, William, 928
Blinkhorn, George, 562
Blissatt, 566
Blissatt, James, 769

Blisset, 566
Blissett, 566
Blomfield, John, 641, 832
Bloomsbury (London):
  Abington, Leonard, 2
  Atwood, Thomas, 25
  Bainbridge, William, 31
  Baker, M., 33
  Baker, William, 33
  Ball, John, 35
  Bankes, William, 37
  Barnes, John, 42
  Bateson, William, 49
  Bennett, Henry, 64
  Bracken, John & Sanders, Ann, 95
  Bran(d)t, Charles, 103
  Brittain, G., 109
  Brookes, Margaret, 11
  Bundock, William, 128
  Davis, John, 231
  Davis, Robert, 232
  Dawes, —, 233
  Dixon, Samuel, 246
  Dover, Charles, 252
  Dover, P.E., 252
  Draycott, Frederick, 256
  Duchemin, Peter, 257
  Dunn, Michael, 260
  Duval, L.C., 263
  Eastgate, Charles, 265
  Edwards, David, 269
  Edwards, Peter, 270
  Emmens, Thomas, 280
  Erskine, William, 282
  Essex, C., 282
  Good, Thomas, 351
  Hall, William, 386
  Harris, Robert, 402
  Harris, Simeon, 402
  Hathwell, Thomas, 410
  Hawkins, John, 413
  Hayne(s), Matthew, 415
  Henderson, James, 420
  Hick, Ben., 427
  Hide, Benjamin, 428
  Hillier, John, 432
  Hill, Samuel, 431
  Holmes, William, 446
  Hopkins, James, 448
  Hopkins, Samuel, 448
  Howell, Charles, 455
  Hubbard, John, 457
  Jeeves, Jeremiah, 482
  Jones, Francis, 494
  Kirby, W., 516
  Lands, David, 524
  Langslow, Edward, 527
  Law, William, 530
  Lawrence, John, 531
  Lewis, William, 541
  Linnell, J., 543
  McClennan & Flint, 564
  Macklin, R., 567

  McLellan, Robert, 568
  Maddox, Ralph, 569
  Marshall, John, 579
  Monkhouse, George, 616
  Mountain, William, 633
  Muddell, Thomas, 634
  Page, Thomas Osborn, 670
  Parkin, John, 676
  Partridge, Francis, 678
  Pastor, James, 679
  Patterson, James, 680
  Perry, Alexander, 691
  Potts, George, 708
  Price, William, 717
  Rathnell, Samuel, 728
  Reid, William, 736
  Remington, George, 737
  Richardson, George, 743
  Roake, Joseph, Samuel, 751
  Sammes, James, 778
  Sands, David, 780
  Sawkins, K., 786
  Smith, Charles, 825
  Stannard, Erasmus, 849
  Stephenson, Sampson, 854
  Sunderland, George, 865
  Taylor, George, 876
  Tompson, John, 898
  Towsey, —, 902
  Tyler, Joseph, 915
  Wallis, Robert, 940
  Wardley Isaac, 944
  Waring, Basil, 945
  Watts, Allen, 951
  Wright, John, 1005
Blount, 842
Blow, John, 281
Blower, J. & B., 588
Blundell, 104
Blunt, C., 134, 731, 811, 929
Blunt, Charles, 609
Blurton, Venables, 136
Bly, Giles, 162
Blyth (Northumb.):
  Davidson, John, 228
  Gates, John, 332
  Hepple, Tristram, 422
  Marshall & Newman, 580
  Maxwell, William, 588
  Tulley, John, Philip, 908
  Wilson, —, 986
Blyth Hall (Notts.): Mayhew, John & Ince, William, 595
Blythe, Richard, 244
Boardman, 363, 647
Boardman, William, 977
Bocking (Essex): Brenes, James, 105
Boconnoc, Lostwithiel (Cornwall): Faradin, Abraham, 289
Boddy, William, 413
Bodham, Philip, 427
Bodingham (Suffolk): Batho, John, 49

Bodmin (Cornwall):
Baron, Thomas, 43
Deacon, Edward, 237
Watkin, John, 947
West, Martin, 960
Williams, M., 981
Bodovine (Paudevin), John, 681
Bogaerts, Peter, 860
Bognor (Sussex):
Richards, Peachey, 742
Smith, Francis, 826
Tate, Thomas, 873
Bolland, William, 754
Bolongaro, 1015
Bolongaro, Dominic, 63
Bolsover (Derbs.):
Shacklock, Francis, 802
Shacklock, John, 802
Bolsterstone (Yorks.): Wainwright,
Joshua, 932
Bolton, James, 960
Bolton, John jnr, 91
Bolton (Lancs.):
Badger, Ellen & Sons, 28
Barrett, John, 44
Brimelow, Zachary, 108
Dixon, George, 246
Dornings, Peter, 251
Eccles, James, 265
Garbut, Francis, 329
Glassbrook, John, 345
Green, William, 368
Grime, George, 375
Grime, Joseph, 375
Grime & Greasdale, 375
Hancock, James, 392
Harrison, John, 404
Harwood, John, 408
Heaton, James, 419
Heaton, Thomas, 419
Heywood, John, 426
Hodgkinson, Samuel, 437
Hope, John, 448
Ingold, Robert, 472
Jackson, James & John, 475
Jackson, Thomas, 477
Leigh, John, 537
Leigh, Richard, 537
Leigh, Thomas, 537
Leigh, William, 537
Marsden, Elizabeth, 576
Morris, Peter, 629
Seddon, Thomas, 798
Smith, John, 829
Walley, Thomas, 940
Whitaker, John, 964
Bolton Hall (Yorks.): Bullock,
George, 127
Bolton-le-Moor (Lancs.):
Badger, Richard, 28
Burrow, Richard, 133
Butler, Abraham, 137
Butler, Benjamin, 137
Dearden, James, 238

Gledhill, Ely, 345
Lomax, William, 554
Bolus, Samuel, 602, 852
Bond, 47
Bond, James, 85, 501
Bond, William, 208, 546
Bonnell, Thomas, 815
Bonner, 318
Bonnett, 979
Bonnington, George, 891
Booden, Thomas, 662
Boore, John, 86
Boorne, Robert, 88
Boot, Aaron, 977
Boote, Alexander, 30, 52, 339
Booth, 66, 141
Boreham House (Essex):
Balch, —, 33
Bladwell, John, 78
Braine (or Brown), James, 101
Chippendale, Thomas snr, 167
Draycott, —, 256
Foyer, James, 315
Garth, James, 331
Harrison, —, 403
Ireland, Richard, 473
Macblane, —, 564
Mayhew, John & Ince, William,
595
Miles, —, 606
Smith, —, 824
Vial(l)(s), Thomas, 922
Watson, —, 948
Boroughbridge (Yorks.):
Brown, John, 116
Gatenby, William, 332
Hardcastle, William, 395
Hird, George, 434
Hird, John, 434
Borver, Joseph, 92
Borwick (Lancs.): Addison, John, 4
Boson, John, 352, 353, 924
Bostock, Edward, 495
Bostock, James, 418
Boston (Lincs.):
Allen, Joseph, 10
Allen, Nicholas, 10
Ashton, Thomas, 21
Atkin(s), Samuel, 23
Bacon, Thomas, 28
Baker, William, 33
Bennett, Joseph, 65
Bogg, William, 83
Brooke, Thomas, 111
Brown, Benjamin, 113
Brumby, Joseph, 121
Bulmer, Benjamin, 128
Burton, Christopher, 134
Elsom, John, 277
Gilson, Robert, 344
Granger, Thomas, 364
Hammersley, William, 391
Hart, Willism, 406
Hunstan, Thomas, 464

Johnson, Thomas, 492
Lamb, John, 522
Lucas, William, 559
Martin, C., 580
Mastin, Charles & Son, 585
Mattison, Quincey, 587
Mountain, John, 633
Mowbray, Ribert, 634
Parratt, Eustace Philip, 677
Pearson, Archer, 684
Pearson, John, 685
Pearson, Thurston, 685
Pearson & Son, 685
Peck, William, 686
Peck & Palmer, 686
Peote, James, 689
Rosilin, Hugh, 766
Rustland, William, 773
Scarfe, Charles & Co., 788
Scott, John, 790
Shikins, Edward, 811
Simpson, Thomas, 816
Smith, Chester, 825
Smith & Tyler, 836
Spi(l)kins, Edward, 844
Stafford, Richard, 847
Stennett, —, 852
Teesdale, Jospeph, 880
Thompson, George, 885
True, Rice, 906
Tuxford, John Lefevere, 914
Tyler, St John, 915
Wake, John, 933
Watson, Edward, 948
Williamson, Ann, 983
Williamson, John, 983
Williamson, Joseph, 983
Wilson, Jekyl, 987
Boswell, 705, 791
Bothman, John, 367
Botley (Hants.): Oughton, Mary,
667
Bottom, Joshua, 349
Bottomley & Walker, 935
Bouch, Thomas, 563
Boucher, John, 91
Boughton (Cheshire): Artingstall,
J., 20
Boughton House (Northants.):
Belchier, John, 59
Davies, Roger, 229
Du Chesne, Gideon, 257
Grimstead, Joseph, 375
Jensen, Gerrit, 486, 487
Lapierre, Francis, 528
Moore, James snr, 618, 619
Parisels, Marie, 673
Paudevin, John, 681
Pelletier, John, 687
Pelletier, Renee, 687
Pelletier, Thomas, 687
Roberts, Thomas & Richard, 753
Stockdale, Mrs Mary, 857
Verhuyck, —, 921

Boulton, Benjamin, 84
Boulton, Charles, 413, 896
Boulton, George, 84
Boulton, I., 814
Boulton, Isaac, 4
Boulton, John, 497, 575, 967
Boulton, Robert, 84
Boulton, Thomas, 84
Boulton, William, 84
Bouran, William, 93
Bourne, 47
Bourne, Lancelot, 458
Bourne (Lincs.):
  Andrew, John, 14
  Bray, John, 104
  Dewey, William, 242
  Phillips, William, 696
Bouvrier, Thomas, 535
Bowditch, George, 417, 497
Bower, Francis, 515
Bowerbank, 941
Bowers, Robert, 241
Bowes, 177
Bowler, Samuel, 587
Bowles, Barnard, 264
Bowood House (Wilts.):
  Adair, John & William, 2
  Cruse, Gabriel, 216
  Gale, Thomas, 327
  Hobcraft, John, 436
  Linfoot, Thomas, 543
  Linnell, John, 545
  Ludgates, —, 560
  Search, —, 792
Bowring, Francis, 261
Bowyer, Thomas, 563
Box, John, 650
Box, Philip, 655
Boyd, Robert Barton, 754
Boydell, 308
Boyden, Thomas, 873
Boyne, George, 53
Boynton Hall (Yorks.):
  Chippendale, Thomas snr, 167
  Cobb, John, 182
Bracey, William, 115, 190
Bracken, John, 782, 784
Brackey (Northants.): Whitmore,
  William, 969
Bradbery, John, 97
Bradbourne Hall (Kent): Levett,
  John, 539
Bradburn, 294, 531
Bradburn, John, 8, 332, 925
Bradburne, John, 316, 924, 927
Braddon (Cornwall): Ward,
  William, 944
Bradford, 815
Bradford (Yorks.):
  Aglen, George William, 5
  Anderson, John Wilson, 13
  Andrew, George, 14
  Archer, Edward, 17
  Aspinall & Fearnley, 22

Barraclough, John, 44
Bedford, William, 58
Boddy, John, 82
Boddy & Wharrie, 82
Booth, Nathan, 87
Brook, Thomas, 111
Dean, Isaac, 237
Driver, Thomas, 257
Graham & Farrer, 363
Green, James, 367
Green, John, 367
Hanson, John, 395
Hepworth, William, 423
Hill, Jonas, 431
Hirst, Jonathan, 434
Holroyd, Squire, 446
Honton, James, 447
Hughgill, John, 461
Hunter, James, 465
Hunton, James, 466
Hutton, James, 469
Illingworth, John, 471
Jackson, Thomas, 477
Kendall, William, 505
King, Daniel, 514
King, John, 514
King, Robert, 515
King, William, 515
Lord, Samuel, 555
Lowe, John, 557
Midgley, Robert, 605
Mills, Thomas, 611
Milnes, Enoch, 611
Miln(e)s, Henry, 611
Muff, William, 634
Newell, John, 642
Newhill, James, 642
Nicholson, William, 647
Nichols, Samuel, 646
Nutter, Joseph, 657
Nutter, Matthew, 657
Philip, Ward, 694
Richardby, James, 741
Sellers, John, 799
Shackleton, Thomas, 802
Shutt, John, 813
Spencer, William, 844
Stephenson, Moses, 854
Swaine, William, 866
Swithenband, John, 868
Thornton, James, 890
Thornton, John, 890
Thorp, George, 891
Velin, John, 921
Weatherill, Joseph, 953
Wilkinson, James, 976
Wilkinson, Thomas Jowett, 977
Williamson, Joseph, 983
Wyrill, Robert, 1011
Yewdale, J., 1013
Bradford, Thomas, 202
Bradford-on-Avon (Wilts.):
  Batchelor, Samuel, 48
  Montague, John, 616

Moore, James, 620
Pluriet, Clem, 703
Pelvin, J., 688
Spackman, Thomas, 841
Bradley, 110, 474
Bradley, George, 117, 828
Bradshaw, 9
Bradshaw, George, 652
Bradshaw, George Smith, 100, 783
Bradshaw, James, 288
Bradshaw, Joseph, 647
Bradshaw, Michael, 460, 764, 782,
  838
Bradshaw, Richard, 756, 783
Bradshaw, William, 98, 590, 592,
  628, 754, 783
Brady, Philip, 951
Braem, Jasper, 104
Brafield, Edward, 97
Bragg, 698
Bragg, William, 487
Brailsford, John, 355
Brailsford, William, 355
Braint, Andrew, 320
Braintree (Essex):
  Barret, Benjamin, 44
  Bianchi, Nicholas, 70
  Joscelyne, Benjamin, 499
  Owens, Thomas, 668
  Parish, Joseph, 673
  Shoobridge, Richard, 812
Braithwaite, 908
Braithwaite, Ebenezer, 497
Braithwaite, Samuel, 751, 756, 907
Braithwaite, William, 190, 238, 346
Braman, William, 575
Bramham (Yorks.):
  Pearson, John, 685
  Wood, John, 997
Bramhope (Yorks.): Baron, Thomas
  jnr, 43
Bramley (Yorks.):
  Midgley, John, 605
  Thompson, John, 887
Brampton (Cumb.):
  Bonnin, James, 86
  Heward, John, 425
  James, Robert, 479
  Latimar, D., 529
  Lattimer, James, 529
  Little, Joseph & Robert, 550
  Parker, John, 674
  Robson, Philip, 761
  Turpin, William, 913
Brampton House (Hunts.):
  Mutton, William, 637
  Snell, William, 836
Brancepeth Castle (Co. Durham):
  Wright, Richard & Elwick,
  Edward, 1008
Brand, George, 225, 508
Brander, Edward, 786
Brandon (Suffolk):
  Garner, James, 331

Green, J., 367
Grief, J., 373
Webber, Benjamin, 954
Brandreth, Charles, 915, 916
Brandsby Hall (Yorks.):
    Reynoldson, George, 740
    Rogers, —, 763
Branson, Richard, 527
Branstore, William Augustus, 103
Brants, George jnr, 102
Brasenose Hall (Oxford): Frogley,
    Arthur, 322
Brathwait, Ebenezer, 101
Brathwaite, 908
Brathwaite, Ebenezer, 101
Brathwaite, Samuel, 101-2
Brathwaite, William, 102, 125, 657
Braughin (Herts.): Pinman, George,
    699
Braxted Park (Essex):
    Burnett, Thomas, 131
    Cross, Edmund, 213
    Gossett, James, 359
    Jarman, Ann, 481
    Kendall, William, 505
    Noon, Lancaster, 651
    Rayner, William, 731
    Sewell, George, 801
    Shakespear, —, 802
    Vile, William, 926
    Williams, Thomas, 982
Bray, Charles, 933
Bray, Jeremiah, 743
Breadeston (Norfolk): Brook,
    William, 111
Breakspear, George, 205
Bream, Samuel, 70, 120, 210, 326,
    858
Brekell, William, 104-5
Brennand, Robert, 40
Brentford (Middlx):
    Dear, Charles & Son, 238
    Heap, Robert, 417
    Lewis, Richard, 540
    Perrott, Thomas, 691
    Pickering, James, 697
    Ratcliff(e), M., 728
Brentwood (Essex): Winterburn,
    John, 993
Brereton, William, 835
Breteuil, John, 597
Brett, 724, 835
Brett, Michael, 16
Brewer, C., 106
Brewood (Staffs.):
    Daw, William, 233
    Price, Thomas, 716
Brice, 433
Bridge, 14
Bridge, John, 72, 711
Bridgen, 328
Bridges, Charles Holme, 334
Bridgewater (Som.): Hartnall,
    Andrew, 407

Bridgnorth (Salop):
    Adams, William, 4
    Ball, Joseph, 35
    Davis, Owen, 232
    Down(e), Edward, 254
    Downes, Edward snr, 254
    Gower, Edward, 361
    Gower & Powell, 361
    Had, Robert, 381
    Hall, Henry, 385
    Haslewood, Henry, 409
    Hunter, —, 465
    Jones, Dodo, 494
    Longford, John, 555
    Meers, John, 600
    Perry & Phillips, 692
    Southwell, Thomas Baker, 840
    Townshend, Thomas, 902
Bridgwater (Som.):
    Barrington, William, 44
    Bult, Robert, 128
    Butt, Robert, 138
    Date, Richard, 227
    Davis, John Giles, 232
    Glover, William, 345
    Higgins, Samuel, 428
    Hobbs, George, 435
    Jerrett, Henry, 487
    Knight, Elizabeth, 519
    Knight, James, 519
    Knight, William Jeffries, 520
    Laroche, William, 528
    Lee, Samuel, 535
    Long, Sarah, 554
    Manchip, John, 572
    Nutt, Thomas, 657
    Priest, William, 717
    Rogers, Samuel, 763
    Roper, Edwin, 765
    Saunders, Alfred, 782
    Slocombe, Thomas, 821
    Trevillian, George, 904
    Williams, Mary, 981
    Williams, Thomas, 982
    Wills, Robert, 985
    Wyburn, Job, John, 1011
Bridlington (Yorks.):
    Allison, Robert, 11
    Bielby, Matthew, 71
    Bielby, William, 71
    Binninton, Foster, 73
    Brown, J., 114
    Dixon, Henry, 246
    Ellis, Burton, 275
    Harrison, William, 405
    Holland, Robert, 442
    Meek, Samuel, 600
    Seller, William, 799
    Wardell, John, 944
    Winteringham, William, 993
Bridport (Dorset):
    Button, William, 139
    Kipping, J., 516
    Loveridge, James, 557

Margrie, Jacob, 574
Orley, Robert, 665
Power & Pavey, 711
Saunders, Henry, 782
Snell, John, 836
Woodward, William, 1001
Bridwell House (Dorset): Seddon,
    George, 796
Brierley (Yorks.): Banks, Benjamin,
    37
Brierley Hill (Staffs.): Gill, William,
    340
Brigg (Lincs.):
    Kennington, William, 508
    Leggott, David, 537
    Parker, Joseph, 674
    Robinson, —, 756
    Robinson, Francis, 757
    Schofield, William, 789
    Schorfell, Thomas, 789
    Smith, Charles, 825
    Thompson, William, 888
    Wood, Thomas, 998
Briggens Park (Herts.): Hutt, John,
    468
Briggins, Griffith, 707
Briggs, John, 605, 972
Brigham, Nicholas, 739
Brighouse (Yorks.):
    Greenwood, William, 369
    Hammerton, George, 391
    Lenton, John, 538
Bright, 33
Brighton (Sussex):
    Ackroyd, Jane & Sons, 2
    Alderton, Henry, 7
    Alderton, J., 7
    Alderton, Thomas, 7
    Alderton, William, 7
    Andre, Edward, 14
    Ashton, A., 21
    Ashton, Simeon, 21
    Atkins, James, 23
    Attree, Henry, 25
    Aucock, T., 25
    Barber, Robert, 39
    Barber, Thomas, 39
    Bartlett, Henry, 46
    Bartlett, T., 46
    Beeves, Josiah, 59
    Bennett, Richard, 65
    Billingshurst, Edward, 72
    Blaber, Oliver, 76
    Bleber, —, 76
    Bloomfield, William, 81
    Boore, Sam(p)son, 87
    Bowman, Robert, 93
    Bowman, William, 93
    Boxall, William, 94
    Brewer, Francis, 106
    Brewer, Joseph, 106
    Brookes, William, 111
    Brown, Thomas, 118
    Brown, William, 119

Brighton

Bryant, Mathew, 122
Bryant, Matthew & Sophia, 122
Bryer, Thomas, 123
Budd, Charles, 124
Buncher, W., 128
Burtenshaw, Richard, 134
Buzzacott, A., 139
Byer, Thomas, 139
Dancaster, George, 225
Davis, Benjamin, 231
Donne, James, 250
Dorney, William, 251
Dudman, John, 258
Dyer, Nicholas, 263
Garbut, Joseph, 329
Garden, William & Co., 329
Gawan, Curtis, 333
Geoff, John, 335
Gites, John jnr, 344
Goddard, Isaac, 346
Goddard, John, 346
Goff, —, 348
Goff, Henry, 348
Gordon, Norman, 357
Grant, Peter, 364
Grantham, George, 364
Gray & Hall, 366
Grover, Robert, 376
Guildford, James, 378
Hammond, William, 392
Harding, Thomas, 396
Hassocks, Nathaniel, 409
Heald, Daniel, 417
Hewlett, Charles, 426
Hill, Edward, 430
Hill, Thomas, 431
Hill, William, 432
Hitchins, —, 435
Hodgson, Thomas, 438
Holmes, William, 446
Houlden, William, 452
House, George, 452
Howell, Robert, 455
Humphrey, C. & George, 463
Humphrey, William, 463
Humphreys, George, 463
Hunt, Benjamin, 464
Hunt, Sarah, 465
Hunt & Marchant, 465
Huskisson, Matthew, 467
Huskisson & Co., 467
Hutchings, Edward, 467
Hutchins, John, 467
Izard, John, 474
Jackson, C., 475
Jackson, Charles, 475
Jackson, John Matthew, 476
Jaffries, Henry, 483
Jarvis, Alfred, 481
Jeffery, Richard, 382
Johnson, Nicholas, 490
Johnson, William, 493
Johnson & Garbutt, 493
Juniper, —, 500

Kilminster, Matthew, 512
Knapp, Thomas, 518
Lansdell, George, 527
Lansdell, James, 527
Lansdell, John, 527
Lansdell, Stephen, 527
Lansdell & Moppett, 528
Lashmar, Charels, 528
Lloyd, James, 550
Lower & Sons, 558
Lulham, Thomas, 560
Mallender, Paul, 571
Marshall, D., 577
Marshall, George, 577
Marshall, James, 578
Marshall, Thomas, 579
Mason, William, 584
Middleton, & Co, 605
Mills, James Henry, 610
Mitchell, George, 613
Mitchell, J., 613
Mitten, William, 614
Morris, Abraham, 627
Morris, Edward, 628
Morris, John Witten, 628
Norman, Gordon, 651
Nye, —, 657
Nye, Isaac, 658
Offord, James, 661
Page, John, 669
Parmer, William, 676
Pasco, William, 679
Patching, Henry, James, 679
Peircey, Gabriel, 687
Penn, Thomas, 688
Pepper, William, 690
Piercy, Gabriel, 698
Pocock, William, 704
Pope, Henry, 706
Pritchard, William, 718
Pruden, Elizabeth, 719
Pyecroft, John, Samuel, 723
Riddles, William, 746
Robertson, George, 755
Robertson, M.A., 755
Robinson, John, 758
Rothwell, James, 767
Rumball, Charles Wilson, 770
Saunders, Edward, 782
Saunders, John, 782
Saunders, Reuben, 785
Saunders, Thomas, 785
Saunders, William, 786
Shearine, —, 806
Shepheard, —, 807
Shoosmith, Robert, 812
Shoulder, James, 812
Sicklemore, Henry, 814
Slight & Robertson, 821
Smith, Edward, 825
Smith, J., 827
Smith, William, 834
Soper, —, 839
Souch, Frederick, 839

Stanbury, Philip, 848
Stepney, Samuel, 854
Stiles, Henry, 856
Stoddard, William, 857
Stubs, —, 863
Thompson & Beves, 888
Toppin, Edwin & Son, 899
Tranter, S., 902
Tully, John, 908
Upton, John James, 918
Upton, William, 918
Verral, —, 922
Verrall, Henry, William, 922
Vick, Christopher Wren, 922
Walker, George, 935
Walker, Lucy, 936
Ward, John, 943
Watts, James, 951
Weller, Samuel, 957
Weller, William, 957
White, Frederick, 965
Wilson, George, 987
Wood, Benjamin, 996
Wood, Frederick, 996
Wood, Thomas, 998
Wood & Sons, 998
Wymark, James, 1011
Wyndham, George, 1011
Brighton: Castle Hotel Assembly
  Rooms: Chippendale, Thomas
  snr, 168
Brighton Pavilion (Sussex):
  Ashlin, William, 21
  Bailey, Edward, 30
  Colbron, William, 186
  Collins, William, 189
  Crace, John & Sons, 206
  Cuff, Thomas, 217
  Elward, George & Marsh,
  William, 277
  Ferraro, Peter, 298
  Folker, Samuel Sheppard, 308
  France & Banting, 317
  Fricker & Henderson, 322
  Goertz, H.L., 347, 348
  Jones, Robert, 496
  Le Gaigneur, Louis Constantin,
  536
  McBean, Anne, 563
  Marshall, John, 579
  Mealing, William, 599
  Miller, William, 609
  Morel, Nicholas and Morel &
  Hughes, Robert, 623
  Newton, James, 644
  Richards, Hugh, 741
  Sanders & Colbron, 779
  Saunders, John, 782
  Saunders, Thomas, 785
  Seddon, George, 797
  Turner, Thomas, 912
  Vick, Christopher Wren, 923
  Watts, James, 951
  Wyatt, Edward, 1010

Brisco, Richard, 376
Bristol:
  Abbott, Thomas, 1
  Abel, William, 1
  Ackery, J., 2
  Adams, Richard A., 3
  Allard, John, 9
  Allen, Anthony, 9
  Allen, Henry Jnr, 10
  Allen, James, 10
  Allen, John, 10
  Allen, Robert, 10
  Allen, Thomas, 10
  Allen & Foster, 10
  Andrewes, Grace, 14
  Andrew(e)s, Mary, 14
  Andrewes, Thomas, 14
  Andrews, John, 14
  Andrews, Matthew, 14
  Annely, John, 15
  Anson, G., 15
  Anson, John, 15
  Anstice, William, 15
  Anstie, Samuel, 15
  Arnold, Richard, 19
  Arthur, William, 20
  Atterbury, Michael, 25
  Attwood, John, 25
  Austin, John, 26
  Badham, John (& Co), 29
  Badham, Richard, 29
  Badham, Thomas, 29
  Bailey, James, 30
  Bailey, William, 30
  Baily, John, 31
  Baker, Edward Jordan, 32
  Baker, James, 32
  Baker, R., 33
  Baker, Richard, 33
  Baker, William, 33
  Ball, G., 35
  Banister, George, 36
  Barnard, James, 42
  Barnes, Samuel, 42
  Barnett, F., 43
  Barr, Mary, 43
  Barrow, Lancelot, 45
  Bartlett, Henry, 46
  Bartlett, James, 46
  Bartlett, James Henry, 46
  Bartley, M.A., 46
  Bastable, Esarhaddon, 48
  Bastable, Jonah, 48
  Bastable, Jonathan, 48
  Batchelor, Walter, 48
  Battle, Joseph, 50
  Baugh, Francis, 50
  Bauley, John, 52
  Bawden, J., 51
  Baxter, Francis, 51
  Bayley, George, 52
  Beard, John, 55
  Beavan, Thomas, 56
  Becks, Frederick, 57

  Beeson, Joseph, 59
  Belcher, Benjamin, 59
  Bell, Francis, 61
  Bennet, Stephen, 64
  Bennett, George, 64
  Bennett, John, 65
  Bennett, Samuel, 65
  Bennett, W.C., 65
  Berrow, Lancelot, 67
  Berry, James, 67
  Berry, John, 67
  Berry, Joseph, 68
  Bevan, John, 69
  Bevan, Richard, 69
  Bidgood, John, 71
  Biggs, John, 71
  Bird, Stephen, 74
  Birtill, Joseph, 75
  Bishop, John, 76
  Bishop, Samuel, 76
  Blackburn, William, 77
  Blatchford, Thomas, 80
  Bliss, William, 81
  Board, Hannah, 82
  Board, James, 82
  Boley, John, 83
  Boley, Robert, 83
  Bolwell, Sarah, 84
  Bolwell, William, 84
  Bowden, Joseph, 92
  Bowen, Matthew, 93
  Bowther, Laurence, 93
  Boyce, John, 94
  Bracey, William, 95
  Bradburn, John, 97
  Brain, John, 101
  Bray, Caleb, 103
  Brett, William, 105
  Brice, Edward, 106
  Brice, Mary, 107
  Bright, William, 108
  Bristow, James, 108
  Brook, Benjamin, 110
  Brookshaw, Ann, 112
  Brookshaw, George, 112
  Broome, Samuel, 112
  Brown, Ebenezer, 113
  Brown, Henry, 114
  Brown, John, 116
  Brown, Joseph, 116
  Brown, Richard, 117
  Brown, Samuel, 118
  Buckle, William Glazeby, 124
  Bucknall, William, 124
  Budd, William, 124
  Bull, Joseph, 125
  Bullen, James, 126
  Bullock, George, 128
  Burchen, W., 129
  Burge, John, 130
  Burnaford, Thomas, 131
  Burnet & Painter, 131
  Burnett, William, 132

  Burroughs, Samuel Adolphus, 133
  Burt, John, 134
  Bush, John, 136
  Bush & Cheppett, 136
  Butler, Hester, 137
  Davie, Ben & Sarah, 228
  Davies, James, 229
  Davies, James Smithers, 229
  Davies, James Swithen, 229
  Davies, John, 229
  Davies, Thomas, 230
  Davis, Benjamin, 230
  Davis, Charles, 231
  Davis, Isaac, 231
  Davis, J., 231
  Davis, Mary, 232
  Davis, Robert, 232
  Davis, Thomas, 232
  Davis, William, 233
  Dawre, George, 234
  Day, Anthony, 236
  De Guidice, Anthony, 238
  Deacon, Zephania, 237
  Dempsey, William, 240
  Dennis, Charles, 240
  Deverell, Joseph, 242
  Dinning, William, 245
  Domer, Robert, 250
  Donovan, Daniel, 250
  Down & Delatouche, 254
  Downing, George R., 254
  Drake, H., 255
  Drew, John, 256
  Driver, John, 256
  Driver, Richard, 256
  Dyke, William, 263
  Eagle, Lot, 264
  Eames, John & Robert, 264
  Eames, Robert, 264
  Earl, Samuel, 264
  Edwards, Charles, 269
  Edwards, George, 269
  Edwards, John, 270
  Edwards, William, 271
  Edy, George jnr, 271
  Elliott, —, 272
  Elliott, William, 274
  Ellis, John, 275
  Ellis, Judith, 275
  Ellis, Walter, 275
  Ellis, William, 275
  Embley, Samuel, 279
  Embley, William, 280
  Emerson, Joseph, 280
  Emery, James, 280
  Eplett, Charles, 281
  Evans, G., 284
  Evans, George, 284
  Evans, John, 284
  Evans, William, 285
  Evatt, John, 285
  Gadd, Thomas, 326
  Gamage, Thomas, 328

Bristol

Gee, John, 334
Geronimo, Peter, 335
Gerrard, G.W., 335
Gibbs, Thomas, 336
Gibson, Robert, 338
Gifford, Joseph, 338
Gillam, Joseph, 340
Gillard, Ann, 340
Gillard, Henry, 340
Gillard, John, 341
Gillard, John Oswald, 340
Gillett, John, 341
Gillett, John jnr, 341
Gilvin, Joshua, 344
Godfrey, Isaac, 346
Godfrey, John, 347
Godfrey, William, 347
Goldsworthy, Robert, 348
Gordon, William, 357
Gorton, William, 358
Gorton & Parker, 358
Goss, Miss Martha, 358
Gough, Abraham, 359
Gould, William, 360
Grainger, Thomas, 363
Grant, Joseph, 364
Grant, Walter, 364
Green, John, 367
Green, Sarah, 367
Green, William, 368
Green & Co., 368
Griffiths, John, 374
Griffiths, Richard, 375
Griffiths, Samuel, 375
Griffiths, Thomas, 375
Grigg, James, 375
Grigg, William, 375
Groves, John, 376
Gulley, John, 378
Gullifer, James, 378
Guyer, Thomas, 381
Haddock, Benjamin, 382
Hague, Josiah, 382
Hall, George, 385
Hall, Jesse, 385
Hall, Joseph, 386
Hall, Joseph Mayor, 386
Hancock, John, 392
Hands, Benjamin, 394
Hands, Jonathan, 394
Handsombody, E.& L., 394
Handsombody, Frederick, 394
Handsombody, J.& L., 394
Hanks, John, 394
Hanson & Parsons, 395
Harris, Francis, 400
Harris, Henry, 400
Harris, John, 401
Harris, Maurice, 402
Harris, Shepherd, 402
Harris, Thomas, 402
Harris, William, 403
Hart, Joseph, 406
Hartland, William jnr, 406

Hartland, William snr, 406
Harwell, Thomas jnr, 408
Haskens, Joseph, 409
Haskins, Edward, 409
Haskins, James, 409
Hathwell, J., 410
Hawker, George, 412
Hawley, —, 413
Hayes, John, 414
Hayes, Shephard, 414
Haynes, William, 415
Heath, Charles, 418
Heness, Richard, 421
Henry jnr., 10
Herbert, Peter, 423
Herring, Ann, 423
Hewlett, John, 426
Hiatt, William, 426
Hicks, Peter, 428
Hillier, Ann, 432
Hill, James, 430
Hill, Jonathon, 431
Hill, William C., 431
Hinds, J., 433
Hingston, James, 433
Hingston, Thomas, 433
Hippisley, Edward & Britten, Stephen, 434
Hiscox, John, 434
Hitchcock, Abraham, 434
Hitchings, John, 434
Hitchings, William & Co., 434
Hobbs, Samuel, 435
Hodges, Joseph, 437
Hodges, Thomas, 437
Holbeach, —, 440
Holbrook, George, 440
Holbrook, Richard, 440
Holbrook, William, 440
Holder, Nathan, 441
Holder, Samuel, 441
Hole, Amos, 441
Hollandish, Andrew, 442
Hollandish, John, 442
Hollister, John, 443
Holman, James, 444
Holman, John, 444
Hooper, H., 447
Hooper, William, 448
Hope, John, 448
Hopkins, John, 448
Hopkins, Richard, 448
Hors(e)ley, Richard, 451
Horsley, John, 451
Hoskins, Charels, 451
Hoskins, Mary, 451
Hoskins, Mrs Rachel, 451
Houlton, Gracious, 452
Howe(l), James, 455
Howell, John, 455
Howell, Mary, 455
Howell & Son, 456
Hoyle, William, 456
Hudson, David, 458

Hughes, John, 461
Hughes, Richard, 461
Hughes, Walter, 461
Hughes, William, 461
Hulbert, Edwin, 461
Humberstone, James, 462
Humberstone, L., 462
Humberstone, Matthew, 462
Humberstone, Thomas Garland, 462
Hunt, Anthony, 464
Hunt, Henry, 464
Hunt, Richard, 465
Ifield, E.C., 470
Illing, Susannah, 471
Inch, John, 471
Ingram, George, 472
Ingram, Stephen, 472
Ivey, J., 474
James, Joseph, 479
James, Richard, 479
James, Robert, 479
James, T.& G., 480
James, Thomas, 480
James, William, 480
Jameson, James, 480
Jarrett, John, 481
Jarrit, Henry, 481
Jayne, John, 481
Jaynes, John, 481
Jeanes, Charles, 482
Jeanes, Richard, 482
Jefferies, James W., 482
Jefferies, William, 482
Jenkins, Francis, 483
Jenkins, James, 483
Jenkins, John, 484
Jenkins & Brock, 484
Jenkins & Speed, 484
Jerritt, James, 487
Jerritt, John, 488
Joacham, James, 488
Johnston, D., 493
Jones, Aaron, 493
Jones, Ann, 494
Jones, George, 494
Jones, James, 495
Jones, John, 495
Jones, Richard, 496
Jones, Samuel, 496
Jones, Thomas, 497
Jones, William, 496, 497, 498
Jones, William Lewis, 498
Joy, Heronles, 499
Keeler, Jabez, 502
Kendall & Son, 505
Kendrick, Edward, 505
Kidson, John, 511, 512
Kilmister, Matthew, 512
Kindon, G. & Co, 513
Kindon, Henry, 513
King, Benjamin, 514
King, Charles, 514
King, Peter, 515

Kingdom, John, 515
Kingston, Thomas, 516
Kingston, William, 516
Kirby, Joseph, 516
Knight, John, 519
Knight, Philip, 519
Lancaster, George, 524
Landcastle, John, 524
Lane, John & Co., 525
Langford, Joseph, 525
Langshaw, William, 527
Lankford, Joseph, 527
Lankford, Robert, 527
Lawrence, Thomas, 531
Lawrence, William, 531
Laycock, G.H., 532
Leach, Martha, 533
Leake, William, 533
Leech, John, 535
Legg, William, 536
Levy, Joseph, 539
Lewis, Isaac, 540
Lewis, John, 540
Lewis, Newton, 540
Lewis, Thomas, 541
Libbey, Richard, 541
Lloyd, Henry, 550
Lockier, James, 552
Locock, W.R., 553
Lombardini, S., 554
London, James, 554
Long, Peter, 554
Maby, Thomas, William, 563
McCarthy, George Packer, 564
M'Carthy, John, 564
M'Donald, G.F., 564
Maddern, John, 569
Maddock, Elias, 569
Male, Robert, 570
Mapleson, Charles, 574
Marshall, James, 577
Marsh, Henry, 576
Marsh, James, 576
Marston, William, 580
Martin, James, 581
Martin, Thomas, 581
Martin, William, 582
Masters, James, 585
Matthew, John, 586
Matthews, John, 587
Matthews, Thomas, 587
Mayers, Morris, 589
Maynard, Braddick, 598
Maynard, Joseph, 598
Mease, Thomas, 600
Melsam, John, 601
Merrick, Joseph, 603
Merrick, William, 603
Millard, William, 607
Miller, John, 608
Miller, Joseph, 609
Millett, Stephen, 609
Mitchell, Francis, 613
Mittens, T., 614

Mitton, John, 614
Mitton, Thomas, 614
Moakes, Isaac, 650
Moffett, James, 615
Mogridge, William, 615
Montague, John, 616
Moody, Joseph, 616
Moor, Dennis, 617
Moore, Demus, 618
Moore, John jnr, 620
Moore, John Lawrence, 620
Moores, John, 622
Morgan, John, 625
Morgan, Miles, 625
Morgan, William, 626
Morris, Ann, 627
Morris, William, 629
Morrow, Richard, 630
Muggleworth, Henry, 634
Nash, Goodwin, 638
Nash, Mrs, 638
Nash, Timothy, 639
Naylor, Henry, 639
Newall, John, 641
Newall, John jnr, 641
Newbery, David, 642
Newbery, Matthew, 642
Newman, James, 643
Newman, William, 644
Northcote, Ann, 655
Northcote, Richard, 655
Norvell, John, 656
Nottingham, John, 656
Nowell, John, 656
Offord, James, 661
Ogborn, Samuel, 661
Okey, Caleb, 662
Onion, Edward, 664
Orchard, William, 664
Owen, Francis, 667
Owen, John, 667
Owen, Samuel Middleton, 668
Paine, John, 670
Painter, Daniel, 670
Painter, Isaac, 670
Painter, Thomas, 670
Painter, William, 670
Pallin, Elias, 671
Pallin, Elizabeth, 671
Pallin, Henry, 671
Palmer, John, 671
Parfit, Owen, 673
Parfitt, Thomas, 673
Park, Walter Archibald, 673
Park, William, 673
Parker, James, 674
Parker, John, 674
Partridge, Thomas, 678
Pater, George, 679
Pater, Henry, 679
Paty, James, 681
Paty, Thomas, 681
Paty, William, 681
Payne, Isaac, 682

Payton, Edmund, 683
Payton, Thomas, 683
Peace, Thomas, 683
Peacock, Robert, 683
Pearce, Joseph G., 684
Pearce, Thomas, 684
Perkins, Thomas, 691
Perrin, William, 691
Perry, James, 691
Perry, Mrs, 691
Pethybridge, Joseph, 692
Petto, John, 693
Phelps, Isaac, 693
Philips, John, 694
Phillips, Benjamin, 695
Phillips, Mrs Benjamin, 694
Phillips, Edmund John, 695
Phillips, Edward, 695
Phillips, George, 695
Phillips, J.W., 695
Phillips, James, 695
Phillips, John, 695
Phillips, Joseph, 695
Phillips, S., 696
Phillips, Thaddeus, 696
Pickford, John, 697
Pidgeon, S., 697
Pike, John, 698
Pilkington, John, 699
Pingstone, John, 699
Point, John, 704
Pollard, John, 705
Pollard, William, 705
Polti, L., 705
Poole, George, 705
Pope, John, 706
Pope, Joshua, 706
Portch, Ambrose, 706
Post, Walter, 707
Potti, Louis, 708
Pottinger, William, 708
Powell, Hopkin, 710
Powell, Joseph, 710
Powell, William, 711
Price, Giles, 715
Prichard, George, 717
Prichard, Richard, 717
Primrose, William Ashton, 717
Proffer, William, 719
Prosser, William, 719
Pugh, William, 721
Pullen, —, 721
Purcell, John, 722
Purnell, John, 722
Purnell, Thomas, 722
Purnell & Lockier, 722
Purrier, Thomas, 722
Racey, Joseph, 725
Rafe, Thomas, 725
Randall, John, 727
Raworth, Thomas, 730
Raymond, Ann & Co., 730
Raymond, Christopher, 730
Reading, J.S., 732

Bristol

Reed, Thomas, 734
Rees, T., 735
Reynolds, Richard, 738
Richards, C.F., 741
Richards, Job, 742
Righton, Thomas, 748
Right, Thomas, 748
Roach, John, 751
Robbins, —, 751
Robbins, James, 751
Robertson, James, 755
Roberts, Thomas, 754
Roberts, William, 754
Robins, Charles, 755
Robins, James, 755
Robinson, William, 761
Rodman, Richmond, 762
Rogers, Francis & Daniel, 763
Rogers, James Sampson, 763
Rogers, William, 764
Roome, Thomas, 765
Rose, Thomas, 766
Routh, James, 768
Rowland, Thomas, 769
Russel, John, 771
Russell, John, 772
Russ, Robert, 771
Sage, George, John, 775
Sainsbury, Mary, 775
Salmon, Robert, 777
Sanders, Frances, 779
Sanders, Richard, 779
Sanders, William, 779
Sangar, Benjamin, 781
Sangar, James B., 781
Sartain, John Frederick, 781
Savery, Thomas, 786
Scantlebury, Thomas & Co., 788
Sceats, Joseph, 788
Scott, Thomas, 790
Scowles, Thomas, 791
Searl, John H., 792
Searle, Nicholas, 792
Searle, William, 792
Sevier, John, 801
Shaw, Daniel, 804
Shearing, —, 806
Shepherd, Henry, 807
Shewring, Daniel, 810
Shewring, Hester, 810
Shewring, Joseph, 810
Shewring, Luke snr, 810
Shewring, Luke jnr, 810
Shilstone, Michael, 811
Short, Isaac, 812
Showring, Daniel, 813
Sidnel, David jnr, 814
Simmonds, Thomas, 815
Simmons, J., 815
Simpson, Richard, 816
Sims, George, 817
Sircom, John, 818
Sircom, Richard, 818
Skinner, Thomas, 820

Small, L. & S., 822
Small, Lydia, 822
Small, Samuel, 822
Smart, Susannah, 823
Smith, Charles, 825
Smith, Fillia, 826
Smith, James jnr, 827
Smith, James snr, 827
Smith, John, 829, 830
Smith, Joseph, 830
Smith, Joseph & Co., 830
Smith, Samuel, 832
Smith, Sarah, 832
Smith, William, 834
Smith & King, 835
Snook, William, 837
Sollis, John, 838
Soloman, Barnet, 838
Solomon, I.L.& B., 838
Solomon, Susanna, 838
Southey, Simon, 840
Southey, W.& S., 840
Southey, William jnr, 840
Sowerby, Thomas, 841
Sparrow, Christopher, 841
Sprod, Elizabeth, 846
Spurrier, Charles, 846
Spurrier, Thomas, 846
Spurrier, William, 846
Stambury, William, 848
Stamp, Samuel, 848
Stephens, James, 852
Stephens, John, 852
Stephens, Nathaniel, 853
Stephens, R.M., 853
Stephens, William, 853
Stinchcomb, James, 856
Stinchcomb, John, 856
Stinchcomb, Sarah, 856
Stinchcomb, William, 856
Stoate, Richard, 857
Stock, George, James, 857
Stockwell, William, 857
Stockwell, William jnr, 857
Stone, George, 858
Stong, Samuel, 859
Stove, George, 860
Strange, S.B., 860
Stratford, Thomas, 861
Stringer, Gabriel, 862
Stringer, Nancy, 862
Stringer, Stephen, 862
Sturge, Harry, 863
Summers, William, 865
Sweet, Samuel, 868
Sweetman, George, 868
Symonds, William, 869
Taylor, James, 876
Taylor, Richard, 878
Thatcher, Joseph, 882
Thomas, Edward, 883
Thomas, Henry, 883
Thomas, John, 883
Thomas, Joseph, 884

Thomas, Mary, 884
Thomas, Robert, 884
Thomas, Susan S., 884
Thomas, William, 884
Thomas & Tucker, 885
Thompson, Simpson, 887
Thom(p)son, Stephen, 887
Thorn, Richard, 889
Tilford, Thomas, 894
Tilly, William, 895
Tindale, Atherlston, 895
Tippet, Francis, 895
Tong, Miss M., 899
Tong(u)e, Sarah, 899
Tool, J., 899
Torr, James, 900
Trapnell, Caleb, 902
Trapnell, Henry, 902
Trenaman, Joseph, 903
Trent, John, 903
Tudway, Charles, 908
Tuftin, Thomas, 908
Turnbull, William, 909
Turner, George, 909
Turner, George jnr, 909
Turner, James, 910
Turner, Joseph, 911
Turner, William Henry, 913
Tustin, Thomas, 914
Tyler, Joseph, 915
Tyndal(l), Athelston(e), 915
Urch, James, 918
Urio, John, 918
Vaughan, Edward snr, jnr, 920
Vaughan, Mary, 920
Vaughan, Robert, 920
Vaughan, Samuel, 921
Vaughan, Thomas, 921
Veal, William, 921
Vigor, M.G., 923
Vigor, Matthew, 923
Vigor, William, 923
Viner, John, 929
Viner, Robert, 929
Viney, Joseph, 929
Viney, Joseph jnr, 929
Vizer, Robert, 929
Voisey, William, 930
Wade, Nathaniel, 931
Waite, John, 932
Wait, Henry, 932
Walker, George, 935
Walker, John, 935, 936
Walley, Thomas, 940
Walters, Thomas, 941
Warner, Henry & Ebenezer,
Henry jnr, 945
Warren, William, 946
Waters, John, 941
Watkins, Christopher, 947
Watson, George, 949
Watts, Thomas, 951
Way, John, 952
Weaver, John, 953

Webb, Charles, 953
Webb, George, 953
Webb, John, 953
Webb, William, 954
Webber, Joseph, 954
Webley, John Clouter, 954
Welsh, Jacob, 958
Wensley, Richard, 958
West, William, 960
Westell, Thomas, 960
Weston, John, 961
Weston, Thomas, 961
Westwood, Thomas, 961
Weymouth, William, 962
White, Joseph, 966
White, Robert, 966
White, William, 967
Whitefield, James, 968
Whitehair, Benjamin Hollister, 968
Whitehair, H., 968
Widdicombe, M., 972
Wilcox, —, 978
Wildman, John, 974
Wilkin, W.& A., 975
Willey, Joseph, 979
Willey, Joseph jnr, 979
Willey, Mary, 979
Willey & Hughes, 979
Williams, Charles, 979
Williams, E., 979
Williams, Elijah, 979
Williams, J., 980
Williams, John, 981
Williams, John Powell, 981
Williams, Nathaniel jnr, 981
Williams, Samuel, 982
Williams, Sarah, 982
Williams, William, 982
Willis, John, 984
Willmott, William, 984
Wilmot, Thomas, 985
Wilmot, William, 986
Wilson, Anthony, 986
Wilway, George, 991
Wimble, William, 991
Winscomb, William, 992
Winter, L., 993
Wise, John, 993
Witherall, John, 994
Withers, John, 994
Wollen, William, 995
Wood, Abel, 995
Wood, James, 996
Wood, John, 997
Woodberry, Richard, 998
Woodeson, Elizabeth, 998
Woodeson, Fane, 998
Woodison, Jane, 999
Woodland, James, 999
Woods, John, 1000
Woods, Thomas, 1000
Woods, William, 1000
Wood, Thomas, 998

Wood, William, 998
Wood, William & Son, 998
Wooles, William, 1001
Wooles & Bailey, 1001
Worboys, G.B., 1002
Wright, Henry, 1005
Wright, Thomas, 1008
Wright, William, 1009
Wrighten, Thomas, 1009
Wyatt, Francis, 1010
Wyman, William, 1011
Yabbicom, William H., 1011
Yandell, Joseph, 1011
Yearbury, George, 1012
Young, James Mates, 1014
Young, John Mates, 1014
Bristol:
  Brislington Church: Landcastle, John, 524
  Christchurch:
    Court, William & Charles, 202
    Paty, William, 681
  7 St George St, for John Pinney (now the Georgian House Museum):
    Court, William & Charles, 202
    Evans, John, 284
    Gorton, William, 358
    Hingston, James, 433
    Wilway, George, 991
  Mansion House:
    Salmon, Robert, 777
    Trapnell, Henry, 902
  Moravian Chapel: Jones, Aaron, 493
  Redland Chapel: Paty, Thomas, 681
  Royal Exchange: Paty, Thomas, 681
  St John's Church: Hippisley, Edward & Britten, Stephen, 434
Bristow, John, 463
Britain, Richard, 929
Britisle, James, 226
Britten, Stephen, 434
Britwell (Oxon.):
  Horne, William, 450
  Hutton, James, 469
  Hutton, William, 469
Brixham (Devon):
  Minnis, James, 612
  Richards, Philip, 742
  Stephens, John, 853
Brixton, John, 754
Brixton (London):
  Harris, William, 403
  Humphrey, J.N. & Joseph, 463
Broadbent, Joseph jnr, 752
Broadbent, William, 72
Broadhurst: Dutton, John, 262
Broadlands (Hants.):
  Daguerre, Dominique, 223
  Harvey, —, 407
  Herve, Francois, 424

Hobcraft, John, 436
King, John, 514
Litchfield & Graham, 549
Mayhew, John & Ince, William, 592, 593, 596
Routledge, Christopher, 768
Simson, George, 817
Soederberg, Thomas, 838
Brocas, Richard, 422
Brock, 484
Brockbank, 737
Brockenhurst Park (Hants.):
  Bromwich, Thomas, 110
  Chippendale, Thomas snr, 167
  Gordon, John & Taitt, John & Richard, 357
  Hudson, —, 458
  Long, —, 554
  Murray, Alexander, 636
  Richardson, Francis, 743
  Thompson, —, 885
  Thompson, James, 886
Brocker, John, 111
Brocket Hall (Herts.): Chippendale, Thomas snr, 165, 166, 167
Broitehall, Henry, 204
Bromfield, Philip, 121
Bromhead, John, 112
Bromley, Edward, 22, 229
Bromley, William, 391
Bromley (Kent):
  Dunn, Edward, 260
  Dunn, Edward E., 260
  Dunn, George, 260
  Dunn, John, 260
  Dunn, Sarah, 260
  Dunn, William, 260
  Hill, James, 430
  Langland, William, 526
  Nettlefold, Abram, 641
  Nettlefold, John, 641
Bromley-St-Leonards (London):
  Lewis, Richard, 540
Brompton (Kent): Arlidge, Abraham, 17
Brompton (London):
  Armour, Henry, 18
  Arnold, George W., 19
  Goulding, Timothy, 360
  Martin, Edward, 580
  Maudsley, Henry, 587
  Thompson, George, 885
Bromsgrove (Worcs.):
  Bayliss, William, 52
  Blent, Charles, 81
  Blunt, Charles, 82
  Brooke, Joseph, 111
  Edwards, Thomas, 270
  Green, William, 368
  Holloway, John, 444
  Parker, Richard, 674
  Poole, Richard, 706
  Tomlinson, Richard, 898
  Webster, John & Richard, 955

Wildsmith, William, 974
Winnall, Richard, 992
Bromwich, Thomas, 474
Bromyard (Herefs.):
  Gough, Richard, 360
  Peell, Walter, 686
  Wilkinson, Thomas, 977
Brook, George, 66, 157, 281, 951
Brooke, 1015
Brooke, Francis, 616, 833
Brooke, Robert, 440, 764, 812
Brooks, 1015
Brooks, Francis, 111
Brooks, Robert, 111
Brooks, William, 111
Brookshaw, 801
Broome Park (Kent): Wyatt, James,
  1010
Broomfield, Philip, 121
Broseley (Salop):
  Gurbett, John, 380
  Hartshorne, George, 407
  Poole, Thomas, 706
Broshfield, William, 122
Brother, Henry, 337
Brotherhood, Samuel, 827
Brothers, John, 489, 584
Brotton (Yorks.): Stonehouse,
  Roger, 859
Brough (Westmld):
  Lambert, Thomas, 523
  Monkhouse, J., 616
Broughton, Christopher, 496, 844,
  991
Broughton, Henry, 471
Broughton (Lancs.):
  Barwick, James, 47
  Barwick, John, 47
  Hartley, George, 406
  Jackson, Henry, 475
  Pickthall, William, 697
  Potts, Thomas, 709
  Young, John, 1014
Broughton Hall (Yorks.):
  Brumfitt, Edward, 121
  Bul(l)man, Robert, 126
  Gillow, 343
  Miles, Henry & Edwards, John,
    606
  Proctor, Christopher, 719
  Syers, John, 869
  Trappes, Robert, 902
Brow Top (Cumb.): Grayson,
  William, 366
Browless, James, 641, 677
Brown, 107, 222, 645, 680, 769, 838
Brown, Anthony, 463
Brown, David, 578
Brown, George, 53, 258, 408
Brown, James, 101, 244, 337, 522,
  1001
Brown, John, 54, 95, 478, 495, 762,
  866, 906
Brown, John Conons, 249

Brown, Joseph, 509, 802
Brown, Ralph, 955
Brown, Richard, 270, 652
Brown, Robert, 613
Brown, Thomas, 160, 172, 191, 198,
  226, 959
Brown, William, 117, 235, 408, 647,
  677, 690, 989, 997
Browne, 862
Browne, Adam, 113
Browne, Benjamin, 819
Browne, E., 117
Browne, Ebenezer, 113
Browne, J.H., 114
Browne, James, 115
Browne, John, 104, 115, 370
Browne, Joshua, 365
Browne, Matthew, 98, 258, 291,
  384, 827, 828, 834, 983
Browne, Matthew snr, 116–17
Browne, Philip, 117
Browne, William, 119
Brownhill, Jonathan, 535
Brownhills (Staffs.): Walker, John,
  936
Brownjohn, George, 59
Brownshill Court (? Gloucs.):
  Viner, Henry, 929
Broxbourne Church (Herts.):
  Warren, Thomas, 946
Broxbournebury (Herts.): Price,
  John, 715
Bruce, 37, 143, 250, 771, 825, 950
Bruce, W., 719, 987, 991
Bruce, William, 23
Bruges (Belgium): Rudd, —, 770
Brumhead, John, 287
Brumley, Edward, 110
Brumwell, John, 287, 999
Brunning, John, 28, 264, 951
Brushfield, William, 157, 290
Bryanstone (Dorset): Mealyard,
  Martin, 599
Brydges, 841
Bryham, Simon, 933
Brynbella (Denbighshire): Mayhew,
  John & Ince, William, 598
Buchanan House (West
  Stirlingshire): Miles, W., 607
Buck, 27, 210
Buck, Henry, 290
Bucket, Joseph, 367
Buckingham, William, 213
Buckingham:
  Blake, Edward, 79
  Gilkes, Thomas, 340
  Gilkes, William, 340
  Haddon, Joseph, 382
  Hains, —, 383
  Jolliffe, Paul, 493
  Mould, Thomas, 633
  Palace, Wyatt, Edward, 1009
  White, John, 966

Willmore, Elizabeth, James &
  Son, 984
Wilmor, James, 985
Buckle, George, 335
Buckle, Joseph, 917
Buckler, Powell, 527
Budden, William, 139
Budleigh (Devon): Patch, Jno., 679
Budleigh Salterton (Devon):
  Hurdle, —, 466
Buggs, James, 460
Bull, James, 875
Bullen, 371, 629
Bullen, Henry, 368
Bullen, Jonathan, 125
Bullen, Thomas, 125
Bullock, George, 204, 371
Bullock, Jeremiah, 497
Bullock, Jeremy, 868
Bulmer, John, 859
Bunaford, Thomas, 131
Bunce, 954
Bungay (Suffolk):
  Leggett, John, 537
  Mayhew, Edward, 589
  Pipe, John, 700
  Rackham, Edward, 725
  Reynolds, John, 738
  Reynolds, Thomas, 738
  Rowe, Robert, 768
  Sears, William, 792
  Taylor, Nathaniel, 878
  Townsend, Samuel, 901
  Waller, John, 940
  Walter, John, 941
Bunny, Joseph, 578
Burbidge, William, 248
Burd, Peter, 254
Burdock, W., 141
Burford (Oxon.):
  Akers, Edward, 6
  Arkell, John, 17
Burge, John, 48
Burgess, 898
Burgoyne, Thomas, 1013
Burghley House (Lincs.):
  Coade, Eleanor and her
    successors, 181
  Cousin, Rene, 202
  Evans, Phineas, 284
  Fell, Lawrence, 295
  Harris, J., 400
  Jensen, Gerrit, 486
  Lapierre, Francis, 528
  Mayhew, John & Ince, William,
    592, 593, 594
  Newton, James, 644
  Searson, Wortley, 793
  Tat(h)am, Henry, 873
  Tipping, Benjamin, 895
  Tymperon, Robert, 915
  Watson, Samuel, 950
  Young, Thomas, 1015
Burkmire, William, 124, 723

Burley, James, 703
Burn, Isaac, 244
Burnell, 314
Burnet, Thomas, 471
Burnet, William, 316
Burnett, Christopher, 157
Burnett, Gilbert, 132
Burnett, James, 674
Burnett, Thomas, 162, 512
Burnham (Norfolk): Wilkerson, Thomas, 975
Burnham Market (Norfolk):
  Norman, Thomas, 653
  Norman, William, 653
  Readwin, Robert, 732
  Roy, William, 769
  Sanctury, James, 778
  Williamson, Robert, 983
Burnley, William, 246, 844
Burnley (Lancs.):
  Birtwistle, William, 75
  Darye, William, 227
  Davye, William, 233
  Gibson, William, 338
  Hargraves, William, 398
  Hargreaves, John, 398
  Hargreaves, Thomas, 398
  Hartley, William, 407
  Hudson, Thomas, 459
  Laycock, Daniel, 532
  Nicholson, John, 647
  Slater, John, 820
  Smith, Richard, 831
  Sutcliffe, William, 865
  Sutcliffe & Hartley, 865
  Whittaker, James, 969
Burns, Thomas, 37
Burnt Yates, Admiral Long's School (Yorks.): Peacock, Joseph, 683
Burrell, Charles, 135, 721
Burrell, Thomas, 1006
Burrough, John, 289
Burroughs, John, 289
Burrowes, Joseph, 914, 1001
Burrows, James, 133
Burrows, James snr, 134
Burrows, John, 727
Burrows, Joseph, 269, 312
Burrows, William, 133
Burslem (Staffs.):
  Barker, Thomas, 41
  Beardmore, George, 55
  Betteley, Henry, 69
  Boon(d),John, 86
  Bosens, Samuel, 88
  Bradburn, William, 97
  Eaton, Thomas, 265
  Mitchell, Richard, 614
  Nicklin, Thomas, 647
  Sant, Aaron, 781
  Stonier, William, 859
  Tittensor, Samuel, 896
  Willmott, John, 984
Burt, William, 204

Burton, Robert, 847
Burton, Samuel, 4, 38, 133, 157, 304
Burton, Thomas, 1003
Burton, William, 758
Burton (Staffs.): Egleston, Thomas, 271
Burton Constable (Yorks.):
  Atkinson, Caleb, 23
  Barry, William, 46
  Bennington, Henry, 66
  Best, George, 68
  Brooks, Thomas, 112
  Brown, Samuel, 118
  Chippendale, Thomas snr, 166, 167
  Chippendale, Thomas jnr, 168, 169
  Church, Thomas, 171
  Cowham & Clark, 203
  Crompton, Samuel, 211
  Dowbiggin(g), Thomas, 253
  Farrer, Richard, 291
  Fletcher, Roun(d)cival, 305
  Foster, Edmund, 311
  Foster, James & Edward, 311
  Hargrave, Jeremiah, 398
  Hargrave, Joseph, 398
  Higham, Thomas, 429
  Howell & Jones, 456
  Kettle, Henry, 511
  Lawson, James, 531
  Litchfield & Graham, 549
  Lowry, John, 558
  Luccock, William, 559
  Martyn, Thomas, 582
  Medforth, Flinton, 600
  Meggitt, Thomas, 600
  Miles, Henry & Edwards, John, 606
  Paulins & Coates, 682
  Piotti, James, 700
  Rawling, Charles, 729
  Reid, John, William, George, Anne(e) & James, 736
  Reynoldson, George, 739, 740
  Richardson, Christopher, 743
  Richardson & Son, 745
  Vial, —, 922
  Walker, Elizabeth, 934
  Walker, Robert, 937
  Walker, Thomas, 937
  Ward, Thomas, 944
  Webber, John, 954
  Wel(l)beloved, Charles, 956
  Wells, Gervase, 957
  Whitfield, Mrs, 969
  Wilton, J., 991
  Winning, John, 992
  Wright, Richard & Elwick, Edward, 1007, 1008
  Wrightson, William, 1009
Burton Court (Herefs.): Gar(d)ner, Samuel, 330

Burton Hall (Lincs.):
  Cobb, John, 183
  Hasert, Peter, 409
  Mayhew, John & Ince, William, 597
  Nix, George, 649
  Price, John, 715
Burton-upon-Trent (Staffs.):
  Appleby, John, 16
  Appleby, Joseph James, 16
  Appleby, Joseph jnr, 16
  Atterbury, James, 25
  Atterbury, Job, 25
  Atterbury, Michael, 25
  Atterbury & Dickinson, 25
  Baxter, William, 52
  Bellatti, Charles, 63
  Dollman, Thomas, 250
  Elliott, Daniel, 274
  Green, T., 367
  Heath, Richard, 418
  Holmes, Thomas, 446
  Hullard, Thomas, 462
  Hunt, John, 464
  Lakin, William, 521
  Lockett, John, 552
  Noon, William, 651
  Prynn, William, 720
  Shorthose, Joshua, 812
  Simpson, William, 817
  Smith, John, 829
  Staley, William, 848
Burwood Park (Surrey):
  Chippendale, Thomas jnr, 169
Bury (Lancs.):
  Appleton, Samuel, 16
  Bentley, John & Joseph, 66
  Brown, —, 113
  Bullen, Henry, 125
  Butterworth, James, 139
  Butterworth, Samuel, 139
  Daniels, Thomas, 225
  Downham, Joseph, 254
  Greenalgh, William, 368
  Hall, John, 385
  Harker, Thomas, 398
  Harrison, William, 405
  Howard, Robert, 454
  Ingold, Robert, 472
  Kay, James, 500
  Nuttall, James, 657
  Parkinson, John, 676
  Rogerson, George, 764
  Summerskill, Charles, 865
  Taylor, O., 878
  Tillott, Henry, 895
  Whittaker, James, 969
Bury St Edmunds (Suffolk):
  Bird, Richard, 74
  Boarsmith, Samuel, 82
  Bradbury, John, 97
  Bryant, William, 122
  Bullen, Ann, J. & T., 125
  Bullen, Mary, 126

Bullen, Thomas, 126
Bullen, Thomas George, 126
Bullon, J.G., 128
Dutton, Alexander, 262
Ely, James, 279
Ely, Joseph, 279
Guest, Ralph, 377
Hammond, William, 392
Hancock, —, 392
Harris, John, 401
Harrison, John, 404
Hill, John, 431
Hunter, Andrew, 465
Hunter, John, 465
Hunter, William, 466
Hunter & Son, 466
Jeneper, Samuel, 483
Macdowell, William, 565
Martin, Rob., 581
Matthews, Edward John, 586
Matthew(s), William, 587
Oakley, Thomas, 660
Oliver, Isaac, John, 663
Oliver, Laver, 663
Ramsey, William, 726
Richardson, Matthias, 744
Sale, William, 776
Shipman, John, 811
Simper, Robert, 815
Singleton, Thomas, 818
Sparrow, John, 841
Spenseley, Thomas, 844
Steward, Henry, 855
Sudbury, William Shipman jnr, 864
Trested, Thomas, 903
Walford, Thomas, 934
Watson, William, 950
Whitlee, Charles, 969
Bury St Edmunds Mansion House (Suffolk): Singleton, Thomas, 818
Bury St Edmunds Town Hall (Suffolk): Singleton, Thomas, 818
Busfield, Anthony, 458
Busfield, John, 458, 563
Bush, 169
Bushell, Edward, 125
Bushell, William, 895
Busswell, 788
Butler, 939
Butler, Philip, 502
Butler, Samuel, 313
Butler, Thomas, 17, 267, 626, 668, 669
Butter, 999
Butterfield, James, 812
Butterfield, Richard, 696
Buttifant, John, 303
Button, John, 488
Buxton (Derbs.):
Hebbirt, John, 419
Johnson, John, 490
Pott, Samuel, 707

Buxton Assembly Rooms (Derbs.):
Brailsford, J.W., 101
Brailsford, William, 101
Buzzard, 143
Byam, Frederick, 5
Byfield, 848
Byfield, Thomas, 139
Byles, John, 416
Bywater, John, 824

C

Cagill, Edward, 4
Calar, William, 266, 609
Calbreath, Robert, 160
Calcutta (India): Seddon, George, 796
Caldecote Hall (Warks.): Cox, Stephen, 205
Caldwell, William, 610
Caledon Castle (Co. Tyrone): Mayhew, John & Ince, William, 592, 596
Calke Abbey (Derbs.): Elward, George & Marsh, William, 279
Calkin, Thomas, 66, 914
Callendar House (Scotland): Davison, Sibella & Deacon, Thomas, 233
Callow, John, 142
Calloway, Henry, 225
Calne (Wilts.):
Lewis, John, 540
Rumming, William, 770
Wheeler, Daniel, 963
Calverley-cum-Farsley (Yorks.):
Jeffery, James, 483
Thompson, Joseph, 887
Wade, Edward, 930
Wade, James, 931
Calvert, Thomas, 577
Camberwell (London):
Allison, Thomas, 11
Barrett, Samuel, 44
Barritt, Samuel, 45
Bennet, J., 64
Bitterton, George, 76
Brock, James, 109
Grantham, John, 364
Griffiths, John, 375
Grimes, John & Thomas, 375
Hayward, James, 415
Hodgson, Richard, 438
Hodgson, Thomas, 438
Ingram, Thomas, 472
Mumford, Joseph, 635
Paine, Sampson, 670
Smith, Edward, 825
Smith, James, 827
Standerwick, G., 848
Standerwick, James, 848
Truscott, James, 906
Vigers, John, 923

Walker, R. jnr, 936
Webber, William, 954
Camborne (Cornwall):
Burall, Paul, 129
Woolcock, John, 1001
Cambridge:
Adams, John, 3
Andrews, John, 14
Ansell, William, 15
Atherton, Humphrey, 23
Austin, Cornelius jnr, 26
Austin, Cornelius snr, 26
Barnot, John, 45
Bath, William, 49
Bedells, John, 58
Bennington, Michael, 66
Benstead, James, 66
Betion, George, 69
Billups, Thomas, 72
Billups, William, 72
Blinkhorn, James Gleed, 81
Blomfield, Anne, 81
Boning, Thomas, 85
Bowman, George, 93
Bradwell, David jnr, 100
Brett, William, 105
Bretton, Stephen, 106
Brooker, George, 111
Bruce, J.H., 121
Brune, George, 122
Burbage, Grain, 129
Burton, Sam., 135
Butler, Jacob, 137
Dalby, William, 223
Davidson, Charles, 228
Day, Charles, 236
Dixon, Thomas Post, 247
Eaves, James, 265
Edwards, David, 269
Edwards, Thomas, 270
Etheridge, Thomas, 282
Evans, John, 284
Golding, Abraham, 348
Goode, William, 351
Gray, John, 365
Gray, John Godfrey, 365
Greaves, Thomas, 366
Greaves, Timothy, 366
Green, Robert, 367
Grubb, William, 376
Hadden, William, 382
Harley, James, 399
Harraden, Jabez Richards, 400
Hazlewood, Thomas, 416
Hills, Joseph, 432
Hills, Robert, 432
Hills, William, 432
Hilton, Richard, 432
Hopkins, William, 449
Hunt, Charles, 464
Hunt, James, 464
Hunt, John Greaves, 464
Hunt, William, 465
Ibberson, William Covey, 470

Isaacson, Philip, 474
Ivory, John, 474
Jarvis, Francis, 481
Johnson, Jeremiah, 490
Johnson, John, 490
Johnson, Robert, 490
Johnson, Thomas jnr, 492
Johnson, Thomas snr, 492
Jones, John, 495
Jones, William David, 498
Kirk, J., 516
Lane, Jacob, 525
Lawson, John, 532
Legge, Thomas, 536
Lunton, John, 561
Martin, William, 581
Mason, Thomas, 584
Mason, William, 584
Matthews, Nicholas, 587
Metcalfe, James, 604
Metcalfe, Robert, 604
Metcalfe, Thomas, 604
Metcalfe & Son, 604
Miller, Nathan, 609
Mills, Robert, 610
Morehen, Henry, 623
Morehen, John, 623
Moulder, Thomas, 633
Munns, Thomas, 636
Mutton, Henry, 637
Mutton, William, 637
Nutter, Thomas, 657
Oliver, William, 663
Peacock, Edmund, 683
Pearl, James Robert, 684
Peters, Thomas, 692
Pinkard, R., 699
Porter, John Barrick, 707
Prigg, Cooper, 717
Proston, Sarah, 719
Pyke, —, 723
Randall, George, 727
Redfarn, Daniel, 733
Reynolds, Thomas, 738
Richardson, Christopher, 743
Richardson, Edward, 743
Robinson, Joseph, 759
Roper, William, 765
Rose, William, 766
Rush, William, 771
Salmon, Robert, 777
Salmon, Samuel, 777
Salmon, William, 777
Saunders, Samuel, 785
Sharpe, C., 803
Sharpe, Thomas, 803
Sharpe, Thomas Edward, 804
Shuter, John, 813
Simkenson, Henry, 818
Simpson, Edward, 816
Smith, Elliot, 826
Smith, John, 828
Smith, Michael Joseph, 830
Smith, S.F., 831

Smith, William Heldon, 835
Smyth, James Samuel, 836
Squires, Samuel, 846
Starimer, Thomas, 850
Starmer, Richard, 850
Starr, Thomas, 850
Stiles, —, 856
Stiles, George, 856
Summers, James, 864
Swan, John, 867
Swan, William, 867
Tall, James, 870
Taylor, William, 880
Thompson, Edward, 885
Thompson, Edward jnr, 885
Thompson, Robert, 887
Thompson, William, 888
Thornton, James, 890
Tofts, William, 897
Turner, Henry, 910
Turner, James, 910
Turner, Thomas, 912
Wagstaff, Charles snr & jnr, 931
Wagstaff, Thomas, 932
Wakeman, Richard, 933
Wall, John, 939
Warland, Thomas, 945
Waterfield, John, 947
Wentworth, Daniel, 958
Wentworth, Joseph, 959
Wonfor, James, 995
Woodland, James, 999
Woodruff, George, 1000
Woodruff, Richard, 1000
Woodward, Francis, 1000
Woodward, John, 1000, 1001
Worseldine, John, 1003
Wright, —, 1004
Yorke, Bridget Nash, 1013
Yorke, Edward & successors, 1013
Cambridge:
  Corporation:
  Day, Charles, 236
  Isaacson, Philip, 474
  Holy Sepulchre Church:
  Wentworth, Joseph, 759
  St Edward's Church: Robinson, Joseph, 759
Cambridge University:
  Christ's College:
  Billups, Thomas, 72
  Billups, William, 72
  Grubb, William, 377
  Lunton, John, 561
  Moulder, Thomas, 633
  Peters, Thomas, 692
  Simpson, Edward, 816
  Divinity Schools:
  Willis, —, 983
  Emmanuel Chapel:
  Austin, Cornelius snr, 26
  Pearce, Edward, 684

Emmanuel College: Willis, John, 984
King's Chapel: Austin, Cornelius snr, 26
King's College Library: Hutt, John, 468
Magdalene College: Sympson, Thomas(?), 869
Pembroke College: Billups, William, 72
St John's College:
  Austin, Cornelius snr & jnr, 26
  Barrnot, John, 45
  Billups, Thomas, 72
  Blomfield, Anne, 81
  Bonnel(l), Thomas, 85
  Burton, Sam., 135
  Butler, Jacob, 137
  Greaves, Thomas, 366
  Greaves, Timothy, 366
  Gwinnel, William, 381
  Hutt, John, 468
  Ivory, John, 474
  Johnson, Thomas snr, 492
  Moulder, Thomas, 633
  Peters, Thomas, 692
  Pinkard, R., 699
  Proston(?), Sarah, 719
  Pyke, —, 723
  Richardson, Christopher, 743
  Smith, Elliot, 826
  Smith, John and successors, 828
  Swan, John, 867
  Williams, Henry, 980
  Woodruff, George, 1000
  Woodward, Francis, 1000
  Woodward, John, 1000
Senate House: Bladwell, John, 78
Sidney Sussex College: Robinson, —, 756
Trinity College:
  Andrews, John, 14
  Austin, Cornelius snr & jnr, 26
  Burton, Sam., 135
  Caiton, William, 140
  Greaves, Timothy, 366
  Grubb, William, 377
  Harraden (or Harredon), —, 400
  Ivory, John, 474
  Johnson, Thomas snr, 492
  Jones, William David, 498
  Lycett, Joseph, 562
  Moulder, Thomas, 633
  Prigg, Cooper, 717
  Pyke, —, 723
  Rayner, Thomas snr, 731
  Robinson, Joseph, 759
  Saunders, Samuel, 785
  Sharpe, C., 803
  Shutter, John, 813
  Smith, John and successors, 828
  Swan, John, 867
  Wakeham, Richard, 933

Wentworth, Joseph, 959
Woodruff, George, 100
Woodruff, Richard, 1000
Woodward, Francis, 1000
Woodward, John(?), 1001
Wright, —, 1004
Cambridge, William, 745
Camden Town (London):
  Edwards, William, 271
  Hammond, William, 392
  Hearne, J., 417
  Walford, C., 934
Came House (Dorset):
  Dobson, Thomas, 248
  Vile, William, 926
Camfield, Richard, 401, 938
Campbell & Bruce, 824, 825
Campfield, Richard, 403
Campion, 835
Campsall Hall (Yorks.): Cobb,
  John, 184
Canada:
  Newfoundland, St John's
  Government House: Pringle,
  John &
    Robert, 718
  Prince Edward Island
  Government House: Seddon,
  George, 797
  Uniacke House (Hants. Co.):
  Adams, George, 3
Canham, Richard, 697
Cannell, Hugh, 263, 834
Cannock (Staffs.): Birch, Geof., 73
Cannon Hall (Yorks.):
  Chippendale, Thomas snr, 167
  Cobb, John, 184
  Hallett, William snr and William
  jnr, 388
  Marshall, John, 578
  Planta, John, 702
  Snowdon, Robert, 837
  Vile, William, 928
  Wright, Richard & Elwick,
  Edward, 1007
Cannons (Middlx):
  French, Thomas, 322
  Pelletier, Thomas, 687
Canons Ashby (Northants.):
  Phill, Thomas, 694
  Vile, William, 925
Cans, Charles, 490
Canterbury (Kent):
  Abbott, John, 1
  Alder, Brian, 6
  Allen, Edward, 9
  Arnold, William, 19
  Arnot, William, 19
  Austin, George, 26
  Back, Stephen, 28
  Baines, Thomas, 32
  Baker, John, 32
  Barber, George, 38
  Bird, Henry, 74

Bodle, John, 83
Boson, John, 89
Bradbridge, John, 95
Bundock, Jonathon, 128
Burnley, Thomas, 132
Delo, William H., 239
Dillow, William, 245
Edisforth, William, 267
Edridge, William, 268
Ellender, Philip, 272
Enstone, Daniel, 281
Epps, Thomas, 281
Gadesby, William, 326
Gardner, John Rayner, 330
Gilham, Frederick, 340
Goulden, Henry, 360
Goulden, James, 360
Goulden, John, 360
Goulden, Thomas, 360
Goulden, William, 360
Greenland, Augustus, 368
Griffey, John, 373
Halladay, Stephen, 387
Hall, John, 385
Halsey, Thomas William, 391
Hammond, George, 392
Harrison, John, 403
Harrison, Theophilas, 404
Harvey, Benjamin, 407
Harvey, Henry, 407
Hobday, William, 436
Hogben, Robert, 440
Holladay, William, 441
Hollingberry, William, 443
Jacobs, F., 477
Jacobs, Jacob, 477
Keeler, John, 502
Kidder, Thomas, 511
Knight, William, 520
Knowles, Daniel, 520
Knowles, William, 520
Ladson, Joseph, 521
Ladson, L., 521
Laggett, James, 521
Laggett, Thomas, 521
Laming, John, 524
Le Cerf, James, 534
Leach, Robert, 533
Leggat, James, 536
Legge, Samuel, 536
Leggett, Josiah, 537
Lepine, Charles jnr, 538
Lepine, John, 538
Lepine, Stephen, 538
Levi, Moses, 539
Litton, Richard, 550
Lyon, George, 562
Marshall, Richard, 579
Matson, Charles, 586
Miles, Henry, 606
Miller, Isaac, 608
Miller, James, 608
Minter, John, 613
Nesbitt, William, 641

Nicholls, Humphrey, 645
Palmer, John, 671
Palmer, William, 672
Pardon, James, 672
Parker, Henry, 674
Parker, Thomas, 675
Parnell, John, 676
Parnell, Thomas, 677
Penn, John, 688
Penn, William, 688
Peters, Charles, 692
Philpott, Stephen, 696
Piddock, Henry, 697
Piddock, John, 697
Plomer, Peter, 703
Pont, Charles, 705
Pont, John, 705
Pout, Charles, 709
Pout, James, 709
Pout, John, 709
Pout, William, 709
Pratt, Martha, 712
Prett, Mrs Walter, 715
Rock, Thomas, 762
Roffway, John snr, 763
Russell, Henry, 772
Russell, Robert, 773
Seath, John, 793
Seeth, John, 799
Sharp, William, 803
Shether, Thomas, 810
Smeed, James, 823
Smeed, John, 823
Soath, John, 838
Southee, George, 840
Southee, John, 840
Spratt, Martha, 846
Stace, Freeguiff, 847
Staines, Richard, 847
Stains, Thomas, 848
Stark, Edward, 850
Stevenson, Richard, 855
Streater, John Sonds, 861
Street, Samuel, 861
Streeter, Sarah, 861
Streeting, Thomas, 861
Strouts, Thomas, 862
T(h)waites, Edward, 893
Tilbe, Spencer, 894
Tol(l)put(t), Joshua, 897
Trestram, John, 904
Vincent, Thomas, 929
Warren, —, 945
Watson, Richard, 950
Webb, James, 953
White, James, 965
White, Samuel, 967
White, Thomas, 967
White & Goulden, 968
Wike, Hougham, 973
Williams, James, 980
Woodhams, George, 999
Worthy, Joseph, 1003
Wright, Richard, 1006

Canterbury Cathedral: Boson, John, 88, 89
Capella, 143
Carline, Thomas, 270
Carlisle (Cumb.):
  Anderson, Thomas, 13
  Baty & Kirkbride, 50
  Beattie, William, 55
  Beaty, George, 55
  Beaty, John, 55
  Bowman, R., 93
  Brockbank & Edmondson, 109
  Brockbank, Ellwood, 109
  Brown, John, 116
  Brown, Richard, 117
  Bullman, Christopher, 128
  Dalston, John, 225
  Dalston, Jonathon, 225
  Denton, William S., 241
  Dent, Thomas, 241
  Dixon, John, 246
  Dodgson, Henry, 249
  Edmond, James, 268
  Edmondson & Creighton, 268
  Gawthorp, Robert, 333
  Graham, J., 361
  Graham, John jnr, 362
  Graham, John snr, 362
  Graham, William, 363
  Hall, Thomas, 386
  Hall, William, 386
  Hardy, James, 397
  Harrison, Edward, 403
  Haugh, John, 410
  Hetherington, George, 424
  Hewitt, Robert, 426
  Hill, James, 430
  Hodgkinson, John, 437
  Hodgson, John, 438
  Holmes, George, 445
  Horsley, Edward, 451
  Irving, John, 473
  James, Edmund, 478
  James, Hugh, 479
  Johnstone, William, 493
  Jollie & Sons, 493
  Kirkbride & Baty, 517
  Little, Thomas, 550
  Little, William, 550
  Macpherson, J., 568
  Milburn, Thomas, 606
  Mullinder, John, 635
  Nelson, William, 641
  Nicholson, William, 647
  Nicholson & Graham, 647
  Norman, Thomas, 653
  Pattinson, John, 680
  Pickup, James, 697
  Richardson, Joseph, 744
  Robson, James, 761
  Saul, David, 781
  Scott, John, 790
  Scott, Joseph, 790
  Scott, William, 791
  Skurr, John, 820
  Snowden, John, 837
  Snowden, Thomas, 837
  Spencer, Christopher J., 843
  Strong, John, William, 862
  Stubbs, John, 863
  Studholme, John, 863
  Studholm, R., 863
  Thompson, John, 887
  Thurman & Son, 892
  Topping, George, 899
  Tweddle, Henry, 914
  Waite, Ezra, 932
  Wallace, William, 939
  Wilson, Daniel, 986
  Wilson, Thomas, 989
  Wilson, William, 990
  Wright, John Martingale, 1006
  Wright, Robert, 1008
  Young, Joseph, 1014
Carlisle House (London): Norman, Samuel, 653
Carlton, Sarah, 66, 116, 251
Carlton Towers (Yorks.): Gillow, 343
Carmichael, John Wilson, 291
Carpenter, 847
Carr, George, 465
Carr, John, 251, 598
Carrall, Richard, 427
Carrick, William, 413
Carrier, John, 645
Carron (Stirlingshire):
  Haworth, Samuel, 413
  Haworth, William, 414
Cartmel (Westmld):
  Elleray, Roger & Sons, 272
  Greenwood, John, 369
  Walker, Thomas, 938
  White, Francis, 965
  White, John, 966
  Whitehead, Robert, 968
Carter, 707, 726, 956
Carter, Elias, 149
Carter, George, 129
Carter, John, 147
Carter, Joseph, 767, 896
Carter, Richard, 63, 452
Carter, Robert, 1004
Carter & Morris, 627
Cartwright, 203, 553
Cartwright, George William, 501
Carver, Matthew, 195
Carver, Robert, 195
Cary, 733
Casbert, John, 698
Cash, Samuel, 150
Cashen, William, 509, 823
Casher, William, 229
Cashin, Charles, 851
Cashin, Henry Edward, 744
Cashin, William, 396, 941
Cassiobury (Herts.): White, Ralph, 966
Castall, John T., 846
Castle Ashby (Northants.): Nixon, James, 650
Castle Bromwich Hall (Warks.): Jensen, Gerrit, 487
Castle Cary (Som.):
  Ash, Hugh, 20
  Lush, George, 561
Castle Coole (Co. Fermanagh): Kennett, Robert & Kidd, William, 507
Castle Donnington (Leics.):
  Gaskill, Thomas, 332
  Pegg, John, William, 687
  Percival, Bosworth, 690
  Thruckley, Thomas, 892
  Thurlby, Richard, 892
  Wright, Richard, 1008
Castle Hedingham (Essex):
  Jarman, James, 481
  Newman, Aaron, 643
Castle Howard (Yorks.):
  Fuhrlohg, Christopher, 321
  Linnell, John, 544
  Lobb, Joel, 551
  Tushaine, —, 914
Castleford (Yorks.):
  England, Matthew, 281
  Hewett, William, 425
  Morton, William, 631
Castletown (Kildare, Ireland): Langlois, Pierre, 526
Catear, Jewel, 833
Catesby, 844
Cathrow, Mary, 516
Cathrow, Thomas, 235, 516
Catignou, James, 696
Caton (Lancs.): Hodgson, John, 438
Catterall, William, 570, 589
Catterick (Yorks.):
  Barwick, Benjamin, 47
  Binks, Thomas, 73
  Smith, William, 834
Catton, 403
Catton, William, 292
Catton (Norfolk): Kew, George, 511
Cattrall, 970
Cattrall & Whittingham, 229, 568, 614, 888, 917, 933
Caukill, 737
Cault, W.J., 263
Caulton, Edward, 810
Cavan, 61
Cavitt, James, 552
Cawdell, James, 6
Cawood (Yorks.):
  Armstrong, Thomas, 18
  Ellison, John, 276
Cawthorne (Yorks.):
  Hemingway, T., 420
  Mosley, Joseph, 632

Cerne Abbas (Dorset):
  Groves, George, 376
  Trim, John, 904
Cerrol, James, 873
Chacewater (Cornwall):
  Hornblower, Jesse, 449
Chadley, 719
Chadley, George, 164, 719
Chadley, Robert, 164, 719
Chadwick, John jnr, 408
Chadwick, Richard, 964
Chaffin, Bob, 188
Chaloner, 243
Chamberlain, Benjamin Storer, 948
Chamberlain, T., 153
Chambers, Richard, 143, 994
Chambers, Timothy, 482
Chambers, William, 579
Chancellor, William, 235
Chandler, George Loudon, 584
Chandler, John, 536
Chandler, Samuel, 899
Chandler, Thomas, 536, 867, 1013
Channon, Hugh, 155
Channon, Otho, 155
Chapel-en-le-Frith (Derbs.):
  Bagshaw, Thomas, 29
  Bennet, Edward, 64
Chaplin, William, 122, 135
Chapman, 52, 403
Chapman, George, 73, 110, 131,
  190, 248, 281, 405, 430, 579, 951
Chapman, Henry, 603
Chapman, John, 54, 73, 131, 157,
  248, 281, 387, 405, 543, 579
Chapman, Sarah, 981
Chappell, 267
Chappell, Daniel, 418
Chard (Som.):
  Bailey, Robert, 30
  Edwards, John Holland, 270
  Radford, Joseph F., 725
  Warren, William, 946
Charing (Kent):
  Humphery, John, 462
  Humphrey, Robert, 463
Charlecote Park (Warks.):
  Bolt, Thomas, 83
  Bott, Thomas, 90
  Buchanan, William, 123
  Emanuel, E., 279
  Graham, Joseph & Partners, 362
  Hooper, Frederick William, 447
  Hume, Robert, 462
  Wilcox, James Morris, 973
  Woodburn, Allen, 998
Charles, Charles, 303, 665, 932
Charles, Edward, 244
Charleston (Lancs.): Walker,
  Aaron, 934
Charleton, John, 517
Charlton, John, 1
Charmbury, Daniel, 688

Charnley, William, 43, 44, 118, 141,
  212, 252, 613, 731, 770, 776, 942
Charnock, Thomas, 724
Charpentier, 756
Chase, Edward, 361
Chatham (Kent):
  Ackworth, William, 2
  Batten, Elizabeth, 50
  Benifold, —, 64
  Benifold, John, 64
  Benifold, Thomas, 64
  Benifold, W., 64
  Burr, John, 132
  Burr, Robert, 132
  Dadd, Isaac, 223
  Denning, Henry, 240
  Dodd, Isaac, 248
  Draycon, Robert, 256
  Drayton, Robert, 256
  Drury, Joseph, 257
  Easton, —, 265
  Harrison, John, 404
  Marrable, John, 575
  Pasco, Thomas, 679
  Roberts, John, 752
  Seaton, Benjamin, 793
  Seaton, Joseph, 793
  Seton, —, 800
  Staples, Thomas, 849
  Tookey, William, 899
  Worth, A.C., 1003
  Wright, John, 1005
Chatham (Kent): Hospital of Sir
  John Hawkins: Bonifold, John,
  85
Chatsworth (Derbs.):
  Barker, John, 40
  Barratt, George, 44
  Bickley, John, 71
  Brailsford, Thomas, 101
  Brailsford, William, 101
  Cobb, Henry, 181
  Cooper, —, 195
  Cowley, William, 203
  Cribb, Robert, 209
  Cuenot, John Antoine, 217
  Davies, —, 228
  Davis, William, 233
  Elliott, Charles, 273
  Fox, Edward, 313
  Freelove, William, 320
  Goodison, Benjamin, 354
  Gordon, John & Taitt, John &
  Richard, 357
  Greaves, —, 366
  Gumley, Elizabeth & John, 380
  Hallam, John, 387
  Hallett, William snr and William
  jnr, 389
  Hancock & Co., 393
  Hancox & Ashlin, 393
  Hayter, George, 415
  Herve, Francois, 424

  Jensen, Gerrit, 486
  Lapierre, Francis, 528
  Lobb, Joel, 551
  Maddox, —, 569
  Mason, —, 583
  Mayhew, John & Ince, William,
  592, 593, 597
  Morrant & Son, 627
  Moseley, Richard, 631
  Nelson, Sefferin, 640
  Orchard, James, 664
  Pavie, Peter, 682
  Radley, Jarvis, 725
  Roberts, Thomas & Richard,
  752, 753
  Smith, William, 833
  Temple, Thomas, 881
  Vile, William, 928
  Wacher, John, 930
  Watson, Samuel, 950
  Wilson, Walter, 990
  Wright, Richard & Elwick,
  Edward, 1008
  Young, Thomas, 1015
  Young, William, 1015
Chatteris (Cambs.):
  Allam, Joseph, 8
  Allan, James, 9
  Bolton, Samuel, 84
Cheadle (Staffs.):
  Browning, John, 120
  Elliott, Charles, 272
  Summerfield, Stephen, 864
Cheater, John jnr, 255
Chelmsford (Essex):
  Abrey, Henry, 2
  Adams, Richard James, 4
  Archer, John, 17
  Bedford, Henry, 58
  Botts, George, 90
  Braton, Frank & Ernest, 103
  Breedford, Henry, 105
  Brown, Charles, 113
  Brown, F.S., 113
  Brown, John, 115
  Brown, Thomas, 118
  Bull, William, 125
  Dowsett, John, 255
  Gilson, Henry, 344
  Gilson, Thomas, 344
  Greene, John, 368
  How(e), —, 453
  How, Samuel, 453
  Johns, George, 488
  Joscelyne, Benjamin jnr, 499
  Keys, James, 511
  Keys, John, 511
  Murrell, Charles, 637
  Myers, Wolfe, 637
  Noon, Lancaster, 651
  Overall, William, 667
  Powell, John, 710
  Rance, Richard, 726
  Ruse, James, 771

Rusher, Benjamin Gilson, 771
Sellons, John, 799
Shoobridge, John, 812
Spite, Robert, 845
Turnage, Samuel, 909
Turner, William, 912
Warner, Richard, 945
Wenley, W., 958
Youxfield, Robert, 1015
Chelsea (London):
Allen, Francis, 9
Atkinson, Edward, 24
Attwood, Thomas, 25
Aves, John, 27
Bilby, Thomas, 71
Bradley, Daniel, 97
Browne, G., 120
Daguerre, Dominique, 223
Draper, John, 255
Eckhardt, Anthony George, 265
Edkins, Thomas, 267
Haines, George, 383
Harwood & Haines, 408
Hawkins, Benjamin, 412
Hawkins, Samuel, 413
Hedley, James, 419
Horsley, Matthew, 451
Humphreys & Atkinson, 463
Kriege, Frederick, 520
Larkin, Philip, 528
Larner, William, 528
Long, John, 554
Lupton, Thomas, 561
Mann, Richard, 572
Mason, William, 584
Mogford, Samuel, 615
Moulton, Francis, 633
Munday, William, 635
Parsons, John, 678
Perry, M.& I., 691
Preston, Francis, 714
Pye, Thomas, 723
Rushworth, Thomas, 771
Rushworth, William, 771
Sarvas, Abraham, 781
Sarvis, A.W., 781
Savage, John, 786
Seaborne, Jno. Henry, 791
Seymour, Samuel, 801
Sims, James, 817
Skelton, Thomas, 819
Smith, John, 829
Soper, E., 839
Steward, Richard, 855
Tann, Mary, 871
Thomas, I., 883
Tichbourne, Isaac, 893
Timbrell, Samuel, 895
Toby, Henry, 896
Waddle, B., 930
Winn, Thomas, 992
Cheltenham (Glos.):
Agle, John jnr., 5
Aglen, George, 5

Alder, John, 6
Arkell & Wheeler, 17
Austin, Robert, 27
Ballard, Charles, 35
Bartholemew, J., 46
Battin, J., 50
Beek, Elizabeth, 58
Berry, Thomas Henry, 68
Bick, Mrs, 70
Bingham, William, 72
Boucher, Daniel, 90
Boucher, George, 90
Boucher, John, 90
Boucher, Thomas, 90
Brighton, T.W., 108
Brooker, James, 111
Butt, John, 138
Dartnall, William, 227
Dawson, Thomas, 235
Eagles, Thomas, 264
Elliott, R., 274
Eyles, Thomas, 286
Eyles, William Henry, 286
Green, Charles, 367
Gunter, Joseph, 380
Haines, George, 383
Haley, Henry, 384
Haselton, William, 408
Hatch, Edward, 410
Hinton, William, 434
Howard, W.H., 455
Hughes, T., 461
Hughes, Thomas, 461
Hundey, Thomas, 464
James, P., 479
Kirkland, George, 517
Lane, T., 525
Lawrence, John, 531
Millard, John & Edward, 607
Millard, Mrs, 607
Moody, Moses, 616
Morris, Richard, 629
Newman, Thomas, 643
Nottingham, John, 656
Oliver, Daniel, 663
Parry, E., 677
Powell, George, 710
Quinton, Jno., 724
Rawlings, Francis, 729
Rich, Timothy, 741
Salmon, Thomas, 777
Slader, Richard, 820
Starr, George, 850
Sweeting, George, 868
Taylor, Joseph, 878
Turnbulls, —, 909
Urch & Seabright, 918
Vaughan, —, 920
Walker, J., J.B., 935
White, William, 967
Williams, T., 982
Williams, Thomas, 982
Williams, William, 983
Wood, Daniel, 996

Wood, James, 996
Wood, Jeremiah, 996
Wood, Thomas, 998
Cheltenham, King St. for Col.
  Redbow: Oakley, George, 660
Chenery, William, 696
Chenn, Joshua, 490
Cheppett, 136
Cherry, John, 244
Chertsey (Surrey):
Abrahams, Nathaniel, 2
Knapp, John, 518
Reed, Richard, 734
Sparrow, John, 841
Sparrow, Joseph, 842
Strudwick, John, 862
Waterer, James, 946
Chesham (Bucks.):
Batchelor, William, 48
Bowden, Jos., 92
Darvell, W., 227
Davey, William, 227
Groves, John, 376
Howard, J., 454
Nickson, —, 647
Potter, John, 708
Prickett, John, 717
Spratley, J., 845
Cheshunt (Herts.):
Godfrey, —, 346
Goodhart, George, 351
Grange, M. & R., 363
Orange, Mary & Rebecca,
  Samuel, 664
Rumball, Charles, 770
Smith, Jno, 830
Smith, Nathaniel Alexander, 830
Worpell, Henry, 1003
Chessey, 700, 730
Chesson, William, 260, 463, 866,
  877, 1008
Chester:
Abbot(t), James, 1
Adams, Robert, 4
Ashton, Peter, 21
Astle, John, 22
Astle, Thomas jnr, 22
Astle, Thomas snr, 22
Austin, J., 26
Barber, John, 38
Barber, Richard, 38
Barker, John, 40
Barlow, John, 41
Barrows, Joseph, 45
Barton, W., 47
Bather, Nathaniel, 49
Beckett, Joseph, 57
Bellis, Edward, 63
Bennett, Thomas, 65
Bennett, William, 65
Bennion, George, 66
Bernard, John Cowley, 67
Berrington, James F., 67
Berrington, William, 67

Berry, William, 68
Bevington, Fletcher, 69
Biggins, Griffith, 71
Billington, George, 72
Bilston, William, 72
Bingley, —, 72
Bingley, Ralph, 72
Bingley, Randle, 72
Binigan, George, 72
Blake, Richard, 79
Bolland, Ralph, 83
Bolland, William, 83
Boulton, Charles, 91
Boulton, Joseph, 91
Bowden, —, 91
Bowers, Robert, 92
Bradley, William, 98
Bresbury, Philip, 105
Bridge, John, 107
Broadbent, William, 109
Broadhurst, Thomas, 109
Brock, John, 109
Bromley, Edward, 110
Brown, Matthew, 117
Brown, Richard, 117
Brown, Thomas, 118
Brown & Lamont, 119
Bunce, William, 128
Burrow(e)s, Joseph, 133
Burton, William, 136
Butler, Robert, 137
Dale, John, 224
Dale, Samuel, 224
Davenport, John, 227
Davenport, William, 227
Davies, John, 229
Davies, Samuel, 229
Davies, Thomas, 230
Dawes, John & Noyes, Edward, 234
Dawson, Perry, 235
Dean, John, 237
Denson, John, 241
Denson, Richard, 241
Diason, John, 243
Dodd, Edward, 248
Dolland, —, 250
Duke, Bartholomew, 258
Dunbar, John, 259
Durbar, John, 261
Dutton, Robert, 263
Dutton, William, 263
Edwards, Edward, 269
Edwards, John, 269, 270
Edwards, Samuel, 270
Ellis, John, 275
Ellis, Matthew, 275
Ellis, William, 276
El(l)rington, John, 276
Erlington, John, 282
Evans, —, 283
Evans, John, 284
Gardner, James, 330
Gardner, John, 330

Gar(d)ner, Mary & Sons, 330
Gar(d)ner, Samuel, 330
Garner, John, 331
Garnett, Thomas, 331
Garratt, G., 331
Garratt, Samuel, 331
Garret(t), Thomas, 331
Gellion, Samuel, 335
Gill, Thomas, 340
Gollion, Samuel, 349
Gorst, Richard, 358
Gough, William, 360
Gray, James, 365
Griffith, —, 373
Griffith, Edward, 374
Griffith, John, 374
Griffith(s), Charles, 373
Griffiths, William, 375
Griffith, Thomas, 374
Groom, William, 376
Habbot, James, 381
Hall, James, 385
Hall, John, 385
Hallowes, James, 390
Hallowes, Thomas, 390
Hallows, John, 390
Hall, Thomas, 386
Hankey, Peter, 394
Hankey, Robert, 394
Harefinch, Peter, 397
Harris, —, 400
Harrison, Samuel, 404
Harrison, William, 405
Harvey, Edward, 407
Harvey, Harvey, 407
Hawkins, E., 412
Hawkins, Edward, 412
Hawkins, Henry, 412
Hawkins, James jnr, 412
Hawkins, James snr, 412
Hawkins, Richard, 413
Heald, William, 417
Heard, William, 417
Henderson, John, 420
Henderson, William, 421
Henshaw, John, 422
Hesketh, Thomas, 424
Hill, J., 430
Hill, John, 431
Hodges, Thomas, 437
Holland, George, 442
Holland, Matthew, 442
Holland, Matthias, 442
Holloway, John, 444
Hooker, Robert, 447
Hughes, James, 460
Hunter, Elizabeth & Catherine, 465
Hunter, James, 465
Huxley, Joseph, 469
Huxley, Thomas, 469
Hyatt, Thomas, 469
Ingham, John, 471
Ingham, Robert, 471

Ingham, William, 471
Jackson, John, 476
Jameson, Peter, 480
Jeffries, Thomas, 483
Johnson, George, 489
Johnson, John, 490
Johnson, Samuel, 491
Johnson, Thomas, 492
Johnstone, James, 493
Jones, James, 495
Jones, John, 495
Jordan, Thomas, 499
Kain, Henry, 500
Keeling, William, 502
Kelly, Henry, 503
Kelly, James, 503
Kelly, Mrs Sarah, 503
Kenna, James, 506
Kettle, John, 511
Key, John, 511
Kirkes, Hamnett, 517
Kirkes, John, 517
Kirkes, Samuel snr, 517
Lanceley, Thomas, 524
Langford, J.L., 525
Langford, Thomas Stringer, 525
Latchford, Thomas, 529
Lawrence, Richard, 531
Lawrence, Thomas, 531
Ledsham, John, 534
Ledsham, Richard, 534
Lee, John, 535
Lee, Richard, 535
Lees, Robert, 536
Leigh, James, 537
Lewis, John, 540
Lindsay, George, 542
Linney, George, John & Peter, 548
Lister, Joseph, 549
Lloyd, George, 550
Lloyd, William, 551
Long, Sarah, 554
Lumber, Charles, 560
McCabe, Thomas, 564
McCan(n)s, Charles, 564
McKay, John C., 566
Maddock, Edward, 569
Maddock, Samuel, 569
Marsden, Henry, 576
Marsh, George Moses, 576
Marsh, Moses, 577
Martin, W., 581
Massey, Thomas, 585
Meacock, Robert, 598
Mercer, J., 602
Mercer, John, 602
Mercer, Samuel, 602
Meredith, John, 602
Miller, Joseph, 609
Milligan, Thomas, 609
Millington, Robert, 609
Monk, Charles Thomas, 616
Moores, Robert, 622

Morgan, William, 626
Morris, James, 628
Morris, Robert & John, 629
Moss, George, 632
Moss, John, 632
Newman, Gilbert, 643
Nicholls, Robert, 646
Nickson, Samuel, 647
Norbury, John, 651
Norbury, Richard, 651
Noyes, Edward, 657
Ormes, John, 665
Ormes, William, 665
Parker, Arthur, 673
Parker, Joseph, 674
Parry, J., 677
Parry, Joseph, 677
Pate, John, 679
Pate, Thomas, 679
Pate, William, 679
Peers, John, 686
Pennington, Edward James, 689
Phenix, James, 693
Phillips, Joseph Jackson, 695
Phillips, William, 696
Podmore, George, 704
Podmore, James, 704
Podmore, Joseph, 704
Podmore, William, 704
Powell, Edward & Thomas, 710
Powell, Edward Frodsham, 710
Powell, John, 710
Powell, Thomas, 711
Powell, Thomas John, 711
Presbury, Philip, 713
Price, John, 715, 716
Price, Samuel, 716
Prince, Thomas, 717
Pritchard, Robert, 718
Randles, George, 727
Ratcliffe, John, 728
Read, William, 732
Rentchall, Jonathon, 737
Richards, Hugh, 741
Ridgeway, William, 747
Roberts, Edward, 751
Roberts, George, 751
Roberts, J., 751
Roberts, James, 751
Roberts, John, 752
Roberts, Lawrence, 752
Roberts, Richard, 752
Roberts, Robert, 752
Roberts, Thomas, 754
Roberts, William, 754
Roby, Richard, 762
Rogers, Robert, 763
Rudgeway, Charles, 747
Sandland, William, 780
Sarratt, Samuel, 781
Scholes, Abner snr, jnr, 789
Seller, John, 799
Seller, Samuel, 799
Sellers, Samuel, 799

Sharman, William, 802
Shaw, John, 804
Shepherd, Joseph, 807
Simpson, Jonathan, 816
Skeat, Henry, 818
Smathers, Samuel, 823
Smith, James, 827
Smith, Samuel, 831
Smith, Thomas, 832
Spencer, Edward, 843
Steele, Charles, 851
Steens, Thomas, 851
Stephens, Ralph, 853
Stretton, John, 861
Stringer, John, 862
Stubbs, Samuel, 863
Summers, John, 864
Sumners, John, 865
Tasker, Charles M., 873
Tasker, Edward M., 873
Taylor, John, 877
Taylor, Richard, 878
Thomas, George, 883
Thomas, John, 883, 884
Thomas, Joseph, 884
Thomas, Robert, 884
Thomson, Charles, 889
Thorley, James, 889
Thrape, George, 891
Tilston, John, 895
Tiltson, Thomas, 895
Todd, George, 896
Todd, James jnr, 896
Todd, Joseph, 896
Turner, Ann, 909
Turner, Edward, 909
Turner, James jnr, 910
Turner, Joseph, 911
Turner, Samuel, 911
Turner, Thomas, 912
Turner, William, 913
Twanbrook(e), Edward, 914
Venable, James, 921
Walker, Edward, 934
Walker, John, 936
Walker, William, 938
Welch, John, 956
Welsh, John, 958
White, Samuel, 967
Whittall, James, 970
Whittingham, James, 970
Wiggens, John, 972
Wilcocks, J., 973
Wilkinson, Joseph snr, jnr, 976
Williams, Ellis, 979
Williams, George, 979
Williams, Griffith, 979
Williams, John, 981
Williams, Joseph, 981
Williams, Peter, 981
Wolfe, John, 995
Wolley, Thomas, 995
Woodfin, William, 999
Woodford, George, 999

Woodins, Joseph jnr, 999
Woodsin, William, 1000
Woods, John, 1000
Woodsworth, John, 1000
Woodsworth, Thomas, 1000
Woodtin, William, 1000
Woodward, John, 1001
Woodward, Thomas, 1001
Woodworth, John, 1001
Woodworth, John jnr, 1001
Woodworth, Thomas, 1001
Wynne, George, 1011
Wynne, Joseph, 1011
Chester Cathedral: Gar(d)ner,
  Samuel, 330
Chester, Charles, 214
Chester-le-Street (Co. Durham):
  Blakey, Thomas, 79
  Brown & Jennings, 119
  Jopling, John, 498
  Jopling, Joseph & Thomas, 498
  Ramsey, Nathan, 726
  Williamson, Martin, 983
Chesterfield (Derbs.):
  Broadhurst, George, 109
  Dyson, Thomas, 263
  Eyre, Joseph, 287
  Glossop, Daniel, 345
  Hall, Henry, 385
  Hodkin, Christopher, 438
  Hodkin, Daniel, 438
  Manknell, William, 572
  Moore, Francis, 618
  Newstead, William, 644
  Parker, George, 674
  Parker, John, 674
  Parker, Thomas, 675
  Pickard, Thomas, 697
  Plant, James, 702
  Roberts, John, 752
  Rodger, William, 762
  Savage, Cephas, 786
  Sharp, Samuel, 803
  Stevenson, Thomas, 855
  Stokes, Samuel, 858
  Tomlinson, Benjamin, 898
  Walker, John, 935
  White, George, 965
  Wilson, Mathias, 988
  Wilson, Samuel, 989
  Wilson, Samuel & Sons, 989
  Wragg, John, 1003
Chesters, John, 489, 557, 602, 637
Chesworth, George, 51
Chevening (Kent):
  Bradshaw, William, 100
  Crompton, Samuel, 211
  Longhurst, —, 555
  Mayhew, John & Ince, William,
  595
  Mitchell, —, 613
  Noller, —, 651
  Norman, Samuel, 653
Chew, 180

Chew, John, 831
Chewter, Thomas, 699
Chicheley Hall (Bucks.):
  Atkins, Henry, 23
  Baxter, Francis, 51
  Goodwin, P., 355
  Hodson, —, 439
  Illison, —, 471
  Kellow, Francis, 503
  Norton, William, 656
  Odell, Mr, 661
  Patterson, —, 680
  Poynter, Edward, 711
  Richards, James, 742
  Spencer, Henry, 843
  Spender, Samuel, 844
  Thompson, —, 885
Chichester (Sussex):
  Alcock, William, 6
  Ball, William, 35
  Barell & Robins, 39
  Bartholemew, William, 46
  Bartlett, John, 46
  Biffin, James, 71
  Binstead, William, 73
  Boxall, Benjamin, 94
  Burrell, W., 133
  Davison, Thomas, 233
  Gale, William, 327
  Garrard, Thomas, 331
  Gray, Drummond, 365
  Knight, James, 519
  Mant, John, 573
  Newman, James, 643
  Pasco, Edward, 679
  Peat, Richard, 685
  Peat, Samuel, 685
  Peat, William, 685
  Robins, Henry, 755
  Russell, James, 772
  Sayers, James, 788
  Sayers, William & Charles, 788
  Sherwin, William, 810
  Shipley, Thomas, 811
  Short, John, 812
  Steele, —, 851
  Trigg, William Henry, 904
  Turner, —, 909
  Turner, Philip, 911
  Tutt, Samuel, 914
  Wade, John, 931
  Weller, John, 957
  Weller, T. & Son, 957
  Wells, Henry, 957
  White, John & Son, 966
  Wright, Henry, 1005
Chiesa, 368
Child, 684
Child, I., 867
Child & Sweet, 867
Chiles, Edward, 379
Chillingham Castle (Northumb.):
  Mayhew, John & Ince, William, 596

Chinnery, William, 527
Chipchase, Henry, 719
Chipchase, Robert, 523, 719
Chipchase & Lambert, 800
Chipchase & Proctor, 719
Chipp, 835
Chippendale, Thomas jnr, 685–6
Chippendale, Thomas snr, 29, 57, 66, 169, 182, 184, 214, 297, 349, 361, 382, 383, 421, 436, 478, 479, 531, 543, 552, 573, 588, 591, 592, 652, 685, 711, 727, 736, 882, 935, 944, 975, 997
Chippendale & Rannie, 831
Chippenham (Wilts.):
  Bishop, Thomas, 76
  Elliott, Paul, 274
  Horton, John, 451
  Mansell, E., 573
  Stockham, James, 857
  Vaisey, Ann Sadlington, 919
  Williams, James, 981
Chippett, 136
Chipping (Lancs.): Windle, John & Joseph, 991
Chipping Camden (Glos.):
  Hartley, John, 407
  Hodgkins, Timothy, 437
  Smith, William, 835
Chipping Norton (Oxon.):
  Birmingham, Fernando, 75
  Day, —, 236
  Hodgkins & Son, 437
  Quartermaine, Joseph, 724
  Quartermaine, Joseph Abraham, 724
  Smith, Thomas, 832
  Wisdom, Philip, 993
Chipping Sodbury (Glos.): Prior, Edwin, 718
Chirk Castle (Denbighshire):
  Croxton, William, 215
  Hasert, Peter, 409
  Mayhew, John & Ince, William, 593, 596
Chiswell, John, 46
Chiswick (London): Wells, Thomas, 958
Chiswick House (London): Boson, John, 89
Chiswick Villa (London):
  Bradshaw, William, 100
Chivers, Noah, 42, 363, 463, 817
Chivers, William, 423, 804
Cholmondeley Castle (Cheshire):
  Bullock, George, 126, 127
Chorley, John, 309
Chorley (Lancs.):
  Ashcroft, Richard, 20
  Bates, Thomas, 49
  Bradshaw, John, 99
  Green, Robert, 367
  Harrison, William, 405
  Kerfoot, John, 509

Kerfoot, Richard, 510
Latham, Henry, 529
Lucas, Richard, 559
M'Cloud, John, 564
Richmond, James, 746
Ward, Richard, 943
Wilkinson, Lawrence, 976
Wilkinson, William, 977
Withnell, Richard, 994
Withnell, William, 994
Chorlton-on-Medlock (Lancs.):
  Ward, Matthew, 943
Christchurch (Hants.):
  Ayles, Benjamin, 27
  Benson, W., 66
  Burden, Thomas, 130
  Gales, Joseph William, 327
  Galliers, Peter, 328
  Gawler, Peter, 333
  Gaylor, Peter, 333
  Holloway, George, 443
  Holloway, William, 444
  Martin, William, 582
  Menty, John, 601
  Miller, W., 609
  Pilgrem, J., 699
  Pilgrim, Thomas, 699
  Pugin, Augustus W.N., 721
Christchurch, Priory Church of Holy Trinity: Pugin, Augustus W.N., 721
Christian, John Houghton, 562
Chubbard, Samuel, 64, 429, 494, 495, 826, 913
Chudleigh (Devon): Searle, William, 792
Churnside, Thomas, 118
Churton & Sons, 179
Cirencester (Glos.):
  Arnold, Daniel, 19
  Bingham, Daniel, 72
  Bingham, David, 72
  Blackwell, Charles, 78
  Blackwell, Edward, 78
  Blackwell, William, 78
  Bradley, Charles, 97
  Brewer, James, 106
  Brewer, John, 106
  Eldborough, William, 271
  Evans, Daniel, 283
  Eycott, William Powlett, 286
  Eyles, William, 286
  Greenwood, William, 369
  Hall, Isaac, 385
  Hampton, John, 392
  Hancock, Thomas, 393
  Hancock & Thomas, 393
  Hart, Stephen, 406
  Harte, John, 406
  Holyoake(s), William, 446
  Jones, William, 498
  Lane, William, 525
  Lawler, William, 530
  Manning, John, 573

Marks, Henry, 574
Marks, James, 574
Mills, John, 610
Morgan, Richard, 625
Padbury, William, 669
Pagett, Thomas, 670
Paine, John, 670
Paish, Charles, 671
Parish, Charles, 673
Pew, John, 693
Savory, Joseph, 786
Slater, William, 821
Southam, Henry, 840
Tull, Samuel, 908
Wills, William, 985
Clapham, William, 45
Clapham (London):
    Adamson, William, 4
    Bartlett, William, 46
    Beville, Charles, 69
    Dodd, James, 248
    Dungate, S., 259
    Hannah, George, 395
    Hitcombe, Thomas, 435
    Ingram, John, 472
    Neal, William, 639
    Rayner, Thomas, 731
    Sherwood, Samuel Oakley, 810
    Thompson, William, 888
    Varden, Frederick, 919
Clappison, John, 244
Clapton (London):
    Kent, William, 509
    Morrice, George, 627
Clare (Suffolk):
    Mortlock, Charles, 630
    Pain, John H., 670
    Smoothy, John, 836
Claremont House (Surrey):
    Snell, William, 838
    Wood, Henry, 996
Clark, 203, 326, 802
Clark, Daniel, 599
Clark, George, 859
Clark, James, 698
Clark, John, 539
Clark, William, 390, 464
Clark, Z., 257
Clarke, 185, 859
Clarke, Cornelius, 173
Clarke, D., 175
Clarke, Francis, 832
Clarke, Job, 66, 251
Clarke, John, 40, 919
Clarke, Joseph Thomas, 664
Clarke, Michael, 857
Clarke, Nicholas, 248
Clarke, Thomas, 674
Clarke, Zachariah, 1
Clarkson, Edward, 302
Clarkson, John, 194
Clarkson, Jos., 752
Clarkson, William, 724
Clay, Henry, 264, 484, 822

Clay, John, 773
Clay, W., 176
Claydon House (Bucks.):
    Chippendale, Thomas snr, 167
    Lightfoot, Luke, 541
Clayton, Robert, 940
Clayton Hall (Lancs.): Gillow, 343
Clearson, 189
Cleator, George, 708
Clegg, James, 674
Cleland, Alexander, 507
Clematson, George, 793
Clements, John, 901
Cleator (Cumb.): Harrison,
    William, 405
Clerkenwell (London):
    Abrahams & Davis, 2
    Adams, William L., 4
    Aland, T. & J., 6
    Alder, Joseph, 6
    Ambrosoni, Francis, 12
    Anderson, Joseph, 13
    Anson, George, 15
    Arnold, Thomas, 19
    Artus, H., 20
    Ashworth, Thomas, 21
    Ayres, Thomas, 28
    Bain, R., 31
    Banbury, William, 36
    Banner, Thomas, 37
    Barfoot, Richard, 39
    Barloni, S.D., 41
    Barratt, Richard, 44
    Beck, J., 56
    Benson, Joseph, 66
    Blunt, J., 82
    Bodington & Thorp, 83
    Bonnington, —, 86
    Bonnington, George, 86
    Bonnington, George & Thorp(e),
    George, 86
    Bosden, Henry, 88
    Bowman, Kemp, 93
    Bowyer, Edward, 93
    Brett, Jn, 105
    Brett, William, 105
    Britten, Sam, 109
    Brown, Peter, 117
    Bryan, I., 122
    Bryant, Francis, 122
    Burgess, Edw., 130
    Butler, Jeremiah, 137
    Butler, William, 138
    Byrne, James, 139
    Daniell, —, 225
    Davies, John, 229
    Dawes, William, 234
    Day, John, 236
    Douglas, Archibald, 251
    Douglas, William, 251
    Eagleso, Peter, 264
    Ebbs, Nathaniel, 265
    Edmonds, John, 267
    Edwards, Charles, 269

    Elliott, —, 272
    Ellison, Thomas, 276
    Emerick, John, 280
    Evans, Benjamin, 283
    Evans, John, 284
    Evans, William, 285
    Gellard, John, 335
    George, Richard, 335
    Gibbs, William, 336
    Gill, John, 340
    Godfrey, Nicholas, 347
    Goode, John, 351
    Goodheart, William, 351
    Goodwin, William, 355
    Gow, Alexander, 361
    Graves, James, 365
    Griffin, William, 373
    Griffiths, William, 375
    Guest, Thomas, 377
    Gunnel, William, 380
    Hammond, H., 392
    Hanson, —, 395
    Hardy, S.C., 397
    Harwood, J., 408
    Helme, Charles, 420
    Hills, Newman, 432
    Hollands, Thomas, 442
    Holmes, Thomas, 446
    Hood, Thomas, 447
    House, Ralph, 452
    Howin, John, 456
    Hutt, Joseph, 468
    James, Stephen, 480
    Johnson, Thomas, 492
    Jones, Thomas, 497
    Kent, Thomas, 509
    Kilburn, Thomas, 512
    Kune, David, 520
    Leech, Robert, 535
    Lee, James, 534
    Linsell, William, 548
    Lock & Richards, 552
    Lowe, Richard, 558
    Lowther, Thomas, 559
    Lyde, John, 562
    Mallet, Francis Peter, 571
    Mantica, Charles, 573
    Mason, Henry R., 583
    Mason, John, 584
    Merrick, William, 603
    Midgley, Thomas, 605
    Mil(l)ward, George, 611
    Milns, Edward, 611
    Mitchel(l), Aylmer, 613
    Molineux, Francis et al, 615
    Mombelli, John Comolli, 615
    Monet, Francis Peter, 616
    Moore, Alexander, 617
    Moore, Charles, 617
    Newell, John, 642
    Newell & Son, 642
    Newnham, Samuel, 644
    Nicholl, Charles, 645
    Nicholls, J., 645

Nicholson, Charles, 646
Nickels, William & Benjamin, 647
Norman, Joseph, 651
Nugent, J., 657
Oates, John, 661
Oldfield, William, 662
Orange, Joseph, 664
Osborn, John, 665
Owen, —, 667
Page, William, 670
Paget, William, 670
Pallant, James, 671
Palmer, Francis, 671
Parkinson, Thomas, 676
Parry, William, 678
Paul, Thomas, 682
Pearson, John, 685
Pedretti, Peter, 686
Periera, John, 690
Phillips, Thomas, 696
Pickford, Hubert, 697
Pinks, William, 699
Porter, Thomas, 707
Pratt, Charles Thomas, 712
Price, S., 716
Prickett, Charles, 717
Rhodes & Goodman, 740
Roberts, Timothy, 754
Robinson, John, 758
Robinson, Joseph, 759
Rouse, Joseph, 768
Scott, Charles, 789
Scott & Boswell, 791
Search, Francis, 792
Search, William, 792
Shaw, William, 805
Simpson, Israel, 816
Sims, Robert, 817
Smith, George, 826
Smith, William, 834
Snell, Frederick, 836
Sutton, Henry, 865
Swindles, R., 868
Thompson, Benjamin, 885
Thompson, Brian Rushworth, 885
Thompson, Frederick, 885
Thorp(e), George, 891
Thwaites, Henry, 893
Tibbetts, Samuel, 893
Tilleard, John, 894
Walford, Samuel, 934
Walker, G., 935
Walsh, John, 941
Watkins, Samuel, 947
Weeks, John, 956
Wilson, D., 986
Windsor, John, 991
Witham, Thomas, 994
Wonter & Benson, 995
Wood, George, 996
Wood, William, 998
Wright, —, 1004

Wright, John, 1006
Cleveland House (London):
Saunders, Paul, 784
Vile, William, 923
Cley (Norfolk):
Boson, John, 89
Crook, Benjamin snr, 212
Dew, Thomas, 242
Gosset, Jacob, 359
Jones, Sandys, 497
Lawrence, Richard, 531
Nix, George, 649
Raven, John jnr, 729
Waller, John, 940
Waller, Samuel, 940
Cliffe, 229
Cliffe, Joseph, 172
Clifton (Bristol):
Jenkins, Thomas, 484
Rogers, Charles, 763
Rogers, Daniel, 763
Clifton Castle (Yorks.): Evans, Benjamin, 283
Clitheroe (Lancs.):
Anderson, William, 13
Arkwright, William, 17
Driver & Satterthwaite, 257
Eastham, James, 265
Hornby, James, 449
Nowell, John, 656
Scott, John, 790
Trappes, Robert, 902
Whittaker, John, 969
Windle, James, 991
Clivedon House (Bucks.):
Boson, John, 88
Bradshaw, William, 100
Cure, George, 220
Dunbar, Robert, 259
Goodison, Benjamin, 353
Pettit, Paul, 692
Cloak, James, 249
Clowes, Joseph, 423
Clubb, Robert, 421
Clubbe, George, 632
Cluderoy, John, 116
Cluley, 675
Clumber Park (Notts.): Burchby, Thomas, 129
Clyatt, Henry, 234
Clyst Hydon (Devon): White, John Albin, 966
Coake, John, 373
Coates, 682
Coates, Daniel, 662
Coates, Edward, 498, 522, 575, 845, 860
Coates, Thomas Bitchfield, 849
Cobb, 201, 389
Cobb, John, 5, 8, 95, 316, 353, 372, 387, 388, 542, 549, 616, 738, 861, 873, 924, 925, 927, 928
Cobb, W., 738
Cobett, William, 814

Cobham Hall (Kent):
Bromwich, Thomas, 110
Cleare, William, 177
Cobb, John, 184
Mayhew, John & Ince, William, 593
Vardy, Thomas, 919
Vial(l)(s), Thomas, 922
Cochran, William, 975
Cockerham (Lancs.): Devis, Anthony, 242
Cockermouth (Cumb.):
Askew, Jonathon, 21
Bell, John, 62
Dean, William, 237
Drewry, Jonathon, 256
Graham, Joseph, 363
Hetherington, Jonathon, 424
Hunter, John, 465
Jenkinson, John, 484
Lawson, Joshua, 532
Nicholson, Isaac, 646
Pearson, John, 685
Ramsay, William, 726
Ritchie, Allan, 750
Ritson, Jonathon, 750
Shilton, John, 811
Slevan, John, 821
Stevan, John, 854
Thompson, Ann, 885
Tickell, John, 894
Waters, Hudson, 947
Wharton, Jeremiah, 962
Wharton, John, 962
Wood, John, 997
Cockfield Hall (Suffolk):
Liret, —, 548
Martin & Parry, 582
Sawyer, Charles, 786
Cockran, John, 337
Codlin, 792
Coggeshall (Essex):
Andrew, Thomas, 14
Bridge, Stephen, 107
Bridge, Susannah, 107
Leaper, Daniel, 533
Mayhew, Thomas Eaton, 589
Rout, William, 768
Stuck, Matthew, 863
Cohen, Henry Pidger, 469
Colbeck, William, 779
Colbron, 779, 785
Colby, James, 864
Colchester (Essex):
Aggio, Paul, 5
Ainsworth, Thomas, 5
Bacon, John, 28
Bacon, Richard, 28
Barlow, Nathaniel, 41
Barnes, Robert, 42
Barritt, James, 44
Barton, Nathaniel, 47
Bearsley, Samuel, 55
Bennell, James, 64

Blyth, Samuel, 82
Blythe, Clarke, 82
Bright, John, 108
Bromley, Thomas, 110
Brown, Mathew, 117
Bunnell, William, 129
Day, William & Son, 236
Dearsley, Samuel, 238
Dodson, George, 249
Ellisdon, Joseph, 276
Gonner, Thomas, 350
Goslin, Byatt, 358
Gosling, George, 358
Gurney, William, 380
Harvey, Charles, 407
Harvey, Christopher, 407
Hutton, Henry F., 469
Jay, William, 481
Jones, Samuel, 496
Keeble, Elizabeth, 502
Kendall, John, 504
Kendall, Robert jnr, 505
Kendall, Thomas, 505
Kendall, William, 505
Lavallin, Michael, 530
Letchworth, Joseph, 539
Lingwood, Isaac, 543
Lodge, Henry, 553
Mannall, John, 573
Marsden, John, 576
Marsden, Reuben, 576
Medowes, Arthur, 600
Minks, J., 612
Minks, Robert, 612
Nicholls, John, 645
Nickels, John Pells, 647
Orrin, Christopher, 665
Orrin, William, 665
Parker, Joseph, 674
Pond, Samuel, 705
Root, John jnr, 765
Ruse, James, 771
Sallows, John snr, jnr, 777
Sallows, Richard, 777
Seager, George, 791
Shave, Philip, 804
Shearcroft, Robert snr, 806
Shellye, John, 806
Shinglewood, William, 811
Shoebridge, Richard, 812
Simmons, John, 815
Street, Joseph, 861
Taylor, John, 876–7
Turner, James, 910
Turner, William, 913
Verlander, Simon, 921
Walford, Timothy, 934
Watty, Joseph, 951
Wife, Richard, 972
Winch, John, 991
Cole, George, 491, 690
Cole, James, 388
Coleman, James, 762
Coleman, Thomas, 684

Collier, William, 752
Collings, 20
Collins, 144
Collins, Charles, 686, 706
Collins, Daniel, 800
Collins, Finch, 216
Collins, Thomas, 694
Collinson, 466
Collinson, George Croyson, 709
Collinson, Thomas, 645
Collinson, William, 141
Collison, William, 157
Collumton (Devon):
    Reynolds, —, 738
    Reynolds, James, 738
    Reynolds, John, 738
Colne (Lancs.):
    Addison, John, 4
    Browne, Benjamin, 120
    Dyson, Roger, 263
    Emmott, William, 280
    Gill, James, 340
    Hargrave, John, 398
    Hargreaves, John, 398
    Hewick, Charles, 425
    Howarth, John, 455
    Ingham, John, 471
    Jones, Charles Edward, 494
    Leeming, Robert, 535
    Robinson, John, 758
    Simpson, Martin, 816
    Smith, Samuel, 832
    Smith, William, 834, 835
    Watson, Peter, 950
Colombine, Paul, 95, 399, 403, 456
Coltishall (Suffolk): Newhouse,
    Thomas, 642
Colton (Yorks.): Swale, Samuel,
    867
Columbine, Paul, 656
Colyton (Devon):
    Major, Samuel, 570
    Street, John, 861
Combe Abbey (Warks.): Mayhew,
    John & Ince, William, 595
Comerbach, Thomas, 471
Compton Verney (Warks.):
    Mayhew, John & Ince, William,
    594
Conder, Samuel, 351
Congleton (Cheshire):
    Alcock, Linney, 6
    Broadhurst, Joseph, 109
    Garside, W., 331
    Locket(t), John, 552
    Plant, Thomas, 702
    Porter, Lewis, 707
    Sutton, Thomas, 866
    Topham, John, 899
    Twemlow, John, 914
    Twemlow, Ralph, 914
Conisbrough (Yorks.):
    Appleyard, George, 16
    Appleyard, Joseph, 16

Handley, Thomas, 393
Morley, John, 627
Smith, William, 835
Tune, William, 908
Connell, John, 550
Connor, Charles, 144
Constable, John, 118, 687
Constable Burton Hall (Yorks.):
    Turner, Thomas, 912
    Turner & Smith, 913
Conway, John, 304
Conway, Joseph, 482
Cook, 43, 500
Cook, Gregory, 665
Cook, James, 37
Cook, John, 915
Cook, Thomas, 194
Cooke, 939
Cooke, Daniel, 60
Cooke, Isaac, 322, 445
Cooke, John, 310, 330, 529, 713
Cooke, Joshua, 625
Cooke, Robinson, 549, 1000
Cooke, Thomas, 176, 193, 363, 418
Cooke, William, 779, 786, 789
Cooper, 424
Cooper, Daniel, 138, 891
Cooper, John, 195, 369
Cooper, Joseph, 195
Cooper, Philip, 230
Cooper, Thomas, 643, 662, 846
Cope, William, 267, 332, 706, 790,
    808, 982
Copeland, John, 233
Copeland, Richard, 50, 442, 732
Copeland, Robert, 118, 461
Copeman, 542
Copland, H., 349
Copland, Henry, 552, 725, 776
Copp, W. & A., 780
Coppell, Richard, 266
Corbett, George, 248
Corbridge (Northumb.):
    Green, William, 368
    Hogarth, John, 440
    Williams, Benjamin, 979
Corbron & Co., 186
Corlass, Henry, 437
Corles, Roger, 732
Corney, 459
Corney, William, 439
Cornish, 341
Cornwall:
    Trefry, John, 903
    Trengrouse, Helston, 903
Corran, Henry, 938
Corrin, Robert, 576
Corry, 1004
Corsham Court (Wilts.):
    Birchell (Birchall?), —, 74
    Bromwich, Thomas, 110
    Chippendale, Thomas snr, 168
    Chippendale, Thomas jnr, 169
    Cobb, John, 182, 184

Cole, George, 187
Dawes, —, 233
Deering, Samuel, 238
Garth, James, 331
Grogan, F.M., 376
Hay, Tempest, 414
Hill, —, 430
Johnson, Thomas, 491, 492
Le Caron, Philip, 534
Main, —, 570
Perkins, —, 690
Sadler, Slacksle, 775
Strangeway & Taylor, 860
Viel, Matthew, 923
Cossins, Robert, 202
Cottingham, Richard, 548
Cottingham (Yorks.):
  Deggitt, John, 238
  Ross, Francis, 766
  Ross, Mary, 766
  Ross, Thomas, 766
  Teal, John, 880
  Todd, John, 896
  Todd, Richard, 897
  Westerman, Joseph, 960
Cottle, George, 954
Cottrell, 523, 931
Cottrell, Richard, 235
Coulstone, R., 879
Coultart, Joseph, 482
Coulton, Thomas, 435
Coupland, Robert, 97
Coventry (Warks.):
  Arnold, John, 19
  Arnold, William, 19
  Ashton, Joseph, 21
  Baker, Amos, 32
  Ball, William, 35
  Barr, John, 43
  Bright, Joseph, 108
  Brothers, George, 112
  Browett, Joseph, 113
  Burden, Richard, 130
  Burgess, Thomas, 130
  Deacon, James, 237
  Dickenson, John, 243
  Dickison, John, 243
  Dry, Samuel, 257
  Gordon, Thomas, 357
  Gray, William, 366
  Grimes, John, 375
  Harald, James, 395
  Hobson, Nathaniel, 436
  Jackson, Henry, 475
  Keene, Robert, 502
  Line, William, 543
  Line & Johnson, 543
  Newark, John, 642
  Palmer, Edward, 671
  Pearman, Thomas, 684
  Sedgely, Arthur, 798
  Taylor, Samuel, 879
  Taylor, Thomas, 879
  Thornbury, William, 889

Trowless, William, 906
White, John, 966
Wright, William, 1009
Cowan, 498
Coward, Henry, 102
Cowell, D. & W., 895
Cowell, Daniel, 385
Cowen, 498
Cowes (Isle of Wight):
  Bayly, E., 52
  Bowes, John, 92
  Donaldson, James, 250
  Hewit, John snr, 425
  Marvin, George, 582
  Moth, William, 632
  Richards, Joseph jnr, 742
  Thomas, Edward, 883
  Wyatt, Frederick, 1010
Cowlam, William, 201
Cowley (Oxon.): Thompson,
  Charles, 885
Cowling (Yorks.): Binns, John, 73
Cowpen Horton (Northumb.):
  Howe, Bennet, 455
Cowper, Robert, 933
Cowper, Thomas, 49, 310
Cowthorpe, William, 3, 832
Cox, 668
Cox, E.T., 204
Cox, James, 378
Cox, John, 110, 134, 222, 281
Cox, Robert, 418
Cox, William Hutton, 859
Coxed, John, 414
Coxed & Woster, 61
Coxter, William, 961
Crace, Frederick, 496
Cragg, 954
Crake, John, 919
Crakehall (Yorks.): Graham,
  William, 363
Cranbrook (Kent):
  Holman, Edward, 444
  Mott, John, 632
  Pawson, Thomas jnr, 682
  Reeves, William Alexander, 736
  Waters, Thomas, 947
Cranburn, 410
Crane, 148
Crane, Edward, 994
Cranford Park (Middlx):
  Chippendale, Thomas snr, 166
Cranwell, 18
Crawford, William, 85
Craymer, 554
Crediton (Devon):
  Dicker, R., 243
  Gover, John, 361
  Tippets, Richard, 895
Creessall, 391
Creighton, 268
Cremer, John, 693
Cressell, John, 11

Crewe Hall (Cheshire):
  Bywater, John, 140
  Cliff, Washington, 179
  Elvey, Elizabeth, 277
  Harris, John, 401
Crewkerne (Som.):
  Bartlett, Susannah, 46
  Bartlett, W., 46
  Bishop, Eli, 76
  Bishop, John, 76
  Howe, George, 455
  Male, Charles, 570
  Oliver, Thomas, 663
  Pearcey, John, 684
  Perry, Henry, 691
Crib, 322
Cribb, 322
Crichel House (Dorset): Mayhew,
  John & Ince, William, 594
Crimes, John, 713
Cripplegate (London):
  Davis, William, 233
  Edmonds, John, 267
  Edwards, Henry, 269
  Harding & Son, 396
  Harland, James, 398
  Hepplewhite, George, 422
  Howard, John & Co., 454
  Hubbard, John, 457
  Lewis, George, 540
  Richardson, John, 744
  Robinson, Richard, 760
  Ryall, Joseph, 774
  Sanderson, James, 779
  Shields, Thomas, 810
  Short, Robert, 812
  Walker, Samuel, 937
  Whytall, Thomas, 972
  Wood, Henry, 996
  Wood, Thomas, 998
Crisp, Samuel, 104
Crispe, Edward, 80
Croft, Isaac, 27
Croft, Joseph, 557
Croft, Samuel, 808
Croft Castle (Herefs.): Seddon,
  George, 796
Crofts, J., 49
Cromar, 607
Crompton, Benjamin, 211, 334
Crool, David, 160
Croome Court (Worcs.):
  Adair, John, 2
  Alken, Sefferin, 8
  Bradburn(e), John, 96
  Brown, James, 114
  Chippendale, Thomas snr, 167
  Chivers, Noah, 170
  Cobb, John, 182, 183
  Crompton, Samuel, 211
  Dermer, William, 241
  Duncombe, Richard, 259
  Edlyn, John & Chappell, 267

Elward, George & Marsh, William, 279
Folgham, John, 307
Gearing, H., 334
Gilbert, John, 338
Gordon, John & Taitt, John & Richard, 356, 357
Graham, Joseph & Partners, 362
Hancock, Colebron, 392
Hobcraft, John, 436
Langlois, Pierre, 526, 527
Linnell, William, 547
Litchfield & Graham, 549
Mayhew, John & Ince, William, 592, 593
Merlin, John Joseph, 603
Morton, John, 630
Morton, Richard, 630
Nelson, Sefferin, 640
Pilton, Thomas, 699
Reynolds, Samuel, 738
Rob(b)ins, John, 756
Smith & Chipp, 835
Spitton, Thomas (?), 845
Taylor, Hynmers, 876
Tousey, John, 900
Vaughan, Samuel, 920
Vile, William, 926
Watts, Thomas, 951
Webb, Henry, 953
Wildsmith, John, 974
Willerton & Roberts, 978
Wood, Henry, 996
Croome D'Abitot (Worcs.), St Mary Magdalen: Adair, John, 2
Crosby, Thomas, 459
Crosby Hall (Lancs.):
    Aldridge, Simon, 7
    Crumpton, —, 216
    Marsh, Moses, 577
    Rigby, Samuel, 747
Crosland (Yorks.): Ro(d)gers, Isaac, 763
Cross, 526, 801, 904
Cross, Aaron, 512
Cross, Adam, 51
Cross, Edmund, 124
Cross, John, 91
Cross, Nicholas, 76, 445, 748, 974
Cross, Thomas, 489
Cross, William, 291
Crossley, 340
Crouch, Ceasar, 164
Crouch, John, 7, 415
Crouch, Stephen, 953
Croughton, John, 161, 492, 511, 715
Crowdell, Isaac, 724
Crowder, Samuel, 789
Crownest (Yorks.): Wright, Richard & Elwick, Edward, 1008
Crowther, 724
Crowther, William, 376

Croxteth Hall (Lancs.): Prescott, Richard, 713
Croydon (Surrey):
    Adams, W., 4
    Bance, George, 36
    Blake, John, 79
    Blake, William, 79
    Hayward, Ebenezer, 415
    Hodder, Richard, 436
    Innes, James, 472
    Plowman, Henry, 703
    Potter, Joseph, 708
    Rowe, William, 768
    Stedhall, Hills, 851
    Streeter, Charles, 861
Cruffall, 391
Crumin, Michael, 494
Crump, Ely, 44, 515, 696
Crump, John, 21, 299
Crump, Richard, 584
Crump, Robert, 921
Crump, Thomas, 870
Crunden, Thomas, 216
Cruse, Gabriel, 857
Crusoe, Charles, 217
Crusoe, Robinson, 408, 662, 929
Cubbins, William, 495
Cubbitt, Paul Springall, 460
Cubett, Benjamin, 144
Cuckfield (Sussex):
    Hamlin, Thomas, 391
    Penfold, Noah, 688
Cuckney (Notts.): Keeton, John, 502
Cuddy, Joseph, 70
Cudland, James, 777
Cudworth, Thomas, 313
Cuenot, John, 271
Cullen, Charles, 218
Cullen, James, 182, 653, 684, 939
Cullen, John, 218
Cullen, Samuel, 218
Cullen, Thomas, 40
Cullingworth (Yorks.): Waddington, John, 930
Cullompton (Devon):
    Davey, John, 227
    Howard, George, 453
    Pratt, Thomas, 712
    Wescombe, William, 959
Culverthorpe Hall (Lincs.): Boson, John, 88, 89
Cumming, 560
Cummings, William, 358
Cuningham, Samuel, 690
Cupis, 629
Cupiss, 629
Cure, George, 401
Currie, Archibald, 736
Curry, Robert, 266
Curtis, William, 602
Cushing, Samuel, 225
Cushion, Samuel, 478
Custance, William, 994

Cusworth Hall (Yorks.):
    Cobb, John, 184
    Graham, Joseph & Partners, 362
    Marshall, James jnr, 578
    Richardson, Christopher, 743
    Wright, Richard & Elwick, Edward, 1007
Cutler, Thomas, 334

D

Daguerre, Dominique, 592, 597, 623, 641, 930
Daguire (Daguerre), Dominique, 641
Dale, George, 376
Dale, Samuel, 358, 704
Dalkeith Palace (Scotland):
    Brayman, Thomas, 104
    Lapierre, Jean, 528
    Moore, James snr, 618
Dalmahoy (Midlothian):
    Chippendale, Thomas snr, 166
Dalquharran (Ayrshire): Hodson, John, 439
Dalston (London):
    Kebbell, —, 502
    Luck, William, 560
    Porters, Thomas, 707
Dalton (Lancs.):
    Hope, John, 448
    Postlethwaite, William, 707
Dalton Hall (Yorks.):
    Chippendale, Thomas snr, 168
    Chippendale, Thomas jnr, 169
    Wright, Richard & Elwick, Edward, 1007, 1008
Dalton-in-Furness (Lancs.): Briggs, George, 107
Danby, John, 859
Dandy, Andrew, 674
Daniel, Edward, 241
Daniel, John, 924
Daniel, Samuel, 102
Dansie, William, 222
Dant, 393
Darby, Thomas, 894
Darby, William, 118
Darbyshire, John, 834
Darkin, James, 802
Darking, George, 108, 306
Darling, William, 956
Darlington (Co. Durham):
    Ainsley, William, 5
    Baker, Jonathan, 33
    Bell, Stephen, 62
    Bellwood, William, 63
    Belton, William, 64
    Bewick, William, 70
    Blackett, Henry, 77
    Botcherby, Robert, 90
    Elgee, Edward, 272
    Garbutt, John, 329

Gibson, Thomas, 338
Gray, James, 365
Hall, William, 386
Hindle, James, 433
Hindle, John, 433
Hobson, William, 436
Hogg, George, 440
Howson, James, 456
Howson, Robert, 456
Jordan, David, 498
Kirton, George, 518
Layfield, Robert, 533
Lindsey, Robert, 543
Lithgo, Robert, 549
Marshall, James, 578
Marshall & Dodds, 579
Martin, E.J., 580
Naylor, Robert H., 639
Oxendale, Thomas, 668
Preston, Matthew, 714
Rimington, Edward, 749
Robinson, George, 757
Robson, Edward, 761
Smith, William, 834
Snaith, William, 836
Spencer, George, 843
Stelling, Robert, 852
Thompson, John, 887
Todhunter, Thomas, 897
Tunstall, George, 908
Tunstall, John, 980
Unthank, William, 917
Wilkinson, Thomas, 977
Wilson, Henry, 987
Wilson, Robert, 989
Windale, Michael, 991
Darnby, John, 859
Darnton, 312
Dartford (Kent):
  Marshall, Charles, 577
  Stidolph, Henry, 856
Dartmouth (Devon):
  Brown, J., 114
  Heard, Charles, 417
  Northcote, William, 655
  Predam, William, 713
  Strange, James, 860
  Veale, Jarvis, 921
  Way, John, 952
  Way, Joseph, 952
Darwen, Thomas, 933
Darwen (Lancs.): Harewood, J., 397
Darwin, Eubulus Thorold, 492
Davenport, John, 862
Davenport, Thomas, 4
Davenport House (Salop): Moore, James jnr, 619
Daventry (Northants.):
  Adams, John, 3
  Smith, Samuel, 832
  Wadsworth, John, 931
  Ward, John, 943
  Winnes, G., 992

Wright, Edward, 1005
Yateman, William, 1012
Davey, 38
David, 134
David, William, 451
Davidson, 5, 902
Davidson, John, 238
Davidson, Peter, 787
Davies, Edward, 230
Davies, Henry, 408
Davies, John, 110, 150, 228, 231
Davies, John Austin, 232
Davies, Joseph, 151
Davies, Peter, 230, 232, 276, 613, 983
Davies, Roger, 228
Davies, Samuel, 179, 230, 381, 970
Davies, Thomas, 197, 228, 229, 408, 895
Davis, 2, 227, 237, 273, 706
Davis, George, 211, 232
Davis, Hugh, 228
Davis, James, 228
Davis, John, 229, 306, 919
Davis, John Austin, 229
Davis, Philip, 388
Davis, Samuel, 229
Davis, T., 229
Davis, Thomas, 230, 231, 284
Davis, William, 228, 230, 783, 800
Davison, 902
Davy, John, 227
Davy, Robert, 227
Dawes, 84, 375, 657, 986
Dawes, Mark, 37, 180, 385, 990
Dawes, Robert, 234
Dawkins, John, 873
Dawlish (Devon):
  Avant, Thomas, 27
  Burt, William Charles, 134
  Stephens, William, 853
Daws, Robert, 234
Daws, William, 234
Daws & Minter, 867
Dawson, Cephas, 808
Dawson, Elizabeth, 151
Dawson, Richard, 226, 235
Dawson, Robert, 743
Dawson, Thomas, 352, 403, 427, 587, 946
Dawson, William, 201
Day, Charles, 867
Day, George, 183
Day, James, 957
De Caux, William, 410
Deacon, B., 237
Deacon, Thomas, 233
Daylesford House (Glos.):
  Mayhew, John & Ince, William, 597
Deal (Kent):
  Denne, Ambrose, 240
  Gillman, David, 341
  Hayman, Richard, 415

Hayman, William, 415
Kingsmill, Comfort, 516
Langley & Denne, 526
Lawrence, William, 531
Parker, John, 674
Smithers, —, 836
Spain, Edmund, 841
Sugden, George, 864
Tilden, M., 894
Wellard, William, 957
Dean, Thomas, 263
Deane, Ambrose, 240
Deare, John, 655
Dearing, Samuel, 725
Debenham (Suffolk):
  Abbot, Joseph, 1
  Levell, John, 539
  Nevell, John, 641
  Pollard, Samuel, 705
  Wyand, John, 1009
Debharms, Peter, 514
Dedham (Essex):
  Grice, Joseph, 373
  Griffiths, Robert, 375
Deeble, John T., 80
Deeble, John Thurston, 994
Deene Church (Northants.): Boson, John, 88
Deene Park (Northants.):
  Bradshaw, William, 100
  Goodison, Benjamin, 354
  Griffith(s), Edward, 374
  Hallett, William snr and William jnr, 389
  Morant, George, 623
  Whittle, James, 971
Deggitt, John, 766
Delafield, Erasmus, 587
Delamere, Abraham, 750
Delatouche, 254
Dell, Benjamin, 760, 1006, 1014
Demee, Daniel, 458, 764
Denby (Yorks.): Lockwood, John, 553
Denham, James, 808
Denham, Thomas, 410, 454
Denne, 526, 707
Dennis, Richard, 53, 75
Dennison, John, 645
Dennison, Joseph, 184
Denson, John, 92
Denton Park (Yorks.):
  Bulkley, —, 125
  Calthrop, —, 142
  Chippendale, Thomas snr, 168
  Ellis, —, 275
  Gillow, 342
  Hacker, —, 381
  Howard, —, 453
  Mayhew, John & Ince, William, 596
  Ryley, George, 774
  Schole, —, 789
  Starkie, —, 850

Turner, Thomas, 912
Turner & Smith, 913
Wade, John, 931
Deptford (London):
Armitage, William George, 18
Bennett, William, 65
Blackshaw, Mary, 78
Bradley, Thomas, 98
Ellis, William, 276
Emmett, Robert, 280
Gibbons, Grinling, 336
Hampshire, George, 392
Langdale, John, 525
Olyett, Robert, 664
Powell, William, 711
Redpath, J., 733
Ridpath, James, 747
Rope, —, 765
Senken, G., 800
Sturdee, William Henry, 863
Walters, John, 941
Wicksteed, Edward, 972
Derbishire, John, 226
Derby, Thomas, 226
Derby:
Adin, John, 5
Ashmole, Benjamin, 21
Ashmole, Richard, 21
Ashmole, Thomas, 21
Baldwin, David, 34
Barnett, George, 43
Barratt, George, 44
Bartholomew, Joseph, 46
Boden, William, 83
Botham, Robert, 90
Bregazzi, Samuel, 105
Bridgen, —, 107
Bromley, William, 110
Brown, Thomas, 118
Burgon, Benjamin, 130
Dale, John, 224
Dudley, Charles
Eaton, John, 265
Gamble & Bridgen, 328
Glazebrook, Paul, 345
Gorse, Joseph, 358
Gravenor, James, 364
Hall, William jnr, 386
Harvey, Samuel, 408
Hewitt, Henry, 425
Hughes, Job, 460
Hughes, John, 461
Jelly, Richard, 483
Johnson, Moses, 490
Johnson, Richard, 490
Kirk, Thomas, 517
Knight, George, 519
Laburn, Thomas, 520
Lauder, John, 529
Lomas, —, 554
Lovat, Samuel, 555
Lovat(t), James, 555
Lovett, Samuel, 557
Lowe, John, 557

Mason, —, 583
Moneypenny, G., 616
Moseley, Robert, 631
Moseley & Tunnicliff, 631
Moss, John, 632
Motherhaw, Thomas, 632
Mottershaw, Thomas, 632
Natt, Joseph, 639
Odams, David, 661
Orme, William, 665
Parrott, John, 677
Pearce, John, 684
Pilkington, Henry, 699
Pool, William, 705
Potter, David, 708
Potter, Edward, 708
Potts, Benjamin, 708
Rickard, George, 746
Rickard(s), George, 746
Robinson, Anthony, 756
Robinson, John, 759
Rutherford, William, 774
Scarlet, S., 788
Shaw, William, 805
Shore, Robert, 812
Silverwood, Theodore, 815
Slater, Robert, 821
Smith, Edward, 826
Smith, George, 826
Smith, John, 830
Soar, George, 838
Storer, William, 859
Taylor, Burder, 874
Taylor, William, 879
Turner, Joseph, 911
Udell, Jacob, 916
Walker & Gadsby, 939
Wathnall, Leonard, 947
Whitehead, John, 968
Wood, John, 997
Woollatt, Joseph, 1002
Woolley, Samuel, 1002
Wright, Thomas, 1008
Derby House (London): Nelson,
Sefferin, 640
Derbyshire, John, 226
Derbyshire, Thomas, 226
Derique, Robert, 241
Derret, Nathanial, 360
Desbrough, Henry, 956
Deschamps, John, 419
Deschamps, Peter, 225, 419
Deschamps, Susanna, 241
Deuguee, Robert, 241
Devey, John, 241
Devignee, Robert, 241
Devizes (Wilts.):
Boys, John jnr, 94
Green, Philip, 367
Jefferys, Charles, 482
Knight, James Thomas, 519
Knight, John & James, 519
Knight, Richard, 519
Lenard, James, 538

Lott, Timothy, 555
Mullins, Benoni, 635
Mullins, James, 635
Pinnock, John, 700
Pontin, Daniel, 705
Reev(e)s, Henry, 736
Reevs, Nicholas, 736
Strugnell, Joseph, 862
Vaisey, Ann, 919
Vaisey, John, 919
Waight, George, 932
White, William, 967
Wilbee, William, 973
Devonport (Devon):
Bennett(s), Richard, 65
Bickley, D., 71
Bishop, William, 76
Blaxell, William, 80
Bodley, John, 83
Bonney, John, 86
Downing, Amos, 254
Easterbrook, William, 265
Elliott, John, 274
Ellis, Thomas, 275
Every, James, 286
Garland, Francis Burrall, 331
Gaul, John, 333
Goad, George, 345
Granville, Robert, 364
Hare, Catherine, 397
Hare, Richard, 397
Harvey, William Henry, 408
Hocking, William, 436
Hodge, Samuel, 437
Holland, —, 441
Howell, Henry, 455
Hughes, —, 460
James, Geoffrey, 478
James, Thomas, 480
Kenning, W., 507
Kimmins, Thomas, 513
Kimmins, William, 513
Knox, John, 520
Lamb, Thomas, 522
Lane, John, 525
Luxmore, John, 561
Mortimore, John, 630
Mortimore, Jos. Pollybank, 630
Niles, Edward, 648
Paddy, Thomas, 669
Phillips, John, 695
Pincombe, Abraham, 699
Pine, Thomas, 699
Prowse, William, 719
Richards, James, 742
Short, Edward, 812
Smith, William, 834
Spray, William, 846
Spry, John, 846
Spry, William, 846
Stevens, J., 854
Stevenson, John, 855
Symons, William, 869
Tyrer, John, 916

Wadelton, Charles, 931
Wakeham, James, 933
Whitford, W., 969
Williams, Joseph, 981
Dewey, William, 590
Dewhurst, John, 757
Dewhurst, Roger, 302
Dewsbury (Yorks.):
  Auty, George, 27
  Balmforth, William, 36
  Bamforth, William, 36
  Brook, Joseph & John, 111
  Brook, Thomas, 111
  Brook, William, 111
  Brown, James, 115
  Ellis, Joseph, 275
  Ellis, Thomas, 275
  Gomersall, Thomas, 349
  Halmshaw, Joseph, 390
  Healey, Benjamin, 417
  Healey, David, 417
  Lister, William, 549
  Marriott, John & Thomas, 575
  Milner, John, 611
  Smith, Joshua, 830
  Smith, Josiah, 830
  Walker, Richard, 937
  Walker, William, 938
  Ward, John, 943
  Wilcock, Edward, 973
Dicken, Edward, 386
Dickenson, William, 371
Dickin, Edward, 244
Dickings, William, 812
Dickinson, 25
Dickinson, Edward, 244
Dickinson, Richard, 847
Dickon, Edward, 82, 131, 243, 604, 827, 882
Dickon, John, 376, 434, 466, 733, 865, 951
Dickson, Edward, 345
Dickson, Thomas, 801
Diglake (Staffs.): Laking, Charles, 522
Dignam, Mo., 783
Dillart, Edward, 159
Dillin, 413
Dilling, 413
Dilworth, Daniel Large, 819
Dingwall, Alexander, 356
Diss (Norfolk):
  Barkham, Thomas, 41
  Battel, William, 50
  Harrison, William, 405
  Lingwood, George, 543
  Parker, John, 674
  Rich, John, 741
  Towell, Robert, 900
  Warne, Henry, 945
  Whaite, James jnr, 962
Ditchley Park (Oxon.):
  Hallett, William snr and William jnr, 389

Moore, James jnr, 619
Ditton (Bucks.): Goodison, Benjamin, 354
Dixon, 446
Dixon, Peter, 754
Dixon, Thomas, 244, 298, 335, 427, 730, 801
Dixon, William, 915
Dobb, Thomas, 333, 382, 677, 749
Dobson, Henry, 706
Dobson, Thomas, 157
Dobyns, Thomas, 199, 425, 519, 819, 954, 960
Dodd, Edward, 72
Dodd, Samuel, 35, 290, 305, 385, 613
Dodds, 579
Dodgson, William, 297
Dodgson, William Fawcett, 223, 443, 932
Doeg, David, 37, 179, 861, 885
Donald, 944
Donaldson, William, 734
Doncaster (Yorks.):
  Adamson, William, 4
  Barton, Thomas, 47
  Belk, John, 60
  Belk, Vincent, 60
  Blumley, —, 82
  Bowling, John, 93
  Bradford, John, 97
  Bradford, Thomas, 97
  Brailsford, William, 101
  Brown, Thomas, 118
  Bunning, James, 129
  Burgan, Benjamin, 130
  Dixon, Jseph, 246
  Everitt, John, 285
  Harrison, Herbert, 403
  Haworth, Thomas, 413
  Hill, Samuel, 431
  Hinchcliffe, John, 433
  King, William, 515
  Kitchin, George, 518
  Leedel, John, 535
  Leggott, Thomas, 537
  Lilley, William, 542
  Malim, Thomas, 571
  Martin, John, 581
  Meens, William, 600
  Morsely, —, 630
  Moss, Matthew, 632
  Mozley, Samuel, 634
  Nicholson, Edward, 646
  Nicholson, Robert, 647
  Norton, John, 656
  Oxley, Daniel, 669
  Oxley, William, 669
  Ramsden, Ann, 726
  Ramsden, John, 726
  Reckard, William & John, 733
  Richardson, Christopher, 743
  Richardson, Robert, 744
  Robeshaw, Levi, 755

Robinson, John, 758
Robinson, William, 761
Robshaw, Levi, 761
Smith, John, 828
Theakston(e), Christopher, 882
Thompson, William, 888
Thornton, Robert, 891
Volanteno, J., 930
Wadworth, P., 931
Walker, Thomas, 938
Waterworth, Thomas, 947
Whitaker, John, 963
Whitehead, John, 968
Wightman, Thomas, 973
Doncaster Mansion House:
  Lilley, William, 542
  Richardson, Christopher, 743
Donnard, Henry, 254
Donne, 428
Donne, Thomas, 706
Donnington (Lincs.): Stanton, Baxter, 849
Doolan, 10, 521
Dorchester (Dorset):
  Bartlett, George, 46
  Beach, William, 53
  Davis, William, 233
  Elford, Lawrence, 272
  Gretton, Thomas & Lake, Richard, 373
  Gritton, Thomas, 375
  Hawkins, James, 412
  Hawkins, William, 413
  Hazard, Mary, 416
  Hazard, Thomas, 416
  Hodder, Benjamin, 436
  Keats, John, 502
  Loder, Thomas, 553
  Nook, Isaac, 651
  Sharren, Robert, 804
  Snook, Robert snr & jnr, 837
  Snook, Samuel, 837
  Treves, William snr & jnr, 904
  Twisse, William, 915
  Wheeler, John, 963
Dore, 366
Dorking (Surrey):
  Ede, Joseph, 266
  Hide, Daniel, 428
  Killick, William, 512
  Lack, James, 521
  Miller, William, 609
  Muggeridge, Frederick, 634
  Raynes, John Smith, 731
  Sayer, Richard, 788
  Sayers, R., 788
  Smith, Samuel, 832
Doughty, Ezra, 146, 504, 917
Doughty, Joseph, 579, 580
Doughty, Martha, 17, 212, 397, 579
Doughty, Thomas, 458
Douglas, John, 490
Douthwaite, Anthony, 160
Dove, John, 850

Dover (Kent):
Allen, F., 9
Allen, John, 10
Beer, James, 58
Bradbridge, John, 95
Broad, Charles William, 109
Burch, Stephen, 129
Byng, Finnis, 139
Emptage, Humphry, 281
Emptage, John, 281
Epps, Thomas, 281
Gibbons, Richard, 336
Harris, William, 403
Harvey, C., 407
Hiller, Frederick John, 432
Horsmaill, William, 451
Lamb, Charles, 522
Lamb, Elizabeth & Sons, 522
Lamb, James, 522
Lamb, William, 522
Lawes, William, 530
Mantle, Thomas, 573
Marlen, William, 575
Marten, William, 580
Munden, Stephen, 635
Orton, Mark & Co., 665
Peake, Henry, 683
Penn, John, 688
Pile, John Trevanion, 698
Pratt, Walter jnr, 712
Pyall, Robert, 722
Reynolds, Thomas, 738
Rutter, Edward, 774
Sclater, E., 789
Shoulden, James, 812
Solly, William Raymant, 838
Stockwell, C., 857
Stockwell, Elizabeth, 857
Timewell, John, 895
Towell, James, 900
Wetherley, Thomas, 961
Wickes, William, 972
Williams, Thomas Stephen, 982
Dovey, John, 895
Dowbiggin, Thomas, 872, 970
Downham Market (Norfolk):
Bird, Benjamin, 74
Burrage, John, 132
Langman, John, 527
Riches, Robert, 745
Tolbot, Michael, 897
Vincent, William, 929
Downhill (Co. Antrim):
Columbani, Placido, 191
Downing, Jos., 770
Downton (Wilts.):
Honeywell, Richard, 447
How, Thomas, 453
Taunton, Jacob, 874
Downton Castle (Herefs.):
Smallman, John, 822
Doyle, 732, 735
Drake, 221
Draper, 645

Draper, Gifford, 161
Draper, Henry, 6
Draper, John, 380
Draper, Thomas, 378
Draper, William, 737
Drayton House (Northants.):
Arbuthnot, Philip, 16
Chisholme, Thomas, 170
Cobb, Henry, 181
Foxhall, —, 315
Greene, John, 368
Jensen, Gerrit, 486
Lapierre, Francis, 528
Penson, Stephen, 689
Rhodes, William, 740
Robinson, Richard, 759
Rymell, Thomas, 774
Sherard, W., 808
Drew, 55
Drew, Richard, 256
Driffield (Yorks.):
Dunning, John, 261
Etherington, George, 282
Grassam, John, 364
Shepherdson, George, 808
Walker, John, 936
White, George, 965
White, John, 966
White, Thomas, 967
Wilson, Francis, 987
Woodmancey, John, 999
Drighlington (Yorks.):
Lawton, Joseph, 532
Rhodes, Joseph, 740
Dring, 174
Driver, Matthew, 256
Droitwich (Worcs.):
Emuss, James, 281
Emuss, William, 281
Noke, Thomas, 651
Stokes, George, 858
Druffil, 53
Drummond Castle (Tayside):
Dowbiggin(g), Thomas, 253
Drury, Edmund, 457
Drury Lane Theatre (London):
Nelson, Sefferin, 640
Smith, Charles, 824
Dublin:
Hopkins, William, 449
Moore, William, 622
Dublin, Leinster House: Kennett,
Robert and Kidd, William, 507
Dublin, Villa Marino: Alken,
Sefferin, 8
Dudley (Staffs.):
Adams, John, 3
Baker, Joseph, 33
Baugh, T & G, 50
Bird, William, 74
Brettell, James, 105
Butler, Edwin, 137
Derecourt, James Greaves, 241
Derecourt, John, 241

Gill, Daniel, 340
Griffin, James, 373
Guest, Zephaniah, 377
Hackitt, John, 381
Hallam, James, 387
Hallam, Samuel, 387
Harris, Thomas, 402
Hipkins, S., 434
Langford, Richard, 525
Morrall, Benjamin, 627
Morrall, William, 627
Nicklin, William, 647
Payton, Joseph, 683
Pensotti, Joseph, 689
Pitt, Samuel, 701
Pitt, Saul, 701
Pyatt, Jos., 722
Pyatt, Joseph, 722
Robinson, J., 757
Seekerson, James, 798
Share, Elizabeth, 802
Share, John, 802
Share, Thomas, 802
Smith, David, 825
Southall, Enoch, 840
Taylor, Richard, 878
Turner, Thomas, 912
Turner & Ellis, 913
Waterson, Joseph, 947
Whitehouse, George, 968
Whitehouse, John & Sons, 968
Williams, Thomas, 982
Wright, Jesse, 1005
Wright, Moses, 1006
Du Flos, Harriet, 56
Duchemin, George, 301
Ducroy, Lewis, 816
Dudds, William, 802
Dueing, Francis, 243
Duffield, 53
Duffield, Francis, 859
Duffield, John, 117
Duffil, 607
Duffill, 53
Duffill, Francis, 63, 114
Duffill, John, 117
Duffs, W.W., 200
Dufill, 32
Dugdale, Joseph, 819
Dugelby, Robert, 747
Dugler, John, 251, 490
Duke, 20, 817
Dukinfield (Lancs.):
Bardsley, John, 39
Haigh, Thomas, 383
Wild, James, 974
Wrigley, James, 1009
Dumfries House (Ayrshire):
Chippendale, Thomas snr, 165, 166
Kerby, Richard, 509
Mercer, George, 601
Moore, Thomas, 621
Smith, Samuel, 831

Dunch, 598
Dunckley, Richard, 891
Dunham Massey (Cheshire):
　Agnew, Thomas & Zanetti,
　　Vittore, 5
　Barber, Thomas, 39
　Bispham, Edward, 76
　Bywater, John, 140
　Cadman, John, 140
　Gregory, John, 370
　Hand, —, 393
　Howard, Robert, 454
　Johnson, John, 490
　Kent, Richard, 508
　Key, James, 511
　Mawson, John, 588
　Norris, John, 654
　Partington, Joseph, 678
　Sayers, John, 788
　Skelhorn, Peter, 818
　Skilbeck, G., 819
　Smith, Samuel, 832
　Swain, Thomas, 866
　Syers, John, 869
　Tratt & Attfield, 902
　Walker, Richard, 937
　Wild, Jacob, 974
　Williams, Harry, 980
　Zanetti, Vittorie, 1015
　Zan(n)etti & Agnew, 1016
Dunholme (Lincs.): Laurance,
　Thomas, 529
Dunkeld Palace (Perthshire):
　Cole, George, 187
　Johnson, Thomas, 492
Dunkinfield (Lancs.):
　Stansfield, William, 849
　Walker, John, 936
Dunlin, 470
Dunmow (Essex):
　Scruby, James, 791
　Smith, William, 835
Dunn, 121
Dunn, John, 306, 975
Dunn, Michael, 136, 739
Dunning, William, 427
Dunns, Michael, 136
Dunstable (Beds.): Mellor, John,
　601
Dunster (Som.):
　Hole, John, 441
　Webber, James, 954
Dunster Castle (Som.): Bromwich,
　Thomas, 110
Dunton, William, 555
Durante, William, 664
Durham, John, 626
Durham:
　Alderson, Joseph, 7
　Anderson, Andrew, 12
　Bilton, Ralph, 72
　Blenkinsop, Peter, 80
　Bolton, John, 84
　Bowes, Thomas, 92

Brown, Matthew, 117
Brown, William, 119
Burdon, Matthew & F.& G., 130
Dixon, William, 247
Douglass, James, 251
Douthwaite, Edward, 252
Goodricke, William, 354
Grieveson, Valentine, 373
Grundy, John, 377
Hawthornthwaite, John, 414
Herrin, William, 423
Hopper, Edmund, 449
Hopper, Michael, 449
Hunter, Matthew, 465
Hutchinson, William, 468
Jefferyes, George, 482
Lightfoot, William, 542
Madoin, John, 569
Mann, James, 572
Marshall, John, 579
Morton, Andrew, 630
Moses, Robert, 631
Padman, John, 669
Peele, T., 686
Preston, Daniel, 714
Richardby, James jnr, 741
Richardby, Thomas, 741
Richardson, John, 744
Richerley, T., 745
Rickaby, James, 746
Rickaby, Thomas, 746
Robinson, Ralph, 759
Robinson, Robert, 760
Sewell, Robert, 801
Sewell, William, 801
Shafto, William, 802
Shaw, John snr & jnr, 804
Shaw, Mary, 805
Sheffield, George F., 806
Shephard, Thomas, 807
Smith, William, 835
Stimpson, William, 856
Stonehouse, George, 859
Thompson, J., 886
Thompson, John & successors,
886
Thompson, Matthew, 887
Thompson, William, 888
Tilly, Thomas, 895
Trotter, Ralph, 906
Turnbull, John, 909
Wallace, John, 939
Wardell, Matthew, 944
Wardell, Thomas, 944
Westgarth, Thomas, 960
White, W., 967
White, William, 967
Whitfield, Lewis, 969
Wilkinson, Thomas, 977
Willey, John, 979
Durley, 502
Durno, 566
Durrant, John, 998
Durrant, Thomas, 456, 857

Dursley (Glos.):
　Halliday, John, 390
　Player, Timothy, 702
　Roe, William, 763
　Rudder, Edmund, 770
　Workman, John, 1003
Durston (Som.): Kingston, Thomas,
　516
Duthoit, James, 369, 899
Dutton, 821
Dutton, John, 22, 358
Dutton, John B., 936
Dutton, M., 262
Dutton, Nathan, 915
Dutton, Thomas, 35, 237, 266, 482,
　622, 636, 664, 726
Dyer, William, 143
Dyrham Park (Glos.):
　Skelton, Humphrey, 818
　Sympson, Thomas, 869
　Trimnell, Charles, 904
Dyson, John, 789

E

Eagles, Thomas, 176
Ealing Grove (Middlx): Mayhew,
　John & Ince, William, 595
Eames, Lynnel, 787
Earl, Elden, 647
Earl, William Elden, 42, 93
Earle, Elden, 122
Earle, W.E., 684, 804
Earle, William Eldon, 835
Earls Heaton (Yorks.): Marriott,
　Luke, 575
Easington (Co. Durham): Sharp,
　Job, 802
Easingwold (Yorks.):
　Atkinson, Thomas, 25
　Dacre, Benjamin, 223
　Holliday, Matthew, 443
　Preston, Thomas, 714
　Rookledge, Francis, 765
　Rooklidge, William, 765
　White, William, 967
East, John, 776
East Bergholt (Suffolk): Jeffery,
　William, 482
East Bridgford (Notts.): Dennis,
　William, 240
East Dereham (Norfolk):
　Brown, Peter, 117
　Eastoe, William, 265
　Elph, Thomas T., 277
　Meal, William, 599
　Minns, William, 612
　Munfort, Peter, 635
　Norton, Matthew, 656
　Riches, Joseph, 745
　Rivett, William, 750
　Roches, Robert, 745
　Self, Thomas James, 799

Smith, Christopher, 825
Smith, John, 829
East Grinstead (Surrey):
  Middleton, Christopher, 605
  Trice, John, 904
  Unicuna, Christopher, 917
  Weller, Thomas, 957
East Ham (London): Hamnett,
  Thomas, 392
East Harling (Norfolk):
  Bailey, William, 31
  Brewen, Francis, 106
East Hoathley (Sussex): Rich,
  Henry, 741
East India House (London): Boson,
  John, 88, 89
East Retford (Notts.):
  Baker, William, 33
  Golland, Joseph, 349
  Hodson, Thomas, 440
  Wright, Richard & Elwick,
    Edward, 1008
East Rudham (Norfolk): Page,
  William, 670
East Stonehouse (Devon):
  Blackwell, F.S., 78
East Sutton Park (Kent):
  Chippendale, Thomas, 166
East Tadcaster (Yorks.): Rockliff,
  Thomas, 762
Eastbourne (Sussex):
  Bindon, Stephen, 72
  Higginson, Francis, 428
  Maynard, Edward, 598
  Maynard, L. & Sons, 598
  Parks, James, 676
  Ranson, Henry, 728
  Stretton, John, 861
Eastbourne, Compton Pl., for
  Frederick, Prince of Wales:
  Richards, James, 742
Eastcheap (London): East, John,
  264
Easterton (Wilts.): Draper, Giffard,
  255
Eastman, John, 105
Eastman, Thomas, 964
Eaton Hall (Cheshire):
  Brown & Lamont, 119
  Gardner, John, 330
  Gillow, 343
Eborall, Thomas, 51
Eccles (Lancs.): Barrett, John, 44
Eccleshill (Yorks.):
  Ingle, Joseph, 471
  Watmough, John, 948
Eccleston (Lancs.):
  Barron, Thomas, 45
  Pythian, John, 723
Echlers, Richard, 754
Eddiesson, 609
Eddleston, 609
Edelson, James, 267
Edelston, James, 267

Eden, John, 70, 141, 199, 263, 640,
  935
Eden, John jnr, 748
Eden, Thomas, 221
Edenfield (Lancs.):
  Pickup, John, 697
  Southerst, Samuel, 840
Edgecote (Warks.): Vile, William,
  927
Edinburgh: Battistessa & Co, 50
Edinburgh, Parliament Close, for
  the Duchess of Buccleuch:
  Sidney, Benjamin, 814
Edmondson, 109
Edmonton (London): Abbis,
  Thomas, 1
Edmunds, Samuel, 267
Edmundson, Berkett, 562
Edmundson, Richard, 293
Edmundson, Robert, 268, 293
Edmundson & Fayrer, 47
Edwards, 253, 433
Edwards, Edward, 388
Edwards, John, 117, 133, 606, 713
Edwards, Oliver, 497
Edwards, William, 270, 284, 959
Edwinstowe (Notts.): Hill, John,
  431
Eggleso, Peter, 264
Egham (Surrey):
  Lovegrove, Richard, 556
  Pitt, Thomas, 701
Egremont (Cumb.):
  Thompson, John, 887
  Thompson, William, 888
Egremont House (London): Vile,
  William, 928
Elder, 696
Elderton, William, 526
Elison, John, 277
Elkins, 663
Elland (Yorks.): Aveson & Henry,
  27
Ellesmere (Salop):
  Baugh, Thomas, 50
  Bough, Thomas, 90
  Edgcombe, George, 266
  Edwards, John, 270
  Jenkins, Edward, 483
  Roberts, John, 752
  Sandland, Robert, 780
  Thom(p)son, Edward, 885
  Weston, James, 961
  Weston, William, 961
Elliot, 233, 240
Elliot, Charles, 783–4
Elliot, David, 451
Elliot, William, 80, 658
Elliott, 197, 368
Elliott, Charles, 332, 554, 659
Elliott, David, 272
Elliott, James, 272
Elliott, John, 573, 711
Elliott, W., 273

Elliott, William, 774
Ellis, 913, 1000
Ellis, Benjamin, 413
Ellis, Francis, 568, 855
Ellis, George, 811
Ellis, John, 41, 666
Ellis, Richard, 666
Ellis, William, 688
Ellisdon, 185
Ellison, John, 229, 251, 990
Ellison, Thomas, 517
Ellys, John, 783
Elmes, Thomas, 666
Elmington (Worcs.): Newman,
  William, 643
Elmley Castle (Worcs.):
  Anderson, Jonathan & Perry,
    Joshua, 13
  Edwards, David, 269
  Ellis, Francis, 275
  Graham, Joseph & partners, 362
  Lock, S., 552
Elms, Joseph, 80
Elrington, John, 72, 276
Elsing (Norfolk): West, Coleman,
  959
Elston (Notts.): Watson, J., 949
Eltringham, John, 459
Elvey, Elizabeth, 530
Elward & Marsh, 321, 626
Elwick, Edward John, 390
Elwick & Robinson, 1007, 1008
Elwin, Charles, 277
Ely (Cambs.):
  Aungier, William jnr, 26
  Aungier, William snr, 26
  Barnard, William, 42
  Bartle, —, 46
  Gotobed, Luke, 359
  Knight, John, 519
  Randall, William, 727
  Read, Joseph, 732
Emett, Michael, 385
Emscote (Warks.): James, Richard,
  479
Emsworth (Hants.):
  Budd, John, 124
  Edney, James, 268
  Preston, Charles, 714
Endsleigh House (Devon):
  Eagles, T.F., 264
  Elward, George & Marsh,
    William, 279
  Hubbard, J.P., 456
  James & Playfair, 480
Enfield (Middlx):
  Oliver, George, 663
  Prior, William, 718
England, Daniel, 110, 951
England, George, 876
England, Thomas, 81, 157
England, William, 951
Englefield House (Berks.): Mayhew,
  John & Ince, William, 596

Englehart, Fran, 881
Engleheart, Thomas, 8
English, William, 204
Enniskillen, 61
Epping (Essex):
  Dorrington, William, 251
  Marsom, John, 580
Epsom (Surrey):
  Butcher, Thomas, 137
  Gardom, Barnabas, 331
  Gardom, James & George, 331
  Gardom, M. & Son, 331
  Holliday, Robert, 443
  Langlands, John, 526
  Young, Abraham, 1014
Epworth (Lincs.):
  Boyes, John, 94
  Johnson, Robert, 491
  Langton, Robert, 527
  Langton, William, 527
Erddig (Clwyd):
  Beckett, Joseph, 57
  Belchier, John, 59–60
  Bingley, —, 72
  Bowden, —, 91
  Downing, —, 254
  Evans, John, 284
  Fentham, Thomas, 296
  France, Edward, 316
  Garding, J., 329
  Gumley, Elizabeth & John, 380
  Hunt, Philip, 464
  Hunter, E. & C., 465
  Hutt, John, 468
  Mathews, —, 586
  Moore, James snr, 618, 619
  Noyes, Edward snr & Edward jnr, 657
  Owen, William, 668
  Pardoe, John, 672
  Powell, John, 710
  Rogers, John, 763
  Smith, Mrs, 824
  Thack(th)waite, Michael, 882
  Wilson, John, 988
Eridge Castle (Sussex): Burrows, Humphrey snr, 134
Erlam, Peter, 664
Essex:
  Wills, William, 985
  Yates, Thomas Smith, 1012
Etherington, John, 391
Eton (Bucks.):
  Barrett, -snr, 44
  Barton, Jacob, 46
  Davids, Charles, 228
  Parker, James, 674
Etruria Hall (Staffs.), for Josiah Wedgwood: Mottershaw, Thomas, 632
Evans, 499
Evans, Ambrose, 667
Evans, Aubrey, 919
Evans, Edward, 205

Evans, H., 283
Evans, J., 998
Evans, John, 232, 271, 285, 384, 408, 536, 658, 660, 727, 964
Evans, Joseph, 358
Evans, Phineas, 283
Evans, S., 283
Evans, Samuel, 772, 919
Evans, William, 499, 812
Evatt, Richard, 496, 971
Everingham Park (Yorks.): Gillow, 343
Everitt, William, 789
Evers, Benjamin, 884
Evers, Charles, 335
Eversley, William, 184, 925
Evesham (Worcs.):
  Agg, George, 5
  Arkles(s), William, 17
  Atkins, John, 23
  Burlingham, Charles, 131
  Jarrett, John, 481
  Jarrett, Thomas, 481
  Jarrot, Thomas, 481
  Kerry, —, 510
  Kerry, John, 510
  Moore, E., 618
  Pratt, George, 712
  Pratt, Joseph, 712
  Tredwell, George, 903
Ewbank, Thomas, 916
Exeter (Devon):
  Alden, Anne, 6
  Alford, Aaron, 7
  Andrews, Edwin, 14
  Anning, Owen, 15
  Arnoll, Eleanor, 19
  Ayres, John, 28
  Badcock, John, 28
  Barber, Thomas, 39
  Barns, William, 43
  Barter, Robert, 46
  Bartlett, William, 72
  Bass, Thomas, 48
  Beard, John, 55
  Bedell, John, 58
  Belcher, Charles, 59
  Bennett, Jaems, 64
  Bickley, William, 71
  Blanchard, William, 80
  Bowcher, John, 91
  Bowden, Andrew, 92
  Bowden, E., 92
  Bowtcher, William, 93
  Brimmacombe, William, 108
  Brinley, Caroline, 108
  Brown, Christopher, 113
  Brown, John, 116
  Buckland, G., 124
  Buckland, W., 124
  Buckland, William, 124
  Bulla Grassi & Pontana, 125
  Burn, William, 131
  Burnaford, Thomas, 131

Burrington, Carter, 133
Burrington, Thomas 133
Burt, James, 134
Dacie, Robert, 223
Dare, Barnard, 226
Dare, John, 226
Davey, David, 227
Davison, S., 233
Davy, William, 233
Daw(e), William, 233
Dean, John, 237
Dingle, Daniel, 245
Discombe, Richard, 245
Dodge, Thomas, 249
Drew, James, 256
Duchemin, George, 257
Dymond, Thomas, 263
Eales, James Thomas, 264
Eales, William, 264
Eales, William Henry, 264
East, John, 264
Edwards, Henry, 269
Edwards, John, 270
Endicott, John jnr, 281
Endicott, Joseph, 281
Eyres, John, 287
Gauntlett, George, 333
Gendall, John, 335
Gidley, John, 338
Gillard, John, 340
Glanfield, John, 344
Glover, William, 345
Godwin, Ian, 347
Goff & Gulley, 348
Gorden, Richard, 355
Gordon, Thomas, 357
Goss, Benjamin, 358
Gove, John, 361
Gove, John Lowton, 361
Gove, Joseph jnr, 361
Gove, Joseph snr, 361
Gove, Robert, 361
Gove, William, 361
Green, William, 368
Gregory, Emanuel, 370
Gregory, J.H., 370
Griffin, Edward, 373
Grove, John Howton, 376
Guest, William, 377
Ham, Elias, 391
Handford, John, 393
Han(n), Elias, 394
Harding, Charles, 396
Hare, Moses, 397
Harris, James, 401
Harris, Samuel, 402
Haynes, William, 415
Heal, Joseph, 417
Heard, Amos, 417
Hedgland, John, 419
Heffer, Samuel, 419
Hele, John, 420
Helsman, Charles, 420
Herbert, Peter, 423

Hitchcock, Thomas, 434
Holland, William, 442
Holman, John, 444
Horrell, George, 450
Horrell, W., 450
Horrill, Thomas, 450
Howell, P., 455
Howell, Philip, 455
Huggins, John, 460
Hunt, Nicholas, 464
Hunt, Samuel, 465
Hurdle, John, 466
Hutchins, Ann, 467
Isaac, Isaac, 473
Isaac, John, 473
Isaacs, Matthew, 474
Ives, William, 474
James, Robert, 479
James, Theodore, 480
Jenkins, John, 482
Jenkins, Uriah, 484
Jones, Thomas, 497
Kent, Gabriel, 508
Kent, Mrs, 508
Kent, Thomas snr & jnr, 508
Kent, William, 509
Kerridge, John, 510
Kingdon, Jane & Son, 515
Kingdon, T.M. & Co, 515
Kinsman, Thomas, 516
Ladd, Richard, 521
Lake, Nathaniel, 521
Lake, William, 521
Lamerton, Julia, 524
Lane, Thomas, 525
Lascelles, Robert, 528
Lascells, Edmund, 528
Laskey, John, 529
Laskey, Robert, 529
Lavallin, John, 529
Lee, Henry, 534
Lester, John, 538
Lightfoot, Joshua, 541
Linscott, John, 548
Lloyd, David, 550
Lloyd, William, 551
Lockyer & Reynold, 553
Lovel, Thomas, 556
Lovell, Thomas, 556
Major, John W., 570
Mann, John, 572
Marker, John, 574
Marsh, William, 577
Marshall, James, 578
Marshall, William, 579
Marshall, William Henry, 579
Martin, G., 580
Martin, George, 581
Martin, Robert, 581
Marwood, John, 582
Matthews, John, 587
Melhuish, Edwin, 601
Mills, William, 611
Mitchamore, Samuel, 613

Moore, Daniel, 617
Moore, Sam., 620
Morgan, Charles, 625
Moxey, James, 634
Moyse, Charles, 634
Mullins, Thomas Owen, 635
Murray, Thomas, 637
Needs, Elizabeth, 640
Nicholls, John snr, 645, 646
Ockford, John, 661
Olford, Gunston, 662
Osment, Edward, 666
Otton, Mr, 666
Oxenham, Henry, 668
Paddon, Cornelius, 669
Page, George, 669
Palk, William, 671
Palmer, Gilbert, 671
Paul, George, 681
Perkins, Mr, 690
Perkins, Mrs, 690
Perkins, William, 691
Perry, Edward, 691
Pincent, Thomas, 699
Pollard, John, 705
Pomeroy, George, 705
Pomeroy, John, 705
Ponett, William, 705
Ponsford, William, 705
Portbury, Edward, 706
Porter, Algernon, 706
Porter, Mrs Ann, 706
Porter, Samuel, 707
Porter, William, 707
Pottenger, John, 708
Presswell, Henry, 713
Presswell, William snr & jnr, 713
Preswell, Joseph, 715
Preswell, William, 715
Pring, William, 718
Pullen, Robert, 721
Rabjohns, William, 725
Raddon, John, 725
Reeve, —, 735
Rex, William, 737
Reynolds, Charles, 738
Reynolds, Robert, 738
Richards, John, 742
Richards, Jonathan, 742
Richards, T., 742
Richards, William, 743
Rider, John, 746
Roberts, William, 754
Rookes, William, 765
Roper, Henry, 765
Rowden, John, 768
Rowe, James, 768
Rowsell, Thomas, 769
Rudd, John, 770
Sage, Samuel, 775
Salisbury, Charles Pyne, 776
Salisbury, John, 776
Salisbury, M.A., 776
Sampson, Thomas, 778

Sanders, John, 779
Sandford, William, 779
Sandover, John, 780
Sanford, John, 781
Sarell, William, 781
Satchell, John, 781
Saunders, William, 786
Saxon, Samuel, 787
Sayer, James, 787
Scanes, Alexander, 788
Sellick, William, 799
Seward, William, 801
Seward, William J., 801
Seymour, Charles, 801
Seymour, John, 801
Shallis, John, 802
Shallis, William, 802
Shapley, Richard, 802
Shobbrook, —, 812
Shooter, Edwin, 812
Shuter, Edwin, 813
Simmons, George, 815
Sinclair, Samuel, 817
Skardon, James, 818
Skardon, Louisa, 818
Skardon, W.N., 818
Smith, Charles, 825
Smith, Thomas, 832
Snell, William, 836
Soper, Elizabeth, 839
Soper, Samuel snr & jnr, 839
Soper, Thomas, 839
Southwood, Edward, 840
Southwood & Martin, 840
Sparkes, Robert, 841
Spiller, John, 844
Splatt, Francis Townsend, 845
Sprague, Daniel, 845
Sprague, John, 845
Staddon, S.H., 847
Stapells, Charles Robert, 849
Stevens, George, 854
Stevens, John, 854
Stocker, Joseph, 857
Stone, —, 858
Stone, John, 858
Stone, Richard, 858
Street, George, 861
Street, Henry, 861
Sugg, James, 864
Symond, John, 869
Tape, John, 871
Taylor, George, 876
Taylor, James, 876
Taylor, John, 877
Taylor, Robert snr & jnr, 878
Thomas, Alexander, 883
Thomas, Alexander & William, 883
Thomas, James, 883
Thomas, Richard, 884
Thomas, Thomas, 884
Thomas, William, 884
Thoms, Alexander, 888

Titherley, J., 896
Toby, James, 896
Toswell, John, 900
Tothill, Ann, 900
Townsend, George, 901
Townsend, John, 901
Tozer, John, 902
Tozer, William, 902
Tripe, Thomas, 904
Trist, Hore Browse, 904
Trist, Nicholas, 905
Trude, Mary, 906
Tucker, Edward, 907
Tucker, Edwin, 907
Tucker, Elias, 907
Tucker, James, 907
Tucker, John, 907
Tucker, W.B. & A., 907
Tucker, William, 907
Turner, John, 911
Twiggs, Edward, 915
Twiggs, Henry, 915
Varguitz, Philip Butz, 920
Vargur, John, 920
Voysey, Alexander, 930
Voysey, William, 930
Waldron, E., 933
Walkey, William, 939
Way, John, 952
Way, William, 952
Webber, Frances, 954
Webber, William jnr, 954
Welsman, George, 958
Welsman, Robert, 958
Wercombe, William, 959
Wescombe, —, 959
West, James, 959
Wheatley, Joseph, 962
White, Benjamin, 965
White, J., 965
White, John, 966
Wicker, Nicholas, 972
Wilcocks & Co., 973
Wilcox, Humphrey, 973
Willey, Abraham John, 979
Willey, John, 979
Williams, Charles, 979
Williams, John snr & jnr, 981
Williams, Nicholas, 981
Williams, Thomas, 982
Williams & James, 983
Wills, Benjamin, 984
Wills, Jasper, 984
Wills, William snr & jnr, 985
Wilson, Edward, 987
Wilson, H., 987
Wilson, John, 988
Wilson, T., 989
Wilson, Thomas, 989
Wilson & Co., 990
Wingyett, Charles, 991
Wolland, John, 995
Woodman, Robert, 999
Yarde, Samuel, 1011

Exmouth (Devon):
  Brown, —, 113
  Brown, John, 116
  Palfrey, Richard, 671
  Palfrey, Robert, 671
  Sheppard, H.M., 808
  Sprague, William, 845
  Stamp, William, 848
Exley, 940
Eye (Suffolk):
  Denny, William, 240
  Penning, John, 688
  Penning, Robert, 689
Eyre, Thomas, 121, 791

F

Fabb, Charles, 581
Fair, Jonathan, 385
Fairbank, Christopher, 287, 321
Fairclough, R., 774
Fairclough, Robert, 55, 118, 641
Fairclough, William, 414, 973
Fairfax House (York): Vile,
  William, 927
Fairhurst, Robert, 30, 99, 311
Fairlawne (Kent): Johnson,
  Thomas, 491
Fakenham (Norfolk):
  Ansell, William, 15
  Leeder, Besome, 535
  Norris, John, 654
  Soame, Henry Thomas, 838
  Winter, George, 992
Fall, 1015
Falmouth (Cornwall):
  Arthur, John, 20
  Ashplant, John, 21
  Bennetto, Edward, 65
  Boulderson, William, 91
  Devonshire, John, 242
  Gwennap, John, 381
  Harvey, Henry, 407
  Harvey & Son, 408
  Hotton, John, 451
  Jacob, Jacob & Co., 477
  Johns, Francis, 488
  Lilly, John, 542
  McDowell, William, 565
  Maclellan, Thomas, 568
  Mankin, Arthur, 572
  Marrack, Alex, 575
  Marrack, John, 575
  Oates, Mark, 661
  Robert(s), Joseph, 752
  Roskilly, John, 766
  Rottenbury, Peter, 768
  Teague, J., 880
  Toms, William, 898
  Treglohan, Philip, 903
  Trenin, William, 903
  Venoe, Charles, 921

Fareham (Hants.):
  Abraham, Edm., 2
  Bell, Augustus, 60
  Nicholson, E.& W, . 646
  Nicholson, Edward, 646
  Silverlock, Richard, 814
  Wells, Richard, 957
  Wills, Richard, 985
  Wrapson, William, 1004
Faringdon (Oxon): Williams,
  William, 983
Farmborough, Hannah, 344
Farmer, Richard, 122, 123, 657,
  740, 773, 791, 807, 889
Farmer, William, 895
Farn, 662
Farnborough, William, 133, 289,
  919
Farnborough Hall (Warks.):
  Morant, George, 622
Farnbrough, Hannah, 289
Farnbrough, William, 133, 289, 290
Farnham, Owen, 289
Farnham (Hants.):
  Ayling, Thomas, 28
  Birch, Thomas, 74
  Birch, William, 74
  Brown, Christian, 113
  Brown, Peter, 117
  Burningham, William, 132
  Earl, James, 264
  Earle(e), William, 264
  Heath, —, 418
  Hewett, James, 425
  Pullen, H. & R., 721
  Turner, Richard, 911
  Whitehouse, Samuel, 968
Farningham (Kent): La Feuillade,
  George, 521
Farnley Hall (Yorks.):
  Carter, Thomas, 148
  Gillow, 343
  Kendell, John, 505
Farnworth, Maurice, 51
Farquhar, John, 494
Farr, Mary Ann, 115
Farrand, S., 290
Farrands, John, 248
Farrer, 363
Farrer, Richard, 331, 739, 827
Farrier, Ann, 291
Farrier, John, 290
Farron, 575
Fassett, William, 92, 756, 1000
Faulkbourne Hall (Essex): Little,
  James, 550
Faulkener, William, 751
Faulkner, William, 442
Faversham (Kent):
  Gillman, James, 341
  Marlen, Francis Thomas, 575
  Minter, Henry, 613
  Minter, Thomas, 613
  Minter, William, 613

Rogers, Richard, 763
Saunders, —, 782
Saunders, James, 782
Seath, William, 793
White, Henry, 965
White, Robert, 966
Fawbert, William, 38, 729
Fawconer, Jonathan, 574, 866, 952
Fawdington, William, 38
Fayrer, 268
Fayrer, John, 47
Fearby, Henry, 299, 940
Fearnan, Owen, 289
Featham, Owen, 289
Featherstone (Yorks.): Mitley,
  Charles George, 614
Feetam, Thomas, 599
Felbrigg Hall (Norfolk):
  Arne, Thomas, 18
  Bellingham, —, 63
  Bernardeau, Daniel, 67
  Bladwell, John, 78
  Chapman, Charles, 157
  Church, G., 171
  Crane, William, 207
  Dixon, Thomas, 246
  Duffour, Rene, 258
  Freeman, Jeremiah, 320
  Haradge, —, 395
  Hetl(e)y, Thomas, 425
  Hogg, —, 440
  Jarman, Ann, 481
  Langthorn, Henry, 527
  Leggett, Samuel, 537
  Middleton, —, 605
  Pattison, James, 680
  Rogers, —, 763
  Roybold, —, 769
  Turene, —, 908
  Watts, Thomas, 951
  Welch, —, 956
Felgate, Andrew, 329
Fell, Lawrence, 644
Fell & Turton, 531, 644
Felto, John, 601
Felton (Northumb.): Richardson,
  Robert, 744
Fendeman, Joseph, 364
Fenham Hall (Northumb.): Cheere,
  Sir Henry, 160
Fenn, Samuel, 602
Fenner, William, 657
Fentham, C.T., 296
Fenton, Charles, 296
Ferguson, 341, 733, 968
Ferguson, John, 550
Ferguson, William James, 341, 342
Ferrand, Thomas, 24, 249
Ferrers, Thomas, 378, 439
Ferris, Samuel, 581
Ferrybridge (Yorks.):
  Hardy, John, 397
  Rayner, William, 731
  Shearwood, Paul, 806

Tree, Anthony, 903
Ferryhill (Co. Durham):
  Richardson, George, 743
Fetherston, 665
Fettiplace, Richard, 309
Few, Thomas, 146
Fewor, Thomas, 58
Fidoe, Thomas, 41
Field, 725
Field, Henry, 940
Field, James, 453
Field, Nicholas, 216
Fields, Eldridge, 962
Filby (Norfolk): Royall, Peter, 769
Fillingley (Northants.): Roe, Roger,
  762
Finch, John, 972
Finch, T., 541
Finkus, Thomas, 298
Finnis, John, 142
Finsbury (London):
  Aylett, Alfred, 27
  Baskerville, Thomas William, 48
  Beaumont, George, 55
  Benton, Edward, 66
  Bonella, —, 85
  Darnell, William, 227
  Davis, George, 231
  Davis, Thomas, 233
  Devereux, T., 242
  Donne, George, 250
  Duplex, George, 261
  Duplex, George jnr & Bowring,
  Francis, 261
  Kirkham, Jno, 517
  Lambert, John, 523
  Lange, Charles, 525
  Langford, William G., 525
  Lawson, James, 532
  Leese, Richard, 536
  Lindsay, Benjamin & Sons, 542
  Lindsey, John, 543
  Linsey, B. & Son, 548
  Loader, Edward, 551
  Loader, Richard, 551
  Lyus, John, 563
  Mason & More, 584
  Maxey, Henry, 588
  Millward, Edward, 611
  Moore, Thomas, 621
  Newson, George William, 644
  Owen, John, 668
  Page, —, 669
  Parker, William, 675
  Price, Joseph, 716
  Prichard & Priest, 717
  Randall, William, 727
  Rivett, Samuel, 750
  Rivett, W., 750
  Robinson, Henry, 757
  Rogers, William, 764
  Rose, William, 766
  Sanders, John, 779
  Sarbearin, C., 781

Scaping, George, 788
Secker, Thomas, 793
Shaw, James, 804
Simpson, Thomas, 816
Simpson, Thomas James, 816
Smith & Madgwick, 835
Southey, Simon, 840
Steward, John, 855
Stewart, Harriet, 855
Stockwell, Stephen, 857
Swainsbury, Samuel, 866
Syer, William, 869
Thimbleby, James, 882
Thorp, Nicholas, 891
Tiddeman, J.S. & Co., 894
Tomkies, John, 897
Tongue, John, 899
Toulmin & Kerr, 900
Townley, William, 901
Turner, D.S., 909
Turner, Edward, 909
Tyler, Henry John, 915
Underwood, A., 917
Weaver, William, 953
Wilkinson, J., 976
Wise, John, 993
Wright, Abel, 1004
Wright, William, 1009
Firth, James, 812
Fish, George, 399
Fisher, 880
Fisher, Francis, 849
Fisher, H., 302
Fisher, James Henry, 301
Fisher, John, 242, 427, 915
Fisher, Joseph, 952
Fisher, Thomas, 413
Fishwick, Edward, 51
Fiske, 889
Fitchett, John, 655
Fitchett, John Starr, 1001
Fitchett, William, 655
Fitter, B.P., 139
Fitzpatrick, William, 579
Flannell, John, 572
Flaxmore, William, 903
Fleetwood, Richard, 159
Fleming, Frederick, 304
Fleming, William, 46
Flesher, 333
Fletcher, 37, 753
Fletcher, Jeremiah, 694
Fletcher, John, 135
Fleuri, 9
Fleuriot, Peter, 427
Fleuritt, Ben, 248
Flewitt, Ben, 248
Fligg, Thomas, 859
Flint, 564, 885
Flood, John, 226
Flower, Henry, 792
Flower, James, 695, 786
Fluck, Abraham, 456
Fluke, Abraham, 231, 456, 730

Fluke, Isaac, 231
Flushing (Cornwall): George, Samuel, 335
Flynn, Michael, 260
Fogg, John, 70
Folds, John, 602
Folds, William, 918
Foley, Richard, 23
Foley, William, 295, 664
Folker, William, 494
Folkestone (Kent):
  Baker, Gilbert, 32
  Elgar, —, 272
  Elgar, Richard, 272
  Elgar, Thomas, 272
  'Gittons, William, 344
  Godden, —, 346
  Jones, Mary, 496
  Jones, Pilcher, 496
  Jones, William, 498
  Kingsford, Edmund, 516
  Moate, William, 614
  Penn, John, 688
  Wraight, John, 1003
Fonmon Castle (Glam.): Johnson, Thomas, 491
Foord, John, 309
Forbes, Peter, 859
Force, Henry, 780
Ford, 429, 543
Ford, J.C., 479
Ford, Samuel, 363
Ford, William, 501
Fordingbridge (Hants.): Honeywell, John, 447
Foreman, Peter, 170
Foremark Hall (Derbs.):
  Chippendale, Thomas snr, 167
  Cobb, John, 184
  Smith, Samuel, 831
Forfar, John, 378, 712
Formstone, John, 193
Forren, 369
Forrest, 438, 773
Forrest, W., 573
Forrest, William, 49
Forst, Alexander, 310
Forster, John Bruce, 311
Fort, Alexander, 551
Foster, 10, 448
Foster, James, 288
Foster, John, 915
Foster, Samuel, 311
Foster, Thomas, 935
Fothergill, George, 133, 385
Fotheringay (Northants.): Marriott, William, 575
Foulger, 863, 954
Foulsham (Norfolk):
  Philips, J., 694
  West, C., 959
Fountain, Nathaniel, 940
Fountaine, George David, 308
Fowler, 749

Fowler, J., 689
Fowler, John, 739
Fowler, Richard, 936
Fowler, Robert, 217
Fowles, John, 307
Fox, 377, 949, 951
Fox, Henry, 488
Fox, John, 131, 410, 586
Fox, William, 921
Foy, John, 315
Foyster, Sam, 881
Framlingham (Suffolk):
  Butcher, George, 137
  Dale, Samuel, 224
  Dennant, Michael, 240
  Leech, William W., 535
  Marshall, John, 578
  Thurlow, Charlotte, 892
  Wightman, Samuel, 973
France, 37
France, Banting & Co., 674
France, Edward, 57, 95, 316
France, William, 8, 57, 95, 96, 117, 167, 353, 588, 924, 927, 955
France & Bradburn, 294, 531
Francis, David, 494
Francis, William, 273
Francis & Elliot, 240
Francklin, John, 199
Franklin, Joseph, 318
Franklyn, Arthur, 318
Fraser, 354
Fraser, Charles, 127
Freame, Ann, 319
Freckleton (Lancs.): Robinson, Benjamin, 756
Freelove, Richard, 354
Freeman, William, 320, 427
Freer, Matthias, 301
French varnisher: Tirpane, Noul, 896
Freshford Manor, Bath (Som.): Fletcher, Richard, 305
Fretton (Norfolk): Nicholas, Henry, 645
The Friars, Winchelsea (E. Sussex): Elliott, Charles, 273
Fricker & Henderson, 904
Friend, George, 193, 513, 607, 861, 951, 969, 971
Frith, William, 676
Frodsham (Cheshire):
  Harvey, George, 407
  Hobson, Henry, 436
  Jones, Edward, 494
  Lee, J., 534
  Lee, John, 535
  Motteram, William, 632
  Nixon, Francis, 649
  Nixon, William, 650
  Outram, John, 667
  Storer, Joseph, 859
  Warburton, Peter, 942

Frogmore House (Berks.):
  Goertz, H.L., 347
  Ponsonby, Thomas, 705
Frome (Som.):
  Bryant, Adam, 122
  Burgess, James, 130
  Davis, William, 233
  Harrold, Edward, 405
  Hooper, Henry, 447
  Kenwood, James, 509
  Kenwood, John, 509
  King, George, 514
  Lacey, John, 521
  Langley, Richard, 526
  Mattocks, Alexander, 587
  Poolman, James, 706
  Pratt, James, 712
  Wilkins, John, 975
Frost, Thomas, 886
Fry, 479
Fry, Thomas, 32, 443
Fry, William, 833
Fryer, 315
Fryer, Ralph Page, 859
Fuhrlohg, Christopher, 411, 482, 544, 548
Fulham (London):
  Davis, John, 231
  Plaw, William, 702
  Richardson, John, 744
  South, Sam., 840
Fuller, 1002
Fulneck (Yorks.):
  Ellis, Joseph, 275
  Planta, John, 702
Furnass, Joseph, 459
Furness (Lancs.): Wilson, Thomas, 989
Furniture design books:
  Saint, Gideon, 775
  Sheraton, Thomas, 808
  Smith, George, 826
Furrance, Jacob, 104

G

Gadsby, 939
Gaffyn, John Benjamin, 140
Gage, Charles, 852
Gainer, Edward, 157
Gaines, Edward, 951
Gainford (Co. Durham): Hart, Thomas, 406
Gainsborough (Lincs.):
  Bass, Samuel, 48
  Bates, John, 49
  Benson, James, 66
  Botamley, William, 90
  Brown, William, 119
  Davison, Thomas, 233
  Dennis, Thomas, 240
  Garland, John, 331
  Headley, Robert, 416

Hind, John jnr, 433
Hind, William, 433
Hooton, John, 448
Hutton, John, 469
Kidd, David, 511
Lister, William, 549
Lowe, Thurston, 558
Makins, Benjamin, 570
Makins, Thomas, 570
March, George, 574
Markham, Thomas, 574
Marsh, George, 576
Morton, John, 630
Offer, Robert, 661
Oliver, William, 663
Page, Henry, 669
Robinson, William, 761
Rollett, William, 764
Rose, Charles, 765
Rose, J., 765
Rose, William, 766
Silverwood, Benjamin, 814
Silverwood, Joseph, 815
Smith, John, 829
Smith, Thomas, 833
Streemson, John, 861
Swift, John, 868
Tall, James, 870
Taylor, George, 876
Thomas, John, 883
Thomas, Richard, 884
Thornham, John, 890
Tomlin, Joseph, 898
Tomlin, William, 898
Torry, Thomas, 900
Watkinson, John, 948
Whelpton, John, 963
Winks, William, 992
Woolsey, William, 1002
Gairdner, 304
Gally & Baker, 82
Gamble, 107
Gamble, Walter, 281
Gamlyn, Thomas, 846
Gamlyn, William, 997
Gammage, Robert, 115
Gamston (Notts.):
    Whitworth, John, 971
    Witworth, —, 995
Gandy, Joseph, 126
Ganinge, Timothy, 751
Ganning, Timothy, 294, 616, 666,
    774
Garbutt, 493
Gardener, 902
Gardener, Thomas, 330
Gardiner, Jno., 478
Gardner, Andrew, 805
Gardner, James, 193, 283, 329, 373
Gardner, Mark, 754
Gardner, Mathew, 564, 913, 983
Gardner, Thomas, 44, 572, 947
Garencieres, Theophilus (William),
    291

Garner, 867
Garner, Mary, 330, 331
Garnons (Herefs.):
    Bishop, —, 75
    Bradford, John, 97
    Farley, G., 289
    Farmer, —, 289
    Garbanati, Joseph, 329
    Mason, —, 583
    Robinson, John & Burton,
    William, 758
    Scambler, Henry, 788
    Snell, William, 836
Garratt, Thomas, 407
Garridge, Robert, 115
Garstang (Lancs.):
    Alston, William, 11
    Beesley, John, 58
    Helme, William, 420
    Wright, Thomas, 1009
Garton, Samuel, 198
Gaston, John, 219
Gates, 263
Gates, William, 95, 352, 636, 677
Gateshead (Co. Durham):
    Bickerdike, John, 70
    Bolam, John, 83
    Bowlt, William, 93
    Bowmer, Michael, 93
    Daglish, William, 223
    Dodd, Joseph, 248
    Donkin, Lewis, 250
    Duke, Robert, 259
    Dunn, Martin, 260
    Harding, John, 396
    Hobson, Michael, 436
    Hudspeth, George, 460
    Hudspeth, John, 460
    Hudspeth, Rachel, 460
    Hudspeth, Robert, 460
    Hudspeth, Thomas, 460
    Mitchi(n)son, Jacob, 614
    Scott, George, 789
    Scott, Robert, 790
    Storey, Matthew, 859
    Talbot, William, 870
    Tate, Adam, 873
    Thompson, William, 888
    Unsworth, Robert, 917
    Walker, John, 936
    Wright, Joseph, 1006
    Young, John jnr, 1014
    Young & Hobson, 1015
Gateshead, Park House:
    Henderson, William, 421
Gatley Park (Herefs.):
    Lewis, Israel, 540
    Mason, —, 583
    Smith, Thomas jnr, 832
Gatliff, Thomas, 247, 615, 944
Gaubert, Guillaume, 482
Gawan, John, 853
Gawthorpe Hall (Yorks.): Kendell,
    Thomas, 505

Gear, Samuel, 765
Gedge, Ambrose, 222
Gee, 27, 913
Gee, Henry, 881
Gee, John, 107
Gee, Richard, 962
Gellion, Samuel, 602, 747
Gendall, John, 186, 187
Geogan, William, 951
George, John, 221
George, Remey, 124, 286, 364, 818
German, Thomas, 480
Germany, Charlottenburg Schloss:
    King, Charles, 514
Gerrard, Peter, 242, 302
Gerrard, Thomas, 708
Gerrard, William, 161, 335
Gervas, Francis, 903
Gibbons, Daniel, 82
Gibbons, Grinling, 531, 619, 695
Giblett, 817
Giblett & Atkins, 817
Gibside (Co. Durham):
    Addison & Davidson, 5
    Alderson, John, 7
    Bickadike, John, 70
    Blenkinsop(p), Peter jnr, 80
    Brown, Ralph, 117
    Brumel & Miller, 121
    Campbell, Daniel, 142
    Clark, George, 173
    Davies (or Davis), T. & Griffin,
    230
    Davis, Thomas, 232
    Dobson, Moses, 247
    Fenton, John, 296
    Greer, William, 369
    Hallett, William snr and William
    jnr, 388
    Harrison, Jonathan, 404
    Lockley, Richard, 553
    Marleys, Robert, 575
    Naish, Catherine, 638
    Palliser, Joseph, 671
    Patterson, James, 680
    Punshon, John, 722
    Richardson, John, 744
    Rose, Joseph, 766
    Sanderson, William, 779
    Say, Francis, 787
    Sheen, James, 806
    Smith, William, 835
    Wand, John, 942
    Willis, John, 984
    Wists, George, 994
Gibson, 220, 563, 779
Gibson, Christopher, 114
Gibson, George, 95, 661, 732, 965
Gibson, H., 786
Gibson, John, 734, 743
Gibson, William, 110, 173, 539
Gibton, 983
Giddings, James, 46

Gidea Hall (Essex): Mayhew, John & Ince, William, 596
Giffard, William, 434
Gigg, George, 1013
Gilbert, 318
Gilbert, John, 378
Gilbert, Sarah, 732, 980
Giles, Richard, 775
Gill, Henry, 576, 599
Gill, James, 70
Gill, John, 53
Gill, Maxey, 340
Gill, Robert, 599
Gillchrist, Bruce, 201
Gillespie, D., 341
Gilling Castle (Yorks.): Reynoldson, George, 740
Gillingham (Kent): Balcomb, James, 34
Gilloch, John, 340
Gillson, John, 898
Girdley, 181
Gisburn (Yorks.):
  Briggs, Ralph, 107
  Duckitt, Christopher, 257
  Harrison, John, 404
  Judson, Jonas, 500
  Wright, Richard & Elwick, Edward, 1008
Gisburn, for Lord Ribblesdale (Yorks.): Wright, Richard & Elwick, Edward, 1008
Glanfield, John, 124
Glanville, John, 344
Glasgow, Duke of Montrose's lodging, Drygate:
  Gumley, Elizabeth & John, 380
  Stanton, Edward, 849
Glastonbury (Som.): Merchant, John, 602
Gleadow, James, 244
Glenstol House (Ireland) (Glenstall Castle, Co. Limerick?):
  Bardwell, William, 39
Glenton, John, 739
Gloucester:
  Bailey, Edward, 30
  Baker, John, 33
  Baker, Richard, 33
  Battin, Isaac, 50
  Bennett, George, 64
  Bennett, Samuel, 65
  Bining, William, 72
  Botham, William, 90
  Brace, —, 94
  Burgoine, Thomas, 130
  Burrup, Richard, 134
  Burrup, Thomas, 134
  Dausell, John, 227
  Davenport, George, 227
  Davenport, J.O., 227
  Davis, Thomas, 232
  Durrett, William, 262

Eggless, William, 271
Evans, —, 283
Halford, John, 384
Halling, William, 390
Harris, William, 403
Hazel, Sampson, 416
Hewlett, John, 426
Hewlett & Warner, 426
Hicks, Thomas, 428
Higgins, Samuel Cook, 428
Higgs, Thomas, 429
Hitches, —, 434
Hitchings, John, 434
Hitchins, John, 435
Hopton, Shadrach, 449
Hughes, John F., 461
Hughes, Thomas, 461
Jeffs, James, 483
Jones, Charles, 494
Jones, Samuel, 496
King, James, 514
Kirk, Joseph Bustle, 517
Morris, R., 629
Murcott, William, 636
Niblett, Edwin, 645
Norris, Joseph, 654
Ockford, Samuel, 661
Opton, Charles, 664
Packer, J.O., 669
Packer, John, 669
Paine, Abel, 670
Peach, —, 683
Pill, Benjamin, 699
Pitt, Benjamin, 700
Pitt, James Thomas, 701
Player, James, 702
Player, William, 702
Poole, James, 706
Powell, Charles, 710
Price, John, 716
Read, J., 732
Ricketts, James, 746
Ricketts, John, 746
Rogers, George, 763
Rudge, Benjamin Johnson, 770
Rudge, James, 770
Savory, John, 786
Sessions, James, 800
Sloman, Robert, 821
Smart, C., 823
Smart, William, 823
Soulsby, James, 840
Stanley, Richard, 849
Stanley, Thomas, 849
Stephens, William, 853
Stratford, John, 861
Tanner, Hannah, 871
Tanner, Thomas, 871
Taylor, John, 877
Tipping, John, 896
Townsend, Benjamin, 901
Townsend, Joseph, 901
Townsend, Richard, 901
Townsend, Thomas, 901

Tucker, Francis, 907
Warner, William, 945
Watts, Stephen, 951
Wheeler, George, 963
Wilcocks, Thomas, 973
Window, William, 991
Wingate, James, 991
Wingate, William, 991
Wingate & Whitehead, 991
Wood, James, 996
Woodward, Thomas, 1001
Woodward & Johnsons, 1001
Gloucester, Claremont House: Dawe(s) (or Daws), Robert, 234
Glover, 50, 845
Goadsby, 377
Godalming (Surrey):
  Harris, Francis, 400
  Lambert, James, 523
  Lyon, George, 562
  Mason, John, 584
  Othen, William, 666
  Peacock, John, 683
  Potter, Richard, 708
  Richardson, Charles, 743
  Richardson & Lyon, 745
Godbold, Francis, 656
Goddard, Thomas, 846
Godfree, Richard, 4
Godfrey, 1014
Godfrey, S., 347
Godmanchester (Hunts.): Dexter, Thomas, 243
Godmersham Park (Kent): Coade, Eleanor and her successors, 181
Goertz, H.L., 563
Goff, William, 768
Goforth, John, 789
Golding, 45
Golding, James, 699
Goldsaddle, Richard, 552
Goldsborough Hall (Yorks.): Chippendale, Thomas snr, 167
Goldsmith, Thomas, 991
Goldsmith, William, 422
Gomersal (Yorks.):
  Holmes, Robert, 445
  Moore, Daniel, 618
  Thornton, George, 890
  Throp, William, 892
Gomm, John, 349
Gomm, Richard, 90, 571
Gomm, William, 571, 763
Gommery, Thomas, 600
Gooch, 853
Gooch, H., 350
Good, Edward, 874
Good, George, 787, 955
Goodbarne, 140
Goodchild, John, 191, 240, 952
Goode, Benjamin, 242
Gooden, Benjamin, 325
Goodfail, John, 354
Goodison, Benjamin, 88, 89, 100,

219, 316, 332, 353, 374, 608, 618, 619, 677, 924, 928

Goodman, 740–1

Goodman, Stephen, 655

Goodnestone Park (Kent):
Chippendale, Thomas snr, 166
Mayhew, John & Ince, William, 593

Goodrich (Herefs.): Weare, Edward, 952

Goodwin, George, 355

Goodwin, Richard, 763–4

Goodwin, Thomas, 347

Goodwood Park (Sussex):
Goodison, Benjamin, 352
Jensen, Gerrit, 486
Riley, John, 749

Goodwyn, Daniel, 407

Gooseman, Robert, 789

Gordon, Thomas, 502

Gordon, William, 356

Gordon & Taitt, 327, 870

Gordon Castle (Moray): Schaw, John, 788

Gorhambury (Herts.):
Bazin (or Basin), —, 53
Beckwith, Samuel, 57
Chipchase, Robert & Henry, 163
Cutter, Charles, 223
Goodwin, —, 354
Graham, Joseph & Partners, 362
Hayley & Co., 415
Kirby, —, 516
Marsh, —, 576
Morgan, —, 625
Reynolds, —, 738
Seddon, George, 797
Simson, George, 817
Thomas, —, 882
Vandiso (or Vandiozo), —, 919

Goring, 193, 199

Gorman, Bryant, 59

Gorst, Richard, 224, 549, 799

Gorton, John, 382

Gorton, Thomas, 262, 284, 1012

Gosfield Hall (Essex):
Bayles, Lucy, 52
Beale (or Beall), George, 54
Cox, John, 204
Ludgater, Benjamin, 560

Gosport (Hants.):
Abraham, Edward, 2
Burnett, Henry, 131
Hayling, Thomas, 415
Mitton, Edward, 614
Stout, John, 860
Todd, Caleb, 896
Toon, John, 899
Warren, Thomas, 946
Winsor, John, 992

Gosling, Thomas, 73

Gosling, William, 694

Gossett, Isaac, 858

Goswell (London): Oates, Reuben, 661

Gouch, 331

Goudhurst (Kent): Shepherd, Jacob, 807

Gough, William, 998

Gould, 504

Gould, Mary, 536

Gould, William, 430, 648

Goulden, 968

Goulding, Joseph, 457

Goulding, Timothy, 160

Gounden, Michael, 360

Gousette, 359

Gover, 756

Government House, Prince Edward Island (Canada): Seddon, George, 797

Gowthorpe (Yorks.):
Armstrong, Charles, 18
Armstrong, John, 18
Dobson, James, 247
Harrison, Benjamin, 403
Turton, James, 914

Graburn, William, 385

Gradwell, 767, 773

Graham, 290, 477, 647, 789

Graham, Frederick, 404

Graham, John, 182, 183, 549, 959

Graham, Joseph, 52, 363, 966

Graham, Nathaniel, 362

Gramlick, William, 696

Grange, Charles, 362, 451, 465, 489, 699, 940, 1002

Grange, James, 170, 309, 610, 812, 941

Grange (Lancs.):
Atkinson, William, 25
Burrow, John, 133

The Grange (Hants.): Morel, Nicholas and Morel & Hughes, Robert, 623

The Grange (Salop): Cotterell, Thomas, 201

Grange (Yorks.), for Sir John Lister Key: Chippendale, Thomas jnr, 169

Grantham (Lincs.):
Akrill, George, 6
Amos, John, 12
Armes, William, 17
Armes & Cranwell, 18
Barston, Thomas, 46
Bettison, William, 69
Bradley, Richard, 98
Brown, John, 116
Brown, William, 119
Dennis, John, 240
Dixon, David, 246
Dixon, Thomas, 247
Doughty, John, 251
Hubbard, John, 457
Johnson, Henry, 489
Lyne, Joseph, 562

Martindale, Hector, 582
Newblatt, William, 642
Newbott, James, 642
Rawlins, Thomas, 730
Scott, John, 790
Shirley, William, 811
Taylor, John, 877
Tilson, Robert, 895
Tompkins, John, 898
Wilson, John, 988

Grannar, Joseph, 863

Grant, 868

Grant, Jacob, 490

Grassam, John, 296

Gravelay, Michael, 335

Gravely, J., 155

Gravenor, James, 385

Graves, 4

Graves, Thomas, 1013

Gravesend (Kent):
Allen, John, 10
Barnaschina, Anthony jnr, 42
Delap, John, 239
Dix, William, 245
Hobcraft, Edward jnr, 435
Hobcraft, John, 436
Hobcraft, John Edward, 436
Johnson, Charles Edward, 489
Johnson, Thomas & Edward, 492
Johnson, Thomas jnr, 492
Johnson & Son, 493
Lukes, Joseph, 560

Gray, 4, 59

Gray, Alexander, 198

Gray, Henry, 366

Gray, Holden, 107, 366

Gray, John, 366

Gray, Joseph, 120

Grayson, 789

Greasdale, 375

Greasley, 972

Great Driffield (Yorks.): Hall, Edward, 385

Great Dunmow (Essex): Taylor, Peter, 878

Great Grimsby (Lincs.): Meeres, John N., 600

Great Lumley (Co. Durham): Young, Peter, 1015

Great Yarmouth (Norfolk):
Allured, John, 11
Audley, Edward, 26
Barford, Richard, 39
Belson, White, 64
Blowers, Mark, 82
Bracey, Jay, 94
Brac(e)y, William, 95
Bream, Samuel, 104
Brooks, William, 112
Brown, John, 115
Brown, John jnr, 115
Brown, John snr, 115
Brown, Pedigrey, 117

Browne, John, 120
Burman, James, 131
Dattman, Robert, 227
Ding, Daniel, 245
Dowing, James, 254
Dyson, Samuel Pagett, 263
Eedy, John, 271
Ellett, James, 272
Ellis, G.T., 275
Ellis, Thomas, 275
Errington, Thomas, 282
Eules, John, 283
Eules, Susanna & Co., 283
Gidney, Samuel, 338
Goodram, John jnr, 354
Gourley, John, 361
Greenacre, Thomas, 368
Greenacre, William, 368
Groome, Edward, 376
Hacon, Henry, 381
Harley, Cornelius, 399
Harley, Robert, 399
Hart, George, 405
Hart, William, 406
Hart, William & John, 406
Haynes, John, 415
Haynes, Joshua, 415
Haynes, Thomas, 415
Haynes, William, 415
Hogg, John, 440
Howard, Maria, 454
Hunt, Charles B., 464
Jackman, William, 475
Johnson, Job, 490
Johnson, Joshua, 490
Kemp, John, 504
Kent, Edward, 508
Leighton, Thomas, 537
Loves, William, 557
Maddison, Samuel, 569
Maddison, William, 569
Mallet, Henry, 571
Mallet, Robert, 571
Millican, Edward, 609
Moon, Philip, 617
Newark, Henry, 642
Nichols, James, 646
Norman, Simon, 653
Page, Nathaniel, 670
Pope, John, 706
Pratt, William, 712
Rackham, John, 725
Reddish, James, 733
Richmond, John, 746
Rivett, John, 750
Rix, Mary, 750
Sallows, John, 777
Seaman, William, 792
Sewell, John, 801
Sharpe, Joseph, 803
Shreeve, G.T., 813
Stanton, Robert, 849
Thirkettle, Nathaniel Palmer, 882
Thirkettle, William D., 882

Thompson, Robert, 887
Thorndick, Charles Kyte, 889
Townshend, John, 901
Townshend, Robert, 901
Townshend, Samuel, 901
Townshend, Thomas, 901
Uting, Samuel, 918
Varley, John, 920
Ward, George, 942
Watson, Edward, 948
West, Henry, 959
Wollverton, E., 1002
Wollverton, Edmund, 1002
Wollverton, Samuel, 1002
Wombwell, Thomas, 995
Woolby, George, 1001
Woolby, John, 1001
Wormald, James, 1003
Wright, William, 1009
Green, 387
Green, Elizabeth, 851
Green, James, 713
Green, John, 123, 391
Green, Joseph, 90, 157
Green, Mrs, 179
Green, Peter, 943
Green, Philip, 414
Green, Sarah, 368
Green, Thomas, 915
Greenwich (London):
  Allen, John, 10
  Biggs, Abraham, 71
  Blake, John, 79
  Bone, Barnabas, 85
  Bone, Samuel, 85
  Briggs, Sarah, 107
  Brooks, George, 112
  Davies, William, 230
  Dolman, George, 250
  Dooks, Thomas, 250
  Gill, Cornelius, 340
  Harris, Jabez, 400
  Harris, William, 403
  Harroway, John, 405
  Hawkins, John, 413
  Hooker, John, 447
  Hughes, Patrick, 461
  Kipps, Henry, 516
  Magor, H., 570
  Major, John Taylor, 570
  Markey, John, 574
  Mason, Isaac & Haygarth,
    James, 583
  Measom, Daniel, 600
  Metzner, W.M., 604
  Moze, James, 634
  Nelson, Henry, 640
  Oakley, James, 660
  Oakley, John, 660
  Pender, Charles, 688
  Pepper, Joseph, 690
  Pettet, George Edward, 692
  Pierce, —, 698
  Poile, Samuel, 704

Powell, T.N., 711
Redpath, J., 733
Seaton, John, 793
Sheperd, Jesse, 807
Shepherd, George, 807
Sly, Bannister, 821
Stickley, John, 856
Storey, William, 859
Stow, John, 860
Stow, William, 860
Taylor, John, 877
Tenlan, Samuel, 881
Teulon, Samuel, 881
Thames, William, 882
Thomas, William, 884
Wells, Thomas, 958
Wheeler, James, 963
Wilson, George, 987
Woodward, Thomas, 1001
Greenwood, 611
Greenwood, Charles, 196, 262, 412,
  538, 774, 800
Greenwood, I., 992
Greenwood, Isaac, 45, 53, 331, 804
Greenwood, J., 77
Greenwood, Thomas, 32
Greenwood, William, 87
Greer, William, 360, 776
Gregory, 271, 739, 815
Gregson, 120
Gregson, M., 86
Gregson, Mathew, 13, 125, 210,
  330, 370, 524, 557, 633, 848, 918,
  956
Gregson, Matthew, 549, 989
Gregson & Bullen, 629
Grendey, Giles, 182
Gretton (Northants.): Dexter,
  Christopher, 243
Grey, Joseph, 365
Greygoose, 366
Grice, Edward, 733
Griffin, 229, 233, 921
Griffin, William Morley, 444–5
Griffith, 835
Griffith, James, 970
Griffith, John, 490
Griffith, Walter, 713
Griffith, William, 374
Griffiths, 835
Griffiths, Charles, 373
Griffiths, Edward, 935
Griffiths, James, 337, 664
Griffiths, Stephen, 375
Griffiths, Thomas, 374, 669
Grifiths, Edward, 352
Grime, Thomas, 951
Grimes, 234
Grimsby (Lincs.):
  Appleby, W., 16
  Dodsworth, Richardson, 249
  Edwards, Edward, 269
  Hall, Charles, 384
  Hollingworth, William, 443

Joys, Richard, 499
Joys, Robert, 499
Langton, Robert, 527
Mansfield, Thomas, 573
Martin, Richard, 581
Pailthorp(e), William, 670
Read, Thomas, 732
Rowson, Thomas, 769
Scholey, John, 789
Scholey, Joseph, 789
Skinner, William, 820
Smith, Thomas, 833
Smith, William, 834
Snowden, Thomas, 837
Snowden, William, 837
Souden, William, 840
Sowden, William, 840
Spring, T., 846
Spring, Thomas, 846
Stovin, William, 860
Urry, William, 918
Webster, Thomas, 956
Grimstead, 337
Grimstead, Joseph, 337
Grimsthorpe Castle (Lincs.):
  Barlow, William, 42
  McLean, John & Son, 568
  Platt, John, 702
Grimston Garth (Yorks.): Jameson,
  Richard, 480
Groce, Sarah, 895
Gronous, James, 108, 223, 418, 510,
  789, 898
Groombridge (Kent): Launder,
  William, 529
The Grove, Watford (Herts.):
  Mayhew, John & Ince, William,
  594
Grove House (Warks.): Bradshaw,
  George Smith, 99
Grover, James Yeall, 244
Groves, William, 114, 431, 585, 940
Grub, W., 561
Grubb, E., 230
Grubb, William, 561
Guanziroli, 50, 1016
Guest, R., 466
Gugeri, 1016
Gugeri, Andrew, 63
Guggiari, Anziani, 377
Guichenet, 446
Guichenett, 446
Guidot, William, 204
Guidott, William, 255, 310, 484,
  719
Guildford (Surrey):
  Boxall, William, 94
  Drury, George, 257
  Holt, George, 446
  Howard, J., 454
  Jones, C.H., 494
  Killeck, William, 512
  Lymposs, William, 562
  Mason, James, 584

Mason, Thomas, 584
Piggott, Ed., 698
Piggott, William, 698
Pimm, William, 699
Powell, John, 710
Ragge, James, 725
Shillick, William, 811
Spencer, Richard, 844
Stanton, John, 849
Stovald, Sam., 860
Strudwicke, Henry, 862
Tiller, Thomas, 894
Turner, John, 911
Valinder, John snr, 919
Vastell, Edward, 920
Warner, John, 945
Wastell, Edward, 946
Weaver, John, 953
Weaver & Whitburn, 953
Whitburn, Thomas, 964
Williamson, William & Son, 983
Winslade, William, 992
Guinn, Daniel, 997
Guisborough (Yorks.):
  Greaves, William, 367
  Harpley, Richard, 400
  Harpley, William jnr, 400
  Johnson, Thomas, 492
  Laing, James, 521
  Small, John, 822
  Small, Thomas jnr, 822
  Taylor, Benjamin, 874
Gulley, 348
Gumbrett, John, 162
Gumley, John, 316, 351, 618, 619,
  908
Gummery, Thomas, 600
Gunby, Day, 795
Gunton Park (Norfolk): Grendey,
  Giles, 372
Guy, James, 915
Guy, Thomas, 438
Guy, William, 315
Gwillyam, Thomas, 229

H

Habberton, S., 590
Habbot, James, 976
Habgood, William, 852
Hackney (London):
  Berry, George, 67
  Bridges, Joseph, 107
  Britten, Daniel, 109
  Goldie, James, 348
  Griffiths, Charles Overton, 374
  Holmes, Robert, 445
  Hutchinson, Richard, 468
  Jay, Jane, 481
  Jay, Joseph, 481
  Jay & Son, 481
  Jennings, Charles, 485
  Jones, Henry, 494

Monk, Samuel, 616
Moore, Thomas, 621
Nunn, William, 657
Page, Thomas, 670
Parsons, William, 678
Reeve, —, 735
Reeves, J., 736
Turfrey, Joseph, 908
Hackwood House (Hants.): Wyatt,
  Edward, 1010
Haddenham (Cambs.): Hutton,
  Robert, 469
Haddon, John, 843
Hadfield, Isaac, 358
Hadkinson, Henry, 247
Hadleigh (Suffolk):
  Lamb, Henry, 522
  Lamb, William Henry, 522
  Oliver, William, 663
  Reeve, Sarah, 735
  Smith, James, 827
  Underwood, Lawrence, 917
  Williams, Samuel, 982
Hafod House (Cardiganshire):
  Bennet, Samuel, 64
  Bullock, George, 127
Hagley Hall (Worcs.):
  Prior, John & Robert, 718
  Underwood, John & Son, 917
Hagues, John, 458
Haig, Thomas, 56
Haig & Chippendale, 29
Haigh, John, 915
Hailsham (Sussex): Piper, Philip,
  700
Haines, 408
Hale, 762
Hale, Ovebury, 861
Hale, Thomas, 74
Hale (Lancs.): Platt, Samuel, 702
Hales, Thomas, 674, 751
Halesowen (Staffs.):
  James, William, 480
  Thomas, Frances, 883
Halesworth (Suffolk):
  Davy, John, 233
  Deekes, John, 238
  Gobbett, Daniel, 346
  Godbold, George, 346
  Goodwin, Stephen, 355
  Grinling, Robert, 375
  Kindred, Phineas, 513
  Rounce, Thomas, 768
Halfhide, Edward, 648
Halford, Robert, 284
Halford, Samuel, 447
Halford, William Henry, 956
Halfpenny, William, 117, 895
Halifax (Yorks.):
  Appleton, C., 16
  Arthington, Joseph, 19
  Bates, James, 49
  Bates, Mary, 49
  Beetham, Joseph, 59

Bell, Jonas, 62
Bland, Matthew, 80
Briggs, James, 107
Briggs, Joseph, 107
Broadbent, William, 109
Bulmer, William, 128
Dawson, William, 235
Denham, James, 240
Dodd, John, 248
Gledhill, John, 345
Glover, Samuel, 345
Greaves, William, 367
Greenwood, Thomas, 369
Hainsworth, Jonathon, 383
Hardisty, John, 396
Hartley, John jnr, 407
Hassall, Samuel, 409
Hawkyard, Henry, 413
Hebblethwaite, James, 419
Hepworth, John, 423
Hepworth, Joseph, 423
Holden, William, 441
Howarth, Jeremiah, 455
Jenkinson, William, 484
Johnston, Robert, 493
Lister, John, 549
Mellin, Thomas, 601
Mellor, James, 601
Melrose, Thomas, 601
Millington, James, 609
Newill & Horsefield, 643
Ogden, Joseph, 661
Park, —, 673
Perkinson, John, 691
Pollard, Austen, 705
Pollard, Esther, 705
Pollard, John, 705
Pollard, William, 705
Pratt, George, 712
Pratt, Joseph, 712
Rhodes, George, 740
Roach, Charles, 750
Rushworth, William, 771
Schofield, John, 788
Scholes, Robert, 789
Shaw, Joseph, 805
Simson, John, 816
Skelton, Joseph, 819
Smith, Benjamin, 824
Spencer, Joseph, 844
Stead, William, 851
Taylor, Samuel, 879
Taylor, William, 880
Taylor & Jenkinson, 880
Thornton, Joseph, 890
Turner, John, 911
Walton, John, 942
Wilson, Isaac, 987
Wood, Benjamin, 996
Young, James, 1014
Hall, 366, 385, 482
Hall, E., 968
Hall, Elkington, 639
Hall, George, 280

Hall, Henry, 234, 399, 441
Hall, James, 248
Hall, John, 312, 361, 719, 895, 936
Hall, John Henry, 203
Hall, Jonathan, 5, 51
Hall, Robert, 51, 292
Hall, William, 63
Hall & Hersant, 386, 466
Hallam, Thomas, 157
Hallett, Samuel, 388
Hallett, William, 269, 651, 652, 738, 970
Hallett, William jnr, 383, 924
Hallett, William snr, 182, 352, 923, 924, 925
Halley, Jonathan, 190
Halliday, 391
Halliday, Henry, 940
Hallier, Charles, 811
Hallot, William, 388
Halls, Edward, 1007
Halse, Richard, 390
Halsey, John, 935
Halstead (Essex):
  Heywood, Martin, 426
  Oakley, James, 660
  Oakley, Richard, 660
Haltwhistle (Northumb.):
  Brown, John, 116
  Glenwright, John, 345
  Liddle, George, 541
  Snowden, Thomas, 837
  Winter, John, 993
Ham, Nicholas, 917
Ham Court (Glos.): Chippendale, Thomas jnr, 169
Ham House (Surrey):
  Barker, William, 41
  Beville, Francis, 69
  Bradshaw, William, 100
  Bullymore, —, 128
  Nix, George, 649
  Paudevin, John, 681
Hambleton, 454, 455
Hames, John, 944
Hamilton, Francis, 367, 517, 611
Hamilton Palace (Lanarkshire):
  Jensen, Gerrit, 487
  Morgan, William, 626
  Paudevin, John, 681
Hammersmith (London):
  Bannard, John, 37
  Barker, James, 40
  Bland, Henry Nicholas, 80
  Eaton, James, 265
  Gardner, Edward, 330
  Gomme, James Chettle, 350
  Hutchings, John, 467
  Longley, Edward, 555
  Longley & Sutton, 555
  Luck, William, 560
  Luck & Co., 560
  Mercers, Long & Sutton, 602
  Mitchell, Thomas, 614

Peirson, Samuel, 687
Radford, Joseph, 725
Robinson, Wilson, 761
Sibley, James, 813
Webb, Henry, 953
Webb, Martha, 954
Webb, William, 954
Webster, George, 955
Hammond, William, 908
Hampstead (London):
  Adams, William, 4
  Bailey, Thomas, 31
  Burgh, James, 130
  Dodd, George, 248
  Ekins, Shadrach S., 271
  Geeves, Ann, 334
  Hook, William, 447
  Hubbard, Zechariah, 457
  Keys, Richard, 511
  Langmead, William, 527
  Moseley, John, 631
  Nash, Henry, 638
  Paxon, George, 682
  Pike, Robert, 698
  Rose, William, 766
  Sell, John, 799
  Soldan, Francis, 838
  Tate, Alexander, 873
  Vile, Joseph, 923
Hampton (Middlx): Rhodes, Robert, 740
Hampton (Middlx), for David Garrick:
  Chippendale, Thomas snr, 166
  Cobb, John, 184
  Coleman, William, 187
Hampton Court (Herefs):
  Bott, Thomas, 90
  Edwards, David, 269
  Edwards, Thomas, 270
  Munns, Richard, 635
  Pratt, Samuel & Henry, 712
  Seddon, George, 797
  Stephens, John snr, 853
  Trollope, George, 905
  Waithman & Co., 933
Hampton Court (Middlx):
  Bailey, Edward, 30
  Baker, William, 33
  Bartlett, G., 46
  Bealing, Richard, 54
  Brumfield, Philip, 121
  Casbert, John, 149
  Cobbett, Pitt & Son, 185
  Cooper, Thomas, 197
  Cousin, Peter, 202
  Elward, George & Marsh, William, 278
  Emmett, William, 280
  Evans, H. Samuel, 284
  Evans, Samuel, 284
  Fletcher, Jeremiah, 304
  Fort, Alexander, 310
  France, William snr, 316

Francis, William, 318
Gilbert, John, 338
Gilbert, Sarah, 338
Goertz, H.L., 347
Goldsmith, Thomas, 348
Goodison, Benjamin, 351, 352
Gumley, Elizabeth and John, 379
Hancock & Rixon, 393
Hill, Thomas, 431
Howard, Gerrard, 453
Jensen, Gerrit, 486
Jones, Samuel, 496
Kingham, Thomas, 515
Lapierre, Francis, 528
Le Sage, John, 538
Lobb, Joel, 551
Malin, Thomas, 571
Malton, Perry, 571
Miles, Henry & Edwards, John, 606
Parran, Benjamin, 677
Pelletier, John, 687
Pitt, Cobbett & Son, 700
Portal, Gilharm, 706
Price, Richard, 716
Reason, William, 733
Rhodes, Robert, 740
Roberts, Thomas & Richard, 752, 753
Russell, John, 772
Seddon, George, 797
Thurston, John, 893
Trotter, John, 906
Vallance, John & Evans, Samuel, 919
Whitby, John, 964
Whitley, John, 969
Williams, Henry, 980
Hanbury Hall (Worcs.):
  Bott, Thomas, 90
  Thurston, John, 893
Hancock, 881
Hancock, W.B., 392
Hand, Thomas, 443, 895
Handalyde, Thomas, 394
Handasyde, Thomas, 394
Handbridge (Cheshire): Peers, James, 686
Handesyde, Thomas, 394
Handiside, Thomas, 339
Hands, Thomas, 63, 274
Handy, William, 639
Handyside, Thomas, 394
Hankey, Robert, 22
Hankins, William, 602
Hanley (Staffs.):
  Audley, William, 26
  Bentley, James, 66
  Betteley, John, 69
  Bossen, Samuel, 89
  Boulton, George, 91
  Bregazzi, C. & S., 105
  Bregazzi, Charles Sebastino, 105
  Broadhurst, John, 109

Edwards, Thomas, 271
Goodall, James, 351
Harris, William, 403
Hollins, George, 443
Johnson, John, 490
Myatt, William, 637
Sadler, Edward, 775
Sarjeant, John, 781
Scarlet, Samuel, 788
Stonier, John, 859
Stonier, Thomas, 859
Tunnicliffe, George, 908
Unwin, William, 917
Walthall, Hugh, 941
Hannebuth, Frederick, 471
Hanson, 297
Harbledown (Kent): White, Hougham, 965
Hardcastle, Thomas, 859
Harden, John, 60
Harding, 974
Harding, Elizabeth, 727
Harding, R., 224
Hardingham, Nicholas, 677
Hardingham (Norfolk): Self, Thomas, 799
Hardman, Thomas, 150
Hardwick, Asty, 217
Hardwick, Asty jnr, 714
Hardwick, Robert, 504
Hardwick Hall (Derbs.):
  Brailsford, J.W., 101
  Goodison, Benjamin, 354
  Lapierre, Francis, 528
  Roberts, Thomas & Richard, 754
Hardy, John, 251, 396, 574, 633, 917
Hare, George, 1005
Hare, Robert, 762
Harefinch, Peter, 517
Harefinch, Samuel, 517
Haresnape, George, 729
Harewood (Yorks.): Wade, Thomas, 931
Harewood House (Yorks.):
  Armitage, William, 18
  Brook(e), John snr, 111
  Brown, John, 115
  Chippendale, Thomas snr, 166, 167
  Chippendale, Thomas jnr, 168
  Crosby, John, 212
  Cutter, Charles, 223
  Fawcett, William, 293
  Gibson, George, 337
  Green, John, 367
  Hardwick, Thomas, 396
  Kendell, John, 505
  Kendell, Thomas, 505
  MacLean, John & Son, 568
  Marshall, James jnr, 578
  Newland & Walker, 643
  Rathbone, Richard, 728
  Reid, William, 736

Riley, John, 749
Smith, Charles, 825
Smith, William, 833
Taprell, Stephen & Holland, William, 871
Tempest, John, 880
Theakston(e), Christopher, 882
Waldron, Thomas, 934
Walker, John, 935
Harleston (Norfolk):
  Barley, James & John, 41
  Barley, John, 41
  Powell, John, 710
  Pulford, Charles, 721
  Thirkettle, Henry, 882
Hargill, 32
Hargrave, Jeremiah, 203
Hargreaves, 188
Harland, 611
Harland, Thomas, 728, 913
Harley, John, 503
Harley, Robert, 222, 504, 792
Harling, Joseph, 70, 213
Harmer, Woodhouse, 190, 456
Harmibe, 268
Harnby (Yorks.): Raper, James, 728
Harper, 1012
Harper, Benjamin, 385
Harper, George, 30, 301
Harper, John, 400
Harper, John Rogers, 385
Harper, Joseph, 698
Harper, Richard, 983
Harper, Samuel, 399–400
Harper, William, 938
Harpsden (Oxon.): Keep, Thomas, 502
Harries, John, 944
Harrimore, James, 366
Harris, 220, 675
Harris, Arthur, 18
Harris, James Camper, 680
Harris, John, 151, 293, 402, 614, 631, 791
Harris, Thomas, 400
Harris, William, 1012
Harrison, 815
Harrison, Cleave, 235
Harrison, Henry, 25
Harrison, James, 656
Harrison, John, 274
Harrison, Michael, 951
Harrison, Samuel, 361
Harrison, Thomas, 940
Harrison, William, 887, 898
Harrogate (Yorks.):
  Hagley, John, 382
  Hardcastle, Aaron, 395
  Horner, Benjamin, 450
  Horner, James, 450
  Horner, Jos., 450
  Lupton, James, 561
  Peacock, Joseph, 683
  Thackwray, Joseph, 882

Thompson, William, 888
Tomlinson & Burgess, 898
Harrow (Middlx): Sandilands,
James, 780
Harrys, John, 112
Hart, Charles, 157
Hart, John, 406
Hart, Thomas, 995
Hartill, 478
Hartlebury Castle (Worcs.):
Mayhew, John and Ince,
William, 592
Hartlepool (Co. Durham):
Brown, Thomas Richardson, 118
Gordon, William, 358
Temple, Jeremiah, 881
Todd, John, 896
Walker, Anthony, 934
Walker, William, 938
Winstanley, William, 992
Worthy, John, 1003
Hartley, 865
Hartshorn, 462
Hartwell House (Bucks.):
Adair, John & William, 2
Thomas, John C., 883
Harvey, Daniel, 614
Harvey, Harwar, 331, 862
Harvey, John, 51, 355
Harvey, Thomas, 563
Harvey, William, 9, 114, 119, 230,
284, 455, 518, 568, 686, 759, 798,
865
Harvie, Harwar, 407, 789
Harwar, Harvey, 407
Harwich (Essex):
Duke, Robert, 259
Hucks, Phil, 457
Hucks, William, 457
Jermyn, Edmund & John, 487
Kendall, Robert, 505
Knight, Robert, 519
Langham, George, 526
Leverett, William, 539
Harwick, Asty, 153
Harwood (Devon): Tucker,
Richard, 907
Haselden, 71
Haslehurst, 366
Haslehurst, Ann, 416
Haslingden (Lancs.):
Heys, Henry, 426
Holden, Henry, 440
Hopkinson, Cunliffe, 449
Kitson, Joshua, 518
Tattersall, John, 874
Tattersil, Thomas & John, 874
Wilkinson, George, 976
Hastings (Sussex):
Arundale, W., 20
Beaney, Thomas, 55
Bragge, Nathaniel, 101
Bravery, Henry, 103
Dracott, Joseph, 255

Ea(s)ton, John, 265
Eldridge, Thomas, 272
Hall, George Thomas, 385
Honiss, William & Edward, 447
Honiss, William Henry, 447
Knight, John, 519
Masters, Stephen, 585
Quinnell, Charles, 724
Ross, Thomas, 767
Stanford, Edward, 848
Walters, George, 941
Whiting, Richard, 969
Willmott & Son, 984
Wingfield, Henry, 991
Woodham, John, 999
Wooll, George, 1002
Hatch, William Proctor, 238
Hatchlands (Surrey): Vile, William,
927
Hatfield House (Herts.):
Beckwith, John, 57
Beckwith & France, 57
Burgh, —, 130
Burrough(s), John, 133
Clarke, William, 175
Elvey, Elizabeth, 277
Folgham, John, 307
Hetl(e)y, Thomas, 424
How, Thomas, 453
Jensen, Gerrit, 487
Kingham, Thomas, 515
Norris, John, 654
Roberts, Thomas & Richard, 753
Savage, William & Co., 786
Tomson, —, 898
Tyrrell, William, 916
Wootton, C., 1003
Hatfield Priory (Essex):
Cobb, John, 184
Hallett, William snr and William
jnr, 389
Hathaway, Thomas, 240, 437, 454
Hatley, Jonathan, 770
Hatley, Thomas, 314
Hatton, John, 25
Haupt, Georg, 324, 544
Haupt, George, 580
Hautboys (Norfolk): Hallock,
John, 390
Hauteville House (Guernsey):
Seddon, George, 796
Havant (Hants.):
Ashford, John, 20
Midlane, Henry, 605
Wheeler, Thomas, 963
Wrapson, James, 1004
Haverhill (Suffolk):
Houghton, Edward, 452
Jolly, Henry, 493
Hawes (Yorks.):
Harker, Richard, 398
Mason, William, 584
Metcalf, Warren, 604
Metcalfe, John, 604

Metcalfe, Thomas, 604
Taylor, John, 877
Hawkesbury (Glos.): Robertson,
James, 755
Hawkhurst (Kent): Harvey,
Richard, 408
Hawkin, William, 63, 302, 413, 891
Hawkins, Captain, 369
Hawkins, David, 754
Hawkins, Edward, 413
Hawkins, James, 615
Hawkins, Parker, 412
Hawkins, Richard, 91
Hawkins, Robert, 412
Hawkins, William, 82, 275, 421
Hawkshead (Lancs.): Ladyman,
George, 521
Hawksworth, 57
Hawksworth, George, 940
Haworth, Samuel, 652
Haworth (Yorks.):
Greenwood, John, 369
Pickles, William, 697
Roper, John, 765
Sugden, Abraham, 864
Sugden, Absalom, 864
Wood, John, 997
Wood, William, 998
Hawxwell, William, 413
Haxby (Yorks.): Bolton, George, 84
Hay, 727
Hay, Jeffrey, 414
Haydon Bridge (Northumb.):
Reed, Ralph, 734
Temperley, John & Ralph, 880
Hayes, Edward, 940
Hayes, John, 847
Hayes, William, 70, 190, 843
Haygarth, James, 583
Hayhurst, Richard, 287, 737
Hayle (Cornwall): Morley, John,
627
Hayman, 229
Haynes, John, 651
Hayward, Henry jnr, 945
Hayward, William, 412, 416
Hayworth, Samuel, 413
Hazehurst, Samuel, 409
Hazelhurst, Samuel, 409
Hazelwood, 154
Hazlehurst, Samuel, 409
Hazzard, John, 1013
Hazzard, Thomas, 806
Heady, Thomas, 416
Heal, 765
Healey, David, 417
Heanor (Derbs.): Watson, Samuel,
950
Hearne, Richard, 92, 741
Hearon, Matthew, 77, 827
Hearsman, John, 55
Hearthseath Park (Flintshire):
Thurston, John, 893
Heasman, Henry, 204, 376, 541

Heath, George, 157
Heath, John, 194, 813
Heath, Thomas, 241
Heath (Yorks.): Haslegrave,
Benjamin, 409
Heath Hall, Manchester: Planta,
John, 702
Heaton, 392
Heaton Hall (Lancs.):
Aycliffe, Thomas jnr, 27
Gee, John, 334
Gillow, 342, 343
Gilpin, John, 344
Glover, John (or Jonathan), 345
Graham, Joseph & partners, 362
Holmes, George & Griffin,
William Morley, 445
Jeacock, Caleb, 482
Linnell, John, 546
Lichfield & Graham, 549
Mayhew, John & Ince, William,
596
Miller, William, 609
Moore, Thomas, 621
Robotham, —, 761
Seddon, George, 796
Smith, Charles, 825
Hebburn Hall (Co. Durham):
Farrington, Richard snr and
Richard jnr, 291
Faulkner, Charles, 291
Fife, George, 299
Lisle, Devergy snr and jnr, 548
Thompson, John and successors,
886
Watson, John snr, 950
Watson, John jnr, 950
Willcox, Elizabeth & Son, 978
Hebden Bridge (Yorks.):
Hollinrake, James, 443
Illingworth, Richard, 471
Lister, George, 548
Pickles, William, 697
Wheelhouse, W., 963
Heckmondwike (Yorks.):
Brierley, Abraham, 107
Lee, Timothy, 535
Hedderley, William, 370
Hedon (Yorks.):
Bond, Matthew, 85
Sanderson, James & Co., 779
Spenceley, George, 843
Heeley, G.D., 263
Heighington (Co. Durham):
Armitage, William, 18
Lancaster, John, 524
Helme, J., 689
Helmsley (Yorks):
Garbutt, George, 329
Johnson, James, 490
Milner, Michael, 611
Shepherd, John jnr, 807
Spark, John, 841
Waines, George, 932

Wanes, George, 942
Wean, George, 952
Helston (Cornwall):
Harvey, John, 407
James & Penberthy, 480
Jennings, John, 485
Johns, Samuel, 488
Pemberthy, William, 688
Hemel Hempstead (Herts.):
Watson, Alfred, 948
Hemingway, Samuel, 590
Hemsworth (Yorks): Banks,
William, 37
Henderson, 19, 321, 322, 717, 904
Henderson, James, 507
Henderson, John, 490
Henderson, Jonathan, 462
Henderson, William, 180, 187, 754,
896, 956
Heneage, Robert, 1005
Henley-on-Thames (Oxon.):
Bevan, James, 69
Birkhead, Philipson, 75
Byles, Henry, 139
Byles, John, 139
Hayward, Richard, 416
Lambden, James, 522
Lambourn, John, 523
Lawrence, Joseph, 531
Lawrence & Owthwaite, 531
Moorhouse, Benjamin, 622
Sayer, John, 787
Sharp, Francis, 802
Stayward, Richard, 850
Henning, 160, 161, 673
Henning, Thomas, 421
Henry, 27
Henshaw, John, 4, 806
Henshaw, William, 510
Hensley, William, 857
Heppel, 138
Heptonstall, 264
Heptonstall (Yorks): Sutcliffe,
William, 865
Hepworth, 315
Hepworth (Yorks): Jackson,
Joseph, 476
Herbert, George C., 73
Herbert, John, 685
Hereford:
Armstrong, Michael, 18
Barber, Charles, 38
Beavan, William, 56
Bishop, William, 76
Bosworth, James, 90
Bradley, William, 98
Brewer, —, 106
Davies, James, 229
Davies, John, 229
Davies, Samuel, 229
Davies, William, 230
Ellam, Peter, 272
Gardiner, John, 329
Garstone, John, 331

Garstone, William, 331
Gwillym, Thomas, 381
Hall, Thomas, 386
Hinksman, Thomas, 433
Hodges, Richard, 437
Holland, James, 442
Holland, Joseph, 442
Hughes, Henry, 460
Humphreys, John, 463
James, William, 480
Jeynes, Joseph, 488
King, Thomas, 515
Lewis, John, 540
Mason, John, 584
Maton, Thomas, 586
Maund, John, 587
Morris, Francis, 628
Morris, James, 628
Norman, Paul, 651
Owen, James, 667
Parker, John, 674
Parker, Mrs, 673
Parker, Philip Joseph, 674
Parker, William, 675
Perkins, Richard, 690
Powell, Henry, 710
Powell, Joseph, 710
Price, Philip, 716
Price, Thomas, 716
Roger(s), John, 763
Seal, John, 792
Senior, John, 800
Skynner, Thomas, 820
Smallman, Joseph, 822
Spencer, Richard, 844
Stephens, John jnr, 853
Stephens, John snr, 852
Symonds, James, 869
Symonds, Joseph, 869
Tims, Thomas, 895
Walker, Thomas, 938
Watkins, Ephraim, 947
Watkins, Thomas, 947
Watkins, William, 947
Watts, George, 951
Wilkes, Thomas, 975
Williams, Charles, 979
Williams, James, 981
Williams, William, 983
Woakes, James, 995
Hernage, Robert, 413, 421
Hernig, Robert, 180
Herriard Park (Hants.): Gatehouse,
John, 332
Herring, Henry, 829
Herring, James, 695
Herring, Robert, 170
Herring, Smith & Slack, 423
Hersant, 386, 466
Hertford:
Brown, Philip, 117
Jackson, George, 475
Kimpton, John Hanyan & Son,
513

Kimpton, William, 513
Molineux, Michael, 615
Molineux, William, 615
Rayment, Jeremiah Joseph, 730
Ruse, James, 771
Sewell, —, 801
Sykes, William, 869
Herve, Daniel, 614
Herve, Francois, 143, 278
Heskin, Sidney, 70
Hesp, 681
Hestercombe House (Som.):
  Chippendale, Thomas snr, 166
Hetton-le-Hole (Co. Durham):
  Pattinson, Thomas, 680
Heveningham Hall (Suffolk):
  Dawe(s) (or Daws), Robert, 234
  Herve, Francois, 424
  Pye, Edward, 723
Hewett, Richard, 426
Hewitt, 432, 641
Hewitt, George, 562
Hewitt, John, 248, 894
Hewitt, Nathaniel, 684
Hewitt, William, 425
Hexham (Northumb.):
  Armstrong, William, 18
  Grant, John & Anderson,
  Christopher, 364
  Hall, Cornelius, 385
  Hutchinson, William, 468
  Lindsey, Robert, 543
  Muse, John, 637
  Nicholson, Dawson, 646
  Nicholson, William, 647
  Platt, Joseph, 702
  Pletts, James, 703
  Potts, John, 709
  Pratt, Joseph, 712
  Pratt, Thomas, 712
  Robson, John, 761
  Rosedon, John, 766
  Shark, John, 802
  Swinburn, Henry jnr, 868
  Swinburn, William, 868
  Walker, James, 935
Heydon, John, 501
Heyland, Charles, 443
Heytesbury House (Wilts.):
  Mayhew, John & Ince, William,
  597
Hibaldstow (Lincs.): Wright,
  Thomas, 1008
Hibberdine, John, 235, 305
Hibberdine, Samuel, 302, 431, 598
Hibbert, 378, 575
Hibbert, John, 83
Hick, 186
Hick, Joseph, 147, 261
Hicklenton, William, 321
Hickling (Norfolk): Ingram,
  Joseph, 472
Hickman, 965, 1014
Hickman, William, 551

Hicks, 240
Hicks, John, 427
Hicks, Joseph, 427
Hicks, Leonard, 654
Hicks Hall (Clerkenwell):
  Gould, Samuel, 360
  Outrem, William, 667
  Spearing, John, 842
  Withers, Daniel, 994
Hide, John, 853
Hidley, Thomas, 911
Higgens, James, 890
Higgins, Henry, 573
Higgs, Samuel, 210
Higgs & Ford, 543
High Park (Worcs.):
  Insull, Henry, 472
  Richards, Joseph jnr, 742
High Wycombe (Bucks.):
  Abram, William jnr., 2
  Abram, William snr., 2
  Allen, Samuel, 10
  Ashold, Amos, 21
  Ashold, John, 21
  Atkins, Richard, 23
  Atkins, William, 23
  Ball, George, 35
  Ball, Henry, 35
  Barrett, Thomas, 44
  Barrett, William, 44
  Barry, William, 46
  Barton, Edmond, 46
  Batten, John jnr, 50
  Batten, William, 50
  Batting, Thomas, 50
  Biggs, Richard, 71
  Bower(s), Robert, 92
  Bravington, Joseph, 103
  Brickwell, John, 107
  Brickwell, Thomas, 107
  Bridgewater, James, 107
  Bridgewater, William, 107
  Bridgewater, William, jnr, 107
  Briggs, Abraham, 107
  Brion, Charles, 108
  Brion, Richard, 108
  Bristow, William, 108
  Brooks, Stephen, 112
  Brown, John, 116
  Brown, Joseph, 116
  Brown, Richard, 117
  Bryant, John, 122
  Buckingham, Michael, 124
  Budd, Joseph, 124
  Buller, John, 126
  Buller, William, 126
  Bullock, Ebenezer, 126
  Bun(ler), John, 129
  Burnet, Alfred, 131
  Burnet, William, 131
  Dannald, Thomas, 250
  Darvil, William, 227
  Davenny, James, 227
  Dennett, Thomas, 240

  Dimmock, John, 245
  Dix, William, 245
  Dixey, George, 245
  Dormer, Thomas, 251
  Dricey, George, 256
  East, Samuel, 265
  East, William, 265
  Edgerly, Thomas, 266
  Ellwood, Joseph, 276
  Evans, Richard, 284
  Gardner, William, 330
  George, George, 335
  Gibbs, William, 336
  Giles, William, 340
  Glenister, Daniel, 345
  Glenister, Joseph, 345
  Gomme, Dinah, 350
  Gomme, James, 350
  Gomme, Lawrence & James, 350
  Graham, John, 362
  Grange, Samuel, 363
  Gray, Henry, 365
  Gray, John, 365
  Gray, William, 366
  Griffin, John, 373
  Grove, Edmund, 376
  Grove, William, 376
  Gurden, John, 380
  Gutteridge, Benjamin, 381
  Hail, John, 383
  Hale, John, 383
  Hamilton, John, 391
  Harding, William & Son, 396
  Harman, George, 399
  Harris, Michael, 402
  Harris, Samuel, 402
  Hart, William, 406
  Hawes, Edmund, 412
  Hawes, William, 412
  Hawkins, Henry, 412
  Haws, Isaac, 414
  Hewitt, John, 425
  Hill, Henry, 430
  Hill, John, 430
  Hill, Richard, 431
  Hitcham, Richard, 434
  Hobbs, William, 435
  Hodgson, Henry, 438
  Holland, Thomas, 442
  Holliday, Thomas, 443
  Hootton, Charles, 448
  Howard, Timothy Thomas, 455
  Howland, Frederick, 456
  Howland, Russen, 456
  Hudson, Edward, 458
  Hudson, Joseph, 458
  Humphrey, Mary, 463
  Hunt, Joseph, 464
  Hutchings, William, 467
  Hutchins, John, 467
  Hutchin(g)s, Jonathan, 467
  Hutchinson, Edmund, 468
  Jackson, William, 477
  James, Martin, 479

Jones, George, 494
Jones, John, 495
King, Edward, 514
Lancaster, Joseph, 524
Lane, Charles, 524
Langley, John, 526
Langley, Thomas, 526
Lee, John, 535
Lisney, James, 548
Macknam, Thomas, 567
Marten, William jnr, 580
Mayo, James, 598
Mead, James, 598
Mead, John, 598
Mealing, Henry, 599
Mealing, John, 599
Mealing, Joseph, 599
Mealing, Thomas, 599
Mealing, William, 599
Menday, James, 601
Miller, James, 608
Miller, John, 609
Miller, William, 609
Milner, Robert, 611
Morris, Whalkin, 629
Morton, Thomas, 630
Mullet, Thomas, 634
Mullet, William, 634
Mullett, James, 634
Mullett, John, 634
Mullett, Samuel, 635
Mullett, Thomas, 635
Mullett, William, 635
Nash, John Downley, 638
Oxlade, James, 669
Oxland, William, 669
Peapal, Thomas, 683
Pepall, Thomas, 690
Pepall, William, 690
Peters, George, 692
Phillips, John, 695
Pierce, Joseph, 698
Pippin, John, 700
Priest, John, 717
Quarterman, James, 724
Rackell, James, 725
Rawlin, James, 729
Reading, John, 732
Reeves, Thomas, 736
Reynolds, John, 738
Ringsell, George, 750
Ringsell, Samuel, 750
Ringshill, Henry, 750
Ringwell, Samuel, 750
Robinson, Thomas, 760
Rogers, William, 764
Rolfe, George, 764
Rothwell, Thomas, 767
Russell, Isaac, 772
Russell, Samuel, 773
Russell, Thomas, 773
Russell, William, 773
Salmon, William, 777
Sammonds, James, 778

Sammonds, John, 778
Sammonds, Samuel, 778
Sammonds, Tom, 778
Saunders, John, 782
Skull, Charles, 820
Skull, Edwin, 820
Skull, John, 820
Skull, Thomas, 820
Smith, James, 827
Smith, John, 829
Standage, William, 848
Standish, William, 848
Stannage, William, 849
Steevens, James, 852
Steevens, John, 852
Steevens, William Henry, 852
Stevens, James, 854
Stevens, John, 854
Stevens, Thomas, 854
Stevens, William, 855
Stiles, Alfred, 856
Stone, James, 858
Stone, John, 858
Strange, Matthew, 860
Stratford, Henry, 861
Tailor, William, 870
Thornton, James, 890
Tilbury, John, 894
Tilby, John, 894
Treacher, Daniel, 902
Treacher, Francis, 902
Treacher, Henry, 902
Treacher, John, 903
Treacher, Samuel, 903
Treacher, Thomas & Co., 903
Treacher, William, 903
Treacher, William Henry, 903
Tucker, Nathaniel, 907
Tumberlick, James, 908
Turner, James, 910
Varney, Thomas, 920
Vollum, Thomas, 930
Walker, Michael, 936
Waller, John, 940
Wallin, Thomas, 940
Walling, Thomas, 940
Walters, Edward, 941
Webb, James, 953
Weeden, John, 956
Weller, John, 957
Westlake, William, 960
Wheeler, William, 963
White, David, 965
White, John, 966
White, Richard, 966
Widgington, Samuel, 972
Widgington, Thomas, 972
Widgington, William, 972
Wilkerson, John, 975
Williams, John, 981
Willoughby, William, 984
Wilson, Ann, 986
Wilson, John, 988
Winch, William, 991

Wooster, Charles, 1002
Wooster, George, 1002
Wooster, James, 1002
Wooster, Timothy, 1002
Wye, Edward, 1011
Youen, Richard, 1013
Youens, James, 1013
Youens, John, 1013
Youens, Robert, 1013
Highfield, George, 557
Highfield, John, 669
Highgate (London):
    Brewen, James, 106
    Hine, Robert, 433
    Sadleir, Thomas, 775
    Wood, Joseph, 997
Highworth (Wilts.):
    Lewis, William, 541
    Litten, James, 549
Hignett, Thomas, 171
Hill, 405, 913
Hill, James, 157
Hill, James jnr, 951
Hill, John, 376, 431, 638
Hill, Samuel, 968
Hill, Thomas, 430, 563
Hill, William, 427
Hill (Warks.): Baily, Richard, 31
Hiller, Edward, 78
Hilliam, 14
Hillier, James, 432
Hills, Robert, 828
Hills Place (Sussex):
    George, Remy, 335
    Linnell, John, 545
Hillsborough House (Co. Down):
    Mayhew, John & Ince, William,
    593
Hinchcliff, 719, 722
Hinckley (Leics.):
    Haddon, William, 382
    Holmes, Mathew, 445
    Lloyd, Joseph William, 550
    Orton, William, 665
    Smith, Job, 828
Hincks, 614
Hind, 476
Hind, John, 866
Hinderwell (Yorks):
    Barton, William, 47
    Skelton, Thomas, 819
Hindle, Joseph, 433
Hindley, Charles, 253
Hindley, Thomas, 637
Hingham (Norfolk):
    Mortlock, J., 630
    Sickling, John, 814
Hingston, James, 984
Hinsley, John, 244, 465, 814
Hinton House (Som.):
    Lock, Matthias, 552
    Wyatt, Edward, 1010
Hipkiss, 822

Hipperholme (Yorks):
  Empsall, Joseph, 280
  Marsden, James, 576
Hitchcock, Joseph, 454
Hitchcock, Peter, 664
Hitchin (Herts.):
  Estwick, William, 282
  Galer, Thomas, 327
  Langford, William, 525
  Lucas, James, 559
  Marks, John, 574
  Paternoster, Jonathan, 679
Hitchin Priory (Herts): Miles,
  Henry & Edwards, John, 606
Hoare, James, 951
Hobden, James, 898
Hobson, 1015
Hockey, George Goldfwyre, 447
Hoddesdon (Herts.): Tingay,
  George, 895
Hodges, 108
Hodges, John, 410, 748
Hodgson, 211, 381, 913
Hodgson, J., 49, 85, 268, 292, 532,
  559
Hodgson, John, 50, 913
Hodgson, William, 783
Hodson, John, 770, 821–2, 837
Hodson, Richard, 200
Hogsdon (Middlx): Noble,
  Nathaniel, 650
Holbeach (Lincs.):
  Bray, Benjamin, 103
  Johnson, William, 493
  Manning, William, 573
  Peck, John, 686
Holborn (London):
  Albina, Clementi, 6
  Albino, E. & Co., 6
  Algar, Joseph, . 8
  Archibald, Adam, 17
  Arthur, John, 20
  Avery, William, 27
  Ayles, Charles, 27
  Bacon, John, 28
  Bainbridge, Thomas, 31
  Baker & Lyal, 33
  Bateson, David, 49
  Bateson, M., 49
  Batley, William, 49
  Beckett, John, 57
  Beech, Samuel, 58
  Best, William, 68
  Binns, Samuels & George, 73
  Bissix & Co., 76
  Blunt, Charles, 82
  Bogle, John, 83
  Bounsall, A., 91
  Bra(i)thwaite, Samuel, 101
  Brees, James, 105
  Brettel(l), Nathan, 105
  Brettel(l), William Guidot, 105
  Brissenden, William, 108
  Brown & Pyner, 119

Browne, Thomas, 120
Browning & Hopkins, 120
Bruce, Henry, 121
Buchop, Johan George, 123
Buck, Ann, 123
Buller, Philip, 126
Burrard, John, 132
Burton, Martin Charles, 135
Butt, Alexander, 138
Buzzard, John, 139
Dallman, Charles, 224
Davies, John, 229
Davis, John, 231
Davis, Thomas, 232
Dawes, Thomas, 234
Donegan, Peter & Co., 250
Duncombe, John, 259
Duryer, Henry Robert, 262
Dwyer, John, 263
Edwards, Thomas, 271
Erwood, Alfred, 282
Erwood, James, 282
Erwood, Solomon, 282
Evans, Maurice Evan, 284
Evans, Samuel Diamond, 284
Gamman, R., 329
Garbanati, Joseph, 329
Gatehouse, John, 332
Gattie, Charles, 333
Godwin, George, 347
Gough, —, 359
Graham & Co., 363
Grange, Charles, 363
Grange, James, 363
Grego, Antonio, 370
Gregory, William, 370
Grey, —, 373
Griggs, Isaac, 375
Grove, John, 376
Guidot Brettrell, William, 378
Gunter, —, 380
Gunter, Barbary, 380
Hall(s)pike, Christopher, 390
Halstaff, John, 391
Handisyde, Thomas, 394
Harkness, Joseph, 398
Harrington, John snr, 400
Harris, Robert, 402
Harrison, John, 404
Hart, Richard, 406
Hatch, John, 410
Hay, Alexander, 414
Hayne, J., 415
Hayward, Thomas, 416
Hearne, Edward jnr, 417
Hearne, John, 417
Hearne, Richard, 417
Herne, Richard, 423
Higby, David, 428
Hill, Jacob, 430
Hill, Josias William, 431
Hobbs, —, 435
Hodgson, George, 438
Holl, Richard, 441

Holston, William, 446
Holt, Richard, 446
Hone, John, 446
Horrocks, Alexander, 450
Houghton, —, 452
Houghton, A., 452
Houghton, Michael, 452
Houghton & Son, 452
Huddleston, George, 457
Ibetson, Jno, 470
Ingmire, B., 472
Ives, Edmund, 474
Jackson, William, 477
Jacques, John, 477
James, John, 479
Jervis & Holl, 488
Jewell, S. & H., 488
Jones, Thomas, 497
Jupp, Stephen, 500
Kaygill, Daniel Mandevil, 501
Keeler, Philip & Butler, Philip,
  502
Killingley, James, 512
Kirk, —, 516
Law, William Henry, 530
Legg, Robert, 536
Leler, Philip, 538
Levy, Joseph, 539
Lewis, C., 539
Licini, P.& F., 560
Lillie, George & Tucker,
  Thomas, 542
Lyon, Hotson & Co., 562
Lyon, Robert, 562
McDonald, John, 564
Mairis, A., 570
Man(n), Robert, 572
Mansford, Daniel, 573
Marshall, Alexander, 577
Masters, Charles, 585
Maybin, Samuel, 589
Mills, John, 610
Molinari, Andrew, 615
Moor, —, 617
Morecock, Michael, 623
Morris, Thomas, 629
Mowsend, John, 634
Nash, Thomas, 638
Neave, John, 640
Newton, James, 644
Norborns, —, 651
Norris, Henry, 653
Norris, John, 654
Norris, Thomas, 654
Norris, Thomas Heaton, 655
Oakes, Richard, 658
Palmer, Jno., 672
Palmer, Matthew, 672
Parker, Charles, 673
Parslow, Henry, 678
Patterson, James, 680
Patterson, W.T., 680
Pattison, Joseph, 680
Paul, Charles & Reuben, 681

Paulin, —, 682
Payne, —, 682
Payne, John, 682
Pennack, Joshua, 688
Pim, Joseph & Co., 699
Pizzala, Joseph, 701
Plukenett, Thomas, 703
Plunkett, William, 703
Poney, Matthew, 709
Ponzini, James, 705
Ponzini, John, 705
Potter, —, 708
Price, John, 716
Prosser, John, 719
Prudie & Hinchcliff, 719
Purkiss, Robert, 722
Radcliffe, Alfred, 725
Ramm, William, 726
Rayment, William, 730
Rayner, Philip, 731
Raynerd, John, 731
Renolds, Francis, 738
Richards, Jacob, 742
Riddoch, David, 746
Ritchie, Hugh, 750
Rivolta, Anthony, 750
Rogers, Richard, 763
Rose, Charles, 765
Rose, Joseph, 766
Rose, Josh., 766
Rumball, Charles, 770
Salleway, John, 777
Selwood, William, 799
Servant, Samuel, 800
Sharp, George, 802
Shew, James, 810
Shoobridge & Phillips, 812
Sim(m)s, William, 815
Simpson, Benjamin, 816
Singleton, Richard, 818
Skelton, Joseph, 819
Slater, Edward, 820
Slatter, William & Gabriel, 821
Smart, John, 823
Smith, Daniel, 825
Smith, John, 828
Smith, Mary, 830
Smith, Thomas, 832
Smith, William, 833
Smith & Son, 836
Southwood, Thomas, 840
Spencer, George & William, 843
Spencer, John & George, 843
Spencer, Peter & John, 844
Stamp, E. & Co., 848
Stampa & Son, 848
Stanley, Bullock, 849
Stanton, William, 849
Steel & Son, 851
Stephens, George, 852
Stevenson, G.& S., 855
Stringer, J.A., 862
Sturton, Arnold, 863
Tarbett, John, 872

Taylor, James, 876
Testi, Joseph, 881
Thomas, John, 883
Tibbatts, William, 893
Topliff, W., 899
Topliff, William, 899
Tucker & Bra(i)thwaite, 908
Tucker & Lil(l)lie, 908
Tucker, John, 907
Tucker, Thomas, 907
Tucker, William, 907
Turner, John, 910
Turner, Samuel & Edmund, 911
Turner, William, 912
Waldron, Thomas, 933
Walker, Joseph, 936
Walker & Steffanoni, 939
Walkington, Robert, 939
Walmsley, James, 940
Walsh & Moody, 941
Watson, George, 949
Wheeler, Mark, 963
Whible, T., 963
White, Nathaniel, 966
Whitehorne, Richard, 968
Wildsmith, Benjamin & Riley, 974
Wills, John, 984
Withey, Samuel, 994
Withy, Susannah, 994
Wood, Henry, 996
Wood, P.& Co., 997
Wood, William, 998
Wyatt, J., 1010
Wyatt, James, 1010
Yale, Elihu, 1011
Holbrow, Daniel, 111, 463
Holden, Samuel, 385, 581
Holden, William, 951
Holdsworth, William, 562
Holebrook, 245
Holkham Hall (Norfolk):
  Armitrage, —, 18
  Banks, —, 37
  Bellamy, —, 63
  Bessant, —, 68
  Best, —, 68
  Birtle, —, 75
  Bladwell, John, 78
  Boson, John, 89
  Bradshaw, George Smith, 98
  Bradshaw, William, 100
  Brettell, —, 105
  Brettingham, Matthew & Lillie, James, 106
  Bromhead, —, 110
  Brown, —, 113
  Burnett, Thomas, 132
  Buttler, —, 139
  Cawdle, —, 152
  Chapman, Charles, 157
  Colombine, Paul, 190
  Cox, John, 204
  Dawson, —, 235

Flatt, —, 303
Gardiner, —, 329
Goodison, Benjamin, 353, 354
Gray, —, 365
Hacket, —, 381
Hackwaite, —, 381
Hales, —, 383
Hallett, William snr and William jnr, 388
Hardman, —, 396
Hodson, —, 439
Hodson, John, 439
Image, —, 471
Jones, Samuel, 496
Kreyer, —, 520
Lee, —, 534
Lillie & Copeman, 542
Marsden, James, 576
Maynard, —, 598
Miller, James, 608
Morgan, —, 625
Neale, John, 640
Nix, George, 649
North, Robert snr, 655
Perrin, Henry, 691
Pugh, —, 720
Roberts, William, 754
Saunders, Paul, 783, 784
Seehausen, —, 798
Smith, Sam., 831
Sowter, J., 841
Spencer, Henry, 843
Spender, Samuel, 844
Staniforth, —, 848
Strode, Edward & John, 862
Surman, Jeremiah, 865
Townson, William, 902
Turing, William, 908
Vile, William, 926
Walford, —, 934
Whitby, John, 964
Whittle, James, 970, 971
Williams, Henry, 980
Woodroffe, Daniel snr and jnr, 999
Woodward, John, 1001
Holland, 20, 46, 252, 254
Holland, Henry, 105, 112
Holland, John, 94
Holland, Matthew, 751
Holland, Samuel, 198
Holland, Thomas, 450
Holland, William, 871
Hollier, C.W., 473
Hollingsworth, 305
Hollingsworth, Samuel, 835
Hollinshed, George, 238
Holliwell, Richard, 426, 625, 911
Holloway, John, 371
Holloway (London):
  Biggs, John, 71
  Huddleston, George, 457
Holme (Yorks):
  Astwick, John, 22

Bottomley, John, 90
Holroyd, John, 446
Jorden, John, 499
Lawson, William, 532
Holme Hall (Yorks.):
Cobb, John, 183
Whitby, John, 964
Holmes, 728, 835, 921, 1003
Holmes, Hezekiah, 480
Holmes, James, 444, 748
Holmes, John, 193, 444, 655
Holmes, Joseph, 557
Holmes, Richard, 40
Holmes, Robert, 444
Holmes, Thomas, 213
Holmes, William, 887
Holmes & Griffin, 445
Holmfirth (Yorks):
Barraclough, William, 44
Broadhead, Benjamin, 109
Grayson, John, 366
Hampshire, Jonas & Brother, 392
Hirst, John, 434
Higgins, George, 428
Jackson, John, 476
Holsworthy (Devon): Ryder, Herbert, 774
Holt, 482, 699
Holt (Norfolk):
Bunnett, S., 129
Dye, James, 263
Dye, Joseph, 263
Mindham & Son, 612
Re(a)dwin, John, 732
Holton (Suffolk):
Aldrich, Richard, 7
Aldridge, Richard, 7
Richards, Tirrell, 743
Holyrood House, Edinburgh:
Bransby, Robert, 103
Morgan, William, 626
Ridge(s), John, 746
Vile, William, 928
Home Market (Westmld):
Whittindale, John, 970
Homerton (London): Nunn, Samuel, 657
Hones, Richard, 731
Honeywell, Richard, 874
Honiton (Devon):
Dodge, John, 249
Hooper, John, 447
Humphrey, Henry, 463
Knight, —, 518
Lowman, Philip, 558
Porter, John, 707
Sydenham, John, 869
Toose, John, 899
Warburton, Henry, 942
Honley (Yorks):
Astwick, Thomas, 22
Holroyd, John, 446
Liversedge, Richard, 550

Hooker, Robert, 713
Hoole (Cheshire): Joynes, John, 499
Hoper, John, 447
Hopetoun House (Lothian):
Cullen, James, 218
Dawes, B., 233
Fleming, William, 304
Gordon, John & Taitt, John and Richard, 355
Guilbaud, John, 378
Hibbert, John, 427
Lawrence, George, 530
Magnus, —, 570
Miles, Henry & Edwards, John, 606
Taylor, David, 875
Hopgood, 381
Hopkins, 120, 532
Hopkinson, James, 494
Hopper, 251
Hoppyland Hall (Co. Durham):
Farrington, Richard snr and jnr, 291
Horksley (Essex): Harris, John, 401
Horn, John, 455
Hornby Castle (Yorks.):
Arrowsmith, James, 19
Whittle, James, 971
Hornby Hall (Lancs.): Channon, John, 156
Horncastle (Lincs.):
Bray, Thomas, 104
Burnett, William, 132
Dawson, Robert, 235
Dawson, William, 235
Dobbs, Thomas, 247
Dodds, Thomas, 249
Harrison & Jiggs, 405
Lenton, John, 538
Linton, John, 548
Marshall, Robert, 579
Middleton, Erasmus, 605
Moore, George, 618
Smith, James, 827
Walker, William, 938
Wells, Wilson, 958
Williams, John, 981
Horne, 303
Horne (Howne?), John, 768
Horner, Thomas, 695
Hornley, George, 997
Hornsea (Yorks): Barr, John, 43
Horocks, John, 442
Horrocks, John, 405, 1000
Horrox, Joseph, 450
Horsant, John, 423
Horseley (Glos.): Burr, John, 132
Horsfall, Samuel, 451
Horsfield, 643
Horsforth (Yorks): Wood, Michael, 997
Horsham (Sussex):
Goldsmith, Joseph, 348

Ireland, John, 473
Morth, John & Son, 630
Penner, John, 688
Philip, Richard & Son, 694
Plumer, John, 703
Plumer, Thomas, 703
Richardson, John, 744
Scrace, Charles, 791
Webber & Taylor, 954
Windham, George, 991
Horsley, William, 363
Horsley (Glos.): Hitchings, Daniel, 434
Horsleydown (London):
Gosby, William, 358
Hayden, William Isaac, 414
Musto, Charles, 637
Norris, Richard, 654
Horsted Keynes (Sussex) for Rector Giles Moore: Cooke, Thomas, 194
Horth, John, 228, 274
Horwood, 232
Hoskins, George, 451
Hotson, 562
Houghs, John, 1008
Houghton, 558
Houghton, John, 674
Houghton, Michael, 816
Houghton, Richard, 456
Houghton, Samuel, 452
Houghton Hall (Norfolk):
Alken, Sefferin, 8
Kite, Ralph, 518
Roberts, Thomas & Richard, 752, 753
Turner, Hill & Pitter, 913
Houghton House (Beds.):
Mayhew, John & Ince, William, 594
Potts, John, 709
Houghton-le-Spring (Co. Durham):
Anderson, Ralph, 13
Ayre, George, 28
Balmer, Pexel, 36
Binks, Arthur, 72
Brown, Isaac, 114
Elstob, Jonathan, 277
Harbron, James, 395
Hunter, William, 466
Nevison, John, 641
Ramshaw, John, 726
Smith, John, 830
Stevenson, William, 855
Watson, John, 950
Houghton-le-Street (Co. Durham):
Todner, Ralph, 897
Houlds, 650
Houldsworth, William, 441
Houndsditch (London):
Barrett, John, 44
Brand, George jnr, 102
Burton, William, 136
Davis, Thomas, 232

Dawson, Thomas, 235
Gale & Seabrook, 327
Golding, Joseph, 348
Gough, William, 360
Goulding, William, 361
Green, Philip, 367
Grove, John, 376
Hall, —, 384
Hickman, —, 427
Lodwick, Jeremiah, 553
Oliver, John, 663
Pinckard, Bridget, 699
Pinckhard, Giles Bly, 699
Purden, John, 722
Quare, Daniel, 723
R-gers, —, 763
Samuel, William, 778
Seabrook, Samuel, 791
Stokes & Wallington, 858
Tantum, Joseph, 871
Torrent, George, 900
Truss, —, 906
Tucker, John, 907
Warren, Edward, 945
White, Bylis, 965
Whiting, Samuel Stewart, 969
Hounslow (Middlx): Woods,
 Thomas, 1000
House, William, 371
Houseman, John, 503, 762
Housley, Peter, 946
How, John, 88–9
How, Samuel, 696
How, Thomas, 299
Howard, 193, 845, 1015
Howard, Edward, 754
Howard, John, 71, 240, 391, 434,
 453, 754, 827
Howard, John jnr, 410
Howard, Joseph, 766
Howard, Thomas, 408
Howard, William, 940
Howarth, John, 413
Howarth, Thomas, 754
Howcraft, Thomas, 759
Howdell, William, 625
Howden (Yorks):
 Armstrong, John, 18
 Brown, Jonathan, 116
 Goulden, John, 360
 Little, John, 550
 Pratt, John, 712
 Sanderson, George, 779
 Shepherd, John, 807
 Vevers, Richard, 922
 Watson, George, 949
 Windle, Thomas, 991
Howell, Hughes, 695
Howell, James, 698
Howell, John, 758
Howes, Joshua, 456
Howitt, William, 455
Howlett, Launcelot, 452
Howlett, Stephen, 262

Howne (Horne?), John, 768
Howton, Thomas, 306
Hoxton (London):
 Arnold, Thomas, 19
 Bailey, William, 31
 Bell, George, 61
 Bethell, Joseph, 69
 Bowden, William, 92
 Bradbear, William, 95
 Buckwell, George, 124
 Butler, John, 137
 Daniel, George, 225
 Donne, George J., 250
 Dunkley, Thomas, 259
 Emmett, John jnr, 280
 Gay, John Daniel, 333
 Gould, William, 360
 Green, James, 367
 Herley, James, 423
 Herring, John, 423
 Jackson, Thomas, 477
 Kitson, Thomas, 518
 Leinaje, Charles, 537
 Lilly, Robert, 542
 Lily, John, 542
 Martin, John, 581
 Moortin, John, 622
 Morrison, D., 629
 Noel, John, 651
 Notbone, —, 656
 Painter, J., 670
 Pearson, —, 684
 Pearson, Thomas, 685
 Poole, Henry, 705
 Poole, Thomas, 706
 Renolds, —, 738
 Renolds, Henry, 738
 Rhodes, J., 740
 Richards, Charles, 741
 Roberts, Edward, 751
 Seal, Josiah, 792
 Sherman, George, 809
 Triggey, John, 904
 Turner, James, 910
 Walker, Martin, 936
 Wooff, Emanuel, 1001
 Young, John, 1014
Hoyle, Isaac, 66, 190, 256, 399
Hubbard, William, 257
Hucknall-Torkard (Notts.):
 Hopewell, George, 448
Huddersfield (Yorks):
 Appleyard, Thomas, 16
 Balmforth, John, 36
 Balmforth, T., 36
 Bamford, John, 36
 Bamford, Thomas, 36
 Bottomley, John, 90
 Briggs, Joseph, 107
 Denby, John, 240
 Denton, William, 241
 Dickinson, Stephen, 243
 Eastwood, Jonas, 265
 Eastwood, Thomas, 265

Ellis, John, 275
Gibson, Abraham, 337
Gibson, Henry, 337
Halmshaw, John, 390
Hanson, John, 395
Hartley, Richard, 407
Heavyse(d)ge, Thomas, 419
Heavyside, Thomas, 419
Hirst, John, 434
Hollingworth, James, 443
Hollingworth, John, 443
Lombardini, John, 554
Machan, Allison, 565
Milner, John, 611
Moorhouse, William, 622
Morrey, John, 627
Morton, Eli, 630
Mos(e)ley, John, 631
Moseley, Joshua & James, 631
Myers, William, 637
Pennington, Fras., 689
Pennington, Matthew, 689
Pennington, Thomas, 689
Reynolds, John George, 738
Rourke, Patrick, 768
Scholes, Benjamin, 789
Shaw, Joseph, 805
Shaw, William, 805
Tate, John, 873
Taylor, Joseph & George, 878
Thornton, Joseph, 890
Tunnicliffe, Robert, 908
Turner, Jonas, 911
Turner, William, 913
Varley, John, 920
Waite, William, 932
Whiteley, Edward, 968
Whiteley, Robert, 968
Wilson, James, 987
Winter, Thomas, 993
Huddestone, Edward, 666
Huddleston, Edward, 665, 935
Hudon, William, 326
Hudson, A., 13
Hudson, Andrew, 458
Hudson, Ann, 838
Hudson, Edward, 841
Hudson, John, 91, 770, 973
Hudson, Joseph, 251, 781
Hudson, Richard, 240
Hudson, Stephen, 459
Hudson, William, 212, 277, 541
Huggett, John, 124, 756
Huggins, 670
Huggins, Henry, 725, 774, 846
Hugh, Thomas, 822
Hughes, 36, 979
Hughes, Hugh, 99
Hughes, Job, 33
Hughes, John, 911
Hughes, Samuel, 915
Hughes, William, 198, 599
Hughes, William jnr, 599
Hull, 365, 366

Hull (Yorks):

Addey, William, 4
Aislabie, Michael, 6
Akam, John, 6
Aldersmith, James, 7
Allison, John, 11
Anderson, W., 13
Appleton, William, 16
Arton, Isabella, 20
Ashworth, John, 21
Atkinson, Bartholomew, 23
Atkinson, John, 24
Atkinson, William, 25
Banks, George, 37
Banks, Thomas, 37
Banks, William, 37
Barnby, Joshua (Wingfield) 42
Barnby, Timothy, 42
Barren, Thomas Richard, 44
Barridger, Laurens, 44
Barry, William, 46
Barton, Matthew, 47
Beach, William, 53
Beale, George, 54
Bealt, Francis, 55
Beaumont, William, 56
Be(i)lby, Thomas, 59
Bennett, Peter, 65
Bennington, George, 65
Bentley, James, 66
Bielby, Richard, 71
Bilton, Peter, 72
Binks, John, 72
Binnington, Christopher, 73
Binnington, James, 73
Binnington, Richard, 73
Bird, John, 74
Blakey, Joseph, 79
Blythe, Richard, 82
Booth, Cath., 87
Bowen, Henry, 92
Bradshaw, Matthew, 99
Brady, Philip, 100
Brian, Peter, 106
Brooks, George, 110
Brooks, Thomas, 112
Brooks, William, 112
Brown, James & Son, 115
Brown, John, 116
Brown, Richard, 117
Brown, Samuel, 118
Brown, William, 119
Bulmer, Mary, 128
Bulmer, Robert, 128
Burn, Isaac, 131
Burnett, Christopher, 131
Butler, Martin, 137
Bywater(s), John, 140
Daggett, John, 223
Daggitt, Robert, 223
Dannatt, John, 225
Darby, Samuel jnr, 226
Darling, William, 227
Davis, John, 231

Davis, William, 233
Dawson, Benjamin, 235
Dawson, Francis, 235
Dean, Joseph, 237
Dewick, George, 242
Dewick, John, 242, 243
Dewick, William, 243
Dickinson, Edward, 243
Dickon, Edward, 244
Dickon, John, 244
Dickson, Thomas, 244
Dixon, John, 246
Dixon, Thomas, 247
Dobson, Isaac, 247
Dobson, Robert, 247
Dobson, Thomas, 248
Dorsey, Robert, 251
Dove, Daniel, 252
Dove, David, 252
Doyle, William, 255
Draysdale, Elias, 256
Drewey, John, 256
Dring, Draper, 256
Dry, Thomas, 257
Duesbery, William, 258
Dunlin, William, 259
Dunning, William, 261
Ellerby, Bartholomew, 272
Ellerker, John, 272
Empson, Thomas, 281
England, William, 281
Everingham, William, 285
Ewbank, Thomas Steel(e), 286
Gace, Nathaniel, 326
Gale, John, 327
Geaves, George, 334
Gell, Richard, 335
Gilder, John, 339
Gleadow, John, 345
Glen, Henry, 345
Godson, George, 347
Godson, Thomas, 347
Gower, Daniel, 361
Graves, Lumley, 365
Gray, John, 365
Grayburn, John, 366
Greasley, Thomas, 366
Gresley, Thomas, 372
Grindall, Thomas Witty, 375
Grocock, James, 376
Grocock, John, 376
Grover, James, 376
Guy, Henry, 381
Guy, Henry Remington, 381
Guy, James, 381
Guy, Thomas, 381
Guy, William, 381
Haddon, George, 382
Haddon, John, 382
Haley, John, 384
Hall, Joseph, 385
Hall, William, 386
Halley, Edmund, 389
Halley, Thomas, 390

Happ(e)y, William, 395
Harbron, John, 395
Hardy, John, 397
Hare, Patrick, 397
Hargrave, —, 398
Hargrave, Jeremiah, 398
Hargrave, Joseph, 398
Harper, George, 399
Harrison, Michael, 404
Hart, Charles, 405
Hartley, Edward, 406
Hartley, Robert, 407
Harvey, Richard, 408
Hawkins, John, 413
Hawkins, Robert, 413
Hayley, John, 415
Haywood, James, 416
Head, Henry, 416
Heall, Joseph, 417
Hempson, John, 420
Hibbeart, John, 427
Hibbert, John, 427
Hick, George, 427
Hick(s), John, 427
Hick(s), Joseph, 427
Hill, James, 430
Hind, William, 433
Hindley, William, 433
Hinds, Peter, 433
Hinsley, George, 433
Hinsley, John, 434
Hoare, James, 435
Hodgson, John, 438
Hodson, John, 439
Holden, William, 441
Holder, W., 441
Holder, William, 441
Holdsworth, Samuel, 441
Holland, R., 442
Holland, William, 442
Hollingsworth, Francis, 443
Hollingsworth, Thomas, 443
Hollingsworth, William, 443
Holmes, Joseph, 445
Holmes, Charles, 444
Holmes, J.H., 445
Holroyd, Tym, 446
Hornby, William, 449
Horrox, Hammond, 451
Hounsworth, Jesse, 452
Howlett, Elija, 456
Howlett, William, 456
Hudson, John, 458
Hudson, Timothy Smithson, 459
Hunter, John, 465
Hunter, William Luddington, 466
Hurst, William, 466
Hustwick, Francis, 467
Hyde, William Wilson, 470
Jackson, James, 475
Jackson, John, 476
Jacobs, Michael, 477
Jakeman, John, 478
Jameson & Smith, 480

Jaques, John, 480
Jaques, Thomas, 480
Jarvis, Benjamin, 481
Jefferson, Henry, 482
Jefferys, James, 482
Jefferys, John & Co., 482
Jeffreys, James jnr, 483
Job, Robert, 488
Johnson, Edward, 489
Johnson, William, 492
Kelsey, James snr & jnr, 503
Kelsey, John, 503
Kenningham, Henry, 507
Kent, Robert, 508
Kent, William, 509
King, John, 514
King, William, 515
Kitching, Mordecai, 518
Kite, Thomas, 518
Knight, John, 519
Lambert, —, 522
Leak, George, 533
Lee, Thomas, 535
Leek, William, 535
Leng, Robert, 538
Lenham, Thomas, 538
Lepsay, William, 538
Leuty, Charles Emanuel, 539
Levett, John, 539
Levett, Mathew, 539
Levett, Robert, 539
Levett, William Day, 539
Levitt, M., 539
Levitt, Richard, 539
Levitt, Thomas, 539
Levitt, William, 539
Lidgett, Elizabeth, 541
Lidgett, Miss Esther, 541
Linsley, William, 548
Lockwood, John, 553
Loggin, Robert, 554
Lonsdale, William, 555
Lovitt, John, 557
Lowry, John, 558
Lowther, John, 559
Luccock, John, 559
Luccock, Marmaduke, 559
Luccock, William, 559
Lumbley, John, 560
Lutherborough, William, 561
Lyel, Joseph, 562
Lyel, Miles, 562
Lyon, Joseph, 562
Lyth, John, 563
Lythe, Robert, 563
McCauley, William John, 564
M'Entire, James, 565
M'Intire, John, 565
M'Kenzie, William, 566
Mallet, William, 571
Maltby, Francis, 571
Malton, Thomas, 571
Manby, William, 572
Manklin, Benjamin, 572

Mann, William, 573
Manzochi, Girolano, 573
Marris, Thomas, 576
Marshall, John, 579
Marshall, Thomas, 579
Marshall, William, 579
Martin, George, 581
Maspoli, Augustus, 585
Maspoli, James, 585
Matson, Benjamin, 586
Matthewson, John Jaques, 587
Maw, George, 588
Medforth, Flinton, 600
Meggitt, Thomas, 600
Meggitt, William, 601
Megson, John, 601
Mercer, John, 602
Metcalf, John E., 603
Metcalfe, Thomas, 604
Meyer, Henry, 604
Milner, Josiah, 611
Milsom, John, 611
Moody, Thomas, 616
Moon, Joseph, 617
Morrod, Joseph, 630
Mounsey, Joseph, 633
Newton, J., 644
Nicholson, Edward, 646
North, Francis, 655
Oates, Bartholomew, 661
Ogilvie, James, 661
Ostler, Henry George, 666
Ounsworth, Benjamin, 667
Ounsworth, Jesse, 667
Ounsworth, John, 667
Ounsworth, Samuel, 667
Parker, Henry, 674
Parker, John, 674
Parkin, James, 676
Parkinson, Charles, 676
Parkinson, William, 676
Paul, William, 682
Payler, Thornton, 682
Peacock, Robert & Co., 683
Peacock, Thomas, 683
Peacock, William, 683
Peck, John, Thomas, 686
Penman, William, 688
Pentith, Francis, 689
Pewlas, Robert, 693
Pexton, William, 693
Philipson, Elizabeth, 694
Pickard, Charles, 697
Picquet, Charles, 697
Pindar, William Thornton, 699
Piotti, James, 700
Portti, James, 707
Postell, Andrew, 707
Potts, John, 709
Poulton, George, 709
Poulton, Robert, 709
Pratt, William, 712
Prescott, James, 713
Prissick, William, 718

Pullan, Jos, 721
Pybus, William, 722
Raliegh, John, 726
Ramsden, Benjamin, 726
Rea, Thomas, 731
Redfearn, John Samuel, 733
Reed, Robert, 734
Reynolds, John, 738
Rhodes, Francis, 740
Rice, Richard, 741
Richards, Simeon, 742
Richardson, Joseph, 744
Richardson, Robert, 744
Richardson, Thomas, 745
Richardson, Tim., 745
Richardson & Son, 745
Richardson & Spence(r), 745
Robinson, John, 758
Robinson, Nicholas, 759
Robinson, Thomas, 760
Robinson, William, 761
Rollit, Richard, 764
Root, William, 765
Rose, John, 766
Ross, Joseph, 766
Rowbotham, Richard, 768
Rutherford, Robert, 773
Ryan, Thomas, 774
Sands, John, 780
Saner, Elias Christopher, 781
Sansby, Richard, 781
Sansby, Robert, 781
Scamen, Allen, 788
Searby & Codlin, 792
Secret, Samuel, 793
Seddon, George, 796
Settle, William, 800
Shackles, John, 801
Shackles, Thomas, 801
Sherwood, William, 810
Sibson, William, 814
Silbon, William, 814
Simpson, David, 816
Simpson, George, 816
Simpson, Thomas, 816
Slingsby, Thomas, 821
Slingsby, William, 821
Smith, James, 827
Smith, Job, 828
Smith, John, 829
Smith, Richard, 831
Smith, Robert, 831
Smith, William, 834
Smith & Richardson, 835
Southern, George, 840
Speck, John, 842
Spenceley, George, 843
Spencer, J., 843
Spencer, John, 844
Spring, Robert, 846
Spurs, William, 846
Staniland, Thomas, 849
Stephenson, Wilberforce, 854
Stockdale, James England, 857

Stockdale, John England, 857
Stockdale, Joseph, 857
Stockton, James, 857
Stokes, Cornelius, 858
Strackles, John, 860
Sunley, William, 865
Sutheran, George, 865
Swann, Thomas, 867
Swewison, Richard, 868
Swinn, F., 868
Tadman, Henry, 870
Taylor, John, 877
Taylor, William, 880
Thairlwall, George, 882
Thompson, Robert, 887
Thorley, Peter, 889
Thornborough, Francis, 889
Tho(r)nham, George, 890
Thornham, Thomas, 890
Thornton, John, 890
Thorp, Bethell, 891
Thorp, R., 891
Tindall, Robert, 895
Todd, John, 896
Turnley, Isaac, 913
Vial, —, 922
Vickerman, James, 923
Wadsworth, Christopher, 931
Waite, John, 932
Wakelin, Henry, 933
Walker, Elizabeth, 934
Walker, George Benison, 935
Walker, John, 936
Walker, Joseph, 936
Walker, Robert, 937
Walker, Thomas, 937
Walker, W., 938
Wallis, Samuel, 940
Walter, John, 941
Walter, Michael, 941
Ward, Benjamin, 942
Ward, Edward, 942
Ward, Thomas, 942
Wardale, Robert, 944
Wardell, John, 944
Watson, George, 949
Watts, John, 951
Watts & Fox, 951
Waugh, James & Co., 951
Waugh, Robert, 951
Webb, John, 953
Webster, —, 954
Webster, James, 955
Webster, Mary, 955
Webster, Peter, 955
Webster, William, 956
Webster & Darling, 956
Webster & Witty, 956
Wells, George, 957
Wells, Robert, 958
Westerdale, George, 960
Wharton, Robert, 962
Whinfield, Joshua, 963
White, William, 967

Whiteley, Eward, 968
Whitfield, Mrs, 969
Wilkinson, Thomas, 977
Wilkinson, William, 977
Williams, James, 980
Wilson, Christopher, 986
Wilson, James, 987
Wilson, John, 987, 988
Wilson, Matthew, 988
Wilson, William, 990
Wilson & Popperwell, 990
Wimble, William, 991
Wintie, George, 993
Wise, William; 994
Withington, Samuel, 994
Wood, Thomas, 998
Worrell & Holmes, 1003
Wray, John, 1004
Wright, Robert, 1008
Wright, William, 1009
Young, George, 1014
Young, William, 1015
Hull:
Corporation: Walker, Thomas, 937
High St and Charlotte St, for Joseph Robinson Pease: Seddon, George, 796
Holy Trinity Church: Chapman, George & John, 157
Trinity House: Walker, Thomas, 937
Hullah, 913
Hulloh, 913
Hulme (Lancs.): Watson, Charles, 948
Hulton, Joseph, 814
Humber, Richard, 300
Humphrey, William, 108
Humphreys, Thomas, 170, 440
Humphreys, William, 614, 776, 787
Humphries, George, 423
Humphrys, Thomas, 699
Hundlebury (Lincs.): Plumtree, George, 703
Hundleby (Lincs.): Ball, John, 35
Hungate (Yorks.):
Bell, John, 62
Howard, William, 455
Wilkinson & Rayson, 978
Hungerford (Berks.):
Pocock, John, 703
Sherman, John, 809
Hunmanby (Yorks.): Dewell, Robert, 242
Hunsley, John, 79, 898
Hunslet (Yorks.): Briggs, Samuel, 107
Hunt, 60, 468
Hunt, James, 828
Hunt, Philip, 468
Hunt, Phillip, 72
Hunt, Thomas, 39, 146, 522, 831, 843

Huntback, John, 944
Hunter, John, 434, 814
Hunter, Jonathan, 465
Hunter, W., 377
Hunter, William, 98, 363
Hunter, William Luddington, 244
Hunter & Hersant, 386
Huntingdon:
Allsop, William, 11
Barnes, James, 42
Barnes, John, 42
Bird, Robert, 74
Garner, Richard, 331
Mackenzie, Ebenizer, 566
Maddison, Francis, John, 569
Moody, John, 616
Mooney, John, 617
Mutton, William, 637
Nodes, Joseph, 650
Ramsey, John, 726
Reany, Robert, 732
Taylor, Thomas, 879
Hunton, John, 940
Huntspill (Som.): Hurdacre, Joseph, 466
Hurley, 364, 868
Hurst, Francis, 611
Hurt, 468
Hurworth (Co. Durham):
Brewster, George, 106
Goldsborough, Richard, 348
Husson, Stephen Lawrence, 955
Hutchins, William, 402
Hutchinson, Thomas, 946
Hutt, Elizabeth, 32, 471
Hutt, J., 32
Hutt, John, 60, 464, 618
Hutton, Charles, 1007
Hutton, Thomas, 946
Hutton (Yorks.): Eland, John, 271
Hux, John, 804
Huxley, 235
Huxley, Thomas Croft, 469, 570, 690, 808, 811
Huxley, William Latham, 469
Hyatt, John, 890
Hyde, Daniel, 428
Hyde, Robert, 971
Hyde (Lancs.): Rogers, Marmaduke, 763
Hythe (Kent):
Gibbons, John, 336
Horne, James, 449
Pilcher, Thomas, 698
Ronalds, John, 765

I

Ickworth (Suffolk):
Banting, France & Co., 37, 38
Bullen, Henry, 125
Bullon, J.G., 128
Columbani, Placido, 190

Jensen, Gerrit, 487
Taprell, Stephen & Holland, William, 871, 872
Ickworth Lodge: Green, William, 368
Ilfracombe (Devon):
 Harris, James, 401
 Slocombe, Thomas, 821
 Stephens, Hugh, 852
Iliffe, J., 288
Iliffe, John, 113, 468, 812
Ilminster (Som.):
 Patch, Wm, 679
 Stringer, Stephen, 862
 Tapscott, Henry, 872
 Towells, Robert, 900
Ince, Charles, 590
Ince, Peter, 593
Ince, William, 99, 959, 971
Ince & Mayhew, 182, 242, 420, 506, 573, 622, 646, 824, 925, 951
Indermaur, Jacob, 471
Ingatstone Hall (Essex): St George, John, 776
Ingham, Thomas, 557
Ingham, William, 914
Inglesant, William, 697
Ingleton (Yorks):
 Holmes, Richard, 445
 Slinger, Thomas, 821
 Wilcock, James, 973
Ingworth (Norfolk): Pierson, William, 698
Innes, 791
Insull, Henry, 895
Invalid furniture:
 Merlin, John Joseph, 602
 Morgan & Sanders, 626
 Plumer, Thomas, 703
 Walker, Thomas, 937
Inveraray Castle (Argyll):
 Girard, —, 344
 Lawrence, Richard, 531
 Linnell, John, 544, 545
 Mercer, George, 602
Ipswich (Suffolk):
 Alexander, John, 7
 Andrews, —, 14
 Baily, John, 31
 Baker, Richard jnr, 33
 Baldry, Foxale, 34
 Bedwell, William, 58
 Bentley, John, 66
 Bloomfield, John, 81
 Board, Nathaniel, 82
 Brame, Benjamin, 102
 Buckingham, William, 124
 Buckingham, William jnr, 124
 Bunage, Thomas, 128
 Burrage, Thomas, 132
 Buxton, Thomas, 139
 Denny, Henry, 240
 Dickenson, Timothy, 243
 Dowsing, J., 255

 Elmer, Samuel, 276
 Ely, Robert, 279
 Goodill, —, 351
 Goodwin, George, 354
 Goodwin, John, 355
 Gordon, Thomas, 357
 Goss, Joseph, 358
 Gow, John, 361
 Green, —, 367
 Greenleaf, Richard, 368
 Harris, Josiah, 401
 Harris, Robert, 402
 Harvey, William, 408
 Hayward, —, 415
 Henshaw, William, 422
 Hill, Isaac, 430
 Howard, William, 455
 Iron, Mark Oliver, 473
 Iron, Nathaniel, 473
 Jeffery, John, 482
 Jeffery, Joseph, 482
 Jennings, Thomas, 485
 Johnson, Nathaniel, 490
 Jones, William, 498
 Keningale, Robert, 506
 King, John, 514
 King, Joseph, 514
 Lee, Thomas, 535
 Leverett, Henry, 539
 Leverett, J., 539
 Lewis, Obadiah, 540
 List, —, 548
 Lockwood, Samuel, 553
 Lockwood, William, 553
 Manning, James, 573
 Manning, William, 573
 Martin, Charles, 580
 Martin, George, 580
 Martin, James, 581
 Mayes, Edward, 589
 Mills, John, 610
 Milne, John, 611
 Morley, David, 627
 Mulley, John, 635
 Neale, Charles, 640
 Noble, Thomas, 650
 Oddie, Henry, 661
 Oliver, Mark, 663
 Payne, George, 682
 Payne, Simon, 683
 Phillips, John, 695
 Pite, Thomas, 700
 Price, William, 716
 Ralph, Daniel, 726
 Rogers, Thomas, 764
 Saul, John, 781
 Selby, Daniel, 799
 Selby, Thomas, 799
 Senton, James, 800
 Setterfield, Thomas, 800
 Shearman, George, 806
 Short, James, 812
 Simpson, Daniel, 816
 Simpson, James, 816

 Singleton, Thomas, 818
 Sparrow, John, 841
 Sparrow, William, 842
 Stevens, William, 855
 Syer, Edward, 869
 Tavell, Charles, 874
 Thompson, William, 888
 Thorne, Edward, 889
 Thurston, Joseph, 893
 Tidman, Thomas, 894
 Tokard, William, 897
 Tunmer, Charles Frederick, 908
 Tunmer, James Robert, 908
 Williams, —, 979
 Worth, Henry, 1003
 Wright, Robert, 1008
Ipswich, Christchurch Mansion: Cox, John, 204
Ireland, 53
Ireland, Sam Booth, 534
Ironbridge (Salop):
 Edwards, Edward, 269
 Lloyd, John, 550
 Rogers, Thomas, 764
Irving, 708
Isaac, John, 397
Isaac & Skardon, 818
Isaacson, Robert, 292
Isherwood, 110
Isleworth (Middlx): Penny, William, 689
Islington (London):
 Allpress, James, 11
 Ames, Samuel, 12
 Atle, Benjamin, 25
 Baker, Daniel S., 32
 Barnes, J.H., 42
 Brown, John, 116
 Daw(e), William, 233
 Dawson, William, 235
 Edlin, Edward C., 267
 Ewins, Daniel, 286
 Hartley, Thomas, 407
 Hawes, M., 412
 Hawes, Mary, 412
 Holbird, James, 440
 Hood, Thomas Frederick, 447
 Jones, Henry, 495
 Keen, D., 502
 Lambert, Joseph, 523
 Longdon, T., 555
 Newell, John, 642
 Newman, J., 643
 Parkes, Joseph & Wells, Thomas, 675
 Perkins, Richard, 690
 Price, Thomas Henry, 716
 Rose, William, 766
 Scholey, William & J., 789
 Scutz, Henry, 791
 Simmons, John, 815
 Stone, Edward, 858
 Stone, Elden, 858
 Stone, G., 858

Tidmarsh, William, 894
Waineright, Robert, 932
Whytall, T., 972
Williams, William, 983
Ismay, 657
Ixworth (Suffolk): Leaman, Samuel, 533

J

Jackson, 31, 237, 931
Jackson, Christopher, 970
Jackson, Francis, 812
Jackson, George, 563
Jackson, John, 572
Jackson, Peter, 475
Jackson, Ralph, 22
Jackson, Rowland, 155
Jackson, Sarah, 475
Jackson, William, 80, 971
Jacobs, John, 796
Jagger, Benjamin, 221, 329
James, 983
James, Charles, 479
James, E., 480
James, Edmund, 479
James, Edward, 366, 971
James, G., 480
James, George, 136, 821
James, James, 976
James, John, 115, 480, 576, 743, 911
James, William, 479, 957
Jamieson, 13
Janson, 808
Japp, William, 751
Jarratt, William, 980
Jarrow (Co. Durham):
    Burlison, William, 131
    Nicholson, William, 647
Jay, Benjamin, 841
Jay, Mathew, 837
Jeacocke, 637
Jean, Dominique, 324, 526
Jebson, Thomas, 263
Jefferson, 425
Jefferson, James, 53, 258
Jefferys, Henry, 839
Jeffries, John, 6
Jeffs, 706
Jellicoe, William, 778-9, 824
Jenkins, 193, 394
Jenkins, John, 861
Jenkins, Samuel, 378
Jenkinson, 880
Jenks, J.M., 484
Jennens & Bettridge, 176
Jenning, John, 752
Jennings, 119, 769
Jennings, Abraham, 541
Jennings, Robert, 969
Jennings, William, 403, 663
Jennings & Walkington, 939

Jensen, Gerrit, 205, 752, 753
Jeremy & Bragg, 698
Jervis, 477
Jiggs, 405
Jinnings, 774
Joad, John, 139, 504
Job, Robert, 313
Johnson, 543, 577, 722, 991, 1001
Johnson, Barry, 363
Johnson, Edward, 29, 137, 492
Johnson, George, 17, 40, 53, 161, 258, 489, 492, 651
Johnson, John, 316, 374, 420, 693, 743, 891, 1001
Johnson, Joseph, 251, 493, 539, 664
Johnson, M., 489
Johnson, Robert, 504-5
Johnson, T., 489
Johnson, Thomas, 110, 157, 187, 214, 227, 345, 349, 776
Johnson, William, 227, 802
Johnstone, John, 507
Jole, William, 821
Jolly, Richard, 438
Jonathan, 405
Jones, 214, 455, 774, 939, 957
Jones, C., 510, 724
Jones, Charles, 535, 615
Jones, Edward, 171
Jones, Hugh, 171, 498
Jones, John, 24, 89
Jones, John jnr, 70
Jones, Matthew, 285
Jones, Morgan, 997
Jones, Richard, 933
Jones, Robert, 557
Jones, Sandys, 128
Jones, Thomas, 576, 693
Jones, Thomas Cason, 949
Jones, William, 91, 101, 648, 684, 720, 971
Jones, William jnr, 63, 92
Jopling, William, 181
Jordaine, John Nathaniel, 285
Jordan, 572
Jordan, John Nathaniel, 285
Joyhnson, Richard, 956
Joynes, John, 517
Jubbergate (Yorks): Ingham, Joseph, 471
Judson, 193
Judson, Farshall, 944

K

Kay, John, 501
Kay, Peter, 303
Kay, Quintin, 787, 978
Kay, Samuel, 915
Keating, 35
Keating, Daniel, 408
Kedleston Hall (Derbs.):
    Alken, Sefferin, 8

Brown, John, 115
Clay, Henry, 177
Crichton & Pitchford, 209
Gamble, —, 328
Gravenor, James, 364
Grendey, Giles, 372
Hall, John, 385
Hall, Joseph, 386
Johnson, William, 492
Linnell, John, 544, 545
Linnell, William, 547
Robinson, Robert, 760
Storer, William, 859
Vickers & Rutledge, 923
Keelby (Lincs.): Everitt, William, 285
Keevil, Robert, 736
Keevill, Robert, 736
Keighley (Yorks):
    Blakey, John, 79
    Dean, William, 237
    Green, Thomas, 368
    Illingworth, James, 471
    Jackson, James, 475
    Judson, John, 500
    Lister, John, 549
    McJay, Barnard, 565
    M'Vay, Bernard, 569
    Midgley, John, 605
    Midgley, Joseph, 605
    Mitchell & Binns, 614
    Preston, James, 714
    Proctor, George, 719
    Robinson, George, 757
    Simpson, Frederick, 816
    Smith, Metcalf, 830
    Spencer, Samuel, 844
    Steel, Fletcher, 851
    Steel, William, 851
    Sugden, William, 864
Kelley, George, 38
Kellow, Francis, 452
Kelly, 172, 305
Kelly, John, 754
Kelsall, Thomas, 820, 836
Kelsey, John, 708
Kelsey & Potter, 708
Kemp, George, 360, 488, 840
Kemp, John, 80, 360, 399, 792, 877
Kemp, William, 65, 251, 757
Kempling, Henry, 853
Kempsey (Worcs.): Haines, John, 383
Kempshott Park (Hants.): De Caix, Alexander, 238
Kempster, Samuel, 140, 275, 709
Kempton Park (Middlx): Collins, William, 189
Kendal (Westmld):
    Atkinson, Francis, 24
    Bateman, William, 49
    Benson, Thomas, 66
    Bland, Isaac, 80
    Burkitt, William, 130

Halhead, Hannah, 384
Halhead, James, 384
Halhead, John, 384
Harker, Jonathan, 398
Holhead, John, 441
Jackson, John, 476
Lewis, William, 541
Mitchel, John, 613
Pedder, Richard, 686
Pennington, Joseph, 689
Railton, Joseph, 725
Redman, Christopher, 733
Stuart, John, 863
Webster, Thomas, 956
Kendall, Edward, 911
Kendall, John, 396, 491
Kendell, John, 851
Kenilworth (Warks.):
　Brown, John, 116
　Robbins, —, 751
Kennedy, William, 576
Kennet & Kidd, 25, 362, 666
Kennett, Robert, 590, 596, 922
Kennett & Kidd, 420, 421, 824
Kennington (London):
　Adams, William, 4
　Dunn, John, 260
　Egerton, George, 271
　Jeffrey, Emanuel, 483
　Morgan, William, 626
　Pratt, Henry, 712
　Robinson, William H., 761
　Rolls, James, 765
Kensington (London):
　Abbott, W., 1
　Abbott, William, 1
　Balls & Hughes, 36
　Burrows, John, 134
　Dickson, W.H., 244
　Dolton, William, 250
　Griffiths, William, 375
　Harris, John, 401
　Humphrey, George, 463
　M'Leland, John William, 568
　Morgan, David, 625
　Moss, Thomas, 632
　Okey, Thomas, 662
　Russell, John, 772
　Smith, George, 826
　Smith, I., 827
　Smith, Robert, 831
　Smith, Thomas & Son, 833
　Smith & Son, 836
　Walter, —, 941
　Walter, Thomas, 941
　Watson, Joseph, 950
Kent, Abbot, 560
Kent, Bartholomew, 833, 978
Kent, John, 102, 989
Kent, Samuel, 509
Kent, William, 580, 685
Kent & Luck, 685
Kentish Town (London):
　Gambee, William Robert, 328

Page, William, 670
Kenure Park (Co. Dublin): Gomm,
　William & Richard, 350
Kenyon, Robert, 748, 935
Kenyon, William, 150
Kepplewhite, 422
Kermode, William, 754
Kerr, 131, 900
Kerrington, Richard, 376
Kerry, Jno., 494
Kerry, John, 30, 724
Keswick (Cumb.):
　Ashburner, John, 20
　Birkett, John, 75
　Dixon, Robert, 246
　Glover, Joseph, 345
　Harrison, Watson, 404
　Harrison, William, 405
　Hogg, John, 440
　Ivison, James, 474
　Ladyman, Thomas, 521
　Lawson, James, 532
　Laydeman, T., 533
　Mawson, J., 588
　Pearson, Joseph, 685
　Postlethwaite, Isaac, 707
　Postlethwaite, Thomas, 707
　Powlay, Henry, 711
　Skurr, William, 820
Kettering (Northants.):
　Brampton, Samuel, 102
　Iliffe, John, 471
　Singleton, Thomas, 818
　Singleton, William, 818
Kettle, Henry, 62, 422, 658
Kettlewell, John, 53, 258
Kettlewell (Yorks): Hill, Charles,
　430
Kew, George, 70
Kew Palace (Surrey):
　Boson, John, 88, 89
　Bradburn(e), John, 97
　Goodison, Benjamin, 351
Key, Benjamin, 957
Key, George, 824
Key, John, 214
Keynsham (Som.): Walter,
　Matthew, 941
Kidd, 25, 362, 420, 421, 666, 824
Kidd, Joseph, 507, 959
Kidd, Richard, 374
Kidd, Robert, 413
Kidderminster (Worcs.):
　Allcock, Charles, 9
　Allcock, William, 9
　Bevan, James, 69
　Dobson, John, 247
　Dounton, S., 251
　Downton, Samuel, 255
　Goodman, Humphrey, 354
　Hill, Walter, 431
　Keyte, John, 511
　Lea, William, 533
　Moore, Robert, 620

Pitt, Francis, 701
　Walters, William, 941
　Watkins, Joseph, 947
Kiddle, John, 59
Kidlington (Oxon.): Sydenham,
　George, 868
Kilburn (London): Prior, Samuel,
　718
Kilkenny Castle (Ireland): Kennett,
　Robert & Kidd, William, 506,
　507
Killerton (Devon): Stone, —, 858
Killingley, Edward, 256
Killingley, Jo., 806
Kilner, John, 513
Kilniddery (Co. Wicklow): Pratt,
　Samuel, 712
Kilnwick Hall (Yorks):
　Platt, John, 702
　Reynoldson, George, 739, 740
　Wright, Richard & Elwick,
　Edward, 1007
Kilpin, William, 322, 463, 628, 788
Kilpin Hall (Yorks.): Tiffin & Sons,
　894
Kilruddery (Co. Wicklow): Froom,
　William, 323
Kilvington, Israel, 536
Kimbolton (Hunts.):
　Quick, John, 724
　Webster, William, 956
　Wright, William, 1009
Kimbolton Castle (Hunts.):
　Mayhew, John & Ince, William,
　592, 595
King, 403, 668, 835
King, James, 275, 515
King, John, 632, 697
King, Michael, 515
King, Thomas, 887
King, William, 62, 216, 514
King, William Alkin, 515
King's Lynn (Norfolk):
　Arbuthnot, Thomas, 17
　Atto, William, 25
　Bailey, George, 30
　Barker, John, 40
　Bones, John, 85
　Bridgman, Jonathan, 107
　Browne, John, 120
　Browne, Oliver, 120
　Bunnett, Jacob jnr, 129
　Bunnett, R., 129
　De Caux, David, 238
　Dewson, James, 243
　Dickerson, John, 243
　Donne, Thomas, 250
　Edwards, Joshua, 270
　Edwards, Thomas, 270
　Eggett, George, 271
　Eggitt, Frances, 271
　Gee, Edward, 334
　Gilbert, William, 339
　Giscard, John, 344

Goddin, Daniel, 346
Goodwyn, Daniel, 355
Greeves, John, 370
Hales, Jonathan, 383
Hardwick, Asty, 396
Harvey, John, 407
Harvey, Thomas, 408
Harwick, Asty, 408
Harwick, Thomas, 408
Hawkins, Alexander, 412
Hawkins, Samuel, 413
Hill, Thomas jnr, 431
Hill, Thomas snr, 431
Hillyard, Maria, 432
Hillyard, S., 432
Innebe, Thomas, 472
Jackson, George, 475
Junipee, Thomas, 500
King, H., 514
King, James, 514
Lyther, James, 563
Moretti, J.C., 625
Morris, R., 629
Morris, Robert, 629
Newman, William, 643
Newsham, Edward, 644
Norton, Hugh, 656
Oldmeadow, Charles, 662
Oldmeadow, James, 662
Payne, Joseph, 682
Pearson, Samuel, 685
Perkins, William, 691
Pope, Henry, 706
Preston, Thomas snr & jnr, 714
Preston, William, 714
Reeve, Charlotte, 735
Reeve(s), James, 735
Rogers, Daniel, 763
Rudd, William, 770
Scott, John, 790
Smith, John, 829
Smith, Richard, 831
Smith, Wainwright, 833
Smith, William, 835
Socket, Jeremiah, 838
Speechly, James, 842
Spencer, Joseph, 844
Swindle, John, 868
Taylor, James, 876
Taylor, John, 877
Taylor, Joseph, 878
Vincent, George Matthew, 929
Voice, John, 930
Wagg, David, 931
West, Joseph Henry, 960
West, Thomas, 960
Whayt, Charles, 962
Whisker, William, 963
White, John, 966
White, T., 967
Young, Henry, 1014
Kingsbridge (Devon):
  Eddy, John, 266
  Hammeth, Robert, 392

Hannaford, W., 395
Kingsbury (Som.): Owsley, Samuel, 668
Kingston (Surrey):
  Beville, Francis, 69
  Bowes, George, 92
  Dawson, John, 235
  Miller, Nathan, 609
  Peake, John, 683
  Peebles, Charles, 686
  Pratt, —, 712
  Russell, Robert, 773
  Walter, John, 941
  Walter, Robert, 941
Kingston Lacy (Dorset): Mayhew, John & Ince, William, 597
Kingswinford (Staffs.): Bent, Daniel, 66
Kington (Herefs.):
  Barrar, Beniah, 44
  Griffiths, Richard, 375
  Griffiths, Thomas, 375
  Hall, Thomas, 386
  Humphreys, Arthur, 463
  Humphreys, Gwynn, 463
  Milner, Henry, 611
  Scandrett, William, 788
Kinross House (Kinross-shire):
  Boyse, Peter Paul, 94
  Vanerba, Cornelius, 919
Kinver (Staffs.): Willmott, William, 984
Kiplin, William, 743
Kirby, 1003
Kirby, James H., 151
Kirby (Westmld): Pedder, Richard, 686
Kirbymoorside (Yorks):
  Berkley, William, 67
  Denney, John, 240
  Denney, Joseph, 240
  Dowthwaite, John, 255
  Haig(h), Thomas, 383
  Johnson, John, 490
  Poole, James, 706
  Potter, George, 708
  Powell, James, 710
  Sigsworth, John, 814
  Stead, Robert, 851
Kirk, Thomas, 305
Kirk Deighton (Yorks): Winter, John, 993
Kirkbride, 50
Kirkburton (Yorks):
  Dyson, Edmund, 263
  Dyson, William, 263
  Earnshaw & Heptonstall, 264
  Kay, John, 500
  Kay, Joseph, 500
  Lockwood, John, 553
  Mitchell, Thomas, 614
  White, Jonadab, 966
  Wilson, William, 990

Kirkby Fleetham (Yorks):
  Henderson, John, 420
Kirkby Lonsdale (Westmld):
  Baines, William, 32
  Bains, John, 32
  Brayshew, William, 104
  Garnett, Thomas, 331
  Russell, John, 772
  Ward, John, 943
  Whittingdale, John, 970
  Willan, William, 978
Kirkby South (Yorks): Ledger, Richard, 534
Kirkby Stephen (Westmld):
  Atkinson, Thomas, 25
  Gibbon, William, 336
  Hutchinson, John, 468
  Jones, John, 495
Kirke, Samuel, 276, 616
Kirkes, John, 499, 537
Kirkes, Samuel, 397, 831
Kirkham, John, 391
Kirkham, William, 585
Kirkham (Lancs.):
  Bamber, James, 36
  Dickson, George, 244
  Sharples, James, 804
  Taylor, Edward, 875
  Ward, Richard, 943
  Ward, Thomas, 944
  Webster, John, 955
  Whalley, John, 962
Kirkland Hall (?Cumbria): Gillow, 343
Kirklees Hall (Yorks.):
  Summerscale, Thomas, 865
  Wright, Richard & Elwick, Edward, 1008
Kirkman, 841
Kirks, Samuel, 27, 159, 616
Kirlew, Thomas, 779
Kirtlington Park (Oxon.):
  Clive, Mr, 179
  Crawley, Gerard, 208
  Gill, John, 340
  Hallett, William snr and William jnr, 389
  Wiseman, —, 994
Kiveton House (Yorks.): Young, Thomas, 1015
Knaresborough (Yorks.):
  Alinson, Thomas, 11
  Anderson, John, 13
  Benson, John, 66
  Benson, William, 66
  Bland, William, 80
  Boldison, Mark, 83
  Buck, Peter, 123
  Bussey, Samuel, 137
  Dawson, Bryan, 235
  Lambert, William, 523
  Lister, William, 549
  Livesey, George, 550
  Marshall, Charles, 577

Mawson, Thomas, 588
Penning, John, 689
Pennington, John, 689
Pullen, Timothy, 722
Rhodes, John, 740
Smithies, William, 836
Temple, Jeremiah, 880
Thompson, George, 885
Umpleby, John, 917
Kneen, Thomas, 408
Knife, John, 284
Knight, 176, 939
Knight, E., 3
Knight, J., 3
Knight, Joseph, 248, 434
Knightsbridge (London):
   Ayling, James, 27
   Ayling, T., 28
   Barker, John, 40
   Bond, S.E., 85
   Brix, Robert, 109
   Deschamps, Francis, 241
   Humphr(e)ys, Robert, 463
   Matthews, John, 587
   Murgatroyd, A., 636
   Pulsford, Robert, 722
   Ram, John, 726
   Room, I., 765
   Rowe, Thomas, 768
   Slater, Edward, 820
   Spedding, Thomas, 842
   Spencer, James, 843
   Stephens, Thomas, 853
Knole Park (Kent):
   Jensen, Gerrit, 487
   Lapierre, Francis, 528
   Roberts, Thomas & Richard,
   752, 753
Knottingley (Yorks.):
   Barwick, Thomas, 47
   Bentley, Michael, 66
   Metcalf, George, 603
   Moore, William, 622
Knowles, 436
Knowles, John Maddock, 754
Knutsford (Cheshire):
   Arde(a)n, Thomas, 17
   Gregson, Robert, 371
   Holde, Willoughby, 441
   Jackson, John, 476
   Kent, Richard, 508
   Kent, T., 508
   Otewell, James, 666
   Oulton, Thomas Clownes, 667
   Read, Georgie, 732
   Read(e), Joseph, 732
   Riade, Joseph, 741
   Turner, Thomas, 912
   Widdal, Samuel, 972
   Woodall, John, 998
Kyre Park (Worcs.): King,
   Benjamin, 514
Kyte, Joseph, 501

L

La Grange, 537
La Porte, Gabriel Laurent, 424
Lace, Henry, 766
Laceby (Lincs.): Burnett,
   Christopher, 131
Lack, Thomas, 1012
Lacock (Wilts.):
   Baker, Charles, 32
   Goodman, John, 354
Ladyman, 1004
Ladyman, Henry, 792, 956
Lago, 139
Lake, Richard, 373
Lamb, Joseph, 181
Lamb, Michael, 465
Lamb, Robert, 141, 292
Lamb, William, 131
Lambe, 957
Lambe, Woolhouse, 114
Lambert, 800
Lambert, Jane, 522
Lambert, Robert, 163
Lambert, Stephen, 837
Lambeth (London):
   Ainge, William, 5
   Allan, Thomas, 9
   Ashman, John C., 20
   Baker, William, 33
   Bayley, Samuel, 52
   Booth, Stephen & J., 87
   Bourne, John, 91
   Brown, J., 114
   Brown, W., 118
   Brown, William, 119
   Browne, George, 120
   Buckman, Edward, 124
   Davis, Edward, 231
   Daws, William, 235
   Dove, —, 252
   Downing, E., 254
   Downing, William, 255
   Dracott, Jos., 255
   Dunn, Edwrad, 260
   Dunn, John, 260
   Dunn, Thomas, 260
   Edwards, P., 270
   Evans, James, 284
   Graves, Isaac Smith, 365
   Greenwood, S., 369
   Griffin, H., 373
   Griffith, H., 374
   Griffiths, Henry, 374
   Gritten, J., 375
   Guthrie, Claud, 380
   Haddrick, —, 382
   Hamilton, Thomas, 391
   Hamilton & Mogany, 391
   Hampton, William, 392
   Harris, —, 400
   Harrison, J., 403
   Headley, Thomas, 416
   Hewetson, John, 425
   Hodder, John, 436
   Hodgson, Septimus, 438
   Holmes, John, 445
   Johnson, Benjamin, 489
   Johnson, George, 489
   Kemp, Matt., 504
   Langford, John, 525
   Lawrence, R. Thomas, 531
   Leach, George, 533
   Lecount, Richard, 534
   Lowe, William, 558
   McLauchlan, Andrew, 567
   Mason, John, 584
   Merrick, George, 603
   Middleton, Thomas, 605
   Miller, John, 608
   Minett, William, 612
   Murrell, John, 637
   Oughton, J., 667
   Oughton, Levi, 667
   Oughton, Samuel, 667
   Oughton, Thomas, 667
   Pattenden, Jeremiah, 680
   Penman, Robert, 688
   Phillips, William, 696
   Pickering, Henry, 697
   Robbins, Edwin, 751
   Rouse, Joseph, 768
   Rowley, Edward, 769
   Sammons, Jer., 778
   Sammons, T., 778
   Saunders, John, 782
   Searle, George, 792
   Senhouse, William Minet, 800
   Shephard, William II, 807
   Simpson, Carrington, 816
   Skinner, John, 819
   Smale, James, 822
   Smith, Joseph, 830
   Smith, Samuel, 832
   Smith, T., 832
   Strudwicke, Henry, 862
   Taylor, Daniel, 875
   Te(a)rnl(e)y, —, 880
   Thorn, Robert, 889
   Thorne, Thomas, 890
   Walker, Robert, 937
   Watson, George, 949
   Watson, George & J., 949
   Watts, William, 951
   Wells, James, 957
   Woodruffe, George snr & jnr,
   1000
   Wybrow, John, 1011
Lambourn (Berks.): Bew, Josiah, 70
Lamont, 119
Lamport Church (Northants.):
   Potter, Thomas, 708
Lancaster, James, 750
Lancaster:
   Addison, John, 4
   Addison, Thomas, 5
   Adlington, Thomas, 5
   Alexander, John, 7

Lancaster

Allen, John, 10
Alston, Thomas, 11
Anderson, Robert, 13
Anderson, William, 13
Anderton, —, 13
Appley, Robert, 16
Appley, William, 16
Armisted, James, 18
Askew, Edward, 21
Askew, William, 21
Atkinson, Edmund, 23
Atkinson, George, 24
Atkinson, James, 24
Atkinson, John, 24
Atkinson, Samuel, 24
Atkinson, Thomas, 24
Atkinson, William, 25
Bagot, Thomas, 29
Bagott, Richard, 29
Bainbridge, Thomas, 31
Baines, Francis Singleton, 31
Baines, Henry, 31
Baines, Thomas, 32
Baldwin, Robert, 34
Ball, Robert, 35
Ball, William, 35
Bamber, Henry, 36
Barber, John, 38
Barker, William, 41
Barr, John, 43
Barrow, John, 45
Barrow, Nicholas, 45
Barrow, Thomas, 45
Barrow, William, 45
Barwick, Henry, 47
Barwick, John, 47
Barwick, Joseph, 47
Barwick, William, 47
Bateman, George, 48
Bateman, John, 48
Bateman, Matthew, 49
Bateman, Redman, 49
Bateson, David, 49
Bateson, James, 49
Battersby, —, 50
Battersby, John, 50
Battersby, Robert, 50
Batty, Edward, 50
Bayley, William, 52
Baynes, Henry, 53
Baynes, James, 53
Baynes, Thomas, 53
Becket, John, 56
Becket(t), William, 56
Beetham, William, 59
Bell, James, 61
Bell, Robert, 62
Bentham, Joshua, 66
Bewes, John, 70
Bidman, Joseph, 71
Birket(t), Henry, 74
Birket(t), Thomas, 74
Blackborne, Edward, 77
Blackbourne, William, 77

Blackburn, Richard, 77
Blackburn, Thomas, 77
Blackburn, William, 77
Blackburn, William jnr, 77
Boardley, William, 82
Bodell, Christopher, 82
Bond, Edward, 85
Bond, Joseph, 85
Bonnel(l), Henry, 85
Boulton, Isaac, 91
Boulton, William, 91
Bowman, William, 93
Brade, John, 97
Brade, Lawrence, 97
Bradley, James jnr, 98
Bradley, John, 98
Bradley, Thomas, 98
Bradley, William, 98
Bradshaw, Isaac, 99
Braithwaite, Thomas, 102
Brian, Samuel, 106
Briscoe, Peter, 108
Briscoe, Thomas, 108
Briscoe, William, 108
Brough, John, 113
Brown, John, 115
Brown, William, 119
Brownrigg, William, 120
Bruce, William, 121
Bryham, Simon, 123
Bure, William, 130
Burrow, John, 133
Burton, James, 135
Burton, James snr, 135
Burton, John, 135
Burton, T., 135
Butler, Robert, 137
Danby, J., 225
Danson, George, 226
Darwen, Thomas, 227
David, Thomas, 227
Davis, Francis & Co., 231
Davis, John, 231
Davis, Thomas, 232
Davis, William, 233
Dawson, Thomas, 235
Dickinson, Thomas, 243
Dickson, James, 244
Dixon, —, 245
Dixon jnr, 245
Dixon, Christopher, 246
Dixon, Hervey, 246
Dixon, James, 246
Dixon, John, 246
Dixon, John Henry, 246
Dixon, Joseph, 246
Dixon, Richard, 246
Dixon, Thomas, 246
Dixon, Thomas jnr, 246
Dixon, Thomas snr, 246
Dobson, James, 247
Dobson, Thomas, 248
Dodson, William, 249
Dowbiggen, John, 252

Dowbiggin, Thomas, 252
Drape, Thomas, 255
Duke, William, 259
Dunderdale, John, 259
Edmondson, James, 267
Edmondson, Richard, 267
Edmondson, Robert I, II & III, 267
Edmondson, Samuel, 268
Edmondson, Thomas, 268
Edmundson, J., 268
Eldson, John, 272
Ellershaw, James, 272
Ellwood, John, 276
Elsdon, John, 277
Elston, Robert, 277
Escolme, Thomas, 282
Eskholme, Richard, 282
Gardner, Daniel, 329
Gardner, James, 330
Gardner, Matthew, 330
Garnett, John, 331
Gelder, Henry, 335
Getskell, John, 336
Getskell, Joseph, 336
Getskell, William, 336
Gibson, Clement, 337
Gibson, Henry, 337
Gibson, Richard, 337
Gibson, W., 338
Gilbanks, M., 338
Gillow, —, 341
Graham, Joseph, 362
Grant, James, 364
Gray, Samuel, 365
Greaves, George, 366
Greenwood, Isaac, 369
Greenwood, John, 369
Greenwood, Peter, 369
Greenwood, Robert, 369
Greenwood, Samuel, 369
Greenwood, Thomas, 369
Gregson, Benjamin, 370
Gregson, Joseph, 370
Gunson, Joshua, 380
Gurnell, Thomas, 380
Hague, Richard, 382
Hague, Robert, 382
Hall, Jonathan jnr, 385
Hall, Richard, 386
Hall, Thomas, 386
Hall, William, 386
Hallhead, James, 390
Hallhead, John, 390
Hamilton, John, 391
Hannibal, John, 395
Hardman, —, 396
Hardy, C., 396
Hardy, William, 397
Hargreaves, Thomas, 398
Harker, Jonathan, 398
Harris, Thomas, 402
Harrison, John, 404
Harrison, Robert, 404

Hartley, James, 406
Haselden, —, 408
Hatton, John, 410
Hatton, Thomas, 410
Hawthornthwaite, John, 414
Helme, William, 420
Herbert, Edward Geoffrey, 423
Herbert, John, 423
Heselden, John, 424
Hesseldon, Isaac, 424
Hesseldon, Isaac jnr, 424
Hesseldon, John, 424
Hewatt, C., 425
Hewitt, —, 425
High, William, 429
Hill, William, 431
Hinde, James, 433
Hodgson, Christopher, 437
Hodgson, David, 437
Hodg(e)son, James, 438
Hodgson, John, 438
Hodgson, Thomas, 438
Hoggart, Barton John, 440
Hoggart, John, 440
Hoggat, William, 440
Holme, Henry, 444
Holme, Thomas, 444
Holmes, Henry, 445
Holme(s), Robert, 444
Horrocks, —, 450
Howard, Charles, 453
Howarth, John, 455
Huck, John, 457
Hudson, Edward, 458
Hully, Christopher, 462
Hunter, Thomas, 465
Hunter, W., 465
Hutton, —, 468
Hutton, George, 469
Hutton, James, 469
Hutton, John, 469
Hutton, Richard, 469
Huttons, —, 469
Ireland, Benson Harrison, 473
Irvin, Richard, 473
Jackson, George, 475
Jackson, Robert, 477
Jackson, Thomas, 477
Jackson, William, 477
Jacobs, —, 477
Jefferson, G., 482
Johnson, Robert, 491
Joynson, —, 499
Kelsey, James, 503
Kelshaw, J., 503
Kendal, John, 504
Kendall, George Knipe, 504
Kendall, James, 504
Kilner, J. jnr, 512
Kilner, John, 512
Kilner, Thomas Earl, 512
King, William, 515
Kirkbride, John, 517
Kitchen, James, 518

Knight, Thomas, 519
Knipe, John, 520
Knott, W., 520
Lambert, John, 523
Lambert, Joseph, 523
Lascelles, William, 528
Lawkland, Thomas, 530
Lawson, James, 532
Lawson, John, 532
Lawson, Robert, 532
Leach, James, 533
Leeming, John, 535
Leeming, Richard, 535
Leeming, William, 535
Leeming, William jnr, 536
Leicester, Thomas, 537
Leighton, —, 537
Leister, Robert, 537
Lindsay, Joseph, 543
Lindsay, Thomas, 543
Lister, John, 549
Lister, Robert, 549
Lister, Thomas, 549
Lodge, Edward, 553
Lodge, James, 553
Lodge & Battersby, 553
Lofthouse, William, 553
Lonsdale, Thomas, 555
Lowther, John, 559
Lowthian, Richard, 559
Lowthian, Thomas, 559
Luny, William, 561
Lupton, —, 561
Lupton, Charles, 561
Lupton, John, 561
Lupton, William, 561
Machell, James, 565
Machell, William, 565
Mackarall, James, 565
Mackereth, S., 566
Malley, John, 571
Malley, Peter, 571
Malley, William, 571
Mally, B.J., 571
Mangenot, N., 572
Mansergh, John, 573
Martin, T., 581
Martindale, Thomas, 582
Mashiter, Gardner, 583
Mashiter, George, 583
Mashiter, Richard, 583
Mason, George, 583
Mason, James, 584
Mason, John, 584
Maychell, —, 589
Maychell, James, 589
Maychell, William, 589
Middlefell, Richard, 605
Middleton, John, 605
Miller, Henry, 608
Miller, James, 608
Miller, John, 608
Miller, Thomas, 609
Mills, William, 611

Minikin, James, 612
Minikin, Thomas, 612
Minshull, —, 612
Mitchell, —, 613
Moizer, Richard, 615
Moon, James Carter, 616
Moon, Thomas, 617
Moon, William, 617
Moor, George, 617
Moore, Marmaduke, 620
Moore, William, 622
Moore & Townley, 622
Moreland, John, 625
Morris, James, 628
Myers, Thomas, 637
Myerscough, Richard, 637
Naylor, James, 639
Naylor, William, 639
Nelson, Thomas, 641
Nevton, John, 641
Newby, Christopher, 642
Newton, John, 645
Newton, Robert, 645
Nightingale, John, 648
Noar, E., 650
Noar, John, 650
Norcross,, Thomas, 651
Oglethorpe, Joseph, 661
O'Neill, John, 664
Ormandy, John, 665
Ormandy, William, 665
Overend, Brian, 667
Overend, Joseph, 667
Padget, John, 669
Padget, Richard, 669
Parker, William, 675
Parkinson, James, 676
Parkinson, Richard, 676
Patefield, Jonathan, 679
Pearson, John, 685
Pedder, Thomas, 686
Pegram, James, 687
Pendleton, John, 688
Pennington, John, 689
Pennington, Miles, 689
Pennington, William, 689
Pinder, John, 699
Polly, Richard, 705
Pool, N., 705
Preston, Joseph, 714
Preston, Thomas, 714
Preston, William, 714
Pritt, Isaac, 719
Pritt, John, 719
Proctor, Christopher, 719
Proctor, George, 719
Proctor, James, 719
Pye, Edward, 723
Ravald, John, 728
Rawes, Christopher, 729
Rawes, Gerrard, 729
Ray, William, 730
Redhead, William, 733
Redmayne, Leonard, 733

Richardson, John, 744
Richardson, Richard, 744
Richardson, Thomas, 745
Richmond, Henry, 745
Richmond, James, 746
Rickarby, John, 746
Rigby, —, 747
Rigby, James, 747
Rigby, Michael, 747
Ripley, James, 750
Roberts, James, 751
Robinson, C., 756
Robinson, Isaac, 757
Robinson, James, 758
Robinson, Joseph, 759
Robinson, William, 760
Romney, George, 765
Romney, Thomas, 765
Rothery, John, 767
Russell, Robert, 773
Sandwick, Robert, 780
Sandwick, William, 780
Sarratt, Samuel, 781
Satterthwaite, Robert, 781
Savage, John, 786
Savage, Michael, 786
Scott, James, 789
Scott, Robert, 790
Seward, P., 801
Sharp, John, 803
Sharples, Richard, 804
Sharples, Robert, 804
Shaw, James, 804
Shawe, John, 806
Shrigley, —, 813
Shuttleworth, Thomas, 813
Silverwood, Thomas, 815
Simpson, Thomas, 816
Singleton, John, 818
Slater, Richard, 821
Slater, William, 821
Slinger, Thomas, 821
Smith, Benjamin, 824
Smith, Hilton, 827
Smith, Richard, 831
Smith, Thomas, 832
Smith, William, 833
Southworth, —, 840
Sowerby, George, 841
Sowerby, Jeremiah, 841
Swainson, John, 866, 867
Swainson, Joseph, 867
Swan, Thomas, 867
Swan, William, 867
Swinburne, John, 868
Sykes, Edmund, 869
Sykes, Edward, 869
Tasker, T., 873
Tate, —, 873
Tatham, Robert, 873
Tatham, Thomas, 874
Taylor, Jonathon, 877
Taylor, John, 877
Taylor, William, 879

Teasdale, Robert, 880
Tennant, James, 881
Tennant, Thomas, 881
Thompson, Marmaduke, 887
Thorney, Robert jnr, 890
Thorney, Robert snr, 890
Thorney, Thomas, 890
Thornton, Christopher, 890
Thornton, John, 890
Thwaite, T., 893
Tinkler, John, 895
Tolley, Richard, 897
Tomlinson, James T., 898
Tomlinson, John, 898
Tomlinson, Richard, 898
Touchet, John, 900
Towers, Thomas, 900
Townley, Richard, 901
Townley, Robert, 901
Townshend, R., 901
Townson, C., John, 902
Townson, John jnr, 902
Townson, Robert jnr, 902
Townson, Thomas, 902
Turner, Anthony, 909
Turner, John, 910
Turner, Richard, 911
Turner, William, 913
Turner, William & Co., 913
Turner & Hodgson, 913
Tyson, Joseph, M., 916
Varley, William, 920
Wainhouse, Edward, 932
Wainhouse, John, 932
Wainhouse, Thomas, 932
Wakefield, John, 933
Walker, Christopher. 934
Walker, H., 935
Walker, Henry, 935
Walker, John, 935
Walker, Thomas, 937
Walling, Henry, 940
Walmesley, Benjamin, 940
Walton, Thomas, 942
Warbrick, Thomas, 942
Warriner, B., 946
Watton, Thomas, 951
Webster, John, 955
West, John, 960
Whinray, Thomas, 963
Whiteside, Edward, 968
Whiteside, James, 969
Whiteside, Thomas, 969
Whittingdale, Thomas, 970
Whormby, William, 972
Wilcock, Crs., 973
Wilcock, James, 973
Wilcock, John, 973
Wilcock, Joseph, 973
Wilcock, Richard, 973
Wilcock, Robert, 973
Wilcock, Thomas, 973
Wilkes, Thomas, 975
Wilkinson, Thomas, 977

Wilks, J., 978
Williams, —, 979
Wilson, Anthony, 986
Wilson, George, 987
Wilson, Henry, 987
Wilson, John, 987, 988
Wilson, Robert, 989
Wilson, Thomas, 989
Wilson, Walter, 989
Winder, Edward, 991
Winder, George, 991
Winder, Thomas, 991
Winder, William, 991
Winston, Charles, 992
Winston, James, 992
Woodall, Robert, 998
Woodcock, William, 998
Woodhouse, James, 999
Woodhouse, Richard, 999
Wrenshall, Joseph, 1004
Wright, David, 1004
Wright, John, 1005
Wright, William, 1009
Lanchester, 125
Lanchester (Co. Durham):
  Mason, William, 584
  Walton, George, 942
Landall, Thomas, 356, 538
Landbeck, 755
Lane, Edward, 655
Lane End (Staffs.):
  Ainsworth, Jos., 5
  Harris, John, 401
  Higginbottom, James, 428
  Higginbottom, John, 428
  Lattimore, —, 529
  Palmer, John, 671
  Rigby, James, 747
  Summer, John, 864
  Vigers, William, 923
  White, William, 967
  Wyatt, Joseph, 1010
Lang, George, 599
Langford Parsonage (Essex):
  Bagster, James, 29
Langley, John Holdenby, 216
Langley, Richard, 272
Langley (Kent): Bradshaw, W., 100
Langley House (Norfolk): Hallett,
  William snr and William jnr, 389
Langley Park (Bucks.): Mayhew,
  John & Ince, William, 595
Langleys (Essex):
  Bridgwater, Thomas, 107
  Davies, Thomas, 230
  Elliott, Charles, 273
  Hasert, Peter, 409
  Turner, John, 910
  Valliant, George, 919
Langlois, Daniel, 482
Langlois, P., 262
Langlois, Pierre, 306, 482, 593
Langmore, William, 468

Langport (Som.):
  Hart, John, 405
  Wyburn, Job, 1011
Langshaw, George, 647
Langton, Daniel, 124
Langton, David, 161, 598, 704, 766, 853
Langton Hall (Yorks.):
  Chippendale, Thomas snr, 167
Lansdale, 945
Lapierre, Francis, 753
Large, Aron, 286
Large, James, 286
Larkin, Samuel, 17
Larter, Thomas, 745
Lartington (Yorks.): Robinson, John, 758
Larzo, 589
Latchford, Thomas, 193
Latchford, Thomas Stringer, 862
Latonstone (Essex): Hart, Balguy jnr, 405
Launceston (Cornwall):
  Bowring, Moses, 93
  Geake, Thomas, 333
  Neck, John, 640
  Rodda, Thomas, 762
Lavenham (Suffolk): Mills, William, 611
Lavington (Wilts.): Tucker, Walter, 907
Law, Thomas, 309
Lawed, Joseph, 371
Lawford, 954
Lawrence, 437
Lawrence, Edward, 530
Lawrence, George, 277
Lawrence, Richard, 8
Laws, William, 530
Lawson, Peter, 531
Lawson, William, 695
Lay, Eleanor, 532
Laycock, Joseph, 695
Le Fousey, John, 359
Leamington (Warks.):
  Abbott, Elizabeth, 1
  Allen, William, 10
  Beley, Henry, 60
  Buck, Edward Jonathan, 123
  Butler, W., 138
  Dowler, John, 254
  Gill, F., 340
  Goodenough, J., 351
  Harte, Jane, 406
  Hooper, Frederick William, 447
  Hooper, M., 447
  Jones, Thomas, 497
  Landor, G., 524
  Lowick, W., 558
  Malvern, Charles, 572
  Robinson, John Kendrick, 759
  Rose, William, 766
  Simmons, George, 815
  Simons, George, 815

Smith, Robert, 831
Stiff, H., 856
Triggery, J., 904
Walker & Cooke's Repository, 939
Watson, Edward Dalby, 948
White, William, 967
Wright, John & Son, 1006
Wright & Son, 1009
Leatherbarrow, William, 562
Leatwood, Charles, 91
Lechdale (Glos.):
  Barr, T., 43
  Wentworth, John, 959
Ledbury (Herefs.):
  Hodges, Richard, 437
  Juckes, Robert, 500
  Matthews, John, 587
  Oakley, Thomas, 660
  Searle, Thomas, 792
Ledieu, Thomas, 690
Ledsham, Richard, 889
Lee, George, 535
Lee, Joseph Richard, 494
Lee, William, 558
Lee Manor House, Lewisham (London):
  Kay, Quintin, 501
  Oakley, George, 659
  Seddon, George, 797
Leech, William, 91, 120, 551
Leeds (Yorks):
  Armitage, William, 18
  Asquith, Christopher, 22
  Asquith, James, 22
  Atkinson, Benjamin, 23
  Atkinson, Francis, 24
  Atkinson, George, 24
  Atkinson, John, 24
  Atkinson, William, 25
  Aveyard & Buck, 27
  Baines, Joseph, 31
  Baiston & Hargill, 21
  Baiston, James, 32
  Baiston & Co., 32
  Balmford, Simeon, 36
  Balmforth, Simeon, 36
  Barker, Edward, 39
  Barker, George, 39
  Barker, William, 41
  Barton, George, 46
  Baslow, Samuel, 48
  Bastow, Samuel, 48
  Bates, Edmund, 49
  Beacock, John, 53
  Bean, Richard, 55
  Beck, Joseph, 56
  Beckwith, Joseph, 57
  Beckwith, Thomas, 57
  Bingham, John, 72
  Black, James, 76
  Blackburn, James, 77
  Blackburn, Robert, 77
  Blenkinsop, Alexander, 80

Blythe, Thomas, 82
Boler, John, 83
Boler, Richard, 83
Bolson, Barker, 83
Bolton, Barker, 84
Borough, John, 88
Boshell, Henry, 88
Bottrell, John, 90
Bradley, William, 98
Braim, Thomas, 101
Brash, John, 103
Brazier, William Henry, 104
Brook, John jnr, 111
Brook(e), John snr, 110
Brown, Robert, 117
Brown, William, 119
Brownfoot, Samuel, 120
Brownhill, James, 120
Bruce, Adam, 121
Bul(l)man, Robert, 126
Bulmer, Samuel, 128
Burrell, Benjamin, 132
Burton, George, 135
Butler, James, 137
Denison, John, 240
Denison, Joseph, 240
Dickinson, Matthew, 243
Diffill, John, 258
Dobson, Hardon, 247
Dobson, William Fawcett, 248
Dolby, John, 249
Drury, James, 257
Duggan, John snr & jnr, 258
Eltoft, Joseph Green, 277
Eltoft & Proctor, 277
Emmott, George, 280
Emmott, James, 280
Emmott, Thomas, 280
Galley, Gregory, 328
Garth, James, 332
Gavins, John, 333
Gawthorp, James, 333
Gawthorp & Flesher, 333
Geldard, William, 335
Gillespie, Andrew, 341
Gillespie, Richard, 341
Gillespie, Robert, 341
Glover, Samuel, 345
Goodall, Elizabeth, 351
Goulden, John, 360
Green, John, 367
Grey, John, 373
Hall, Thomas, 386
Hampshire, James, 392
Handley, Henry jnr, 394
Handley, Henry snr, 394
Handley, John, 394
Handley, William, 393
Hardwick, Thomas, 396
Hardwick & Waddy, 396
Hargrave, Josephus, 398
Hargraves, —, 398
Hargrave & Co., 398
Hargreaves, J., 398

Leeds

Hargreaves, William & John, 398
Harland, John & William, 398
Harland, John jnr, 398
Harland, John snr, 398
Harland, Joseph, 398
Harland, William, 398
Harley, David, 399
Hartley, David, 406
Hartley, George, 406
Hartley, James, 406
Hartley, John, 407
Hartley, Robert, 407
Hartley & Littlewood, 407
Head, Thomas, 416
Hewitt, Thomas, 426
Hick, —, 427
Hick, Joseph, 427
Hicks, Joseph, 428
Hill, Mary, 431
Hilton, Richard, 432
Hindle, John, 433
Hindle, Patrick, 433
Hirst, Joseph, 434
Hobson, George, 436
Hobson, John, 436
Holdforth, Joseph, 441
Holey, Thomas, 441
Holmes, John, 445
Holmes, William, 446
Hope, Edward, 448
Hope, Frances, 448
Hope & Foster, 448
Hopkins, William, 449
Horton, John, 451
Huddleston, William, 457
Hunter, William, 466
Hurst, Joseph jnr, 466
Hutchinson, Anthony, 468
Hutton, James, 469
Ikin, Abel, 470
Ingle, Joseph, 471
Isle, Susanna, 474
Jackson, James, 475
Jackson & Wood, 477
Jenkinson, Joseph, 484
Johnson, William, 493
Jordan, James, 498
Kendel, Thomas, 505
Kendell, John, 505
Kendell, Thomas, 505
Kirk, Samuel, 517
Kitchen, David, 518
Lambert, John, 523
Lawrance, William, 530
Lawrence, Thomas, 531
Liley, Joseph, 542
Lindsley, John, 543
Littlewood, Joseph, 550
Littlewood, Thomas, 550
Littlewood & Smith, 550
Lodge, Robert, 553
Longbottom, J., 555
Lord, Jonathan, 555

Lumb, William & Thomas, 560
Lumby, John, 560
Malorie, Thomas, 571
Manby, George, 572
Marcroft, John, 574
Marriot(t), Thomas, 575
Marshall, John, 579
Marshall, Thomas, 579
Mason, Joseph, 584
Massey, William, 585
Matthews, Thomas, 587
Mawson, John, 588
Mawson, William, 588
Maygill, John, 589
Meadows, John, 599
Milner, Samuel, 611
Mitchell, James, 613
Moody, Thomas, 616
Moon, Joseph, 617
Moseley, Elizabeth, 631
Moseley, Robert, 631
Moseley, Thomas, 631
Motley, Daniel, 632
Mountain, Peter, 633
Mountain, Richard, 633
Moxon, John, 634
Natt, Joseph, 639
Naylor, John, 639
Nicholson, Joash. W., 646
Nicholson, Jonah Walker, 647
Norton, George, 656
Norton & Shuttleworth, 656
Oates, Joseph, 661
Oliver, Christopher James, 663
Orridge, John, 665
Overend, Joseph, 667
Parker, John, 674
Pearson, Edward, 684
Penney, Samuel, 688
Penniston, Thomas, 689
Penny, Samuel, 689
Pettinger, Isaac Lyth, 692
Picard, Esther, 697
Pickard, Thomas, 697
Pinder, Robert, 699
Plant, James, 702
Platt, Joseph, 702
Pointer, William, 704
Polti, Jno., 705
Polti, Joseph, 705
Powell, Robert, 711
Preston, John, 714
Prince, William, 718
Proctor, John, 719
Rabner, Matthias, 725
Railton, William, 725
Rawson, Gervas, 730
Rawson, Thomas, 730
Reid & Caukill, 737
Render, John, 737
Rhodes, James, 740
Rhodes, John, 740
Rhodes, Joseph, 740
Richardson, Joseph, 744

Richardson, Joshua, 744
Riley, John, 749
Roberts, J.& T., 751
Roberts, James, 752
Roberts, John, 752
Robinson, Christopher, 756
Robinson, John, 758
Robinson, Peter, 759
Rodwell, James, 762
Rogers, John, 763
Rowland, John, 769
Russell, Thomas, 773
Sadler, James, 775
Saltonstall, William, 777
Scholes, George, 789
Scholes & Askey, 789
Senton, James, 800
Senton, John, 800
Senton, Thomas, 800
Senton, William, 800
Shaw, James, 804
Shaw, John, 805
Shepherd & Janson, 808
Shiers, Theophilus, 811
Shires, John, 811
Shute, Henry, 813
Shuttleworth, James, 813
Simpson, James, 816
Simpson, Michael, 816
Simpson, Thomas, 816
Simpson, Wharton, 816
Singleton, Jane, 818
Singleton, John, 818
Singleton, Martha, 818
Slawin, John, 821
Smith, John, 829
Smith, Joseph, 830
Smith, Thomas & Son, 833
Smithson, John, 836
Snowden, Joshua, 837
Sowden, Joshua, 840
Speight, Jervis, 842
Spence, Ann, 843
Spence, Anne & Sons, 843
Spence, George, 843
Spence, William, 843
Stead, Joseph, 851
Stead, Samuel, 851
Stead, Thomas, 851
Stead, William, 851
Stead & Atkinson, 851
Steel, Thomas, 851
Stonehouse, Ann & Sons, 859
Stooks, Thomas, 859
Stoppani, Anthony, 859
Storey, Benjamin, 859
Stroud, John, 862
Stubbs, John, 863
Swain, James, 866
Swan, Robert, 867
Sykes, Jonathan, 869
Talbot, Joseph, 870
Tarrone, John B., 872
Taylor, T., 879

Taylor, Thomas, 879
Teale, John, 880
Teale, Josiah, 880
Teale, Thomas, 880
Tempest, John, 880
Thackray, James, 881
Thackray, Joseph, 881
Theaker, Joseph, 882
Thornton, Joseph, 890
Tinning, Mary, 895
Todd, John, 896
Townsend, George, 901
Townsend, John, 901
Trencham, William, 903
Turlay, James, 909
Turlay, Hannah, 909
Turner, William, 913
Umpleby, John, 917
Waddy, Thomas Charles, 930
Wainwright, Charles, 932
Waite, William, 932
Walker, Benjamin, 934
Walker, Charles, 934
Walker, John, 936
Ware, Robert, 944
Watson, Emanuel, 949
Weare, Robert, 952
West, Thomas, 960
Westerman, Samuel, 960
Westmoreland, Edward, 961
Westmoreland, William, 961
Whatson, Samuel, 962
Whitwell, Charles, 971
Wilkinson, William, 977
Wilson, James, 987
Wilson, John, 988
Wilson, Joseph, 988
Wilson, Mary, 988
Wilson & Wilkinson, 990
Winn, John, 992
Wood, Elizabeth, 996
Wood, George, 996
Wood, Richard, 997
Wood, Robert, 997
Wood, William, 998
Wormald, William, 1003
Worswick, Richard, 1003
Wright, David, 1004
Wright, Robert, 1008
Wynn, Francis, 1011
Wynn, John, 1011
Leeds, Oxford Pl. Methodist
   Chapel:
   Constantine, William & Co., 192
   Worswick, Richard, 1003
Leek (Staffs.):
   Barnes, Jonathan, 42
   Bassett, William, 48
   Booth, John, 87
   Booth, William, 87
   Davenport, Uriah, 227
   Em(m)erson, Robert, 280
   Harrison, Samuel, 404
   Hide, Ralph, 428

Johnson, Thomas, 492
Joinson, Thomas, 493
Nixon, Allan, 649
Pratt, Thomas, 712
Shufflebotham, Jesse, 813
Travis, John, 902
Turnock, Daniel, 913
Wain, Richard, 932
Washington, Thomas, 946
Wright, Thomas, 1008
Leeming, Thomas, 733
Lees, Joseph, 549
Leeson, Morgan, 501
Legg, Samuel, 580, 786
Legge, Thomas, 284
Legge, Thomas jnr, 154
Leggett, 559
Leicester:
   Allcock, William, 9
   Al(l)kin, Sampson, 8
   Atkins, Thomas Illiff(e), 23
   Bailey, John, 30
   Bailey, William, 31
   Bakewell, William, 33
   Barnes, Robert, 42
   Barnes, William, 43
   Barracluff, J., 44
   Bateman, John, 48
   Bellamy, John, 63
   Bettoney, John, 69
   Birchnall, James, 74
   Birtchnall, James, 75
   Birtchnall, John, 75
   Blackwell, W., 78
   Botham, John, 90
   Boulter, Henry, 91
   Bradley, Henry, 98
   Bradley, W., 98
   Brewin, J., 106
   Brothers, John, 112
   Brown, R., 117
   Bruce, Charles, 121
   Bruce, Elizabeth, 121
   Bruce, John, 121
   Bruin, Samuel, 121
   Brydone, Charles, 122
   Bucknall, William, 124
   Burbage, Joseph, 129
   Burton, Mevil, 135
   Daft, David, 223
   Dennis, John, 240
   Douglas, John, 251
   Elliott, John, 274
   Elliott, Michael Cooke, 274
   Gamble, John, 328
   Gee, George, 334
   Glover, William, 345
   Goodrich, William, 354
   Green, James, 367
   Green, John, 367
   Green, Joseph, 367
   Green, Joshua, 367
   Haines, John, 383
   Halfpenny, Joseph, 384

Hall, Francis, 385
Harrison, James, 403
Holden, John, 440
Holland, John & Sons, 442
Hollingworth, William, 443
Holmes, Thomas, 446
Houlden, John, 452
Howes, George, 456
Inchley, Claypole George, 471
Inchley, George, 471
Iron, John, 473
Issit(t), Mary, 474
Jee, Samuel, 482
Jelley, Richard, 483
Johnson, Emanuel, 489
Johnson, Henry William, 489
Johnson, John, 490
Johnson, Joseph, 490
Johnson, Moses, 490
Johnson, Thomas, 492
Johnson, William, 493
Jordan, Thomas, 499
Kindon, James, 513
Kingston, James, 516
Leeson, William, 536
Lewin, John, 539
Locker, William, 552
Mans, Joseph, 573
Marton, Ellis, 582
Mason, Thomas, 584
Meadows, John, 599
Measures, John, 600
Measures, William John, 600
Moore, William, 622
Morton, Ellis, 630
Oliver, Iron, 663
Oliver, Mark, 663
Onely, John, 664
Palmer, Edward, 671
Palmer, James, 671
Palmer, William, 672
Payne, Benjamin, 682
Perkins, Joseph, 690
Porter, Arnold, 706
Porter, Edward, 706
Porter, John, 707
Powell, Joseph, 710
Powell, William George, 711
Powell, William John, 711
Powers, Edmund, 711
Prime, George, 717
Raven, Edward, 729
Raven, John, 729
Ricketts, J., 746
Riley, Thomas, 749
Rouse, Joseph, 768
Saxton, Nathaniel, 787
Seward, Thomas, 801
Shardlow, Edward, 802
Sherwin, Ann, 810
Shewan, Alian, 810
Shipley, Ann, 811
Shipley, Jno., 811
Shipley, John snr & jnr, 811

Shipley, L., 811
Shipley, Richard, 811
Smith, James, 827
Smith, John, 830
Smith, Richard, 831
Smith, Richard Clay, 831
Smith, Thomas, 833
Smith, W.B., 833
Smith, William, 834
Smith, William Bootham, 834
Smith & Campion, 835
Spencer, James, 843
Spencer, Joseph, 844
Spencer, Thomas, 844
Steeples, John, 851
Steere, John, 851
Stevenson, T., 855
Stewart, William, 856
Stockton, Elitzer Thomas, 857
Sutton, Jehu, 866
Sutton, William, 866
Thickpenny, Thomas, 882
Tip(p)ler, Thomas, 895
Tissitt, Mary, 896
Towers, Thomas, 900
Townsend, John, 901
Townsend, William, 901
Tunney, Charles, 908
Tunney, Thomas, 908
Wale, William, 934
Walker, Robert, 937
Warren, Richard, 946
Watkinson, Thomas, 948
Webster, W., 956
Whitehead, Susannah, 968
Whitewood, Arthur, 969
Wilkinson, John, 976
Wilkinson, Joshua, 976
Winrow, Richard, 992
Wright, Benjamin, 1004
Wright, Henry, 1005
Leigh, James, 517
Leigh, Leonard, 110
Leigh (Lancs.):
  Kay, James, 500
  Knowles, John, 520
Leighton, John, 311
Leighton Buzzard (Beds.):
  Avelin(e), George, 27
  Inwood, John, 473
  Mathews, J.F., 586
  Mathews, Thomas, 586
  Matthews, —, 586
  Matthews, John Felix, 587
  Matthews, Thomas, 587
  Mead, Thomas, 598
  Poole, George, 705
Leighton Mansion House:
  Head, William, 416
  Mead, William, 598
  Stone, J., 858
Leinster House (Dublin): Kennett,
  Robert & Kidd, William, 507

Leith (Midlothian): Reid, Charles,
  736
Lemaitre, John, 378
Lenden, William, 524
Lenn, Andrew, 809
Leominster (Herefs.):
  Bee, Henry, 58
  Davis, Thomas, 232
  Doody, Joseph, 250
  Hickin, James, 427
  Holmes, Henry, 445
  Nash, James, 638
  Phillips, James, 695
  Smith, Thomas jnr, 832
Leonard, Peter, 866
Levens Hall (Cumbria): Jensen,
  Gerrit, 486
Levet, 325
Levett, John, 110, 173
Lewes, Colin Mackenzie, 664
Lewes (Sussex):
  Adams, John & Son, 3
  Alderton, William, 7
  Bartlett, George Frederick, 46
  Bishop, John, 76
  Blower, Richard, 82
  Boor(e), Charles, 86
  Boore, Charles jnr, 86
  Boore, Edward, 87
  Boore, Frederick, 87
  Boore, Samuel, 87
  Dedhart, —, 238
  Dillart, Edward, 244
  Drawbridge, David, 256
  Dunstone, John, 261
  Dunstone, Thomas, 261
  Earle, Thomas, 264
  Edwards, Abraham, 269
  Edwards, John, 269
  Gates, Thomas, 332
  Hartley, John, 406
  Hill, Richard, 431
  Holde, Stephen, 441
  Holler, William, 442
  Holt, John, 446
  Hook, Richard, 447
  Hother, William, 451
  Humphreys, George, 463
  Hylt, John, 470
  Jennings, John, 485
  Kelter, William, 503
  Keston, William, 510
  Lambe, Richard, 522
  Marten, John, 580
  Marten & Adams, 580
  Medhurst, George, 600
  Miles, W., 607
  Nye, William, 658
  Penfold, George, 688
  Philcox, George, 694
  Ridge, Timothy, 747
  Shelley, Thomas, 806
  Simmons, Thomas, 815
  Smart, Henry, 823

  Smart, William, 823
  Spittall, Elizabeth, 845
  Spittall, Hannah, 845
  Spittall, William, 845
  Steadman, James, 851
  Stevens, Edward, 854
  Stevens, William, 855
  Stone, Thomas, 859
  Swaysland, Thomas, 867
  Tankard, William, 871
  Veral(l), George, 922
  Verrall, George jnr, 922
  Verrall, George Henry, 922
  Vinall, John, 929
  Weller, Stephen, 957
Lewes County Hall (Sussex):
  Morgan & Sanders, 626
Lewin, John, 490
Lewis, 648
Lewis, David, 485
Lewis, Israel, 580
Lewis, James, 924
Lewis, John, 774
Lewis, Joshua, 630
Lewis, Lewis, 205
Lewis, Richard, 328, 599
Lewis, Thomas, 929
Lewisham (London):
  Bone, James, 85
  Stickley, Thomas, 856
  Strickley, John, 862
Lewtas, Richard, 562
Leyburn (Yorks): Winsby, Thomas,
  992
Leyton (London): Pocock, W., 703
Leytonstone (Essex):
  Brigham, Thomas, 107
  Pennyfeather, Charles, 689
  Williams, Richard, 982
Lichfield (Staffs.):
  Arnold, Joseph, 19
  Brassington, Stephen, 103
  Bull, William, 125
  Dennis, James, 240
  Dennis, Thomas, 240
  Dennitts, Thomas, 240
  Denston(e), Thomas, 241
  Dicken, Francis, 243
  Gee, William jnr, 334
  Harper, Robert, 400
  Harris, Ratcliff, 402
  Harris, Richard, 402
  Harris, W.& Son, 402
  Lawley, Thomas jnr, 530
  Maddox, Charles, 569
  Parker, Jane, 674
  Prynn, William, 720
  Pynn, William, 723
  Richdale, George, 745
  Rigby, James, 747
  Rushton, Samuel, 771
  Stafford, Joseph, 847
  Tunnadine, William, 908
  Turnadine, William, 909

Wakelin, Hugh, 933
Walker, Charles, 934
Walmesley, Gilbert, 940
Winter, Samuel, 993
Winter, William, 993
Lidard Millicent (Wilts):
    Kebblewhite, Thomas, 502
Lidbitter, 515
Liddell, Gilbert, 459
Lideard, Joseph, 430
Lidgley, John, 997
Life-saving apparatus: Trengrouse,
    Helston, 903
Light, John, 906
Light, William, 418
Like, Thomas, 909
Lilburn Tower (Northumb.):
    Humble, Messrs, 462
Lilie, 908
Lilley, 132
Lillie, 908
Lillie, George, 907
Lillie, James, 106
Limehouse (London):
    Bennett & Co., 65
    Deane, John, 237
    Deane, Richard, 238
    Eden, Michael, 266
    Linton, Richard, 548
    Livesay, John, 550
    Lloyd, Samuel, 551
    Morrow, John, 630
Limpsham (Som.): Tranter, Joseph,
    902
Lincoln:
    Appleby, William, 16
    Askwith, George, 22
    Atkinson, William, 25
    Audley, Erasmus, 26
    Bassett, Thomas, 48
    Beach, Richard, 53
    Borrows, David, 88
    Bracebridge, George, 94
    Braceby, William, 94
    Bruce, Henry, 121
    Brumby, John, 121
    Darwin, Eubulus Thorold, 227
    Dimoline, Abraham, 245
    Dimoline, Abraham snr, 245
    Gandy, William, 329
    Gundy, William, 380
    Hardy, George, 397
    Harvey, George, 407
    Hickson, Mathew jnr, 428
    Horner, James Beck, 450
    Horner, M., 450
    Horner, Samuel, 450
    Johnson, Thomas, 492
    Johnson, William, 492
    Key, John, 511
    Kirk, Paul, 517
    Kirton, John, 517, 518
    Knowles, John, 520
    Knowles, Richard, 520

Lamb, John, 522
Lewis, George, 539
Locking, William, 553
Mann, H., 572
Moss, George, 632
Pearson, John, 685
Plumtree, George, 703
Porter, Sarah, 707
Porter, William, 707
Potter, William, 708
Powell & Reynolds, 711
Preston, John, 714
Preston, Robert, 714
Preston, Thomas, 714
Reynolds, James, 738
Robson, Joseph, 761
Roughton, Henry, 768
Rowton, Henry, 769
Sempers, John, 799
Sharpe, John, 803
Simpson, William, 817
Somerscales, John, 838
Stanley, Henry, 849
Stimpson, William, 856
Stimson, William, 856
Swallow, James, 867
Taylor, Ralph, 878
Tindall, Samuel, 895
Todd, William, 897
Trotter, Samuel, 906
Usher, James, 918
Vickers, Samuel, 923
Walker, William, 938
Wallace, William, 939
Wilson, George, 987
Wilson, William, 990
Wright, Stephen, 1008
Lindfield (Sussex):
    Murrell, James, 637
    Pierpoint, J., 698
Lindrick (Notts.): Drabble, James,
    255
Line, William, 429
Linfoot, Thomas, 940
Linfoot, William, 812
Ling, John, 65, 158
Lingereux, M.E., 223
Lingon, Henry, 638
Linnell, 970
Linnell, John, 324, 411, 482, 547,
    548, 588, 593, 972
Linnell, Richard, 974
Linnell, William, 85, 95, 104, 543,
    544, 545, 588
Linney, John, 713
Linning, Johann Christian, 324
Lipper, William, 421
Liskeard (Cornwall): Littleton,
    John, 550
Lisle, Devergy, 845
Lisle, Devergy snr, 558
Lismore Castle (Co. Waterford):
    Moore, William, 622
Lissel, 416

Lissington (Lincs.): Bray, Charles,
    103
Lister, Joseph, 358
Lister, T., 93, 97, 247, 699, 909
Lister, Thomas, 386, 477
Litchfield, 182
Litchfield, William, 362
Litherlad, William, 192
Litherland, William, 371, 918
Little, 851, 908
Little, Thomas, 915
Little Bolton (Lancs.):
    Davies, Richard, 229
    Nicholson, William, 647
    Pearson & Metcalfe, 685
    Wroe, John, 1009
Little Brickhill (Bucks.): Martin,
    Richard, 581
Little Britain (London):
    Ray, Thomas, 730
    Selby, James, 799
    Yale, Elisha, 1011
Little Haugh Hall (Suffolk): Ross,
    Thomas, 767
Little Walsingham (Norfolk):
    Buchan, Henry, 123
Littlehampton (Sussex):
    Denyer, William, 241
    Gray, Joseph, 365
    Millard, James, 607
    Osborn, William Arthur, 665
    Piddell, Mrs S., 697
    Richardson, K., 744
Littlewood, 407
Littlewood, Samuel, 422
Liverpool:
    Abbot, Anthony & Sons, 1
    Abbott, Anthony, 1
    Abbott, Nehemiah, 1
    Abbott, Samuel, 1
    Abbott, Thomas, 1
    Ackers, James, 2
    Adams, David, 3
    Adams, John, 3
    Aigby, Samuel, 5
    Alcock, William Roscoe, 6
    Aldridge, Simon, 7
    Alexander, John, 7
    Allan, John, 9
    Allanson, William, 9
    Allen, Thomas, 10
    Almond, Joseph, 11
    Almond, Thomas, 11
    Amery, Samuel, 12
    Anders, Jonathan, 12
    Anderson, John, 12
    Anderson, Robert, 13
    Anderson, Thomas, 13
    Anderton, —, 13
    Anderton, Henry, 13
    Anderton, John, 13
    Anderton, Thomas, 13
    Anthony, William, 15
    Appleton, John, 16

Liverpool

Archer, Jane, 17
Archer, Ralph, 17
Ardran, Ann, 17
Arger, George, 17
Armstrong, John, 18
Arnold, David, 19
Arnold, John, 19
Arrowsmith, Thomas, 19
Ashcroft, Joshua, 20
Ashton, George, 21
Ashton, James, 21
Aspinall, Henry, 22
Aspinall, James, 22
Aspinall, Robert, 22
Aspinall, William jnr, 22
Aspinall, William snr, 22
Atherton, James, 23
Atherton, Joseph, 23
Atherton, William, 23
Atkinson, John, 24
Atkinson, Peter, 24
Atkinson, Richard, 24
Atkinson, William, 25
Aven, Charles, 27
Avery, Edward, 27
Avon, Charles, 27
Avon, Edward, 27
Avon, Margaret, 27
Awty, Richard, 27
Backhouse, Bartholomew, 28
Backhouse, James, 28
Backhouse, John, 28
Backhouse, Thomas, 28
Bagot, William, 29
Bagott, Thomas, 29
Bailey, Francis, 30
Bailey, Henry, 30
Bailey, John, 30
Bailey, Joseph, 30
Bailey, Robert Manners, 30
Bailey, Rodney, 30
Bailey, Thomas, 30
Baivan, Edward, 32
Baker, Edward, 32
Baker, Thomas, 33
Baker, William, 33
Baldwin, Robert, 34
Ball, Henry, 35
Ball, John, 35
Ball, Mary, 35
Ball, William, 35
Ballantine, David, 35
Ballard, Robert, 35
Balmer, Daniel, 36
Balmer, Thomas, 36
Bancroft, David, 36
Bancroft, Joseph, 36
Banister, John, 36
Bankes, Margaret, 37
Banks, Henry, 37
Banks, Thomas, 37
Banner, J.L., 37
Banner, Thomas, 37
Bardswell, G., 39

Barker, Mary, 40
Barlow, John, 41
Barndale, Josiah, 42
Barnes, George, 42
Barnett, Thomas, 43
Barret(t),William, 44
Barrington, James, 44
Barrington, John, 44
Barron, Richard, 45
Barrow, Margaret, 45
Barrow, Richard, 45
Barrow, Samuel, 45
Barton, James, 46
Barton, Miss Mary, 47
Barton, Thomas, 47
Barton, Thomas jnr, 47
Barwick, William, 47
Basendale, Lloyd, 47
Basnett, Edward, 48
Basnett, Thomas, 48
Basnett, Thomas P., 48
Bates, William, 49
Bather, Nathaniel, 49
Bathgate, Archibald, 49
Baxendale, Gamaliel, 51
Baxendale, Joseph, 51
Baxendale, Josiah, 51
Baxendale, Lloyd, 51
Baxter, John, 51
Baxter, Thomas, 52
Bayley, Francis Allen, 52
Bayley, John, 52
Bayley, Rodney, 52
Bayley, Rubin, 52
Beard, Daniel, 55
Beard, David, 55
Beardwood, Henry, 55
Beatty, Edward, 55
Beatty, William, 55
Beckwys, Benjamin, 58
Beech, Thomas, 58
Beesley, Nicholas, 59
Beetham, Joseph, 59
Beetham, Thomas, 59
Beethorn, Joseph, 59
Belcher, Elisha, 59
Bell, James, 61
Bell, John, 62
Bellard, Robert, 63
Bellino, John, 63
Bellys, Benjamin, 63
Belshaw, Edmund jnr, 64
Belshaw, William, 64
Bennet, John, 64
Bennett, John, 65
Bennet(t), Joseph, 64
Bennett, William, 65
Benson, Abram, 66
Benson, William, 66
Bernard, John, 67
Berrington, John, 67
Berry, Edward, 67
Berry, John, 68
Bettys, Benjamin, 69

Bevan, Edward, 69
Bevan, Thomas, 69
Bevington, Henry, 69
Bibby, George, 70
Bibby, Hannah, 70
Bibby, Harriet, 70
Bibby, Thomas, 70
Bickerstaff(e), Edward, 70
Bickerstaff(e), William, 70
Biggam, William, 71
Biggin, William, 71
Biggins, Samuel, 71
Biggs, Ambrose, 71
Birchall, Daniel, 74
Birchall, Sophia, 74
Birchall, Thomas, 74
Birchall, William, 74
Bird, Samuel, 74
Birkett, Edmundson, 75
Birkett, Henry, 75
Birkmeyer, Joseph, 75
Bisbrown, Cuthbert, 75
Bispham, Edward, 76
Bissell, Joseph, 76
Bissell, Thomas, 76
Bissett, Thomas, 76
Blackburne, Elizabeth, 77
Blackburn(e), John, 77
Blackburne, Margaret, 77
Blackburn, Thomas, 77
Blackley, John, 77
Blain, Arthur, 78
Blain, Thomas, 79
Blair & Sons, 79
Blamer, Thomas, 79
Blanchard, James, 80
Bland, James, 80
Blaney, Thomas, 80
Blease, Peter, 80
Blinkhorn, George, 81
Blossom, George, 81
Bloxham, Samuel, 82
Boaler, James Box, 82
Boardman, Henry, 82
Boardman, William, 82
Bolland, Thomas, 83
Bolton, John, 84
Bonney, Richard, 86
Booker, Thomas, 86
Boon, John, 86
Boor(e),John, 86
Bootham, Joseph, 87
Booth, John, 87
Booth, Nathan, 87
Borrows, William, 88
Bostock, Edward, 89
Borwick, William, 88
Bottomley, Thomas, 90
Boulton, Charles, 91
Bourn, George, 91
Bourn, James, 91
Bourne, Peter, 91
Bouvrier, Thomas, 91
Bower, Thomas, 92

Bowker, Thomas, 92
Bowman, Isaac, 93
Bowman, James, 93
Bowman, Robert, 93
Bowman, Thomas, 93
Bowman, William, 93
Boyd, Robert Barton, 94
Brabazon, Edward, 94
Brabner, Samuel, 94
Bradburn, John, 97
Bradbury, Bob, 97
Bradbury, Richard, 97
Bradbury, Thomas, 97
Bradley, Thomas, 98
Bradshaw, James jnr, 99
Bradshaw, James snr, 99
Bradshaw, Samuel, 99
Brandreth, Charles, 102
Brandreth, Robert, 102
Brandreth, Thomas, 103
Brannagan, William, 103
Branston, Abram, 103
Bratherton, William, 103
Brattan, James, 103
Brawley, Alexander, 103
Breakhill, Thomas, 104
Brearley, William, 104
Breckell, John, 105
Breely, William, 105
Breer, John, 105
Brekell, William, 104
Brenson, Abram, 105
Brent, Ann, 105
Bretherton, William, 105
Brew, John, 106
Brew, Thomas, 106
Brew, William, 106
Bridge, William, 107
Brierley, William, 107
Briggs, Amos, 107
Bright, George, 107
Broadbent, Joseph, 109
Broadbent, Samuel, 109
Broadhurst, Samuel, 109
Brodie, John, 109
Broley, Alexander, 110
Bromfield, —, 110
Bromfield, Francis, 110
Broom, John, 112
Broom, Robert, 112
Broome, David, 112
Broster, William, 112
Brotherton, Charles, 113
Brotherton, Thomas, 113
Brotherton, William, 113
Brough, William, 113
Browless, James, 113
Brown, Elizabeth, 113
Brown, George, 114
Brown, James, 115
Brown, John, 116
Brown, Joseph, 116
Brown, Mary, 116
Brown, Matthew, 117

Brown, Thomas, 118
Brown, W., 118
Brown, William, 119
Brown(e), William, 119
Brownbill, Jonathan, 120
Brownhill, Johnathon, 120
Brownless, James, 120
Bruffell, Thomas, 121
Brussells, Thomas, 122
Bryan, Peter, 122
Bryce, David, 122
Bryden, Michael, 122
Bryden, Nicholas, 122
Bryde, Thomas, 122
Bryde, William, 122
Bryling, Robert, 123
Bryson, James, 123
Buchannan, John, 123
Bullen, —, 125
Buller, Jonathon, 126
Bullock, George, 126
Bullock, William, 128
Bullock & Stoakes, 128
Bunderson, George, 128
Burgess, Henry, 130
Burham, John jnr, 130
Burland, John, 130
Burland, Thomas, 130
Burland, William, 130
Burnett, George, 131
Burns, James, 132
Burns, Thomas, 132
Burrows, Henry, 133
Burrows, John, 134
Burton, John, 135
Burton, Wilson, 136
Burton & Watson, 136
Butterworth, John, 139
Button, Jane, 139
Byrom, Patrick, 139
Byron, T., 139
Dagnall, Thomas, 223
Dale, John, 224
Dalrymple, James, 224
Danson, Edward, 225
Danson, James, 226
Danson, Richard, 226
Danson, Robert, 226
Danson, Stephen, 226
Danvers, Margaret, 226
Darbyshire, John, 226
Darbyshire, Thomas, 226
Darwent, A., 227
Dauber, Thomas, 227
Daulby, George, 227
Daulby, Robert, 227
Davidson, John, 228
Davidson, Thomas, 228
Davidson, William, 228
Davies, David, 228
Davies, Edward, 228
Davies, George, 228
Davies, Henry, 228
Davies, John, 229

Davies, Joseph, 229
Davies, Margaret, 229
Davies, Robert, 229
Davies, Thomas, 230
Davies, William, 230
Davies, William Woodburn, 230
Davies, William Woodburne, 230
Davis, Benjamin, 230
Davis, Peter, 232
Davis, T. & Beamish, 232
Dawes, Ann, 233
Dawes, John, 234
Dean, Thomas, 237
Dempsey, John, 240
Dennett, William, 240
Denton, William, 241
Derbyshire, Edward, 241
Devey, John, 242
Dewer, Peter, 242
Dewhurst, John, 242
Dewhurst, Roger & Gerrard,
Peter, 242
Dickenson, Thomas, 243
Dickinson, Thomas, 243
Dickson, Abraham, 244
Dickson, James, 244
Dickson, Robert, 244
Dillart, Edward, 244
Dilworth, Daniel Large, 245
Dixon, Hugh, 246
Dixon, James, 246
Dixon, Mrs, 245
Dixon, Peter, 246
Dixon, William, 247
Dobb, Thomas, 247
Dobson, Lawrence, 247
Dobson, William, 248
Dodd, Thomas, 249
Douglas, Adam, 251
Doyle, Charles, 255
Doyle, Mrs, 255
Doyle, William, 255
Duckett, William, 257
Duckworth, Richard, 257
Dugdale, Joseph, 258
Duke, John, 258
Dunbabin, John, 259
Dunbabin, William, 259
Duncley, John, 259
Dunn, James, 260
Durrant, William, 262
Dutton, John, 262
Dutton, Joseph, 262
Dutton, Nathan, 263
Dutton, Nathaniel & Son, 263
Dutton, Thomas, 263
Dutton, William, 263
Dyer, William, 263
Easton, Robert, 265
Eaton, John, 265
Eaves, Richard, 265
Eccles, William, 265
Echlers, Richard, 265
Ed(d)en, John jnr, 266

Liverpool

Eden, Christopher, 266
Edmondson, Peter, 267
Edmondson, Peter & Sons, 267
Edmondson, Robert, 268
Edmunds, John, 268
Edmundson, —, 268
Edmundson, James, 268
Edmundson, Rachel & Sons, 268
Edmundson, Richard, 268
Edmundson, Robert, 268
Edmundson, Thomas, 268
Edon, John, 268
Edwards, Alexander, 269
Edwards, George Barrister, 269
Edwards, John, 270
Edwards, Thomas, 271
Ehlers, Richard, 271
Elliot, David, 272
Elliot, James, 272
Ellis, Evan, 275
Ellis, John, 275
Ellis, Michael, 275
Ellis, Richard, 275
Ellis, Thomas, 275
Ellis, William, 276
Ellishaw, James, 276
Ellison, Edward, 276
Ellison, T., 276
Ellison, Thomas, 276
Ellison, William, 276
El(l)ston, Thomas, 277
Elsmere, —, 277
Elston, William, 277
Elsworth, Israel, 277
Emery, Thomas, 280
Emmorson, Peter, 280
Empson, Henry, 280
Ennis, Thomas, 281
Erlam, Peter, 280
Evans, Ambrose, 283
Evans, George, 284
Evans, John, 284
Evans, Joseph, 284
Evans, Richard, 284
Evans, Robert, 284
Evans, William jnr, 285
Eversedge, Thomas, 286
Every, Edwards, 286
Every, Henry, 286
Eyes, John, 286
Eyos, Charles, 286
Eyos, John, 286
Galletti, William Anthony, 327
Garbett, Robert, 329
Garbit, Robert, 329
Gardener, Matthew, 329
Gardner, John, 330
Gardner, Matthew, 330
Gardner, Samuel, 330
Garner, John, 331
Garner, Thomas, 331
Garrett, John, 331
Gaskell, John, 332
Gatcliffe, Thomas, 333

Gatcliffe, Thomas jnr, 332
Gatcliffe, Thomas snr, 332
Gee, Thomas, 334
Gerard, Joseph, 335
Gerrard, Thomas, 335
Gibbons, Daniel, 336
Gibson, John, 337
Gibson, Mary, 337
Gibson, Richard, 338
Gibson, William, 338
Gilbert, Robert, 338
Gildard, William, 339
Giles, Isaac jnr, 339
Gill, Benjamin, 340
Gill, Henry, 340
Gill, James, 340
Gill, Richard, 340
Gill, Robert, 340
Gill & Crossley, 340
Gillespie, William, 341
Gitter, John, 344
Gleave, John jnr, 345
Gledhill, Jonathon, 345
Glover, John, 345
Glover, Thomas, 345
Golding, James, 348
Gondy, John Mill, 350
Gordon, George, 355
Gordon, Joseph, 357
Gordon, Thomas, 357
Gore, John, 358
Gore, Joseph, 358
Gorman, Henry, 358
Gornall, John, 358
Gorstage, Henry, 358
Gorton, James, 358
Gorton, John, 358
Gorton, John Muir, 358
Gorton, Joseph, 358
Gorton, Thomas jnr, 358
Gorton, William, 358
Goudy, —, 359
Gough, Thomas, 360
Gouldie, James, 360
Grace, James, 361
Gradwell, John, 361
Graham, Jane, 361
Graham, John, 362
Graham, T.D. & T., 363
Graham, Thomas, 363
Graham, William, 363
Grant, Ellen, 364
Gray, Richard, 365
Gray, Thomas, 366
Green, Ellen, 367
Green, John, 367
Green & Parkinson, 368
Greener & Chiesa, 368
Greetham, James, 370
Gregson, Charles, 370
Gregson, Joseph, 370
Gregson, Mathew, 370
Grey, William jnr, 373
Griffiths, Charles, 374

Griffiths, James, 374
Griffiths, John, 375
Griffiths, Robert, 375
Griffiths, Thomas, 375
Griffiths, William, 375
Griggi, Joseph, 375
Guest, Joseph, 377
Guy, —, 381
Guy, Richard, 381
Guy, Thomas, 381
Guy, William jnr, 381
Hacking, William, 381
Haddon, William, 382
Hadfield, Isaac, 382
Hadkinson, Hebry, 382
Haigh, John, 383
Hale(s), Thomas, 383
Hale, William, 383
Halfpenny, Thomas, 384
Hall, John, 385
Halliday, Andrew, 390
Hallsall, Charles, 390
Hallso, William, 390
Halsall, William, 391
Halton, Richard, 391
Hamer, John, 391
Hammond, Henry, 392
Hammond, John, 392
Hammond, John & Henry, 392
Hammond, Joseph, 392
Hampson, Henry, 392
Hand, John, 393
Hand, Stephen, 393
Hankens, James, 394
Hanley, John, 394
Hanley, Stinsil, 394
Hannah, William, 395
Hanns, George, 395
Hannys, John, 395
Hanser, John, 395
Hanson, Abram, 395
Hanson, John, 395
Hardern, James, 396
Hardman, Richard, 396
Hardman, Robert, 396
Hardman, Thomas, 396
Hardwick, Richard, 396
Hardwick, Robert, 396
Harford, Benjamin, 397
Harford, Charles, 397
Hargreaves, Francis & Co., 398
Hargreaves, Thomas, 398
Harling, John, 399
Harling, Joseph, 399
Harness, William, 399
Harpe, Thomas, 399
Harper, George, 399
Harper, Thomas, 400
Harris, John, 401
Harris, Robert, 402
Harris, Thomas, 402
Harrison, George, 403
Harrison, Henry, 403
Harrison, Henry Wood, 403

Harrison, Isaac, 403
Harrison, James, 403
Harrison, John, 404
Harrison, Joseph, 404
Harrison, Richard, 404
Harrison, Thomas, 404
Harrison, William, 405
Harrocks, John, 405
Hart, Charles, 405
Hart, Henry, 405
Hart, Peter, 406
Harterton, William, 406
Hartley, Lawrence, 407
Harvey, John, 408
Harvey, William, 408
Harwood, James, 408
Harwood, John, 408
Haslehurst, Samuel, 409
Haslet, David, 409
Hatton, John, 410
Haven, Edward, 411
Haven, Margaret, 411
Hawkins, David, 412
Hawkins, James, 412
Haworth, Henry, 413
Haworth, Thomas, 414
Hay, Peter, 414
Hayes, J., 414
Hayes, James, 414
Hayes, John, 414
Hayes, Thomas, 414
Hayes, William, 414
Hayhurst, Richard, 414, 415
Hayward, Edward, 415
Hayward, Robert, 416
Hazelhurst, John, 416
Hazlehurst, Ann, 416
Hazlehurst, Hannah, 416
Hazlehurst, John, 416
Head, —, 416
Head, Jeremiah, 416
Head, Jonathon, 416
Head, Joseph, 416
Head & Lissel, 416
Heald, William, 417
Heap, George, 417
Heap, Samuel, 417
Heathcote, John, 419
Heaton, Thomas, 419
Hedges(s), William, 419
Hegan, Samuel Van, 419
Helme, William, 420
Helsby, George, 420
Henderson, John Burdett, 420
Henessy, John, 421
Heskin, Sidney, 424
Hewett, John, 425
Hewit, John, 425
Hewit & Tryer, 425
Hewitt, George, 425
Hewit(t), John, 425
Hewit(t), Thomas, 426
Heyes, Ann, 426
Heyes, J., 426

Heyland, Charels, 426
Heywood, Ann, 426
Heywood, Edward, 426
Hickson, Henry, 428
Higgin, Samuel, 428
Higgins, Thomas, 428
Higginson, Henry, 428
Highfield, George, 429
Highfield, John, 429
Hignet, Thomas, 429
Higson, William, 429
Hill, Ambrose, 430
Hill, Edward, 430
Hill, James, 430
Hill, John, 430, 431
Hilton, James, 432
Hind, John, 433
Hindle, Charels, 433
Hindley, Thomas, 433
Hinds, John, 433
Hitchcock, Peter, 434
Hodge, James, 436
Hodges, Thomas, 437
Hodgkinson, Francis, 437
Hodgson, Elizabeth, 437
Hodgson, Isaac, 438
Hodgson, John, 438
Hodgson, Joseph, 438
Hodgson, Leonard, 438
Hodgson, Mary, 438
Hodgson, Mrs, 438
Hodgson, Richard, 438
Hodson, John, 439
Hodson, Thomas, 440
Holden, John, 440
Holden, Thomas, 441
Holden, Thomas Patrick, 441
Holdsworth, William, 441
Holiday, Geirge, 441
Holinshade, —, 441
Holland, Alice, 441
Holland, Thomas, 442
Holland & Roberts, 442
Hollingsworth, Thomas, 443
Holliwell, Richard, 443
Holme(s), James, 444
Holmes, Joseph, 445
Holmes, Thomas, 445
Holmes, William, 446
Holt, Edward, 446
Holt, Rachel, 446
Holt & Morris, 446
Hones, Richard, 446
Hope, Robert, 448
Hope, Samuel, 448
Hopkins, Richard, 448
Hopper, Mary, 449
Hopperton, Edward, 449
Horrocks, John, 450
Horton, Walter, 451
Hough, Edward Fletcher, 452
Hough, Robert, 452
Hough, Thomas, 452
Houghton, James, 452

Houghton, John, 452
Houghton, John Christian, 452
Hovell, Richard, 453
Howard, Edward, 453
Howard, Henry jnr, 454
Howard, Henry snr, 454
Howard, John, 454
Howard, Peter, 454
Howard, Richard, 454
Howard, Thomas, 454
Howard, William, 455
Howards, Henry, 455
Howarth, Joseph, 455
Howcraft, Thomas, 455
Howe, Thomas, 455
Howell, John, 455
Huddleston, Edward, 457
Huddleston, Edward John, 457
Huddlestone, John, 457
Hudson, Joseph, 458
Hughes, Alice, 460
Hughes, James, 460
Hughes, John, 461
Hughes, Joseph, 461
Hughes, Robert, 461
Hughes, Samuel, 461
Hughes, Thomas, 461
Hughes, Timothy, 461
Hughes, William, 461
Hughes, William & Richard, 461
Hunt, Joseph, 464
Hunt, Rachael, 464
Hunter, James, 465
Hunter, Thomas, 465
Hunter, William, 466
Hutchon, John, 468
Hutchon, Richard, 468
Huxley, Thomas, 469
Huxley, Thomas Croft, 469
Huxley, William Latham, 469
Hyde, Daniel, 469
Hyde, James, 470
Hyde, Jonathan, 470
Ingham, Thomas, 471
Inman, James, 472
Inman, Joseph, 472
Introvino, Antonio, 472
Irvin, Thomas, 473
Irwin & Potter, 473
Isaac, John, 473
Jackson, George, 475
Jacques, Catherine, 477
Jamar, S., 478
James, John, 479
Jameson, James, 480
Jebson, Thomas, 482
Jeffreys, Richard, 483
Jenkins, Matthew, 484
Jenkins, Thomas, 484
Jepson, Charles, 487
Jess, George, 488
Johnson, Archibald, 489
Johnson, Edmund, 489
Johnson, George, 489

Johnson, John, 490
Johnson, Joseph, 490
Johnson, Robert, 490, 491
Johnson, Thomas, 492
Johnson, William, 492
Johnston, Archibald, 493
Johnston, Ellen, 493
Johnston, James, 493
Johnston, Stanley J., 493
Johnston, Thomas, 493
Johnston, William s., 493
Joliffe, James, 493
Jolley, Richard, 493
Jolly, Richard, 493
Jones, Ann, 494
Jones, C., 494
Jones, Daniel, 494
Jones, David, 494
Jones, Edward, 494
Jones, George, 494
Jones, Hugh, 495
Jones, James, 495
Jones, John, 495
Jones, M., 496
Jones, Margaret, 496
Jones, Owen, 496
Jones, Richard, 496
Jones, Robert, 496
Jones, Thomas, 497
Jones, Thomas jnr, 497
Jones, William, 498
Jones & Parry, 498
Jones & Perkins, 498
Jump, Richard, 500
Kay, James, 500
Kay, Peter, 500
Kay, Samuel, 501
Kaye, James, 501
Kaye, John, 501
Kaye, Joseph, 501
Kaye, Richard, 501
Kaye, William, 501
Keating, Daniel, 502
Keating, David, 502
Keating, William, 502
Kelly, Charles, 503
Kelly, Martin, 503
Kelly, Robert, 503
Kelsey, John & Co., 503
Kelshaw, James, 503
Kendall, John, 504
Kendall, Robert, 505
Kendrick, James, 505
Kennedy, Josiah, 506
Kennedy, William, 506
Kennell, Hugh, 506
Kenyon, John, 509
Kenyon, William, 509
Kerfoot, Daniel, 509
Kerfoot, Richard, 510
Kerr, George, 510
Kewley, John, 511
Kibble, John, 511
Kilshaw, James, 513

Kindell, John, 513
Kirby, Henry, 516
Kirkes, Samuel, 517
Kirkham, Thomas, 517
Kirkpatrick, James, 517
Kirks, Samuel, 517
Kitchen, Joseph, 518
Kitchen, Robert, 518
Kneen, Ellen, 518
Kneen, Thomas, 518
Knight, George, 519
Knowles, Robert, 520
Knowles, William, 520
Knowles, William Maddock, 520
Knox, James, 520
Lace, Henry, 521
Laidley, William, 521
Lambert, John, 523
Lambert, Robert, 523
Lancaster, William, 524
Lang, George, 525
Lassell, Thomas, 529
Latchford, Thomas, 529
Latham, James, 529
Law, John, 530
Lawson, George, 531
Layton, William, 533
Leace, Catherine, 533
Leach, William, 533
Leadbetter, Thomas, 533
Leatherbarrow, William, 534
Leather, John, 534
Ledger, Richard, 534
Lee, James William, 534
Lee, John, 534, 535
Lee, Nicholson, 535
Leech, William, 535
Leigh, Alexander, 537
Leighton, Alexander, 537
Lennard, —, 538
Lenton, John, 538
Lester, Joseph, 539
Lester, Thomas, 539
Levi, Samuel, 539
Lewis, Thomas, 541
Libbey, Henry, 541
Libbey, John, 541
Libbey, Richard, 541
Lindop, Richard, 542
Linfey, William, 543
Linsey, William, 548
Litherland, William, 549
Little, Thomas, 550
Lloyd, Thomas, 551
Lockhart, Andrew, 552
Logan, Hugh, 553
Logan, James, 554
Lollie, William, 554
Loney, James, 554
Long, George, 554
Longshaw, John, 555
Longworth, Richard, 555
Lord, Ann, 555
Lortin, Thomas, 555

Lovelady, Edward, 556
Lovelady, Lawrence, 556
Lovelady, Thomas, 556
Lovett, Edward, 557
Lovett, James, 557
Loving, Thomas, 557
Lowe, Edward, snr & jnr, 557
Lowe, James, 557
Lowe, Thomas, 558
Lowe, William, 558
Lowe & Houghton, 558
Lowe & Parry, 558
Lowndes, Joseph, 558
Lowther, John, 559
Loxham, Edward, 557
Lunt, Luke, 5461
Lurton, Joseph, 561
Lurton, Thomas, 561
Luxham, Edward, 561
Lyden, John, 562
Lyon, George, 562
Lyon, George jnr, 562
Lyon, George Philander, 562
Lyon, George Frederick, 562
Lyon, James, 562
Lyon, John, 562
Lyon, Thomas, 562
Lyons, Charles, 562
Lyons, Samuel, 563
Mabrey, John, 563
McAlister, John, 563
McAllester, John, 563
Macalpine, Hugh B., 563
McBeth, Alexander, 564
McBride, George, 564
McComb, John, 564
McConnell, John, 564
McConvill, Peter, 564
McCoomb, John, 564
McCormick, Charles Hinten, 564
McCourt, Thomas, 564
McCreary, Isabella, 564
McDaniel, 564
McDonald, Archibald, 564
McDonald, Hugh, 564
McDonald, John, 564
McDowell, James, 565
McGill, Ralph, 565
McGoulrick, George, 565
Mackenzie, George, 566
McKenzie, Thomas, 566
McLachlan, James, 567
McLaughlin, James, 567
McMay, John, 568
McMillan, John, 568
McMullin, Robert, 568
McNab, Neil, 568
McNabb, Archibald, 568
McNay, John, 568
McNeill, J. & Co, 568
McNicol, Alexander & Lewis, 568
Macom, Alexander, 568
M'Phearson, J., 568

Mactaggart, Alexander, 569
M'Taggart, John, 569
Mactaggart, Robert Carson &
Alexander, 569
Maddock, Samuel, 569
Maddock, Thomas, 569
Maddox, John, 569
Maddox, Joseph, 569
Maddox, Samuel, 569
Magill, Ralph, 570
Maguire, Richard, 570
Major, Samuel, 570
Malkin, Thomas, 571
Mann, John, 572
Marchese, Lewis, 574
Margerson, Joseph, 574
Marriner, Christopher, 575
Marriner, George, 575
Marsden, William, 576
Marsh, Isaac, 576
Marsh, James, 576
Marsh, John, 576
Marsh, Peter, 577
Marshall, Edward, 577
Martin, Hugh, 581
Martin, John, 581
Martin, Robert, 581
Martin, William, 582
Martlew, William, 582
Mashiter, George, 583
Mashiter, John, 583
Mason, Alice, 583
Mason, Edward, 583
Mason, Sophia, 584
Mason, Thomas, 584
Massey, John, 585
Massey, Mathew, 585
Massey, Robert, 585
Mather, William, 586
Mathews, William, 586
Mathieson, Robert, 586
Mathson, Robert, 586
Matthews, William, 587
Maxwell, Benjamin, 588
May, J. & S.W., 589
May, James, 589
May, John, 589
May, John & William, 589
May, Solomon William, 589
May, William, Sharp, Peter, &
Wilson, Isabella, 589
Maybrick, John, 589
Mayer, George, 589
Mayer, John, 589
Meares, George, 599
Mears, George, 599
Mears, John, 599
Mears, Thomas, 600
Meineke, John, 601
Meller, John, 601
Mellineaux, George, 601
Melling, George, 601
Melton, John, 601
Mercer, John, 602

Mercer, Samuel, 602
Mercer, Thomas, 602
Mercer, William, 602
Metcalf, Anthony, 603
Metcalf, Cuthbert, 603
Metcalf, Richard, 603
Miles, Edward, 606
Miller, George, 608
Miller, James, 608
Miller, John, 608
Miller, Joseph, 609
Mil(l)ne, George, 609
Mills, Robert, 610
Mills, William, 611
Milner, James, 611
Mitchell, Joseph, 614
Mitchell, Robert, 614
Moffatt, Samuel, 614
Mollineaux, George, 615
Mollineaux, John, 615
Molyneux, Henry, 615
Molyneux, John, 615
Moncas, Thomas, 616
Moncaster, John, 616
Moody, David, 616
Mooney, Elizabeth, 617
Mooney, Ellen, 617
Moore, Samson, 620
Moore, Thomas, 621
Moran, Thomas, 622
Morcar, William, 623
Moreton, Thomas, 625
Morgan, Edward, 625
Morris, John, 628
Morris, Joseph, 628
Morris, Robert, 629
Morris, Rowland, 629
Morris, Thomas, 629
Morris, William, 629
Morrison, Robert, 628
Morton, Thomas, 630
Moss, Robert, 632
Moss, Robert jnr, 632
Moss, Thomas, 632
Moss, William, 632
Mottram, William, 632
Moulson, —, 633
Moulton, Ann, 633
Mowett, Peter, 634
Muir, Nathan, 634
Murie, Mary, 636
Murphy, John, 636
Murray, Thomas Slater, 637
Musgrove, Edwin Duckworth,
637
Musker, Robert, 637
Mutch, John, 637
Myers, Edward, 637
Myers, Richard, 637
Nairn, Thomas, 638
Navin, Thomas, 639
Naylor, James, 639
Naylor, Thomas, 639
Neal, John, 639

Needham, Richard, 640
Nelson, Joseph, 640
Nelson, Samuel, 640
Nevett, Samuel, 641
Newall, Mathew, 641
Newell, Nathan, 642
Newitt, Samuel, 643
Newton, John, 645
Nice, Mary, 645
Nichols, James, 646
Nichols, Paul, 646
Nicholson, Christopher, 646
Nicholson, Neile, 647
Nickson, Thomas, 648
Nicol, Alexander, 648
Nicol & Lewis, 648
Nightingale, John, 648
Noble, Henry, 650
Noble, Mary, 650
Norman, Henry, 651
Norris, Robert, 654
Norris, Thomas, 655
Nowland, Martin, 656
Nowland, Mrs Mary Anne, 656
Oakey, —, 658
O'Hara, Thomas, 661
Okell, George, 661
Oldham, Daniel, 662
Ollis, Thomas, 663
O'Neal, Francis, 664
O'Neill, Charles, 664
O'Neill, James, 664
O'Neill, Jane, 664
O'Neill, John, 664
O'Neill, Mary 664
Orme, John, 665
Orrell, —, 665
Orrell, John, 665
Orrell, Thomas, 665
Osborn, William, 665
Osborne, William, 666
Ottley, John, 666
Otty, John, 666
Otty, Samuel, 666
Overend, William, 667
Owen, Catherine, 667
Owen, J., 667
Owen, John, 667, 668
Owen, Owen, 668
Owen, Thomas, 668
Owen, William, 6668
Owens, Joseph, 668
Owens, Thomas, 668
Oxton, Thomas, 669
Page, Mathew, 669
Painter, John, 670
Panting, Thomas, 672
Parke, John, 673
Parke, Joseph, 673
Parke, Richard, 673
Parker, Edmund, 673
Parker, Edward, 673
Parker, Edwin, 673
Parker, George, 674

Liverpool

Parker, James, 674
Parker, John, 674
Parker, John & James, 674
Parker, Richard, 674
Parker, Thomas, 675
Parker, William, 675
Parkinson, James, 676
Parkinson, Richard, 676
Parkinson, Thomas, 676
Parkinson, William, 676
Parkinson, William jnr, 676
Parlior, Thomas, 676
Parr, William, 677
Parry, Henry, 677
Parry, James, 677
Parry, John, 677
Parry, Samuel, 677
Parry, Thomas, 677
Paton, Alexander, 679
Patten, William, 680
Paul, John, 682
Pearson, James, 685
Pearson, Peter, 685
Pearson, William, 685
Peeling, Henry, 686
Peers, George snr & jnr, 686
Peet, William, 686
Pemberton, Charles, 688
Pemberton, John, 688
Pendlebury, Collins, 688
Penketh, Thomas, 688
Penn, Joseph, 688
Pennington, Christopher, 689
Pennington, Lawrence, 689
Pennington, Seth, 689
Pennington, Thomas Matthew, 689
Peppitt, Robert, 690
Percy, William Carter Stafford, 690
Perkins, Thomas, 691
Perry, Henry, 691
Perry, John, 691
Pether, Thomas, 692
Phenix, James, 694
Phillips, Margaret, 695
Pickering, Henry & Pollard, William, 697
Pickthall, William, 697
Pilkington, Aston, 699
Pilkington, Charles, 699
Pilkington, Henry, 699
Pinder, Thomas, 699
Pirkin, Thomas, 700
Plant, Joseph, 702
Plasket, John, 702
Platt, Thomas, 702
Plunkett, Luke, 703
Poole, William, 706
Pope, Samuel, 706
Porteous, George, 706
Porteous, George M. & Henry J., 706
Porteous, Henry, 706

Potter, John, 708
Potter, Thomas, 708
Potter & Irving, 708
Potts, James, 708
Povah, Daniel, 710
Pover, Michael, 710
Powell, Edward, 710
Power, Michael, 711
Pozzi, Charles, 711
Prebble, Stehano, 713
Prenson, Abraham, 713
Prenton, Thomas, 713
Prescott, Richard, 713
Preston, John, 714
Price, Arthur, 715
Price, Edward, 715
Price, Horatio, 714
Price, John, 715, 716
Price, Martha, 716
Priest, David, 717
Priest & Co., 717
Pritchard, Edward, 718
Pritchard, James, 718
Pritchard, John, 718
Prola, Francis, 719
Pye, Brian, 722
Pye, Bryan, 723
Quay, James, 724
Quay, John, 724
Quick, Joseph, 724
Quiggin, John, 724
Quin, William, 724
Quint, Joshua, 724
Quirk, Henrietta, 724
Quirk, Thomas, 724
Quirk, William, 724
Rainford, —, 726
Rainford, Stretch & Co., 726
Rainford, Thomas, 726
Rainford, William, 726
Rankin, Richard, 727
Rasbury, Stephen, 728
Ratcliffe, John, 728
Ratcliffe, Thomas, 728
Rathbone, John, 728
Rawlsham, Richard, 730
Ray, John, 730
Ray, Robert, 730
Raymond, Mary, 731
Rea, William, 731
Read, Charles, 731
Read, Robert, 732
Read, Roger, 732
Reader, Henry, 732
Reader, Thomas, 732
Reader & Doyle, 732
Red(d)ish, John, 733
Redfearn(e), John, 733
Reed, James, 734
Reed, William, 734
Reede, Henry, 734
Reede & Doyle, 735
Reeder, Mrs, Henry, 735
Reely, George, 735

Reid, John, 736
Reid, Robert, 736
Ren, William, 737
Reynolds, John, 738
Reynolds, Joseph, 738
Reynolds, William, 739
Rice, Richard, 741
Richards, Benjamin Tapley, 741
Richardson, George, 743
Richardson, John, 744
Richardson, Thomas, 745
Richmond, Henry, 746
Richmond, James, 746
Richmond, William, 746
Riddiogh, James, 746
Rielly, George, 747
Rigby, Charles, 747
Rigby, Henry, 747
Rigby, Peter, 747
Rigby, Samuel, 747
Rigby, Thomas, 748
Rigby, William, 748
Rigg, Edward, 748
Rimmer, Henry, 749
Rimmer, James, 749
Rimmer, John, 749
Rimmer, Joseph, 749
Rimmer, Thomas, 749
Rimmer, William, 749
Rim(m)ington, Edward, 749
Rimmington, John, 750
Ritson, John, 750
Robb, John, 751
Robbs, John, 751
Roberts, Archibald, 751
Roberts, Edward, 751
Roberts, Henry, 751
Roberts, John, 752
Roberts, John William, 752
Roberts, Joseph, 752
Roberts, Rice, 752
Roberts, Robert P., 752
Roberts, Thomas, 754
Roberts, William, 754
Roberts, William John, 754
Robertson, Archibald, 755
Robertson, George Valentine, 755
Robertson, J. & D., 755
Robertson, Samuel, 755
Robinson, Archibald, 756
Robinson, George, 757
Robinson, Henry, 757
Robinson, James, 757
Robinson, Jane, 758
Robinson, John, 758
Robinson, John & Joseph, 758
Robinson, Joseph, 759
Robinson, Richard, 760
Robinson, Samuel, 760
Robinson, Thomas, 760
Robinson, William, 761
Robson, Thomas, 761
Ro(d)gers, Margaret, 763

Rodick, John, 762
Rofe, Thomas, 763
Rogerson, John, 764
Rome, David, 765
Rome & Turner, 765
Rose, Isaac, 765
Rose, Thomas, 766
Rose, William, 766
Roskell, James, 766
Ross, David, 766
Rossall, Thomas, 767
Rossall & Gradwell, 767
Rosson, Andrew, James, 767
Rothwell, Daniel, 767
Rouths, James, 768
Rowland(s), Edward, 769
Royle, John, 770
Russell & Gradwell, 773
Ryan, Richard, 774
Rycroft, John, 774
Ryley, George, 774
Ryley, John, 774
Sadler, George, 775
Sadler, William, 775
Sampson, Thomas, 778
Sampson, William, 778
Sandbach, William, 778
Sanderson, John, 779
Sandrino, John Baptist, 780
Sandys, William, 780
Santley, Joseph, 781
Santley, Thomas, 781
Sartorio, John, 781
Saul, Edward & Co., 781
Sayer, John, 787
Sayer, William, 788
Sayers, John, 788
Scales, James, 788
Scales, William, 788
Scevery, James, 788
Schiavi, Antonio, 788
Schiavi, Francis, 788
Schiavi, James, 788
Schiavi, Margaret, 788
Schiavi, William, 788
Scott, Alexander, 789
Scott, John, 790
Seddon, Henry, 798
Seddon, Richard, 798
Seddon, William, 798
Seed, John, 798
Seel, George, 798
Seel, James, 798
Seers, Mathew, 798
Sefton, William, 799
Sergeant, James, 800
Serjeant, John, 800
Service, Thomas & David, 800
Shacklady, Henry, 801
Sharp, John, 802
Sharp, Peter, 803
Sharpe, John, 803
Sharples, George, 804
Sharples, John, 804

Sharples, Thomas, 804
Sharples, William, 804
Sharrat, Samuel, 804
Sharrock, George, 804
Shaw, James, 804
Shaw, Nicholas, 805
Shaw, Thomas, 805
Shepherd, Thomas, 808
Shepherd, Thomas Walter, 808
Sherlock, George, 809
Sherlock, John, 809
Sherrat, Samuel, 809
Sherwood, James, 810
Shillito, James, 811
Shipman, Thomas, 811
Sim(m)s, Thomas, 815
Simner, John, 815
Simson, William, 817
Sinclair, Edward, 817
Single, Philip, 818
Skeat, Henry, 818
Skeleton, Joshua, 818
Skellicorn, Robert, 818
Skillicorn, John, 819
Skillicorn, Robert, 819
Slater, Edward, 820
Slater, John, 820
Slater, Richard, 821
Slater, William, 821
Slatyer & Dutton, 821
Sloan, John, 821
Sloan, Robert, 821
Smart, James, 823
Smith, Charles, 825
Smith, Ellen, 826
Smith, George, 826
Smith, Hugh, 827
Smith, James, 827
Smith, John, 829
Smith, Margaret, 830
Smith, Richard, 831
Smith, Samuel, 832
Smith, Samuel & Thomas, 832
Smith, Thomas, 832, 833
Smith, William, 833, 834, 835
Sommervale, Adam, 839
Southart, Richard, 840
Southel & Wilson, William, 840
Southwell & Wilson, 840
Southworth, John, 840
Sparrow, John, 841
Sparrow, Mrs Hannah, 841
Sparrow & Blount, 842
Speakeman, John, 842
Speakman, Henry, 842
Spence, Thomas, 843
Spence, William, 843
Spencer, Thomas, 844
Spencer, William, 844
Spikins, Benjamin, 844
Spurr, William, 846
Stalker, John, 848
Stanaway, Ann, 848
Stanley, Charles, 849

Starkie, Arrowsmith, 850
Starkie, John, 850
Steel, John jnr, 851
Stephenson, Robert, 854
Stephenson, William, 854
Stevenson, Thomas, 855
Stevenson, William, 855
Stewart, Joseph, 856
Stinson, Handley, 856
Stoakes, William, 857
Stockdale, Thomas, 857
Stopperton, John, 859
Strap, John, 861
Stretch & Rainford, 861
Strode, Byslet, 862
Suddert, John, 864
Suddorth, John, 864
Sudlow, James, 864
Summer, John, 864
Summers, John, 865
Summers, Ralph, 865
Summers, Robert, 865
Sumner, John, 865
Sumner, Thomas, 865
Sumners, John, 865
Sumners, Robert, 865
Sutton, Leigh, 866
Swain, John, 866
Swain, Luke, 866
Swaine, William, 866
Swan, John, 867
Swan, William, 867
Swan, William & Co., 867
Swinburn, Henry, 868
Swinburn, John, 868
Swinderton, James, 868
Swinnerton, Joseph, 868
Tankard, William, 871
Tarbuck, Henry, 872
Tarleton, Robert, 872
Tarleton, William, 872
Tate, Richard, 873
Tate, Richard Seddon, 873
Taylor, Ann, 874
Taylor, Charles, 874
Taylor, Edward, 875
Taylor, Edward William Whinfield, 875
Taylor, George, 876
Taylor, James, 876
Taylor, John, 877
Taylor, Peter, 878
Taylor, Thomas, 879
Taylor, William, 879
Thewler, Samuel, 882
Thistleton, Daniel, 882
Thomas, Edward, 883
Thomas, James, 883
Thomas, John, 884
Thomas, William, 884
Thomason, Thomas, 885
Thompson, Clelland, 885
Thompson, James, 886
Thompson, John, 886, 887

Liverpool

Thompson, John & Isaac, 886
Thompson, Joseph, 887
Thompson, Messrs, 888
Thompson, Robert, 887
Thompson, Samuel, 887
Thompson, Thomas, 887, 888
Thompson, William, 888
Thomson, Joseph, 889
Thorburn, Samuel, 889
Thorney, Robert, 890
Threlfall, James, 891
Tiddowson, George, 894
Tidensor, George, 894
Tilling, Edward, 894
Tipping, George, 895
Tipping, Josiah, 896
Tittenson, George, 896
Tittenson, James, 896
Titterson, James, 896
Titterson, Joseph, 896
Tobin, Michael, 896
Tolbott, Thomas, 897
Tomlin, Robert, 898
Topping, John, 900
Toulmin, Robert, 900
Townley, James, 901
Townsend, Robert, 901
Travis, James, 902
Trelford, James, 903
Tristram, Henry, 905
Tristram, Thomas, 905
Trotter, James, 905
Trotter & Magill, 906
Troughton, Thomas, 906
Tudor, Cornelius, 908
Tudor, John, 908
Tudor, Robert, 908
Tunstall, James, 908
Turbett, Thomas, 908
Turnbull, John, 909
Turner, John, 911
Turner, John Ward, 911
Turner, Joseph, 911
Turner, Robert Conway, 911
Turner, William, 913
Tute, William, 914
Tyne, Banjamin, 915
Tyrer, Bartholomew, 915
Tyrer, George, 915
Tyrer, James, 916
Tyrer, Martin, 916
Tyrer, Richard, 916
Tyrer, Robert, 916
Tyrer, Thomas S., 916
Tyrer, William, 916
Underwood, Francis, 917
Unsworth, Edward, 917
Urmston, John, 918
Urquart, Thomas, 918
Usher, Ralph, 918
Usherwood, John, 918
Usherwood, Samuel, 918
Vanhegan, Samuel, 919
Vaughan, Alexander, 920

Vere, Joseph, 921
Veree, Joseph, 921
Vincent, William, 929
Wainwright, Duncan, 932
Wainwright, James, 932
Wainwright, John, 932
Wainwright, William, 932
Wakefield, Thomas, 933
Walker, George, 935
Walker, James, 935
Walker, John, 935
Walker, Joseph, 936
Walker, Thomas, 938
Walker, Thomas, 938
Walker, Thomas, 938
Walker, William, 938
Walker, William Longworth, 938
Walker & Jones, 939
Waller, John, 939, 940
Waller, Richard, 940
Waller, William, 940
Wallis, John, 940
Waln, Robert, 941
Walters, Miles, 941
Warburton, John, 942
Ward, Thomas, 942, 943
Wardlaw, George, 944
Wardley, Isaac, 944
Waring, John, 945
Waring, Michael, 945
Waring, Richard, 945
Waring, William, 945
Warlow, William, 945
Warren, George, 946
Waters, Samuel, 947
Waterworth, Joseph, 947
Watson, Bingley, 948
Watson, G., 949
Watson, George, 949
Watson, John, 950
Watson, Samuel, 950
Watson, William, 950
Watt, John, 951
Wattleworth, John, 951
Watts, John, 951
Wealing, John, 952
Weatherell, John, 952
Webb, Alfred, 953
Webber & Sparrow, 954
Webster, J., 955
Webster, John, 955
Webster, Thomas, 956
Webster & Carter, 956
Wells, Alexander, 957
Wells, Henry, 957
Wells, W.& Penn, 958
Westbury, Daniel, 960
Wetherall, John, 961
Whalley, John, 962
Wharton, James, 962
Whatton, William, 962
Wheatley, Joseph, 962
Whitaker, Samuel, 964
Whitby, John, 964

Whitby, Samuel, 964
Whitby, Solomon, 964
White, George, 965
White, James, 965
White, John, 966
White, Ross, 967
White, Stephen, 967
White, Thomas, 967
White, William, 967
Whitehead, Joseph, 968
Whitehead, Thomas, 968
Whitelaw, Joseph, 968
Whitley, Solomon, 969
Whittingham, Thomas &
Cattrall, 970
Whyatt, W.G., 972
Wickstead, William, 972
Wilcock, Richard, 973
Wild, John, 974
Wilde, Walter, 974
Wilding, Robert, 974
Wilding, Thomas, 974
Wildridge, John, 974
Wilkes, John, 975
Wilkes, Thomas, 975
Wilkin, John, 975
Wilkinson, Lawrence, 976
Wilkinson, William, 977
Wilks, John, 978
Willcox, Richard, 978
Williams, Edward, 979
Williams, George, 979
Williams, Hugh, 980
Williamson, Edward, 983
Williamson, John, 983
Williams, Richard snr & jnr, 982
Williams, Robert snr & jnr, 982
Williams, Thomas, 982
Williams, William, 983
Wilson, Henry, 987
Wilson, Isabella, 987
Wilson, John, 988
Wilson, Jonathan, 988
Wilson, Richard, 989
Wilson, Robert, 989
Wilson, Thomas, 989
Wilson, William, 990
Windspere, Edward, 991
Winn, Matthew, 992
Winskel, Benjamin, 992
Winskel, Thomas, 992
Winstanley, John, 992
Winstanley, William snr, 992
Winterbottam, James Blundell,
993
Winterbottam, James, 993
Winterbottam, Thomas, 993
Wison, Newman, 988
Witham, Lawrence, 969, 994
Wood, Robert, 997
Woodbridge, James, 998
Woodman, —, 999
Woods, Henry, 1000
Woods, John, 1000

Woods, Joseph, 1000
Woods, William, 1000
Woodward, James, 1000
Woolfield, Thomas & John, 1001
Woolridge, James, 1001, 1002
Wooten, Charles, 1002
Worrell, John, 1003
Wright, John, 1006
Wright, Joshua, 1006
Wright, Samuel, 1008
Wyatt, William, 1010
Wymp, George, 1011
Yates, Charles, 1012
Yates, Henry, 1012
Yates, William, 1012
Yeeds, Elizabeth, 1013
Youd(s), Elizabeth, 1013
Young, George, 1014
Young, Thomas, 1015
Zerbon & Co., 1016
Liverpool:
  St Peter's Church: Prescott, Richard, 713
  Town Hall:
    Edmundson, Rachel & Sons, 268
    Gill, Benjamin, 340
    Hand, John, 393
    Miller, Joseph, 609
Liversedge (Yorks):
  Brook, William, 111
  Hey, John, 426
  Hirst, John, 434
  Walker, William, 938
Livesey, Francis, 754
Llanblodwel (Salop): Griffiths, John, 374
Lloyd, Charles, 274
Lloyd, Thomas, 535, 911
Lloyd, William, 550
Loader, 24
Loader, John, 723
Lobb, Henry, 310
Lobb, Joel, 233
Lock, Edward, 552
Lock, James, 552
Lock, John, 552
Lock, Matthias, 165, 198, 218, 349, 499, 776
Lock & Foulger, 863, 954
Locke, John, 559
Lockey, 998
Lockey, George, 553
Lockey, John, 432
Lockier, 722
Lockwood (Yorks):
  Auty, G., 27
  Rushworth, John, 771
Lodden (Norfolk): Pipe, Edward, 700
Lodge, Edward, 50, 719, 987
Lodge, Henry, 898
Lodge, William, 385
Lodge & Battersby, 438
Lodsley, 961

Lofthouse, John, 136
Lofthouse (Yorks):
  Dobson, John, 247
  Wake, John, 933
  Walker, John, 936
Loftus, 589
Logan, 360
London, William, 895
London, see individual districts, eg Mayfair, Westminster
London Houses, Churches etc.:
  Adderbury House: Mayhew, John & Ince, William, 594
  Adelphi: Mayhew, John & Ince, William, 596
  Albemarle St, for Charles Mellish: Mayhew, John and Ince, William, 595
  Albion Club: Taprell, Stephen & Holland, William, 872
  Apsley House: Dowbiggin(g), Thomas, 253
  Arlington St:
    for Henry Pelham:
      Barlow, William, 41
      Murray, George, 636
      Neale, John, 640
    No. 16, for the Gage family: Banting, France & Co., 37
    No. 17, for Lord Pelham: Richards, James, 742
    No. 19, for Sir Lawrence Dundas:
      Allwood, Thomas, 11
      Bradburn(e), John, 95, 96
      Fell, Lawrence, 294
      France, William snr, 316
      Laughton, Henry, 529
      Lawson, James, 531
      Norman, Samuel, 652, 653
      Vile, William, 927
  Armourers and Brasiers' Co.: Wilkinson, William, 978
  Arthurs Club: Taprell, Stephen & Holland, William, 872
  Athanaeum: Taprell, Stephen & Holland, William, 871, 872
  Bank of England:
    Baxland, Henry & Sons, 51
    Bruce, David, 121
    Kent, Abbot, 508
    Oakley, George, 660
    Rob(b)ins, John, 756
  Bath House, Piccadilly: Collins, William, 189
  Bedford House:
    Allwood, Thomas, 11
    Ellis, B., 275
    Eyre(s), James & Large, James, 287
    Goodison, Benjamin, 354
    Guibert, Philip, 377
    Hertoch, Jacob, 423
    Hibbert, John, 427

  Hutchins, Abraham, 467
  Hutchins, Abigail, 467
  Hutchin(s), Hassall, 467
  Malin(e), Thomas, 571
  Mayhew, John & Ince, William, 594
  Norman, Samuel, 652
  Peyrard, Jean, 693
  Plukenett, Thomas, 703
  Sammes, James, 778
  Saunders, Paul, 785
  Soederberg, Thomas, 838
  Wood, Henry, 996
  Berkeley Sq.:
    for 3rd Duke of Ancaster: Platt, John, 702
    for Lord Jersey: Elwick, George & Marsh, William, 279
    for 4th Duchess of Beaufort: Mayhew, John and Ince, William, 596
  Berners St.:
    for James Alexander, 1st Earl of Caledon: Mayhew, John and Ince, William, 595
  Bond St.: for Duke of Montrose:
    Crofts, Henry, 211
    Guidot, Anthony, 378
    Gumley, Elizabeth & John, 380
    Hodson, Robert, 440
    Marshall, John, 578
    Moor(e), Richard, 620
    Sheers, —, 806
    Tombes, Henry, 897
    Turing, William, 909
    Turrin, William, 914
  Bridgewater House: Morant, George, 622
  British Museum:
    Taprell, Stephen & Holland, William, 872
    Vile, William, 926
  Brook St, for George Bowes: Bradshaw, William, 100
  Browne's House, Fulham, for Sir Gilbert Heathcote:
    Chippendale, Thomas snr, 167
    Dallain, Isaac, 224
  Bruton St, for Sir William Beauchamp Proctor:
    Hallett, William snr and William jnr, 389
    Vile, William, 925
  Buckingham House:
    Bradburn(e), John, 95, 96
    Elliott, Charles, 273
    Mayhew, John & Ince, William, 595
    Norman, Samuel, 652, 653
    Tait(t), Richard, 870
    Vile, William, 928
  Buckingham Palace:
    Adair, William, 2
    Adair, William Robert, 2

London

Bailey, Edward, 30
Baker, William, 33
Beckwith, William, 57
Beckwith & France, 57
Branston, —, 103
Brown, J., 114
Browne & Co., 120
Coade, Eleanor and her
successors, 180
Crace, Frederick & Son, 206
Cripps, John, 209
Dadd, Robert, 223
Dickson, John, 244
Dowbiggin(g), Thomas, 254
Faraday, Robert, 289
Francis, H., 317
Francis, William, 318
Gates, William, 332
Goertz, H.L., 348
Gosset, Jacob, 359
Jackson, George, 475
Jennens & Bettridge, 485
Marshall, John, 579
Mealing, William, 599
Ponsonby, Thomas, 705
Robson & Hale, 762
Snell, William, 836
Spencer, James, 843
Turner, J., 910
Turner, Thomas, 912
Vick, Christopher Wren, 923
Waterhouse, —, 947
Wyatt, Edward, 1010
Burlington House:
Bradshaw, William, 100
Chippendale, Thomas snr, 166,
167
Coward, John, 203
Fox, Benjamin, 313
France, Edward, 315
Kerby, Richard, 509
Mathews, —, 586
Mayhew, John and Ince,
William, 595
Moore, James snr, 619
Naish, Catherine, 638
Richards, James, 742
Burlington St, for Sir John Griffin
Griffin:
Gordon, John and Richard, 356
Saunders, Paul, 785
Bushy Lodge:
Baker, William, 33
Evans, Samuel, 284
Camden House: Whitby, John, 964
Canonbury House, Islington:
Farlam, Jonathan, 289
Carlisle House:
Chippendale, Thomas snr, 166
Cullen, James, 218
Norman, Samuel, 652, 653
Carlton House:
Allwood, Thomas, 11
Ashlin, William, 21

Bailey, Edward, 29–30
Boggaert(s), Peter, 83
Bran(d)t, Charles, 103
Brookshaw, George, 112
Campbell, John, 142
Campbell, Robert, 143
Chippendale, Thomas jnr, 169
Clay, Henry, 177
Coade, Eleanor and her
successors, 181
Crace, John & Sons, 206
Cure, George, 220
Daguerre, Dominique, 223
De Caix, Alexander, 238
Delabriere, Louis A., 239
Elward, George & Marsh,
William, 277, 279
France & Banting, 317
Freiker & Henderson, 321
Fuhrlohg, Christopher, 324
Goertz, H.L., 348
Goodison, Benjamin, 353
Hancock, —, 392
Hancox, Nicholas, 393
Herve, Francois, 424
Hopkins, William, 449
Jean, Peter Dominique, 482
Kibble, John, 511
Le Gaigneur, Louis Constantin,
536
Mayhew, John & Ince, William,
592, 597
Morel, Nicholas & Hughes,
Robert, 623, 624
Nelson, Sefferin, 641
Prussurot, John, 719
Ravald & Morland, 729
Vulliamy, Benjamin L., Messrs
& Son, 930
Wacher, John, 930
West, John, 960
Wood, Henry, 996
Wyatt, Edward, 1010
Carrington House, Whitehall:
Thacker, Benoni, 881
Chapel Royal, Whitehall:
Bailey, Edward, 30
Loerhuick, Anthony, 553
Charles St, for John Chute:
Bradburn(e), John, 96
Chiswick House:
Almond, William, 11
Badger, —, 28
Boson, John, 88, 89
Hallett, William snr and Willian
jnr, 389
Hancock & Co., 393
Wilson, Walter, 990
Chiswick Villa: Bradshaw, William,
100
Clapham, Henry Hoare's house:
Alken, Sefferin, 8
Prihorn, —, 717

Clarence Club: Taprell, Stephen &
Holland, William, 872
Clarence House:
Bailey, Edward, 30
Casement, William, 149
Clarges St, for 5th Duke of
Bedford: Mayhew, John and
Ince, William, 597
Cleveland Court, for George
Selwyn: Chippendale, Thomas
snr, 167
Cleveland House:
Alken, Sefferin, 8
Bradshaw, William, 100
Cuenot, John Antoine, 217
Richards, James, 742
Roberts, William, 754
Saunders, Paul, 784
Vile, William, 925
Wood, Henry, 996
Coal Exchange: Webb, Tesdale, 954
College St, No. 13 for John Bruce:
Chippendale, Thomas jnr, 169
Conduit St, for Duke of Gordon:
Gordon, John and Taitt, John
and Richard, 357
Covent Garden, for James West:
Whittle, James, 971
Wormell, Joseph, 1003
Covent Garden Church: Langley &
Cross, 526
Coventry House: Mayhew, John
and Ince, William, 592, 593
Derby House:
Mayhew, John and Ince,
William, 592, 593
Nelson, Sefferin, 640
Devonshire House: Mayhew, John
& Ince, William, 597
Devonshire Place, for Lord
Deerhurst: Seddon, George, 797
Dilettanti, Society of:
Haddock, Elka, 382
Vial(l)(s), Thomas, 922
Divinity School: Cleer(e), William,
177
Downshire House, 20 Hanover Sq.:
Mayhew, John & Ince, William,
593
Dover House:
Bradshaw, William, 100
Goodison, Benjamin, 352
Griffith(s), Edward, 374
Wing, Matthew, 991
Dover St:
No. 14 for 7th Baron Digby:
Mayhew, John and Ince,
William, 593
for Robert Harley, 1st Earl of
Oxford: Hasert, Peter, 408, 409
for Duchess of Marlborough:
Goodison, Benjamin, 352
for Robert & Anne Nugent:
Cox, John, 204

Ludgater, Benjamin, 560
Drury Lane Theatre:
King, John, 514
Linnell, John, 544
Nelson, Sefferin, 641
Smith, Charles, 824
The Duke's House, Dorset Gdns:
Gibbons, Grinling, 336
East India House:
Boson, John, 88, 89
Chesson, William, 161
Cooper, Joseph, 197
Gibson, Christopher, 337
Gilbert, John, 338
Sherwin, George, 810
Smallwood, Joseph, 823
Egremont House:
Haworth, Samuel, 413
Vile, William, 928
Fishmongers' Co. Hall:
Ovenston, John, 667
Pearce, Edward, 684
Foundling Hospital:
Linnell, William, 547
Sanderson, John, 779
Fulham, North End, for Sir Gilbert
Heathcote: Stuart, Henry, 862
Glasshouse St, for Sir William
Robinson: Chippendale, Thomas
snr, 166
Gloucester House: Chippendale,
William snr, 166
Gloucester Pl., for Robert
Clavering Savage:
Edwards, David, 269
Ellis, Francis, 275
Graham, Joseph & partners, 362
Lock, S., 552
Goldsmiths' Hall: Wilkinson,
William, 978
Grand Lodge of Freemasons:
Kennett, Robert & Kidd,
William, 506, 507
Great George St, for Alexander
Copeland: Oakley, George, 660
Great Russell St, for Joseph
Harrington: Harrison, Richard,
404
Greenwich Hospital:
Collins, William, 189
Lawrence, Richard, 531
Osborn, Arthur, 665
Grosvenor Pl. House, for Lord
Whitworth: Morel, Nicholas and
Morel & Hughes, Robert, 624
Grosvenor Sq.:
for Lord Belgrave: Davis, John,
231
No. 20 for 3rd Duke of
Buccleuch: Mayhew, John and
Ince, William, 594
No. 2 for Marquis of
Carmarthen: Bradburn(e), John,
97

for Earl of Coventry: Alken,
Sefferin, 8
No. 23 for 12th Earl of Derby:
Mayhew, John and Ince,
William, 595
No. 38 for Duke of Dorset:
Crichton, David, 209
for Earl of Guildford:
Saunders, Paul, 784
Saunders, Paul & Trotter, John,
785
for Sir Gilbert Heathcote:
Alken, Sefferin, 8
Chippendale, Thomas snr, 167
Stuart, Henry, 863
for Lady Mary Saunderson:
Heasman, Henry snr and jnr, 418
No. 18 for 8th Earl of Thanet:
Mayhew, John and Ince,
William, 594
Hamilton Pl., for Duke of Bedford:
Davis, David, 231
France, William jnr, 317
Haw, William, 412
Thornton, John, 890
Watson, David jnr, 948
Hanover Sq.:
for Duke of Montrose: Moor(e),
Richard, 620
No. 22 for 2nd Viscount
Palmerston: Mayhew, John and
Ince, William, 596
Harcourt House: Moore, James
snr, 619
Harewood House:
Beaumont, —, 55
Bogaert(s), Peter, 83
Child, Robert, 162
Chippendale, Thomas jnr, 168
Claridge, Robert, 173
Cutter, Charles, 223
Elliott, Charles, 273
Elward, George & Marsh,
William, 279
Morel, Nicholas and Morel &
Hughes, Robert, 624
Norman, Joseph, 651
Norris, William, 655
Oakley, George, 659
Pailey, —, 670
Piercy, John, 698
Rathbone, Richard, 728
Rittener, Mrs, 750
Stephens, William, 853
Harrington House:
Baker, William, 33
Goertz, H.L., 348
Hatfield House ('The Casino',
Aldborough):
Beckwith, John, 57
Beckwith & France, 57
Henrietta St, for Richard Crosse:
Channon, John, 156

Hertford St, for Sir John Geers
Cotterell:
Bradford, John, 97
Coleman, William, 187
Farley, G., 289
Farmer, —, 289
Mason, —, 583
Robins, —, 755
Robinson, John and Burton,
William, 758
Scambler, Henry, 788
Snell, Robert, 836
Hicks Hall: Knight, William, 519
Hind Lodge: Goertz, H.L., 348
Hill St, Mayfair: Linnell, William,
547
Hoare's Bank: Blunt, Charles, 82
Holdernesse House: Saunders, Paul,
784
Holy Trinity Church, Marylebone
Rd: Quintus, —, 724
Home House: Nelson, Sefferin, 640
Horse Guards: Richards, James,
742
Houses of Parliament:
Bealing, Richard, 54
Elliott, Charles, 273
Evans, Samuel, 284
Farmborough, Hannah, 289
Farmborough, William, 289
Fletcher, Jeremiah, 304
Gilbert, Sarah, 338
Goodison, Benjamin, 352
Jensen, Gerrit, 486
Lowry, Sarah, 558
Morris, Robert, 629
Parran, Benjamin, 677
Phill, Thomas, 694
Price, John, 715
Reeve(s), Ham(b)den, 735
Russell, John, 772
Trotter, John, 906
Vallance, John & Evans, Samuel,
919
Whitby, John, 964
Williams, Henry, 980
Wyatt, Edward, 1009
Joiners' Co. Court Parlour:
Newman, Edward, 643
Kensington Palace:
Bailey, Edward, 30
Banting, France & Co., 38
Bealing, Richard, 54
Carpenter, Andrew, 146
Catignou, James, 151
Derignee, Robert, 241
Emmett, William, 280
Evans, H. Samuel, 284
Evans, Robert H., 284
Farmborough, William, 289
Ferguson, John, 297
Ferguson, Mary, 297
Fort, Alexander, 310
France, William snr, 316

France & Banting, 317
Francis, William, 318
Freeman, Ant(h)ony, 320
Gilbert, Sarah, 338
Goodison, Benjamin, 353
Guibert, Philip, 377
Gumley, Elizabeth & John, 379
Jensen, Gerrit, 486, 487
Lapierre, Francis, 528
Le Sage, John, 538
Lobb, Henry, 551
Malton, Perry, 571
Moore, James snr, 619
Moore, James jnr, 619
Pelletier, John, 687
Pic, Nicholas, 696
Reason, William, 733
Reeve(s), Ham(b)den, 735
Richards, James, 742
Roberts, Thomas and Richard, 753
Robson & Hale, 762
Russell, John, 772
Snell, William, 836
Trotter, John, 906
Vallance, John & Evans, Samuel, 919
Williams, Henry, 980

Kenwood House:
Channon, John, 155
Chipchase, Robert & Henry, 163
Chippendale, Thomas snr, 167
Elward, George & Marsh, William, 279
Faulding, R., 292
Fell, Lawrence, 294
France, Edward, 315
France, William snr, 316
Goodison, Benjamin, 353
Luttich von ('Merlin'), 561
Merlin, John Joseph, 603
Minshall, John, 612
Morel, Nicholas and Morel & Hughes, Robert, 624
Nelson, Sefferin, 640
Seddon, George, 797
Twaddel, William, 914

Kew Palace:
Bailey, Edward, 30
Boson, John, 88, 89
Bradburn(e), John, 97
Cure, George, 220
Farmborough, Hannah, 289
Goertz, H.L., 348
Goodison, Benjamin, 353
How, John, 453
Jones, Samuel, 496
Richards, James, 742
Russell, John, 772
Seddon, George, 797
Spencer, James, 843
Trotter, John, 906

King's Lodge: Goertz, H.L., 347

Lansdowne House:
Boyle, James, 94
Buhl, John, 125
Chippendale, Thomas snr, 167
Chippendale, Thomas jnr, 169
Gilbert, John, 338
Linfoot, Thomas, 543
Linnell, John, 545
Mayhew, John & Ince, William, 594
Perfetti, Joseph, 690

Laurence Pountney Lane, for Charles Rogers:
Bradshaw, Michael, 99
Fraser, —, 319
Gibbs, —, 336
Gilbert, John, 338
Wood, Thomas, 997

Leicester House:
Boson, John, 89
Cure, George, 220
Goodison, Benjamin, 353
Naish, Catherine, 638
Trotter, John, 906

Lichfield House: Wyatt, Edward, 1010

Little Ormond St, for Paul Foley:
Gumley, Elizabeth & John, 380
Howard, John, 454
North, Robert snr, 655
Overton, Philip, 667
Padbury, Jon., 669
Perkins, Francis, 690
Phillmore, John, 696
Strode, Edward & John, 862
Winston, Sibill, 992

Lower Grosvenor St:
for 9th Earl of Exeter: Mayhew, John and Ince, William, 594
for Thomas Foley: Whitby, John, 964

Lower Lodge: Goertz, H.L., 347

Ludgate, St Martin's Church:
Arnold, —, 19

Mansfield St, for William Constable: Chippendale, Thomas snr, 167

Mansion House:
Adye, Thomas, 5
Andrewes, Thomas, 14
Chesson, William, 161
Gilbert, John, 338
Goodison, Benjamin, 354
Grange, Charles, 363
Kippin, William, 516
Oakley, George, 660
Saunders, Paul, 784
Walker, John, 935
Willis, John, 984

Marine Society: Hanway & Co., 395

Marlborough House:
Mayhew, John & Ince, William, 595

Moore, James snr, 619
Melbourne House: Chippendale, Thomas snr, 165, 167
Middle Temple, for Samuel and Rebecca Tufnell:
Davies, Thomas, 230
Hamford, James, 391

Montagu House:
Pelletier, John, 687
Verhuyck, —, 921

New Burlington St, for Sir John Griffin Griffin:
Adair, John & William, 2
Adair, William Robert, 3
Aycliffe, Thomas jnr, 27
Belcher, Thomas, 59
Belcher & Gray, 59
Chipchase, Robert & Lambert, Robert, 163
Fox, Solomon, 314
Hudson, Solomon, 459
Lambert, Robert, 523
Mayhew, John and Ince, William, 594
Ravald & Morland, 729
Seaton, Frederick, 793
Tomkins, J.F. or J.T., 897
Welsh, Jacob, 958

Norfolk House:
Cuenot, John Antoine, 217
Cure, George, 220
Edwards, William, 271
Metcalf, Joseph, 603
Metcalfe, Joseph, 604
Stuart, George, 862
Swift, Grant & Hurley, 868

Northumberland House:
Chippendale, Thomas snr, 166
Cullen, James, 218
Jenkins, John, 483
Mayhew, John & Ince, William, 592, 595
Morel, Nicholas and Morel & Hughes, Robert, 624, 625
Pavie, Peter, 682
Reilly, Henry, 737
Reilly, Peter, 737
Walle, Henry & Reilly, Peter, 939

Oxford and Cambridge Club:
Taprell, Stephen & Holland, William, 872

Pall Mall:
Nos 49 & 112 for Duchess of Bedford:
Dodds, William, 249
Dunn, Michael, 260
Elward, George & Marsh, William, 279
Grews & Wright, 373
Ireland, E. & Hollier, C.W., 473
Knight, James, 519
Mayhew, John and Ince, William, 591, 597

Tait(t), Richard, 870
for Duke of Buckingham:
Lawrence, Richard, 531
for James Calthorpe: Gosset,
Isaac, 359
for Earl Fitzwalter: Richards,
James, 742
for the Prince of Wales:
Goodison, Benjamin, 353
The Pantheon: Knight, Thomas,
519
Park Lane:
for Earl of Breadalbane: Taylor,
David, 875
No. 17 for Edward Morant:
Murray, Alexander, 636
Park Pl., for the Prince of Wales:
Goodison, Benjamin, 353
Pembroke House:
Chippendale, Thomas snr, 166
Metcalf, Joseph, 603
Piccadilly, Nos 29 & 106 for 6th
Earl of Coventry:
Bradburn(e), John, 96
Mayhew, John and Ince,
William, 593
Portman Sq.:
for 3rd Earl of Athol: Chipchase,
Robert & Henry, 163
for 3rd Earl of Kerry: Mayhew,
John and Ince, William, 594
for James Leigh: Marshall, John,
578
No. 22 for Mrs Elizabeth
Montagu: Seddon, George, 796
Queen Ann St, for Lord Cork:
Gordon, John and Taitt, John
and Richard, 357
Queen's House:
Gates, William, 332, 333
Russell, John, 772
Vile, William, 924
Reform Club: Taprell, Stephen &
Holland, William, 872
Richmond Lodge:
Bradburn(e), John, 96
Farmborough, William, 289
France, William, 316
Jones, Samuel, 496
Royal Adelphi Terr., for David
Garrick: Chippendale, Thomas
snr, 167
Royal Hospital, Chelsea:
Allen, William, 10
Dawes, Thomas, 234
Farmborough, William, 289
Ferguson, John, 297
Gamlyn, Thomas jnr, 328
Heasman, Henry snr & jnr, 418
Lapierre, Francis, 528
Marshall, Thomas, 579
Morgan, William, 625
Shelton, Humphrey, 806
Wildman, Thomas, 974

Royal Model Repository,
Woolwich: Wyatt, Edward, 1010
Royal Yachts:
Bailey, Edward, 30
Bywater, John, 140
Casbert, John, 149
Elward, George & Marsh,
William, 278
Evans, Samuel, 284
Guibert, Philip, 377
Jensen, Gerrit, 486
Roberts, Thomas & Richard, 753
Smith, Charles, 824
Trotter, John, 906
Whitby, John, 964
St Bartholomew's Royal Hospital:
Freelove, —, 320
Jones, William snr, 497
St Dunstan-in-the-East Church:
Wyatt, Edward, 1010
St George's Church, Bloomsbury:
Boson, John, 88, 89
St George's Hall: Baker, William,
33
St James's Palace:
Adair, William Robert, 3
Bailey, Edward, 29, 30
Beckwith, James, 57
Beckwith & France, 57
Boson, John, 89
Bradburn(e), John, 97
Cure, George, 219
Elliott, Charles, 273
Evans, H. Samuel, 284
Evans, Samuel, 284
Farmborough, Hannah, 289
Ferraro, Peter, 298
Ferrers, Thomas, 298
Fort, Alexander, 310
France, William snr, 316
Francis, William, 318
Gilbert, Sarah, 338
Goertz, H.L., 348
Goodison, Benjamin, 352, 353
Gumley, Elizabeth & John, 379
Henderson, James, 420
Howard, —, 453
Jackson, Mary, 476
Jensen, Gerrit, 486
Jones, Samuel, 496
Lawrence, Richard, 531
McBean, Anne, 563
Marshall, John, 579
Naish, Catherine, 638
Parran, Benjamin, 677
Price, Elizabeth, 715
Reason, William, 733
Reeve(s), Ham(b)den, 735
Roberts, Thomas and Richard,
753
Robson & Hale, 762
Russell, John, 772
Seddon, George, 797
Spencer, James, 843

Tait(t), Richard, 870
Thurston, John, 893
Trotter, John, 906
Turner, Thomas, 912
Vallance, John & Evans, Samuel,
919
Vile, William, 927, 928
Williams, Henry, 980
Wyatt, Edward, 1010
St James's Park:
Boson, John, 89
Crompton, William, 211
Wyatt, Edward, 1010
St James's, for Duke of Schomberg:
Lapierre, Francis, 528
St James's Sq.:
for Duke of Bedford:
Ashlin, William, 21
Eagles, T.F., 264
Ellis, B., 275
France, William jnr, 317
for Peter Du Cane:
Gosset, James, 359
Jarman, Ann, 481
Moreland, Robert, 625
Spark & Brydges, 841
No. 4 for Duke of Kent: Boson,
John, 88, 89
for 2nd Earl of Rosslyn: Pocock,
William, 704
No. 20 for Sir Watkin Williams
Wynn, 4th Bt:
Collins, Richard, 189
Mayhew, John and Ince,
William, 595
St John Horseleydown, Southwark:
Boson, John, 89
St John's Church, Westminster:
Boson, John, 89
St Lawrence Jewry: Pearce,
Edward, 684
St Luke's Church, Old St: Boson,
John, 89
St Martin-in-the-Fields:
Bridgewater, Thomas, 107
St Mary's Lutheran Church, Savoy:
Alken, Oliver, 8
St Mary-le-Bow: Pearce, Edward,
684
St Mary-le-Strand: Phill, Thomas,
694
St Olave's Church, Southwark:
Boson, John, 89
St Paul's Cathedral:
Belchier, John, 60
Bernard, John, 67
Clackson, William, 172
Cleer(e), William, 177
Fanshaw, Edward, 289
Osborn, Arthur, 665
St Stephen's Church, Coleman St:
Newman, William, 643
St Stephen's, Walbrook: Rolf,
Samuel, 764

Salisbury House: Putt, —, 722
Schomberg House:
  Bolar, Samuel, 83
  Bradshaw, William, 100
  Howard, Gerrard, 453
  Jones, Sandys, 496
  Spurret, William, 846
  Stephenson, Luke, 854
  Versovile, —, 922
  Waters, William, 947
Shelburne House:
  Adair, John & William, 2
  Boyle, James, 94
  Bright, —, 107
  Bromwich, Thomas, 110
  Chambers, Samuel, 154
  Hakewell, John, 383
  Herve, Francois, 424
  Langley, —, 526
  Mayhew, John & Ince, William,
  592, 594
  Nelson, Sefferin, 640
  Panton, John, 672
  Search, —, 792
  Tousey, John, 900
  Vial(l)(s), Thomas, 922
  Walle, Henry & Reilly, Peter,
  939
  Wharton, —, 962
  Wybrow & Barnard, 1010
  Young, —, 1014
Soane Museum: Bruce, David, 121
Society for Propagation of
  Christian Knowledge (SPCK):
  Heardson, —, 417
  Wood, John, 996
  Woodroffe, James, 1000
Soho Sq., No. 26 for Sir William
  Robinson: Chippendale, Thomas
  snr, 166
Somerset House:
  Alken, Sefferin, 8
  Alken, Samuel, 8
  Casbert, John, 149
  Jensen, Gerrit, 486
  Lawrence, Richard, 531
  Lay, Henry, 532
  Le (or La) Grange, —, 537
  Price, Richard, 716
  Williams, Henry, 980
South Audley St:
  No. 75 for Duke of Buccleuch:
  Morel Nicholas and Morel &
  Hughes, Robert, 624
  for Mrs Henrietta Howard:
  Barnard, John, 42
  Cobb, John, 184
  Crabtree, James, 206
  Saunders, Paul, 785
Southampton St, for David
  Garrick: Chippendale, Thomas
  snr, 167
Spencer House:
  Gordon, John and Taitt, John
  and Richard, 356

Vardy, Thomas, 919
Stafford House:
  Butt, —, 138
  Dowbiggin(g), Thomas, 253
  Hughes, —, 460
  Miles, Henry & Edwards, John,
  606
  Morant, George, 622
  Pratt, Samuel & Henry, 712
  Seddon, George, 796, 797
  Taylor, —, 874
  Town & Emanuel, 901
  Tratt & Attfield, 902
Stanhope St:
  for Duke of Bedford:
  France, William jnr, 317
  Haw, William, 412
  for Sir George Cornewall:
  Graham, Joseph & partners, 362
  Hayward, —, 415
  Holmes, —, 444
  Kelly, —, 503
  Van Gelden, —, 919
Stratford Pl.: No. 2 for 2nd Earl
  Stanhope: Mayhew, John and
  Ince, William, 595
  for Sir Richard Worsley Bt:
  Chippendale, Thomas jnr, 168
Streatham Manor House: Lee, —,
  543
Swin(d)ley Lodge:
  Elliott, Charles, 273
  France & Banting, 317
  Williams, Henry, 980
The Temple, for Paul Foley:
  Gumley, Elizabeth & John, 380
  Howard, John, 454
  North, Robert snr, 655
  Overton, Philip, 667
  Padbury, Jon., 669
  Perkins, Francis, 690
  Phillmore, John, 696
  Strode, Edward & John, 862
  Winston, Sibill, 992
Tower of London: Evans, Samuel,
  284
Treasury:
  Roberts, Thomas and Richard,
  753
  Sapp, Robert, 781
  Seddon, George, 796
Union Club: Taprell, Stephen &
  Holland, William, 872
United Services Club: Taprell,
  Stephen & Holland, William, 872
Upper Brook St:
  for Sir Charles Hanbury-
  Williams: Vile, William, 927
  for William Weddell:
  Chippendale, Thomas jnr, 168
Upper Grosvenor St, for Duke of
  Gordon:
  Dingwall, Alexander, 245

Gordon, John and Taitt, John
  and Richard, 355, 357
Uxbridge House: Linnell, John,
  544, 546
Vintner's Hall:
  Bell, —, 60
  Graham, Joseph & Partners, 362
  Halford, —, 384
  Hall, Benjamin, 384
  Newman, Mr, 643
Virginia Water:
  Goertz, H.L., 348
  Spencer, James, 843
Westminster:
  Fort, Alexander, 310
  France, William snr, 316
  France & Banting, 317
  Gilroy, John, 344
  Lawrence, Richard, 531
  Reeve(s), Ham(b)den, 735
  Riley & Fowler, 749
  Russell, John, 772
Westminster Abbey:
  Boson, John, 88, 89
  Goodison, Benjamin, 352
  Phill, Thomas, 694
  Roberts, Thomas & Richard, 753
  Ryland, A., 774
Westminster Fire Office: Mayhew,
  John & Ince, William, 592, 598
Whitehall Palace:
  Allen, William, 10
  Bealing, Richard, 54
  Beckwith, James, 57
  Brumfield, Philip, 121
  Casbert, John, 149
  Farmborough, William, 289
  Ferrers, Thomas, 298
  Fort, Alexander, 310
  France & Banting, 317
  Guilliband, John, 378
  Jackson, Mary, 476
  Jensen, Gerrit, 486
  Le (or La) Grange, —, 537
  Malin (or Malyn), Thomas, 571
  Morris, Robert, 629
  Parran, Benjamin, 677
  Paudevin, John, 681
  Phillips, Henry, 695
  Price, Elizabeth, 715
  Price, Richard, 716
  Puckle, Thomas, 720
  Roberts, Thomas & Richard, 753
  Rouseau, —, 768
  Russell, John, 772
  Sapp, Robert, 781
  Traherne, Edward, 902
  Whitby, John, 964
Whitehall Yard, for the Gage
  family: Banting, France & Co.,
  37
Wimbledon House: Wotton, C.,
  1003

York Buildings, for Samuel Pepys:
  Sympson, Thomas(?), 869
Long, 602
Long, Charles, 43
Long, Enoch, 853
Long, William, 652, 653, 833, 970
Long Melford (Suffolk): Browning,
  William, 120
Long Sutton (Lincs.):
  Amory, Jno., 12
  Longlands, Joseph, 555
Longdendale (Lancs.): Dekin,
  George, 238
Longford Castle (Wilts.):
  Addinet, —, 4
  Beaumont, —, 55
  Beyer, James, 70
  Bradley, —, 97
  Bradshaw, William, 100
  Chipchase, Robert & Henry, 163
  Clay, Henry, 177
  Costar, Henry, 200
  Duffour, William, 258
  Elfe, —, 272
  Elliott, —, 272
  Finschard (?), —, 300
  Garth, James, 331
  Goodfellow, Lall, 351
  Goodison, Benjamin, 352, 353
  Green, —, 367
  Grendey, Giles, 371, 372
  Griffith(s), Edward, 374
  Habgood, William, 381
  Hodson, John, 439
  Hodson, Robert, 440
  Holloway, —, 443
  Kay, Quintin, 501
  Kilpin, William, 513
  Krampf, —, 520
  Mercer, George, 601
  Nickells, John, 647
  Page, —, 669
  Ricknoll (?), —, 746
  Ridler, —, 747
  Roger, —, 763
  Sandorby (?), —, 780
  Seddon, George, 797
  Seehausen, —, 798
  Smagg, Peter, 822
  Smith, George, 826
  Snow, Thomas, 837
  Taunton, Jacob, 874
  Turner, —, 909
  Vial(l)(s), Thomas, 922
  Vile, William, 927
  Walkins, —, 939
  Walle, Henry & Reilly, Peter,
  939
Longford Hall (Salop): Kettle,
  Henry, 511
Longtown (Cumb.):
  Park, James, 673
  Wright, George, 1005
Lord, John, 932

Lorimer, 163
Lorimer, David, 919
Lostwithiel (Cornwall):
  Bar(r)ron, John, 45
  Jenkins, Joseph, 484
Lothbury (London):
  Bennet(t), Samuel, 65
  Benyon, John, 67
  Brown, William, 119
  Eckford, John, 265
  Helderbrant, 419
  Langham, Henry, 526
  Mercer, John, 602
  Saltmarsh, William, 777
Lotherton Hall (Yorks.): Staveley,
  William, 850
Lough (Lincs.): Ashton, John, 21
Loughborough (Leics.):
  Abel, Samuel, 1
  Ball, W., 35
  Barnside, Edward, 43
  Blood, Robert, 81
  Booth, John, 87
  Dawkins, John, 234
  Dewberry, Daniel, 242
  Dewberry, Thomas, 242
  Dexter, Robert, 243
  Hack, William, 381
  Harding, James, 396
  Harrison, Thomas, 404
  Hill, Thomas, 431
  Hull, Edwin, 462
  King, Daniel, 514
  King, William, 515
  Kirk, Thomas, 517
  Lewell, William, 539
  Mills, John, 610
  Mitchell, Thomas, 614
  Pegg, William, 687
  Smith, John, 829
  Start, J., 850
  Sudbury, J., 864
  Sudbury, John, 864
  Wale, William, 934
  Wardle, John, 944
  Warner & Sudbury, 945
Loughton Hall (Essex): Freame, —,
  319
Louth, Daniel, 261
Louth (Lincs.):
  Anderson, William, 13
  Ashton, Richard, 21
  Ashton, Samuel, 21
  Atkin, Joseph, 23
  Atkin, Moses, 23
  Bell, George, 61
  Boothby, Henry, 87
  Brown, John, 116
  Burman, John, 131
  Butters, John, 138
  Dales, George, 224
  Dales, Joseph, 224
  Dales, Sam., 224
  Davis, William, 233

Dixon, John, 246
Edwards, William, 271
Elvin, Isaac, 277
Emerson, George, 280
Emerson, William, 280
Goddard, William, 346
Green, Robert, 367
Hewison, Richard, 425
Hubbard, John, 457
Hudson, William, 459
Ingoldby, James, 472
Johnson, William, 493
Leak, William, 533
Middleton, George, 605
Miller, Devereux, 608
Moakes, James, 614
Moody, Thomas, 616
Pell, George, 687
Pinder, James, 699
Pinner, Robert, 700
Pool, Robert, 705
Preston, William, 714
Reed, Mat(t)hias, 734
Rushforth, Isaac, 771
Stevenson, John, 855
Stockton, William, 857
Tara, Innocent, 872
Taylor, James. 876
Taylor, John, 877
Trotter, George, 905
Walker, William, 938
Whaley, Henry, 962
Wilcockson, Joseph, 973
Willerton, Robert, 978
Wright, John, 1006
Louth Searge (Lincs.): Seaman,
  Allen, 792
Lovejoy, William, 945
Loveland, Richard, 1
Lovell, William, 541
Lovett, Richard, 602
Lovitt, Thomas, 557
Low Ackworth (Yorks): Mason,
  Allan, 583
Lowestoft (Suffolk):
  Brewster, John, 106
  Brewster, Robert, 106
  Edmonds, Robert, 267
  Ellett, James, 272
  Gill, Henry, 340
  Goose, William, 355
  Hogg, William Johnson, 440
  Scarll, William, 788
  Titlow, William, 896
  Wright, John, 1006
Lowater, Richard, 256
Lowe, 105
Lowe, Edward, 25, 48, 51, 161, 429,
  445, 452, 471, 569, 751, 760,
  964, 974, 982
Lowe, Thomas, 557
Lowes, 788
Lowes, George, 548
Lowry, John, 992

Lowth, Henry, 762
Lowther, James, 110
Lowther, John, 669, 934
Lowther Castle (Westmld):
  Wilkinson, William, 977
Lowys, Sarah, 732
Lucas, Thomas, 891
Luck, Samuel, 508, 509, 552, 685, 897
Ludford, James, 371
Ludlow (Salop):
  Bowen, George, 92
  Brompton, John, 110
  Davies, John, 229
  Davies, William, 230
  Davis, Jonathon, 232
  Grosvenor, John, 376
  Harper, Joseph & Samuel, 399
  Howton, Benjamin, 456
  Lewis, Samuel, 540
  Massey, Jonathon, 585
  Poole, John, 706
  Price, Edward, 715
  Smith, Ann(e), 824
  Smith, William, 834
  Tilley, George, 894
  Tilley, Samuel, 894
Lumley, 666
Lumley, Leonard, 637
Lund, Charles John, 812
Lund, Edward, 54
Lund, John, 859
Lund, Robert, 53, 258
Lunton, John, 377
Lupton, John, 293
Lupton, Thomas, 739, 740
Luscombe Castle (Devon):
  Chippendale, Thomas jnr, 169
Luthys, W., 524
Luton (Beds.): Smith, Robert, 831
Lutterworth (Leics.):
  Baines, John, 31
  Hales, William, 384
  Smith, George, 826
Lyal, 33
Lyme Park (Cheshire): Moore, John, 620
Lyme Regis (Dorset):
  Anning, John, 15
  Govis, William, 361
  Knight, John, 519
  Lee, James, 534
  Margrie, George, 574
  Owen, Michael, 668
Lymington (Hants.):
  Banks, W., 37
  Baskett, J., 48
  Bowler, William, 93
  Brackston, Charles, 95
  Gattrell, John, 333
  Gattrell, Joseph, 333
  Gerrard, James, 335
  Lee, Thomas, 535
  Mitchell, James, 613

Silverlock, William, 814
  Turner, William, 913
Lyncombe (Som.): Biggs, William, 71
Lynes, 154
Lynham, James, 972
Lyon, 745
Lyon, George Philander, 75, 79, 81, 171, 425, 441, 625, 880
Lyon, Thomas, 534
Lyons, William Sharp, 664
Lytham (Lancs.):
  Lupton, William, 561
  Tomlinson, Richard, 898
Lytham Hall (Lancs.): Gillow, 343
Lyther, James, 90, 408, 431, 475
Lytholl, John, 830

M

McBean, Anna, 589, 1009
McBean, Thomas, 563
Mcbout, Thomas, 18
McCabe, Thomas, 626
McCaddon, Jane, 238
McClelland, John William, 568
Macclesfield (Cheshire):
  Dean, John, 237
  Dunn, John, 260
  Goodwin, Noah, 355
  Hamson, James, 392
  Hibbert, Charles, 427
  Hollinshed, Daniel, 443
  Ingleton, Joseph, 471
  Laurence, Alexander, 529
  Lediard, Thomas, 534
  Leicester, Charles, 537
  Liddiard, Thomas, 541
  Mellor, Hugh, 601
  Patefield, Lydia, 679
  Porter, Joseph, 707
  Riding, James, 747
  Schofield, William, 789
  Smallwood, Thomas, 823
  Smith, William, 834
  Stonehewer, Samuel, 859
  Thorley, John, 889
  Underhill, Timothy, 917
  Verga, John Marie, 921
  Whitaker, George, 963
  Wilkson, —, 978
  Willmott, John, 984
  Wyate, Richard, 1009
McComb, John, 913
McCormack, Charles Hinton, 677
Maccrummin, 494
McDonald, 306
Macdonald, 743
Machin, Lancelot, 501
Mackenzie, 81, 851
Mackenzie, Ebenizer, 617
Mackenzie, John, 720
McKenzie, Lawrence, 887

Mackery, George, 842
Mackett, 24
McKinnon, 173
Mackintyre, George, 565
McLauchlan, 498
McLean, William, 567
McLellan, 306
Maclellan, 706
McMay, John, 408
McNabb, Neil, 151
Macnamara & Brett, 724
Maddock, Samuel, 789
Maddocks, Edward, 704
Maddocks, Thomas, 557
Madeley (Salop):
  Evans, Robert jnr, 284
  Evans, Robert snr, 284
  Perks, George, 691
  Williams, James, 981
Madge, Matthew, 833
Madgwick, 835
Madgwick, John, 674
Madingley Hall (Cambs.):
  Aycliffe, Thomas jnr, 27
  Cobb, John, 182
  Foxhall, —, 315
  Gilbert, John, 338
  Godfrey, Richard, 347
  Harraden (or Harredon), —, 400
  Mayhew, John & Ince, William, 598
  Oakley, George, 659
  Sherrer (or Sherran), —, 809
  Swan, John, 867
  Yorke, Edward and successors, 1013
Magill, 416, 906
Magill, Ralph, 151, 637
Maguire, Richard, 642
Maidenhead (Berks.):
  Bensley, John, 66
  Hardy, William, 397
  Harris, Ralph, 402
  Henderson, Robert, 420
  Lock, James, 551
  Silver, James, 814
  Summers, George, 864
  Wyatt, Charles, 1009
Maidstone (Kent):
  Argles, Edward, 17
  Argles, Thomas, 17
  Barden, Isaac, 39
  Beaumont, John D, 56
  Bellingham, Edward, 63
  Bishop, John, 76
  Bishop & Terry, 76
  Box, George, 94
  Box, James, 94
  Bradshaw, W., 100
  Burch, James, 129
  Busendon, James, 136
  Day, William, 237
  Denne, William, 240
  Edmett, Thomas, 267

Gegan, James, 335
Godding, John, 346
Godling, Samuel, 347
Godon, Samuel, 347
Green, William, 368
Haddrick, Thomas, 382
Harrison, Thomas, 404
Hartridge, John, 407
Hughes, William, 461
Hurtridge, John, 466
Jury, Edward, 500
Lake, Thomas, 521
Martin, John, 581
Morris, —, 627
Morris, Henry, 628
Morris, John, 628
Morris, Samuel, 629
Nye, Carter, 657
Nye, George, 657
Olive, Nicholas, 663
Oliver, Walter, 663
Parks, Thomas, 676
Pett, Thomas, 692
Pexton, Alfred, James, 693
Pilbrow, J., 698
Pope, John, 706
Rand, William, 726
Reeve(s), William A., 736
Roffway, James, 763
Sawer, Joseph Philip, 786
Shreeves, William jnr, 813
Smallman, Robert, 822
Smith, John Martin, 830
Stephenson, Thomas, 854
Stubberfield, John, 863
Taylor, John, 876
Taylor, Thomas, 879
Tilbe(e), John snr, 894
Welleson, George, 957
Willson, George, 985
Wills, William, 985
Wood, James, 996
Young, Henry, 1014
Major, S., 876
Major, Samuel, 469
Malbone, John, 691
Maldon (Essex):
 Barwell, Robert, 47
 Beale, James, 54
 Dyer, William, 263
 Hodgson, John, 438
 Jefferies, Benjamin, 482
 Orrell, Stephen, 665
 Pattison, I.K.B., 681
 Sach, John, 775
 Stratford, George, 861
Mallet, Francis Peter, 349, 350
Malmesbury (Wilts.):
 Kayns, Ayliff(e), 501
 Nelmes, George, 640
 Odge, —, 661
Malpas (Cheshire):
 Baxter, Samuel, 52
 Tomkins, Edward, 897

Tomkinson, Edward, 898
Malster, Robert, 572
Malton (Yorks):
 Ash, George, 20
 Ash, James, 20
 Beverley, George, 69
 Bradley, Arthur, 97
 Douthwaite, John, 252
 Garencieres, John, 331
 Goodhill, John, 351
 Goodrick, John, 354
 Hall, George, 385
 Hill, John, 431
 Jackson, John, 476
 Jefferson, John, 482
 Lee, John, 535
 Lee, William, 535
 Lincett, Ash, 542
 Marshall, Richard, 579
 Monkman, William, 616
 Nelson, John, 640
 Nelson, Richard, 640
 Nelson, Robert, 640
 Pycock, George, 722
 Sellers, James, 799
 Sowman, Richard, 841
 Spurr, Harwick, 846
 Stamper, John, 848
 Stokehill, George, 858
 Sunman, Richard, 865
 Thompson, James, 886
 Tomlinson, George, 898
 Wardill, John, 944
Malyn, Thomas, 571
Mamhead (Devon): Morant,
 George, 623
Manchester:
 Abrams, John & Robert, 2
 Abram(s), William & John, 2
 Adams, John & Robert, 3
 Agnew, Thomas & Zanetti, 5
 Alferi, Charles, 7
 Alton, John, 11
 Alton, Mat(t)hew & John, 11
 Anderson, James, 12
 Anderson, Richard, 13
 Andrew, Philip, 14
 Antrobus, James, 15
 Appleyard, Thomas, 16
 Arrowsmith, Simon, 19
 Asheton, William, 20
 Aspinwall, John Francis, 22
 Aspinwall, Thomas William, 22
 Assheton, Ralph, 22
 Atkinson, James, 24
 Atkinson, John, 24
 Atkinson, Joseph, 24
 Atkinson, Robert, 24
 Axton, Thomas, 27
 Bagshaw, William, 29
 Baker, James, 32
 Ball, Benjamin, 35
 Ballard, Henry, 35
 Bamber, Thomas, 36

Bancks, Jacob, 36
Bancroft, C., 36
Bancroft, Sarah, 36
Bancroft, William, 36
Barber, John, 38
Barber, Samuel, 39
Barber, Thomas, 39
Barborough, Matthew, 39
Barker, Thomas, 41
Barlow, Edward, 41
Barnasconi, Anthony, 42
Barnes, Robert, 42
Barnett, William, 43
Barraclough, Richard, 44
Barron, Elizabeth, 45
Barron, John, 45
Barron, Peter, 45
Barron, Thomas, 45
Barrowclough, John, 45
Barrowclough, Richard, 45
Barton, John, 47
Barton, Thomas, 47
Barton & Bond, 47
Bates, John, 49
Batty, John, 50
Baxendale, James, 51
Baxendale, John, 51
Beaumont, John, 56
Beaumont, William, 56
Bebbington, Richard, 56
Beckett, Samuel, 57
Beddon, John, 58
Bell, Elizabeth, 61
Bellard, Henry, 63
Bellhouse, David jnr, 63
Belongaro, Dominic, 63
Bennett, Joseph, 65
Bennion, Joseph, 66
Bennison, John, 66
Benyon, Joseph, 67
Benyon, Richard, 67
Bernard, Arthur, 67
Beswick, Matthew, 68
Bethel, John & E., 68
Bewsher, William, 70
Beynon, Rowland, 70
Bianchi, John, 70
Bibby, John, 70
Billington, Thomas, 72
Birch, Charles, 73
Birch, John, 73
Birch, Thomas, 74
Birks, Richard, 75
Bisham, John, 75
Blackburn, Thomas, 77
Blomley, Robert, 81
Bolongaro, Dominic, 83
Booth, Thomas, 87
Booth, William Aspinall, 87
Boothman, John, 87
Bowcock, William, 91
Bowman, William, 93
Bradbury, Robert, 97
Bradley, James, 98

Manchester

Bramley, John, 102
Brasgirdule, John, 103
Bridge, Walter snr, 107
Bridgford, John, 107
Brierley, John, 107
Broadhurst, Joshua, 109
Bromley, John, 110
Brown, George, 114
Brown, James, 115
Brownhill, James, 120
Brumfitt, John, 121
Brundrett, William, 122
Buchanan, Peter, 123
Bullard, Henry, 125
Burkett, Thomas, 130
Burrows, John, 134
Burton, George, 135
Burton, William, 136
Bushell, William, 136
Butterworth, John, 139
Dale, Thomas, 224
Daniel, John, 225
Darnton, Frederick, 227
Darnton, George, 227
Darnton, John, 227
Davenport, Thomas, 227
Davies, Edward, 228
Davi(e)s, Hugh, 228
Davies, Hugh, 228
Davies, James, 229
Davies, John, 229
Davies, John Austin, 229
Davies, Thomas, 230
Davis, Edward & Thomas, 231
Dawson, Samuel, 235
Dean, Thomas, 237
Dean & Steele, 237
Dent, Robert, 241
Dewhurst, James, 242
Dey, Peter, 243
Dibb, James, 243
Dickenson, Henry, 243
Dickenson, Jonathan, 243
Dickenson, William, 243
Ditchfield, William, 245
Dixon, John, 246
Dixon, Richard, 246
Dodd, Thomas, 249
Dodson, George, 249
Doughty, Thomas, 251
Doveston, George, 252
Drinkwater, Eliza, 256
Drinkwater, James, 256
Du Fort, John, 258
Dunbar, William, 259
Dutton, Maria, 263
Dyson, Gibson, 263
Dyson, William, 263
Eagle, John, 264
Eccles, Henry, 265
Eccles, Thomas, 265
Edge, Richard, 266
Edwards, Thomas, 271
Eglin & Gregory, 271

Eglington, Richard, 271
Elder, John, 271
Ellam, William, 272
Elliott, John, 274
Ellis, John, 275
Esplin, William, 282
Etherington, Francis, 282
Evans, Charles, 283
Evans, Richard, 284
Evans & Movette, 285
Gadsby, William, 326
Gale, John, 327
Gale, Joseph, 327
Galley, John, 328
Garbitt, Joseph, 329
Gard(e)ner, James, 329
Garfoot, Robert, 331
Gibb & Thomas, 336
Gibson, Charles, 337
Gilbank, Thomas, 338
Gilbert, William, 339
Gilchrist, John, 339
Gill, John, 340
Gillbank, William, 341
Gillbanks, Thomas, 341
Gillespie, Andrew, 341
Gilpin, John, 344
Glossop, John, 345
Golburn, John, 348
Goodwin, Edward, 354
Goodwin, George, 354
Goulburn, John, 360
Gratix, Robert, 364
Gray, John, 365
Gray, Thomas, 366
Grayson, Henry, 366
Greenhalgh, Samuel, 368
Greenough, James, 368
Gregory, John, 370
Gregory, William, 370
Grocott, William, 376
Grundy, John Clowes, 377
Grundy & Fox, 377
Grundy & Goadsby, 377
Hackett, William, 381
Hague, Mary, 382
Hague, Thomas, 382
Haigh, John, 383
Hampson & Heaton, 392
Hampson, James, 392
Hampson, Thomas, 392
Hancock, John, 392
Hancock, Thomas, 393
Hand, Charles, 393
Hand, John, 393
Hand, Joseph, 393
Hand, Thomas, 393
Handford, Samuel, 393
Hanson, Herbert, 395
Harden, G.B., 395
Harding, William, 396
Hardman, Benjamin, 396
Hardman, William, 396
Harker, Ralph, 398

Harker, William, 398
Harris, Samuel, 402
Harrison, John, 404
Hartley, Richard, 407
Hartley, Thomas, 407
Hartley, William, 407
Hattlebarrow, Samuel, 410
Hawkins, Joseph, 413
Hawkins, Matthew, 413
Hayes, John, 414
Hays, John, 415
Hayton, Joseph, 415
Haywood, Thomas, 416
Heaton, John, 419
Heron, J.& T., 423
Heron, John, 423
Heron, Thomas, 423
Herrol, John, 423
Hetherington, Francis, 424
Hewitt, Thomas, 426
Hewkins, Henry, 426
Heyes, John, 426
Heywood, John, 426
Hilitch, Eliza, 429
Hill, Henry, 430
Hinde, Thomas, 433
Hindley, John, 433
Hockney, John, 436
Hodges, Thomas, 437
Hodgson, William, 438
Hodson, Samuel, 440
Hodson, William & Co., 440
Hoit, William, 440
Holden, James, 440
Holding, Henry & Sons, 441
Holland, James, 442
Holt, William, 446
Horatio, Samuel, 819
Horne, S. & Co., 450
Horne, Samuel, 450
Horner, Hannah, 450
Horner, James, 450
Horner, John, 450
Horner, Mary, 450
Horner, Peter, 450
Houlton, James, 452
Howard, John, 454
Howard & Whitehead, 455
Howorth, John, 456
Howson, Charles, 456
Hoyle, James, 456
Hoyle, John, 456
Hughes, James, 460
Hulme, Joseph, 462
Hulme, Thomas, 462
Hulme, William, 462
Hume, Joseph, 462
Hume, William, 462
Hunter, Thomas, 465
Hunting, William, 466
Hutton, Samuel, 469
Hyde, G.B., 469
Hyde, John, 470

Introvino, Antonio & Gaspar, 472
Irlam, Jane, 473
Jackson, Daniel & Peter, 475
Jackson, Edward, 475
Jackson, Peter, 476
Jackson, Ralph, 476
Jennings, David, 485
Jones, Edward, 494
Jones & Cowen, 498
Kay, George, 500
Kay, John, 500
Kay, William, 501
Kaye, John, 501
Kaye, William, 501
Kearsley, James, 501
Kellam, Richard, 503
Kellett, John, 503
Kelsall, Edward, 503
Kendall, Robert, 505
Kenworthy, J.B., 509
Kershaw, Thomas, 510
Kewley, John, 511
Kirkham, Thomas, 517
Kitchen, George, 518
Knebworth, James, 518
Knight, Joseph, 519
Laing, —, 521
Lamb, Daniel, 522
Landsall, Matthew, 524
Lansdale, Matthew, 527
Latham, William, 529
Lawton, John, 532
Lawton, Samuel, 532
Lawton, William, 532
Leach, Henry, 533
Leadbeater, John, 533
Leadbeater & Barlow, 533
Lee, John, 535
Lee, Thomas, 535
Lees, Thomas, 536
Leftwich, Thomas, 536
Leigh, Thomas, 537
Lever, Mary, 539
Lewis, John, 540
Lewtas, John, 541
Lingard, John, 543
Linney John, 548
Litchfield, Jonathon, 549
Livingston, John, 550
Lloyd, Edward, 550
Lofthouse, George, 553
Lomas, William, 554
Lomax & Nightingale, 554
Lorthwick, Samuel, 555
Lowe, Isaac, 557
Lowndes, James, 558
Lowndes, William, 558
Lyon, John, 562
McCann, Andrew, 564
McDonald, Archibald, 564
McKinley, Thomas, 566
Macom, James, 568
Maddock, Samuel, 569

Makinson, I., 570
Malone, Thomas, 571
Marland, John, 575
Marsden, George B., 576
Marsden, Mary, 576
Marsden, Thomas Barton, 576
Marsh, John, 576
Martin, William, 582
Matti(n)son, John, 587
Mawn, Benjamin Hardman, 588
Maybury, William, 589
Meakin, James, 599
Mellor, John, 601
Merone, Joseph, 603
Middleton, William, 605
Molteni, Innocent, 615
Monaghan, John, 615
Moore, Richard, 620
Moors, Joseph, 622
Morland, John, 627
Mosley, Charles, 632
Mosley, Thomas, 632
Moss, Joseph, 632
Mossley, James & Co., 632
Mottershead, Henrietta, 632
Mountain, Joseph, 633
Munro, William, 636
Mush, John, 637
Natt, Thomas, 639
Nelson, Thomas, 641
Nelson, William, 641
Newton, Edward, 644
Newton, Gabriel, 644
Newton, James & Son, 644
Nicholson, Isaac, 646
Nicholson, William, 647
Nightingale, John, 648
Nixon, Isaac, 649
Nixon, William, 650
Normansell, James, 653
Normansell, Robert, 653
Norris, Edward, 653
Norris, John, 654
North, James, 655
North, Joseph, 655
Nuttall, James, 657
Nuttall, John, 657
Nuttall, Richard, 657
Ogden, Thomas, 661
Ogg(s), Charles Morris, 661
O'Hara, Thomas, 661
Oldham, Anthony, 662
Oliver, Joseph, 663
Oliver, William, 663
Orford, John, 664
Orme, Thomas, 665
Owen, John, 668
Parke, Jonathon, 673
Parker, William, 675
Parker & Wragg, 675
Parkin, Joseph, 676
Partington, John, 678
Patterson, Samuel, 680
Paul, William, 682

Peach, William, 683
Pearson, Christopher, 684
Pearson, William, 685
Peartshire, Richard, 685
Ped(d)uzzi, Anthony, 686
Ped(d)uzzi, James, 686
Peerce, Edward, 686
Peirt, Richard, 687
Perkins, Thomas, 691
Petrie & Walker, 692
Phenix, James, 693
Pickard, William, 697
Pickford, Adam, 697
Pickford, Esther, 697
Pickford, John, 697
Pickford, Thomas, 697
Pigott, Thomas, 698
Pitts, John, 701
Pizotti, John, 702
Plant, James, 702
Poole, Robert, 706
Porter, David John, 706
Porter, John, 707
Porter, William, 707
Potter, David John, 708
Powlay, Thomas, 711
Predary, James, 713
Priestly, Joseph, 717
Radley, Joseph, 725
Rawson, Thomas, 730
Reany, William & Adam, 732
Renshaw, James, 737
Resbury, Stephen, 737
Reynolds, R., 738
Reynolds, Robert, 738
Reynolds & Gregory, 739
Richards, John, 742
Richardson, Henry, 743
Richardson, Stephen, 745
Roberts, I.& T., 751
Roberts, Thomas, 754
Robinson, Eleanor, 756
Rogerson, Edward, 764
Ronchetti, Joseph, 765
Ronchetti, Joshua, 765
Rooker, Thomas, 765
Roskell, John, 766
Roskill, Gilbert, 766
Ross, David, 766
Rothwell, —, 767
Rothwell, Mrs, 767
Rothwell, James, 767
Rothwell, John, 767
Rothwell, Lydia, 767
Rothwell & Marsden, 767
Royale, William, 769
Royle, John, 769
Royle, William, 770
Rushworth, James, 771
Rushworth, William, 771
Sampson & Shaw, 778
Sanderson, John, 779
Scholes, Henry, 789
Scholes & Grayson, 789

Scholfield, Arthur, 789
Scorah, Joseph, 789
Seddon, John, 798
Seel, George, 798
Seel, Sarah, 798
Seel, Thomas, 798
Seymour, Thomas, 801
Sharples, James, 804
Sharrock, James, 804
Shayler, James, 806
Sherratt, James, 809
Shiers, Richard Peart, 810
Shires, Mary, 811
Shore, John, 812
Shore, Roger, 812
Sillo & Co, 814
Singleton, James, 818
Skeer, Thomas, 818
Skerratt, Samuel, 819
Skerrit, Robert, 819
Slack, John, 820
Slater, Joseph, 820
Smethurst, Samuel, 823
Smith, George, 826
Smith, John, 829
Smith, William, 834
Southall, William, 840
Spencer, William, 844
Stapleton, Ann, 849
Stapleton, Thomas, 849
Steel(e), George, 851
Steel, William, 851
Stoakes, William, 857
Stra(c)han, Francis, 860
Strahan, William, 860
Stretch, Joseph, 861
Stringer, John, 862
Sudlow, John, 864
Swallow, Joseph, 867
Swarbrick, John, 867
Swinnerton, Joseph, 868
Syers, John, 869
Syers, Joseph, 869
Tayloer, Hector, 874
Taylor, Acten, 874
Taylor, Brian, 874
Taylor, George, 876
Taylor, John, 877
Taylor, Samuel, 879
Taylor, Thomas, 879
Thomas, Charles, 883
Thomas, James, 883
Thomas, Joseph, 884
Thomas, Nathaniel, 884
Thompson, Elizabeth, 885
Thompson, Robert, 887
Thompson, Thomas, 887
Thorne, Mary, 890
Thornes, James, 890
Tieurcono, Caspar, 894
Tipping, George, 895
Tootell, Joshua, 899
Topham, George, 899
Travis, James, 902

Travis, Thomas, 902
Treble, John & Sykes, 903
Trees, John, 903
Trubshaw, Richard, 906
Tunbrell, William, 908
Turner, George, 909
Turner, Henry, 910
Turner, John, 911
Turner, Richard, 911
Turner, Samuel, 911
Turner, Thomas, 912
Turner, W., 912
Turner, William, 913
Upton, David, 917
Ursell, Edward, 918
Uttering, Samuel, 918
Vernon, Richard, 922
Vittore & Marone, 929
Vittory, I. & V., 929
Vitty, George Ascough, 929
Wainhouse, Thomas, 932
Wainright, Edward, 932
Wainwright, Alice, 932
Waite, John, 932
Wakefield, John, 933
Walker, John, 936
Walker, Nicholas, 936
Walker, Richard, 936
Wallis, James, 940
Walmsley, Robert, 941
Warburton, Thomas, 942
Ward, Abraham, 942
Waring, James, 945
Waring & Lansdale, 945
Washington, Samuel, 946
Waterhouse, Thomas, 947
Watmough, James, 948
Watmough, John, 948
Watson, George, 949
Watson, John, 950
Webster, James, 955
Weddall, John, 956
Weller, John, 957
Wells, William, 958
Whaite, Henry, 962
Whalley, Thomas, 962
Wheatley, Thomas, 962
Wheeldon, Benjamin, 963
Wheeldon, William, 963
White, Henry, 965
Whitehead, John, 968
Whiteley, James, 968
Whiteley, Thomas, 968
Whiteley, William, 968
Whittaker, Dinah, 969
Whittaker, Josiah, 969
Whittaker, William, 969
Whitworth, Benjamin, 971
Whitworth, John, 971
Whitworth, Mary, 971
Wild, Jacob, 974
Wild, John, 974
Wild, Thomas, 974
Wild, William, 974

Wilde, Joseph, 974
Wilde, Thomas, 974
Wildin, James, 974
Wilding, Benjamin, 974
Wilkinson, James, 976
Wilkinson, John, 976
Williams, George, 979
Williams, James, 980
Williams, Job, 981
Williamson, Richard, 983
Willmott, John, 984
Wilmot, John, 985
Wilson, John, 988
Wilson, Peter, 989
Wilson, Richard, 989
Wilson, William, 990
Wimbles, William, 991
Wolfenden, John, 995
Wolstencroft, Joshua, 995
Wommels, William, 995
Wood, John, 997
Wood, William, 998
Woodworth, John, 1001
Worrall, Catherine, 1003
Worrall, William, 1003
Worsley, William, 1003
Wright, Clayton, 1004
Wroe, James, 1009
Wroe, John, 1009
Wroe, Joseph, 1009
Yates, Edward, 1012
Yates, Thomas, 1012
Yates, William, 1012
Young, John, 1014
Zandra, George, 1015
Zanetti, Bolongaro & Agnew, 1015
Zanetti, Joseph, 1015
Zanetti, Vinc(i)ent, 1015
Zanetti, Vittorie, 1015
Zan(n)etti & Agnew, 1015
Manchett, 173
Mander, Joseph, 807
Manet, Francis Peter, 616
Manlove, Richard, 696
Mann, James, 804, 805
Mann, Samuel, 475
Mann, Thomas, 767, 873
Manningham (Yorks): Waugh, William, 952
Manningtree (Essex):
  Arthy, William, 20
  Goodwin, Robert, 355
  Self, Robert, 799
Mansfield (Notts.):
  Al(l)sop, Peter, 11
  Alsop, Charles, 11
  Ashby, Richard, 20
  Ashford, John, 20
  Day, William, 236
  Hallam, Richard, 387
  Harrison, John, 404
  Lellan, William M., 538
  Lester, John, 539

M'Lellan, Elizabeth & Son, 568
M'Lellan, John, 568
M'Lellan, William, 568
Peet, John, 686
Pegg, James, 687
Platt, Joseph, 702
Sansom, Richard, 781
Sansom, Thomas, 781
Taylor, William, 880
White, Samuel, 967
Woodhead, Joseph, 999
Manthorpe, James, 428
Marazion (Cornwall): Ham, John, 391
March, William, 623
March (Cambs.):
  Graves, Robert, 365
  Throssell, William, 892
  West, Joseph, 960
Marchand, 775
Marchant, 465
Marchant, George, 464
Margate (Kent):
  Bassett, Henry, 48
  Brett, William, 105
  Brown, John, 116
  Bytham, Henry, 139
  Goddin, Richard, 346
  Hammond, Henry, 392
  Ladson, W.B., 521
  Lovelock, Henry, 556
  Lovelock, J., 556
  Marsh, —, 576
  Minter, George, 612
  Noakes, Robert, 650
  Pindar, John, 699
  Pyle, Henry William, 723
  Roasway, John, 751
  Roffway, John jnr, 763
  Simcock, James, 815
  Sinnock, Henry, 818
  Walker, James, 935
  Wormsley, —, 1003
Mariner, William, 779
Maris, Samuel, 293
Market Bosworth (Leics.): Thorpe, William, 891
Market Deeping (Lincs.):
  Allam, Thomas, 9
  Allam, William, 9
Market Drayton (Salop):
  Bate, —, 48
  Gad, Thomas, 326
  Gadd, Richard, 326
  Grant, Thomas, 364
  Griffith, Isaac, 374
  Griffiths, Isaac, 374
  Griffith(s), Thomas, 374
  Harper, George, 399
  Jarvis, George, 481
  Jervis, Henry, 488
  Millward, James, 611
  Mo(u)ntford, Thomas, 633
  Noden, William, 650

Ray, Uriah, 730
Roden, Samuel, 762
Smith, Thomas, 832
Swinchall, Charles, 868
Swin(e)chatt, Charles, 868
Swine(c)hatt, Job, 868
Swinehat, Mrs, 868
Taylor, T., 879
Trentham, Timothy, 903
Trevor, James, 904
Market End (Essex): Barrows, Richard, 45
Market Harborough (Leics.):
  Bosworth, Robert, 90
  Burditt, David, 130
  Hamshaw, William, 392
  Hind, W., 433
  Holloway, William, 444
  Hughes, John, 461
  Kilbourn, John, 512
  Martin, John, 581
  Over, James, 667
  Paillet, Melchior, 670
  Russell, John, 772
  Shipley, Richard, 811
  Thompson, John, 886
  Thomson, —, 889
  Warrington, John, 946
Market Lavington (Wilts.): Bartlett, James, 46
Market Rasen (Lincs.):
  Bell, William, 63
  Benton, Charles, 66
  Dean, John, 237
  Kendall, Joseph, 505
  Sellers, Richard, 799
  Shearman, John jnr, 806
  Tarrey, Thomas, 872
  Torry, George, 900
  Wallis, James, 940
  Walsham, William, 941
  Ward, George, 942
Market Weighton (Yorks):
  Barron, Robert, 45
  Mackley, William, 567
  Pool, Thomas, 705
  Pottage, Thomas, 708
  Saltmire, Rd., 777
  Smith, Thomas, 833
  Wray, Thomas, 1004
  Young, George, 1014
Marks, John, 397, 738
Marks, Sterry, 91, 840
Marland, James, 575
Marlborough (Wilts.):
  Broom, Francis, 112
  Hancock, James, 392
  Hill, —, 430
  Hill, Henry, 430
  Hilliker, Samuel, 432
  Luff, John, 560
  Newman, William, 644
  Reeve, —, 735
  Reeve, J., 735

Shrimpton, John, 813
Shrimpton, Thomas, 813
Simonds, John, 815
Marlow (Bucks.):
  Blake, Richard, 79
  Bond, William, 85
  Daniels, George, 225
  Maddox, Robert, 569
  Mealing, Edward, 599
Marlow Hill (Bucks.): Treacher, Samuel, 903
Marly (France): Van Opstal, Louis, 919
Marone, 929
Marot, Daniel, 486, 487, 491, 528, 752
Marples, Thomas, 800
Marquis, Spencer, 837
Marr, Henry, 180
Marriot, Samuel, 102
Marsden, 767–8
Marsden, William, 1007
Marsh, 321
Marsh, Isaac, 200, 340, 479, 506, 585, 637, 688, 715, 866, 911
Marsh, John, 757
Marsh, Joseph, 118, 292, 398, 911
Marsh, Samuel, 842
Marshall, 251, 542
Marshall, Edward, 915
Marshall, George, 9
Marshall, James, 113, 131, 431, 579
Marshall, Josiah, 236
Marshall, Martha, 397
Marshall, Thomas, 157, 270, 287
Marshall, William, 578, 873
Marshe, George, 749
Marske (Yorks): Herbert, Thomas, 423
Marston, John, 948
Marston, William, 509, 540, 747
Marston House (Som.): Alken, Sefferin, 8
Martin, 840, 858, 951
Martin, Carl Gustav, 324
Martin, Charles, 19, 762, 806
Martin, Hugh, 754
Martin, Samuel, 287, 298, 441, 745, 821, 929
Martin, Thomas, 580
Martinoff, Theo, 648
Martock (Som.): Passley, Wm, 679
Marton (Yorks): Higham, Thomas, 429
Maryland (USA): Pennington, John, 689
Marylebone (London):
  Anderson, William, 13
  Ansell, John, 15
  Banton, T., 38
  Batchelor, William, 48
  Bateman, John, 49
  Bennett, J., 64
  Boucher, John, 90

Bow, Charles, 91
Bow, Robert, 91
Butterworth, Joseph, 139
Buttler, C.H., 139
Desassarts, Henry, 242
Dickens, William, 243
Gibson, James, 337
Gough, John, 360
Gregson, Mary, 370
Hall, Joseph, 386
Harris, Ralph, 402
Harvey, Henry, 407
Henderson, William James, 421
Hensell, Charles, 422
Higgs, Thomas, 429
Hillier, Charles, 432
Hudson, Richard, 458
Hyland, James, 470
Iley, Mary, 470
Iley, William, 471
Johnson, James, 489
Keenan, Nicholas, 502
Kelley, William, 503
Kengall, Charles, 506
Kilvington, Israel, 513
King, Peter, 514
Laverick, James, 530
Lee, George, 534
Leeds, Levi, 535
Linderbusch, H., 542
Livett, Richard, 550
Lomax, Frederick, 554
Lovell, James, 556
Low, Stephen, 557
McIlraith, John, 565
Mantle, Thomas, 573
Marcuccis, Charles, 574
Mathews, William, 586
Mills, Charles, 610
Mills, John, 610
Mills, William, 611
Moir, William, 615
Monk, Thomas, 616
Morton, James, 630
Moses, Samuel, 632
Murray, John, 636
Nelson, David, 640
Newbery, John, 642
Nicholl, Thomas, 645
Parnell, John, T.& H., 676
Pecquer, Louis & Son, 686
Perfetti, Joseph, 690
Piper, Christopher, 700
Randall, John, 727
Reid, Richard, 736
Reid, William, 737
Roberts, Thomas & Richard, 752
Robinson, Charles, 756
Robinson, Elizabeth, 756
Scarfe, Samuel, 788
Seyer, David, 801
Spencer & Catesby, 844
Stephens, John, 852
Stephens, William, 853

Stevens, Thomas, 854
Swan, Thomas, 867
Talbert, —, 870
Telfer, John, 880
Thack(th)waite, Michael, 882
Thompson, William, 888
Thurnell, William, 892
Tiffin & Son, 894
Walker, Richard, 937
Walker, William, 938
White, Robert, 967
Wilkinson, John, 976
Wison, Edward, 994
Wood, John, 996
Maryport (Cumb.):
  Allan, John, 9
  Brown, Anthony, 113
  Brown, George, 114
  Brown, Thomas, 118
  Eaglesfield, Charles, 264
  Graham, John, 362
  Hinde, Robert, 433
  Kirkby, Thomas, 517
  Lowther, John, 559
  Millican, John, 609
  Nelson, William, 641
  Nicholson, H., 646
  Nicholson, Joseph, 647
  Park, Thomas, 673
  Payne, John, 682
  Penn, Joseph, 688
  Ritson, William, 750
  Slater, Abraham, 820
  Tickel, William, 894
Maschwitz, 53
Masey, Abram, 573
Masey, Thomas, 585
Masham (Yorks):
  Alton & Atkinson, 11
  Metcalfe, James, 604
  Musgrave, George, 637
  Myers, Thomas, 637
  Pullen, Thomas, 722
  Towler, John, 900
Mashiter, R., 246, 438, 523, 767, 879
Maskall, Hugh, 349
Mason, 160
Mason, Daniel, 436
Mason, James, 154
Mason, Nicholas, 366
Mason, Thomas, 216
Massey, Mathew, 576
Massey, W., 952
Masterman, Benjamin, 376
Mather, G., 576
Mather, William, 314
Mathews, William, 754
Mathue, Samuel, 776
Matson, Benjamin, 760
Matthews, John, 276
Matthews, Richard, 541
Matthews, Timothy, 239
Mattindale, Thomas, 582

Maudlen, James, 904
Maudlin, James, 235
Maugham, William, 764
Maulden, James, 78, 93
Maunders, John, 459
Mauson, John, 588
Maw, Marmaduke, 63
Maxey, 340
Maxwell, 207
May, John, 853
May, William, 803, 987
Maybreck, John, 151
Maychell, William, 933
Mayfair (London):
  Buist, William, 125
  King, —, 513
  King, John, 514
  Robinson, John Thomas, 758
  Smith, Thomas, 832, 833
  Thornton, William, 891
  Weston, J., 961
Mayhew, 182, 242, 420, 506, 573, 622, 646, 925, 951
Mayhew, Bartholomew, 590
Mayhew, John, 99, 959, 971
Mayhew, William, 652
Maynard, Charles, 146
Mayow, Richard, 427
Mead, Thomas, 866
Meade, William, 527
Meadley, Richard, 294
Meakins, William, 538, 662
Meakins, William jnr, 615
Mear, Catherine, 600
Mear, Richard, 600
Mears, Catherine, 600
Mears, John, 18, 461, 525, 540, 589, 615, 750, 774, 914, 945
Measures, John, 801, 843
Mecomb, John, 330
Medbourne (Leics.):
  Exton, John, 286
  Rowe, William, 769
Medcalf, Christopher, 603
Meers, John, 340
Megson, John, 857
Meineke, John, 754
Melbourne (Derbs.): Ault, John, 26
Melbourne Hall (Derbs.): Watson, Samuel, 950
Melford Hall (Suffolk): Morant, George, 623
Melksham (Wilts.): Wheeler, C., 963
Mellerstain (Berwicks.):
  Hambley, Peter, 391
  Turin, —, 908
Melling (Lancs.): Walker, T., 937
Melrose, Thomas, 413
Melton Mowbray (Leics.):
  Barton, Thomas, 47
  Burton, Langley, 135
  Burton, Thomas, 135
  Butlin, Thomas, 138

Gamble, Edward, 328
Langley, Thomas, 526
Orson, John, 665
Sheffield, James, 806
Townsend, Edward, 901
Townsend, John, 901
Waddington, J., 93–0
Wragg, Zachariah, 1003
Mendlesham (Suffolk):
    Day, Daniel, 236
    Day, Richard, 236
Mercer, John, 161, 295, 948, 995
Mercer, Ralph, 602
Mercer, Samuel, 752, 911
Mercer, William, 307, 945
Meredith, Richard, 39, 84, 221, 394, 557
Mere (Wilts.): Light, Thomas, 541
Meres, John, 745
Merle, John, 667
Merrill, Golding, 366
Merryman, Joseph, 3, 158, 881, 960
Mersham-le-Hatch (Kent):
    Burroughs & Watts, 133
    Chippendale, Thomas snr, 165, 166, 167
    Crawford, William, 208
    Gilbert, John, 338
    Graham, Joseph & partners, 362
    Hansan, George, 395
    Hassan, George, 409
    Heming, George & Co., 420
    Lawson, James, 531
    Piddock, John, 697
Merton (Devon): Bennett, William, 65
Merton (Surrey), Lord Nelson's House:
    Morgan & Sanders, 626
    Ward, Thomas, 943
Mervin, Philip, 712
Merwyn, Phillip, 773
Meschain, John, 424
Metcalf, Robert, 986
Metcalfe, 651, 685
Metcalfe, James, 58
Metcalfe, Joseph, 51
Metcalfe, Robert, 603
Metcalfe, Thomas, 244
Methley (Yorks): Braime, William, 101
Meynell, George, 54
Michon, Peter, 696
Micklegate, York:
    Gibson, Malby, 337
    Gregg, Christopher, 370
    Rayson, Henry, 731
Middleham (Yorks):
    Harrison, Thomas, 404
    Hogg, George, 440
    Raper, Henry, 728
    Sturdy, Stephen, 863
    Walker, John, 936

Middlesborough (Yorks):
    Garnett, Thomas, 331
    Rivers, Joseph, 750
    Westwick, William, 961
Middlesex Hospital:
    Almond, William, 11
    Chippendale, Thomas snr, 166
    Haworth, Samuel, 413
Middleton, Billy, 1008
Middleton, John, 5, 107
Middleton (Manchester): Wrigley, James, 1009
Middleton Park (Oxon.):
    McLean, John & Son, 568
    Mewkill, Josiah, 604
Middleton-in-Teesdale (Co. Durham): Pinkey, Joseph, 699
Middlewich (Cheshire):
    Andrew, John, 14
    Beckett, Henry, 57
    Drinkwater, George, 256
    Earl, Charles, 264
    Edge, Samuel, 266
    Egerton, John, 271
    Higginson, Nathaniel, 428
    Hough, James, 452
    Hughes, Daniel, 460
    Steel, George, 851
    Steel, John, 851
    Wolf, Isaac, 995
Middup, Elijah, 377
Midhope (Yorks): Thompson, Jonathon, 887
Midhurst (Sussex):
    Higginson, Francis, 428
    Higinson, Francis, 429
    Knight, Richard, 519
    Mercer, William, 602
    Peat, George, 685
Midlane, George, 605
Midsomer Norton (Som.): Smith, William, 833
Milburn, James, 605
Mildenhall (Suffolk): Woodland, Samuel, 999
Miles, Edward, 802
Miles & Edwards, 253, 433
Milford (Pembrokeshire): Bowen, Thomas, 92
Milhum, Andrew, 322
Millar, George, 608
Millar, John, 608
Miller, 121, 1001
Miller, George, 696
Miller, James, 607, 609
Miller, William, 608
Milligan, Thomas, 141
Millne, George, 864
Mills, 43
Mills, John, 363
Mills, W., 283
Mills, William, 754
Milne, George, 609
Milner, 6, 746

Milner, John, 43, 728, 913
Milner, Richard, 611
Milner, Robert, 466, 786
Milnthorpe (Westmld): Thompson, Anthony, 885
Milsom, John, 391, 601
Milton (Kent): Pain, James, 670
Milton (Northants.): Mello, —, 601
Milton Manor (Berks): Lawrence, Richard, 531
Milward, Benjamin, 933
Milward, William, 780, 873
Minchinhampton (Glos.): Browning, Samuel, 120
Minter, 867
Missenden (Bucks.): Hart, Mary, 406
Misson, John, 248
Misterley (Essex):
    Self, Robert, 799
    Self, Thomas, 799
Misterton (Notts.): Sefton, Thomas, 799
Mistley (Essex): Paskell, John, 679
Mitcham (Surrey): Warrimer, William, 946
Mitchell, Alexander, 82
Mitchell, James, 160, 229
Mitchell, Joseph, 151
Mitley, Charles, 198, 816
Mitton (Lancs.): Morris, Peter, 628
Mixbury (Oxon.): Morgan, Daniel, 625
M'kewan, 560
Mobray, Christopher, 633–4
Moccas Court (Herefs.):
    Collett, Jonathan, 188
    Graham, Joseph & partners, 362
    Hayward, —, 415
    Holmes, —, 444
    Kelly, —, 503
    Symonds, James, 869
    Van Gelden, —, 919
Moditonham House (Cornwall):
    Cole, Charles, 186
Moffett, Samuel, 599
Mogany, 391
Mold, John, 906
Moline, Anthony, 615
Molineux, Francis, 412
Molineux, Thomas Gisborne, 412, 615
Molteni & Guanziroli, 50
Molyneux, Henry, 754
Molyneux, John, 333
Mombray, Paul, 494
Momet, Francis Peter, 616
Moncas, Thomas, 517
Moncaster, John, 47
Monday, 200
Monday, Thomas, 635
Mondey, 200
Money, Thomas, 715, 999

Money, Tim, 181
Money, Timothy, 111, 329
Monro, David, 636
Montacute (Som.): Spencer, Henry, 843
Montford, Thomas, 633
Moody, 941
Moon, George, 617
Moon, James Carter, 733
Moor, Paul, 620
Moor, Thomas, 621
Moor Hall Park (Essex): Labbett, H., 520
Moor Park (Herts.):
  Allwood, Thomas, 11
  Almond, William, 11
  Brown, Richard, 117
  Fell, Lawrence, 294
  France, William snr, 316
  Haworth, Samuel, 413
  Lawson, James, 531
  Norman, Samuel, 652, 653
  Roberts, Thomas & Richard, 753
  Sidney, Benjamin, 814
  Taylor & Sons, 880
  Vile, William, 927
Moore, 366
Moore, James, 316, 351, 379, 677
Moore, James jnr, 618, 742
Moore, John Stamford, 236
Moore, Joseph, 617
Moore, M., 679
Moore, Richard, 857
Moore, Robert, 480
Moore, Simpson, 620
Moore, Thomas, 61, 866
Moore, William, 590
Moorecroft, James, 617
Moorehouse, James Blisset, 623
Moorfields (London):
  Barr, William, 43
  Bell, M., 62
  Bennett, James, 64
  Besset, John, 68
  Bolter & Dawes, 84
  Branston, William, 103
  Bratt, Sm., 103
  Buskins, —, 136
  Dawes, Mark, 234
  Dell, Benjamin, 239
  Derrett, Nathaniel, 241
  Dodgson, George, 249
  Draper, Thomas & Co., 255
  Gibbs, David, 336
  Gibbs, Robert, 336
  Gibson, George, 337
  Gillock, Thomas, 341
  Goulding, Richard, 360
  Grantham, John, 364
  Greville, Henry & Co., 373
  Griffiths, John, 375
  Guidot, William snr, 378
  Hall, Henry, 385
  Hall, William, 386

Hallows, John, 390
Hammond, Edward, 392
Hammond, John, 392
Harding, Richard, 396
Harris, —, 400
Harrison, William, 405
Hatton, Leonard, 410
Hayes, Robert, 414
Hersant, John, 423
Hersant, W., 423
Holmes, Alexander, 444
Horsley, James, 451
Horsley, John, 451
Horsley, Mary, 451
Howel, William, 455
Hubbard, John, 457
Hunter, W., 465
Hunter, William, 466
Inglish, M., 472
Ingram, Benjamin, 472
Johnson, Edmund, 489
Kemp, John, 504
Langford, Richard, 525
Ledger, Richard, 534
Light, John, 541
Loader, Edward snr & jnr, 551
Markham, Gregory, 574
Meek, William, 600
Metcalf, Henry & Son, 603
Meymott, Thomas, 604
Miles, Frederick, 606
Mullett, James, 634
Mullett, Paul, 635
Newbury, Francis, 642
Palliser, William, 671
Parkey, Arthur, 676
Perry, William, 692
Pettit & Oliver, 692
Phene, jnr & Rickett, 693
Phene, Samuel, 693
Pitt, James, 701
Pitt, John, 701
Pitt & Son, 701
Price, Charles, 715
Prothero, William & Spraggon, 719
Pullen, Joseph, 721
Ravner, William, 729
Rayner, William, 731
Reeves, J., 736
Reid, Thomas, 736
Rivett, J., 750
Robertson & Landbeck, 755
Rotheray, Joseph, 767
Rumball, Thomas, 770
Rusbridge(r), Richard, 771
Russell, —, 771
Russel(l), John, 772
Russell, John, 772
Sadgrove, Thomas, 775
Scaping, Joseph, 788
Sels, W., 799
Shepperd, Richard, 808
Smart, William, 823

Spraggon, William, 845
Staunton, —, 850
Stevenson, Daniel, 855
Stinton, —, 856
Stoddart, George, 858
Stubbs, John S., 863
Swain, Charles, 866
Swain, Elizabeth, 866
Swain, Samuel, 866
Swain, William, 866
Taylor, Isaac, 876
Thomequay, —, 885
Tomkies, Richard, 897
Tomkins, Philip, 897
Tomkins, Samuel, 897
Tomkins, William, 897, 898
Tompkins, Francis, 898
Tompkins, Jane, 898
Turner, David, 909
Turner & Hullah, 913
Wakefield, James, 933
Wareup, William, 945
Watts, James, 951
Webb, Arthur, 953
White, William, 967
Wilkinson, Joseph, 976
Wilkinson, Joshua jnr, 976
Wilkinson, Thomas & Co., 977
Wilkinson, William, 977
Wilkinson, William & Thomas, 977
Willis, John, 984
Willis, William, 984
Wilson, Benjamin, 986
Woodward, William, 1001
Wright, Charles, 1004
Wright, J., 1005
Wright, Joseph, 1006
Wright, Richard, 1006
Wright, William, 1009
Moorgate (London):
  Goulds, William Ellis, 361
  Lambert, George, 523
  Senols, James, 800
Moppett, 528
More, 584
Morel, Nicholas, 549, 795
Morel & Seddon, 252, 435, 721, 766, 808, 970
Moreley, Richard, 455
Moreten, Henry, 630
Moreton, Thomas, 443
Moreton-in-Marsh (Glos.): Keck, John, 502
Moretonhampstead (Devon):
  Heard, —, 417
  Rowden, John, 768
Morgan, Charles, 156, 194
Morgan, John, 627
Morgan, Thomas, 138, 263, 668
Morgan, William, 280, 564
Morgan & Ravald, 627
Morgan & Sanders, 129, 261
Morland, John, 728, 729

Morley (Yorks):
  Dearnley, William, 238
  Lord, James, 555
  Waterhouse, William, 947
Morpeth (Northumb.):
  Bryson, Robert, 123
  Daglish, Anthony, 223
  Gair, William, 327
  Grieve, William, 373
  Haswell, William, 410
  Jackson, Henry, 475
  James, Wilson, 480
  Manner, John, 573
  Noble, William, 650
  Ord, John, 664
  Potts, Thomas, 709
  Robinson, Christopher, 756
  Todd, Thomas, 897
  Wilson, James, 987
  Young, John, 1014
Morris, 148, 446, 627, 704
Morris, Alfred, 627
Morris, Sargeant Witten, 627, 628
Morrison, Robert, 911
Morrison, Thomas, 540
Morris's, 161
Morrow, 446
Mortlake (Surrey):
  Gray, Stephen, 365
  Storr, John, 860
Morton, 201, 294, 368
Morton, Isaac, 366
Morton, Richard, 44, 733
Moseley, Richard, 401
Mosley, John, 631
Moss, John, 180
Mote Park (Kent): Wood, Henry, 996
Moteni, 1016
Mouland, William, 627
Moulder, Thomas, 26, 692
Moules, William, 634
Moulsham Hall (Essex):
  Bagley, John, 29
  Bell, Daniel, 61
  Bolar, Samuel, 83
  Bradshaw, William, 100
  Broumhead, Rob., 113
  Cox, John, 204
  Dawson, Mrs, 235
  Dowyer, —, 255
  Dunton, William, 261
  Fletcher, Joseph, 304
  Gainge, —, 327
  Gosset, Jacob, 359
  Haddock, Elka, 382
  Hallett, William snr and William jnr, 389
  Holford, —, 441
  Howard, Gerrard, 453
  Jarman, —, 481
  Jones, Sandys, 496
  Lucera, Anthony, 560
  Moline, —, 615

Moore, Thomas, 621
Murray, George, 636
Newman, Edward, 643
Nix, George, 648, 649
Noon, Lancaster, 651
Pickover, Richard, 697
Prestage, John, 713
Richards, James, 742
Roberts, Thomas & Richard, 753, 754
Rodwell, William, 762
Shipman, Robert, 811
Spurnet, William, 846
Steinfield, H., 852
Stephenson, Luke, 853
Tailors, Mrs, 870
Tooley, James, 899
Toomes, Mrs, 899
Versovile, —, 922
Walters, William, 941
Waters, William, 947
Moulton (Norfolk): Lammas, Edmund, 524
Mount Clare (Surrey): Columbani, Placido, 190
Mount Stewart (Co. Down):
  Blackwell, William, 78
  Crow, Robert, 214
  Daniel, William, 225
  Reid, John, 736
  Robson & Hale, 762
  Smith, George, 826
Mountford, Henry, 733
Mountier, Thomas, 891
Mountsorrel (Leics.): Harris, Ralph, 402
Movette, 285
Mowain, William, 899
Mowbray, Paul, 615
Mowbray, William, 66, 116, 251
Mower, 520
Mower, William, 305
Moysant, Jacques, 615
M'Shane, 572
Mulley, Benjamin, 635
Mure, Hutchenson, 623
Murray, George, 531
Murray, John, 263
Murthly Castle (Perths.): Pugin, Augustus W.N., 721
Musgrove, 242
Mush, Frederick, 940
Musker, Robert, 161
Mycroft, George, 482
Myers, Edward, 70, 433, 570, 576, 752, 911
Myers, Watt, 458

N

Nafferton (Yorks): Preston, Francis, 714
Nailor, John, 4

Naish, Catherine, 980
Nantwich (Cheshire):
  Audley, William, 26
  Baker, John, 33
  Barker, John, 40
  Barton, George, 46
  Beckett, Charles, 56
  Binns, John, 73
  Birch, William, 74
  Bithell, Joseph, 76
  Blears, Joseph, 80
  Boles, Peter, 83
  Bolland, John W.J., 83
  Boughey, George, 90
  Boughey, Samuel, 90
  Boughton, George, 91
  Bowler, George, 93
  Burgess, Joseph, 130
  Burgess, William, 130
  Burroughs, Thomas, 133
  Dean, John, 237
  Dutton, Joseph, 262
  Gillion, Samuel, 341
  Hall, Thomas, 386
  Haywood, William, 416
  Heath, John, 418
  Heath, Randle, 418
  Heath, William, 419
  Hulms, John, 462
  Ikin, William, 470
  Jackson, George, 475
  Jackson, Joseph, 476
  Jeffrys, Thomas, 483
  Jennings, John, 485
  Jennings, Robert, 485
  Jennings, William, 485
  Judson, Thomas snr & jnr, 500
  Kay, Samuel, 501
  Kitchen, Henry, 518
  Kitchen, Richard, 518
  Latham, Joseph, 529
  Latham, Samuel, 529
  Leversage, Thomas, 539
  Maddock, James, 569
  Manchester, John, 572
  Millar, Henry, 607
  Newton, George, 644
  Owen, John Edward, 668
  Owen, Richard, 668
  Page, Joseph, 669
  Parkes, John snr & jnr, 675
  Parkes, William, 676
  Potovine, John, 707
  Pratchett, Thomas, 712
  Prince, Richard, 717
  Pritchard, Robert, 718
  Ravenscroft, James, 729
  Ravenscroft, John, 729
  Roberts, Samuel, 752
  Rogers, Andrew, 763
  Sherrett, Joseph jnr, 819
  Skerrett, Joseph snr, 819
  Spark(e)s, John, 841
  Speed, William, 842

Taylor, Thomas, 879
Tilsley, John, 895
Tomkinson, Charles, 898
Topham, George, 899
Turbitt, Johnson Thomas, 908
Vaughan, George, 920
Vaughan, George jnr, 920
Wade, George, 931
Walker, Thomas jnr, 938
Walley, Samuel, 940
Ward, G., 942
Welch, Charles, 956
Welch, John, 957
Whittle, Robert, 971
Wilkinson, George, 976
Wilkinson, James, 976
Willet, James, 978
Williams, James, 980
Williamson, Nicholas, 983
Wilson, John, 988
Wright, John, 1005
Wright, Richard, 1006
Yates, Isaac, 1012
Nash, Hall & Whitehorne, 385
Nash, Harry, 543
Nash, J., 756, 968
Nash, Thomas, 807
Neat, William, 430
Needham Market (Suffolk):
  Adams, John, 3
  Sadd, John, 775
  Steverson, William, 855
Needin, 983
Neill, J., 49, 390, 438
Nelson, John, 640
Nelson, S., 223
Nelson, Samuel, 266
Nelson, Thomas jnr, 81
Nelson (Lancs.): Ideson, Francis, 470
Neswick Hall (Yorks): Wright, Richard & Elwick, Edward, 1008
Neton, 234
Nevitt, Samuel, 287
New, Edward, 641
New, Frederick, 641
New Malton (Yorks): Dowthwaite, William, 255
New Romney (Kent): Bridge, William, 107
New Sleaford (Lincs.): Durham, Robert, 262
New Walsingham (Norfolk): Purdy, Robert, 722
Newall, Mathew, 113
Newall, Nathan, 908, 982
Newark (Notts.):
  Allice, William, 10
  Allin, William, 10
  Alliss, William, 11
  Barber, James, 38
  Barber, John Foster, 38
  Barber, Joseph Foster, 38
  Barber, Peter, 38

Barker, James, 40
Bellat(t)i & Sons, 63
Bettison, William, 69
Bostock, Edward, 89
Bradfield, Charlotte, 97
Bradfield, John, 97
Brooks, Andrew, 111
Brown, William, 119
Bugg, Thomas, 124
Derry, William, 241
Doubleday, George, 251
Ellis, J., 275
Harston, William, 405
Hulley, James, 462
Hutchinson, Henry, 468
Hutchinson, Thomas, 468
Jameson, Daniel, 480
Kelk, William, 503
Mercer, —, 601
Miles, William, 607
Morris, Robert, 629
Mycroft, John, 637
Newborn, Mary & Matilda, 642
Pearce, James, 684
Pettefor, Robert, 692
Ridge, John, 747
Ridge, Samuel, 747
Rippingale, Francis, 750
Stansall, Thomas, 849
Talbot, John, 870
Thompson, John, 887
Thompson, John jnr, 887
Turpin, Richard, 913
Watkin, John, 947
Wells, John, 957
Wells, Joseph, 957
Wells, William, 958
Williamson, William, 983
Winn, John, 992
Wynn, John, 1011
Newark Town Hall: Bellison, —, 63
Newberry, Francis, 1006
Newberry, George, 469
Newbery, Francis, 826
Newburgh Priory (Yorks.):
  Johnson, Thomas, 491
Newbury, Hannah, 601
Newbury, John, 83
Newbury (Berks.):
  Adler, George, 5
  Baker & Bright, 33
  Blugrove, Ann, 82
  Davies, William, 230
  Doe, John, 249
  Edmonds, Thomas, 267
  Elliott, George, 274
  Elliotts, James, 274
  Golding, Joseph, 348
  Gosling, John, 358
  Hircombe, Thomas, 434
  Jacobs, John, 477
  Kent, Richard, 508
  Knight, T.W., 519

Lamdin, Charles, 523
Lamdin, Joseph, 524
Merrick, Philip, 603
Merrick, William, 603
Palmer, William, 672
Prince, John, 717
Tooley, William, 899
Triggs, Messrs William, 904
Waller, William, 940
Webb, John, 953
Wright, Charles, 1004
Newby Hall (Yorks.):
  Adamson, Robert, 4
  Chippendale, Thomas snr, 165, 166, 167
  Chippendale, Thomas jnr, 168, 169
  Dodsworth, Thomas, 249
  Gomm, William & Richard, 350
  Reid, William, 736
Newby Park (Yorks.):
  Barker, William, 41
  Bradshaw, William, 100
  Chippendale, Thomas jnr, 169
  Hawkin(s), William, 413
  Reynoldson, George, 740
Newcastle:
  Aderson, Thomas, 5
  Alder, Caleb, 6
  Alderson, John, 7
  Alderson, Thomas, 7
  Amry, George, 12
  Anderson, J., 12
  Anderson, J. jnr., 12
  Anderson, John, 13
  Anderson, John jnr, 13
  Angus, Abraham Cooke, 15
  Angus, John, 15
  Angus, William, 15
  Annet, Thomas, 15
  Appleby, John, 16
  Appleton, William, 16
  Armstrong, Lawson, 18
  Armstrong, John, 18
  Atkinson, Robert, 24
  Avery, John, 27
  Aynsley, Robert, 28
  Baird, Thomas, 32
  Baker, Ann, 32
  Baker, John, 32
  Balmar, Adam, 36
  Bancks, Adam, 36
  Baptist, Alexander, 38
  Baptist & Angus, 38
  Barclay, Jacob, 39
  Barker, John, 40
  Baron, Robert, 43
  Barras, William, 44
  Barron, A.F., 45
  Bell, John, 62
  Bell, Richard, 62
  Bezilley, George, 70
  Bickadike, John, 70
  Blagburn, Willliam, 78

Blenkinsop, Thomas, 81
Bolam, John, 83
Bolam, Ralph, 83
Bolam, Robert, 83
Bolam, William, 83
Bollam, Robert, 83
Bolton, Ralph, 84
Booth, Nathaniel, 87
Bourne, Lancelot, 91
Brockbank, John, 109
Brown, —, 113
Brown, George, 114
Brown, Jacob, 114
Brown, Jacon jnr, 114
Brown, John, 116
Brown, Matthew, 117
Brown, Ralph, 117
Brown, Thomas, 118
Brown, William, 119
Brum(m)ell, George, 121
Brumwell, Jonathon, 122
Bulman, Hesilrigg, 128
Bulmer, —, 128
Bulmer, George, 128
Bulmer, Joseph, 128
Burnand, Richard, 131
Burrell, Samuel, 133
Davidson, Thomas, 228
Davis, —, 230
Dean & Jackson, 237
Delap, John, 239
Dennis, William, 240
Dixon & Waters, 247
Dobson, John, 247
Donaldson, William, 250
Donkin, William, 250
Dotchin, James, 251
Dotchin, Thomas & James, 251
Douglas, George, 251
Douthwaite, Anthony, 252
Downie, Alexander, 254
Duncan, William, 259
Dunn, John, 260
Dunn, Richard, 260
Dunn, William, 260
Duxfield, Ralph, 263
Easten, James, 265
Eastern, James, 265
Easton, George, 265
Eden, Francis, 266
Eden, Thomas, 266
Edgar, James, 266
Edon, —, 268
Eilkie, William, 975
Elliott, Ebenezer, 274
Elliott, Walter, 274
Elsdon, John, 277
Eltringham, John, 277
Embleton, John, 279
Garret, John, 331
Gibson, John jnr, 337
Gibson, John snr, 337
Gill, Joshua, 340
Glover, Jane, 345

Glover, Joseph, 345
Glover, Richard, 345
Glover, William, 345
Goodrick, John, 354
Graham, John, 361
Graham, Thomas, 363
Green, Denton, 367
Guthrie, J., 380
Hague, John, 382
Hall, Bentham, 384
Hall, Edward, 385
Hall, John, 385
Hall, Matthew, 386
Hall, Thomas, 386
Hardy, James jnr, 397
Hardy, R., 397
Hardy, Robert, 397
Harle, William, 398
Harrison, George, 403
Harrison, John, 403, 404
Hazelrigg, Medcalf, 416
Henderson, Andrew, 420
Henderson, Christopher, 420
Henderson, William, 421
Henzell, Gabriel, 422
Henzell, William, 422
Hills, William, 432
Hindmarsh, Matthew, 433
Hobson, James, 436
Hodgson, Daniel, 437
Hodgson, Philip, 438
Hogg, William, 440
Hopper, Richard Mandeville, 449
Hornsby, Thomas, 450
Horsley, Luke, 451
How, Bennett, 453
How, Charles, 453
Hudson, James, 458
Hudson, John, 458
Hudson, Joseph, 458
Hudson, William, 459
Hudspeth, John & Thomas, 460
Humbles, Messrs, 462
Hunt, Thomas, 465
Jacksom, James, 475
James, John, 479
James, Mathew, 479
Johnson, —, 489
Johnson, Edward, 489
Johnson, James, 489
Johnson, Robert, 490, 491
Johnson, William, 493
Jopling, William, 498
Jordan, George, 498
Kent, Bartholomew, 508
Kent, Samuel, 508
Kent, Thomas, 509
Kidd, Joseph, 511
King, James, 514
Lambert, John, 523
Lamb, Joseph, 522
Lamb, Michael, 522
Lamb, Nathaniel, 522
Lamb, Ralph, 522

Langley, George, 526
Langstaffe, Joseph, 527
Liddell, Gilbert, 541
Lisle, Devergy, 548
Lisle, John, 548
Lister, Jacob, 548
Lockley, Richard, 553
Lowes, George, 558
Lowes, Richard, 558
Lumsden, George, 560
Lumsdon, James, 560
Lunsdale, —, 561
McKay, James, 566
Mackenzie, Alexander, 566
Maddison, John, 569
Maddison, Michael, 569
Makepeace, Joseph, 570
M'Allister & Gibson, 563
Manners, Matthew, 573
Marr, Henry, 575
Marr, James, 575
Marr, Thomas, 575
Mather, Robert, 586
Medcalfe, Hesilrigg, 600
Melvin, J., 601
Metcalfe, Richard, 604
Metcalf(e), Robert, 603
Milbourne, Thomas, 606
Milburn, John, 606
Milburn, Joseph, 606
Milburn, Robert, 606
Millar, —, 607
Miller, James, 608
Miller's, 609
Mitchell, George, 613
Mitchell, James, 613
Mitchell, Patrick, 614
Mood, —, 616
Moor, George, 617
Moore, William, 622
Newton, John, 645
Nixon, William, 650
Pal(l)ister & Barkas, 671
Palmer, Robert, 672
Palmer, William, 672
Parker, Edward, 673
Parker, John, 674
Parker, Thomas, 675
Parker & Amry, 675
Parkinson, Joshua, 676
Parkinson, William, 676
Parson, William, 678
Pattison, John, 680
Pattison, Robert, 680
Pattison, Thomas, 681
Pearson, William, 685
Peers, Thomas, 686
Percival, N., 690
Perkins, Lewes, 690
Pether, Thomas, 692
Pigg, Cuthbert, 698
Plasket, Robert, 702
Pochaine, John, 703
Preston, Gawen, 714

Preston, William, 714
Pringle, William, 718
Priestman, Robert, 717
Punshon, John, 722
Quincey, Lawrence, 724
Rankin, John, 727
Ratcliff, John, 728
Rays(t)on, James, 731
Redford, Burdus, 733
Redford, Robert, 733
Redhope, John, 733
Reed, Henry, 734
Reed, John, 734
Reed, Joseph, 734
Reed, Robert, 734
Renwick, Robert, 737
Revely, Cuthbert, 737
Richardson, David, 743
Richardson, Francis, 743
Richardson, John, 744
Richardson, John & Thomas, 744
Richardson, Nathaniel, 744
Ridpeth, John, 747
Robertson, Adam, 755
Robinson, Cuthbert, 756
Robson, Anthony, 761
Robson, Benjamin, 761
Robson, Christopher, 761
Robson, David, 761
Robson, Dawson, 761
Robson, John, 761
Robson, Matthew, 761
Robson, Robert, 761
Robson, Timothy, 762
Robson & Spark, 762
Rosedon, Joseph, 766
Row, John B., 768
Rumford, C., 770
Rumford, Cuthbert, 770
Rumney, Robert, 770
Russel, James, 771
Rutherford, William, 773
Rut(t)ledge, William, 774
Saint, Thomas, 776
Salmon, Robert, 777
Sanderson, George, 779
Sanderson, William, 779
Sapwith, Thomas, 781
Scott, Nicholas, 790
Scott, Robert Sadler, 790
Scott, William, 791
Semple, —, 799
Sheen, James, 806
Sheen, Thomas, 806
Sheerwood, —, 806
Shields, George, 810
Shortridge, Christopher, 812
Shotton, William, 812
Simonton, Robert, 815
Small, Thomas Bell, 822
Smiles, James, 823
Smiles, William, 824
Smith, Edward, 825

Smith, John, 830
Smith, William, 833, 834
Sopwith, Jacob, 839
Sopwith, James, 839
Sopwith, T.J., 839
Sopwith, Thomas, 839
Spark, James, 841
Spark, John, 841
Spence, William, 843
Spencer, Robert, 844
Spooner, Joseph Henry, 845
Spoor, Amor, 845
Spour, George, 845
Stephenson, Adam, 853
Stephenson, George M., 853
Stephenson, George, 853
Stephenson, John, 853
Stephenson, Thomas, 854
Stokoe, John, 858
Story, William, 860
Straker, Jof., 860
Strickett, George, 861
Sturdy, George, 863
Talintyre, William, 870
Tate, George, 873
Tate, John, 873
Tate, Peter, 873
Taylor, William, 880
Thir(l)well, Robert, 882
Thompson, Mark, 887
Thompson, Robert, 887
Thompson, Thomas, 887
Thornhill, George, 890
Thurlston, Benjamin, 892
Todd, Robert, 897
Turnbull, Robert, 909
Turner, James, 910
Vickerson, Ralph, 923
Wallace, Charles, 939
Walton, Joseph, 942
Walton, Robert, 942
Wanless, John, 942
Ward, John, 943
Wardale, H., 944
Wardle, John, 944
Wardle, Ralph, 944
Wardle, Richard, 944
Watson, John jnr, 950
Watson, John snr, 949
Watson, Joseph, 950
Webster, Elizabeth, 955
Webster, Robert, 955
Webster, Simon, 955
Webster, Thomas, 955
West, Bryan, 959
West, George, 959
West, Joseph, 960
Wigham, Richard, 973
Wightman, Ralph, 973
Wilcox, Elizabeth & Son, 978
Wilkinson, John, 976
Wilkinson, Thomas, 977
Wilkinson, William, 977
Wilson, Robert, 989

Woodruff, Thomas, 1000
Young, George, 1014
Young, John, 1014
Newcastle Society of Antiquaries:
Farrington, Richard snr and jnr, 291
Newcastle-under-Lyme (Staffs.):
Audley, William jnr & John, 26
Beech, James, 58
Bentley, John, 66
Berrisford, John, 67
Betteley, Thomas, 69
Broomhall, John, 112
Ditchfield, John, 245
Eccles, Bowyer, 265
Edwards, Samuel, 270
Edwards, Thomas, 270
Gallimore, Robert, 328
Goodall, Joseph, 351
Goodall, Samuel, 351
Goodall, Thomas jnr, 351
Goodall, Thomas snr, 351
Goodall, William, 351
Greatbatch, Daniel, 366
Hand, Uriah, 393
Hand, Uriel, 393
Hand, William, 393
Hele, John, 420
Hill, Harry, 430
Hill, Josiah, 431
Hill, Thomas, 431
Hill, William, 431
Hollins, John, 443
Hunt, John, 464
Hutchinson, Thomas, 468
Jackson & Stalvies, 477
Lott, Timothy, 555
Lowe, George, 557
Ludlow, Thomas, 560
Mason, Theophilus, 584
Molineux, Joseph, 615
Palmer, John, 671
Parr, Richard, 677
Parr, Thomas, 677
Redshaw, John, 734
Redshaw, Thomas, 734
Robinson, John, 759
Russell, Joseph, 772
Sault, Joseph, 781
Sault, Richard, 782
Scarlet, Samuel, 788
Sheppard, John, 808
Sheppard, Richard, 808
Stalvies, John, 848
Stanway, Henry, 849
Stelves, John, 852
Stockton, John, 857
Stonier, Hugh, 859
Stonier, John, William, 859
Sudlow, T., 864
Taylor, Joseph, 878
Taylor, Michael, 878
Taylor, William, 880
Tew, Joseph, 881

Tittensor, Benjamin, 896
Tittensor, George, 896
Tittensor, John, 896
Toose, John, 899
Vyse, George, 930
Wilks, Thomas, 978
Newell, Nathan, 570
Newent (Glos.):
Merrett, Thomas, 603
Merritt, Robert, 603
Newham (Glos.):
Hook, John, 447
Shortman, Samuel, 812
Newington (London):
Bonsall, Richard, 86
Bunnett, W.& A., 129
Day, —, 236
Dickson, William, 244
Doke, Samuel, 249
Dolby, George, 249
Gardner, James, 330
Gee, William Charles, 334
Glover, W.J., 345
Goddard, William, 346
Hare, —, 397
Harrison, Samuel, 404
Herring, Joseph, 423
Hogg, —, 440
James, John & William, 479
Jones, William, 496
Luck, William, 560
Miller, James, 608
Pennell, Thomas, 688
Plumpton, John, 703
Sam(p)son, John, 778
Simmons, Samuel, 815
Skinner, David, 819
Smith, —, 824
Smith, William, 834
Staples, Thomas, 849
Talbor, Edward, 870
Turner, Robert, 911
Turner & Co., 913
Walker, Jasper, 935
Wear, John, 952
Webb, William, 954
West, John, 960
Willson, Joseph, 985
Wilson, William, 990
Young, Abraham, 1014
Young, James, 1014
Newington Butts (London):
Davies, John, 229
Herring, George, 423
Hillary, Thomas, 432
Jones, James, 495
Miller, Peter, 609
Mugg(e)ridge, Robert, 634
Oughton, Clement, 667
Price, Thomas, 716
Williams, William, 983
Young, Godfrey, 1014
Newman, 580

Newmarket (Suffolk):
Hull, Henry & Son, 462
Newman, William, 644
Rawlinson, Stephen, 730
Tait, William, 870
Newmarket Palace:
Elliott, Charles, 273
Jensen, Gerrit, 486
Parran, Benjamin, 677
Paudevin, John, 681
Russell, John, 772
Newnham Paddox (Warks.): King,
Benjamin, 514
Newns, Thomas, 542
Newport (Isle of Wight):
Abraham, David, 2
At(t)well, Thomas, 25
Brook, John, 111
Dashwood, Henry, 227
Deacon, William, 237
Douglas, Robert, 251
Exton, —, 286
Exton, Barnabas, 286
Horton, Richard, 451
Jenkins, Mary, 484
Jenkins, Thomas, 484
Jupe, Henry, 500
Kelly, James, 503
Lawrence, James, 531
Love, John, 556
Mew, Richard, 604
Milward, Stephen, 611
Morris, George, 628
Paine, Joseph, 670
Pember, Joseph, 688
Poore, John, 706
Poor, W., 706
Rayner, W., 731
Rayner, William, 731
Rowland, William, 769
Saunders, Stephen, 785
Silverlock, William, 814
Stoneley, Richard, 859
Sweet, Richard, 868
Tucker, B.B., 907
Turner, Joseph, 911
Urry, H.R., 918
Urry, Thomas, 918
Wavell, Jonathon, 952
Whitehouse, Joseph, 968
Newport Church (Essex): Grendey,
Giles, 372
Newport House (Herefs.):
Chapman, Edward, 157
Chebsey, John, 160
Gumley, Elizabeth & John, 380
Howard, John, 454
North, Robert snr, 655
Overton, Philip, 667
Padbury, Jon., 669
Perkins, Francis, 690
Phillmore, John, 696
Strode, Edward & John, 862
Winston, Sibill, 992

Newport Pagnell (Bucks.):
Knibb, George, 518
Miller, William, 609
Rose, Robert, 766
West, John, 960
Newsham, Henry, 601
Newton, 233, 234
Newton, George, 737
Newton, Isaac, 469
Newton, James, 294, 295, 645, 1010
Newton, John, 147, 240
Newton, Robert, 644
Newton, Stephen, 427
Newton Abbot (Devon):
Balsam, John, 36
Bartlett, Robert, 46
East, William, 265
Giles, Henry, 339
Hatchwell, Robert, 410
Henley, —, 421
Martin, Thomas, 581
Snelling, John, 836
Newton Bushel (Devon): Hendy, —
, 421
Newton Park, Bristol: Durant, I.,
261
Newton-upon-Ouse (Yorks.):
Hawitt, William, 412
Newtown Linford (Leics.):
Johnson, William, 492
Nias, Benjamin, 433
Nias, Benjamin Merriman jnr, 971
Nicholl & Brown, 645
Nicholls, 172
Nicholls, Henry, 45
Nicholls, Thomas, 99
Nicholls, Thomas the elder, 89
Nicholls, William, 919
Nichols, 68, 646
Nicholson, 191
Nicholson, John, 119, 647
Nicholson, Joseph, 497
Nicholson, W., 646
Nicholson & Boardman, 647
Nickalls, Thomas, 99, 952
Nicoll, Thomas, 700
Nicols, 666
Nies, Mary, 645
Nightingale, 23, 554
Nixon, Richard, 394
Noake, 863
Nockolds, Samuel, 264
Nodin, Samuel, 650
Norbury, John, 489
Norfolk: Townson, William, 902
Norgrove, 78
Norman, 645
Norman, Albert, 764
Norman, John, 808
Norman, Joseph, 856
Norman, Samuel, 11, 99, 117, 218,
387, 413, 531, 554, 555, 590,
592, 783, 784, 928, 959, 970, 971,
999

Norman & Metcalfe, 651
Normanton Park (Rutland):
    Alken, Sefferin, 8
    Bradburn(e), John, 96
    Chippendale, Thomas jnr, 169
    Dallain, Isaac, 224
    Mills, —, 609
    Stuart, Henry, 863
    Tat(h)am, Henry, 873
    Vile, William, 927
Norris, 441, 584
Norris, John, 428, 790
Norris, Samuel Taylor, 654
Norris, Thomas, 813, 996
Norris, William, 354, 445, 678
North, Benjamin, 727
North, Robert, 94, 238, 302
North, Robert snr, 525
North Cray (Lincs.):
    Goodison, Benjamin, 353
    Moore, James snr, 619
North Curry (Som.): Linton,
    Arthur, 548
North Scarle (Lincs.): Taylor,
    George, 875
North Shields (Northumb.):
    Ainsley, John, 5
    Alexander, John, 7
    Appleby, Robert, 16
    Aynsley, John, 28
    Bell, Thomas, 62
    Broderick, Henry, 109
    Dawson, Thomas, 235
    Dennis, John, 240
    Doninson, James, 247
    Gibson, John, 337
    Greenwell, Walter, 368
    Greenwell, William & John, 369
    Hall, James, 385
    Hall, Thomas, 386
    Hardy, James, 397
    Harriot, Archibald & John, 400
    Holder, George, 441
    Hudson, John, 458
    Hudson, Mrs, 458
    Kennedy, John, 506
    Kennedy, Thomas, 506
    Makepeace, Mark, 570
    Ornsby, William, 665
    Patrick, John, 680
    Pringle, William, 718
    Rae, John, 725
    Reay, George, 733
    Skipsey & Rutherford, 820
    Smith, Jackson, 827
    Spoor, —, 845
    Stewart, James, 856
    Stewart, Matthew, 856
    Stewart, William, 856
    Stonebanks, Robert, 859
    Stuart, Matthew, 863
    Swan, James, 867
    Swan, John, 867
    Trotter, Henry, 905

    Turnbull, John, 909
    Turnbull, William, 909
    Turner, William, 913
    Turpin, Robert, 913
    Usher, John, 918
    Young, Robert, 1015
North Walsham (Norfolk):
    Barwood, William, 47
    Goose, William, 355
    Hewitt, William, 426
    Kiddle, Charles, 511
    Kiddle, George, 511
    Lacey, John, 521
    Lacey, Richard Culley, 521
    Mace, John, 565
    Mace, Joseph, 565
    Mayer, Edward, 589
    Paul, William, 682
    Randell, John, 727
    Rice, Charles, 741
    Sillett, George, 814
Northallerton (Yorks.):
    Atkinson, John, 24
    Breckin, Thomas, 105
    Raw, Christopher, 729
    Robinson, William Stevinson,
    761
    Snowden, Robert, 837
    Tanfield, William, 871
    Thompson, Thomas, 888
    Wharton, George jnr, 962
Northampton:
    Ager, Josiah, 5
    Aman, George, 12
    Aman, Richard, 12
    Ash, Charles, 20
    Ashton, Jeremiah, 21
    Ashton, John, 21
    Barker, James, 40
    Barker, John, 40
    Barker, William, 41
    Brownsgrave, Arthur, 121
    Bryan, Mark, 122
    Bull, Ebenezer, 125
    Davis, William, 233
    Dexter, John Charles, 243
    Douglas, John, 251
    Edmonds, William, 267
    Eldridge, Thomas, 272
    Goodman, Benjamin, 354
    Hand, Daniel, 393
    Harris, Richard, 402
    Horn, Benjamin, 449
    Inwood, Benjamin, 472
    Kershaw, Charles, 510
    Kew, John, 511
    Kirshaw, Charles, 517
    Lee, William, 535
    Lenoir, Peter, 538
    Lewis, Jos. Ekins, 540
    Marriott, Willianm, 575
    Marshall, James, 578
    Mold, Thomas, 615
    Moon, James, 616

    Moore, William Henry, 622
    Nason, Charles William, 639
    Parbery, Thomas, 672
    Peirce, John Warwick, 687
    Peirce, Joseph, 687
    Peirce, William Warwick, 687
    Pierce, James, 698
    Pierce, Joseph, 698
    Pierce, Wm, 698
    Pitts, Ebenezer, 701
    Powell, Charles, 710
    Powell, John, 710
    Powell, Joseph, 710
    Richardson, John, 744
    Roberts, Thomas, 754
    Roddis, John, 762
    Russel(l), George, 771
    Smalley, John, 822
    Smith, William, 834
    Spokes, Thomas, 845
    Syred, Edward, 869
    Triggey, John jnr, 904
    Triggey, Joseph Fielding, 904
    Underwood, James, 917
    Vores, John, 930
    Westley, John, 961
    Wright, John, 1005, 1006
    York, Thomas, 1013
Northleach (Glos.): Bee, John jnr,
    58
Northouse, Joseph, 739
Northowram (Yorks.): Northend,
    John, 655
Northwich (Cheshire):
    Anderson, George, 12
    Bowden, James, 92
    Bratton, Edward, 103
    Burgess, John, 130
    Edge, Samuel, 266
    Heald, John, 417
    Hughes, Hugh, 460
    Percy, William, 690
    Sandbach, William, 778
    Skerrett, Joseph, 819
    Smith, George, 826
    Weston, William, 961
Norton, H., 176
Norton Conyers (Yorks.): Wright,
    Richard & Elwick, Edward, 1008
Norton Falgate (London):
    Elliott, Francis, 274
    Tate, William, 873
    Woolford, R., 1002
Norway, Ulefoss Manor House, nr
    Posgrunn: Seddon, George, 797
Norwich:
    Abel, Anthony, 1
    Abel, William, 2
    Alexander, John, 7
    Allwood, Thomas, 11
    Andrews, Henry, 14
    Arnold, George, 19
    Ashley, George, 20
    Atkins, —, 23

Bacon, Daniel, 28
Bagg, Charles Johannes, 29
Bailey, John jnr, 30
Bailey, Leonard, 30
Bales, Simon, 34
Baletti, Anthony, 35
Baltis, Matthew, 36
Barnaby, Edward Elden, 42
Barnard, John, 42
Barnham, James, 43
Barnham, John, 43
Barrant, Thomas, 44
Barrett, James, 44
Barroth, James, 45
Barwick, John, 47
Batley, William, 49
Baxter, Thomas, 52
Bell, Edmund Hurst, 61
Bell, Edward, 61
Bell, John, 62
Bennett, Thomas, 65
Bentle, James, 66
Besfield, R. & J., 68
Best, Samuel, 68
Bexfield, J., 70
Bexfield, James, 70
Bexfield, John, 70
Bexfield, Joseph, 70
Bexfield, Richard, 70
Bexfield, William, 70
Bitton, William, 76
Blazeby, James, 80
Blazeby, John, 80
Blomfield, John, 81
Blumfield, James, 82
Boltz, Thomas, 84
Bone, John, 85
Bore, Robert, 87
Boswell, William, 90
Bowles, Bernard, 93
Bowles, John S., 93
Bracey, William, 95
Brackett, William Bury, 95
Bradbury, John, 97
Brettingham, Robert, 106
Briggs, James, 107
Britisle, James, 108
Broitehall, Henry, 110
Brooke, Francis, 111
Brooke, William, 111
Brooke(s), William, 111
Brown, Gregory, 114
Brown, John, 116
Browne, Jonas, 120
Browne, Joshua, 120
Browne, Peregrine, 120
Brownes, Matthias, 120
Brunning, John, 122
Brunton, James, 122
Brunton, Thomas Page, 122
Bull, Henry, 125
Bullidge, William, 126
Burcham, Peter, 129
Burrage, John, 132

Burt, David, 134
Burt, William, 134
Bush, Henry, 136
Bush, Robert, 136
Butter, John, 138
Buttifant, John, 139
Buttifant, Jonathan, 139
Buttifant, Thomas, 139
Dady, James, 223
Dansie, William, 225
Darkin, George, 226
Darkin, James, 226
Darkin, Robert, 227
Darkins, Robert, 227
David, William Heron, 228
Dawson, Samuel, 235
De Caux, William, 238
Deeker, James, 238
Dell, Nathaniel, 239
Demee, Daniel, 240
Ding, John, 245
Downing, Jos., 254
Driver, Sam., 256
Drury, Edmund, 257
Duckett, William, 257
Dunning, Thomas, 261
Durrant, Thomas jnr, 262
Durrant, Thomas snr, 262
Earl, Elden, 264
Earl, William Eden, 264
Earle, Thomas, 264
Easter, William, 265
Edwards, William, 271
Elden, William, 271
Elliott, David, 274
Elvin, Robert, 277
Emmens, Edward jnr, 280
Emmes, Edward snr, 280
English, William, 281
Ganning, Timothy, 329
Gardiner, John, 329
Gedge, Ambrose, 334
Gidney, Christopher, 338
Gill, James Carver, 340
Gill, William, 340
Gillman, John, 341
Gillman, William, 341
Gilney, Christopher, 344
Girling, James, 344
Gobart, John, 346
Gobart, Thomas, 346
Godman, John, 347
Gooch, James, 350
Goodman, Stephen, 354
Goreham, Edward, 358
Grant, William, 364
Gray, Joseph, 365
Gray, Robert, 365
Gray, William Holden, 366
Green, Thomas, 367
Greenfinch, Benjmain, 368
Greenwood, Erasmus, 369
Gridley, Timothy, 373
Grimmer, Thomas, 375

Gulley, John, 378
Gunton, James, 380
Gurney, Samuel, 380
Gynne, George snr & jnr, 381
Hales, James, 383
Hall, William, 386
Halls, William jnr, 390
Hamm, Henry, 391
Hanison, Henry, 394
Hardingham, Nicholas, 396
Hardy, John jnr, 397
Hare, Robert, 397
Harmer, Wodehouse, 399
Harold, John, 399
Harold, Thomas, 399
Harold, William, 399
Harper, Joseph, 399
Harrison, —, 403
Harrison, James, 403
Harrison, William, 404
Harston, Standish, 405
Hart, William, 406
Hartstongue, Robert, 407
Hartstongue, Standish, 407
Harwood, Thomas, 408
Hatch, William, 410
Hatch, William Proctor, 410
Hawkins, —, 412
Hawkins, Parker, 413
Hawkins, Robert, 413
Helmes, Robert, 420
Helsdon, Langley, 420
Hicklenton, William, 427
Hicks, Leonard, 428
Higgins, Henry, 428
Higgins, Maria, 428
Hogg, John, 440
Holl, Samuel, 441
Holmes, James, 445
Holmes, John, 445
Homer, William, 446
Hoothe, John, 448
Horn, Edward, 449
Horner, James Horner, 450
Horsley, William, 451
Horth, John, 451
Houghton, Richard, 452
Howell, James, 455
Howes, Simon, 456
Howlett, Charels, 456
Howlett, Heasman Thomas, 456
Howlett, Henry, 456
Howlett, Launcelot, 456
Howlett, Stephen, 456
Howlett, Thomas, 456
Hoyle, Isaac, 456
Hubbard, —, 456
Hubbard, James, 456
Hubbard, William, 457
Huby, Henry, 457
Huby, Richard, 457
Huby, William, 457
Huggins, Henry, 460
Huggins, Richard, 460

Hutton, Robert, 469
Huwood, Thomas, 469
Ireland, Richard, 473
Ivory, Thomas, 474
Jagger, Benjamin, 478
James, Charles, 478
Jarvis, Henry, 481
Jarvis, Thomas, 481
Jary, Roger, 481
Jenny, Winslow, 485
Jones, C., 494
Kemp, James, 504
Kemp, Thomas, 504
Kendall, Robert, 505
Kendall, William, 505
Kerr, J., 510
Kerr, James, 510
Kerry, John, 510
Kettle, James, 511
King, —, 514
King, Elizabeth H., 514
King, William, 515
Kinnebrook, David, 516
Kinnebrook, William, 516
Kitten, John, 518
Kittle, James, 518
Ladbrooke, Robert, 521
Laddell, Robert Stephen, 521
Laeth, Samuel, 533
Lake, Thomas Constable, 521
Lake, William, 521
Lancaster, James, 524
Lander, Paul, 524
Lane, Israel, 525
Lane, Richard, 525
Lane, Robert, 525
Lannder, Paul, 527
Larrance, Samuel, 528
Larter, Thomas, 528
Larter, William, 528
Latten, James, 529
Latton, James, 529
Lawes, Samuel, 530
Lawrance, Samuel, 530
Lay, William, 532
Leggett, Samuel, 537
Lewes, Edward Tyler, 539
Lincoln, Robert, 542
Lindsay, William, 543
Lindsey, Sarah, 543
Ling, Mrs Elizabeth, 543
Ling, John T., 543
Ling & Son, 543
Linger, James, 543
Loader, Obadiah, 551
Lord, Aaron, 555
Lovewell, T.S., 557
Manthorpe, James, 573
Margarom, Robert William, 574
Marks, John, 574
Martin, —, 580
Martin, Charles, 580
Martin, Samuel, 581
Martin, Thomas, 581

Martin & Perry, 582
Martin & Smith, 582
Mason, George, 583
Mason, Henry John, 583
Mason, William, 584
Mason & Norris, 584
Mathue, Samuel, 586
Matser, Robert, 572
May, Edward, 589
Meens, John, 600
Mien, Robert, 605
Miles, Joseph, 607
Miller, Ruth, 609
Mills, David, 610
Mills, Joseph, 610
Mills, William, 611
Mingay, John, 612
Minns, James jnr, 612
Molden, Edward, 615
Molden, Nathaniel, 615
Money, Timothy, 616
Monk, John, 616
Monsear, Robert, 616
Monthorpe, James, 616
Moore, Mary, 620
Moore, Stephen, 621
Moore, William, 622
Morris, John, 628
Morris, William, 629
Mounsear, Robert, 633
Mowain, William, 633
Mumford, William, 635
Nelson, Thomas jnr, 641
Newdigate, Christopher, 642
Newson, John, 644
Nichols, Henry, 646
Nickolds, Samuel, 647
Norfor, James, 651
Norris, James, 654
Norris, John, 654
Norris, John jnr, 654
Norris, Paul, 654
Norris, Samuel, 654
Norris, Thomas, 654, 655
Norris, William, 655
Northern, J., 655
Norton, John, 656
Norton, Robert, 656
Notley, William, 656
Nurse, Robert, 657
Osborn, Robert, 665
Osborne, John, 666
Page, Thomas, 670
Palmer, Benjamin, 671
Palmer, William, 672
Parke, Luke, 673
Parnell, Joseph, 676
Parot, James, 677
Partridge, Nathaniel, 678
Paul, William, 682
Pawsey & Smith, 682
Pearce, William, 684
Pearson, David, 684
Peete, Richard, 686

Peete, Robert, 686
Pennington, John, 689
Philips, John jnr, 694
Pigg, Joseph, 698
Pleasants, Robert, 703
Pool, Richard, 705
Pooley, John, 706
Pope, Thomas, 706
Punchard, Jeremiah, 722
Punchard, Robert, 722
Purdy, Richard, 722
Quilley, William, 724
Rackham, James, 725
Rackham, John, 725
Rainer, Thomas, 726
Rayner, Thomas III, 731
Rayner, Thomas jnr & snr, 731
Rayner, William, 731
Record, John, 733
Reeve, Samuel, 735
Renton, George, 737
Reynolds, John, 738
Rice, Zachariah, 741
Riches, Robert, 745
Riches, Robert jnr, 745
Rickard, John, 746
Ringer, Mrs Elizabeth, 750
Ringer, James, 750
Robbins, Joseph, 751
Roberts, Richard, 752
Robins, John, 755
Roe, Benjamin Hambling, 762
Rogers, Thomas, 764
Roope, James, 765
Rossi, George, 767
Rudd, Francis, 770
Rudd, John, 770
Rudd, Thomas, 770
Rudd, William snr & jnr, 770
Rullidge, Charles, 770
Rullidge, William, 770
Runnage, William, 771
Rutter, Gascoigne, 774
Ryder, Francis, 774
Sabberton, Joshua, 774
Sadler, George, 775
Safreey, Thomas, 775
St Quinton, Percy, 776
Salmon, Abraham, 777
Salmon, Isaac, 777
Salmon, Richard, 777
Salmon, Sarah, 777
Sancroft, Joshua Baker, 778
Savory, David, 786
Scott, John, 790
Scott, Robert, 790
Scott, Samuel, 790
Scott, William, 791
Scotter, Joseph, 791
Secker, Thomas, 793
Self, James, 799
Self, Thomas Coswll, 799
Sewter, Robert, 801
Sharp, Edward, 802

Sharp, John, 803
Sharp, Samuel, 803
Sharp, William, 803
Sharwood, James, 804
Shaw, William Henry, 806
Sheen, Edmund Henry, 806
Shenfield, John, 807
Shreeve, William, 813
Silcock, Jacob, 814
Silcock, Obadiah, 814
Slater, Charles, 820
Slater, John, 820
Smee, Samuel, 823
Smith, - jnr, 824
Smith, Benjamin, 824
Smith, Christopher Hill, 825
Smith, Edward, 825
Smith, J., 827
Smith, Thomas, 832
Smith, William, 833
Smith, Wright, 835
Soloman, John, 838
Solomon, John, 838
Solomon, Joshua Edward, 838
Solomon, Samuel, 838
Sowter, Robert, 841
Spooner, Richard F., 845
Springall, Cubitt Paul, 846
Stannard, R., 849
Stannard, Richard, 849
Staveley, Thomas, 850
Stevens, William, 854
Steward, Richard, 855
Steward, Robert, 855
Stocking, John, 857
Stone, Charles, 858
Sudbury, James, 864
Tabb, Charles, 869
Tagge, Henry Cowell, 870
Tagger, Benjamin, 870
Tallack, William, 870
Tarte, Frederick James L., 873
Taylor, Charles, 874
Taylor, Thomas Paston, 879
Taylor & Utting, 880
Terry, Robert, 881
Thirtle, John, 882
Thompson, James, 886
Thompson, Thomas jnr, 887
Thorn, Edward, 889
Thorne, —, 889
Thorpe, Edward, 891
Thursby, William, 892
Thurston, Samuel, 893
Thurtle, Thomas, 893
Tillyard, Susan, 895
Titter, Benjamin Palmer, 896
Tomlinson, William, 898
Tompson, Jacob, 898
Tooke, William Barber, 899
Tubb, Samuel, 906
Tubby, Samuel, 906
Tunney, Thomas, 908
Turner, Henry, 910

Turner, James, 910
Turner, John Swanton, 911
Twiddy, George, 914
Twiddy, James, 914
Utting, Henry, 918
Utting, James Henry snr & jnr, 918
Vincent, John, 929
Vincent, William, 929
Wade, John, 931
Wade, John Wright, 931
Waite, James, 932
Wardell, Gilbert, 944
Waterson, John, 947
Watson, Gilbert, 949
Watts, Samuel, 951
Watts, Samuel Moses, 951
Webster, George, 955
Wells, John, 957
Wellsman, Henry, 958
Wheeler, James, 963
White, Dean, Edward, 965
Wiles, Samuel, 975
Wilsea, Samuel, 986
Wilson, John snr & jnr, 987
Wilson, William, 990
Witherington, Richard, 994
Withers, Henry, Maria, 994
Wollverton, Edmund, 1002
Wolverton, Edward, 995
Wood, Edward, 996
Wood, Philip, 997
Wooltorton, Edmund, 1002
Wooltorton, James Poston, 1002
Yallop, Jeremiah, 1011
Yallop, Jeremiah Grindley, 1011
Nostell Priory (Yorks.):
  Barker, Robert jnr, 41
  Chippendale, Thomas snr, 165, 166, 167
  Chippendale, Thomas jnr, 168, 169
  Disney, John, 245
  Reid, William, 736
  Vaughan, Samuel, 920
  Ward, Thomas, 944
  Wright, Richard & Elwick, Edward, 1007
Notley, 574
Notley, William, 403
Notloy, William, 190
Nottingham:
  Adderton, John, 4
  Addicot, Edward, 4
  Addicot, John, 4
  Allen, Silas, 10
  Allen, William, 10
  Anderton, —, 13
  Appley, Robert snr, 16
  Armstrong, Francis, 18
  Ashby, William, 20
  Ashmole, David, 21
  Ashton, John, 21
  Asling, William, 22

Attenborough, George, 25
Attenborough, Job, 25
Atterbury, Job, 25
Avison, William, 27
Bacon, Mark, 28
Bagshaw, John, 29
Bailey, Gilbert, 30
Ball, William, 35
Banks, Joseph, 37
Barker, John, 40
Barnett, C., 43
Barnsdall, Edward, 43
Barnsdall, Joseph, 43
Barton, Frank, 46
Bartram, William, 47
Barwick, James, 47
Beedham, James, 58
Bell, Thomas, 63
Berles, Rob., 68
Bestall & Widley, 68
Betson, John, 69
Binkley, George, 72
Bird, William Edward, 74
Birtles, Robert, 75
Black, John, 76
Blackwell, William, 78
Bonsor, Henry, 86
Boot, Aaron, 87
Breckels, Thomas, 105
Bregazzi, Innocent & Peter, 105
Bretland, George, 105
Broadhurst, George, 109
Brooksbank, Timothy, 112
Brotherhood, Samuel, 112
Brothers, Benjamin, 112
Brothers, Mary, 112
Brough, Mrs, 113
Brown, James, 115
Bruntnell, William, 122
Brydone & Son, 123
Bull, George, 125
Bull, William, 125
Burchby, Francis, 129
Burden, Anne, 129
Burden, Robert, 130
Burrows, Francis, 133
Burton, Robert, 135
Butcher, John, 137
Butler, Robert, 137
Darker, John Lomas, 226
Dawson, William, 235
Dean, William, 237
Dennis, James, 240
Dennis, William, 240
Dickinson, Richard, 243
Dixon, Moses, 246
Dodd, Samuel, 248
Dodsley & Weston, 249
Drewry, Benjamin, 256
Drewry, John, 256
Drewry, William, 256
Eden, John, 266
Eden, William, 266
Eley, John, 272

Elliott, Francis, 274
Elliott, John, 274
Elliott, Thomas, 274
Elsey, William, 277
Ely, —, 279
England, George, 281
England, John, 281
Everitt, John, 285
Gear, Samuel, 333
Gee, Edward, 334
Gilsthorpe, George, 344
Goadby, John, 345
Goodrich, William, 354
Greasley, John, 366
Green, Jospeh, 367
Green & Elliott, 368
Greenshield, David, 368
Greenwood, Thomas, 369
Gregory, Robert, 370
Grundy, Joseph, 377
Grundy, William, 377
Guggiari, Domenico, 377
Guzziari, Domenico, 381
Halfpenny, John, 384
Halfpenny, Joseph, 384
Hall, James, 385
Hall, John, 385
Hallam, E., 387
Hallam, Edward, 387
Hallam, John, 387
Hallam, Joseph, 387
Hallam, Thomas, 387
Hallam & Green, 387
Hallam & Pid(l)ock, 387
Hallert, John, 387
Hallet, J.M., 387
Hallet(t), JOhn, 387
Hallum & Pidcock, 390
Hammond, William, 392
Harrison, John, 404
Harrison, William, 405
Hawksley, Francis, 413
Hawley, William, 413
Hazard, Thomas, 416
Heald, John, 417
Heard, John, 417
Hedderley, Thomas, 419
Hedderley, William, 419
Hemsley, William, 420
Henshaw, John, 422
Hill, Charels, 430
Hodgkinson, Isaac, 437
Holmes, Edward, 444
Holmes, Rob, 445
Hopewell, John, 448
Horne, John, 449
Housley, Peter, 452
Hunt, John, 464
Hunter & Wyles, 466
Hutchinson, George, 468
Hutchinson, Thomas, 468
Hutton, Thomas, 469
Inglesant, William, 471
Jackson, John, 476

Jalland, John, 478
James, Thomas, 480
Jebb, Joshua, 482
Johnson, A.E., 489
Johnson, Edwin, 489
Johnson, William, 492
Jones, Edward, 494
Jones, William, 498
Kayes, Michael snr & jnr, 501
Keys, Michael, 511
Killingley, Edward, 512
Killingley, Joseph, 512
Kirkham, William, 517
Knight, Elizabeth, 519
Knight, John, 519
Knighton, William, 520
Lackenby, William, 521
Lakin, Thomas, 521
Laking, Thomas, 522
Larking, Thomas, 528
Laughton, Henry, 529
Lawson, —, 531
Lawson, Elizabeth, 531
Lawson, James, 532
Lawson, Matthew, 532
Lawson, Thomas, 532
Leader, George, 533
Leake, William, 533
Lee, James, 534
Lees, George, 536
Lees, James, 536
Lees, John, 536
Lees, Philip, 536
Lees, Thomas, 536
Lees & Redgate, 536
Levitt, John, 539
Lock, William Cook, 552
Lomas, Jos., 554
Machen, Lancelot, 565
Maltby, William, 571
Malton, Thomas, 572
Mann, John, 572
Marr, William, 575
Marriott, Mrs, 575
Mather, H., 585
Mather, John, 585
Mather, Mrs, 585
Mather & Son, 586
Maudsley, Henry, 587
Meadows, Samuel, 599
Meller, Richard, 601
Milligan, Thomas, 609
Millington, Matthew, 609
Milner, William, 611
Misson, John, 613
Mitchell, J., 613
Mitchell, John, 613
Moore, —, 617
Mosley, Henry, 632
Moss, John, 632
Muggleston, Isaac, 634
Newell, James, 642
Newton, William, 645
Nightingale, William, 648

Osborn, Joseph, 665
Osborne, Joseph, 666
Owen, John, 668
Pell, Thomas, 687
Pidcock, William, 697
Poole & Jeffs, 706
Porter, Joseph, 707
Potter, Samuel, 708
Poynton, Edward, 711
Radcliffe, Albert, 725
Richards, Sam., 742
Richardson, Henry, 743
Rider, Francis, 746
Rippon, John, 750
Rushworth, William, 771
Russell, Richard, 773
Sands, Benjamin, 780
Saxton, Joshua, 787
Saxton, Thomas, 787
Sharp, Thomas, 803
Sharpe, Frederick George, 803
Shelton, John, 806
Shepherd, William, 808
Sheraton, Ninian John, 808
Sheraton, Ralph, 808
Shipley, John, 811
Simmons, William, 815
Simons, William, 815
Skerrett, Samuel, 819
Skinner, Thomas, 820
Smart, Daniel, 823
Smart, Francis, 823
Smart, Sarah, 823
Smart, Thomas, 823
Smith, James jnr, 827
Smith, James snr, 827
Smith, Job, 828
Smith, John, 830
Smith, John & William, 830
Spencer, William, 844
Stainrod, Samuel, 847
Stainrod & Byfield, 848
Stevens, Isaac, 854
Stevenson, Ann, 855
Stevenson, Nathaniel, 855
Stocks, Robert, 857
Stokes, George, 858
Stone, Thomas, 859
Stoney, Benjamin, 859
Stoney, William, 859
Swan, William, 867
Tann, William, 871
Taylor, David, 875
Taylor, James, 876
Taylor, James & William, 876
Taylor, Thomas, 879
Taylor, William, 879
Taylor & Son, 880
Thornhill, William, 890
Thurman, Thomas, 892
Thurman & Attenborough, 892
Tiddiman, George, 894
Tiddiman, Joseph, 894
Tilley, John, 894

Torr, Thomas, 900
Tort, Thomas, 900
Towle, W., 900
Towle, William, 900
Toyne, John, 902
Trubshaw, James, 906
Trustwell, Joseph, 906
Unwin, John, 917
Walker, Robert, 937
Ward, John, 943
Ward, Sam, 943
Warrick, Joseph, 946
Webster, Thomas, 956
Welch, John, 957
Wells, Joseph, 957
Weston, Field, 961
Weston, George, 961
Weston, Stephen, 961
Weston & Lodsley, 961
Wheatley, William, 962
Whitby, James, 964
Whitby, John, 964
Whitby, Stephen, 964
Whitworth, John, 971
Whitworth & Greasley, 972
Wightman, William, 973
Wild, Nathaniel, 974
Wild, William, 974
Wildey, John, 974
Wilkinson, Caleb, 975
Wilkinson, John, 976
Wilkinson, Richard, 977
Wilkinson, Samuel, 977
Wilkinson, Stephen, 977
Williamson, Richard, 983
Wilson, Joseph, 988
Wood, Thomas, 998
Woodford, John, 999
Woodhall, John, 999
Woodsend, John & William, 1000
Woodward, Samuel, 1001
Woodward, Thomas, 1001
Wright, Henry, 1005
Wright, John, 1005, 1006
Wright, Joseph, 1006
Wright, Robert, 1008
Noutners : Wapshott, Robert, 942
Noyes, Edward, 234
Nuneaton (Warks.):
  Ballard, J., 35
  Barrowclough, William, 45
  Burrowclough, William, 133
  Haddon, Joseph, 382
  Payne, William, 683
  Randle, Charles, 727
  Swan, Thomas, 867
  Wheway, James, 963
Nunnykirk House (Northumb.):
  Humble, John, 462
Nye, Edmund, 295
Nye, James, 295

O

Oakey, Thomas, 1012

Oakham (Leics.):
  Baines, William, 32
  Hand, Thomas, 393
  Pennistone, —, 689
  Sharpe, Nathaniel, 803
  Smith, Henry, 826
Oakley, 845
Oakley, Benjamin, 660
Oakley, George, 274, 510, 661, 662
Oakley, H., 660
Oakley Park (Beds.):
  Erwood, James, 282
  Kerr, John, 510
  Mayhew, John & Ince, William, 597
  Wood, Henry, 996
Oates, Christopher, 859
O'Donnell, Hugh, 150
Ody, John, 662
Officer, James, 101
Offord, 817
Ogleby, Richard Gorse, 22
Ogleforth (Yorks.):
  Hubie, John, 457
  Hubie, William, 457
  Layton, Thomas, 533
Okeover Hall (Staffs.):
  Hallett, William snr, 388
  Patrick, —, 679
Okey, Charles, 950
Old, Thomas, 86
Old Bethlem (London): Rawlings, William, 730
Old Brentford (Middlx): Atwell, Richard, 25
Old Malton (Yorks.): Spaven, Simpson, 842
Oldbury (Birmingham): Downing, Joseph, 254
Older, George, 662
Oldham (Lancs.):
  Bancroft, John, 36
  Brock, John, 109
  Hudson, William, 459
  Lawson, William, 532
  Read, George, 732
  Read, John, 732
  Snowden, Thomas, 837
Oldmeadow, James, 181, 197, 217, 685, 1014
Olive, William, 33
Oliver, 161, 692
Oliver, John, 315
Oliver, Mark, 473, 844
Oliver, William, 760
Ombersley Court (Worcs.): Elward, George & Marsh, William, 279
O'Neill, 453
O'Neill, Alan Francis, 664
O'Neill, Charles, 911
O'Neill, J., 330
O'Neill, John, 74, 261, 263, 281, 307, 434, 706
Onely, John, 490

Ongar (Essex): Scruby, James, 791
Oram, 946
Orchard, John, 664
Orierie, Adam Wilkinson, 161
Orme, John, 159
Orme, Thomas, 482
Ormskirk (Lancs.):
  Balshaw, Charles, 36
  Balshaw, John, 36
  Blundell, John, 82
  Davies, James, 228
  Goore, Charles, 355
  Goore, James, 355
  Goore, Thomas, 355
  Gore, James, 358
  Heald, William, 417
  Highton, William, 429
  Huyton, William, 469
  Lawson, James, 532
  Lolli, John, 554
  Martin, John, 581
  Martin, Thomas, 581
  Martlew, Richard, 582
  Martley, Richard, 582
  Moor(e)croft, James, 617
  Morefly, Henry, 623
  Moresly, Henry, 625
  Nuttall, Thomas, 657
  Scott, James, 789
  Sourbuts, William, 840
  Twist, Samuel, 915
  Wainwright, Richard, 932
  Walker, L.W., 936
  Watkinson, Henry jnr, 948
Orton, Robert, 787
Osborn, 575
Osborn, Arthur, 43, 291, 463, 495
Osborn, John, 45, 276
Osborn, Robert, 192
Osborne, Arthur, 453
Osborne, James, 908
Osborne, John, 329
Osborne, John Benjamin, 77
Osborne, Thomas, 881
Osborne, William, 457
Osborne House (Isle of Wight):
  Taprell, Stephen & Holland, William, 872
Osbourne, Arthur, 898
Osmotherly (Yorks.): Weighill, Christopher, 956
Ossett (Yorks.): Brook, Richard, 111
Osterley Park (Middlx):
  Beck, Arnold Frederick, 56
  Clay, Henry, 177
  Gilbert, John, 338
  Haupt, Georg, 411
  Jean, Peter Dominique, 482
  Linnell, John, 544, 545
  Linnell, William, 547
  Moore, Thomas, 621
  Newton, James, 644
  Ravald & Morland, 729

Webb, Henry, 953
Oswald & Nichols, 646
Oswestry (Salop):
 Arnold, William, 19
 Brougall, James, 113
 Edwards, W., 271
 Gabriel, James, 326
 Hughes, Richard, 461
 Hughes, William, 461
 Jones, Ellis, 494
 Jones, J., 495
 Jones, John, 495
 Maddox, Richard, 569
 Mellor, William, 601
 Morris, Griffith, 628
 Parry, John, 677
 Parry, Joseph, 677
 Price, George, 715
 Price, Griffith, 715
 Price, John, 716
 Pritchard, John, 718
 Pritchard, Samuel, 718
 Smallman, Edward, 822
 Southall, John, 840
 Taylor, John, 877
 Taylor, Richard, 878
 Vaughan, Edward, 920
Otley (Yorks.):
 Aspinal, John, 22
 Bowling, John, 93
 Brown, John, 116
 Burley, Thomas, 131
 Burrow, William, 133
 Dawson, James jnr, 235
 Dawson, William, 235
 Harrison, John, 404
 Kendall, James, 504
 Kendall, John, 505
 Kendall, Nathaniel, 505
 Kendall, William, 505
 Mountain, John, 633
 Rhodes, Richard, 740
 Richardson, Jonathon, 744
 Rollinson, Richard, 764
 Saxton, William, 787
 Smith, John, 830
 Smith, Samuel, 832
 Smithson, John, 836
 Spence, Joseph, 843
 Stubbs, Joseph, 863
 Taylor, Matthew, 878
 Thompson, Abraham, 885
 Thompson, Richard, 887
 Thompson, Robert, 887
 Waddington & Wood, 930
 Walker, John, 936
 Wood, William, 998
 Yates, James, 1012
Ottery St Mary (Devon):
 Harris, —, 400
 Harris, William, 403
 Kenwood, William, 509
 Pocock, L., 703
Otty, John, 275

Oulton (Cumb.): Mitchinson, John, 614
Oundle (Northants.):
 Bevan, George, 69
 Bevins, John, 69
 Gann, John, 329
 Ganns, Richard, 329
 Hosted, Samuel, 451
 Smith, Benjamin, 824
 Vickers, J., 923
Ourdie, Andrew, 722
Ouseburn (Newcastle): Goodall, David, 351
Ousegate (York): Brown(e), Matthew snr, 116
Outhwaite, 461
Ovenston, J., 44
Overlove, J., 602
Overlove, John, 722, 931
Overton, 366
Owen, 200, 974
Owen, Henry, 376
Owen, John, 27, 283
Owens, Edward John, 664
Owston (Lincs.):
 Temperton, Edward, 880
 Waterhouse, Solomon, 946
Owthwaite, 531
Oxenham, Samuel, 669
Oxenham, Thomas, 138, 626
Oxenthorpe (Yorks.): Pollard, William, 705
Oxford:
 Adames, Charles James, 3
 Adams, George snr., 3
 Adams, James, 3
 Archer, Robert, 17
 Ashold, John, 21
 Atkins, John, 23
 Badcock, Charles, 28
 Badcock, Francis, 28
 Badcock, John, 28
 Badcock, Martha, 28
 Badcock, Richard, 28
 Badcock, Thomas, 28
 Bardin, Samuel, 39
 Beckett, John, 57
 Beckett, William, 57
 Bishop, Samuel, 76
 Bletsoe, James, 81
 Bletsor, William, 81
 Blettsoe, William, 81
 Blofeld, —, 81
 Braithwaite, John, 101
 Bush, William, 136
 Davis, Philip, 232
 Day, Michael, 236
 Day & Parker, 236
 Dicks, William Andrew, 244
 Edmonds, William, 267
 Evans, James, 284
 Evins, James, 286
 Gee, Richard, 334
 Giles, James, 339

Goolding, Henry, 355
Green, John, 367
Halfe, James, 384
Halfe, Thomas, 384
Halse, James, 391
Hanwell, John, 395
Hartley, Edward, 406
Hastings, John, 409
Hayes, James, 414
Higgins, John, 428
Holder, William, 441
Holloway, Richard, 444
Ivory, Richard, 474
Jackman, Paul, 474
James, George, 478
Jones, David William, 494
Keel, William, 502
Keele, Arthur, 502
Kirtland, John, 517
Knibb, —, 518
Leach, Charles, 533
Linnell, William, 547
Linsell, George, 548
Litchfield, William, 549
Mallam, Robert & Charles, 571
May, Charles, 588
Melsham, Joseph, 601
Merrick, William, 603
Messenger, Charles, 603
Millsham, Joseph, 611
Milsham, Thomas, 611
Munday, Thomas, 635
Newell, John, 642
Newman, John, 643
Newman, Ralph, 643
Newman, Robert, 643
Newman, Thomas, 643
Orson, John, 665
Parker, William, 675
Paviour, John, 682
Payne, John, 682
Payne, Mary, 682
Payne, William, 683
Phillips, Matthew, 695
Powell, Richard, 710
Prother, Hugh, 719
Ransford, Charles, 727
Rause, Richard, 728
Reynolds, John, 738
Richards, Benjamin, 741
Roberts, Adrian, 751
Robinson, William, 760
Rouse, Richard, 768
Rowell, George Auguste, 769
Ryman, James, 774
Saunders, Edward, 782
Saunders, Peter, 785
Saunders, Thomas, 785
Seabright, Joseph, 791
Seabright, Mark, 791
Selstone, John, 799
Sergeant, Thomas, 800
Shepherd, Richard, 808
Shury, Robert, 813

Simms, W., 815
Slatter, Gabriel, 821
Slatter, Thomas, 821
Smith, John, 830
Smith, William, 833
Stevens, William, 855
Tawney, Robert, 874
Taylor, John, 876
Taylor, Joseph, 878
Taylor, William Smith, 879
Thompson, —, 885
Thompson, Guy, 885
Thom(p)son, James, 886
Thompson, Thomas, 887
Thompson, William, 888
Trotman, William, 905
Varney, Frederick, 920
Vincent, Edward jnr, 929
Ward, John, 943
Ward, Philip, 943
Waren, Joseph, 944
Watts, Thomas, 951
West, John, 959
West, Sephrend, 960
West, William, 960
Wharton, Robert & Gee,
Richard, 962
Wharton, Thomas, 962
Wilkins, Robert, 975
Williams, John, 981
Willis, James, 983
Winter, William, 993
Wise, Richard, 993
Wood, John, 997
Wyatt, James, 1010
Wyatt, Thomas, 1010
Young, Richard, 1015
Oxford University:
  All Souls College:
    Chadwell, —, 153
    Osborne, —, 666
    Riggins, H.(?), 748
    Rouse, Richard, 768
    Taprell, Stephen & Holland,
    William, 872
    Tawney, Robert, 874
  Christ Church:
    Chippendale, Thomas snr, 167
    James, George, 479
    Jones, David William, 494
    Powell, Richard, 711
    Wilkins, Robert, 975
    Williams, John, 981
  Codrington Library, All Souls
  College:
    Butler, J., 137
    Franklin, Jeremiah, 319
    Riggins, H.(?), 748
    Tawney, Robert, 874
  Jesus College: Powell, Richard,
  711
  Lincoln College: Cooke, William,
  194

Pembroke College: Prother,
  Hugh, 719
Queen's College: Powell,
  Richard, 711
Radcliffe Asylum: Gee, Richard,
  334
Radcliffe Camera: Linnell,
  William, 547
St Edmund's Hall: Frogley,
  Arthur, 322
St John's College:
  Munday, Thomas, 635
  Williams, Samuel, 982
Sheldonian Theatre:
  Cleer(e), William, 177
  Frogley, Arthur, 322
Trinity College Chapel: Frogley,
  Arthur, 322
University College: Adams,
  George snr, 3
Worcester College: Munday,
  Thomas, 635
Oxnop (Yorks.): Ogden, Nathan,
  661

P

Pachon, George, 429
Packington Hall (Warks.): King,
  Benjamin, 514
Paddington (London):
  Berry, Henry, 67
  Elliott, Charles, 273
  Musgrave, Thomas, 637
  Parmee, Jno., 676
  Pettitt, John, 693
  Prisk, Richard, 718
  Rower, Thomas, 769
  Tyler, William, 915
Padget, J., 901
Padiham (Lancs.): Holland,
  Williamson, 442
Padstow (Cornwall): Ham, John,
  391
Page, John, 919
Page, Mathew, 375
Page, Thomas, 689
Paget, 923
Paignton (Devon): Beard, Thomas,
  55
Paine, Elizabeth, 670
Paine, Thomas, 972
Painswick (Glos.):
  Bryan, John, 122
  Merrett, Joseph, 603
Painter, 131
Painter & Huggins, 670
Pajon, James Lewis, 541
Palfrey, Ellen, 671
Palgrave (Suffolk): Thurlow,
  Abraham, 892
Pallant, Thomas, 636
Palliser, William, 578

Palmer, 78, 148, 686
Palmer, Thomas, 671
Palmer, William, 671
Panshanger (Herts.):
  Cooper, George, 196
  Jackson, George, 475
  Kimpton, William, 513
  Marshall, —, 577
  Miles, Henry & Edwards, John,
  606
  Sewell, —, 801
  Smith, Charles, 824
  Tait(t), Gordon, 870
  Taylor, David, 875
  Vaughan, George, 920
  Woodburn, Allen, 998
Pape, Isaac, 63
Papworth Hall (Cambs.): Oakley,
  George, 660
Parham Park (Sussex):
  Coade, Eleanor and her
  successors, 181
  Hopkins, William, 448
Parke, 345
Parke, James, 270
Parke, Joseph, 77
Parke, Reuben, 946
Parke, Samuel, 421
Parke & Henning, 673
Parker, 180, 236, 358
Parker, Andrew, 727
Parker, George, 175, 177, 292, 383,
  452, 747
Parker, James, 569
Parker, Joseph, 979
Parker, Robert, 131
Parker, Thomas, 155, 674, 999
Parkes, John, 903
Parkes, Thomas, 322
Parkinson, 368
Parlby, George, 683
Parlington (Yorks.):
  Dixon, John, 246
  Gillow, 343
  Myers, Thomas, 637
  Thornton, Osborn, 891
Parot, James, 396
Parran, Benjamin, 332, 352, 772
Parratt, Alexander, 598
Parry, 498, 558, 582
Parry, John, 113, 119, 247, 564,
  641, 873
Parry, William, 446
Parsons, 395
Partney (Lincs.): Smith, Joseph, 830
Partridge, Nathaniel, 655
Pascall, James, 767
Pastor, 410
Patching, 428
Patching & Wood, 679
Paten, 317
Patrick, Nicholas, 645, 776
Patrington (Yorks.): Robson,
  Thomas, 761

Patten, George, 946
Pattenden & Brown, 680
Pattendon, 119
Patton, Francis, 919
Paudevin, John (Poitevin, Jean),
753
Paul, Charles, 682
Paul, James, 671, 779
Paul, Reuben, 681
Paul, Robert, 56
Pavey, 711
Pawlett, Robert, 151
Paxton, 809
Paxton, Sherard, 353
Paxton House (Berwick):
Chippendale, Thomas snr, 166,
167
Chippendale, Thomas jnr, 168,
169
Payne, 374
Payne, Bartholomew, 723, 930
Peacock, Josiah, 847
Pearce, 15, 162
Pearce, Edward, 373
Peareth, 685
Peareth, John, 169
Pearman, Ambrose, 187, 425, 497,
921, 995
Pearse, 401
Pearse, William, 264
Pearson, 747, 978
Pearson, George, 141
Pearson, John, 312
Pearson, Samuel, 662
Pearson, William, 915
Peart, John, 686
Peasegood, Thomas, 789
Peck, John, 903
Peckham (London): Hull, —, 462
Peell, Jeremiah, 875
Peers, George, 408
Peet, William, 25
Peirson, Thomas, 191
Pelletier, John, 241, 618
Pelly, 421
Pember, Joseph, 859
Pemberton, 891
Pemberton, Charles, 576, 829
Pemberton, John, 61, 276
Penberthy, 480
Pender, Thomas, 348
Pendlebury (Lancs.): Barlow, John,
41
Pendleton (Lancs.):
Holmes, Robert, 445
Jackson, John, 476
Penfold, George, 936
Penistone (Yorks.):
Haley, John, 384
Tinker, Uriah, 895
Penman, Robert, 697
Penn, J., 958
Penning, 159
Penning & Charmbury, 688

Pennington, John, 670
Pennington, M., 986
Pennington, Myles, 47
Pennington, Nicholas, 442
Penrhyn Castle (Caernarvonshire):
Boulnois, John, 91
Penrice Castle (Glam.):
Allen, John, 10
Hill, Henry, 432
Kay, Quintin, 501
Penrith, John jnr, 816
Penrith, John snr, 816
Penrith (Cumb.):
Akitt, John, 6
Atkinson, John, 24
Bird, Isaac, 74
Bird, Robert, 74
Bowman, John, 93
Dawson, James, 235
Edmondson, William, 268
Elliot, John, 272
Elliott, William, 274
Ewbank, William, 286
Gibson, John, 337
Green, Joseph, 367
Herring, William, 423
Hindson, Joseph, 433
Hodgson, William, 438
Hornsby, Nicholas, 450
James, Robert, 480
Kendal, John, 504
Kirkbride, J., 517
Mallinson, John, 571
Mason, Jos., 584
Mawson, J., 588
Mawson, Joseph F., 588
Mayson, Joseph, 598
Nicholson, Thomas, 647
Noble, James, 650
Richardson, John, 744
Rimington, J.& W., 749
Rimington, William, 749
Rogers, Thomas, 764
Salkeld, John, 776
Sanderson, Joseph, 779
Scott, John, 790
Thompson, Thomas, 888
Thompson, William, 888
Tolson, John, 897
Ubank, William, 916
Penryn (Cornwall):
Edgcombe, William, 266
Hosken, William Veal, 451
Mansell, William, 573
Williams, Nicholas, 981
Penshurst Place (Kent): Roberts,
Thomas & Richard, 753
Pentonville (London):
Banks, Thomas, 37
Barwick, William, 47
Brunton, James, 122
Butcher, Philip, 137
Edwards, —, 269
Edwards, Richard, 270

Godarth, Herbert, 346
Hardcastle, Thomas, 395
Harrison, John, 404
Hewitt, Thomas, 426
Hinds, T.W., 433
Lawrence, Matthew, 531
Parsons, John, 678
Phillips, Cornelius, 695
Pickering, Benjamin, 697
Powell, James, 710
Prindle, John, 718
Reynolds, Thomas, 738
Shrewsbury, Thomas, 813
Simmons, John, 815
Waterhouse, Joseph, 947
West, Daniel, 959
Wills, F., 984
Winmill, Charles, 992
Penwortham (Lancs.): Townley,
Robert, 901
Penzance (Cornwall):
Dennis, John, 240
Hambleton & Son, 391
Harvey, James & Edward, 407
Lugg, Francis, 560
Matthews, Henry, 586
Moyle, Hugh Mason, 634
Pascoe, William, 679
Pearce, Michael, 684
Read, Thomas, 732
Richards, William, 743
Tregerthen, George, 903
Wallis, John, 940
Wallis, Thomas & Josh., 940
Weymouth, William Paul, 962
Peppitt, Joseph, 915
Peppitt, Robert, 469
Percy, 698
Perit, Richard, 687
Perkins, 432, 498
Perkins, John, 369
Perkins, Thomas, 700
Perring, George, 756
Perrot, Thomas, 570
Perrott, Thomas, 917
Perry, 472, 582
Perry, I., 691
Perry, Jno. 472
Perry, Joshua, 13
Perry Hall (Warks.): Pugin,
Augustus W.N., 721
Pershaw (Worcs.): Dovey, Samuel,
252
Pershore (Worcs.):
Blake, James, 79
Blake, William, 79
Peterborough (Northants.):
Bevis, John, 70
Boulton, William, 91
Bristow, George, 108
Bristow, John, 108
Edwards, John, 270
Holmes, George, 445
Horden, William, 449

Leicester, John, 537
Norris, Frederick Augustus, 653
Phillips, Edward, 695
Phillips, Robert, 696
Phipps, Edward, 696
Trowell, William, 906
Wakelin, John, 933
Wilkinson, Edward, 975
Wright, William, 1009
Petergate, York:
  Bollans, Francis, 83
  Smith, William, 834
Peters, Thomas, 72, 633
Petersfield (Hants.): Hoar, Richard, 435
Petfield, Christopher, 371
Petherton (Som.): Ban(d)fiels, John, 36
Pettegrew, Anthony, 804
Pettit, 161
Pettitt, 217
Petworth (Sussex):
  Austin, Thomas, 27
  Drewett, William, 256
  Knight, George, 519
  Row, James, 768
  Selden, John, 799
  Steer, George, 851
  Steer, James, 851
  White, Thomas, 967
Petworth House (Sussex):
  Chippendale, Thomas snr, 166, 168
  Cousin, Peter, 202
  Cousin, Rene, 202
  Crompton, Samuel, 211
  Duffour, Joseph, 258
  Elward, George & Marsh, William, 279
  Finch & Smith, 300
  Gerrard, Charles, 335
  Gosset, Gideon, 358
  Gosset, Isaac, 358
  Greene, Isaac, 368
  Harmer, B., 399
  Harrison, Mrs, 403
  Havre, John, 412
  Hindes, James, 433
  Huet, Michael, 460
  Hutton, —, 468
  Jensen, Gerrit, 487
  Johnson, Robert, 490
  Kay, Quintin, 501
  Kerr, John, 510
  Malton, Perry, 571
  Paudevin, John, 681
  Pavie, Peter, 682
  Ritson, Jonathan, 750
  Saunders, Paul, 783, 784
  Selden, John, 799
  Vaughan, Samuel, 921
  Waid, —, 932
  Ward, Thomas, 943
  Waters, William, 947

Watts, John, 951
  Whittle, James, 970, 971
Peyton, Bladwell, 208, 962
Phelps, Joseph, 590
Phene, Samuel, 497, 700
Philadelphia (USA):
  Mears, John, 599
  Seddon, George, 797
  Webster, John, 955
Philips, T., 696
Phill, Thomas, 189, 304
Phill and Fletcher, 753
Phillips, 692
Phillips, Frederick, 49
Phillips, Henry, 310
Phillips, J., 840
Phillips, John, 306, 423, 450, 460, 626, 733
Phillips, Richard Carlton jnr, 695
Phillips, Richard Carlton snr, 695
Phillips, Samuel, 502
Phillips, Thomas, 216, 319, 812
Phillips, William, 895
Phillipson, Nicholas, 822
Philp, Richard, 727
Phipp, Josiah, 441
Phipps, John, 572
Phipps, Josiah, 747
Phipps, Robert, 26, 49, 138, 363, 453, 608
Phipps, Thomas, 161
Phipps, William Philip, 694
Phipps & Shepherd, 696
Phoenix, James, 490
Pick, 39
Pick, Robert, 61
Pickering (Yorks.):
  Beswick, Anthony, 68
  Bielby, William, 71
  Brown, William, 119
  Dalton, John, 225
  Dalton, Thomas, 225
  Ellis, Thomas, 275
  Hesp, John, 424
  Hodgson, James, 438
  Johnson, Robert, 491
  Kirby, George, 516
  Kirby, Thomas, 516
  Newsome, John, 644
  Parke, Thomas, 673
  Stordy, Thomas, 859
  Sturdy, Thomas, 863
  Walker, John, 936
  Wilson, John, 988
  Wilson, Thomas, 989
Pickford, Joseph, 632
Pickstone, Thomas, 32
Picnot, A., 223
Pidcock, 390
Pidlock, 387
Pidock, 387
Pigg, Joseph, 399, 455, 770
Pigg, Thomas, 698
Pigou, Mark Anthony, 243

Pike, Thomas, 151
Pike, William, 888
Pilton (Som.): Barrow, James, 45
Pimlico (London):
  Allen, William, 10
  Anyon, John & Co., 16
  Bye, George, 139
  Bye, Jacob, 139
  Davis, J., 231
  Davis, T.H., 232
  Davis, Thomas, 2233
  Deschamps, John, 241
  Ellis, Benjamin, 275
  Goff, James Copeland, 348
  Gordon, Henry, 355
  Griffiths, Thomas, 375
  Hewetson, John, 425
  Hogg, George, 440
  Jennings, Henry Kickweed, 485
  Mares, William & J., 574
  Mill, Michael, 607
  Murgatroyd, A., 636
  Newman, Samuel, 643
  Pishot, John, 700
  Prentice, Richard, 713
  Smith, Edward, 826
  Thurnell, Samuel, 892
  Tijou, Sophia, 894
  Warren, William, 946
  Wilson, Jasper, 987
Pimm & Holt, 699
Pinckney, William, 363, 463
Pinkney, John, 248
Piotti, James, 944
Piqueret, Charles, 697
Pirewich (Hants.): Eyles, Joseph, 286
Pitchford, 209
Pither, 913
Pitt, 185
Pitt, Cecil, 731
Pitt & Chessey, 700, 730
Pitt (Wilts.): Madin, Mathew, 569
Pitter, 913
Pitts, Carill, 757
Pizzala, M., 701
Plaistowe, Thomas, 924
Plastow (Essex): Ehrliholtzer, Felix, 271
Playfair, Thomas, 480
Pleasance, John, 325
Pluckrose, Joseph, 130
Plunkett, Luke, 263
Plymouth (Devon):
  Algar, John, 7
  Algar, William & Sons, 8
  Badge, —, 28
  Baker, Edward, 32
  Baron, James, 43
  Baron, William jnr, 43
  Baron, William snr, 43
  Baxter, Mary, 51
  Beasley, Robert, 55
  Beer, John, 58

Bellet, A., 63
Belletti, Anthony, 63
Besley, Robert, 68
Blackwell, E.&j., 78
Bray, —, 103
Browne, J.E., 120
Brown(e), J.H., 114
Budge, Thomas, 124
Bullin, F., 126
Bullin, Thomas, 126
Burgoine, Aaron, 130
Burgoine, John, 130
Bussel(l), Joseph, 136
Dickerson, James, 243
Dyer, Adolphus, 263
Emery, D., 280
Giles, Samuel, 340
Gray, Robert, 365
Gray & Co., 366
Hare, William, 397
Harris, J., 400
Hearder, Cath., 417
Hobbs, John, 435
Hocking, John jnr, 436
Hodge, James, 436
Holland, —, 441
Holland, J., 442
Holland, John, 442
Honey, H. & W., 447
Honey, R., 447
Howard, Charlotte, 453
Howard, Nathaniel, 454
Hundrey, John, 464
James, George, 479
James, James, 479
Johnson, J., 489
Johnson, Samuel, 491
Lane, Thomas, 525
Leach, William, 533
Leverton, John, 539
Lott, Ann, 555
Lovell, Abraham, 556
Madge, Mat(t)hew, 569
Marshall, John, 579
Marshall, Mrs, 577
Martin, John, 581
Martin, Solomon, 581
May, —, 588
May, Joseph Ball, 589
May, Joseph, 589
May, Mrs, 588
Mewton, —, 604
Mewton, R., 604
Mewton, William, 604
Midleton, —, 605
Miller, Thomas, 609
Mitchell, John, 613
Morcombe, D., 623
Morcombe, Thomas, 623
Morcombe, William, 623
Oliver, Jonathan, 663
Parsons, Sophia, 678
Pascoe, William, 679
Peck, John, 686

Pilditch, Philip, 698
Price, William, 717
Puleston, Edward, 721
Quint, William, 724
Randle & Williams, 727
Reeby, James, 734
Rendle, Henry, 737
Rider, Joseph, 746
Rogers, Robert, 763
Saunders, Samuel, 785
Sinclair, William, 818
Skardon, James, 818
Skardon, Joseph, 818
Smith, John, 829
Smith, Sidney, 832
Smith, Thomas, 833
Stephens, John, 853
Stephens, Robert, 853
Stephens, Walter, 853
Style, Thomas, 863
Sutherland, Alexander, 865
Tapscott, G., 872
Thomas, Samuel, 884
Thomas, William, 884
Thomas & Son, 885
Thompson, John, 887
Thompson, S.S., 887
Trevenen, Henry, 904
Tymwoll, Edward, 915
Vivian, W., 929
Webb, William, 954
Were, James, 959
Westaway, Messrs, 960
Westlake, William, 960
White, John, 966
Williams, —, 979
Williams, George, 979
Wills, James, 984
Wills, John, 985
Worth, William, 1003
Wyatt, James, 1010
Wyatt, John, 1010
Wyatt, Samuel, 1010
Plymouth Dock (Devon):
  Baxter, A., 51
  Dingle, Joseph, 245
  Haley, Philip, 384
  Haley, Robert, 384
  Hancock, T., 393
Pocklington (Yorks.):
  Beal, Thomas, 54
  Hagyard, Thomas, 382
  Hardy, David, 397
  Judson, Robert, 500
  Judson, William, 500
  Nicholson, Thomas, 647
  Richardson, William, 745
  Robinson, William, 761
  Swan, Clifford, 867
  Ward, John, 943
Podmore, William, 224, 569, 628, 710, 711
Podmore & Morris, 704

Podmore & Powells, 628, 704, 710, 711
Podvine (Paudevin), John, 681
Poictevine (Paudevin), John, 681
Poitevin, Jean (Paudevin, John), 753
Poland, Nieborow Palace, Warsaw: Campbell, Robert, 143
Polhill, Edward, 87, 527
Pollard, William, 697
Ponder's End (Middlx): Bradley, Benjamin, 97
Pontana, 125
Pontefract (Yorks.):
  Athorn, John, 23
  Barber, Thomas, 39
  Dickinson, William, 243
  Glover, Samuel, 345
  Harrison, George, 403
  Hartley, Bernard, 406
  Hewitt, William, 426
  Hurtley, Barnard, 466
  Hutchinson, James, 468
  Lawcock, John, 530
  Lowcock, Mary, 557
  Lowcock & Wing, 557
  Marshall, Benjamin, 577
  Marshall, Dorothy, 577
  Marshall, William, 579
  Nellteton, Thomas, 640
  Nettleton, Thomas, 641
  Pease, John, 685
  Pease, Midgley, 685
  Pease, William, 685
  Sykes, Samuel, 869
  Tattersal, —, 874
  Teal, —, James, 880
  Turner, John, 911
  Turpin, Thomas, 913
  Wing, —, 991
  Wright, James, 1005
Poole, Elizabeth, 174
Poole, Jeremiah, 189
Poole, Rid., 99
Poole (Dorset):
  Bond, J.H.B., 85
  Drew, William, 256
  Gallop, George, 328
  Gollop, George, 349
  Gustar, John, 380
  Hayward, John, 415
  Hewlett, Robert, 426
  Hewlett, Stephen, 426
  Holland, Robert, 442
  James, William, 480
  Knight, Charles, 519
  Layton, Edward, 533
  Major, John Taylor & Samuel, 570
  Marsh, Cornelius, 576
  Randall, Robert, 727
  Reeks, William, 735
  Reeve(s), William, 735
  Ricks, William, 746

Scaplen, John jnr, 788
Seapton, John, 792
Seymour, James, 801
Seymour, Richard, 801
Sharp, James, 802
Smith, William, 835
Taylor, J. & Major, S., 876
Tullock, John, 908
Waterman, William, 947
Wormald, James, 1003
Pope, Samuel, 664
Popevine (Paudevin), John, 681
Poplar (London):
    Gibbs, John, 336
    Hayward, James, 415
    Hill, Henry William, 430
    Jeves, William, 488
    Morton, Andrew, 630
    New, Harvey, 641
    Ramsey, Isaac & Son, 726
    Ramsey, J.& E., 726
    Ramsey & Co., 726
    Ramsey & Carter, 726
    Rose, John, 766
    Shrimpton, Joshua, 813
Popperwell, 990
Porden, W., 51
Portch & Davis, 706
Porteous, George Mathew, 819
Porter, Arnold, 768
Porter, James, 198, 247
Porter, William, 760
Portesham House (Dorset):
    Wholler, Benjamin, 972
Portsea (Hants.):
    Barnes & Cook, 43
    Bell, George, 61
    Brett, James & Eastman, 105
Portsmouth (Hants.):
    Atkins, G.H., 23
    Bacon, William, 28
    Ball, Robert, 35
    Bastard, John, 48
    Blake, George, 79
    Breet, James, 105
    Brooks, James Philip, 112
    Budden(n), Robert, 124
    Daglish, William, 223
    Deacon, Richard, 237
    Dermott, Dominick, 241
    Digby, Joseph, 244
    Douglass, Francis, 251
    Eastman, James, 265
    Eastman, Thomas, 265
    Elford, Samuel, 272
    Emanuel, E., 279
    Garnett, William, 331
    Garratt, Dingley, 331
    Gilbert, John, 338
    Govan, James, 361
    Grist, Edward, 375
    Headdon, Benjamin, 416
    Hill & Perkins, 432
    Hodder & Son, 436

Horsey, Joseph, 451
Houghton, George, 452
Howey, Joseph, 456
Jarvis, Thomas, 481
Jerome, Jas., 487
Jerome, Josh., 487
Jones, John, 495
Knapp, George, 518
Knapp, John, 518
Lavender, James, 530
Levett, George Alms, 539
Lock, Thomas, 552
Luff & M'kewan, 560
Martin, William, 582
Marvin, Edward, 582
Marvin, R., 582
Miall, William, 604
Mitchell, William, 614
Orange, Joseph, 664
Palmer, James, 671
Piguinett, James, 698
Pratt, George, 712
Sabine, —, 774
Shaw, James, 804
Shortland, Richard Watson, 812
Simmons, John, 815
Smith, James, 827
Smith, Joseph, 830
Somkins, Jonathon, 839
Stevens, George, 854
Taplen, John & William, 871
Tarrant, John, 872
Tom(p)kins, Jonathon, 897
Upton, William, 918
Ward, William, 944
Wellcome, John, 957
Wendover, G., 958
Whitbread, George, 964
Williams, J., 980
Wilson, Alexander, 986
Wilton, Edward, 990
Woodhouse, I.A., 999
Woodruff, John, 1000
Woods, T., 1000
Wright, Charles Britannia, 1004
Portwood, John, 492
Potevine (Paudevin), John, 681
Pots, John, 816
Pott, 240
Potter, 473
Potter, James jnr, 871
Potter, John, 754
Potter, Samuel, 808
Potter, Thomas, 51, 177, 335
The Potteries (Staffs.):
    Beech, George, 58
    Eaton, Thomas, 265
    Humphreys, Charles, 463
    Lees, John, 536
    Saint, Aaron, 775
    Shenton, Matthew, 807
    Wedgwood, Aaron, 956
Potternewton (Yorks): Wade, John, 931

Potton (Beds.):
    Hagger, Thomas, 382
    Hearne, Edward snr, 417
    Hearne, Richard, 417
    Youd, George, 1013
Potts, 189
Potts, William, 942
Potts, Son & Collinson, 709
Potvin (Paudevin), John, 681
Poulton (Lancs.): Harrison, Robert, 404
Poulton-le-Fylde (Lancs.):
    Lewtas, Edward, 541
    Topping, William, 900
    Whiteside, Henry, 968
Powderham Castle (Devon):
    Avant, Thomas, 27
    Channon, John, 155, 156
    Channon, Otho, 156
    Channon, T., 157
    Elward, George & Marsh, William, 279
Powell, 361, 628, 835
Powell, Benjamin, 261, 474
Powell, Edward Frodsham, 704, 711
Powell, John, 704, 715
Powell, Joseph, 229, 704
Powell, Richard, 808
Powell, Thomas, 241, 576, 679, 704, 1007
Powell, Thomas John, 710
Powers, Maurice, 263
Powick Court (Worcs.):
    Anderson, Jonathan & Perry, Joshua, 13
    Insull, Henry, 472
    Read (or Read), Thomas, 734
Powle, Mrs, 710
Powle, William, 723, 1006
Powys Castle: Burrey & White, 133
Pratt, 176, 288, 437
Pratt, Andrew, 310, 936
Pratt, Christopher, 657
Pratt, Michael, 733
Presbury, Philip, 4, 269, 447, 548, 632, 754, 780
Prescot (Lancs.):
    Banks, Benjamin, 37
    Dickson, William, 244
    Houghton, Isaac & Samuel, 452
    Jump, Edward Tryor, 500
    Robinson, Samuel, 760
    Sedgwick, Thomas, 798
    Sedgwick & Son, 798
    Swift, John, 868
    Traverse, John, 902
    Welsby, Jonathon, 958
    Woods, Jonathon, 1000
    Woods, Thomas, 1000
    Wood, Thomas, 998
Prescott, James, 890
Prestbury, Philip, 193
Preston, John, 65, 723, 901
Preston, Thomas, 408

Preston (Lancs.):
Abbot, William, 1
Addison, Richard, 4
Ainsworth, George, 5
Anderson, Robert, 13
Aspindle, Richard, 22
Aspinwall, Rhodes & Co., 22
Atkinson, John, 24
Aughton, Richard, 26
Backhouse, Richard, 28
Bamber, William, 36
Barnes, Thomas jnr, 42
Barnes, Thomas snr, 42
Blackhurst, Robert, 77
Bowerbank & Bamber, 92
Brade & Storey, 97
Bradshaw, William, 100
Bray & Winder, 104
Broughton, Thomas, 113
Brown, John, 116
Brown, Richard, 117
Brown, Robert, 117
But(t)ler, —, 137
Butler, John, 137
Dandy, James, 225
Dewhurs, Ralph, 242
Dewhurst, Thomas, 242
Dixon, Thomas, 247
Dugdale, Robert & Co., 258
Eccles, Edward, 265
Ellison, Edward, 276
Ellison & Co, 276
Emett, Michael jnr, 280
Emett, Michael snr, 280
Emmett, Thomas, 280
Gardner, John, 330
Gornal, John, 358
Grundy, Isaac, 377
Hall, George, 385
Hamilton, Jacobus, 391
Hamilton, Willus, 391
Hilton, George, 432
Hodgson, Robert, 438
Holme(s), James, 444
Holme(s), John, 444
Howard, George, 453
Hubbersley, William, 457
Hughes, Peter, 461
Johnson, James, 489
Johnson, John, 490
Jones, Alexander, 494
Jones, Thomas, 497
Kay, John, 500
Kay, Joseph, 500
Kilner, John, 512
Kilner, Thomas, 512
Kilner, William, 513
Ladyman, Thomas, 521
Latus, William, 529
Leeming, Thomas, 535
Lees, John, 536
Leyland, Samuel, 541
Livesay, John & William, 550
Lupton, Thomas, 561

Luvate, Dominic, 561
McKenzie, Daniel, 566
May, Richard, 589
Milsom, Arthur, 611
Mitchell, Matthew, 614
Money, Thomas, 616
Nightingale, John, 648
Oakey, Caleb, 658
Oxendale, William, 668
Parker, John, 674
Parkinson, T. & R., 676
Parr, Henry, 677
Pemberton, John, 688
Pemberton, Richard, 688
Pennington, Garnett, 689
Pritchard, James, 719
Riding, William, 747
Riley, —, 748
Riley, John, 749
Robinson, John, 758
Robinson, Joseph, 759
Robinson, Joshua, 759
Rogers, Robert, 763
Roper, John, 765
Rose, William, 766
Rushton, John & Son, 771
Rushton, Samuel, 771
Ryley, John & Son, 774
Salthouse, Richard & Riding,
William, 777
Saul, Robert, 781
Scolcroft, Robert, 789
Shannon, Martin, 802
Singleton, Thomas, 818
Slater, Robert, 821
Stocks, Joseph, 857
Sudell, Margaret, 864
Sudell, Thomas, 864
Sutton, James, 865
Sutton, Richard, 866
Thornton & Pemberton, 891
Timmins, Robert, 895
Towers, William, 900
Townsend, Charles, 901
Townsend, Joseph, 901
Tyrer, Wilkinson & Co., 916
Verscragen, James, 922
Verscragen, John, 922
Walker, Peter, 936
Walker, Salthouse & Butler, 939
Waller, Richard, 940
Walmesley, William, 940
Walmsley & Bowerbank, 941
Wareing, Thomas, 944
White, John, 966
White, Nicholas, 966
Whittle, Peter, 971
Whittle, Thomas, 971
Wilkinson, —, 975
Wilkinson, Matthew, 976
Williams, James, 981
Williams, John, 981
Wilson, Arthur, 986
Wilson, George, 987

Wilson, John, 988
Winder & Johnson, 991
Woodcock, William, 998
Wray, Thomas, 1004
Wren, Timothy, 1004
Price, Francis, 915
Price, Hilton, 827
Price, John, 6, 158, 616, 710, 730
Price, Joseph, 715–16
Price, Philip, 948
Price, Richard, 752
Price, Richard F., 255
Price, Thomas, 720, 731
Priest, 717
Priestland, John, 80
Priestley, 968
Princes Risborough (Bucks.):
Slaughter, Richard, 821
Pringle, 296
Pritchard, William, 745
Proctor, 153, 277
Proctor, Francis, 562
Proctor, Samuel, 997
Proctor, William Grosvenor, 164
Proctor & Chadley, 164
Prosser & Bassana, 719
Proudman, John, 378, 811
Proviss, William, 481
Prussurot, John, 482
Pryce, William, 497, 997
Pryer, 566, 844
Pryer, George, 720
Pryor, 851
Pryor, William, 718
Puddletown (Dorset): Kiddle, John,
511
Pugh, Charles, 720, 721
Pugin, A.W.N., 76, 796
Pulham St Mary (Norfolk): Valiant,
George, 919
Pullan, Timothy, 722
Pullen, Joseph, 133
Pullon, Henry, 38
Punchard, Robert, 799, 846
Purcell, 322
Purdie & Hinchcliff, 722
Purdon, John, 244
Purnell, John, 852
Pursseveill, J.B., 667
Purves, 410
Purvis, 425
Putney (London):
Layton, Samuel, 533
Nicholson & Walker, 647
Stewart, James, 856
Stewart, Jno., 856
Walker, Adam, 934
Watkin, Robert Smart, 947
Pye, Edward, 933
Pyner, Francis, 124, 551, 682, 710,
714
Pyner, Francis jnr, 1002
Pyner, Francis snr, 1002
Pyner, James, 118

Q

Queenhithe (London): Knight, James, 519
Queen's Elm (London): Reefe, G.C., 735
Quelch, 242
Quernmore Park (Lancs.): Richardson, John, 744
Quick, Joseph, 752
Quilley, William, 494, 510
Quin, William, 160, 176
Quincey, Lawrance, 955
Quirke, William, 864

R

Rabett, Edward, 921
Raby Castle (Co. Durham): Gosset, Jacob, 359
Rackham, James, 460
Radcliffe (London): Beddine, David, 58
Radford, 707
Radford & Field, 725
Radford (Notts.):
   Brutnell, William, 122
   Halfpenny, John, 384
   Locke, William, 552
   Simons, William E., 815
   Smith, John, 830
   Smith, William, 835
   Taylor, John H., 877
   Wilson, Samuel, 989
Radway Grange (Warks.): King, Benjamin, 514
Rainford, 64, 804, 861
Rainford & Sharples, 726
Rainford (Lancs.): Hall, Thomas, 386
Rainper, 729
Raistrick (Yorks):
   Booth, John, 87
   Booth, Jonas, 87
   Hepworth, James, 423
   Marsden, James, 576
Ramsgate (Kent):
   Abbott, Stephen, 1
   Bennett, Charles, 64
   Bradfield, George, 97
   Greey, Frederick, 370
   Grey, T.B., 373
   Hammond, H., 392
   Harrison, William, 405
   Hinds, George, 433
   Hooper, George, 447
   Horton, William, 451
   Hurst, William, 466
   Joad, John, 488
   Ladson, James, 521
   Mairne, Charles, 638
   Moorehead, —, 622
   Norton, John, 656

Rayner, George Thomas, 731
Robinson, George, 757
Styles, James, 863
Thornton, F., 890
Twyman, Stephen, 915
Walker, Richard, 937
Warman, Henry, 945
Ranceford, Charles, 727
Randall, 946
Randall, Matthew, 694
Rannie, 831
Rannie, James, 164, 167, 297, 382
Ranshall, John, 284
Raper, Edward, 301
Rastrick (Yorks):
   Bintcliff, Charles, 73
   Brook, Emanuel, 110
Ratcliffe, John, 916
Ratcliffe (London):
   Doyle, William, 255
   Gill, George, 340
   Grimsey, Rowning, 375
   Household, Robert, 452
   Rathbone, Philip, 728
   Selby, James, 799
   Taylor, John, 877
   Tindale, M.F., 895
   Webster, Barnabas, 954
Ravald, John, 627
Ravauld, John, 627
Ravenhill, 842
Ravis & Rickman, 729
Rawcliffe (Yorks): Watson, Richard, 950
Rawden, Christopher, 292
Rawdon (Yorks):
   Naylor, James, 639
   Thompson, Richard, 887
Rawes, G., 210, 457, 989
Rawlins, 835
Rawlins, Charles, 729, 937
Rawlins, William, 715, 866
Rawlinson, Stephen, 1013
Rawtenstall (Lancs.): Atkinson, Thomas, 25
Rayer, Moses, 306
Rayleigh (Essex): Grigg, William, 375
Rayley, John, 726
Rayment, William, 1011
Rayner, 663
Rayner, L., 529
Raynes, 315
Raynham Hall (Norfolk): Chippendale, Thomas jnr, 169
Rayson, 978
Rayson, James, 160
Rea, William, 446
Read, 68, 118, 119, 990
Read, Joseph, 787, 840
Read, Thomas, 734
Reader, Richard, 735
Reading (Berks.):
   Abery, Christopher, 2

Aldridge, Robert, 7
Allaway, George & James, 9
Avery, William, 27
Baker, John, 32
Benwell, Charles, 67
Blanch, Thomas, 79
Bunce, Robert, 128
Dewe, J., 242
Dewe, Musgrove & Quelch, 242
Eyre, Richard, 287
Grossmith, William, 376
Hewlings, Samuel, 426
Higgs, - jnr, 428
Higgs, Benson, 428
Higgs, Holland Thomas, 428, 429
Higgs, T. Holland, 429
Higgs, Thomas, 429
Higgs & Ford, 429
Hodgson, Thomas, 438
Holland, Thomas, 442
Illsley, Charles, 471
Jackson, Richard, 477
Jacob, Edward, 477
Jacob, John, 477
Jessop, Mrs Ann, 488
Knowles, Edward, 520
Lambden, Edward, 522
Lambdon, Charles, 522
Line, William, 543
Masters, Richard, 585
Monk, William, 616
Osmond, William, 666
Plummer, George, 703
Poulton, Charles, 709
Quelch, William, 724
Robinson, John, 758
Round, Thomas, 768
Saunders, James, 782
Silver, Elizabeth, 814
Silver, James, 814
Simmonds, William, 815
Simmons, Joseph, 815
Simpson, William, 817
Sims, Richard L., 817
Stevens, Samuel, 854
Tagg, Charles, 870
Truss, Thomas, 906
Tyrell, Timothy, 916
White, John, 966
White, Joseph, 966
Whiting, Richard, 969
Whiting, Thomas, 969
Wiggins, William, 973
Wray, Benjamin, 1004
Wright, Ellis, 1005
Reason, William, 338, 352, 558
Redbourne Hall (Lincs.): Lovitt, John, 557
Redbraes Castle (Berwicks.): Hallett, William snr, 389
Redding, Edward, 630
Redding, Samuel, 633

Redenhall (Norfolk): Plain, James, 702
Redfearn, John Samuel, 244
Redgate, 536
Reding, William, 630, 712, 975
Redknap, William, 373
Redman, Leonard, 297
Redmayne, Leonard, 11, 38, 45, 297, 341, 365, 423, 444, 473, 491, 512, 608, 616, 617, 773, 881, 890, 968, 973
Redmayne, Whiteside & Ferguson, 341, 733
Redruth (Cornwall):
  Bray, James, 104
  Dunge(r)y, Thomas, 259
  Nicholls, Benjamin, 645
  Pearce, —, 683
  Raseigh, John, 728
  Watkinson, William John, 948
Redshaw, 803
Redshaw, George, 695
Redwin, John jnr, 732
Reed, 989
Reed, Henry, 250, 337, 909
Reed, John, 806, 918
Reed, Joseph, 732
Reed, Robert, 732
Reed, Roger, 21, 732
Reed, Thomas, 732
Reeder, 732
Reedham (Norfolk): Briggs, James, 107
Reeks, William, 904
Reeve, Sam, 271, 584
Reid, Anne, 736
Reid, George, 736
Reid, James, 220
Reid, Roger, 23, 199, 732
Reid, William, 167, 935
Reider, Edward, 735
Reigate (Surrey):
  Jepps, William Henry, 487
  Keasley, Ann, 501
  Keasley, John, 501
Reilly, Peter, 939
Relph, 646
Ren, William, 414
Renolds, William, 738–9
Renwick, 254
Restell, Henry, 245
Retford (Notts.):
  Billyard, William, 72
  Hill, Benjamin, 430
  Hodgkinson, Richard, 437
  Hopkinson, Francis jnr, 449
  Hopkinson, Francis snr, 449
  Kippax, George, 516
  Kirkby, George, 517
  Lambert, Cornelius, 523
  Lambert, Henry, 523
  Leadbeater, William, 533
  Liller, John, 542
  Richardson, John, 744

Saunders, John, 782
Saunderson, James, 786
Scorah, William, 789
Shaw, John, 804
Shaw, Thomas, 805
Standage, Peter, 848
Stock, Thomas, 857
Stocks, Thomas, William, 857
Stubbin(g)s, Francis, 863
Stubbins, Thomas, 863
Tate, George, 873
Tomlinson, Thomas, 898
Watson, James, 949
Watson, Jarvis, 949
Wheatland, William, 962
Whitaker, Thomas, 964
Whitlam, Benjamin, 969
Whittam, John, 970
Willey, Richard, 979
Revell, Thomas, 482
Rew, 737
Reynold, 553
Reynolds, 344, 711
Reynolds, John, 574
Reynolds, Samuel, 182, 183, 184, 185, 388, 389, 924, 925
Reynolds, William, 737
Reynoldson, George, 107, 260, 291, 312, 655, 780, 826, 1012
Reynoldson, Henry, 739
Reynoldson, Joseph, 9
Rhodes, 22, 413
Rhodes, Henry, 54
Rhodes, William, 290, 315, 982
Riade, Joseph, 732
Ribchester (Lancs.):
  Alston, William, 11
  Robinson, William, 760
Riccall (Yorks): Pratt, Richard, 712
Rice, Vincent, 104
Rich, 421
Richards, 552
Richards, Charles, 417
Richards, James, 41, 353, 531, 619, 636
Richards, Joseph, 203
Richards, William, 741
Richardson, 433, 835
Richardson, Edward, 104, 804, 981
Richardson, Henry, 879
Richardson, John, 150, 743, 747, 878
Richardson, Joseph, 820
Richardson, R., 743
Richardson, Thomas, 744
Richardson, William, 185, 258
Riches, Robert, 581
Riches, Robert jnr, 528
Richmond (Surrey):
  Best, George, 68
  Bid(d)en & Moorey, 71
  Bromage, William, 110
  Eggleston, William, 271
  Evans, William, 285

Gregory, Richard, 370
Gumbrell, John & Chiles, Edward, 379
Gumbrell, William, 379
Hunter, John, 465
Keep, Richard, 502
Kemp, Richard, 504
Loader, John, 551
Low, John, 557
Luckett, William, 560
Miles, Henry, 607
Mivart, John, 614
Norris, John, 654
Norris, John Frederick, 654
Pennington, William, 689
Piggott, Frederick, 698
Piggott, James, 698
Pigott, James jnr, 698
Remington, William, 737
Robertson, William, 755
Robinson, John, 758
Rowland, Thomas, 769
Sandall, Thomas, 778
Snowden, Thomas, 837
Steere, Alfred George, 851
Stevens, William, 855
Webster, John, 955
Richmond (Yorks):
  Addison, John, 4
  Alderson, John, 7
  Arrowsmith, James, 19
  Atkinson, Richard, 24
  Barker, John, 40
  Bates, Samuel, 49
  Bell, Marchant M., 62
  Bell, Thomas, 62
  Brown, Robert, 118
  Burn, George, 131
  Dunn, Isaac, 260
  Glenston, James, 345
  Greathead, Matthew, 366
  Groves, John, 376
  Harrison, Robert, 404
  Heslop, Thomas, 424
  Ibbotson, J.M., 470
  Irvin, George, 473
  Langstaff, Francis, 527
  Lonsdale, Joseph, 555
  Metcalfe, James, 604
  Norman, George, 651
  Norman, James, 651
  Norman, Matthew, 651
  Parkin, George, 676
  Parkinson, Thomas, 676
  Redstone, Jane, 734
  Robinson, John, 759
  Rosewassa, Thomas, 766
  Smith, Jeffrey, 827
  Smith, Thomas, 833
  Spedding, Snowden, 842
  Vitty, William snr & jnr, 929
  Walker, William, 938
  Wharton, George, 962
  Wright, George, 1005

Wright, William, 1009
Richmond House: Platt, John, 702
Richmond Park (Surrey):
    Chippendale, Thomas jnr, 169
Rickett, 693
Rickett, Edward, 135
Rickman, 729
Rickmansworth (Herts.): Pricket(t),
    John, 717
Ridge, Timothy, 580, 696
Ridgeway, Charles, 335
Ridgeway, Thomas, 980
Ridgeway & Rolleston, 747
Riding, William, 777
Ridpath, John, 744
Ridpeth, John, 959
Ridsdales, 962
Rigby, Charles, 674
Rigby, Mary, 748
Rigby, Thomas, 444
Rigby, William, 213
Rigg, Ellen, 266, 748
Righton, John, 824
Righton, Richard, 437
Riley, 974
Riley, Peter, 737
Rimill, John, 678
Rimmer, James, 247
Rimmer, William, 599
Rimmington, Edward, 804
Ring, 119
Ringer, James, 524
Ringmer (Sussex): Weller, Henry,
    957
Ringshall (Suffolk): Sissons, —, 818
Ringwood (Hants.):
    Bull, Joseph, 125
    Darley, Henry, 227
    Lock, George, 551
    Morland, William, 627
Riorto, James, 239
Ripley (Yorks.): Mason, Thomas,
    584
Ripon (Yorks.):
    Arrowsmith & Son, 19
    Atkinson, William, 25
    Beckwith, Richard, 57
    Bedford, William, 58
    Brown, William, 119
    Davidson, Thomas, 228
    Dodsworth, Thomas, 249
    Drake, John, 255
    Gowing, Ralph, 361
    Harrison, Matthew, 404
    Heslop, George, 424
    Hindley, Thomas, 433
    Howell, William, 455
    Husband, Christopher, 466
    Ireland, William, 473
    Jackman, James, 474
    Johnson, George, 489
    Judson, Charles, 500
    Kearsley, John, 501
    Metcalf(e), John, 604

Moss, Henry, 632
Norman, James, 651
Poppleton, Thomas, 706
Poppleton, William, 706
Rawson, John, 730
Ray, Andrew, 730
Roy, Andrew, 769
Steel, William, 851
Turner, Thomas, 912
Whitehouse, Thomas, 968
Wilson, Mary, 988
Wilson, Thomas, 989
Rise Hall (Yorks.): Wright, Richard
    & Elwick, Edward, 1008
Rishworth (Yorks.):
    Baines, Samuel, 32
    Hebden, William, 419
    Northend, Joseph, 655
    Sharp, William, 803
Rixon, 393
Roades, Robert, 191
Robbins, John, 755–6
Robbs, John, 557
Robert, James, 1008
Roberts, 442, 978
Roberts, Adrian, 993
Roberts, Edward, 383, 708, 778,
    1000
Roberts, Ellis, 409
Roberts, Henry, 281
Roberts, J., 174, 676, 818
Roberts, James, 292, 442
Roberts, John, 602, 724
Roberts, Joseph, 109, 938
Roberts, Josiah, 485
Roberts, Richard, 694, 735, 980
Roberts, Robert, 637
Roberts, T., 751
Roberts, Thomas, 83, 421, 454, 713,
    864
Roberts, William, 83, 99, 708
Roberts, William John, 94, 246,
    265, 412, 453, 455, 520, 581,
    586, 601, 611, 615, 875, 879, 902
Robertson, 20, 821
Robertson, D., 755
Robertson, John, 163
Robins, 39
Robins, John, 691
Robins, Joseph, 102, 292, 329, 755
Robins, William, 102
Robinson, 121, 1007
Robinson, Benjamin, 460
Robinson, Charles, 157
Robinson, Christopher, 99
Robinson, George, 576, 758
Robinson, George Valentine, 755
Robinson, James, 455, 504, 550,
    701, 875
Robinson, John, 576, 756, 757,
    1007, 1008
Robinson, Joseph, 408, 757, 758
Robinson, Mark, 309
Robinson, Richard, 455, 847

Robinson, Thomas, 51, 239, 557,
    586, 942
Robinson, William, 507, 758, 764
Robson, 173, 761
Robson, John, 955, 959
Robson & Knowles, 436
Roby, Thomas, 452
Rochdale (Lancs.):
    Ashton, Edward, 21
    Barton, William, 47
    Davenport, James, 227
    Gray, John, 365
    Gulielmus, Newill, 378
    Hoyle, Henry, 456
    Hoyle, John, 456
    Murray, Martin, 637
    Newill, Gulielmus, 642
    Nuttall, James, 657
    Oddy, William, 661
    Rim(m)ington, Edward, 749
    Rushforth, William, 771
    Stott, John, 860
    Taylor, John, 877
    Whipp, John, 963
    Whitaker, James, 963
    Whitaker, William, 964
    Williamson, George, 983
    Wrigley, Edmund snr & jnr, 1009
    Wrigley, Robert, 1009
Rochester (Kent):
    Affiter, Thomas, 5
    Assiter, Thomas, 22
    Austen, J., 26
    Batten, T., 50
    Batten, Edward, 50
    Batten, John, 50
    Batten, Latitia, 50
    Benifold, W., 64
    Burnett, R., 131
    Burr, Robert, 132
    Burr, Thomas, 132
    Butten, John, 138
    Dawson, Elizabeth, 235
    Dawson, John, 235
    Dunning, Henry, 261
    Ellender, Daniel, 272
    Elvee, Robert, 277
    Goodred, Jonas, 354
    Hales, John, 383
    Kidwell, Cole, 512
    Kidwell, J., 512
    Kidwell, Robert, 512
    Leith, John, 537
    Marrable, John, 575
    Middleton, R., 605
    Pymm, Hammond, 723
    Seath, John, 793
    Sharp, George, 802
    Snook, Jane, 837
    Taylor, John, 877
    Thomas, F., 883
    Thomas, Franklen Matthew, 883
    Thomas, S., 884
    Watson, Joseph, 950

Wilkinson, Thomas, 977
Wood, Edward, 996
Rochford (Essex):
Gay, Thomas, 333
Gay, William, 333
Quy, Thomas, 725
Rockley (Notts.):
Nicholson, George, 646
Walker, Frederick, 934
Rockwood, 419
Rodgers, Isaac, 763
Rodgers, Margaret, 763
Rodwell, 700
Rodwell, James, 730, 779, 866,
897–8
Rodwell, William, 115
Roe, Benjamin Hambling, 397
Roentgen, Abraham, 156, 349
Rogers, Thomas, 3, 994
Rogers, William, 99, 111, 240
Rogers & Solly, 764
Rokeby Park (Co. Durham):
Ridsdale, Benjamin, 747
Rolleston, 747
Rollet, William, 872
Rollett, William, 48, 66, 587, 651,
761, 870, 900
Romford (Essex):
Allen, John, 10
Dawson, William, 235
Moore, William Lacey, 621
Workham, John, 1003
Romsey (Hants.):
Berry, Thomas, 68
Jervis, John, 488
Lejeune, Thomas, 537
Masters, M., 585
Maunder, Thomas, 587
Routledge, Charles, 768
Routledge, Christopher, 768
Routledge, Thomas, 768
Rutledge, Christopher, 774
Sharp, Clement, 802
Shergold, Thomas, 809
Sparkman, Jas., 841
Ronalds, 300
Rook, William, 333
Root, William, 333
Roper, William, 1013
Roscoe, Philip, 62
Rose, 835
Rose, John, 267
Rose, Thomas, 915
Rose, William, 527, 771
Ross, Francis, 238, 767
Ross, Joshua, 679
Ross, Thomas, 148, 766, 880, 897,
960
Ross & Mann, 767
Ross-on-Wye (Herefs.):
Bailey, William, 31
Beavan, George, 56
Evans, William, 285
Hoale, Amos, 435

Hoale, Moses, 435
Hole, Amos, 441
Jordan, J.L., 498
Morgan, John, 625
Parry, Ann, 677
Rossen, R., 988
Rosson, Andrew, 51
Rostill, 386
Rostilt, 386
Rothbury (Northumb.):
Anderson, Alexander, 12
Burn, Thomas, 131
Hall, William, 386
Mattison, Thomas, 587
Rotherel, Richard, 767
Rotherham (Yorks.):
Athey, John, 23
Beeley, Edmund, 58
Beeley, Joseph, 58
Bell, J Bell, James William, 61
Bell, John, 62
Bell, Jonathan, 62
Bell, Thomas, 62
Berry, Robert, 68
Blackmoor, John, 78
Davenport, James, 227
Hallam, Thomas, 387
Heathcote, Thomas, 419
Hill, Benjamin, 430
Jubb, William, 499
Kitchen, Joseph, 518
Lent, George, 538
Peninston, Joseph, 688
Shore, Richard, 812
Turton, John, 914
Turton, Jos., 914
Wright, William, 1009
Yates, John, 1012
Rotherhithe (London):
Amber, Francis, 12
Bacon, Thomas, 28
Barnard, Robert, 42
Batten & Glover, 50
Batton, Edward, 50
Brannon, James, 103
Burrough, Thomas, 133
Drayton, Edmund, 256
Drayton, Richard, 256
Ember, Francis, 279
Emery, William, 280
Gardner, Charles, 329
Gardner, Henry, 330
Gathereole, B.&C., 333
Grayfoot, J., 366
Groves, George, 376
Hall, Robert, 386
Henderson, John, 420
Hopkins, Henry, 448
Hurwood, John, 466
Keegan, John, 502
Knowles, Mrs Elizabeth, 520
Lawson, Stephen, 532
Montraves, John Samuel, 616
Nyles, William, 658

Pearce, Thomas, 684
Scales, Samuel, 788
Turner, Peter, 911
Wiles, John, 974
Willson, Robert, 985
Rothwell (Yorks.): Morley, Joshua,
627
Rouse, Joseph, 706
Rouse, Richard, 821
Rousham House (Oxon.):
Cartwright, Mr, 149
Chippendale, Thomas snr, 166
Davis, —, 230
Davis, J., 231
Guibert, Philip, 378
Haddock, Elka, 382
Hallett, William snr and William
jnr, 388
Pritchard, William, 718
Row, 373
Row, Benjamin, 19, 580
Row, Benjamin Hambling, 762
Rowe, Charles, 997
Rowe, George, 762
Rowe, Isaac, 765
Rowe, James, 952
Rowes, Isaac, 765
Rowlands, James, 716
Rowley, 516
Rowley, Edward, 81
Rowling & Brown, 769
Rowsley (Derbs.): Barker, John, 40
Royston (Herts.):
Abbott, William, 1
Andrew, Charles, 14
Bunyan, Robert, 129
Good, John, 351
Green, Charles, 367
Johnson, Josiah, 490
Stredder, Edward, 861
Rudd, John, 698
Rudding Park (Yorks.): Kendell,
John, 505
Ruddock, William, 859
Rudyard, 440
Rudyard, Lawrence, 439, 458
Rudyeard, Lawrence, 458
Rugby (Warks.):
Beasley, George, 55
Eyles, William, 286
Goode, John, 351
Harrowell, William, 405
Ladkin, William, 521
Usher, Robert, 918
Wright, William, 1009
Rugeley (Staffs.):
Barton, John, 47
Bickley, John, 71
Brickley, John, 107
Bullock, Robert, 128
Keyte, William, 511
Remmington, Alexander, 737
Tunnicliffe, Robert, 908
Turner, Daniel, 909

Rullidge, William, 254
Rummer, Michael, 763
Rumney, Robert, 160
Runcorn (Cheshire): Rigby,
    William, 748
Rusby, 276
Rusby, Hugh, 74, 395, 568, 855, 886
Rush, William, 766
Russel, Richard, 469
Russell, 789
Russell, Charles, 773
Russell, I., 773
Russell, J., 773
Russell, James, 305
Russell, John, 677, 773
Russell, R., 49, 310
Russell, Robert, 936
Russell, Thomas, 771, 783
Russell, William, 290
Russell & Bruce, 771
Russia (Empress of): Seddon,
    George, 796
Rutherford, 820
Rutherford, John, 950
Rutherford, Joseph, 154
Rutledge, 31, 923
Rutledge, Christopher, 768
Rutledge, William, 959
Rutt, Thomas, 274
Rutter, Gasgoine, 329
Rutterford, 820
Ryan, 210
Rycroft, John, 599
Rydal Hall (Westmld.):
    Harker, Jonathan, 398
    Littledale, Joseph, 550
Ryde (Isle of Wight):
    Ball, T., 35
    Hansford, William, 395
    Marvin, Edward, 582
    Pearce, George, 684
    Purnell, James, 722
    Riddrett, George, 746
    Shorland, Richard, 812
    Wheeler, Emanuel, 963
    Wiltshire, Thomas, 991
Ryder, Francis, 460
Ryder, Joseph, 746
Ryder & Scribe, 456
Rye (Sussex):
    Blackman, James, 77
    Brazier, Blundell & Tutt, 104
    Brazier, James, 104
    Brazier, William, 104
    Hilder, Edward, 429
    Hoil, Thomas, 440
    Sampson, Thomas, 778
    Seymour, James, 801
    Seymour, John, 801
    Tamset, John, 870
    Tutt, Henry, 914
    Tutt, John, 914
    Worsell, Richard, 1003
Rylance, John, 68

Rylands, Joseph, 230
Ryley, 747
Ryley, John, 749
Ryther, Francis, 1015
Ryton, Obadiah, 774
Ryton, William,.774
Ryton (Co. Durham): Mordue,
    John, 623

S

Sabourin & Marchand, 775
Sadborow (Dorset):
    Horris, —, 450
    Knight, —, 518
Saddleworth (Yorks.):
    Beaumont, John, 56
    Blackburn, Richard, 77
    Ogden, William, 661
    Thorp, Daniel, 891
Saffron Walden (Essex):
    Brown, Francis, 114
    Brown, J., 114
    Burrows, Richard, 134
    Bush, Richard, 136
    Dunn, Hannibal, 260
    Dunn, Henry, 260
    Hutchinson, —, 467
    Leverett, William, 539
    Paul, Robert, 682
    Reed, William, 734
    Saggers, John, 775
    Searle, John, 792
    Searle, R.C., 792
    Smart, David, 823
    Smart, Jonathan, 823
    Spefford, William, 842
    Whitmore, Thomas, 969
Sagar, Stephen, 40
Sage, T., 775
Saint, Thomas, 160
St Albans (Herts.):
    Haynes, Edward, 415
    Munday, Thomas, 635
    Nicholls, James, 645
    Richardson, James Christopher,
    744
    Richardson, John, 744
    Sparrow, Jeremiah, 841
    Wood, J., 996
St Austell (Cornwall):
    Bennett, Jonathon, 65
    Bullen, Thomas, 126
    Glanville, Julian, 344
    Thomas, William, 884
St Columb (Cornwall):
    Best, John, 68
    George, Thomas, 335
    Hawey, —, 412
    Morcomb, John, 623
    Whitford, John, 969
St Day (Cornwall):
    Hawke, Richard, 412

Hosken, William, 451
St Giles (Middlx): Kemp, William,
    504
St Giles's (Dorset): Hallett, William
    snr, 389
St Helens (Lancs.):
    Hall, Joseph, 386
    Halsall, Richard, 391
    Hawksey, Andrew, 413
    Latham, James, 529
    Lawrenson, John, 531
    Penketh, John, 688
    Shaw, Thomas, 805
    Varley, Henry, 920
St Ives (Cornwall):
    Allpress, John, 11
    Dexter, John, 243
    Starmar, John, 850
St Ives (Hunts.):
    Balling, Timothy, 35
    Goodyer, William, 355
    Green, John, 367
    M'Kenzie, William, 566
    Quilton, Henry, 724
    Sanders, William, 779
    Saunders, William, 786
    Skeeles, George, 818
    Townsend, Richard, 901
    Townsend, Richardson, 901
St Leonards-on-Sea (Sussex):
    Bragg, Nathaniel, 101
    Drury, James, 257
    Smith, James, 827
St Luke (Middlx): Bateman, John,
    48
St Mary's Kalendar (Hants.):
    Hayes, John, 414
St Neots (Hunts.):
    Atkins, John, 23
    Banks, Thomas, 37
    Burgin, Richard, 130
    Dunkley, John, 259
    Dunkley, William, 259
    Gurry, Ebenezer, 380
    Gurry, Samuel, 380
    Key, Thomas, 511
    Oliver, Joseph, 663
    Paxton, Joseph, 682
    Quincey, William, 724
    Webster, Edward, 955
St Pancras (London):
    Abbey, Thomas, 1
    Lawrence, George, 530
    Steains, Cs., 851
    Steward, Richard, 855
    Tiffin, C., 894
    West, F., 959
St Quintin, Percy, 586
Saladine, Thomas, 312
Sale, Phineas, 369, 1009
Salford (Lancs.):
    Armitage, George, 18
    Atkinson, Francis, 24
    Badcock, Thomas, 28

Bancroft, David, 36
Bancroft, John, 36
Barlow, Henry, 41
Baxendale, Richard, 51
Beaumont, William, 56
Bebbington, Ralph, 56
Booth, James, 87
Booth, Ralph, 87
Bostock, Mary, 89
Brancroft, J. & D., 102
Brown, Joseph, 116
Daniel, William, 225
Davies, Thomas & Edward, 230
Dixon, Thomas 247
Dodgson, George, 249
Drape, Thomas, 255
Gaskell, John, 332
Hardman, Benjamin, 396
Hart, Pater, 406
Hart, Thomas, 406
Hassall, William, 409
Heron, John & Son, 423
Heywood, John, 426
Hindley, John, 433
Hindley, Mrs, 433
Hodgkinson, Francis, 437
Holcroft, Richard, 440
Hopkins, Thomas, 448
Hort, Peter, 451
Hudson, Elizabeth, 458
Hulme, Joseph Hilton, 462
Hunt, J., 464
Hunt, James, 464
Irlam, John, 473
Irlam, Mary, 473
Isaacs, Henry, 474
Jackson, George, 475
Jones, Isaac, 495
Kay, William, 501
Kearsley, William, 501
Knipe, William Garnet, 520
Latham, Pater, 529
Leigh, Ralph, 537
Losdale, Matthew, 555
McCann, William, 564
Makin, John, 570
Marsland, James, 580
Millne, George, 609
Monro, William, 616
Mooney, James, 617
Moore, William, 622
Mouncey, William, 633
Naylor, John, 639
Ormrod, John, 665
Ormrod, Richard, 665
Petrie, James, 692
Plant, John, 702
Powell, Richard, 710
Rimmer, George, 749
Robinson, Thomas, 760
Royle, James, 769
Rymer, George, 774
Savage, John, 786
Smith, Edward, 825

Starkey, Charles, 850
Statham, Benjamin, 850
Steele, William, 851
Stratham, Benjamin, 861
Sumner, Daniel, 865
Sutton, Daniel, 865
Sutton, Elizabeth, 865
Thomas, William, 884
Thorley, William, 889
Upton, James, 918
Walker, James, 935
Wharton, Robert, 962
Whitefield, Francis, 968
Whitehead, Thomas, 968
Wild, Thomas, 974
Wilkinson, George, 976
Williamson, Henry, 983
Wilson, John, 988
Wood, Thomas, 998
Woodstock, James, 1000
Young, Benjamin, 1014
Salisbury, John, 264, 781
Salisbury (Wilts.):
  Acton, John, 2
  Argall, William, 17
  Ball, Jonathan, 35
  Barry, James, 46
  Barter, John, 46
  Begbie, James, 59
  Begbie, Joseph, 59
  Bigbie, James, 71
  Blachford, Robert, 76
  Brownjohn, George, 120
  Bucket, Joseph, 123
  Davis, Richard, 232
  DuChemin, John, 257
  Edsall, Henry, 268
  Elderton, William, 272
  Elkins, Charles, 272
  Goodfellow, Lall, 351
  Goolding, Walter, 355
  Green, John, 367
  Green, Samuel, 367
  Heyley, William, 426
  Honeycroft, —, 447
  Howe, James, 455
  Hudson, John, 458
  Jay, Benjamin, 481
  Jeary, A.H. & Co., 482
  Kemm, William, 504
  Keynes, William, 511
  Kirk, Mary, 517
  Knight, William, 519
  Langley, Richard, 526
  Lewis, Benjamin, 539
  Long, Charles, 554
  Marshall, Michael, 579
  Norton, Charles, 656
  Parker, James, 674
  Powell, Robert, 710
  Salmon, Thomas, 777
  Salph, Elias, 777
  Simmonds, William, 815
  Skeats, Highmore, 818

Skilton, George, 819
Sleat, Robert, 821
Smith, Richard, 831
Snow, John, 837
Snow, Thomas, 837
Soper, Charles, 839
Streat, William, 861
Stuart, Charles, 862
Troubridge, John, 906
Vidler, Joseph, 923
Vilder, Joseph, 923
Sallows, Aldred, 801
Sallows, John, 801
Salter, John, 482
Saltford (Som.): Allen, William, 10
Salthouse, 939
Salthouse, Richard, 747
Saltram House (Devon):
  Campbell, Robert, 143
  Chippendale, Thomas snr, 167
  Crichton, David, 209
  Kettle, Henry, 510
  McLean, John & Son, 568
  Perfetti, Joseph, 690
Sampson, 954
Samuel, James, 71
Sandbach (Cheshire):
  Dickinson, John, 243
  Eaches, Peter, 263
  Steele, Richard, 851
  Steele, Thomas, 851
  Stringer, Joseph, 862
  Swinton, William, 868
Sandell, Samuel, 726
Sanders, 129, 261
Sanders, Frances, 779
Sanders, Joseph, 138, 668
Sanderson, 29, 144
Sanderson, Alexander, 779
Sanderson, Harry, 681
Sanderson, John, 136, 186, 438,
  517, 574
Sandford, William, 308
Sandon Hall (Staffs.):
  Bell, Daniel, 61
  Bell, Philip, 62
  Cable, —, 140
  Chippendale, Thomas snr, 166
  Cobb, John, 184
  Hilker, Anthony, 430
  Linnell, John, 545
  Linnell, William, 548
  Moore, Thomas, 621
  Morehouse, —, 623
  Reeves, —, 736
  Sherman, —, 809
  Silk, Thomas, 814
  Vile, William, 926
  Ward, James K., 943
Sands, Daniel, 420
Sandwell, Henry, 873
Sandwell, Joseph, 612
Sandwell Park (Staffs.): Mayhew,
  John & Ince, William, 593

Sandwich (Kent):
  Anston, Daniel, 15
  Baker, John, 32
  Baker, John F., 32
  Denne, John, 240
  Enston, Daniel snr, 281
  Hicks, John jnr, 428
  Howard, Joseph jnr, 454
  Miles, William, 607
  Pott, William, 707
  Pott & Denne, 707
  Rutter & Jinnings, 774
  Slaughter, Thomas M., 821
  Taylor, David F., 875
  Terry, Edward, 881
  Walker, James, 935
  Walker, Richard, 937
  Woodhams, George, 999
Sandys, Martin, 739
Sangar, 984
Sanston House: Gordon, John &
  Tait J. & R., 355, 357
Sargeant, James, 438
Sargent, 233
Sargood, 329
Sarnesfield Court (Herefs.):
  Calldicolt, —, 141
  Mapey (or Masey), Abram, 573
  Packer, Thomas, 669
  Parker, Mrs, 673
  West, John, 959
Satterthwaite, 257
Saunders, 263, 414
Saunders, Ann, 95
Saunders, Henry, 785
Saunders, John, 785
Saunders, Joseph, 840
Saunders, Paul, 98, 99, 100, 554,
  652, 653, 835
Saunders, Richard, 30
Saunders, Thomas, 782
Saunders & Colbron, 785
Saunier, Julia, 786
Savage, Michael, 546
Savage, Purbeck, 194
Savage, Walter, 611
Savile, Thomas, 65, 933
Savill, 136
Savill, Thomas, 306, 536
Saville, 937
Saville, Thomas, 102
Sawick: Robinson, James, 758
Sawston Hall (Cambs.):
  Eyre(s), James & Large, James,
  287
  Hasert, Pater, 409
Sawtry (Hunts.): Stafford, Joshua,
  847
Sawyer, 421
Saxmundham (Suffolk):
  Bright, Jerome, 107
  Bromwich, Thomas, 110
  Cobb, John, 184
  Crompton, Samuel, 211

Hewitt, John, 425
Hynmers Taylor, —, 470
Mo(w)bray, Christopher, 633
Ridley & Son, 747
Seddon, George, 796
Wright, James, 1005
Saxton, Alfred, 787
Saxton, George, 787
Saxton, Henry, 787
Saxton, Nathaniel, 811
Say, Frances, 500
Say, Francis, 228, 350, 732
Say, Richard, 730, 969, 994
Scafe, William, 859
Scarborough (Yorks.):
  Archer, Isaac, 17
  Archer, Thomas, 17
  Archer, Tristram, 17
  Bassick, A., 48
  Berwick, Anthony, 68
  Burton, William, 136
  Daggett, John, 223
  Davison, Thomas, 233
  Haigh, Francis, 383
  Jameson, Daniel, 480
  Kingston, John, 516
  Lawson, Thomas, 532
  Lee, James, 534
  Lord, William & Son, 555
  Lunn, Thomas, 561
  Pearson, Hewland, 684
  Percy, Robert, 690
  Perry, Robert, 692
  Simpson, William, 817
  Smailes, John, 822
  Smith, Thomas, 833
  Suggitt, David, 864
  Thornton, Samuel, 891
  Tindale, George, 895
  Tissiman, Peter, 896
  Underwood, Hugh, 917
  Waite, Matthew, 932
  White, Daniel, 965
Scawby Hall (Lincs.): Chippendale,
  Thomas jnr, 169
Scholefield, John, 788–9
Scholes, Abner, 72
Scholes, Benjamin, 263
Scholes (Lancs.): Holding, George,
  441
Scholey, Joseph, 215, 286
Scholey, Robert, 836
Schouten, William, 376
Scoles, Abner, 407, 569
Scone Palace (Perthshire): Bullock,
  George, 127
Scorton (Lancs.): Parkinson, Robert
  jnr, 676
Scotney Castle (Kent): Wyatt,
  Edward, 1010
Scott, 319
Scott, Charles, 38
Scott, George, 637
Scott, Samuel, 654

Scott, Thomas, 198, 637
Scratby Hall (Norfolk): Oliffe,
  Robert, 662
Scribe, 456
Scrimshire, Matthew, 290
Scrimshire, William, 287, 401, 647,
  819, 859, 894
Scriven, William, 855
Scruton (Yorks.): Dunn, Richard,
  260
Sculptor: Bullock, George, 126
Seabright, 918
Seabrook, 327
Seager, 200
Seal, Richard, 298
Seaman, William, 11, 399, 504
Search, Samuel, 521
Searson, William, 983
Searson, Wortley, 37, 983
Sebire, 369
Sedan chairmakers:
  Vaughan, George, 920
  Vaughan, Samuel, 920
Sedburgh (Yorks.): Dodgson, John,
  249
Seddon, 75, 252, 282, 435, 721, 766,
  808, 867, 970
Seddon, George, 6, 178, 372, 562,
  624, 653, 658, 688, 728, 780, 954
Seddon, Henry, 408
Seddon, Richard, 408
Seddon Sons & Shackleton, 643,
  699, 794, 796, 797
Sedgley (Staffs.):
  Law, Joseph, 530
  Law, William, 530
  Mainwaring, William, 570
Sedgwick, Christopher, 759
Sedgwick, John, 798
Sedwell, William, 965
Seely, Abraham, 864
Selby (Yorks.):
  Andrew, Nathaniel, 14
  Armstrong, Christopher, 18
  Bairsto, George, 32
  Banks, James, 37
  Bentley, James, 66
  Garbut, Robert, 329
  Jackson, Thomas, 477
  Pratt, Philip, 712
  Staniland, Joseph, 849
  Staniland, Robert, 849
  Tomison, Jackman, 897
  Ullathorne, John, 916
  Ward, John, 943
Seller, Christopher, 398
Sellers, John, 358
Semple, Alexander, 802
Semple, John, 802
Senols, James, 233, 369, 1012
Serlby Hall (Notts.): Wright,
  Richard & Elwick, Edward, 1007
Settle (Yorks.):
  Hallpike, V., 390

Harger, Robert, 398
Moorhouse, John, 622
Wilcock, James, 973
Wilkinson, George, 976
Wilman, Stephen, 985
Wilson, Christopher, 986
Sevenoaks (Kent):
  Kipps, Thomas, 516
  Middleton, James & Henry, 605
  Pett, —, 692
  Sanders, Benjamin, 779
  Stanger, James, 848
Severn, Samuel, 10, 863, 876
Severn End (Worcs.):
  Crump, John snr, 216
  Ward, William, 944
Severn Stoke (Worcs.): Jackson,
  William, 477
Sewell, John, 7, 777
Sewerby House (Yorks.): Taylor,
  John, 877
Shackleton, 643, 699, 796, 797
Shackleton, Thomas, 658, 659, 660,
  794, 795, 1008
Shackleton (Yorks.): Parker, John,
  674
Shadbolt, Charles, 800
Shadbolt, William, 800
Shadwell (London):
  Eyles, Charles, 286
  Morgan, Thomas, 625
  Osmond, S., 666
  Plowman, J., 703
  Shipman, Coleman, 811
  Smith, Henry, 827
  Smith, Thomas, 832
Shaftesbury (Dorset):
  Beale, Dan., 54
  Blanchard, James, 80
  Buckland, R., 124
  Downs, Richard, 255
  Higham, George, 429
  Hiscock, Jos., 434
  Knight, James, 519
  Mansfield, Thomas jnr, 573
  Meader, William, 599
  Oborne, W.& I., 661
  Pinhorne, Charles, 699
  Reynolds, Joseph Hiscock, 738
  Spearing, David, 842
  Sweet, James, 867
  Usher, James, 918
  West, Robert, 960
Shakels, Thomas, 244
Shakespear, Henry, 731
Shaldon (Devon):
  Buckland, William, 124
  Norsworthy, William, 655
Shardeloes (Bucks.):
  Adair, John, 2
  Alken, Sefferin, 8
  Gale, Thomas, 327
  Lawrence, Richard, 531
  Linnell, John, 544–5

Linnell, William, 546, 547
Quirke, Tom, 724
Whitcomb, John, 964
Wicksted, John, 972
Sharp, 481
Sharp, Ann, 803
Sharp, James, 803
Sharp, John, 606
Sharp, Joseph, 173
Sharp, Peter, 589, 987
Sharp, Robert, 802
Sharp, Samuel, 416
Sharp & Clark, 802
Sharpe, Charles, 803
Sharpe, Christopher, 803
Sharpe, Edward, 226–7
Sharpe, Thomas, 743
Sharples, Thomas, 726
Sharples & Rainford, 64, 804
Sharrat, Samuel, 64
Sharrington, Ralph, 387, 388
Sharwood, James, 264
Shaw, 778
Shaw, John, 572
Shearar, Thomas, 737
Shearer, Thomas, 810
Sheen, Edmund Henry, 580
Sheerness (Kent):
  Attwater, James Thomas, 25
  Burlingham, John, 131
  Mantle, James, 573
  Rose, —, 765
  South, George, 840
Sheffield (Yorks.):
  Adams, Francis, 3
  Adams, William, 4
  Aray, Robert, 16
  Armitage, William, 18
  Badger, Joseph, 28
  Bailey, Edward, 29
  Bardwell, Ann, 39
  Bardwell, Edward, 39
  Barker, Hugh, 40
  Barton, Thomas, 47
  Bell, James, 61
  Bertie, William, 68
  Bertie & Nichols, 68
  Binge, John, 72
  Bings, John, 72
  Blackburn, John, 77
  Blackwell, James, 78
  Blagden, Williamn, 78
  Bland, James, 80
  Bonnett, John, 86
  Booth, James, 87
  Booth, John Henry, 87
  Bower, Benjamin, 92
  Bower, Charles, 92
  Bowling, Thomas, 93
  Boylyn, Caesar, 94
  Brailsford, J.W., 101
  Brailsford, Joseph Hill, 101
  Brailsford, Thomas, 101
  Brailsford, William, 101

Brocklehurst, Joseph, 109
Brown, George, 114
Burnard, Robert, 131
Burton, George, 135
Burton, John, 135
Burton, Thomas, 135
Bussey, William, 137
Dawson, William, 235
Dean, Joseph, 237
Ditchfield, William, 245
Dobbs, Thomas, 247
Doughty, William, 251
Downing, William, 254
Drury, Edward, 257
Drury, Thomas, 257
Eadon, George, 263
Ellis(s), John, 275
Gill, David, 340
Gill, James, 340
Gill, Richard, 340
Gillatt, George, 341
Gillott, George, 341
Glossop, Nathan, 345
Goodlad, John, 354
Goodwin, John, 355
Gosling, George, 358
Green, George, 367
Green, Joseph & Joshua, 367
Green, William, 368
Green & Morton, 368
Greenwood, James, 369
Greenwood, Jonathan, 369
Gregory, Joseph, 370
Grinold, William, 375
Guest, Thomas, 377
Guggiari, Charles, 377
Hall, John, 385
Hall, William, 386
Harrison, James, 403
Hartshorn, Michael, 407
Hawksworth, Hannah, 413
Hayes, John, 414
Hayne(r)s, Roger, 415
Henderson, Robert, 421
Hill, John, 431
Hill, Joseph, 431
Hobson, Joseph, 436
Horrocks, Barnard E., 450
Horrocks, Joseph, 450
Ibbotson, Thomas, 470
Ingham, Peter, 471
Jackson, John, 476
Jackson, William, 477
Jenkinson, John, 484
Jessop, James, 488
Jessop, Thomas, 488
Johnson, William, 493
Jones, J., 495
Keates, Joseph, 502
Keats, Joseph, 502
Knott, Thomas, 520
Landers, James, 524
Latham, William, 529
Lee, James, 534

Lee, William, 535
Lister, John, 549
Lister, William, 549
Lucas, John, 559
Lucas, Mrs, 559
Mackenzie, P., 566
Mackenzie, W., 566
Mackenzie, William, 566
Marples, William Edward, 575
Marples & Hibbert, 575
Marsden, Thomas, 576
Martin, James, 581
Mawrice, Joseph, 588
Miller, Thomas & Son, 609
Miller, William, 609
Mills, George, 610
Morley & Co., 627
Morris, Joseph, 628
Morton, Thomas, 630
Mosley, Robert, 632
Moss, George, 632
Moxon, William, 634
Nevill, William, 641
New, Thomas, 641
Newton, Ann, 644
Newton, Thomas, 645
North, John, 655
Norton, J., 656
Oram, Skidmore & Co., 664
Outram, Richard, 667
Outram, Thomas, 667
Outram, William, 667
Parker & Cluley, 675
Pearsey, John snr, 684
Prandi, Francis, 712
Ramsay, Robert, 726
Rawson, John, 730
Redfern, Samuel, 733
Rippon, Reuben, 750
Robinson, John & William, 758
Rodgers, Robert, 762
Rodgers, Thomas, 762
Rogers & Shimmeld, 764
Rose, John, 766
Ryan, Thomas, 774
Saunders, Thomas, 785
Saville, Peter, 786
Scantlebury, John, 788
Scantlebury, Thomas, 788
Shemeld, Charles, 807
Shepherd, John, 807
Shepherd, Malin & Son, 807
Sheppard, John, 808
Sherwood, W., 810
Singleton, Thomas, 818
Smith, John, 829, 830
Smith, Sampson, 831
Smith, William, 835
Spacey & Wragg, 841
Steer, Edward, 851
Sterkey, J., 854
Stevenson, Charles, 855
Stevenson, John, 855
Styring, George, 863

Styring, James, 863
Styring, Richard W., 863
Styring, Robert, 864
Swan, Henry, 867
Taylor, Micah, 878
Thirnbeck, Richard, 882
Thrinbeck, Richard, 892
Titley, John, 896
Todd, John, 896
Tyson, George, 916
Tyson, James, 916
Unwin, Charles, 917
Vickers, Samuel, 923
Wade, Frederick, 931
Wade & Jackson, 931
Wainwright, Joseph, 932
Walker, Benjamin, 934
Walker, Robert, 937
Walker, William, 938
Ward, Thomas, 942
Watson, George, 949
Whildon, Joseph, 963
White, William, 967
Wills, William, 985
Wilson, James, 987
Wolstenholme, John, 995
Woodhead, William, 999
Wragg & Wigfall, 1003
Wright, George, 1005
Yates, Benjamin, 1012
Yates, David & Son, 1012
Shelbrook (Yorks.): Wright,
   Richard & Elwick, Edward, 1008
Sheldon, 498
Shelf (Yorks.): Barker, Robert, 41
Shelford (Notts.): Howett, John,
   456
Shellingford Manor (Berks.):
   Hodson, John, 439
Shelton, John, 422, 501
Shelton (Staffs.):
   Bailey, William, 31
   Bolton, George, 84
   Davies, Edward, 228
   Heath, Thomas, 419
   Johnson, John, 490
   Parton, Daniel, 678
   Parton, David, 678
   Wyatt, William, 1010
Shene, Thomas, 734
Shenton, John, 834
Shepard, 53, 304
Shepard, William, 572, 838, 956
Shephard, J., 161
Shepherd, 73, 304, 696
Shepherd, Daniel, 205
Shepherd, John, 290, 961
Shepherd, Richard, 710
Shepherd, Simpson, 808
Shepherd, Thomas Walker, 469
Shepherd, William, 240, 376
Sheppard, 304
Shepton Mallet (Som.):
   Earl, Elijah, 264

Gaite, David, 327
Holliwell, John, 443
Mansford, John, 573
Ruddock, William, 770
Slocombe, Chas., 821
Wilcox, Edward, 973
Sheraton, Thomas, 143, 422, 573
Sherborne, William, 371
Sherborne (Dorset):
   Bastard, Thomas, 48
   Ellis, Thomas, 275
   Geake, Thomas, 333
   Gent, George, 335
   Hawkins, Richard, 413
   Hebdish, Charles, 419
   Higgens, James, 428
   Hoddinet, —, 436
   Hoddinot(t)(s), James, 436
   Hyatt, John, 469
   Jeffery, Samuel, 482
   King, John, 514
   Langlois, Pierre, 526
   Moore, George, 618
   Percy, Joseph, 690
   Pitman, John, 700
   Rawlings, George, 730
   Rogers, James, 763
   Short, William, 812
   Sturges & Noake, 863
   Thorne, George, 889
   Thorne, John, 890
   Thorn(e), Thomas, 890
   Vincent, John, 929
   Winter, Benjamin, 992
Sherborne Castle (Dorset):
   Chippendale, Thomas snr, 167
   Gosset, Isaac, 359
   Hughes, —, 460
   Isherwood, —, 474
   Langlois, Pierre, 527
   Mayhew, John & Ince, William,
   592, 593
   Vaughan, Samuel, 920
   Ward, Thomas, 943
   Williams, Thomas, 982
Sherborne House (Glos.):
   Blackwell, Norgrove & Smagge,
   78
   Bladwell, John, 78
   Lockyer, —, 553
   Moore, James jnr, 619
   Richards, James, 742
   Smagg, Peter, 822
   Williams, Henry, 980
Sheringham Hall (Norfolk):
   Phillips, Thomas, 696
Sherman, John, 901
Sherrard St (Middlx): Draper,
   James, 255
Sherwood, John, 853
Sherwood, John Hallett, 806
Shifnal (Salop):
   Barke, Thomas, 39
   Burke, Thomas, 130

133

Bullock, William, 128
Halley, George snr & jnr, 389
King, Charles, 514
Pointon, William, 704
Reynolds, James, 738
Shildon (Co. Durham): Brown,
  Matthew, 117
Shillington (Beds.): Eames, Samuel,
  264
Shillito, James, 469
Shimmeld, 764
Shipley, Ann, 787
Shipley, John, 43, 129, 146, 199,
  661, 787, 834, 843, 844
Shipley (Yorks.):
  Hainsworth, James, 383
  Teale, John, 880
Shipman, 365
Shipman, Edward, 64, 390, 719
Shipman, James, 856
Shipton, 400
Shire Hall (Sussex): Lambe,
  Richard, 522
Shobden Court (Herefs.):
  Bradshaw, —, 98
  Pember, Joseph snr, 688
S(?)holl, Thomas, 510
Shore, James, 827
Shore, William, 363, 471
Shoreditch (London):
  Abbott, Henry, 1
  Agland, William, 5
  Archer, John, 17
  Atkinson, George, 24
  Bailey, J., 30
  Bailey, William, 31
  Barber, William, 39
  Bath, John, 49
  Benton, J., 67
  Bertin, James Charles, 68
  Bird, Benjamin, 75
  Bowden, George, 92
  Bransby, Samuel, 103
  Bret, J., 105
  Bull, Obadiah, 125
  Bullock, James, 128
  Bunn, Henry, 129
  Burton, Joshua, 135
  Darnell, John, 227
  Davies, David, 228
  Deadman, James, 237
  Deadman, Samuel, 237
  Denham, James, 240
  Dodd, John, 248
  Downes, —, 254
  East, Benjamin, 264
  Gillach, John, 340
  Gillock, Thomas, 341
  Goldsmith, Charles, 348
  Goodbody, William, 351
  Goulding, J., 360
  Grantham, John, 364
  Gray, Charles, 365
  Gray, Joshua, 365

Groves, Micael, 376
Harris, William, 403
Heathcott, I., 419
Hindle, John, 433
Hopkins, William, 449
Hopkins, William Frederick, 449
Horner, Charles, 450
Horsley, James, 451
Hoy, William, 456
Ivory, Robert, 474
James, Philip, 479
Jones, Charles, 494
Keith, William, 502
Kirk, John, 516
Langridge, John, 527
Leveridge, William, 539
Lewin, John Thomas, 539
Lilly, Richard, 542
Lindsay, Benjamin, 542
Luff, Charles, 560
Manchee, John, 572
Martinelli, Peter, 582
Merchant, John, 602
Miller, E., 608
Miller, Henry, 608
Mills, Charles, 610
Milton, John, 611
Morris, Joseph, 628
Mould, E., 633
Mower, John, 634
Nickells, James, 647
Olive, William, 663
Owen, Richard, 668
Parker, Henry, 674
Payne, William, 683
Pears, Richard, 684
Pearson, John, 685
Philip, James, 694
Pineh, John, 699
Pitches, Thomas, 700
Pritchard, Richard, 718
Ranshall, John, 728
Redfarn, William Robert, 733
Rose, S., 766
Sabourin, George, 774
Saevent, William, 775
Salisbury, William, 776
Samuel, S.J. & P., 778
Sanders, John, 779
Seager, George, 792
Shearman, James, 806
Smith, Nathaniel, 830
Smith, Thomas, 833
Sprague, Saul, 845
Spurgeon, John, 846
Stanton, James, 849
Steadman, Robert, 851
Stewart, John, 856
Trigg, John, 904
Troughton, John, 906
Valentino, Dan., 919
Walker, John, 936
Watson, —, 948
Webb, John, 953

Welch, Joseph, 957
Welch, Nathaniel, 957
White, George Morris, 965
Wicking, Benjamin, 972
Wride, William, 1004
Wryde, Peter, 1009
Yarrow, Ridley, 1012
Shores, Arthur, 301, 568, 855, 877
Shores, John, 779
Short, James, 138
Short, William, 84
Shotter, 111
Shotter, Gawn, 285, 779
Shotter & Evans, 812
Showbridge, John, 61
Shrewsbury (Salop):
  Adams, Charles, 3
  Adams, Henry, 3
  Adams, James Evan, 3
  Allen, John, 10
  Allison, William, 11
  Anslow, Thomas, 15
  Badger, James, 28
  Baker, Thomas, 33
  Baker, William, 33
  Baxter, Richard, 52
  Bernard, Charles, 67
  Betton, Richard, 69
  Bevan, William, 69
  Birch, John, 73
  Blakeway, Robert, 79
  Blower, John, 81
  Bratton, Richard, 103
  Bratton, Thomas, 103
  Brereton, James, 105
  Brew, Thomas, 106
  Brown, Edwin, 113
  Burleigh, Thomas, 130
  Burrey, James, 133
  Burrey & White, 133
  Davies, —, 228
  Davies, Adam, 228
  Davi(e)s, Evan, 228
  Davies, Peter, 229
  Davies, Thomas & Son, 230
  Davies, William, 230
  Devey, James, 242
  Dixon, —, 245
  Donaldson, John, 250
  Donaldson, Peter Evans, 250
  Donaldson, Thomas, 250
  Durnford, John, 262
  Goucher, James, 359
  Green, Charles, 367
  Griffiths, Charles, 374
  Hall, Henry, 385
  Hall, Joseph, 386
  Hall, Thomas, 386
  Harris, Arthur, 400
  Harrison, John, 404
  Hartshorn, J., 407
  Harwood, John Philip, 408
  Harwood, John Philip jnr, 408
  Haynes, Thomas, 415

Hewett, —, 425
Hewit(t), Thomas, 425
Hewlett, Charles, 426
Hewlett, William, 426
Hewlitt, William, 426
Hill, Thomas, 431
Hill, William, 432
Hill & Hewitt, 432
Hodges, George, 437
Hodges, John, 437
Hodges, Richard, 437
Hodges & Lawrence, 437
Hood, John, 447
Hughes, Richard, 461
Hughes, Thomas, 461
Ireland, Edward, 473
Jones, Richard, 496
Kinaston, —, 513
Kingley, Gabriel, 516
Lacey, T., 521
Lacy, Tenant, 521
Lawrence, —, 530
Lawrence, Joseph, 531
Lawrence, Thomas, 531
Leake, Eileen, 533
Leake, Eslem, 533
Leake, George Edward, 533
Leake, James, 533
Lee, —, 534
Lee, George, 534
Lee, William, 535
Leicester, William, 537
Leigh, John, 537
Lewis, William, 541
Lloyd, William, 551
Lomax, Francis, 554
Lomax, George, 554
Mallard, Edward, 571
Mansell & Son, 573
M'Cready, John, 564
Morley, Henry, 627
Morris, John, 628
Murray, Richard, 637
Nelson, —, 640
Nicholls, Richard, 646
Oliver, John, 663
Pearce, Edward, 684
Pearson, Benjamin, 684
Penrhyn, Thomas, 689
Perason, J., 685
Perry, Jonathan, 691
Pitchford, John, 700
Pugh, Edward, 720
Pugh, Thomas, 720
Revall, Champ., 737
Reynolds, Ralph, 738
Richards, James, 742
Richards, John, 742
Richards, Thomas, 742
Ridgeway, Hugh, 747
Roe, George, 762
Sandford, Thomas, 779
Scoltock, John & Richard,
Jonathan, 789

Smith, William, 834
Steventon, John, 855
Tempson, J., 881
Thomas, John, 883
Thomas, Joseph, 884
Thomas, William, 884
Thornton, —, 890
Tit(t)ensor, John, 896
Tudor, Samuel, 908
Wade, George, 931
Watkiss, Richard, 948
White, Henry, 965
White, John, 966
White, Timothy, 967
Williams, Edward, 979
Wood, —, 995
Wood, John, 996
Wood, Richard, 997
Shrigley, Robert, 889
Shrubland Park (Suffolk): Bullock,
    George, 128
Shuffrey, William, 654, 825
Shugborough (Staffs.):
    Adair, John, 2
    Collins, William, 189
    Reynier, Charles, 737
    Smith, Charles, 825
Shute, James, 813
Shute, William, 813
Shuter, William, 1002
Shuttleworth, 656
Shuttleworth, Barton, 418
Sibley, John, 775
Sidbury, Worcester:
    Reed, Thomas, 734
    Wellsman, John, 958
    Wesman, Nicholas, 958
Siddall, Samuel, 462
Siddon, George, 178
Siddons, 1
Sidmouth (Devon):
    Denby, Edward, 240
    Holmes, John, 445
    Pile, Michael, 698
    Potbury, George, 707
    Potbury, Gregory, 707
    Saunders, J., 782
    Slader, R., 820
    West, John, 960
Silbon, William, 79, 434, 465
Silcock, Obadiah, 965
Silk, Thomas, 199, 292
Silkstone (Yorks.): Swift, John, 868
Silsden (Yorks.): Laycock, William,
    532
Silverwood, 213
Simcock, John, 704
Simecock, John, 647
Simmonds, William, 85
Simmons, William, 85, 881
Simmons & Gregory, 815
Simms, Joseph, 355
Simonburn (Northumb.): Bell,
    George, 61

Simpson, 128, 258
Simpson, George, 817
Simpson, Giblett & Atkins, 817
Simpson, James, 371
Simpson, Michael, 291
Simpson, Richard, 689
Simpson, Samuel, 257
Simpson, William, 806, 916
Simpson & Duke, 817
Simpson & Giblett, 817
Sinclair, Edward, 47
Sindrey, 835
Sion House (Worcs.): Bishop,
    William Henry, 76
Sipling, Nicholas, 767
Sittingbourne (Kent):
    Drayson, John, 256
    Hooper, —, 447
    Hopper, Edward, 449
    Ironmonger, William, 473
    Jordan, William, 499
    Knowles, Thomas, 520
    Peacock, —, 683
    Peacock, Robert & Parlby,
        George, 683
    Reason, Thomas Filmer, 732
    Williams, John, 981
Skeel, Thomas, 688
Skegg, 835
Skeldergate, York:
    Jennings, Thomas, 485
    Pollard, John, 705
Skeldon, William, 818
Skelmanthorpe (Yorks.):
    Hampshaw & Thomas, 392
Skelton, Arthur, 335
Skelton, Humfrey, 409
Skelton, Humphrey, 973
Skelton, Samuel, 120, 791
Skelton (Yorks.): Appleton,
    William, 16
Skerrett, John, 819
Skerton (Lancs.): Hall, Richard,
    386
Skilbeck, John, 54
Skillicorn, John, 245, 258
Skillicorn, Richard, 159
Skinner, Harry, 248, 954
Skinner, Timothy Matthew, 837
Skipton (Yorks.):
    Brown, John, 116
    Brown, William, 119
    Brumfitt, Edward, 121
    Brumfitt, William, 121
    Demaine, Christ., 239
    Ellison, James, 276
    Ellison, William, 276
    Gyer, John, 381
    Hagg, Thomas, 382
    Hail, William, 383
    Hall, John, 385
    Hogg, Thomas, 440
    Hull, Christopher, 462
    Lister, Robert, 549

Lowcock, John, 557
Lowcock, William, 557
Matron, John, 586
Peacock, James, 683
Peacock, John, 683
Pearson, James, 685
Peason, William, 685
Proctor, Christopher, 719
Proctor, George, 719
Pullan, Thomas, 721
Reader, John, 732
Smith, William, 834
Thompson, Joseph, 887
Wade, Thomas, 931
Walsh, William, 941
Watson, Henry, 949
Watson, John, 950
Watson, Thomas, 950
Wilkinson, Alexander, 975
Wilson, Henry, 987
Wilson, John, 988
Skircoat (Yorks.): Dyson, Joseph, 263
Slack, 423, 829
Slade, Josh. N., 14
Slades, 513
Slater, 829, 906
Slater, Edward, 834
Slatford, Edward, 463
Slatter, Gabriel, 479
Sleaford (Lincs.):
  Brand, John, 102
  Hackett, Thomas, 381
  Halford, Edward, 384
  Marsh, Thomas, 577
  Mason, Ann, 583
  Payne, John, 682
  Payne, William, 683
  Simpson, William, 817
  Singleton & Son, 818
  Tapster, Stephen, 872
  Watson, John, 950
  Wright, William, 1009
Sledmere (Yorks.):
  Platt, John, 702
  Robbins, John, 751
Sleigh, Samuel, 493, 581, 870
Sleight, H., 764
Slingsby (Yorks.): Smith, Thomas, 833
Slodden, 123
Slough (Bucks.):
  Hewitt, Richard, 426
  Lovegrove, Henry, 556
  Pitt, John, Paul, 701
Slyne (Lancs.): Boardley, William, 82
Smagge, 78
Smagget, P., 439
Small, 696
Small, James, 694, 696
Smart, Abraham Chubb, 869
Smart, James, 150
Smart, John, 730

Smee, Samuel, 906
Smethurst, John, 215
Smith, 208, 300, 423, 474, 480, 493, 514, 515, 550, 582, 588, 634, 664, 671, 682, 863, 913, 933, 961, 962
Smith, Abraham, 748
Smith, Alexander, 833
Smith, Anthony, 53, 258
Smith, Captain, 832
Smith, Charles, 590, 831, 925
Smith, Edmund, 826
Smith, Edward, 813, 944, 961
Smith, Elliot, 432, 464, 731, 867, 1003, 1013
Smith, Elliot Macro, 828
Smith, Fillia, 834
Smith, G., 99
Smith, George, 168, 171, 642
Smith, H.T., 504
Smith, Henry, 739, 740
Smith, Henry Barrows, 536
Smith, J., 831
Smith, James, 244, 415, 454, 971
Smith, Jeremiah, 77, 98, 117, 291
Smith, John, 71, 86, 423, 688, 732, 834, 835, 852, 1005
Smith, John C., 830
Smith, Jos., 882
Smith, Joseph, 27, 940
Smith, Lucy, 344, 824
Smith, Richard, 408, 465, 563
Smith, Robert, 162
Smith, Robert Donald, 824
Smith, Samuel, 831, 914
Smith, T., 827
Smith, Thomas, 81, 151, 174, 202, 244, 430, 487, 569, 631, 828, 829, 831, 834, 835, 915
Smith, Trower & Co., 829
Smith, Trower & Slater, 829
Smith, William, 55, 111, 117, 143, 150, 224, 226, 444, 508, 514, 552, 611, 646, 807, 820, 829, 830, 851, 864, 881, 961
Smith, Wright, 264
Smith & Elliot, 828
Smith & Key, 824
Smith & Latterfield, 832
Smith & Slack, 829
Smithfield (London):
  Bennett, Thomas, 65
  Bodham, Philip, 83
  Brown, Thomas & Pyner, James, 118
  Browning, —, 120
  Butcher, James, 137
  Butler, Thomas, 137
  Davis, N., 232
  Dawes & Grimes, 234
  Dibble, Andrew, 243
  Edwards, Thomas, 270
  Gardner, J., 330
  Gomm, William & Richard, 349
  Gracey, William, 361

Griffith, William & Co., 374
Griffith & Payne, 374
Hambleton, —, 391
Hamilton, Francis, 391
Hamilton, Joseph, 391
Harding, C., 396
Heather, William, 419
Howard, John, 454
Howard & Hambleton, 455
Killick, John, 512
King, William, 515
Kirkham, John, 517
Lad, Richard, 521
Laurikens, Mark Anthony, 529
Lawton, John, 532
Medhurst, —, 600
Medhurst, David, 600
Meras, Henry, 599
Mills, Thomas D., 610
Molinare, James, 615
Molinari, J., 615
Pailthorpe, G., 670
Partridge, William, 678
Peachey, Thomas, 683
Pearce, B., 684
Powell, John Henry, 710
Pyner, James, 723
Reed, Shakespear & Wainwright, George & Charles, 734
Rippin, Richard, 750
Robinson, Thomas, 760
Simpson, John, 816
Smartfoot, Benjamin, 823
Springweiler, Andrew Barnard, 846
Strugnell, Charles E., 862
Tallantire, Thomas, 870
Taylor, —, 874
Taylor, George, 876
Watson & Martin, 951
Welborn, Joseph, 956
Wenborn, Josiah, 958
Willett & Blandford, 979
Zuardri, Joseph, 1016
Smithson, Robert, 940
Snaith (Yorks.):
  Batley, Richard, 49
  Dickinson, William, 243
  Drake, Joseph, 255
  Hepworth, Thomas, 423
  Turton, Joseph, 914
Snell, 1005
Snell, Edward, 836
Snell & Wright, 836
Snettisham (Norfolk): Rix, George, 750
Snow, John, 458
Snow, Thomas, 458
Snow, William, 376
Snow Fields (London):
  Longbotham, Henry, 555
Snowfield (London): Ready, John, 732

Snowhill (London):
  Bunyard, William, 129
  Dell, Nathan, 239
  Gower, Thomas, 361
  Hoby, James, 436
  Jarvis, Samuel, 481
  Jordan, Thomas, 499
  King, Thomas William & Co, 515
  King, William, 515
  Millard, W., 607
  Owen, Thomas, 668
  Rawbone, Thomas, 729
  Rawbone & Rainper, 729
  Randall & Hay, 727
  Robbins, William, 751
  Robins, William, 756
  Robinson, Henry 757
  Robinson, Henry Sacheverall, 757
  Smith, William, 834
  Walker, Matthew, 936
  Want, George S., 942
  Wicks, Charles, 972
Snuggs, H., 838
Sodd, Sam, 859
Soham (Cambs.):
  Bailey, Thomas, 31
  Levet, Jospeh, 539
Soho (London):
  Adair, John & William, 2
  Adair, William Robert, 2
  Adam, James, 2
  Adams, Robert & Co., 4
  Aike, James, 5
  Ainsworth & Milner, 6
  Aitken, Alexander, 6
  Akers, C., 6
  Akers, Mark, 6
  Anderson, Geroge, 12
  Andrews, John W., 14
  Appletree, John, 16
  Ashby, John, 20
  Bailey, James & Boote, Alexander, 30
  Baldie, John, 34
  Baldwin, John, 34
  Bales, Samuel, 34
  Ball, William, 35
  Banks, Benjamin, 37
  Bardolph, James, 39
  Baret, W., 44
  Barker, Robert, 41
  Barrett, James, 44
  Barrett, John, 44
  Barrett, T. & Wickstead, 44
  Bartington, S., 46
  Bartlett & Co., 46
  Bartlington, S., 46
  Bates, Richard, 49
  Baugham, William, 50
  Bayley, James & Boote, Alexander, 52
  Beale, John, 54

Bellingham, John, 63
Bertram, William, 68
Biers & Stringer, 71
Bigelston, William, 71
Bird, Thomas, 74
Black, Robert, 77
Black, Thomas, 77
Blackburn, William, 77
Blain, Joshua, 79
Blanch, Samuel, 79
Bobbitt, William, 82
Bogue, John, 83
Bond, S.G., 85
Bond, Stephen, 85
Bonham, William, 85
Booker, William, 86
Boone, Thomas, 86
Boote, Alexander, 87
Boston, J., 89
Bowles, George, 93
Bowman, Robert, 93
Brader, John, 97
Breteuil(e), John, 105
Bull, William, 125
Bunyan, —, 129
Burgis, William, 130
Burn & Kerr, 131
Burroughs & Watts, 133
Butler, James, 137
Byfield, James, 139
Byfield, Thomas, 139
Dalrimple, H., 224
Daniel, Edward, 225
Davies, John, 229
Davis, Henry Hart, 231
Davis, John, 231
Davis & Newton, 233
Dawes, B., 233
Dawes, Bartholomew, 233
Daws, Edward, 234
Daymond, Edward James, 236
Daymond, Sophia, 236
De Labertauche(s), Stephen, 239
De Labertauche, T.U., 239
De Labertauche, W., 239
Deacon, Samuel, 237
Deals, Joseph, 237
Deeker, James, 238
Demar(s), James, 239
Deschamps, Peter, 241
Dods, Andrew, 249
Doyle, Michael, 255
Dubois, Julian, 257
Dudley, Thomas, 258
Edmonds, John, 267
Edmondson, Matthew, 267
Edwards, Francis, 269
Elcock, John, 271
Eldrick, Stephen, 272
Eldridge, Henry, 272
Ellis & Co., 276
English, Thomas, 281
Eyles, James, 286
Garrett, John Alexander, 331

Gasley, George Alexander, 332
Gastard, J., 332
Gee, John, 334
George, Thomas, 335
Gerrard, Charles, 335
Gibson, —, 336
Gibson, John, 337
Gilchrist, Andrew, 339
Goate, John, 346
Goddard, Ralph, 346
Goddart, Peter, 346
Goodhall, John, 351
Gosset, James, 359
Gosset, Matthew, 359
Graham, James, 361
Graham & Son, 363
Grant, W., 364
Gray, George, 365
Green, Thomas, 368
Green & Walker, 368
Grey, W.P., 373
Griffin, —, 373
Griffith(s), Edward, 374
Guillet, James Charles, 378
Hale, Richard, 383
Hanson, Samuel, 395
Harding, Charles, 396
Harding, Richard, 396
Harley, Alexander, 399
Harratt, Thomas, 400
Harris, John, 401
Harris, Thomas, 402
Harris, William, 403
Harrison, John, 404
Hart, Aaron Hyam, 405
Hawkins, Edward, 412
Hawkins, H., 412
Hawkins, William, 413
Hayman, Christopher, 415
Hebdersley, T., 419
Hedges, John, 419
Hedges, K., 419
Hele, John, 419
Hen(n)ekin, Simon, 421
Henniker, Sir John, 421
Henning, George, 421
Henning, John, 421
Henningham, J.& G., 421
Herford, —, 423
Herman, Julius David, 423
Hermann, Louis, 423
Herring & Co., 423
Hilder, James, 429
Hildersley, Francis, 429
Hildersley, William & Martha, 429
Hoare, Thomas, 435
Hodson, John, 439
Hodson, Robert, 439
Hodson & Rudyard, 440
Holding, J., 441
Holt, Richard, 446
Hopkins, William, 449
Horner, —, 450

Howard, Thomas, 454
Hurst, George, 466
Hyde, Hannah, 470
Hyfield, —, 470
Ireland, Hugh, 473
Jackson, Benjamin, 475
Jamar, Jervais, 478
James, Andrew, 478
James, John, 479
Jeffery, Benjamin, 482
Jennings, John, 485
Jennings, Thomas, 485
Johnson, Robert, 490
Johnson, Thomas, 491
Jones, J., 495
Jones, John, 495
Jones, Richard, 496
Jones, William, 498
Joseph, B., 499
Keating, William, 502
Keith, George, 502
Kelham, John, 503
Kellett, John Patrick, 503
Kensett, E., 508
Kensett, John, 508
Kirk, Thomas, 517
Knight, C., 518
Knowles, Henry Sidney, 520
Lambert, John, 523
Lane, Henry, 525
Lano, W., 527
Lauder, David, 529
Laughton, Henry, 529
Lawrence, John, 531
Lawrence, Richard, 531
Lay, E., 532
Lay, Henry, 532
Leake, A., 533
Lee, William, 535
Levington, Henry, 539
Lewis, Jno., 540
Lewis, Robert, 540
Like, Thomas & Turner, Henry, 542
Leith, James, 537
London, C.P., 554
Long, John, 554
Lonsdale, William, 555
Lough, Robert, 555
Lowe, Jno, 557
Lowe, Musgrave, 557
Luke & Turner, 560
Lyons, —, 562
McCliesh, Andrew, 564
McDonald, A., 564
Mackenzie & Wakeling, 566
Macklin, Thomas, 567
Makie, Robert, 566
Marin, Stephen, 574
Marshall, Matthew, 579
Mash, —, 582
Mash, Thomas, 582
Maskens, Adrian, 583
Maskens, John, 583

Maskins, Ernest, 583
Maxwell, L., 588
Messinger, John, 603
Metcalfe, Charles, 604
Michelin, Nicholas, 604
Mill, —, 607
Millard & Son, 607
Miller, Joseph, 609
Milne, David, 611
Milner, Michael, 611
Miniken, Thomas, 612
Minter, George, 612
Minter, John, 613
Mitchell, William, 614
Mitchell(s), William, 614
Molton & Son, 615
Moore, John, 620
Morehead, James, 623
Morris, —, 627
Neilson, Lawrence, 640
Newby, John, 642
Newton, Robert & James, 645
Nicholls, Thomas, 646
Nicholls, William, 646
Noscotti, Charles Andrea, 656
Nott, James, 656
Olive, John Daniel, 662
Orchard, James, 664
Orme, Thomas, 665
Osborne, John Benjamin, 666
Osborne, William, 666
Overton, —, 667
Owen, Samuel, 668
Pain, J., 670
Palmer, William, 672
Parkinson, William, 676
Parry, Thomas, 677
Patrick, Nicholas, 680
Paul, James, 682
Pavie, Jacob, 682
Payle, —, 682
Pether, Thomas, 692
Phelps, George, 693
Plant, George, 702
Poole, John, 706
Pope, Joseph, 706
Potts, William, 709
Powell, John, 710
Presland, John, 713
Price, Richard, 716
Purver & Johnson, 722
Rackstraw, James, 725
Ramuz, Alexander, 726
Ramuz, Henry, 726
Randall, James, 727
Randall, William, 727
Ravald & Morland, 728
Reason, Thomas, 732
Reich, Christian, 736
Reilly, Henry, 737
Renolds, George, 738
Rich, Joseph, 741
Richman, John, 745
Richmond, John, 746

Rickman, John, 746
Rielly, T., 747
Rigby, John, 747
Robertson, Charles, 755
Robinson, —, 756
Robinson, S., 760
Rogers, William Gibbs, 764
Rolin(g), Edward, 764
Rook, J., 765
Rosenburgh, Fred., 766
Rudyerd, Launcelot, 770
Ruffell, John, 770
Salter, Thomas, 777
Sanderson, & Gibson, 779
Sands, David, 780
Sargood, Joseph, 781
Saul, John, 781
Saunders, Paul, 782
Sawyer, James, 786
Scott, John, 790
Scott, R., 790
Seagrave, Thomas, 792
Seaton, Frederick, 793
Selway, Thomas & Joseph, 799
Servies, James, 800
Sidney, Benjamin, 814
Simpson & Co., 817
Sloman, Bartlett, 821
Sloman, Benjamin, 821
Sloman, Samuel, 821
Smagg, Peter, 821
Smart, Thomas, 823
Smith, Benjamin, 824
Smith, John, 829
Smith, Samuel, 831
Smith, Thomas, 833
Smith, William, 834
Smith Bradshaw & Saunders, 835
Smythurst, Robert, 836
Speare, James, 842
Speer, Thomas, 842
Spence, John, 843
Spencer, John, 843
Spinnage, William, 845
Stalon, John, 848
Stannard, Edward, 849
Stannard, J., 849
Stanton, James, 849
Stark, James, 850
Stark, William, 850
Steedham, William, 851
Stephens & Co., 853
Stevenson, William, 855
Stoker, James, 858
Stone, Rene, 858
Strachan, James, 860
Strutton, —, 862
Styfield, Thomas, 863
Summers, John, 865
Symonds, Joseph, 869
Taylor, David, 875
Taylor, John, 876
Temple, William, 881
Thatcher, William, 882

Thomas, William, 884
Thomas & Flint, 885
Thomas & Wallace, 885
Tijou & Son, 894
Tissott, L., 896
Todd, —, 896
Towler, James, 900
Townsend, W., 901
Townshend, George, 901
Treherne, T., 903
Trotter, John, 905
Trotter, William, 906
Turk, John, 909
Turner, —, 909
Turner, Henry, 909
Turner, John, 910
Turner & Watkins, 913
Van Dem Helm, —, 919
Vaughan, William, 921
Voble, John, 929
Wachers, Thomas, 930
Wakeling, Giles, 933
Walker, John, 936
Walkins, Thomas, 939
Walters, —, 941
Wansell, John, 942
Waples, Sam, 942
Ward, Charles & Co., 942
Ward, James K., 943
Ward, Thomas, 944
Ward, William, 944
Watchers, Thomas, 946
Waterhouse, Joseph, 947
Waters, William, 947
Watkins, John, 947
Watkins, Philip, 947
Watson, —, 948
Watson, Hanchett, 949
Watts, John, 951
Watts, Thomas, 951
We(a)therall, John, 961
Weir, James, 956
Wells, James, 957
Wellsman, John, 958
Welsh, Jacob, 958
Wheeler, Joseph, 963
Whitcomb, John, 964
White, Jeremiah, 965
Wickham, J.H., 972
Wilcox, Leonard James, 973
Wildey, Thomas & H., 974
Williams, William, 982
Willshire, Leonard, 985
Wilson, Andrew, 986
Winnpenny, William, 992
Winter, James, 992
Wood, John, 997
Wrag, John, 1003
Wright, Charles, 1004
Wright, Daniel, 1004
Wright, William Thrale, 1009
Young & Trotter, 1015
Soho Manufactory (Birmingham):

Mayhew, John & Ince, William, 595
Solby, William, 807
Solihull (Staffs.): Bellamy, Henry, 63
Solitt, John, 859
Solly, 764
Solly, Isaac, 99, 974
Soloman & Brown, 838
Somerville, William, 24
Somersham (Hunts.): Ibbot, Francis, 470
Somerstown (London):
  Bennett, John, 65
  Bradley, James, 98
  Dansie, William, 225
  Edwards, Richard, 270
  Gawan, John, 333
  Gray, James, 365
  Griffiths, Henry, 374
  Harris, John, 401
  Heffer, Edward, 419
  Hiffer, Edmund, 428
  Mummery, Stephen, 635
  Neate, John, 640
  Roberts, James, 752
  Turner, William, 913
  Turrell, J.W., 913
  Wade, William, 931
  Wilson, George, 987
  Woodall, Edward, 998
Somerton (Som.):
  Burford, William, 130
  Gill, John, 340
  Hedges, John, 419
Sonderberg, Thomas, 838
Sotherley, John, 839
Sotwell (Berks.): Bradford, Samuel, 97
Souldern (Oxon.): Effery, Henry, 271
Soundy, Benjamin, 49, 575, 782
South, Peter, 970
South Carolina (USA):
  Lord, John, 555
  Lupton, William, 561
  McClellan, James, 564
  McGrath, Richard, 565
South Collingham (Notts.):
  Nicholson, Thomas, 647
South Molton (Devon):
  Dunn, John, 260
  Hacche, John, 381
  Hunt, John, 464
  Kelly, Richard, 503
  Oram, William, 664
  Rossiter, Henry, 767
  Smythe, James, 836
  Snow, Robert, 837
South Ormsby Hall (Lincs.):
  Burton, —, 134
  Cross, William, 214
  Lupton, —, 561
  Mais, —, 570

Pinner, Robert, 700
Preston, John, 714
Redmond, Mrs, 733
Seddon, George, 797
Weston, Stephen, 961
Wilcockson, Joseph, 973
South Shields (Co. Durham):
  Anderson, Robert, 13
  Bennet(t), William, 64
  Burlison, Isaac, 131
  Deavey, William, 238
  Duncan, George, 259
  Ellison, John, 276
  Ellison, Thomas, 276
  Gedling, Robert, 334
  Grieves, Thomas, 373
  Hall, Richard, 386
  Hiers, Joshua, 428
  Mattinson, James, 587
  Phillips, Henry, 695
  Railton, Thomas, 725
  Reed, Thomas, 734
  Robertson, William, 755
  Robinson, Thomas, 760
  Robson, John, 761
  Sawkill, John, 786
  Shevill, William, 810
  Smith, William, 834
  Spoor, Michael, 845
  Whatton, James, 962
Southampton (Hants.):
  Aldridge, Thomas, 7
  Alford, Jock, 7
  Allen, Andrew, 9
  Ball, Edwin, 35
  Batchelor, Samuel, 48
  Bence, John, 64
  Benwell, Thomas, 67
  Blake, Benjamin, 79
  Blundell, Thomas, 82
  Bownd, John, 93
  Boyce, John, 94
  Brooks, Charles, 111
  Brown, Charles, 113
  Brown, George, 114
  Buchan, Henry, 123
  Buchan & Slodden, 123
  Bulbrook, J., 124
  Bullrock, James, 128
  Butterfield, Richard, 138
  Dell, —, 239
  Dermott, Henry, 241
  Douglas, J., 251
  Douglas, Joseph, 251
  Dufautey, Charles, 258
  Dunning, William, 261
  Dusautoy, Charles, 262
  Eldride, Thomas, 272
  Etheridge, E., 282
  Gold, James, 348
  Hart, William, 406
  Hatcher, Robert, 410
  Hewett, G., 425
  Hitchcock, Thomas, 434

Hobbs, John, 435
Hookey, George, 447
Hookey, George Goldwyre/er, 447
Hutchings, John, 467
Kingwill, Joseph, 516
Knight, Edward, 519
Leach, George, 533
Legune, Thomas, 537
Lejeune, Edward, 537
Lejeune, Thomas, 538
Mecey, John, 600
Monday, Richard, 616
Moor(e), Joseph, 617
Muspratt, Thomas, 637
Newman, Charles, 643
Newman, G., 643
Norman, J., 651
North, James, 655
Oakley, J.& H., 660
Oakley, John & Benjamin, 660
Ockleford, G., 661
Okleford, George, 661
Olford, William, 662
Peacock, Robert, 683
Peaty, Charles, 685
Perkins, Richard H., 690
Pettfield, Christopher, 692
Petty, Ashley, 693
Pink, Joseph, 699
Pollard, James, 705
Purkis, C., 722
Purkiss, Charles, 722
Roberts, William, 755
Rogers, Robert, 763
Russell, W.& I., 773
Russell, William & John, 773
Shakell, Edward, 802
Shepherd, I., 807
Shepherd, Isaac, 807
Simkins, John, 815
Simpkins, John, 815
Skinner, James, 819
Skinner, Joshua, 819
Smith, John, 830
Snelgrove, W.& J., 836
Stead, John, 851
Stevens, Thomas, 854
Storror, William, 860
Street, Joseph, 861
Sturdy, John, 863
Symonds, Charles, 869
Syms, Charles, 869
Thompson, Alexander, 885
Treadwell, Humphrey, 903
Triggs, James, 904
Tucker, J.T., 907
Valentine, T., 919
Ward, Stephen, 943
Weeks, John, 956
Weeks, Thomas, 956
Weston, John R., 961
Weston, William, 961
Whitcher, W., 964

Williams, H., 980
Wright, Richard, 1008
Yeoman, J., 1013
Southeram, John, 504
Southgate (London):
  Anty, Joseph, 16
  Auty, Joseph, 27
Southill (Beds.):
  Delabriere, Louis A., 239
  Elward, George & Marsh, William, 278, 279
  Litchfield & Graham, 549
  Morel, Nicholas and Morel & Hughes, Robert, 623
  Robinson, —, 756
Southport (Lancs.): Scott, James, 789
Southsea (Hants.):
  Blanchard, W., 80
  Shaw, Joseph, 805
Southwark (London):
  Aderne, Ralph Henry, 5
  Alford, Robert, 7
  Allnutt, Francis, 11
  Angell, Thomas, 14
  Arderne, Ralph Henry, 17
  Ashelford, Joseph, 20
  Baker, Samuel, 33
  Baker, William, 33
  Bansall, Richard, 37
  Barber, John, 38
  Barrett, Robert, 44
  Barrow, William, 45
  Barton, Joseph, 47
  Barton, W., 47
  Barton, William, 47
  Bates, James, 49
  Bates, John James, 49
  Bayly, Thomas, 53
  Baynes & Co, 53
  Baynes & Ireland, 53
  Beagle, James, 53
  Beltshire, Thomas, 64
  Bensley, Thomas, 66
  Betley, Samuel, 69
  Bittleston, George, 76
  Blacknell, John, 78
  Blackwell, John, 78
  Blake, Benjamin, 79
  Bonsal(l), Thomas, 86
  Bradley, John, 98
  Braithwaite, Benjamin, 101
  Breckels, Sam., 105
  Brockbridge, Henry, 109
  Broom, John, 112
  Bryan, William, 122
  Bubb, John, 123
  Buckingham, Henry, 123
  Buckley, William, 124
  Buckman, James, 124
  Bulbrook, Charles, 125
  Bull, Henry, 125
  Bull, Joseph, 125
  Bunney, Thomas, 129

Burges, B., 130
Burrage, John Calvin, 132
Busfield, Josh., 136
Butcher, Michael, 137
Byrne, Edmund, 139
Dallas, Robert, 224
Darby, Thomas, 226
Davis, Thomas, 232
Daws, Thomas, 235
Day, Philip, 236
Day, Theophilus, 236
Day, William, 236
Dear, John, 238
Dennis, Benjamin, 240
Docker, John, 248
Doolan & Co., 250
Dore, Frederick, 251
Draper, John, 255
Draper, Thomas, 256
Dunn, —, 259
Edwards, James, 269
Edwards, Samuel, 270
Eling, James, 272
Evans, Thomas, 285
Everidge, John, 285
Gates, Stephen, 332
Gill, —, 340
Gill, John, 340
Glanvill, James, 344
Gough, —, 359
Gould, John, 360
Graham, Frederick Henry, 361
Green, Bainer & Co., 368
Griffith, J., 374
Griffiths, John, 374
Griffith(s), John, 374
Griffiths, Joseph, 375
Guibert, —, 377
Hall, Joseph, 386
Hanebuth, Frederick & Co., 394
Hare, Valentine, 397
Harper, John, 399
Harris, E., 400
Harris, Edward, 400
Harris, George, 400
Harris, Thomas, 402
Harris, William, 403
Harrison, Samuel, 404
Hart, John, 405
Hays, William, 415
Hewitt, Nathaniel, 425
Hiller, Robert, 432
Hillier, Mary, 432
Hodder, Charles, 436
Hodges, Richard, 437
Hodges, Thomas, 437
Hodgson, Thomas, 438
Holford, J., 441
Holland, Thomas, 442
Homersham, Thomas, 446
Hood, Robert, 447
Hornblow, William, 449
Houghton, Henry, 452
Hubbard, —, 456

Hudson, Joseph, 458
Indermaur, Frederick, 471
Ireland, Richard, 473
Jackson, Joseph & William, 476
James, Thomas, 480
James & Wise, 480
Jenks, Robert, 484
Jepps, Samuel, 487
Johnson, J., 489
Joseph, Benjamin, 499
Joseph, William, 499
King, Edward, 514
King, Susan, 515
King & Lidbitter, 515
Knowles, James Spencer, 520
Knowles, John, 520
Lawrence, James, 531
Lee, John, 535
Lewis, Josiah, 540
Lightfoot, —, 541
Lightfoot, Luke, 541
Looker, Francis, 555
Looker, John, 555
Lowdell, —, 557
Lowry, Henry, 558
Luson, William, 561
McCathey, Charles, 564
McGowen, Alexander, 565
Mack, William, 565
Macklecan, John, 567
McLean, Charles, 567
Marchant, S., 574
Marchant, Samuel, 574
Markey, Cornelius, 574
Marks, M., 574
Marshall, Mary Ann, 579
Marsh, William, 577
Martinelli, Lewis & Son, 582
Massey, Thomas, 585
Masterman, John, 585
Mathison, Richard, 586
Maulden, James, 587
May, —, 588
May, John, 589
Meredith, John, 602
M'Ewen, John, 565
Miller, —, 608
Miller, James, 608
Miller & Woodward, 609
Mills, William, 611
Mitchell, William, 614
Monk, Samuel, 616
Morgan, Isaac, 625
Morris, John, 628
Morris, William, 629
Mote, Edward, 632
Mulligan, Robert, 635
Myers, Michael, 637
Neale, Philip, 640
Nicklin, Thomas, 647
Noakes, Robert, 650
Norris, W., 655
Ogborn, William, 661
Oldner, George, 662

O'Neil & Smith, 664
Page, Thomas, 670
Parker, James, 674
Pearman, Ambrose, 684
Pedley, John, 686
Peerman, Ambrose, 686
Penman, William, 688
Perrin, John, 691
Plucknett, John, 703
Potter, Henry, 708
Price, Charles, 715
Price, John, 715
Price, Thomas, 716
Pugh, William, 720
Pugh, William & Charles, 720
Reed, William, 734
Reeper, George Cornelius, 735
Rider & Milner, 746
Rix, James, 750
Robinson, Samuel, 760
Rodd, William, 762
Rokes, George, 764
Ruckman, J., 770
Ruckman & Winter, 770
Russell, Thomas, 773
Sams, Samuel, 778
Saul, W., 781
Saunders, Joseph, 782
Scott, Thomas, 790
Seward, Henry, 801
Shaw, William, 805
Shears, Ambrose, 806
Shepherd, George, 807
Sherwood, Robert, 810
Simpson, James, 816
Smith, Abraham, 824
Smith, John, 829
Smith, Joseph, 830
Smith, T., 832
Smith, Thomas, 833
Smith, William, 834
Snuggs, John, 838
Southey, John, 840
Spencer, Samuel, 844
Stephens, —, 852
Stevenson, Thomas, 855
Stickner, John, 856
Stokes, Thomas, 858
Storey, William, 859
Strugnell, Charles, 862
Such, John, 864
Sutton, Charles, 865
Sutton, Thomas, 866
Taylor, Benjamin, 874
Taylor, Saul, 879
Taylor, William, 880
Terret(t), Jos., 881
Terveld, Pet., 881
Tervella, James, 881
Thornton, Christopher, 890
Thornton, E.N., 890
Tickner, J., 894
Tijou, Thomas, 894
Tizon, T.& I., 896

Trevett, James, 904
Truman, Jonah, 906
Turner, W.R., 912
Turnley, John Samuel, 913
Villeneau, Josias, 929
Wagstaff, Anthony, 931
Walter, William, 941
Ward, Thomas, 943
Waters, William, 947
Watkins, E., 947
Watson, Thomas, 950
Way, Thomas, 952
Wear, Hannah, 952
Weatherstone, Thomas, 953
Webb, George, 953
Webber, John Thomas, 954
Whale, William, 962
Wharton, Charles, 962
Wheeler, Michael, 963
Whitaker, —, 963
Whitaker, Joseph, 964
Whitley, David, 969
Williams, George, 979
Williams, Henry, 980
Williams, John, 981
Willmott, W., 984
Wilson, John, 987
Wilson, Joseph, 988
Wilson, S.W., 989
Wilson, Samuel, 989
Wilson, Thomas, 989
Wilson & Read, 990
Witton, William, 995
Wollett, Charles, 995
Wollett, Ralph, 995
Wood, Alexander, 995
Wood, Stephen, 997
Woodward, J., 1000
Woodward & Miller, 1001
Woollett, Ralph, 1002
Woollett, Thomas, 1002
Wray, Thomas, 1004
Wright, James, 1005
Southwell, John, 732
Southwell (Notts.):
  Auls(ey)brook, John, 26
  Breckels, Thomas, 105
  Brown, Joshua, 116
  Dolby, Abraham, 249
  Dutton, Edward, 262
  Gilbert, John, 338
  Nicholson, James, 646
  Parr, Jonathon, 677
  Phipps, John, 696
  Pleasant, Stephen, 703
  Reville, George, 737
Southwold (Suffolk):
  Osborne, Robert, 666
  Roune, —, 768
  Sawyer, Charles, 786
Sowerby, J., 233
Sowerby, Jeremiah, 458, 786
Sowerby, John, 841
Sowerby & Kirkman, 841

Sowerby Bridge (Yorks.): Stubbs,
James, 863
Spain (King of): Seddon, George,
797
Spalding (Lincs.):
  Ashton, John, 21
  Bailey, Joseph, 30
  Barker, Charles, 39
  Barker, Mrs, 39
  Bennet, Henry, 64
  Brainsby, Fraser, 101
  Kingston Samuel, 516
  May, Robert, 589
  Oliver, Charles, 663
  Roughton, William, 768
  Rowton, William, 769
  Shaw, Waltham, 805
  Spilkins, Jos., 844
  Stanton, Edward, 849
  Stanton, Hammond, 849
  Tory, George, 900
Spark, 762
Sparrow, 729, 954
Sparrow, Elizabeth, 84
Sparrow, James, 847
Sparrow, Robert, 999
Speare, 354
Speare, James, 566
Spearing, Perrias, 577
Speechly, James, 960
Speed, 484
Speke Hall, Liverpool:
  Bullock, George, 127
  Gregson, Mathew, 371
Spence, 745
Spence, William, 465
Spenceley, George, 382, 427, 564,
  951
Spencely, George, 441
Spencer, 745
Spencer, Alexander, 151
Spencer, John jnr, 632
Spencer, Joseph, 23, 600
Spencer, Samuel, 843
Spencer, Thomas, 917
Spencer, William, 25, 843
Spender, Samuel, 843
Spice & Pryer, 844
Spicer, John, 655, 790
Spicer, Thomas, 811
Spilsby (Lincs.):
  Andrew, William, 14
  Asher, William, 20
  Ashton, John, 21
  Ashton, Robert, 21
  Ashton, Samuel, 21
  Ashton, William, 21
  Aster, William, 22
  Ball, John, 35
  Baslington, John, 48
  Hall, James, 385
  Hastings, John, 409
  Rainey, Edward, 726
  Rainy, Edward, 726

Ratenbury, William, 728
Rattenbury, William, 728
Richardson, Thomas, 745
Swinn, John, 868
Ward, Dymoke, 942
Spindler, Nathaniel, 220
Spinnage, 211
Spinnage & Howard, 845
Spinning wheel makers:
  Barber, John, 38
  Bardin, William, 39
  Rickaby, James, 746
  Rickaby, Thomas, 746
  Thompson, J., 886
Spital (Cheshire): Taylor, John, 877
Spitalfields (London):
  Ashworth, Thomas, 21
  Balley, William, 35
  Barritt, James, 44
  Barritt, Samuel, 44
  Battey, William, 50
  Beaumont, W., 56
  Benson, Obadiah, 66
  Blair, Thomas, 79
  Blizzard, Robert, 81
  Bolter, James, 84
  Bouskell, George, 91
  Bowden, Joshua, 92
  Bradbear, William, 95
  Brett, Thomas, 105
  Brown, William, 119
  Bunn, J.& W., 129
  Bunn, John Henry, 129
  Burbridge, John, 129
  De Steffani, William, 242
  Dibble, Andrew, 243
  Dibble, J., 243
  Dibon, Charles, 243
  Dodd, George, 248
  Duck, John, 257
  Elliot(t), David, 272
  Emmett, John, 280
  Etheridge, Thomas, 282
  Evans, P., 284
  Garbett, Joseph, 329
  Gazely, Joseph, 333
  Greville, George, 373
  Griffiths, G., 374
  Groves, John, 376
  Hale, William, 383
  Hall, William, 386
  Hartdrig, William, 406
  Harwood, Thomas, 408
  Harwood, William, 408
  Hewson, Thomas, 426
  Hobbs, John, 435
  Hogben, John, 440
  Horne, William, 450
  Hubbard, James, 457
  Imray, George, 471
  Jones, J., 495
  Jordan, J., 498
  Jordan, John, 498
  Jordan, Thomas, 499

Keen, John, 502
Kidston, T., 512
Knight, Francis, 519
Lakeman, William, 521
Latleff, John, 529
Lawley, John, 530
Lawson, J., 531
Lawson, James, 532
Lyne, John, 562
Mason, John, 584
Morris, John, 628
Morton, John, 630
Norris, John, 654
Parker, Arthur, 673
Parrott, Thomas, 677
Pether, Robert, 692
Pickering, William, 697
Sadler, Robert, 775
Shew, James, 810
Short, James, 812
Smith & Brett, 835
Spearman, Mr, 842
Spicer, Lewis, 844
Stocker, John, 857
Sykes, Edward jnr, 869
Tagg, Thomas, 870
Thomas, Samuel, 884
Tilney, George, 895
Turfrey, John, 908
White, Ann, 965
White, Richard, 966
White, William, 967
Willmott, Robert, 984
Wolfe, James, 995
Wright, Thomas, 1009
Spondon (Derbs.): Kirkland,
  William, 517
Spooner, Joseph Henry, 181
Spoor, Amor, 548
Spraggon, 719
Spurling, Nathaniel, 346, 722
Spurreet, William, 197
Spurrier, Thomas, 862
Spurriergate, York: Ellis, Francis,
  275
Stables, William, 760
Stacey, Joseph, 683
Stafford, John, 815
Stafford:
  Devell, James, 242
  Dudley, Francis, 258
  Dudley, James, 258
  Goodall, Henry, 351
  Keeling, Benjamin, 502
  Moseley, William, 631
  Rider, Samuel, 746
  Rogers, William, 764
  Smith, Jane, 827
  Smith, Thomas, 833
  Stanton, John, 849
  Trubshaw, Richard, 906
  Trubshaw, Thomas, 906
  Wiggin, Jane, 972
  Wood, William, 998

Stafford House: Seddon, George, 797
Stain, Samuel, 848
Staindrop (Co. Durham):
  Atkinson, Thomas, 25
  Hutchinson, Peter, 468
  Robinson, Thomas, 760
  Spooner, James Henry, 845
  Tailor, Thomas, 870
  Taylor, John, 877
  Taylor, William, 879
  Thompson, Michael, 887
  Wade, William, 931
  Walton, Robert, 942
Staines (Middlx):
  Adams, James, 3
  Alexander, Thomas, 7
  Allman, John, 11
  Atkinson, Daniel, 23
  Bardin, Samuel, 39
  Butler, Thomas, 137
  Hopkins, E., 448
  Layton, William, 533
  Richards, Emanuel, 741
  Stranson, W., 861
  Sumner, Robert, 865
  Yeaxley, William, 1013
Staithes (Yorks.):
  Burton, William, 136
  Roddam, Thomas, 752
Stalbridge (Dorset):
  Harris, Robert, 402
  Taylor, Thomas, 879
Stalvies, 477
Stalybridge (Lancs.):
  Bentley & Booth, 66
  Booth, John, 87
  Gordon, Thomas, 357
  Hadfield, Robert, 382
  Hardman, Samuel, 396
  Ousey, George, 667
  Prosser, James, 719
  Whaley, Matthew, 962
Stamford (Lincs.):
  Abbott, William, 1
  Addington, John, 4
  Andrews, Thomas, 14
  Andrews & Hilliam, 14
  Atton, James, 25
  Banks, —, 37
  Banks, Thomas, 37
  Banks, William, 37
  Barrow, John, 45
  Bishop, Thomas, 76
  Booth, John, 87
  Bromhead, Thomas Boyall, 110
  Broughton, John, 113
  Broughton, William, 113
  Brown, John, 116
  Burton, —, 134
  Burton, Edwin, 135
  Burton, Frederick Thomas, 135
  Butcher, Henry, 137
  Butcher, John, 137

  Dixon, John, 246
  Edwards, William, 271
  Gamble, John, 328
  Gilbert, Henry snr, 338
  Goodwin, James, 354
  Hare, Thomas, 397
  Haughton, Thomas, 410
  Hicks, John, 428
  Hilliam, John, 432
  Hillingham, John, 432
  Hind, William, 433
  Hunter, William, 466
  Lamson, Thomas, 524
  Laughton, Saunders, 529
  Lowe, Thomas, 558
  Lowe, William, 558
  Mann, John P., 572
  Maugham, Thomas, 587
  Mills, C.E., 610
  Mills, Samuel, 610
  Murray, William, 637
  Pears, Thomas, 684
  Pollard, Zaccheus, 705
  Robertson, James, 755
  Robinson, Thomas Wilkinson, 760
  Rooe, John, 765
  Screens, Wortly, 791
  Sealy, H.W., 792
  Searson, George, 792
  Searson, Robert, 792
  Searson, William, 792
  Searson, Wortley, 792
  Snow, John, 837
  Snow, Thomas snr & jnr, 837
  Staplee, Thomas, 849
  Studwell, W., 863
  Tat(h)am, Henry, 873
  Tilley, James, 894
  Tipping, Benjamin, 895
  Tymperton, Robert, 915
  Whitehead, Francis, 968
  Whitley, William, 969
  William, John, 979
  Williamson, Thomas, 983
  Wortley, William, 1003
  Wright, Henry, 1005
Stamford: St Michael's Church:
  William, John, 979
  Town Hall: Dixon, John, 246
Stamford Baron (Lincs.): Mason, Edward, 583
Stanaway, Henry, 849
Stanbridge, Mary, 814
Standen (Sussex): Jewell, S. & H., 488
Stanfield (Suffolk): Heffer, John, 419
Stanger, 236
Stanier, John, 847
Staniland, Thomas, 956
Stanley, Henry, 301
Stanley, William, 849

Stanmer Park (Sussex):
  Riley, John, 749
  Tonge, R., 899
Stanningley (Yorks.): Whittam, John, 970
Stanton, 974
Staples, James, 849
Staples, John, 74, 434
Stapleton, Edward, 808
Starcross (Devon): Barton, Jos., 47
Starimer, James, 850
Statham, John Henry, 281
Staveley, John, 39, 73, 252
Staveley, William, 73, 252
Stayner, Charles, 850
Stayner, George, 850
Stayner, James, 850
Stead, Samuel, 505
Steains, 566
Steains, James, 720
Steane, Richard, 457
Steel & Little, 851
Steele, 237
Steele, John jnr, 150
Steffanoni, 939
Stephens, Edward, 381
Stephens, George, 84
Stephens, John, 363, 722, 829, 854
Stephens, Joseph, 527
Stephens, Samuel, 527
Stephens, William, 854
Stephens & Gooch, 853
Stephens & Wilson, 853
Stephenson, 588
Stephenson, Ann, 855
Stephenson, George, 767
Stephenson, John, 19, 76, 333, 428, 482, 589
Stephenson, Michael, 933
Stephenson, Nathaniel, 808
Stephenson, William, 137, 339
Stepney (London):
  Allbritan, Samuel, 9
  Allcock, William, 9
  Bayman, Francis, 53
  Billington, Thomas, 72
  Binns, Nimrod, 73
  Bonnet, Adrian, 86
  Burns, Nimrod, 132
  Leadman, John, 533
  Morgan, Philip, 625
  Pixley, Samuel, 701
  Prictor, William, 717
  Snowde, John William, 837
  Taylor, John, 876
  Thornton, Joseph, 890
  Wheatley, Edward, 962
Sterling, Humphry, 745
Sterridge, James, 856
Sterry, James, 856
Sterry & Amphlett, 854
Stevens, 1009
Stevens, Edward, 2
Stevens, Thomas, 852

Stevens, William, 7
Steward, 885
Steward, Edward, 301, 568, 812, 877
Stewart, James, 388
Stewart, Richard, 1002
Stewerton (Berks.): Butler, Thomas, 137
Steyning (Sussex):
  Bawcombe, Harry, 50
  Parsons, Thomas, 678
  Sone, Thomas, 839
Stidston, William, 1
Stirridge, James, 811
Stoakes, 126, 128
Stockbridge (Northumb.):
  Bell, William, 63
  Mould, William, 633
Stockdale, James England, 601
Stockham, James, 216
Stockholm (Sweden): Haupt, Georg, 410
Stocking, John, 262
Stockport (Cheshire):
  Barnes, Robert Wilkinson, 42
  Barrow, Joseph, 45
  Bolton, Richard, 84
  Bolton, Robert, 84
  Davis, John Austin, 231
  Dodge, Robert, 249
  Etchells, John, 282
  Etchells, Robert, 282
  Etchells, William, 282
  Evans, Ann, 283
  Evans, Edwards, 283
  Evans, William, 285
  Exley, William, 286
  Gaywood, William, 333
  Gough, Thomas, 360
  Gouldthorpe, John, 361
  Lain, James, 521
  Mellor, Hugh, 601
  Mills, John, 610
  Moore, John, 620
  Nightingale, James, 648
  Partington, Robert, 678
  Partington, Thomas, 678
  Pownall, Thomas, 711
  Price, John, 716
  Rotherel, James, 767
  Rothwell, Richard, 767
  Roylane, Ellen, 769
  Roylane, John, 769
  Roylane, P., 769
  Schofield, John, 789
  Siddelley, James, 814
  Skelborne, Peter, 818
  Spence, John, 843
  Stopford, William, 859
  Tomlinson, Samuel, 898
  Wainwright, George, 932
  Wallington & Exley, 940
  Wildgoose, Joseph, 974
  Wilson, John, 988

Stockton (Co. Durham):
  Allam, James, 8
  Allen, James, 10
  Appleby, —, 16
  Armstrong, William, 18
  Atkinson, Benjamin, 23
  Atkinson, George, 24
  Beckwith, Henry, 57
  Bell, J., 61
  Bell, John, 62
  Best, Martin, 68
  Braillwaite, John, 101
  Dob(b)ing, Anthony, 247
  Douthwaite, William, 252
  Dunn, Lawson, 260
  Gregory, Benjamin, 370
  Hall, John, 385
  Hart, William, 406
  Heaviside, John, 419
  Hewitt, William, 426
  Horlton, William, 449
  Hunton, Christopher, 466
  Johnson, James, 490
  Johnson, William, 493
  Johnson & Smith, 493
  Kirby, William Henry, 516
  Kirkup, Simpson, 517
  Kirton, John, 518
  Manners, Robert, 573
  Martindale, John, 582
  M'Donald, Donald, 564
  Metcalf, John, 603
  Moses, Thomas Metcalfe, 632
  Newham, Robert jnr, 642
  Peacock, Francis, 683
  Perkins, Christopher, 690
  Potts, John, 709
  Richlieu, Robert, 745
  Scurfield, Robert, 791
  Semfield, Robert, 799
  Smith, John, 830
  Smith, William, 834
  Sudron, James, 864
  Taylor, Robert, 879
  Thompson, Thomas, 888
  Unthank, William, 917
  Walton, Thomas, 942
  Williams, Charles, 979
Stockwell, E.P., 857
Stockwell, John, 791
Stockwell (London):
  Hewitt, Philip, 426
  Walshaw, John, 941
  Wilkins, Charles, 975
Stoddard, 144
Stoke Damerell (Devon):
  Brooking, John, 111
  Halley, George, 389
Stoke Edith Park (Herefs.):
  Ody, John, 661
  Whitby, John, 964
Stoke Gifford House (Glos.):
  Mayhew, John & Ince, William, 596

Stoke-on-Trent (Staffs.):
  Bentley, James, 66
  Brinsley, John, 108
  Brinsley, Richard, 108
  Greatbatch, Henry, 366
  Hay(e)s, Jeffrey, 414
  Hullard, Thomas, 462
  Lake, Thomas, 521
  Luke, Thomas, 560
  Marlow, James, 575
  Steel, Samuel, 851
  Taylor, Peter, 878
Stokenchurch (Oxon.): Burgess, Robert, 130
Stoker, John, 345
Stokesley (Yorks.):
  Jeram, Francis, 487
  Pounder, Robert, 709
  Richlieu, Thomas, 745
Stolworthy, Edmund, 104
Stolworthy & Martin, 858
Stone, 254
Stone, William, 688
Stone (Staffs.):
  Ainsworth, John, 5
  Halmarack, Richard, 390
  Turner, William, 913
Stonegate, York:
  Brocklebank, Joseph, 109
  Parkinson, Nathaniel, 676
Stoneleigh (Warks.): Hallot, William, 390
Stoneleigh Abbey (Warks.):
  Burnett, Thomas, 132
  Burrough(s), John, 133
  Chipchase & Proctor, 164
  Clay, Henry, 177
  Davies, Thomas, 230
  Devey, John, 242
  Dobyn(s), Thomas, 248
  Fox, Deveareux, 313
  Frost, Daniel, 323
  Gee, John, 334
  Gomm, William & Richard, 350
  Gordon, Thomas, 357
  Grimes, John, 375
  Hallot, William, 390
  Hands, Humphrey, 394
  Harles, Henry, 399
  Hearsy, John, 418
  Hensman, Thomas, 422
  Hoarsy, John, 435
  Keene, Robert, 502
  Lenoir, Peter, 538
  Litchfield & Graham, 549
  Marshall, John, 578
  Morgan & Sanders, 626
  Oakley, George, 660
  Pardoe, John, 672
  Pratt, Samuel & Henry, 712
  Proctor & Chadley, 719
  Rob(b)ins, John, 756
  Seddon, George, 797
  Smith, Richard, 830

Strawbridge, Thomas, 861
Thack(th)waite, Michael, 882
Woolley, George Outram, 1002
Wyatt, Edward, 1010
York, John, 1013
Stones, D., 21
Stones, George, 128, 227, 258, 323
Stonestreet, Henry, 791
Stoney & Clarke, 859
Stoney Stratford (Bucks.):
Aveline, Frederick, 27
Day, Thomas, 236
Inwood, Jno, 473
Kent, John, 508
Lambert, John, 523
Pierce, Richard, 698
West, George, 959
West, William snr, 960
Storer, 67
Storey, 97
Storey, Francis, 745
Story, William, 181
Stourbridge (Staffs.):
Allport, James, 11
Ashbourn(e), Ann, 20
Bent, Daniel, 66
Bird, Peter, 74
Burton, Charles, 135
Gaddick, Thomas, 326
Haynes, Richard, 415
Holloway, J., 443
Lees, Benjamin, 536
Lees, James, 536
Middleton, Warren, 605
Mills, Thomas, 611
Nash, Thomas, 639
Nock, Thomas, 650
Parker, Richard & Thomas, 674
Payne, Francis, 682
Payne, Thomas, 683
Payton, James, 683
Tidmarsh, Richard, 894
Underwood, William, 917
Stourhead (Wilts.):
Alken, Sefferin, 8
Barton, I., 46
Boson, John, 88, 89
Brent & Lowe, 105
Buck, Henry, 123
Chippendale, Thomas jnr, 168, 169
Davis & Co., 233
Duffour, Rene, 258
Folgham, John, 307
Gilding, Edmund, 339
Grendey, Giles, 371, 372
Hill, —, 430
Linnell, William, 546
Pascall, James & Ann, 679
Potter, Thomas, 708
Tideman, 894
Stout, John, 229
Stow-on-the-Wold (Glos.):
Bartlett, William, 46

Blizard, Richard, 81
Stowe House (Bucks.):
Blugrove, Ann, 82
Chippendale, Thomas snr, 166
Collinson, George Croyson, 190
Dell, Tom, 239
Dishon, John Baptist, 245
Dryhurst, James, 257
Hanson, William, 395
Jafensen, —, 478
Keybold, Edward, 511
Linnell, William, 547
Marshall, Jo., 578
Morris, Joseph, 628
Saunders, Paul, 784
Sawyer, Thomas, 787
Sheard, Jaxton & Co., 806
Willmore, James & Son, 984
Stowmarket (Suffolk):
Adams, Daniel, 3
Bailey, William, 31
Bloomfield, William, 81
Downing, Henry Shuckforth, 254
Downing, J., 254
Downing, James, 254
Elliott, Robert, 274
Joscelyne, John, 499
Keeble, Robert, 502
King, William, 515
Payne, James, 682
Read, John Parish, 732
Squirrell, Robert, 847
Strahan, James, 860
Strait (Lincs.):
Hawson, John jnr, 414
Webster, Thomas, 956
Strateon, John, 599
Stratford, Thomas, 322
Stratford (Essex):
Hawkins, John, 413
Hill, William, 431
Lawson, James, 532
Lloyd, Thomas, 551
Maddison, Charles, 569
Martin, Frederick, 580
Matthews, William, 587
Moore, John, 620
Moore, Thomas, 621
Nicheles, J., 645
Nickels, James, 647
Prigg, Daniel, 717
Rogers, Richard, 763
Tovey, John, 900
Watts, Thomas, 951
Stratford-upon-Avon (Warks.):
Bernard, Abraham, 67
Hancox, James, 393
Harris, Thomas, 402
Harte, George, 406
Mills, Joseph, 610
Phipps, John, 696
Stratford-upon-Avon Corporation:
Davies (or Davis), T. & Griffin, 230

Stratton & Waddingham, 861
Stratton Park (Hants.): Mayhew, John and Ince, William, 591
Strawberry Hill (Middlx):
Beaumont, William, 56
Bromwich, Thomas, 110
Cobb, John, 184
Edwards, Edward, 269
Hallett, William snr and William jnr, 389
Lawrence, Richard, 531
Nicholls, William, 646
Strickland & Jenkins, 861
Vile, William, 927
Strawbridge, Thomas, 133
Strawder, Charles Ward, 249
Streatham (London):
Lockwood, John, 553
Shaw, Sophia, 805
Shawe, John F., 806
Shew, John, 810
Streatham Park (Surrey):
Gillow, 343
Hutchins, Abigail, 467
Streatlam Castle (Co. Durham):
Bott, Thomas, 90
Busby, Joseph, 136
Clark, John, 173
Gradon, Thomas, 361
Harrison, Jonathan, 404
Strenshall (Yorks.): Linfoot, Ralph, 543
Stretch, 726
Stretton Hall (Staffs.):
Eyre(s), Thomas, 287
Folgham, John, 307
Gilding, Francis, 339
Hynmers Taylor, —, 470
Langlois, Pierre, 526
Reynier, Charles, 737
Seddon, George, 796
Smith, Charles, 825
Smith, Mary, 830
Strickland, 483
Strickland, William, 924–5
Stridder, Edward, 861
Stringer, 71
Stringer, J., 525
Stringer, John, 227, 407
Stringer, Nancy, 846
Stringer & Browne, 862
Strood (Kent):
Burch, Thomas, 129
Horsmail, Thomas, 451
Howard, Henry, 454
Stroud (Glos.):
Dunning, Henry, 260
Egginton, Josiah, 271
Engley, John, 281
Gregory, John, 370
Hambridge & Halliday, 391
Jay, William, 481
Merredith, John, 603
Mynett, George, 638

Powell, James, 710
Pugh, John, 720
Purcell, John, 722
Rudge, John, 770
Thornbury, Nathaniel, 889
White, Henry, 965
Stuart, Henry, 800
Stubbs & Smith, 863
Studley Royal (Yorks.): Mitley,
    Charles George, 614
Sturdy, Marmaduke, 381
Styning, R., 287
Sudbury, 945
Sudbury, James, 186
Sudbury (Suffolk):
    Brand, Benjamin, 102
    Dupont, Richard, 261
    Joscelyne, Samuel, 499
    King, John & William, 514
    King & Smith, 515
    Murrell(s), Ambrose, 637
    Oliver, John, 663
    Oliver, Joseph & Co., 663
    Oliver, William, 663
    Sillitoe, William, 814
    Spring, John, 846
    Wallet, Robert, 940
    Wilsmore, Edward M., 986
Sudbury Hall (Derbs.):
    Grew, John, 373
    Pearce, Edward, 684
    Young, William, 1015
Suddlow, Joseph, 562
Suddorth, John, 429
Sugg, 556
Suggett, Benjamin Linto, 377
Sulivan, Sarah, 216
Sullivan, John, 216
Summer, John, 76, 609, 724, 754,
    835
Summers, Ralph, 159
Summers, Robert, 408
Summerscales, John, 838–9
Summertown, Oxford: Rouse,
    Robert, 768
Sumner, John, 307, 864
Sun shades: Dawes, Thomas, 234
Sunbury (Middlx): Layton,
    Frederick, 533
Sunderland (Co. Durham):
    Alcock, Samuel, 6
    Allinson, John, 11
    Armstrong, Thomas, 18
    Atkinson, George, 24
    Barnet, John jnr, 43
    Bates, William, 49
    Bell, John, 62
    Billam, Edward, 71
    Binns, Joseph, 73
    Binns, Thomas, 73
    Blacket, John, 77
    Blakey, George, 79
    Browell, John, 113
    Brown, George, 114

Brown, Joseph, 116
Davie, Jurdison, 228
Davison, Joseph, 233
Dodds, William, 249
Dowel, Richard, 254
Dowel & Renwick, 254
Drysdale, William, 257
English, William, 281
Gibson, Edward, 337
Godling, Robert, 347
Gowland, —, 361
Graham, William, 363
Grecian, Thomas, 367
Harrison, Andrew, 403
Harrison, Ralph, 404
Hartforth, John, 406
Hewett & Jefferson, 425
Hewitt, John F., 425
Hogg, James F., 440
Hudson, Thomas, 459
Jefferson, Robert, 482
Kirkbride, John, 517
Kirkup, John, 517
Lee, —, 534
Lindsay, J., 542
Lindsay, James, 543
Lindsay, John, 543
Lonie, Douglas, 555
Lumsdon, John, 560
Martin, Thomas, 581
Moore, Thomas, 621
Munro, Thomas, 636
Nicholson, Richard, 647
Oliver, George, 663
Oliver, John, 663
Park, Edward, 673
Penrith, John snr & jnr, 689
Pringle, John, 718
Reay, Robert, 733
Reay, Thomas, 733
Renton, George, 737
Salvin, Robert, 777
Shields, John, 810
Simpson, Richard, 816
Stokell, Nicholas, 858
Turnbull, George, 909
Turner, Adam, 909
Turner, Robert, 911
Walker, Andrew, 934
Wanless, George, 942
Weatherill, William, 953
Wedderal, William, 956
Wilson, Henry, 987
Wray, Richard, 1004
Sunley, William, 244
Surrey House, Littlehampton
(Sussex):
    Denyer, William, 241
    Lear, James, 533
    Millard, James, 607
    Osborn, William Arthur, 666
    Piddell, Mrs S., 697
    Richardson, K., 744
    White, Edward, 965

Sutton, 20, 194, 301, 555, 602
Sutton, Jehu, 274
Sutton, John, 293
Sutton, Lee, 55, 433
Sutton, Leigh, 51, 55, 433
Sutton, Thomas, 538, 598
Sutton (Yorks.):
    England, Daniel, 281
    England, Thomas, 281
Sutton-in-Ashfield (Notts.):
    Knighton, George, 520
Sutton Scarsdale House (Derbs.):
    How, Thomas, 453
    Poynton, Edward, 711
Swaffham (Norfolk):
    Avington & Beckett, 27
    Balders, William, 34
    Dickenson, J., 243
    Dix, Robert, 245
    Godman, Michael, 347
    Harwin, Robert, 408
    Horne, Enoch, 449
    Kiddle, George, 511
    Moneyment, Matthew, 616
    Overton, Richard, 667
    Sudbury, John, 864
    Sudbury, William, 864
    Watling, Thomas, 948
    White, John, 966
Swain, George, 775
Swain, Luke, 288
Swain, Samuel, 752
Swain, William, 916
Swaine, John, 576
Swaine, S., 360
Swaine, Samuel, 621, 730, 1008
Swaine, Thomas, 756
Swale, John, 509
Swale, Joseph, 599
Swalewell, George, 258
Swalwell, George, 53
Swan, John, 106, 826, 828
Swan, Sir John, 236
Swan, William, 154
Swan & Garner, 867
Swanage (Dorset): White, William,
    967
Swann, William, 915, 933
Swarthmoor (or Swarthwood?)
    Hall (Lancs.): Wilson, Thomas,
    989
Swayne, William, 997
Sweden, Palace of Tullgarn:
    Wilmott, Thomas, 986
Sweet, 162
Swerford (Oxon.): Blea, —, 80
Swift, Gerwas, 1005
Swindale, Isaac, 946
Swindon (Wilts.):
    Eyles, William, 286
    Reeve, Jonah, 735
    Smith, Thomas, 833
Swineshead (Lincs.): Thompson,
    Noah, 887

Swinley, Alexander, 128
Swinton (Yorks.): Birtes, William,
  75
Swinton Park (Yorks.): Wright,
  Richard & Elwick, Edward, 1008
Sworder, 865
Syers, 903
Symes, Charles, 823
Syon House (Middlx):
  Adair, John, 2
  Davies (or Davis), T. & Griffin,
    230
  Davies (or Davis), Thomas, 230
  France, William snr, 316
  Jenkins, John, 483
  Linnell, John, 545
  Mayhew, John and Ince,
    William, 595
  Moore, Thomas, 621
  Morel, Nicholas and Morel &
    Hughes, Robert, 624, 625
  Ponsonby, Thomas, 705

T

Tabor, Robert, 821
Tabley Hall (Cheshire):
  Davies (or Davis), Samuel, 229
  Ellick, —, 272
  Harden, G.B., 395
  Jackson, Daniel & Peter, 475
  Kaye, John, 501
  Leicester, Charles, 537
  Martindale, —, 582
  Powell, Thomas, 711
  Sherrett, —, 809
  Spinnage, William, 845
  Walker, Richard, 937
  Wheeldon, Benjamin, 963
Tadcaster (Yorks.):
  Archbell, John, 17
  Archbell, Thomas, 17
  England, Thomas, 281
  Hogget, John, 440
  Hurscroft, William, 466
  Husband, John, 467
  Huscroft, William, 467
  Marshall, William, 579
  Muscroft, John, 637
  Pannett, Marmaduke, 672
  Rawson, John, 730
  Rockcliff, Henry, 762
  Rodwell, John, 762
  Simpson, Thomas, 816
  Smith, Richard, 831
  Waterhouse, Henry, 947
Taitt, John, 327
Taitt, Richard, 356
Taitt, William, 356
Tall, James, 764, 1013
Tamworth (Staffs.):
  Allsop, William, 11
  Ensar, George, 281

Hards, Thomas, 396
Hare, James, 397
Harris, Thomas, 402
Holloway, Charles, 443
Horton, George, 451
Jones, Edward, 494
Marshall, John, 579
Moore, Henry, 618
Mouseley, John, 633
Pickering, Thomas, 697
Robinson, Robert, 760
Stretton, Samuel, 861
White, John, 966
Tandell, Samuel, 726
Tanfield (Co. Durham): Storey,
  William, 860
Tantum, 934
Tantum & Walker, 871
Tarleton (Cheshire): Dandy, James,
  225
Tarn, 662
Tarn, Joseph, 872
Tarporley (Cheshire):
  Holland, Thomas, 442
  Mahanah, John, 570
  Mehanna, John, 601
  Sheen, William, 806
  Wilkinson, John, 976
Tarporley Hunt Club: Wilkinson,
  John, 976
Tarrey, Thomas, 764
Tarry, George, 612, 780, 881
Tasker, 634
Tatam, Henry, 915
Tate, John, 572
Tate, Richard Seddon, 677
Tatham, Thomas, 30, 544, 930
Tatham & Co., 647
Tatham & Bailey, 544
Tatnall, John, 350
Tattem, Henry, 873
Tattenhall (Cheshire): Butler, Jos.,
  137
Tattershall (Lincs.): Hidrid,
  Thomas, 428
Tatton Park (Cheshire):
  Coade, Eleanor and her
    successors, 181
  Gillow, 343
  Kilner, J. jnr, 512
  Pye, Edward, 723
Taunton, Jacob, 447
Taunton (Som.):
  Atlee, Samuel, 25
  Baker, William, 33
  Bryer, Robert, 123
  Dollen, Thomas, 250
  Drake, Richard, 255
  Garway, William, 332
  Gridley, Charles, 373
  Harman, Joseph, 399
  Hiett, William, 428
  Joggett, William, 488
  Line, William, 543

Linton, Arthur, 548
Linton, Robert, 548
Lowe, James, 557
Lucraft, Benjamin, 560
Mockeridge, Henry, 614
Pearcey, —, 684
Pearcey, Thomas, 684
Perry, William, 692
Preddy, J., 713
Preddy, James, 713
Rowsell, Henry, 769
Shannon, Thomas, 802
Shepherd, —, 807
Sheppard, John, 808
Stevens, John, 854
Toggett, William, 897
Tytherleigh, Arthur, 916
Webber, James, 954
White, James, 965
White, Richard, 966
Woodford, William, 999
Wyburn, Robert, 1011
Tavistock (Devon):
  Geake, Thomas, 333
  Gordon, William, 357
  Jessop, Thomas, 488
  Maygor, —, 589
  Wonnacot, —, 995
  Worden, William, 1002
Tayler, Joseph, 877
Tayler, Joshua, 878
Tayler, Matthew, 878
Tayler, Richard Walker, 773
Tayler & Wright, 877
Tayloer, George, 876
Taylor, 341, 586, 587, 860–1, 942,
  954
Taylor, Charles, 879, 918
Taylor, David, 877, 879
Taylor, Edward, 758
Taylor, Edward William Whinfield,
  754
Taylor, Elias, 686
Taylor, G., 263
Taylor, George, 125, 878
Taylor, Isaac, 929
Taylor, James, 74, 916
Taylor, John, 323, 438, 452, 579,
  630, 812, 875, 878, 879, 883, 912
Taylor, Joseph, 504
Taylor, Major, 877
Taylor, Richard, 744, 877
Taylor, Thomas, 754, 874, 876, 918
Taylor, William, 562, 875, 876
Taylor & Fisher, 880
Taylor & Jones, 774
Taymouth Castle (Perths.):
  Newton, James, 644
  Robertson, Charles, 755
  Taylor, David, 875
  Wyatt, Edward, 1010
Tayspill (London): Daniell, George,
  225
Teal, John, 767

Teddington (Middlx): Black,
  Henry, 76
Teignmouth (Devon):
  Hubbard, —, 456
  Hubbard, John Peters, 457
  Linter, R., 548
  Nichols, J., 646
  Nosworthy, William, 656
  Partridge, William, 678
  Searle, John, 792
  Seward, —, 801
  Tucker, William, 907
Temple Newsam (Yorks.):
  Allen, J., 10
  Amos, John, 12
  Bancroft, John, 36
  Beard, T., 55
  Bray, Joseph, 104
  Channon, John, 155
  Chippendale, Thomas snr, 167
  Cooper, H.W., 196
  Coulthirst, Robert, 202
  Dyson, James, 263
  Edmonds, John, 267
  Evans, Benjamin, 283
  Farmb(o)rough, William, 289
  Fell, Lawrence, 294
  Foster, Thomas, 312
  Freelove, Richard, 320
  Gatehouse, John, 332
  Gee, John, 334
  George, Remy, 335
  Green, Thomas, 368
  Guibert, Philip, 377
  Hallett, William snr and William
    jnr, 388
  Hardy, James, 397
  Hodson, Robert, 440
  Hudson, Francis, 458
  Hull, James, 462
  Ikin, Abel, 470
  Isaac, A., 473
  Johnson, Thomas, 491
  Kennedy, John, 506
  Kerby, Richard, 509
  Kerry, —, 510
  Kirton, James, 518
  Leicester, Charles, 537
  Marshall, James jnr, 577
  Moore, James jnr, 619
  Moor(e), Richard, 620
  Nash, Robert, 638
  Newman, Edward, 643
  Pascall, James & Ann, 679
  Pearson, William, 685
  Peareth, John, 685
  Planta, John, 702
  Price, Richard, 716
  Semple, John & Alexander, 800
  Simpson, Michael, 816
  Spencer, J., 843
  Tomkins, John, 897
  Trott, Thomas snr, 905
  Trott, Thomas jnr, 905

  Turner, Joshua, 911
  Webb, Thomas, 954
  Whitney, Abraham, 969
  Wills, John, 985
  Wilson, A., 986
  Wright, Richard & Elwick,
    Edward, 1006, 1007
Temple Sowerby (Westmld):
  Harrison, George, 403
Tenterden (Kent):
  Barns, James, 43
  Benzie, James, 67
  Drury, John, 257
  Grisbrook, William, 375
  Hall, John, 385
  Masters, David, 585
  Masters, James, 585
  Symes, William, 869
Tentmaker: Bagster, James, 29
Terry, 76, 109, 1011
Terry, Henry, 334, 603
Tetbury (Glos.):
  Hancock, Thomas, 393
  Mill, Thomas, 607
  Oldham, Thomas, 662
  Sealy, Alexander, 792
  Smith, William, 834
  Woodward, Christopher, 1000
Tettenhall Wood (Wolverhampton):
  Easthope, George, 265
  Giusani, Peter, 344
Tewkesbury (Glos.):
  Archer, Charles, 17
  Archer, George, 17
  Bagley, Edward, 29
  Bethell, James, 69
  Brewer, James, 106
  Bucherfield, John, 123
  Butt, John, 138
  Edgecombe, Handy, 266
  Edgecombe, Mrs, 266
  Edgecombe, Richard F., 266
  Edgecombe, William, 266
  Glover, Joseph, 345
  Hart, Thomas, 406
  Hart, William, 406
  Hayes, George, 414
  Hodges, Richard, 437
  Hooper, Richard, 447
  James, Edward, 478
  James, William, 480
  Knight, George, 519
  Moore, Samuel, 621
  Nible, Henry, 645
  Potter, Joseph, 708
  Rhodes, William, 740
  Richardson, John, 744
  Roads, James, 751
  Sander, Thomas, 779
  Smith, Thomas, 833
  Story, Ralph, 860
  Wheeler, Joseph, 963
  Yarnall, Richard, 1011
  Yarnall, William, 1011

Thacker, George, 316
Thairlwall, George, 244
Thame (Oxon.): Randel, —, 727
Thames Ditton (Surrey):
  Mathew(s), Samuel, 586
  Wardell, John, 944
Thaxted (Essex):
  Baynes, George, 53
  Harris, John, 401
Theakstone, Christopher, 935
Thermometers: Battistessa & Co,
  50
Thetford (Norfolk):
  Atkins, William, 23
  Gostling, John S., 359
  Mann, Charles, 572
  Oldman, John, 662
  Vinsen, W., 929
Theweneti, 836
Thickpenny, Thomas, 393
Thirsk (Yorks.):
  Gainforth, Richard, 327
  Gamble, Richard, 328
  Gamble, William, 328
  Hambleton, Joseph, 391
  Peacock, William, 683
  Peat, Joseph, 685
  Richmond, John, 746
  Rose, Robert, 766
  Tindall, George, 895
Thistleton, Daniel, 915
Thomas, 305, 336, 392, 393
Thomas, Joseph, 554
Thomas, Moreton, 562
Thomas, Philip, 174
Thomas, William, 883
Thomas & Tucker, 884
Thompson, 259
Thompson, Charles, 534
Thompson, George, 249
Thompson, Henry, 910
Thompson, Isaac, 886
Thompson, J. & S., 887
Thompson, James, 323
Thompson, John, 275
Thompson, Matthew, 886
Thompson, Richard, 956
Thompson, Samuel, 405
Thompson, Thomas, 151, 328
Thompson, William, 137, 887, 899
Thompson, William Hall, 886
Thoms, W., 888
Thomson, Guy, 885
Thomson, James, 886
Thomson, Simpson, 887
Thomson, Stephen, 887
Thoresby Park (Notts.):
  Chippendale, Thomas snr, 167
Thorganby-cum-Cottingworth
  (Yorks.): North, John, 655
Thorn, Thomas, 890
Thorndon Hall (Essex):
  Bracken, —, 95
  Crabtree, James, 206

Saunders, Paul, 785
Ward & Donald, 944
Thorne, George, 290, 813
Thorne, Thomas, 428, 469
Thorne (Yorks.):
Barnet, John, 43
Bowling, John, 93
Gill, Richard, 340
Harrison, John, 404
Hawksworth, John, 413
Hinchcliffe, John, 433
Kitchen, Jonathan, 518
Middlebrooke, Richard, 604
Norton, John, 656
Pepper, William, 690
Pullen, Robert, 721
Robinson, William, 761
Todd, William, 897
Wade, William, 931
Thorner (Yorks.):
Dalby, George, 223
Harrison, Robert, 404
Thorney, R., 16, 243, 366, 688, 714,
758, 760, 821, 895, 898
Thorney, Robert, 369
Thornham, George, 713, 890
Thornham, Thomas, 686
Thornhill, Birmingham:
Bullock, George, 127, 128
Wilcock, Robert, 973
Thornton, William, 859
Thornton (Norfolk): Hooks,
Robert, 447
Thornton Watlass (Yorks.): Wright,
William, 1009
Thorold, John, 259
Thorp, 83
Thorp, Bethel, 951
Thorp, George, 86
Thorp, William, 413
Thorpe, Francis, 285
Thorpe, George, 86, 490, 1001
Thorpe, Robert, 490, 633
Thorpe (Essex): Brooke, Daniel,
111
Thorpe Hall (Yorks.): Wright,
Richard & Elwick, Edward, 1008
Thoverton (Devon): Rowe, T.B.,
768
Thrapston (Northants.):
Bucknell, John, 124
Dicks, Joseph, 244
Hensman, W.D., 422
Threlfall, James, 51
Thringston (Leics.): Moore, John,
620
Thurkettle, Nathaniel Palmer, 882
Thurkettle, William D., 882
Thurston, 1002
Thurtle, John, 882
Tickhill (Yorks.):
Godfrey, Edward, 346
Hudson, James, 458
Tidmarsh, Wall, 1, 226, 894

Tildesley, 386
Tillier, John, 791
Tilston, John, 385, 696
Tiltson, John, 230
Timberlake, James, 908
Timings, 203
Timmings, 216
Timmings, John, 136, 252, 472, 554
Tims, Joseph, 482
Tindale, Athelstane, 53
Tipler, Thomas, 393
Tipping, Josiah, 938
Tippler, Thomas, 9, 309
Tipton (Staffs.):
Jones, William, 498
Leech, Joseph, 535
Peacock, Henry, 683
Tissington Hall (Derbs.): Hobcraft,
John, 436
Titter, Benjamin P., 791
Tiverton (Devon):
Boden, —, 82
Bowden, —, 91
Gill, John, 340
Hewett, James, 425
Hobbs, Nocholas, 435
How, J., 453
James, George, 479
Land, Samuel, 524
Quick, James, 724
Radford, John, 725
Sharland, William, 802
Skinner, Richard, 820
Striling, W., 862
Tucker, John, 907
Tucker, Richard, 907
Turner, John, 911
Todd, George, 421
Todd, John, 91, 148
Todd, Richard, 767
Todd, Thomas, 1008
Toddington (Beds.): Potts, John,
708
Todmorden (Yorks.):
Ashworth, John, 21
Ashworth, William, 21
Baron, Henry, 43
Butterfield, John, 138
Holt, James, 446
Horsfall, James, 451
Ingham, John, 471
Roberts, Timothy, 754
Scholfield, Abraham, 789
Scholfield, James, 789
Shackleton, Isaac, 801
Sutcliffe, James, 865
Walton, Thomas, 942
Toft (Cambs.): Harris, Benjamin,
400
Tolputt, 207
Tomkins, 509
Tomkins, Thomas, 898
Tomkins, William, 762
Tomlin, Roger, 376

Tomlinson, 222
Tomlinson, Robert, 61, 79, 297,
464, 750
Tomlyn, James, 371
Tomlyn, Roger, 553
Tompson, Jacob, 404
Toms, Richard, 888, 889
Tonbridge (Kent):
Borsman, John, 88
Diplock, Thomas, 245
Gasson, William, 332
Gorringe, Charles, 358
Harris, William, 403
Hill, Thomas, 431
Holmes, W., 446
Inman, S., 472
Laker, William, 521
Langley, John, 526
Morgan, Henry, 625
Morgan, John, 625
Morgan, William, 626
Nye, John, 658
Saker, J., 776
Stidolph, Edward, 856
Stidolph, George, 856
Stidolph, George Lambert, 856
Wise, George snr & jnr, 993
Wise, Thomas, 994
Woodham, Thomas, 999
Tooke, Barber William, 633
Toplis, James, 262
Toplis, Samuel, 893
Topping, 37
Topsham (Devon):
Bennet, Richard, 64
Hayward, J., 415
Rodd, John, 762
Torquay (Devon):
Bailey, J., 30
Burt, Charles William, 134
Burts, —, 136
Hearder, Gilbert, 417
Hearder, Sarah, 417
Jenkins, John, 484
Matthews, John R., 587
Oliver, Thomas, 663
Poulton, Henry, 709
Stark, William, 850
Waren, I., 946
Torrington (Devon):
Lee, J., 534
May, William Morris, 589
Torry, George, 764
Tothill, John, 809
Totnes (Devon):
Angel, John jnr, 14
Bennet(t), Thomas, 64
Bowden, William, 92
George, Thomas, 335
Holland, John, 442
Jackson, Edward, 475
Pulling, William, 722
Teasell, Henry, 880
Teasell, Joseph, 880

Trist, Browse, 904
Tottenham (London):
  Bradbear, William, 95
  Burton, James, 135
  Dennison, James, 240
  Dewer, James, 242
  Dickenson, Thomas, 243
  Dixon, Charles, 245
  Dobbs, —, 247
  Dodd, James, 248
  Eichel, George, 271
  Eichel, John, 271
  Gagnon, Alexander John, 327
  Gasson, James, 332
  Gill, James, 340
  Newton, Thomas, 645
  Noon, —, 651
  Norman, George William, 651
  Reid, R., 736
  Richards, Samuel, 742
  Ware, Charles, 944
Totteridge Church (Herts.): Leader,
  George, 533
Toulmin, Robert, 77
Touzey, Jacob, 775
Towcester (Northants.):
  Blaxley, John, 80
  Blaxley, William, 80
  Inns, William, 472
  Jeffs, John, 483
  Jeffs, Thomas, 483
  Lovell, George, 556
  Lovell, Thomas, 556
  Webb, John, 953
Towneley Hall (Lancs.):
  Gillow, 343
  Hathwell, —, 410
  Reynoldson, George, 740
  Riley, —, 748
  Rothwell, —, 767
  Seddon, George, 796
  Skerrett, Thomas, 819
  Stephenson, William, 854
  Syers, Joseph, 869
  Turner (or Turno(u)r), Thomas,
  912
  Williams, Samuel, 982
Townley, 622
Townsend, John, 178
Townsend, William, 809
Townshend, John, 546
Townson, John jnr, 754
Trafford Hall (Lancs.): Gillow, 343
Tredegar House (Mons.):
  Gumley, Elizabeth, 379
  Hasert, Peter, 409
Tregothnan (Cornwall): Vile,
  William, 927
Trevett, Samuel, 587
Trewin, William, 903
Trim, John, 735
Trimnell, Arthur, 33
Trimnell, Thomas, 904

Tring (Herts.):
  Griffin, William, 373
  Higgs, William, 429
  Jones, Garnett, 494
Trollope, John Amos, 905
Trother & Magill, 416
Trotter, 1015
Trotter, Coutts, 906
Trotter, James, 888
Trotter, John, 10, 56, 784, 785
Trowbridge (Wilts.):
  Butcher, Philip, 137
  Hilps, George, 432
  Knee, William, 518
  Moore, Benjamin, 617
  Newton, J., 644
  Newton, Thomas, 645
  Rawlins, James, 730
  Sargeant, Jacob, 781
  Tucker, John Samuel, 907
Trower, 829
Troy House (Mons.): Kensett,
  William, 508
Trubshaw, James, 585
Truro (Cornwall):
  Baynard, John, 53
  Blake, William, 79
  Bone, Henry, 85
  Down(e), William, 254
  Halse, William, 391
  James, William, 480
  Jordan, John, 499
  Mawton, Richard, 588
  Mudge, W., 634
  Nicholls, Richard, 646
  Symonds, Robert Walter, 869
  Syms, —, 869
  Teague, John, 880
  Thomas, John, 883
  Thomas, Richard, 884
  Trebilock, Richard, 903
  Tregonning's Repository, 903
  Vice, John, 922
  Whitford, W., 969
Truro Cathedral: Bone, Henry, 85
Trusted, Thomas, 903–4
Trusthead, Thomas, 903–4
Tubby, Samuel, 823
Tucker, 884, 885
Tucker, A., 907
Tucker, John, 146
Tucker, Richard, 157
Tucker, Thomas, 102, 542
Tudgey, John, 371
Tudor, Cornelius, 911
Tudor, Robert, 911
Tunbridge Wells (Kent):
  Beale, John, 54
  Bennett, George, 64
  Berry, William, 68
  Brisenden, Thomas, 108
  Brissenden & Hodges, 108
  Burrows, George & James, 133
  Burrows, Humphrey jnr, 134

  Burrows, Humphrey snr, 133
  Burrows, Thomas, 134
  Burrows, William & James, 134
  Downard, Henry, 254
  Dyer, Benjamin, 263
  Goodiham, John, 351
  Goodrham, John, 354
  Hicks, Frederick, 427
  Hodges, Thomas, 437
  Knight, Joseph, 519
  Lancaster, Henry, 524
  Latter, James, 529
  Noyes, Henry, 657
  Nye, Edmund, 657
  Nye, Henry, 658
  Rason, Henry, 728
  Roberts, Christopher, 751
  Saltmarsh & Wicking, 777
  Sammons, Thomas, 778
  Sharp, John, James & Ann, 803
  Stapley, Henry, 850
  Stapley, John Baker, 850
  Stapley, Michael, 850
  Strange, Nicholas, 860
  Ubsdell, John Talbot, 916
  Wicking, —, 972
Tunbridge-ware:
  Bennett, George, 64
  Browning & Hopkins, 120
  Burrows, George & James, 133
  Burrows, Humphrey jnr, 134
  Burrows, Humphrey snr, 133
  Burrows, Thomas, 134
  Burrows, William & James snr,
  134
  Evans, John, 284
  Gibson, John, 337
  Halford, F.W., 384
  Heath, Robert, 419
  Hewlin(s), Peter, 426
  Hodges, Richard, 437
  Hollyer, Matilda, 444
  Jacques, Thomas, 477
  Knight, Joseph, 519
  Latter, James, 529
  Lecount, Richard, 534
  Marshall, Martha, 579
  Merrick, William, 603
  Morris, John Witten, 628
  Nesbitt, William, 641
  Nye, Edmund, 657
  Nye, Henry, 658
  Nye, John, 658
  Roberts, Christopher, 751
  Robinson, John, 758
  Sharp, John et al, 803
  Souch, Frederick, Webster, 839
  Upton, William, 918
  Wise, George snr & jnr, 993
  Wise, Thomas, 994
Tunnicliff, 631
Tunstall, James, 642
Tunstall (Staffs.):
  Eardley, Samuel, 264

Hulse, Charles, 462
Nickson, George, 647
Walker, John, 936
Wood, Hugh, 996
Turing, William, 379
Turnbrooke, Edward, 133
Turnbull, 7
Turnbull, Robert, 734
Turndall, Athelston(e), 915
Turner, 163, 523, 560, 765, 836, 975
Turner, Charles, 873
Turner, Edmund, 911
Turner, Edward, 1
Turner, Henry, 542, 912, 955
Turner, John, 456
Turner, John Ward, 35, 433, 443, 461, 479, 551, 576, 629, 637, 664, 908, 932, 947
Turner, Joseph, 602
Turner, Josiah, 4
Turner, Thomas, 551, 682, 745
Turner, William, 171, 564
Turney, James, 371
Turnham Green (Surrey): Bullock, John, 128
Turnor, Thomas, 912
Turnour, Thomas, 912
Turpin, 675
Turton, 531, 644
Turton, William, 294
Turvey, John, 900
Tuson, Robert, 998
Tustian, William, 858
Tute, William, 599
Tutop, Charles, 64
Tutt, 104
Tuxford (Notts.):
  Blenkhorne, James, 80
  Hannah, John, 395
  Johnson, William, 493
  Marples, William, 575
  Shaw, William, 805
Twaites, Edward, 893
Twanbrook, Edward, 471, 831
Twanbrooke, Edward, 141
Tweedmouth (Northumb.):
  Denham, William, 240
  Hood, James, 447
  Lough, Francis, 555
  Murray, George, 636
  Sandilands, George, 780
Twickenham (London):
  Anderson, Robert, 13
  Barr, James, 43
  Bromage, William, 110
  Brown, —, 113
  Brown, Henry, 114
  Dunn, Joseph, 260
  Jones, Joseph, 496
  Pritchard, Samuel, 718
  Thorne, Lewis, 890
  Thorne, William, 890
Twitty, James, 715, 832
Tydder, Samuel, 908

Tyler, 836
Tylston, Thomas, 895
Tymperon, Robert, 192
Tyndal, 129
Tyndall, Athelstane, 53
Tyrer, 425
Tyrer, Bartholomew, 64, 102, 263, 302, 383, 461, 501, 550, 685, 766, 882, 916
Tyrer, Benjamin, 577
Tyrer, James, 916
Tyrer, Richard, 159
Tyrer, Robert, 728, 866
Tyrer, Thomas Savage, 80, 102, 876, 915
Tyrer, Thomas Savage jnr, 915
Tyrer, Thomas Savage snr, 916
Tyrrell, Timothy, 917
Tyson, J., 66, 154
Tyson, Joseph, 91, 898
Tysse, James, 916
Tyte, Richard, 935
Tyte, William, 816, 935
Tythegston Court (Glam.):
  Court, Charles, 202
  Deering, —, 238
  Derring, —, 241
  Edwards, —, 268
  Elward, George & Marsh, William, 279
  Hill, —, 430
  Mayhew, John & Ince, William, 595
  Perfetti, Joseph, 690
  Richards, James, 742
  Saunders, Richard, 785
  Say, Francis, 787
  Trotter, John, 906
  Watson, —, 948
  Wynne, —, 1011

U

Ubaine, Thomas, 51
Uckfield (Sussex): Rice, Henry, 741
Ulverston (Lancs.):
  Ashworth, James, 21
  Atkinson, Matthew, 24
  Barwick, James, 47
  Brocklebank, John jnr, 109
  Dodgson, John, 249
  Duke, William, 259
  Duke & Ashbuner, 259
  Gaskell, —, 332
  Gastrell, Miles, 332
  Law, William, 530
  Lewis, Thomas, 541
  Marr, Thomas, 575
  Spencer, John Liddel, 843
  Webster, Thomas, 956
  White, Francis, 965

Underwood, Frances, 151
Underwood, James, 251
Underwood, John, 1, 124, 391, 691, 844, 916
Uppark (Sussex):
  Bladwell, John, 78
  Cobb, John, 182
  Elward, George & Marsh, William, 279
  Entwistle, Mrs, 281
  Hallett, William snr and William jnr, 388, 389
  Saunders, Paul, 783, 784
  Vile, William, 928
Uppingham (Leics.):
  Abbot, Matthew & Richard, 1
  Baddely, Thomas, 28
  Baines, Edward & Henry, 31
  Baines, John, 31
  Baines, Robert, 32
  Birch, Francis, 73
  Holmes, James, 445
  Jackson, John, 476
  Langley, William, 526
  Reynolds, William, 739
  Twigg, William, 915
Upton, John, 906
Upton (Norfolk):
  Davey, John, 227
  Shepherd, Thomas, 808
Upton Scudamore (Wilts.): Grist, Samuel, 375
Upton-upon-Severn: (Worcs.)
  Bartlett, Stephen, 46
  Bick, John, 70
Ure, William, 918
Urmson, Elizabeth, 371
Urmson & Gregson, 633
Utting, 880
Utting, Henry, 874, 879
Uttoxeter (Staffs.):
  Al(l)kins, John, 8
  Atkins, John, 23
  B(l)urton, Venables, 136
  Daken, William, 223
  Deakin, John, 237
  Evans, William, 285
  Goodall, Richard, 351
  Jessop, Benjamin, 488
  Jessop, John, 488
  Lee, Nathaniel, 535
  Manlove, Rowland, 572
  Morley, Thomas, 627
  Mottram, Joseph, 632
  Roberts, Edward, 751
  Smith, Lewis, 830
  Stone, John, 858
  Taylor, Robert, 879
  Taylor, William F., 879
  Tomlinson, George, 898
  Wakefield, Thomas, 933
  Weston, John, 961
  Wilcocks, William, 973
  Woodroffe, John, 1000

Uxbridge (Middlx):
  Burgiss, William, 130
  Dunham, Richard, 259
  Godbold, Francis, 346
  Jepps, William Henry, 487
  Keyte, Richard, 511
  Moore, George B., 618
  Mor(e)ten, Henry, 630
  Morten, Thomas & Charles, 630
  Murray, Charles & Son, 636
  Norton, Daniel & Godbold,
  Francis, 656
  Prior, John & Robert, 718
  Saunders, Jos., 782
  Stransom, William, 861

V

Valence (Kent): Vardy, Thomas,
  919
Vallance, J., 772
Van der Stein, John, 919
Vanderbank, John, 783
Varley, William, 458
Vaudvine (Paudevin), John, 681
Vauxhall (London):
  Ball, David, 35
  Giles, James, 339
Vecchio, 706
Venables, John, 684
Venn, 554
Vennor, 136
Venson, 946
Venson, William, 929
Ventris, William, 67, 314, 725
Verers, Richard, 922
Vernal, John, 216
Vernon, Thomas, 506
Versailles (France): Van Opstal,
  Louis, 919
Verscragen, James, 242
Vialls, Thomas, 56
Vials, Thomas, 925
Vicars & Rutledge, 31
Vickard, 995
Vile, William, 95, 182, 183, 184,
  316, 352, 353, 387, 388, 389, 713,
  738, 824, 861
Vile & Cobb, 95, 388, 389, 924,
  925, 926, 927, 928
Vincent, George Mathyson, 217
Vinson, 945
Vinton, 322
Vipond, Nicholas, 581
Virginia (USA): Lindsay, John, 543
Vizard, Isaac, 108, 541, 876
The Vyne (Hants.):
  Bradburn(e), John, 97
  France, William snr, 316
  Prestage, John, 713
  Vile, William, 925
  Zurn, —, 1016

W

Wacker, John, 482
Waddilove, James, 682
Waddingham, 861
Waddle, Daniel, 143
Wade, William, 667
Waggoner, William, 53, 258
Wagner & Cottrell, 523
Wainfleet (Lincs.):
  Audas, William, 26
  Beal, Francis, 54
  Ordas, William, 664
Wainwright, Charles, 734
Wainwright, George, 159, 734
Wainwright, James, 35, 911
Wainwright, Thomas, 224
Wakefield, J., 73, 123, 197, 565,
  650, 867
Wakefield, Thomas, 151
Wakefield (Yorks.):
  Allat, Thomas, 9
  Allat, William, 9
  Arson, E. & Sons, 19
  Balmforth, Jos, 36
  Billington, John, 72
  Billington, William, 72
  Beaumont, Joseph, 56
  Burton, Thomas, 135
  Byewater, George, 140
  Dodgson, William, 249
  Drew, Samuel, 256
  Drew, William, 256
  Elwick, Edward jnr & Son, 279
  Elwick, Edward snr, 279
  Elwick, John & Robinson, John,
  279
  Everingham, John, 285
  Everingham, Richard & John,
  285
  Goodwin, Jonathan, 355
  Grace, William, 361
  Green, John, 367
  Halley, George Henry, 389
  Hirst, James, 434
  Izott, Joseph, 474
  Lee, Robert, 535
  Machan, Matthew, 565
  Machan, William, 565
  Marsden, John, 576
  Marsden, Thomas, 576
  Marsden, William, 576
  Mat(t)hewman, George, 586
  Middleton, John, 605
  Middleton, Robert, 605
  Middleton, William, 605
  Milnes, Edward, 611
  Musgraves, George, 637
  Noble, John, 650
  Olivant, Edward, 662
  Powell, Thomas jnr, 711
  Priestly, Stephen, 717
  Rayner, Joseph, 731
  Reading, Thomas, 732
  Richardson, William, 745
  Roach, Charles, 751
  Roberts, William, 754
  Robinson, John, 758
  Rushworth, Constantine, 771
  Scholes, Richard, 789
  Scholfield, —, 789
  Schurry, William, 789
  Scott, Francis & Son, 789
  Scott, William, 791
  Shaw, William, 805
  Shillitoe, Daniel, 811
  Shurray, William, 813
  Shuttleworth, Thomas, 813
  Skilito, Daniel, 819
  Skurray, William, 820
  Stewart, William, 856
  Strafford, William, 860
  Summerscale, Thomas, 865
  Terry, William, 881
  Torbutt, Charles, 900
  Tunstall, Thomas, 908
  Walker, Samuel, 937
  Walsh, Robert, 941
  Ward, Nehemiah, 943
  White, Janadab, 966
  White, Matthew, 966
  Whitehead & Priestly, 968
  Whitehead, Thomas, 968
  Whittaker, Ann, 969
  Whittaker, J., 969
  Wilby, Samuel, 973
  Wilkinson, Thomas, 977
  Wraith, Sarah, 1004
  Wraith, William, 1004
  Wright, Richard & Elwick,
  Edward, 1006
  Yeamans, Edward, 1012
Wakefield Masonic Lodge (Yorks.):
  Wright, Richard & Elwick,
  Edward,
  1007
Wakefield Town Hall (Yorks.):
  Bul(l)man, Robert, 126
Wakelin, Henry, 63, 103
Wakeling, 566
Wakeling, Thomas, 933
Wakeman, Thomas, 496
Walbrook (London): Ran(s)ford,
  John, 727
Walcott (Som.): Madden, John, 569
Waldergrave, Samuel, 786
Waldron, Thomas, 138, 418
Walker, 162, 293, 368, 467, 611,
  643, 647, 692, 871, 949
Walker, Charles, 695
Walker, Christopher, 337, 453, 664
Walker, Elizabeth, 936, 937
Walker, George, 857, 916
Walker, Henry, 455, 937
Walker, John, 266, 312, 336, 385,
  391, 457, 520, 882, 938
Walker, Mary, 194
Walker, Milicent, 517

Walker, Millicent, 773
Walker, Richard, 262, 313, 581,
  688, 712, 773, 950, 975, 1002
Walker, Robert, 934, 936, 937
Walker, Samuel, 802
Walker, T., 375
Walker, Thomas, 1, 119, 272, 641,
  729, 806, 934
Walker, William, 507, 934
Walker, William Longworth, 200,
  752, 896
Walker & Saville, 937
Walkington, 485
Walkington, John, 997
Wallace, 23, 885
Wallace, John, 34
Walle, Henry, 737
Waller, Richard, 51, 939–40
Wallin, Richard, 363
Wallingford (Berks.):
  Arnould, Robert, 19
  Belcher, John, 59
  Belcher, Joseph, 59
  Dyer, William, 263
  Maxey, Charles, 588
  Maxey, George, 588
  Ponking, Francis, 705
Wallington, 858
Wallis, 885
Wallis, James Wilkinson, 944
Walls, Thomas, 299, 312, 376, 390,
  413, 466, 637
Wallsend (Northumb.): Garbutt,
  John, 329
Walmgate, York: Hague, Thomas,
  382
Walsall (Staffs.):
  Aulton, Abraham, 26
  Bayley, William, 52
  Bayliss, Thomas, 52
  Bloomfield, J., 81
  Brooks, Joseph, 112
  Duncalfe, Henry, 259
  Harrison, John, 404
  Hulton, Abraham, 462
  Lates, John James B., 529
  Livesay, Samuel, 550
  Lucas, William, 559
  Moore, Napthali, 620
  Murray, Richard, 637
  Nock, Edward, 650
  Nock, Thomas, 650
  Pearson, Samuel, 685
  Reynolds, Thomas, 738
  Richardson, J. & R., 743
  Roberts, Thomas, 754
  Stokes, William, 858
  Taylor, Thomas, 879
  Willatt, Anthony, 978
  Willett, Anthony, 978
Walsh, John, 363
Walsingham (Suffolk):
  Burcham, Henry, 129
  Lovick, Samuel, 557

Playford, Thomas, 702
Tagge, William Little, 870
Walters, William Miles, 150, 941
Walthamstow (Essex):
  Heath, James, 418
  Humphreys, John, 463
  Rawlings, Ann, 729
  Rawlings, George, 730
  Waller, John, 940
  Williams, Henry, 980
Walton, 880
Walton, Benjamin, 774
Walton, Humphry, 709
Walton, Robert, 160
Walworth (London):
  Anderson, John, 12
  Ault, John, 26
  Ball, James, 35
  Brown, James, 115
  Brown, Richard, 117
  Bubkrook, Thomas, 123
  Burroughs, R., 133
  Day, Thomas, 236
  Dixon, Henry, 246
  Eginton, Mary, 271
  Elder, Alexander, 271
  Griffith, John, 374
  McCarthy, Dennis, 564
  Monat, John, 616
  Mouat, John, 632
  Mount, J., 633
  Mount, John, 633
  Newcomb, Alexander, 642
  Nicks, —, 647
  Potter, G.A., 708
  Prebble, J., 713
  Prew, William, 715
  Redward, —, 734
  Taylor, Joshua, 878
  Trent, John, 903
  Trew, James, 904
  Turner, William, 913
  Venn, Henry, 921
  Ward, John, 943
  Ward, William, 944
Wandsworth (London):
  Herrington, H., 423
  Mold, William, 615
Wantage (Oxon.):
  Jones, James, 495
  Wilder, Leonard, 974
  Youse, William, 1015
Wapping (London):
  Baxter, John, 51
  Britain, Richard, 108
  Dunlop, George, 259
  Goddard, William, 346
  Hubart, Adam, 456
  Hume, James, 462
  Jones, James, 495
  Jones, Richard, 496
  Kerrison, Peter, 510
  Lancaster, John, 524
  Leycock, Thomas, 541

Nash, James, 638
Parker, Robinson, 675
Pigg, John, 698
Robinson, John Edwin, 758
Sanders, Daniel, 779
Sandilands, James, 780
Simson, Francis, 817
Smith, William, 833
Thompson, Alexander, 885
Ward, 293
Ward, Benjamin, 760
Ward, James, 944
Ward, John, 38, 300
Ward, R., 943
Ward, Thomas, 51, 130, 376, 676
Ward, William, 26
Ward, William snr, 465
Wardale, Thomas, 601
Wardle, Ralph, 825
Wardley, Isaac, 333, 973
Ware (Herts.):
  Bland, John, 80
  Elkins, George, 272
  Hitch, James, 434
  Jenks, Robert, 484
  Smart, William, 823
  Stevens, John, 854
  Webb, Thomas, 954
  Webster, J., 955
  Webster, Robert, 954
Wareing, Michael, 602
Waring, Cruis, 507
Waring, John, 599
Warley Hall (Worcs.): Bullock,
  George, 128
Warminster (Wilts.):
  Barnes, John, 42
  Edwards, George, 269
  Morgan, John, 625
  Park, John, 673
  Tucker, Walter, 907
  Warren, Stephen, 946
  Wyatt, John, 1010
Warne & Vinson, 945
Warner, 426, 978
Warr, Richard, 945
Warren, Edward, 206, 367, 465
Warren, Isaac, 864
Warren, James, 674
Warren, John, 235
Warrington (Lancs.):
  Anderson, John, 12
  Ashton, John jnr, 21
  Atherton, James, 23
  Atherton, Thomas, 23
  Blundell, Ellis, 82
  Booth, Samuel, 87
  Bradley, Richard, 98
  Bradley, Robert, 98
  Bradley, Thomas, 98
  Bratherton, Thomas, 103
  Broadhurst, John, 109
  Edwards, Hannah, 269
  Elcock, Jos., 271

Garnett, Robert & Sons, 331
Gent, Samuel, 335
Geover, John, 335
Glover, James, 345
Glover, John & Co., 345
Harrison, James, 403
Harrison, John, 404
Harrison, William, 405
Haslep, Pater, 409
Hendrich, John, 421
Hurst, Henry, 466
Jolly, Edward, 493
Jolly, James, 493
Keenan, Nicholas, 502
Kendrick, John, 505
Kendrick, Peter, 505
Lawton, Joseph, 532
Leigh, Thomas, 537
Mercer, Joseph, 602
Phillips, Nancy, 695
Phillips, Peter, 695
Rawlinson, Anne, 730
Rigby, Charles, 747
Roughley, Mary, 768
Rowe, John, 768
Stirrup, James, 856
Urmson, Elizabeth, 918
White, Stephen, 967
Worrell, James, 1003
Yates, Richard, 1012
Warsop (Notts.):
  Hallam, Edward, 387
  Sansom, William, 781
Warwick:
  Arnold, John, 19
  Beatty, Thomas, 55
  Davies, T. & Griffin, 229
  Dowler, John, 254
  Dowler, William, 254
  Dunn, John, 260
  Durham, Thomas, 262
  Gummery, Thomas, 380
  Hands, Humphrey, 394
  Hartley, William, 407
  Hawkins, John, 413
  Hyatt, Thomas, 469
  Jones, James, 495
  Joyner, Thomas, 499
  Kibler, William, 511
  King, Benjamin, 514
  King, Francis, 514
  Levens, John, 539
  Manton, Edward, 573
  Meeks, John, 600
  Nicks, J., 647
  Penn, Joseph, 688
  Pichford, Josiah, 696
  Pickford, John, 697
  Pickford, Josiah, 697
  Pratt, William, 712
  Purden, William, 722
  Redfearn & Cary, Charles, 733
  Sharpe, Thomas, 804
  Southey, Thomas, 840

Sparrow, William, 842
Tew, William, 881
Thompson, James, 886
Wadsworth, Thomas Rawbone, 931
Ward, Benjamin, 942
Watkins, William, 948
Watt, John, 951
Wilcox, James Morris, 973
Willins, John, 983
Wood, James, 996
Woolley, William, 1002
Warwick Castle:
  King, Benjamin, 514
  Mayhew, John & Ince, William, 595
Waterhouse, Joseph, 63
Waterloo (London): Elkin, Samuel, 272
Waters, James, 305
Waters, Samuel, 911
Watford (Herts.):
  Lewin, John Field, 539
  Mitchell, John, 614
  Pinnock, John, 700
  Seager, George, 791
  Sims, David, 817
  Sparrow, J., 841
  Sparrow, Philip, 842
  Wilkinson, Henry, 976
Wath (Yorks.): Nailor, Thomas, 638
Watkins, 143, 154, 913
Watkins, William, 716
Watlin, Robert Sharp, 947
Watlington, Isaac, 602
Watlington (Oxon.):
  Maxey, Thomas, 588
  Sadler, John, 775
  Sibley, John, 813
  Tallant, James, 870
Watson, 136, 774
Watson, Alexander, 241
Watson, Bingley, 949
Watson, David, 949
Watson, G., 948
Watson, Henry, 467, 950
Watson, John, 497
Watson, Joseph, 949
Watson, Robert, 798
Watson, Samuel, 233
Watson, Thomas, 936
Watson, W.D., 146
Watson & Fox, 949, 951
Watson & Walker, 949
Watton (Norfolk):
  Barker, William, 41
  Buxton, Charles, 139
  Hubbard, William, 457
  Stebbings, T., 851
  Tillett, Richard Tallot, 894
Watts, John, 590
Watts, Moses Samuel, 122
Wattson, John, 322

Waugh, Robert, 100, 110, 157, 244, 281, 404, 430, 435, 441, 891
Waylett, John III, 302
Weald Hall (Essex): Baker, Barnard, 32
Weale, Daniel, 692
Wear, Richard, 647
Weare, Thomas, 585
Weare, William, 293
Wearg, Daniel, 768
Wearg, George, 952
Wearmouth (Co. Durham): Alcock, John, 6
Weatherall, John, 961
Weatherby, Crowther & Windle, 724
Weaverham (Cheshire):
  Mason, S., 584
  Rogers, Robert, 763
Webb, 27, 32, 880
Webb, J. & R., 954
Webb, John Richman, 842
Webb, M., 953
Webb, Richard, 954
Webb, Robert, 248, 819
Webb, Samuel, 806
Webb, William, 863
Webb & Bunce, 954
Webb & Cragg, 954
Webb & Lawford, 954
Webster, 271
Webster, Edward, 350, 467, 909, 956
Webster, Elizabeth, 117
Webster, John, 54, 70
Webster, Robert, 18, 761
Webster, Simon, 724
Webster, T., 955
Webster, Thomas, 421
Webster, William, 849, 955
Wednesbury (Staffs.):
  Duncalfe, Henry, 259
  Jones, Henry, 495
  Sutton, John, 866
  Taylor, Joseph, 878
  Taylor, Thomas, 879
  Walters, Thomas, 941
  Wright, John, 1006
Wednesfield (Staffs.):
  Adey, Walter, 5
  Basford, John, 47
  Homer, Benjamin, 446
  Lees, Thomas T., 536
Weedon, Henry, 384, 807, 955
Weightman, William, 973
Welbeck Abbey (Notts.):
  Brown, Benjamin, 113
  Coward, John, 203
  Fox, Solomon, 314
  Herve, Francois, 424
  Hill, William, 431
  Hyde, Robert, 470
  Jensen, Gerrit, 487
  Mathews, John, 586

Moore, William, 622
Welburn (Yorks.): Thompson,
William, 888
Welch, John, 39
Wellbeloved, Charles, 956
Weller, 498
Wellgate (Lancs.): Driver &
Satterthwaite, 257
Wellingborough (Northants.):
Abbott, John, 1
Green, William, 368
Hume, John, 462
Maule, William, 587
Mitton, John, 614
Pendered, Joseph, 688
Spong, William, 845
Thompson, Josh., 887
Wellington (Salop):
Anslow, James, 15
Anslow, John, 15
Greedy, William, 367
Groom, John, 376
Heaford, Thomas, 417
Large, Thomas, 528
Miles, Charles, 606
Moore, Elizabeth, 618
Moore, Richard, 620
Moore, William, 622
Page, Francis, 669
Scadding, Thomas, 788
Sheppard, Robert, 808
Southwood, James, 840
Turner, Thomas, 912
Webb, John, 952
Wellow (Notts.):
Goodwin, John, 355
Ralphs, John, 726
Wells, 522
Wells, Alexander, 67, 498
Wells, James, 749
Wells, Thomas, 675
Wells & Lambe, 957
Wells (Som.):
Beaver, George, 56
Bence, George, 64
Dabine, Josiah, 223
Davies, John, 229
Hansford, John, 395
Keary, Daniel, 501
Leslie, John, 538
Lessley, James, 358
Levi, Emanuel, 539
Lovell, George, 556
Magnus, Richard, 570
Maynard, Joseph, 598
Melmoth, John, 601
Melmouth, John, 601
Melnoth, John, 601
Mindham, John, 612
Mindham, Robert, 612
Morehouse, James Blisset, 623
Nicholls, Jacob, 645
Parfitt, Thomas, 673
Plowman, George Aram, 703

Smith, William, 833
Sparks, Peter, 841
White, William, 967
Wells-next-the-Sea (Norfolk):
Betts, Edward, 69
Bouch, Thomas, 90
Dunsbye, Richard, 261
Welsh, Joseph, 236, 511, 963
Welsh, William, 664
Welton (Yorks.): Ogilvie, Edward
Johnson, 661
Welton Grange (Yorks.): Wright,
Richard & Elwick, Edward, 1008
Wem (Salop):
Abbott, William, 1
Betteley, William, 69
Garbet, James, 329
Hales, John, 383
Hales, William, 383
Lee, John, 535
Machin, George, 565
Mason, James, 584
Mason, John, 584
Newns, Richard, 644
Nicholas, Edward, 645
Owen, Francis, 667
Owen, William, 668
Sandford, Thomas, 779
Sandland, Thomas, 780
Taylor, George, 875
Wemmergill (Yorks.): Bayles,
William, 52
Wenlock (Salop):
Beckett, Thomas, 57
Hewlett, George, 426
Nicholas, William, 645
Wensleydale (Yorks.):
Little, Thomas, 550
Thompson, M. jnr, 887
Wentworth, Joseph, 3
Wentworth Castle (Yorks.):
Godier, Jonathan, 347
Wright, Richard & Elwick,
Edward, 1007
Wentworth Woodhouse (Yorks.):
Brailsford, William, 101
Wright, Richard & Elwick,
Edward, 1007
West, George, 362, 511, 747, 774
West, James, 773
West, John, 248, 590, 603, 971
West, Thomas, 842
West Auckland (Co. Durham):
Howe, David, 455
Potter, William, 708
West Bromwich (Staffs.):
Bromfield, Mary Ann, 110
Danks, John, 225
Green, Henry, 367
Hackett, John, 381
Halsall, Anthony, 390
Russell, John, 772
Stokes, Thomas, 858

West Halton (Lincs.): Maugham,
William, 587
West Ham (London):
Balch, Edward snr, 34
Hammett, James, 392
Pick, William, 696
West Melton (Yorks.): Blackburn,
Joseph, 77
West Retford (Notts.): Baker,
William, 33
West Wycombe (Bucks.):
Aldrid, John, 7
Ashalls, John, 20
Bavin, John, 50
Bavin, William, 50
Biggs, Thomas, 71
Bowden, John, 92
Bowler, Charles, 92
Bowler, James, 93
Bryant, William, 122
Edmonds, George, 267
Gray, Charles, 365
Gray, Richard, 365
Gray, William, 366
Grimsdell, James, 375
Hardin(g), Joseph, 396
Harris, Caleb, 400
Harris, Edmond, 400
Harris, Henry jnr, 400
Harris, Henry snr, 400
Harris, Jubas, 402
Harris, Thomas, 402
Harris & Catton, 403
Hawes, James, 412
Hobson, Joseph, 436
Hodgkinson, James, 437
Hodson, Charles, 439
Holson, Joseph, 446
Keen, Joseph, 503
Lambden, John, 522
Langles, John, 526
Lindsay, John, 543
Linford, William, 543
Lipskin, Joseph, 548
Mase(lon), Philip, 582
Mead, Samuel, 598
Mead, Thomas, 598
Meade, Abraham, 598
Miggs, John, 605
Moore, Charles, 617
Moorecroft, Joseph, 622
Mouston, James, 633
Plumridge, James, 703
Plumridge, John, 703
Plumridge, William, 703
Powell, James, 710
Rolfe, John, 764
Rolfe, Robert, 764
Sewell, William, 801
Smith, Daniel, 825
Smith, Joseph, 830
Steel, William, 851
Stevens, John, 854
Stiles, James, 856

Treacher, James. 902
Veary, James, 921
Wooster, John, 1002
West Wycombe Park (Bucks.):
Coade, Eleanor and her
successors, 181
Hudson, Solomon, 459
Westbridge, Leicester: Birtchnall,
James, 75
Westbury on Trym (Glos.):
Hopkins, David, 448
Phillips, Richard, 696
Westerham (Kent): Davis,
Nathaniel, 232
Westerleigh (Glos.): Shrewring,
Jos., 813
Westerman, Joseph, 767
Westham (Essex): Grant,
Zachariah, 364
Westminster (London):
Abbott, Andrin, 1
Abbot(t), Philip, 1
Abegg, John Henry, 1
Adams, William, 4
Affleck, James, 5
Afflecks, —, 5
Albert, Thomas, 6
Alexander, William, 7
Alken, Martyn, 8
Allem, Thomas, 8
Allen, Randolph, 10
Anderson, John, 12
Angland, William, 15
Archibald, Alex., 17
Arnold, Michael, 19
Arrow, John Henry, 19
Ashton, Thomas, 21
Atkin, Alexander, 23
Atkins, William, 23
Backhouse, Robert, 28
Barret, John, 44
Bary, William Lonsdale, 50
Bates, George, 49
Bayley, William, 52
Beachcroft, Samuel, 53
Beale, George, 54
Bendall, John, 64
Billings, John, 72
Bott, Samuel, 90
Bromwell, John, 110
Brown, Joseph, 116
Brown, Lucy, 116
Brown, Thomas, 118
Brown, William, 119
Buist, Henry Seaton, 125
Burrows, John, 134
Butterfield, James, 138
Daniel, Samuel, 225
Darley, Robert, 227
Dawes & White, 234
Dawson, John, 235
De Hoare, —, 238
Dempster, James, 240
Dickson, John, 244

Dillworth, Edward, 245
Dobson, John, 247
Douglas, John, 251
Douglas, Joseph, 251
Dunkley, Thomas, 259
Dunno, James, 261
Durno, James, 262
Edwards, Thomas, 270
England, Thomas, 281
Galloway, Edward, 328
Garbett, Thomas, 329
Gardner, John, 330
Garwood, John, 332
Geatenby, George, 334
George, John, 335
Gilroy, John, 344
Godfrey, Richard, 347
Goff, William, 348
Gore, Thomas, 358
Gosse, —, 358
Gowing, James, 361
Graveley, Michael, 364
Gray, Joseph, 365
Green, Richard, 367
Greer, William, 369
Griffiths, John, 374
Guillot, James Lewis, 378
Hall, John, 385
Harding, Abraham, 396
Harris, Isaac, 400
Hart, William, 406
Hathwell, John, 410
Hawkins, Charles, 412
Hawkins, Edward, 412
Hayley, William, 415
Henden, Robert, 420
Henderson, Alexander, 420
Higgs, Joseph, 429
Higgs, Samuel, 429
Hillman, Edwain, 432
Hills, William, 432
Hinder, Robert, 433
Hockmill, Daniel, 436
Hocknill, H., 436
Hodgson, Thomas, 438
Holbart, Thomas, 440
Hopkins, David, 448
Horner, —, 450
Horner, George, 450
Horner, William, 450
Horrod, James, 451
Hose, John, 451
How, Thomas, 453
Howell, William, 455
Hudson, John, 458
Hudson, Robert, 459
Hulton, Robert, 462
Iron, John, 473
Jack, Richard, 474
Jackson, Ephraim, 475
Jelfe, Peter, 483
Jones, Aaron, 493
Jones, Elizabeth, Farquhar, John
& Crumin, Michael, 494

Jones, Hugh, 495
Jones, William, 498
Keir, John, 502
Kelsey, John, 503
Kenton, John, 509
Kirby, W., 516
Kirkwood, John, 517
Kishere, Joseph, 518
Kitty, Robert, 518
Knibbey, John, 518
Lamb, Henry, 522
Lamb, Woolhouse, 522
Landall, Thomas, 524
Lane, James, 525
Lane, Joseph, 525
Lane, Samuel, 525
Lawson, Gilbert, 531
Lee, John, 535
Lenden, William, 538
Lever, —, 539
Linney, Joseph, 548
Livingstone, James, 550
Lloyd, John, 550
Lowther, Isaac, 559
Lynham, James, 562
Lyon, Alexander, 562
Mackley, John, 567
Marrian, Thomas, 575
Maxwell, Robert, 588
Maxwell, William, 588
Mear(s), Richard & Catherine,
600
Meere, Richard, 600
Mellet(t), John, 601
Mitchell, Martha, 614
Mitchell, William, 614
Morley, Henry, 627
Morley, William, 627
Morris, George, 628
Morris, Joseph, 628
Moucar, James, 633
Mumford, Henry, 635
Murray, William, 637
Naisbett, John, 638
Neate, John, 640
Nelthorpe, Thomas, 641
Newman, John, 643
Newton, Thomas, 645
Nichol, James, 645
Ogilvy, Thomas, 661
Oldfield, John, 662
Oldmeadow, W., 662
Ore, William, 664
Oswell, Andrew, 666
Paine, Joseph, 670
Palmer, Mr, 671
Panner, —, 672
Parish, John, 673
Parkinson, Stanfield, 676
Parran, Benjamin, 677
Parrey, Jacob, 677
Parry, George, 677
Pattison, James, 680
Pattison, William Henry, 681

Patty, Paul, 681
Pearson, Edward, 684
Phillips, —, 694
Phipps, James, 696
Phipps, John, 696
Piercey, Thomas, 698
Preamer, John, 713
Prince, George, 717
Pullen, James, 721
Pyner, George, 723
Rhodes, John, 740
Roberts, Henry, 751
Robillion, Jan Baptiste, 755
Robinson, George, 757
Row(e), Charles, 768
Russell, William, 773
Sainsbury, Philip, 775
Salmon, Charles, 777
Sama, James, 778
Saunderson, John, 786
Savile, Thomas, 786
Scobie, James, 789
Scotland, Lawrence, 789
Scudworth, Rudolph, 791
Sculthorpe, John, 791
Seager, William, 792
Seal, John, 792
Shaclesworth, Roger, 802
Shaw, William, 805
Sherrard & Paxton, 809
Sidey, John, 814
Simpson, Joseph, 816
Skeate, William, 818
Skelton, Joseph, 819
Skinnor, David, 820
Smith, Andrew, 824
Smith, George, 826
Smith, James, 827
Smith, Joseph, 830
Smith, William, 835
Stack, William, 847
Starling, Henry, 850
Stevens, George 854
Strife, Joachim, 862
Strong, Francis, 862
Stuart, Charles, 862
Stuart, Francis, 862
Thack(th)waite, Daniel & William, 881
Thompson, Stephen, 887
Tripp, John, 904
Tripp, William, 904
Truscott, John, 906
Tucker, George, 907
Tull, Samuel, 908
Tutoft, Charles, 914
Tyler, Joseph, 915
Valois, Gabriel, 919
Vaut, Thomas, 921
Walker, David, 934
Walker, Jane, 935
Walker, William, 938
Wallis, James, 940
Walsh, Lawrence William, 941

Walter, William, 941
Water, David, 946
Waters, James, 947
Watkins, John, 947
Watson, David jnr, 948
Watson, Thomas, 950
West, John, 960
White, John, 966
Whitroe, Abraham, 969
Whitrow, George, 969
Willer, William, 978
Wilshed, Daniel, 986
Wilson, James, 987
Wood, Edward, 996
Wood, John, 997
Woodin, Thomas, 999
Worthy, John, 1003
Wright, George, 1005
Wright, John, 1005, 1006
Wright, Timothy, 1009
Wright & Stevens, 1009
Weston, 249
Weston, A.H., 961
Weston, John, 974
Weston House (Warks.): Pugin, Augustus W.N., 721
Weston Longville (Norfolk), for Rev. James Woodforde:
Brooke(s), William, 111
Coles, Roger jnr, 188
Freeman, Edward, 320
Hart, William, 406
Rice, Charles, 741
Thorne, —, 889
Weston Park (Staffs.): Morel, Nicholas and Morel & Hughes, Robert, 624
Westwood, Charles, 205, 825
Westwood Park (Worcs.):
Anderson, Jonathan & Perry, Joshua, 13
Crisp, William, 171
Colley, Richard, 188
Cowell, Daniel, 203
Hodson, John, 439
Hubbard, John, 457
Kingdon, Jane & Son, 515
Norman, Samuel, 653
Pearse, Samuel, 684
Stark, William, 850
Wetherby (Yorks.):
Bulmer, William, 128
Dacre, Benjamin, 223
Dacre, William, jnr, 223
Green, Samuel, 367
Hudson, William, 459
Kitchen, Kelita, 518
Whitfield, David, James, 969
Weymouth (Dorset):
Bartlett, John, 46
Blin, Joshua, 81
Bowman, Robert, 93
Buck, Avery, 123
Elliott, O., 274

Geare, James, 334
Goodwin, Christopher, 354
Green, Henry, 367
Hagley, William, 382
Hancock, —, 392
Hancock, Anthony, 392
Hancock, J.& W.B., 392
Hancock & Son, 393
Hodges, Jesse, 437
Honeywell, John, 447
Inkpen, Joshua, 472
Isaac, William, 473
Lee, Robert, 535
Masters, John, 585
Milledge, John, 607
Royal, John, 769
Sherren, James, 809
Sturney, James, 863
Syms, Charles, 869
Syms, James, 869
Voss, George, 930
Watkins, Thomas, 947
White, James, 965
White, John, 966
Whale, William, 251
Whalley, Charles, 693
Whalley (Lancs.):
Birtwistle, Daniel, 75
Birtwistle, James, 75
Pilling, John, 699
Waddington, W., 930
Whalley Church (Lancs.):
Charpentier, Benjamin, 160
Whally, John, 952
Wharrie, 82
Wharton, 334
Wheatley, 446
Wheatley, John, 467
Wheeler, 483, 899
Wheeler, Constable, 373
Whickham (Co. Durham):
Nicholson, Relph, 647
Oliver, John, 663
Tweedy, Joseph, 914
Whistler, John, 957
Whitbread, George, 265
Whitburn, 953
Whitby, John, 153
Whitby, Thomas, 327
Whitby (Yorks.):
Agar, Robert, 5
Bell, John, 62
Bennison, William, 66
Burn, William, 131
Dobson, Thomas, 248
Estill, Thomas, 282
Gill, James, 340
Hazelwood, Moses, 416
Hey, William, 426
Hezlewood, Moses, 426
Hill, Thomas, 431
Hirst, Robert, 434
Hodgson, John, 438
Hubbock, William, 457

Iley, William, 471
Jackson, John, 476
Lord, William, 555
Lund, Thomas, 561
Medd, William, 600
Pyman, John, 723
Scott, John, 790
Sedman, John, 798
Simpson, David, 816
Smith, Thomas, 832
Tate, David, 873
Turner, Edward, 909
Weatherill, George, 953
Weatherill, Joseph, 953
Weatherill, William, 953
Whitchurch (Salop):
  Arrowsmith, —, 19
  Arrowsmith, Thomas, 19
  Benham, Harvey, 64
  Davis, Benjamin, 230
  Hughes, George, 460
  Lakin, Benjamin & Sons, 521
  Lakin, William & Abraham, 521
  Moore, John, 620
  Moores, John, 622
  Morgan, William, 626
  Philips, William Philip, 694
  Price, —, 715
  Roughey, William, 768
  Sadler, I., 775
  Welach, George, 956
  Welsh, George, 958
White, 133, 234
White, Edward, 798, 814
White, Francis, 966
White, George Norris, 337
White, John, 352, 422, 967
White, Richard, 362
White, Samuel, 965
White, William, 91
White & Hickman, 965
The White House, Oakley
  (Norfolk): Freeman, John, 321
Whitechapel (London):
  Atkinson, Henry, 24
  Bates, John, 49
  Beaumont, William, 56
  Beeson, Joseph, 59
  Benson, Thomas, 66
  Brand, George snr, 102
  Brown, Joseph, 116
  Bush, Thomas, 136
  Doggett, Thomas, 249
  Duncombe, Joseph, 259
  Dunn, Charles, 260
  Durrant, John, 262
  Edwards, Adam, 269
  Edwards, Joseph, 270
  Edwards, William, 271
  Elliston, Henry, 276
  Ewbank, John, 286
  Gadbury, George, 326
  Gardner, James, 330
  Goud, William, 359

Hale, William, 383
Hamilton, —, 391
Hamilton, William, 391
Hammond, Richard, 392
Herring, John, 423
Higgs, Edward, 428
Higgs, Thomas, 429
Hornzee, George, 450
Kelly, Richard, 503
Leith, James, 537
Lingard, I., 543
Mascitti, P., 582
May, Robert, 589
Meyer, Elias, 604
Molineux, John, 615
Moore, John, 620
Moor(e), Thomas, 621
Moss, Moses, 632
Myers, Emanuel, 637
Owen, Sarah, 668
Pennock, Joshua, 689
Petty, Henry, 693
Phillips, Edward, 695
Robinson, John, 758
Smallwood, John, 822
Smallwood, Joseph, 822
Steward, William, 855
Temple, T.& J., 881
Thurnall, —, 892
Turstian, William, 914
Walker, Roger, 937
Warner, R., 945
Wortley, William, 1003
Whitefield (Lancs.): Longworth,
  John, 555
Whitefriars (London):
  Gambling, James, 328
  Smith, Edward, 825
Whitehaven (Cumb.):
  Bragg, John, 100
  Bragg, William, 101
  Brooke, Robert, 111
  Brownrigg, Samuel, 120
  Burton, Thomas, 135
  Burnyeat, Jonathan, 132
  Dickinson, David, 243
  Douglas, John, 251
  Eilbeck, John, 271
  Eilbeck, Robert, 271
  Gamwell, A., 329
  Glaister, William, 344
  Hardie, John, 396
  Harrison, Jonathan, 404
  Hartley, Christopher, 406
  Hassall, Charles, 409
  Hetherington, Michael, 424
  Holmes, William, 446
  Hudleston, Mrs, 458
  Ismay, Joseph, 474
  Jefferson, M., 482
  King, William, 515
  Kirkbride, Isaac, 517
  Kitchen, William, 518
  Landells, George, 524

Little, George, 549
Littledale, Joseph, 550
Littledale, Mary, 550
Lyon, James, 562
McKnight, Alexander, 567
McKnight, Robert, 567
Martin, James, 581
Martindale, Thomas, 582
Maxwell, Joseph, 588
Metcalf, Thomas, 604
Myers, Christopher, 637
Nutsford, George, 657
Nutsford & Ismay, 657
Opra, Richmond, 664
Ormandy, Richard, 665
Osborn, George, 665
Osborne, John, 666
Pearson, John, 685
Pearson, Joseph, 685
Pennington, - jnr, 689
Postlethwaite, William, 707
Potts, Thomas, 709
Race, William, 725
Reed, John, 734
Reed, Thompson, 734
Reed & Son, 734
Reep, Thompson, 735
Reid & Brockbank, 737
Richardson, Joseph, 744
Scott, Adam, 789
Selby, Isaac, 799
Sherwen, William, 810
Sim, William, 815
Spedding, William, 842
Thompson, —, 885
Thompson, John, 886
Welsh, Hugh, 958
Young, William, 1015
Whitehead, 455, 477, 991
Whitehead, Francis, 610
Whitehorne, 385
Whitehorne, Richard, 639
Whiteknights (Berks.): Mayhew,
  John & Ince, William, 595
Whiteside, 341, 733
Whiteside, Edward, 297, 341
Whiteside, Henry, 297
Whithorn, Lawrence, 787
Whiting, Samuel, 322, 485, 569
Whiting, Thomas, 427
Whitmore, William, 205
Whitney House: Potts, Thomas,
  709
Whitred, Marmaduke, 366
Whittaker, Samuel, 557
Whittam, George, 1008
Whittam, John, 1008
Whittingham, 229, 614, 888, 917,
  933
Whittingham, James, 229
Whittingham, Thomas, 151, 589
Whittle, James, 554, 590, 651, 652,
  653, 928, 959
Whittle, John, 102

Whittle, Thomas, 970
Whittle & Norman, 970–1
Whittlesey (Cambs.):
　Harpham, Ishmael, 400
　Hollis, Robert, 443
　Russell, Jabez, 772
Whitworth, John, 1012
Whitworth, Thomas, 322
Whitworth Hall (Co. Durham):
　Wright, Richard & Elwick,
　Edward, 1008
Whyte, James jnr, 434
Wickham (Northumb.): Reed,
　Henry, 734
Wickham Market (Suffolk):
　Hill, David, 430
　Rouse, William, 768
Wicking, 777
Wicks, Cullum, 300
Wickstead, G., 44
Wickwar (Glos.): Howell, Mathew,
　455
Widcombe (Som.): Whiteacre,
　Stephen, 968
Widnes (Lancs.):
　Hales, Thomas, 383
　Patten, William, 680
Wigan (Lancs.):
　Ackerley, John, 2
　Bolton, Thomas, 84
　Dorling, Peter, 251
　Glassbrook, Edward, 345
　Glazebrook, Edwrad, 345
　Harrison, William, 405
　Haworth, John, 413
　Hayes, William, 414
　Holden, John, 440
　Holding, Charles, 441
　Holding, John, 441
　Howarth, John, 455
　Irvin, —, 473
　Johnson, Ellen, 489
　Johnson, Jonathan, 490
　Kearsley, James, 501
　Kearsley, John, 501
　Kearsley, William, 501
　Latham, Peter, 529
　Lenthall, Francis, 538
　Lenthall, James, 538
　Marsden, John, 576
　Marsden, Robert, 576
　Postlethwaite, William, 707
　Sassi, Peter, 781
　Slack, Seth, 820
　Taylor, James, 876
　Watmough, James, 948
　Winnard, William, 992
　Winstanley, William, 992
Wigfall, 1003
Wightman, George, 141
Wightman, Ralph, 458
Wigton (Cumb.):
　Armstrong, John, 18
　Barnfather, David, 43

Bell, Allan, 60
Blackburn, William, 77
Brisco(e), Joseph, 108
Graham, John, 362
Gunson, Anthony, 380
Hartley, William, 407
Hodgson, William, 438
Hutton, John, 469
Irving, Edward, 473
Nixon, Simpson, 650
Pape, James, 672
Pearson, J., 685
Rigg, R., 748
Salkeld, James, 776
Smith, John, 830
Stoddart, John, 858
Todd, John, 896
Topping, Charles, 899
Topping, George, 899
Wright, Elizabeth, 1005
Wikeley, William, 973
Wilcock, Richard, 287, 944
Wilcox, Humphrey, 6
Wilcox, Richard, 949
Wilcox, Thomas, 765, 958
Wilcoxon, 849
Wildey, 68
Wilding, 338
Wilding, Robert, 213
Wilding, Thomas, 557
Wilford, James, 333
Wilke, Friedrich, 973
Wilkes, Thomas, 733
Wilkie, Friedrich, 973
Wilkins, George, 260, 936
Wilkinson, 109, 916, 990
Wilkinson & Turner, 975
Wilkinson, Charles, 977
Wilkinson, Fenwick, 977
Wilkinson, Joseph, 381
Wilkinson, Joshua, 829
Wilkinson, Thomas, 976
Wilkinson, William, 82, 951–2, 976
Willcox, B. Kent, 978
Willcox, Bartholomew Kent, 508
Willcox, Elizabeth, 508
Willenhall (Staffs.):
　Homer, Benjamin, 446
　Lees, Thomas T., 536
　Rowley, Joseph, 769
Willersley Castle (Derbs.): Wilson,
　Walter, 990
Williams, 509, 727
Williams, Charles, 320, 621
Williams, David, 979
Williams, Edward, 193
Williams, Edward John, 150
Williams, Griffith, 674
Williams, I., 979
Williams, Jacob, 664
Williams, James, 747
Williams, John, 559, 743
Williams, Joseph, 158
Williams, Richard, 557

Williams, Robert, 642
Williams, Theophilus, 541
Williams, Thomas, 198, 980, 981
Williams, William, 330, 740
Williamson, 693
Williamson, Edward Henry, 155
Williamson, George, 229
Williamson, John, 666
Williamson, Reuben, 117
Williamson, Thomas, 792, 1005
Williamstrip Park (Glos.): Oakley,
　George, 659
Willis, William, 985
Willis & Sangar, 984
Wills, John, 136
Willson, J., 985
Willson, Matthew, 985
Wilmslow (Cheshire): Barlow,
　Daniel, 41
Wilsden (Yorks.):
　Barker, George, 40
　Hartley, Thomas, 407
Wilsford (Wilts.): Jarvis, Thomas,
　481
Wilson, 58, 119, 230, 634, 653, 734,
　840, 853, 961
Wilson, A., 990
Wilson, Ann, 990
Wilson, Benjamin, 603
Wilson, Charles, 996
Wilson, Edward, 990
Wilson, Harry, 150, 564
Wilson, Isabella, 589, 803
Wilson, Joseph, 40
Wilson, Mary, 985
Wilson, Matthew, 985
Wilson, Thomas, 508, 985
Wilson, Walter, 986
Wilson, William, 66, 116, 234, 251,
　859, 987
Wilson & Brown, 990
Wilson & Dawes, 986
Wilson & Reed, 989
Wilton (Wilts.): Ingram, George,
　472
Wilton House (Wilts.):
　Chippendale, Thomas snr, 166
　Haddock, Elka, 382
　Hallett, William snr and William
　jnr, 389
　Metcalf, Joseph, 603
　Vial(l)s, Thomas, 922
Wimborne (Dorset):
　Barfoot, William, 39
　Blanchard, James, 80
　Golding, James, 348
　Habgood, Henry, 381
　Hart, Robert jnr, 406
　Hayward, Richard, 416
　Moore, Stephen, 621
　Moore, William, 622
　Talbott, John, 870
　Wheeler, John, 963

Wimborne Minster (Dorset):
  Hewlett, Robert, 426
Wimpenny, William, 113
Wimpole Hall (Cambs.):
  Chippendale, Thomas snr, 168
  Chippendale, Thomas jnr, 169
  Davies, Thomas, 230
  Foxhall, Edward, 315
  Hasert, Peter, 408, 409
  Leivers, William, 537
Wincanton (Som.):
  Dowden, Robert, 254
  Green, Elias, 367
  Hussy, Edmund, 467
  Hutchins, George, 467
  Mathews, William, 586
  Pond, Uriah, 705
  Thorn, Robert, 889
Winch, John, 44
Winchester (Hants.):
  Bale, James, 34
  Basepool, Robert, 47
  Betts, J., 69
  Betts, James, 69
  Binste(a)d, Peter, 73
  Blake, Henry, 79
  Bo(o)rman, William, 87
  Brereton, Thomas, 105
  Brown, Henry Carey, 114
  Brown, William, 119
  Godwin, James, 347
  Godwin, Thomas, 347
  Grantham, John, 364
  Gudgeon, Robert & Son, 377
  Hayes, William, 414
  Henderson, John, 420
  Hurll, William, 466
  Jourd, William Handel, 499
  Mant, John, 573
  Marsh, Thomas, 577
  Mould, Benjamin, 633
  Mould, Henry, 633
  Muspratt, Thomas, 637
  Peacock, James, 683
  Pistell, William, 700
  Purchell, Thomas, 722
  Rangecroft, John, 7727
  Shergold, John, 809
  Stevens, George, 854
  Urquart, William, 918
  Wells, William, 958
Winder, 104
Windle, 724
Windsor (Berks.):
  Atlee, John, 25
  Baker, William, 33
  Barton, John, 47
  Bell, James, 61
  Bradley, Henry, 98
  Dunn, Richard, 260
  Goertz, H.L., 347
  Hill, Arthur, 430
  Hill, John, 430
  Hobbs, George, 435

Horniman, Richard, 450
Horniman, William, 450
Hutchings, John, 467
Jenkins, Alexander, 483
Jenner, Thomas, 485
Jones, Benjamin, 494
Kennedy, John, 506
Kimberley, William, 513
Leggat, Alexander, 536
Leike, Thomas, 537
McBean, Anne, 563
McBean, James, 563
McBean, Thomas, 564
Macdougall, Alexander, 565
Miller, John, 608
Morris, Alexander, 627
Newman, Thomas, 643
Russel, Seaton, 771
Smith, Daniel, 825
Spencer, James, 843
Starkey, John, 850
Stevens, John, 854
Sumner, Robert, 865
Taylor, David, 875
Tebbott, Robert, 880
Watkins, John, 947
Wier, Hugh, 972
Witney, George, 994
Wright, William, 1009
Windsor Castle (Berks.):
  Adair, William Robert, 3
  Adron, W. & C., 5
  Bailey, Edward, 29, 30
  Baker, William, 33
  Banting, France & Co., 38
  Bealing, Richard, 54
  Bennington & Co., 66
  Bream(e), Jasper, 104
  Bywater, John, 140
  Casbert, John, 149
  Coade, Eleanor and her
  successors, 181
  Cooper, George, 195
  Cooper, Thomas, 197
  Cousin, Rene, 202
  Crouzet, Joseph, 214
  Dadd, Robert, 223
  Dowbiggin(g), Thomas, 252, 254
  Elward, George & Marsh,
  William, 278
  Farmborough, William, 289
  Fletcher, Jeremiah, 304
  Francis, William, 318
  Gibbons, Grinling, 336
  Goertz, H.L., 347, 348
  Goodison, Benjamin, 353
  Guibert, Philip, 377
  Henderson, E., 420
  Henning, David, 421
  Hermow & Son, Richard, 423
  Herve, Francois, 424
  Hoare, Thomas, 435
  Jenner, Thomas, 485
  Jensen, Gerrit, 486, 487

Jones, Samuel, 496
Lawrence, Richard, 531
Le Gaigneur, Louis Constantin,
536
Le (or La) Grange, —, 537
McBean, Anne, 563
Mealing, William, 599
Miller, William, 609
Morant, G., 622
Morel, Nicholas and Morel &
  Hughes, Robert, 624
Norman, Samuel, 652, 653
Paudevin, John, 681
Pelletier, John, 687
Phill, Thomas, 694
Phillips, Henry, 695
Pratt, Samuel, 712
Price, Richard, 716
Pugin, Augustus W.N., 721
Reeve(s), Ham(b)den, 735
Roberts, Thomas and Richard,
  752, 753
Rosier, —, 766
Seddon, George, 795, 796, 797
Sheppard, T., 808
Snell, William, 836
Spencer, James, 843
Tebbott, Robert, 880
Thurston, John, 893
Turner, Thomas, 912
Van Opstal, Louis, 919
Weston, J., 961
Whitby, John, 964
Williams, Henry, 980
Wyatt, Matthew, 1010
Windsor Corporation: Stevens,
  John, 854
Wing, 557
Winslade, Hyde, 992
Winlaton (Co. Durham):
  Nicholson, John, 647
Winslow (Bucks.):
  Mayne, George, 598
  Todd, James, 896
Winston (Co. Durham): Dodds,
  Matthew, 249
Winter, 770
Winter, Benjamin, 1012
Winterbottom, George, 562
Winton, Henry, 154, 298, 327
Winton (Hants.): Brenton, Thomas,
  105
Wiormo, John Peter, 972
Wirksworth (Derbys.):
  Greatrix, William, 366
  Maplebeck, John, 574
Wisbech (Cambs.):
  Ashton, John, 21
  Ashton, Thomas, 21
  Barnes, W., 42
  Bray, Charles, 104
  Bray, George, 104
  Bray, H., 104
  Bray, James, 104

Briggs, Luke, 107
Denton, Octavius, 241
Harrison, Matthew, 404
Harrison, Robert, 404
Jackson, George, 475
Leedel, William, 535
Morris, Robert, 629
Mowles, William, 634
Moyses, John, 634
Nicholls, Charles, 645
Norton, H., 656
Platt, Thomas, 702
Powell, John, 710
Preston, Robert, 714
Rawlinson, James, 730
Richars, William, 745
Self, John, 799
Short, Joseph, 812
Talbot, William, 870
West, J.H., 959
Wise, 480
Wise, Elizabeth, 993
Wise, Richard, 751
Wiseman, Richard, 994
Wisker, Daniel, 787
Wiskersley (Yorks.): Marsh,
   William, 577
Wiston (Sussex): Pickett, Jesse, 697
Witham (Essex): Harvey, Robert,
   408
Withers, Henry, 207, 222, 764
Withers, William, 238
Withers & Deeble, 994
Withnee, Thomas, 650
Witney (Oxon.):
   Bolton, George, 84
   Edney, John, 268
   Gardiner, T., 329
   Langford, William, 526
   Skinner, John, 819
Witton, William, 74, 684
Witton-le-Wear (Co. Durham):
   Watson, John, 950
   Watson, William, 950
Wittridge, Henry, 618
Witty, 956
Wiveliscombe (Som.):
   Thorne, William, 890
   White, David, 965
   Wring, William, 1009
.PN488
Woakes, James, 199
Woburn (Beds.):
   Devey, John, 242
   Devey, John Spencer, 242
   Devey, T.S., 242
   Gardner, Andrew, 329
   Shaw, Robert, 805
   Shaw, Thomas, 805
Woburn Abbey (Beds.):
   Alken, Sefferin, 8
   Bastard, John & William, 48
   Bealing, Richard, 54
   Bladwell, John, 78

Breteuil(e), John, 105
Bridgman, Thomas, 107
Buttery, John, 139
Daguerre, Dominique, 223
De Caix, Alexander, 238
Eagles, T.F., 264
Elward, George & Marsh,
   William, 279
Erwood, James, 282
Erwood, Solomon, 282
Eston, Negus, 282
Gardner, Andrew, 329
Herve, Francois, 424
Hollin(s)worth, William, 443
Hutchins, Abraham, 467
Hutchins, Abigail, 467
Hutchin(s), Hassall, 467
Kean, John, 501
Kerr, John, 510
King, Benjamin, 514
Langlois, Pierre, 526, 527
Laughton, Henry, 529
Linnell, William, 546, 547
Mayhew, John and Ince,
   William, 592, 593, 597
Nelson, Sefferin, 641
Norman, Samuel, 652, 653
Norman, William, 653
Pelliseur, Leon, 687
Plukenett, Thomas, 703
Potts, John, 709
Rittener, E., 750
Saunders, Paul, 785
Seddon, George, 797
Shaw, Robert, 805
Shaw, Thomas, 805
Shipley, John snr, 811
Tatham, J., 873
Vial(l)(s), Thomas, 922
Vile, William, 928
West, John, 960
Whittle, James, 970, 971
Wood, Henry, 996
Woburn Parish Church: Potts,
   John, 709
Wokingham (Berks.):
   Bennett, William, 65
   Goodwin, John F., 355
   Holmes, Joseph, 445
   Johnson, Emanuel, 489
   Johnson, William, 493
   Parsons, Thomas, 678
Wolfe, James, 406, 602
Wollaton (Notts.): Hewson, J.
Bothomley, 426
Wolseley Hall (Staffs.): Pearce,
   Edward, 684
Wolsingham (Co. Durham):
   Dobinson, Mark, 247
   Hodgson, Richard, 438
   Nicholson, Jos., 647
   Robinson, Jos., 759
   Thompson, John, 887
Wolly, G., 51

Wolverhampton (Staffs.):
   Anderson, James, 12
   Aston, John, 22
   Aston, William, 22
   Barns, Edward, 43
   Bate, George, 48
   Benstone, Daniel, 66
   Burton, Joseph, 135
   Derver, John, 241
   Devey, James, 242
   Devey, John, 242
   Donnithorne, Isaac, 250
   Easthope, George, 265
   Evans, James, 284
   Evans, Poynton, 284
   Evans, W.H., 285
   Evans, William, 285
   Eykin, James, 286
   Gardener, Thomas, 329
   Gascoigne, Edward, 332
   Giusani, Peter, 344
   Gough, Thomas, 360
   Gough, Benjamin, 359
   Grassey, Stephen, 364
   Green, Richard, 367
   Gregory, Benjamin, 370
   Heath, Charles, 418
   Hewitt, Catherine, 425
   Holloway, John, 444
   Illidge, Thomas, 471
   Jones, John, 495
   Kent, Thomas, 509
   Lockley, F.R.& W., 553
   Lockley, Francis, 553
   Lockley, T. & Co. 553
   Lockley, William, 553
   Lockley & Cartwright, 553
   Mander, Benjamin, 572
   Marlton, John, 575
   Marston, John, 580
   Mills, John, 610
   Moore, Thomas, 621
   Moore, William, 622
   Mosedale, Edward, 631
   Murray, Richard, 637
   Owen, Robert, 668
   Pettit, Joseph, 692
   Plant, William, 702
   Ryton & Walton, 774
   Smallwood, William, 823
   Smith, John, 829
   Thomas, Henry Walter, 883
   Thomas, Robert, 884
   Thomas, W.H., 884
   Walford, Obadiah, 934
   Walker, John Smith, 936
   Walker, R., 936
   Walker, William, 938
   Whitby, Joseph, 964
   Whitehouse, Joseph, 968
   Wilshe, William, 986
   Wyatt, James, 1010
   Wynn, James, 1011
   Yardley, Samuel, 1011

Wolverley House (Worcs.):
  Chippendale, Thomas snr, 166
  Chivers, Noah, 170
  Kettle, Henry, 511
  Mason, Richard, 584
  Peacock, Robert, 683
  Pilton, Thomas, 699
Wood, 213, 477, 679, 930
Wood, Edward, 40, 86, 654, 986
Wood, Francis, 951
Wood, James, 530
Wood, John, 192, 760, 768
Wood, Josiah, 458
Wood, Richard, 66, 164, 328, 496,
  720, 866, 939
Wood, Stephen, 995
Wood, Thomas, 869
Wood, William, 262, 284, 360
Woodbridge, James, 1002
Woodbridge (Suffolk):
  Baker, John, 33
  Baynham, Thomas, 53
  Buckingham, William, 124
  Gennills, John, 335
  Giles, Thomas, 340
  Goodwin, George, 354
  Goodwin, William Bezant, 355
  Hartridge, W., 407
  Hawtridge, William, 414
  Hayward, Robert, 416
  Hayward, Miles, 416
  Hayward & Son, 416
  Head, Samuel, 416
  Jennings, John, 485
  Land, Benjamin Cole, 524
  Miles, —, 606
  Miles, Edmund, 606
  Miles, Francis, 606
  Miles, Richard, 607
  Morgan, John, 625
  Osborne, William, 666
  Sherwood, William, 810
  Simpson, James, 816
Woodburn, John, 833
Woodford (Essex): Hawkins, John,
  413
Woodhall House (Herts.): Parker,
  Robert, 674
Woodhouse (Salop): Linnell, John,
  546
Woodin, 983
Woodin, Thomas, 651, 652, 784,
  932
Woodroffe, Daniel, 121, 616, 707,
  842, 1000
Woods, George, 962
Woods, William, 192
Woodstock (Oxon.):
  Dewdney, Francis, 242
  Eldridge, Charles, 272
  Gulliver, John, 378
Woodward, 609
Woodward, James, 450
Woodward, John, 244, 303

Woodworth, Thomas, 133, 891
Woolcock, Thomas, 391
Wooler (Northumb.):
  Elliot, Richard, 272
  Hume, John, 462
  Law, Robert, 530
  Short, James, 812
Woolfit, 899
Woolfitt, 899
Wooll, G., 20
Woollen, William, 995
Woollett, Ralph, 936
Woolley, 432, 786
Woolley, George, 723
Woolley, William, 879
Woolley Hall (Yorks.):
  Drew, William, 256
  Hartley, Bernard, 406
  Herring, James, 423
  Mosley, Samuel, 632
  Swithenband, John, 868
  Whitaker, Thomas, 964
  Wright, Richard & Elwick,
    Edward, 1007, 1008
Woolton Hall (Lancs.): Prescott,
  Richard, 713
Wooltorton, Edmund, 855
Woolverton, Edward, 298
Woolwich (London):
  Adams, John Atlie, 3
  Akers, William, 6
  Armitage, William, 18
  Bayliss, William, 52
  Binchs, J.D., 72
  Grundy, William, 377
  Gudd, Robert, 377
  Hall, George, 385
  Healey, John, 417
  Hitchcock, Robert, 434
  Hubbard, James, 457
  Judd, Robert, 500
  Moore, Thomas, 621
  Palfreman, Thomas, 671
  Redpath, James, 733
  Shepherd, William, 808
  Tandy, Charles, 871
  Tandy, Edward, 871
  Tandy, Robert, 871
  Taylor, Samuel, 879
  Thompson, Charles, 885
  Thorley, John, 889
  Wallace, James, 939
  Walters, James jnr, 941
  Wates, James snr & jnr, 947
  Wiles, T.H., 978
  Wilson, John, 988
Woore, Joseph, 580
Wootin Bassett (Wilts.):
  Woodward, Paul, 1001
Wootton, James, 363
Worboys, G.B., 505
Worcester, James, 1002
Worcester:
  Amphlett, Thomas, 12

Anderson, John, 13
Anderson, Jonathan & Perry,
  Joshua, 13
Andrews, Jonathan, 14
Ashton, William, 21
Auster, John, 26
Balld, Robert, 35
Bannister, John, 37
Bardin, John, 39
Bardin, Samuel, 39
Bardin, Thomas jnr, 39
Bardin, Thomas snr, 39
Bardin, William, 39
Barret, William, 44
Barrett, James, 44
Bickley, William, 71
Bird, John, 74
Bolus, Henry, 84
Bolus, Samuel, 84
Bolus, Susanna, 84
Bradley, J., 98
Bradley, James, 98
Brewer, Francis, 106
Briscoll, —, 76
Bushell, William, 136
Davies, Henry, 228
Davis, John, 231
Dawson, William, 235
Dovey, John, 252
Dovey, William, 252
Edmunds, Isaac, 268
Evans, Frederick, 283
Evans, John, 284
Gardner, William, 330
George, William, 335
Gough, —, 359
Grainger, George, 363
Hall, James, 385
Hall, John Henry, 385
Handy, William, 394
Hankins, William, 394
Hanley, Peter, 394
Harris, James, 401
Harris, William, 403
Harrop, Philip jnr, 405
Harrop, Philip snr, 405
Harrop, William, 405
Hickes, James, 427
Hickey, —, 427
Hill, John, 430
Hill, Thomas, 431
Howton, Thomas, 456
Hulland, Samuel, 462
Humphreys, George, 463
Hunt, Joseph, 464
Huntback, John, 465
Insull, Henry, 472
Insull, William, 472
Jones, James, 495
King, William, 515
Knight, Thomas, 519
Lane, Samuel, 525
Langford, R., 525
Langford, Richard, 525

Lewis, Thomas, 540
Lindon, Malachi, 542
Lingon, Henry, 543
London, William, 554
Lovett, Richard, 557
Lowe, Richard, 557
Mallam, Charles Richard, 571
Malvern, Charles, 572
Marks, William, 575
Martin, Ann, 580
Mason, James, 584
Mason, Thomas, 584
Meredith, Richard, 602
Michael, William, 604
Morton, J., 630
Morton, James, 630
Morton, John, 630
Morton, Richard, 630
Morton, William, 630
Mountford, Henry, 633
Nash, Harry, 638
Nayers, John, 639
Nicholas, John, 645
Nicholls, John, 646
Nichols, John, 646
Osborn, Watkin, 665
Pardoes, William, 672
Pember, Joseph snr & jnr, 688
Phillip, H.T., 694
Phillips, Thomas, 696
Pratt, Michael, 712
Price, Francis, 715
Price, Thomas, 716
Prosser, Frederick, 719
Rayer, Moses, 730
Rea, John, 731
Redding, Edward, 733
Redding, Samuel, 733
Reding, William, 733
Reed, Charles, 734
Short, Edwin, 812
Short, John, 812
Smale, J., 822
Smith, Thomas, 832
Stephens, George, 852
Sterry, George, 854
Stone, William, 859
Summerfield, John, 864
Tanner, Benjamin, 871
Tate, Alexander, 873
Taylor, Robert snr, 878
Taylor, Thomas, 879
Thomas, Benjamin, 883
Thorne & Yarnold, 890
Thornton, Thomas, 891
Tim(m)ings, John, 895
Tupe, John, 908
Turner, William Macdonald, 913
Twitty, James, 915
Tyler, George, 915
Tyler, Mary, 915
Vernal, John, 921
Wakefield, Richard, 933
Ward, William, 944

Wilkes, Thomas, 975
Woodward, John, 1001
Woodward, William, 1001
Young, John, 1014
Worcester, The Palace: Mayhew, John and Ince, William, 592
Workington (Cumb.):
Askew, H., 21
Atkinson, Wilson, 25
Bell, Johnson, 62
Brown, William, 119
Eliot(t), James, 272
Garrard, William, 331
Grayson, Joseph, 366
Grayson, Thomas, 366
Grayson & Moore, 366
Harrison, T., 404
Hayson, James, 415
Hodgson, Joseph, 438
Marley, John, 575
Moore, —, 617
Moore, Isaac, 618
Nealey, Matthew, 640
Nicholson, Henry, 646
Ormandy, John, 665
Osbourne, Joseph, 666
Osbourne, William, 666
Rule, James, 770
Sewell, Jacob, 801
Slee, Joseph, 821
Tallentire, John, 870
Tallantire, Jonathan, 870
Tate, Thomas, 873
Todd, Jonathan, 896
Twentyman, Daniel, 914
Walker, Richard, 937
Waugh, James, 951
Wheawell, John, 962
Wilson, Thomas, 989
Younghusband, John, 1015
Workington Hall (Cumb.):
Fisher, John, 302
Gillow, 343
Worksop (Notts.):
Broomhead, John, 112
Brown, Benjamin, 113
Gabbitass, Elizabeth, 326
Gabbitas(s), John, 326
Haslop, Isaac, 409
Hyde, Richard, 470
Hyde, Robert, 470
Markham, John, 574
Mathews, John, 586
Meller, John, 601
Miller, John, 608
Moss & Alsop, 632
Sharp, Samuel, 803
White, William, 967
Wright, John, 1006
Worksop Manor (Notts.):
Fenton, Francis, 296
Hyde, Robert, 470
Miller, John, 608
Richardson, Christopher, 743

Wright, Richard & Elwick, Edward, 1007
Wormell, Benjamin Lane, 1003
Worrell, John jnr, 951
Worseldine, John, 828
Worswick, 208
Worthing (Sussex):
Burtenshaw, Thomas, 134
Eadson, Joseph, 263
Ede, George, 266
Groves, William, 376
Hide, Edward, 428
Hide & Patching, 428
Lansdell, Stephen, 527
Martin, Thomas, 581
Martin & Bennett, 582
Perkins, Charles, 690
Philips, Charles, 694
Rich, Henry, 741
Snewin, William, 836
Stubbs, William, 863
Vaile, J.P., 919
Verrall, William, 922
Worthington & Kirby, 1003
Wortley, Thomas, 837
Wosbury (Salop): Edwards, William, 271
Woster, 61
Woster, Thomas, 205
Wotton House (Surrey): Gibbons, Grinling, 336
Wotton-under-Edge (Glos.):
Ellis, John, 275
Evans, Thomas, 285
Hunt, John, 464
Parsons, Thomas, 678
Short, Shirley, 812
Wragby (Lincs.): Gell, William, 335
Wragg, 675, 841
Wragg, Zachary, 135
Wray (Lancs.): Grime, Thomas, 375
Wren & Corry, 1004
Wren & Ladyman, 1004
Wrench, Thomas, 958
Wrest Park (Beds.):
Bransby, Robert, 103
Chippendale, Thomas jnr, 169
Dowbiggin(g), Thomas, 253
Wrexham (Clwyd):
Biggins, George, 71
Griffiths, William, 375
Wright, 109, 373, 836, 877, 990
Wright, Charles, 536
Wright, David, 148
Wright, Francis, 1009
Wright, Henry, 983
Wright, J., 293, 440, 637, 645, 651, 719, 977
Wright, John, 397, 413, 421, 697
Wright, Joseph, 575
Wright, Lawrence, 733
Wright, M., 1008

Wright, Richard, 133, 239, 304, 1004, 1009
Wright, Samuel, 866
Wright, Timothy, 776
Wright, William, 843, 1005, 1006
Wright & Snell, 1005
Wyatt, 174, 176
Wycliffe (Yorks.): Harrison, George, 403
Wye (Kent): Howard, William, 455
Wylde, Nathaniel, 974
Wylde, Richard, 838, 974
Wylde, William, 501
Wyles, 466
Wymondham (Norfolk):
  Harvey, William, 408
  Howes, William, 456
  Kent, Jacob, 508
  Kett, Jacob, 510
  Poll, J.C., 705
Wynnstay (Denbighs.): Mayhew, John & Ince, William, 595
Wynyard Park (Co. Durham):
  Alcock, John, 6
  Anderson, John, 12
  Beckwith, Henry, 57
  Crow, Robert, 214
  Dob(b)ing, Anthony, 247
  Dowbiggin(g), Thomas, 253
  Flintof(f)t, James, 306
  Grace, Henry, 361
  Horton, David, 451
  Lindsay, John, 543
  McDonald, D., 564
  Miles, Henry & Edwards, John, 606
  Morant, George, 622
  Orchard, James, 664
  Paul & Co., 682
  Ponsonby, Thomas, 705
  Sopwith, Jacob, 839
  Taylor, —, 874
  Thompson, W., 888
Wythenshawe Hall, Manchester:
  Hollister, John, 443

Y

Yardley, Samuel, 175
Yarm (Yorks.):
  Darwent, Andrew, 227
  Darwent, Henry, 227
  Ewbank, John W., 286
  Langdale, John, 525
  Smith, James, 827
  Smith, John, 829
  Taylor, George, 876
Yarmouth (Norfolk):
  Aldred, John, 7
  Aldred, William, 7
  Goffin, Robert, 348
Yarnold, 890

Yarpole (Salop): Doody, Joseph, 250
Yate, 286
Yate, Elisha, 1011
Yateman, William, 662
Yates, Henry, 358
Yates, John, 739
Yealmpton (Devon):
  Husband, Philip, 467
  Millman, William, 609
  Selly, William, 799
Yearby (Yorks.): Scott, Wrighton, 791
Yeovil (Som.):
  Allen, Moses, 10
  Geake, Robert & Thomas, 333
  Geake, Thomas, 333
  Geare, —, 333
  Langford, John, 525
  Male, James, 570
  Male, Joseph, 570
  Oliver, Thomas, 663
  Phelps, Thomas, 693
Yolland, 972, 994
York, Edward, 730, 870
York, Thomas, 730
York:
  Abbey, Harry C., 1
  Agar, Edward, 5
  Aldersmith, James, 7
  Allanson, Thomas, 9
  Allen, George, 9
  Allison, John, 11
  Almand, Thomas, 11
  Archer, Thomas, 17
  Arundel, Charles, 20
  Arundel, Hannah, 20
  Ashworth, T., 21
  Atkinson, Richard, 24
  Bacon, John, 28
  Bailes, Matthew, 29
  Baines & Dufill, 32
  Balmer, John, 36
  Banks, Thomas, 37
  Barber, John, 38
  Barker, George, 39
  Barker, John, 40
  Barker, John snr, 40
  Barker, Matthew, 40
  Barker, Robert jnr, 41
  Barker, Robert snr, 40
  Barker, William, 41
  Barnett, Henry Mark, 43
  Basfield, John, 47
  Baskett, Joseph, 48
  Battler, Mathew, 50
  Bawtry, Barnaby, 51
  Bawtry, Joseph, 51
  Baynes, Richard & Duffield, 53
  Beadle & Perfect, 53
  Beal, George, 54
  Beal(e), Thomas, 54
  Bean, Samuel, 55
  Beedham, John, 58

  Beedham, William, 58
  Beilby, John Alexander, 59
  Bell, John, 61
  Bell, Thomas, 62
  Bellerby, John, 63
  Bellerby, John jnr, 63
  Bellerby, Thomas, 63
  Bellerby, William, 63
  Benson, Thomas, 66
  Best, George, 68
  Billerby, John, 71
  Binnington, James, 73
  Birdsall, Thomas, 74
  Blackburn, Christopher, 77
  Blake, Robert, 79
  Blakesly, William, 79
  Blakey, John, 79
  Boddy, William, 82
  Bolton, Richard, 84
  Boocock, Benjamin, 86
  Bootley, William, 87
  Brabs, William, 94
  Bracken, Henry, 95
  Bradley, George, 98
  Braithwaite, John, 101
  Bridgewater, Thomas, 107
  Briggs, John, 107
  Brigham, Nicholas, 107
  Broad, William, 109
  Brocklebank, David, 109
  Brown, George, 114
  Brown, James, 115
  Brown, John, 115
  Brown, Richard, 117
  Brown, Robert, 118
  Brown, W., 118
  Brown & Co., 119
  Browne, John, 116
  Bulmer, James, 128
  Bulmer, John, 128
  Burnett, George, 131
  Burniston, John, 132
  Burrell, Jane, 133
  Bus(s)field, John, 136
  Butler, Matthias, 137
  Dalby, William, 223
  Dall, Joseph, 224
  Dalton, Christopher, 225
  Darling, Philip, 227
  Darnby, John, 227
  Davies, —, 228
  Davies, Peter, 229
  Davies & Wilson, 230
  Davis, John, 231
  Davison, William, 233
  Dempster, Anthony, 240
  Dempster, Thomas, 240
  Dickinson, William, 243
  Digby, James, 244
  Disney, John, 245
  Dixon, Christopher, 246
  Dodgson, William, 249
  Dodgson, William Fawcett, 249
  Doeg, David, 249

Doughty, George, 251
Doughty, Joseph & Maria, 251
Doughty, William, 251
Dove, Arthur, 252
Dove, John, 252
Drake, Thomas, 255
Duffield, Francis, 258
Duffill, James, 258
Duffill, John, 258
Dugelby, Robert, 258
Dunn, Michael, 260
Dunning, William, 261
Edwards, William, 271
Ellis, Benjamin, 275
Ellis, John, 275
Ellis, Robert Stephen, 275
Ellis, Wilfred, 275
Ellis, William, 276
Ellis & Rusby, 276
Ellison, John, 276
Elston, —, 277
Eshelby, George, 282
Etty, William, 282
Evers, Benjamin, 286
Ewbank, Thomas, 286
Garencieres, William, 331
Gell, Thomas, 335
Gibson, George, 337
Graham, Thomas, 363
Gray, Henry, 365
Gray, Thomas, 366
Greenwood, William, 369
Gregory, Catherine, 370
Groce, Joshua, 376
Groves, George, 376
Groves, William, 376
Halfpenny, Joseph, 384
Halfpenny, William, 384
Halliday, Henry, 390
Hands, Thomas, 394
Hansom, Henry, 395
Hansom, Richard, 395
Hardcastle, John, 395
Hardy, Charles, 396
Hardy, John, 397
Hardy, Seth, 397
Hare, George, 397
Harely, John, 397
Hargitt, Richard, 398
Hargrave, William, 398
Harland, Thomas, 398
Hauxwell, —, 411
Hawkin(s), William, 413
Hawkswell, William, 413
Hawksworth, George, 413
Heneage, Robert, 421
Hill, John, 431
Hill, Josias, 431
Hilstrip, William, 432
Hodgson, George, 438
Hodgson, Ralph, 438
Hodgson, Thomas, 438
Hollins, George, 443
Holmes, Norman, 445

Holmes, William, 446
Horner, John, 450
Houl(d)gate, Thomas, 452
Houlgate, Robert, 452
Houlgate, William, 452
Hudson, Francis, 458
Hudson, T., 459
Hunsley, John, 464
Hunter, John, 465
Hunton, John, 466
Hustcroft, Samuel, 467
Ingram, William, 472
Jameson, John, 480
John, John, 61
Johnson, H., 489
Jones, Dorothy & Ashworth, 494
Kaye, Henry, 501
Kaye, Robert, 501
Kendall, John, 504
Kibblewhite, James, 511
Kibblewhite, John, 511
King, James snr, 514
King, John, 514
King, Thomas, 515
Kirlew, Thomas, 517
Lambert, George, 523
Lawrence, Christopher, 530
Lawrence, James, 530
Lawrence, Thomas, 531
Lawson, George, 531
Lawson, Richard, 532
Lawson, William, 532
Lee, Harman, 534
Letchemond, Francis, 539
Linfoot, Mark, 543
Lockey, John, 552
Lockley, George, 553
Lonsdale, Robert, 555
Lowther, Henry, 559
Lupton, John, 561
Lyth, George, 563
Lythe, George, 563
McLean, William, 568
Mailor, Robert, 638
Mann, Thomas, 572
Mariner, William, 574
Marsh, Joseph, 576
Marsh & Johnson, 577
Marshall, Charles, 577
Marshall, George, 577
Marshall, James snr & jnr, 577
Marshall, John, 579
Marshall, Martin, 579
Marshall, Matthew Chitty, 579
Marshall, Thomas, 579
Marshall & Doughty, 579
Masterman, Benjamin, 585
Maw, Marmaduke, 588
Meadley, William, 599
Metcalfe, Joseph, 604
Meynell, George, 604
Middleton, John, 605
Mills, Ambrose, 609
Milner, John, 611

Milner & Harland, 611
Mitchell, James, 613
Moore, Christina, 617
Moore, Joseph Wright, 620
Morritt, John, 630
Mosley, Benjamin, 632
Mountain, Francis, 633
Mountain, Richard, 633
Mowbray, William, 634
Mowbray & Wilson, 634
Moxon, Hewley, 634
Mush, Frederick, 637
Musham, Frederick, 637
Myres, Watt, 638
Nothouse, Joseph, 655
Officer, James, 661
Oldfield, Jonathon, 662
Palfryman, John, 671
Pape, Isaac, 672
Pattison & Hesp, 681
Peirson, John, 687
Pentith, William, 689
Phillips, John, 695
Pivett, Christopher, 701
Powell, Thomas, 711
Raper, John, 728
Raper, Thomas, 728
Ratcliffe, John, 728
Rawden, Christopher, 729
Rayson, George, 731
Rhodes, Henry, 740
Richardson, Harman Henry, 743
Richardson, William, 745
Ridsdale, Thomas, 747
Riley, Thomas, 749
Rippon, George Calvert, 750
Robinson, Leonard, 759
Robinson, Mark, 759
Robinson, Richard, 760
Rumfitt, William, 770
Rusby, U., 771
Ryley, Robert, 774
Sagar, Stephen, 775
Salmon, Samuel, 777
Sanderson, John, 779
Sandys, Martin, 780
Saunderson, John, 786
Scholey, John, 789
Scholey, Nathaniel, 789
Scott, Charles, 789
Scott, Thomas, 790
Scott, Walter, 790
Seager, Stephen, 792
Sedgwick, Christopher, 798
Sedgwick, Thomas, 798
Sedgwick, William, 798
Segar, Stephen, 799
Seller, Christopher, 799
Settle, John, 800
Severs, Samuel, 800
Shelton, Thomas, 807
Shores, Anthony, 812
Shores, Arthur, 812
Sidwell, William, 814

Simpson, John, 816
Simpson, William, 816
Skelton, Elizabeth, 818
Skelton, John, 819
Skelton, Thomas, 819
Smith, Henry, 826
Smith, Jeremiah, 827
Smith, William, 834
Stables, William, 847
Staveley, John, 850
Staveley, William, 850
Stead, John, 851
Steel, William, 851
Stephenson, Timothy, 854
Steward, Edward, 855
Stokoe, William, 858
Stones, D., George, 859
Strawder, Charles Ward, 861
Sutherland, John, 865
Swaile, Joseph, 866
Tatam, Thomas, 873
Tate, John, 873
Taylor, John, 877
Tennercliffe, Joseph, 881
Terry, Thomas, 881
Thomas, James, 883
Thomas, John, 884
Thompson, George, 885
Thompson, John, 886, 887
Thompson, John Atkinson, 887
Thompson, Ralph, 887
Thomson, Alexander, 889
Thornton, William, 891
Thorp, William, 891
Threapland, Rt., 891
Thrisk, Henry, 892
Tinddall, John, 895
Tiplady, Stephen, 895
Todd, John, 896
Tomlinson, Robert, 898
Turner, James, 910

Turner, John, 911
Turner, Robert, 911
Turner, Thomas, 912
Turner, William, 913
Ubank, Thomas, 916
Underwood, Thomas, 917
Walker, John, 935
Walker, Richard, 937
Walker, Thomas & William, 938
Walker, William, 938
Walls, Joseph, 940
Walls, Thomas, 940
Walton, John, 942
Ward, John, 943
Warham, —, 945
Watehouse, Joseph, 946
Waud, John Chapman, 951
Webster, John, 955
Weightman, Anthony, 956
Whitehouse, Robert Bland, 968
Wikeley, Benjamin, 973
Wilcock, Thomas, 973
Wilkinson, Edward, 975
Wilkinson, Matthew, 976
Wilkinson, Stephen, 977
Williamson, George, 983
Williamson, Reuben, 983
Wilson, William, 990
Winfield, James, 991
Wisker, Robert, 994
Wolstenholme, Francis, 995
Wolstenholme, Thomas, 995
Wood, Edward, 996
Wood, Richard, 997
Wright, John snr & jnr, 1005
Yates, John, 1012
Yeoman, Adam, 1013
Yeoman, William, 1013
Young, William, 1015
York:
  Assembly Rooms:
    Barker, Robert snr, 40

Reynoldson, George, 739, 740
Barr Convent: Chippendale,
  Thomas jnr, 169
City House:
  Etty, William, 282
  Reynoldson, George, 739
Mansion House:
  Farrer, Richard, 291
  Forster, Thomas, 310
  Reynoldson, George, 739, 740
  Thrisk, Henry, 892
Mayor's House: Wilkinson,
  Stephen, 977
Minster:
  Allanson, Thomas, 9
  Mitley, Charles George, 614
Retreat Quaker Asylum:
  Boocock, Benjamin, 86
  Fisher, James, 302
  Gregory, Catherine, 370
  Taylor, John, 877
  Wood & Lockey, 998
St Saviour's Chapel: Hands,
  Thomas, 394
Yorke, Edward, 154, 366, 765, 947
Yorke, Samuel, 828
Yorke, Thomas, 154
Youlgrave (Derbs.): Staley,
  Thomas, 848
Young, Henry, 662
Young, Neal, 239
Young & Godfrey, 1014
Young & Hickman, 1014
Yoxford (Suffolk): Edwards,
  Robert, 270

Z

Zanetti, Vittore, 5

SUPPLEMENT OF 'C' and 'F'

Surnames omitted from English City and Town entries,
due to a computer sorting error

A

Abingdon (Berks.):
Crew, Edward, 209
Crew, Robert, 209

Ackworth (Yorks.): Clarebrough,
Joseph, 172

Alcester (Warks.): Franklin, Richard,
319

Aldermanbury (London): Field,
James, 299

Aldgate (London):
Coleman, Robert, 187
Fern, Geoffrey, 297

Allendale (Northumb.):
Fairlamb, Michael, 288
Fairlamb, Nicholas, 288

Alnwick (Northumb.):
Carr, Adam, 146
Carr, Thomas, 147
Forester, William, 310
Forster, William, 310
Fothergill, Joseph, 312

Ambleside (Westmld): Cousins, John,
202

Ambrosden (Oxon.): Cockerill,
Henry, 185

Amersham (Bucks.): Climpson,
Edward, 179

Ansford (Som.):
Clarke, William 'Painter', 175
Coles, Roger jnr, 188

Arnold (Notts.): Challand, W., 153

Arundel (Sussex): Cooper, T., 197

Ash (Kent): Fells, John, 295

Ashburton (Devon): Croydon,
William N., 215

Ashby-de-la-Zouch (Leics.): Farmer,
Edward, 289

Ashton-under-Lyne (Lancs.):
Cock, James, 185
Crabtree, John, 206

Attleborough (Norfolk):
Childerhouse, Charles, 162

B

Banbury (Oxon.):
Cockerill, Robert, 185

Crosby, Thomas, 212
Fox, Charles, 313

Barbican (London):
Farmer, Thomas, 290
Fouke, —, 312

Barnard Castle (Co. Durham):
Clifton, Joseph, 179
Fidler, Harvey, 298

Barnstaple (Devon):
Carter, Robert Burgess, 148
Chamberlayne, James, 154
Crook, Richard, 212
Ford, Thomas, 309

Barton-on-Humber (Lincs.):
Cradleton, Thomas, 207

Basingstoke (Hants.): Chapman, C.,
157

Bath (Som.):
Calder, John, 141
Caleborne, Thomas, 141
Callan & Booth, Mesdames, 141
Cannings, William, 143
Carpenter, Robert, 146
Champneys, Edmund, 154
Chead, Joseph, 160
Chippett, E., 169
Cogan, John, 186
Coleborne, Thomas, 187
Cook, G., 192
Cooke, Isaac, 193
Cooke, J., 193
Cooper, J., 196
Cottle, J., 201
Coxhead, Robert, 206
Croft, William, 211
Cross, William, 214
Cullimore, Daniel, 219
Farmer, W., 290
Farrell, James, 290
Fennell, J., 295
Flower, John, 306
Foot, T., 308
Ford, William, 309
Fox, William, 315
Francies, Jane, 317

Battle (Sussex): Croft, Samuel, 210

Beccles (Suffolk):
Clarke, Stephen, 175
Creed, Samuel, 208
Cudden, John, 217

Cutting, William, 223
Fletcher, Samuel, 305

Bedale (Yorks.): Clark, George, 173

Bedford:
Coleman, William, 188
Franklin, William, 319
Frohock, John, 322

Berkhamstead (Herts.): Cox, William,
205

Bermondsey (London):
Cook, S., 192
Fall, Jonathan, 288

Berwick-upon-Tweed (Northumb.):
Carr, John, 146
Chartres, David, 160
Chartres, Francis, 160
Fair, William, 287
Ford, James, 309

Bethnal Green (London):
Clarke, Henry, 174
Clemmans, William, 178
Fisher, James, 302
Framingham, C., 315
Framington, Christ., 315

Beverley (Yorks.):
Cade, Robert, 140
Cockerill, John, 185
Farrah, John, 290
Farrah, Richard, 290
Farrah, William, 290
Fenteman, Joseph, 296
Fernot, William, 297
Foster, John, 311

Bewdley (Worcs.):
Cooke, Thomas, 194
Coombes, William, 195
Crutchley, John, 217

Bicester (Oxon.): Clements, Joseph,
178

Bideford (Devon): Chapman, John,
158

Biggleswade (Beds.): Conder, Samuel,
191

Billericay (Essex): Curtis, William jnr,
221

Bilston (Staffs.):
Cheshire, William, 161
Corbitt, John, 199

Bingham (Notts.): Clifton, Thomas,
179

Bingley (Yorks.):
Cryer, John, 217
Foulds, Thomas & William, 312
Birmingham:
Callow, Martin, 141
Campini & Capella, 143
Carpenter, Joseph, 146
Carr, Thomas, 146
Carrington, Joseph, 147
Cartwright, Joseph, 149
Chambers, Samuel, 154
Chatterton, Thomas, 160
Child, John, 162
Churley, William, 172
Clare, Richard, 172
Clare, Sarah, 172
Clark, William, 174
Clark & Wyatt, 174
Clarke, Thomas Hardeman, 175
Clarke & Wyatt, 176
Clay, Henry, 176
Clayton, James, 177
Clowes, Daniel & Samuel, 180
Colborne, Joseph, 186
Colbourne, Thomas, 186
Colder, James, 186
Cole, Thomas, 187
Cole, William, 187
Coleman, William, 188
Cook, Betsey, 192
Cook, Elizabeth, 192
Cooke, Henry, 193
Cooke, John, 194
Cooper, Joseph, 197
Corns, Joseph, 200
Cotterell, Thomas, 201
Cotton, William, 201
Cottrell, Samuel, 201
Cox, Joseph, 204
Cox, Samuel, 205
Cox, William, 205
Cox, William Farmer, 205
Crampton, Ellis, 207
Cresshall, James, 208
Cresswell, James, 208
Crompton, Ellis, 211
Crompton, John, 211
Crompton, Joseph, 211
Crosby, William, 212
Cross, William, 214
Faherty, John, 287
Fahetty, John, 287
Falciola, Barnard, 288
Falciola, Benjamin, 288
Fallows, Thomas, 288
Fantham, James, 289
Farmer, Richard, 290
Fawdry, Thomas, 293
Fellows, Thomas, 295
Fernyhough, Robert, 297
Field, John, 299
Field, Matthew, 299
Field, Thomas, 299
Finch, Thomas, 300

Fisher, Henry, 301
Flavell, William, 303
Fleming, William, 304
Flint, Abraham, 305
Flower, Samuel, 306
Ford, James, 309
Fowell, Benjamin, 312
Fowell, George, 312
Fowell, Thomas, 312
Fretwell, William, 322
Fretwill, Mary, 322
Fulluck, Edmund, 325
Furber, Jonathan, 325
Birstal (Yorks.): Furness, George, 326
Bishops Waltham (Hants.): Churcher, J.M., 171
Bishopsgate (London):
Campion, George, 143
Clarke, Thomas, 175
Clifton, William, 179
Collier, Francis, 188
Collins & Co., 189
Cooper, Henry L., 196
Cooper, Joseph, 197
Curtis, P., 221
Fickling, R., 298
Field, Benjamin, 298
Finer, William, 300
Fisher, James, 301
Ford, William, 309
Fox, Thomas, 314
Furneaux, John, 326
Blackburn (Lancs.): Craven, John, 208
Blackfriars (London):
Chilevier, —, 162
Cook, Isaac, 192
Cooper, William, 197
Cordy, William, 199
Cross, William, 214
Faulkner, James, 292
Fawley, John, 293
Franks, James, 319
Blackheath (London):
Coleman, Robert, 187
Couchman, Henry, 201
Blackpool (Lancs.): Cookson, James, 195
Blandford (Dorset):
Cantrill, Joseph, 144
Carpenter, Stephen, 146
Charmbury, Daniel, 159
Coles, F.E., 188
Fry, Thomas, 323
Blandford St Mary (Dorset): Clarke, John, 175
Bloomsbury (London):
Caldecott, William Edward, 141
Chupain, Elijah, 171
Cock, J., 185
Collison, Thomas, 190
Coningsby, Bennet & Barnes, Elizabeth, 191
Cooper, J., 196

Cooper, Thomas, 197
Cope, Richard & Gray, Alexander, 198
Cousens, Thomas, 202
Couzens, Thomas, 203
Cugnett, Peter, 217
Fabry, John George, 287
Fellows, Robert, 295
Fidler & Son, 298
Flint, T., 305
Flint, Thomas, 305
Fogarty, Edward, 306
Foggitt, Ann, 307
Fuhrlohg, Christopher, 323
Fuller, James, 325
Flint & Co., 306
Blyth (Northumb.): Fenwick, Thomas, 296
Bolton (Lancs.):
Campbell, Samuel, 143
Cryer, Anthony, 217
Fray, John, 319
Boston (Lincs.):
Caistor, Thomas, 140
Collins, Aaron, 189
Cooper, John, 196
Creasy, Thomas, 208
Foster, —, 311
Foster, William, 312
Boston (Yorks.): Chippendale, A., 164
Botesdale (Suffolk):
Clark, James, 173
Clarke, Thomas M., 175
Boughton (Cheshire): Cartledge, N., 149
Bradford (Yorks.):
Cansick, Robert, 144
Clayton, John, 177
Cockshut, Martin, 186
Crabtree, Benjamin, 206
Farrer, David, 290
Fawthorp, Richard, 293
Fearnley, Henry, 293
Braintree (Essex): Fordham, Thomas jnr, 309
Brentford (Middlx): Cock, Samuel, 185
Brentwood (Essex): Cox, Edward, 204
Brewood (Staffs.): Fox, George, 313
Bridgnorth (Salop):
Cartwright, F. & R., 149
Cartwright, Francis, 149
Cartwright, Richard, 149
Cartwright, William, 149
Colley, James, 188
Bridgwater (Som.):
Culverwell, Robert, 219
Furze, Mrs, 326
Bridlington (Yorks.):
Collinson, Benjamin, 189
Forth, Thomas, 311
Bridport (Dorset):
Cawley, James, 152

Curme, H., 220
Brighton (Sussex):
  Caffyn, Henry, 140
  Caffyn, John Benjamin & Charles, 140
  Carbon, John, 144
  Carden & Stoddard, 144
  Carley, Jesse, 145
  Carley, Stephen, 145
  Carly, J., 145
  Carly, S., 145
  Carly, Samuel, 145
  Carly, Stephen, 145
  Chamberlain, John, 153
  Chapman, Thomas, 158
  Cheesman, Thomas, 160
  Childs, William, 162
  Clark, Henry, 173
  Clark, John, 173
  Colbron, William, 186
  Collins, Edward, 189
  Connard, Edward, 191
  Cooke, Thomas, 194
  Coppard, Lawrence, 199
  Corben, Thomas, 199
  Corbin, John, 199
  Crane, William, 207
  Cruden, Thomas, 216
  Cuthbertson, John, 222
  Featherstone, Abraham, 294
  Fitch, William, 302
  Foard, E., 306
  Folker, Samuel Sheppard, 307
  Foster, John, 311
  Franklin, J., 318
  Franklin, Thomas, 319
  Fry, Richard, 323
  Furse, John, 326
Bristol:
  Campbell, John, 142
  Campbell, Richard, 142
  Carpenter, Abraham, 146
  Carpenter, John, 146
  Carter, John, 148
  Case, John, 149
  Castle, Thomas, 150
  Ceulas, Marmaduke, 152
  Chandler, Thomas, 154
  Chaplin, Joseph, 157
  Chaplins & Co., 157
  Chapman, Walter, 158
  Chapman, William, 159
  Chappell, Daniel, 159
  Charnock, John, 160
  Cheary, William, 160
  Cherry, David, 161
  Cherry, Henry Granger, 161
  Cherry, J.L., 161
  Cherry, John, 161
  Cherry, William, 161
  Chippett, —, 169
  Chivers, James, 170
  Church, George, 171
  Clark, Henry, 173

Clark, James, 173
Clark, John, 173
Clark, Joseph, 174
Clark, Samuel, 174
Clarkson, George, 176
Clifford, Mrs, 179
Cock, William, 185
Cocks, George C., 185
Code, A., 186
Code, Richard, 186
Colbatch, George, 186
Colbatch, Harry, 186
Cole, James, 187
Coleman, Edward, 187
Coles, Benjamin, 188
Coles, John, 188
Collins, John, 189
Collis, George, 190
Collis, Mrs H., 190
Cook, James, 192
Cook, Samuel, 193
Cornish, William, 200
Cornock, Thomas, 200
Cosens, Hannah, 200
Cottle, 201
Cotton, Ann, 201
Cotton, Benjamin, 201
Cotton, Mary, 201
Cotton, William, 201
Cottrell, J.F., 201
Coules, Marmaduke, 201
Coulsting, James, 202
Court, Charles, 202
Court, Esther, 202
Court, James, 202
Court, John, 202
Court, William & Charles, 202
Craig, Colton, 207
Crane, Peter, 207
Crew, William jnr, 209
Crew, William snr, 209
Cross, John, 213
Cubitt, Jonah, 217
Cummings, John, 219
Cummins, Charles, 219
Cummins, Thomas, 219
Curles & Harris, 220
Curtis, Joseph, 221
Felt, John, 295
Ferrier, Richard, 298
Fisher, John E., 302
Fishpool, William, 302
Fone, Samuel, 308
Foot, George, 308
Foot, William, 308
Ford, John, 309
Ford, W., 309
Fore, Samuel, 309
Foster, Henry, 311
Foxhall, Martin, 315
Frances, William, 317
Franklyn, Margaret, 319
Freeman, Edward, 320
Frost, Thomas, 323

Fry, Thomas, 323
Fry, William, 323
Fryer, Benjamin, 323
Fryer, Richard, 323
Fungus, John, 325
Brixton (London): Conway, C., 192
Bromley (Kent): Carpenter, Jabez, 146
Bromsgrove (Worcs.): Cotton, William, 201
Broroughbridge (Yorks.): Cawood, Henry, 152
Broseley (Salop): Colley, Joseph, 188
Brough (Westmld): Fawcett, John, 292
Broughton (Westmld): Casson, John, 150
Bryanston (Dorset):
  Carpenter, Stephen, 146
  Cartwright, Thomas, 149
Buckingham: Collingridge, Thomas, 188
Bude (Cornwall): Fish, William, 301
Budleigh Salterton (Devon): Cawley, James, 152
Bunbury (Cheshire): Cathrall, William, 151
Bungay (Suffolk):
  Cooper, John, 196
  Cudden, James, 217
Burnley (Lancs.):
  Chaffer, Benjamin, 153
  Chaffer, William, 153
Burslem (Staffs.):
  Copeland, Thomas, 198
  Copeland, William, 198
  Ford, William, 309
Burton-upon-Trent (Staffs.):
  Coplep, John, 199
  Copley, John, 199
Bury (Lancs.):
  Cleminshaw, John, 178
  Fell, Benjamin, 294
  Fletcher, Thomas, 305
  Fletcher, William, 305
Bury St Edmunds (Suffolk):
  Capon, J., 144
  Capson, John, 144
  Cox, John, 204
  Fenton, Thomas, 296
  Frost, Samuel, 323

C

Calne (Wilts.):
  Chivers, John, 170
  Chivers, Matthew, 170
Calverley-cum-Farsley (Yorks.):
  Craven, Ambrose, 208
Camberwell (London):
  Carter, Gabriel, 147
  Carter, Samuel, 148

Clarke, Thomas, 175
Froy, William, 323
Cambridge:
Caiton, William, 140–1
Chamberlain, Dixon, 153
Chandler, John, 154
Chandler, Thomas, 154
Chandler & Hazelwood, 154
Chinn, Charles, 163
Clare, Thomas, 172
Cole, William, 187
Cooke, Joseph, 194
Coote, William, 198
Cracknell, William Francis, 206
Fox, John, 314
Canterbury (Kent):
Cacket, Thomas, 140
Castle, Daniel, 150
Castle, Thomas, 150
Catchmead, John, 151
Chapman, John, 158
Claris, William, 173
Collins, Edward, 189
Collison, William, 190
Cooper, Henry, 196
Corkham, Joshua, 199
Cradock, Robert, 207
Cullen, Thomas, 218
French, John, 321
Friend, Thomas, 322
Frost, Thomas, 323
Fuller, Robert, 325
Carlisle (Cumb.):
Capstick, Thomas, 144
Carruthers, Reginald, 147
Compston, John, 191
Creighton, James, 208
Cumpston, John, 219
Fleming, Joshua, 304
Forster, John, 310
Foster, William, 312
Chard (Som.):
Coles, John, 188
Collins, Philip Alford jnr, 189
Charing Cross (London):
Collett, Jonathan, 188
Collins, H., 189
Crompton, James, 211
France, Edward, 315
Chatham (Kent):
Chickley, Richard, 162
Cosier & Seager, 200
Crockford, Jon., 210
Fletcher, Thomas, 305
Chatsworth (Derbs.): Cooper, —, 195
Chatteris (Cambs.): Feast, John, 294
Cheadle (Staffs.): Flint, Abraham, 305
Cheapside (London):
Chandle, Thomas, 154
Clarke, Samuel, 175
Cock, William, 185
Copland, Henry, 198
Cowdall, Samuel, 203

French, John, 321
Fryer, Francis, 323
Fryer, Robert & Ralph, 323
Chelmsford (Essex):
Cohen, Jacob, 186
Cook, William, 193
Chelsea (London):
Caswell, Thomas & W., 151
Chandler, —, 154
Collett, James, 188
Ferguson, Matthew, 297
Firby, John, 301
Flack, Thomas, 303
Fulcher, Nathaniel, 325
Cheltenham (Glos.):
Challenor, J., 153
Chandler, Charles, 154
Chreiman, Olive, 170
Coke, T. & J., 186
Cooke, Thomas, 194
Cooke, Thomas & John, 194
Cooke & Co., 194
Cowling, T., 203
Creed, William, 208
Curry, William, 221
Fruin, William, 323
Fry, H., 323
Fry, James, 323
Chertsey (Surrey): Coolridge, William, 195
Chesham (Bucks.):
Cox, Cabel, 204
Freeman, William, 321
Chester:
Calkin, Thomas, 141
Cartwright, John, 149
Cartwright, Thomas, 149
Challiner, Thomas, 153
Chantler, William, 157
Chester, Charles, 214
Chesters, Charles, 161
Chubbe, Robert, 171
Churton, William, 172
Clare, John, 172
Clayton, Thomas, 177
Cliffe, Charles, 179
Cliffe, Joseph, 179
Clubbe, Robert, 180
Coake, John, 181
Coleclough, William, 187
Collins, Pendlebury, 189
Cooke, John, 193
Cooper, J., 196
Cooper, Philip, 197
Cottingham, Richard, 201
Crawford, W., 208
Critchley, John, 210
Crofts, William, 211
Crosby, Samuel, 212
Cross, William, 214
Croughton, John, 214
Croxton, Thomas, 215
Croxton, William, 215
Culm, John jnr, 219

Farnworth, Samuel, 290
Faulkner, William, 292
Fletcher, Edward, 304
Floyd, Thomas, 306
Formstone, John, 193, 310
Fothergill, George, 312
Foulkes, Thomas Bennet, 312
Frost, Richard, 323
Chester-le-Street (Co. Durham):
Coatsworth, John, 181
Corner, Mat., 200
Chewton (Som.): Curtis, Hipsley, 221
Chichester (Sussex):
Clement, Henry, 178
Cloyde, John, 180
Fleet, Francis, 303
Fleet, James, 303
Chorley (Lancs.):
Chorley, James, 170
Farrington, Thomas, 291
Christchurch (Hants.): Cranston, George, 207
Cirencester (Glos.):
Carr, John, 146
Chappell, Job, 159
Clappen, F., 172
Cook, George, 192
Cook, John, 192
Cooke, Charles, 193
Clapham (London):
Cogger, John George, 186
Frost, George, 323
Frost, James, 323
Clare (Suffolk): Cox, John, 204
Clerkenwell (London):
Cameron, Charles, 142
Carpenter, James, 146
Carpenter, John, 146
Castell, John, 150
Chalk, Charles, 153
Chalk, James T., 153
Chapman, John, 158
Chapman, R., 158
Cheatham, J., 160
Cheesewright, Joshua, 160
Cheltman, John, 161
Clare, F. Knight, 172
Clare, William, 172
Clark, William, 174
Clarke, Henry, 174
Clarke, James & Son, 175
Cole, William, 187
Cooke, Robert, 194
Cooper, Edward, 195
Corbett, Thomas, 199
Coventon, Joseph, 203
Crasby, —, 208
Creak, William, 208
Cullimore, Daniel, 219
Fitt, James, 303
Forse, C., 310
Fowler, Thomas, 313
Franklin, Thomas, 319
Fraser, George, 319

Friend, George II, 322
Friend, George III, 322
Cley (Norfolk): Christmas, Joseph, 171
Clitheroe (Yorks.): Cottam, John, 200
Cockermouth (Cumb.):
Cape, William, 144
Cape, William & George, 144
Fleming, Jonah, 304
Fletcher, Peter, 305
Colchester (Essex):
Calver, James, 142
Carrington, Richard, 147
Cary, John, 149
Chignall, Charles, 162
Cobb, Nathaniel, 184
Cobb & Ellisdon, 185
Cook, Jeremiah, 192
Couch, William, 201
Crisp, Samuel, 210
Cross, Edmund, 213
Cross, John Wainwright, 213
Cross, Joseph, 213
Cross, Peter, 213
Fenton, Francis, 296
Fuller, John, 325
Colne (Lancs.):
Crankshaw, Edward, 207
French, Thomas, 322
Congleton (Cheshire):
Clegg & Bowes, 177
Crew, Samuel, 209
Cornhill (London):
Crawley, Gerard, 208
Farthing, John H., 292
Cottingham (Yorks.): Ford, John, 309
Covent Garden (London):
Carey, Peter, 145
Cartwright, Richard, 149
Champion & Watkins, 154
Chissham, William, 170
Clark, —, 173
Clark, James, 173
Clark, John, 173
Clarke, R., 175
Collett, Jonas, 188
Cook, Henry, 192
Cook, Samuel, 192
Cowie, John, 203
Cox, John, 204
Crackerode, John, 206
Cribb, William, 209
Cumming, Alexander, 219
Finch & Smith, 300
Fleming, Hannah, 304
Fleming, William, 304
Flem(m)ing, John, 304
Fontaine, George David, 308
Ford, George, 309
Coventry (Warks.):
Chambers, Samuel, 154
Cherry, James, 161
Clarke, John & Yardley, Samuel, 175

Clarke, Samuel, 175
Clay, William, 177
Connor, James, 191
Ford, Joseph, 309
Cranbrook (Kent): Foord, William, 308
Crewkerne (Som.): Coussins, Robert, 202
Cripplegate (London):
Cave, Robert, 152
Clemapon, George, 178
Cumber, Peter, 219
Croydon (Surrey):
Cattaneo, Pasqual, 151
Clark, J., 173
Fusedale, Thomas, 326
Cullompton (Devon):
Fowler, George, 312
Frost, Richard, 323

D

Darlington (Co. Durham):
Champney, Robert Nelson, 154
Chapman, John, 158
Charlton, Michael, 159
Chisman, John, 170
Clark, James, 173
Cundell, Joseph, 219
Curry, Robert, 221
Daventry (Northants.):
Cattall, Samuel, 151
Cox, William, 205
Field, John, 299
Deal (Kent)
Castle, Richard, 150
Clark, George, 173
Cramp, Enoch, 207
Debenham (Suffolk):
Cook, George, 192
Fisk, William, 302
Denton Park (Yorks.): Calthrop, 142
Derby:
Cartlich, Thomas, 149
Cholerton, Matthew, 170
Cole, William, 187
Coleman, John, 187
Collambell, Thomas, 188
Collumbell, Thomas, 190
Cooper, John, 196
Cooper, Joseph, 197
Crayne, Thomas, 208
Cunliffe, Henry, 219
Finney, Charles, 300
Finney, John, 300
Ford, —, 309
Ford, Humphrey, 309
Ford, Thomas, 309
Ford, William, 309
Foster, Edward, 311

Devizes (Wilts.):
Cadby, Joel, 140
Crockett, Joseph, 210
Cruse, Gabriel, 216
Ferris, J., 298
Ferris, John, 298
Devonport (Devon): Carter, Richard John, 148
Dewsbury (Yorks.):
Chadwick, Jeremiah, 153
Fawcett, George, 292
Fawcett, Thomas, 292
Firth, Joseph, 301
Doncaster (Yorks.):
Catley, James, 151
Crowther, Joseph, 215
Donyatt (Som.): Chedsey, Mathew, 160
Dorchester (Dorset):
Comings, Matthew, 191
Curme, Charles, 220
Curme, Thomas, 220
Foot, John, 308
Dorking (Surrey):
Curtis, William, 221
Fontaine, George Daniel, 308
Fontaine, George David, 308
Dover (Kent):
Caspall, James Austen, 150
Clement, John, 178
Flashman, George, 303
Frazer, William, 319
Downham Market (Norfolk):
Casebow, William, 149
Downton (Wilts.): Field, James, 299
Dudley (Worcs.):
Cassera, Charles, 150
Child, Thomas, 162
Colley, Thomas, 188
Dunstable (Beds.): Cheshire, Stanbridge, 161
Durham:
Caldcleugh, Robert, 141
Caldcleugh, Thomas, 141
Clark, George, 173
Clark, John, 173
Clarke, 173
Forster, Barnabas, 310
Forster, John, 310
Dursley (Glos.): French, George, 321

E

Easingwold (Yorks.): Clemetshaw, Thomas, 178
East Spa Fields (London): Fenner, Samuel, 295
Easterton (Wilts.):
Cheater, John jnr, 160
Draper, Gifford, 160

Egham (Surrey): Farrant, Thomas, 290
Ely (Cambs.): Chambers, James, 154
Epsom (Surrey): Churchill, Frederick, 171
Evesham (Worcs.):
  Fields, Simon Henry, 299
  Fowler, Henry, 312
Exeter (Devon):
  Canes, William, 143
  Carpenter, John, 146
  Carter, B., 147
  Carter, Burrington, 147
  Carter, Elias, 147
  Carter, Robert, 148
  Carter & Son, 149
  Cawley, James, 152
  Challice, Richard, 153
  Chamberalin, John, 153
  Chandler, Richard, 154
  Channon, Atho, 155
  Channon, John, 156
  Channon, Otho, 156
  Chaplin, John, 157
  Chapple, Charles, 159
  Chub, Stephen, 171
  Churchward, George, 172
  Churchward, John, 172
  Churchward, Robert, 172
  Clark, Robert, 174
  Clode, William, 179
  Coffin, Edmund, 186
  Cole, Charles, 186
  Cole, John, 187
  Cole, Thomas, 187
  Comroy, John, 191
  Cook, Frederick, 192
  Coombe, J., 195
  Creasy, James, 208
  Crofts, John, 211
  Crook, Richard, 212
  Cross, John, 213
  Cross, Richard, 213
  Cross, William, 214
  Crudge, Thomas, 216
  Cruse, Daniel, 216
  Cullimore, Thomas, 219
  Culverwell, Robert, 219
  Ferguson, William S., 297
  Finch, John Williams, 300
  Fisher, Jabez Henry, 301
  Flashman, George, 303
  Flashman, Henry, 303
  Force, Charles, 308
  Force, Henry, 308
  Foster, John, 311
  Frool, Henry, 322
  Frost, Henry, 323
  Frost, Matthew, 323
  Frost, William, 323
  Fry, James, 323
  Furguson, William, 326
  Furse, Christopher, 326
Exmouth (Devon): Crudge, Thomas, 216

F

Fakenham (Norfolk):
  Colman, William, 190
  Constance, William, 191
  Custance, William, 222
Falmouth (Cornwall): Crew, Samuel, 209
Fareham (Hants.): Fry, Edward, 323
Faringdon (Oxon.): Fidel, John & Sons, 298
Farnham (Surrey): Cowdry, Richard, 203
Farnley (Yorks.): Chippendale, William, 169
Faversham (Kent):
  Freeman, William, 321
  Frost, Thomas, 323
Ferrybridge (Yorks.): Freare, John, 319
Finsbury (London):
  Cain, John, 140
  Camfield, John Thomas, 142
  Clarkson, Edward, 176
  Clemman, J., 178
  Farrer, Edwin, 290
  Flamston, Richard, 303
  Freeman, Elizabeth, 320
Fletching (Sussex): Cooke, Thomas, 194
Folkstone (Kent): Franklyn, —, 319
Freckleton (Lancs.): Coulbourn, Richard, 201
Frodsham (Cheshire): Forster, John, 310
Frome (Som.): Cox, Thomas, 205

G

Gainsborough (Lincs.):
  Campbell, John, 142
  Carter, John, 148
  Carter, William, 148
  Cod(d)ington, John, 186
  Corrington, John, 200
  Cross, George, 213
  Foster, William, 312
Gateshead (Co. Durham):
  Clark, Lancelot, 174
  Clark, Richard, 174
  Colling, George, 188
  Coltman, Thomas, 190
  Corner, William & Son, 200
  Foggin(s), John, 307
  Forster, John, 310
Gibside (Co. Durham): Campbell, Daniel, 142
Gloucester:
  Case, George, 149
  Case, John, 149
  Clutterbuck, Obadiah, 180
  Cocks, James, 186

  Cocks, Thomas, 186
  Collett, Thomas, 188
  Connibeare, George, 191
  Con(n)ibeare, R., 191
  Cooks, James, 195
  Cooks, Thomas, 195
  Cox, James, 204
Godalming (Surrey):
  Court, James, 202
  Ford, Mary, 309
  Ford, William, 309
Goodman's Fields (London):
  Cook, Samuel, 192
  Crowley, John, 215
Gorhambury, St Albans (Herts.):
  Chipchase, Robert & Henry, 163
Gosport (Hants.):
  Castleman, Richard, 151
  Crook, James, 212
Grantham (Lincs.): Fell, Valentine, 295
Gravesend (Kent): Cocks, John, 186
Great Driffield (Yorks.): Carter, William, 148
Great Yarmouth (Norfolk):
  Carsey, James, 147
  Carsey, William, 147
  Chapman, John, 158
  Church, Thomas, 171
  Clements, Valentine, 178
  Colby, Rouse, 186
  Cory, George, 200
  Cozens, James, 206
  Cozens, William, 206
  Crabtree, Edward, 206
  Creed, John & Co., 208
  Creed, William, 208
  Crisp, Samuel, 210
  Crow, Charles, 214
  Crow, John, 214
  Crow, William, 215
  Cushing, James M., 221
  Fish, John, 301
  Furrance, Jacob, 326
Green Street (Middlx): Furneaux, John, 326
Greenwich (London):
  Coltman, Robert, 190
  Compton, Robert W., 191
  Crosty, James, 214
  Crosty, Robert, 214
Grimsby (Lincs.):
  Carr, John E., 146
  Cooke, Thomas, 194
  Cousins, John, 202
  Crowder, Samuel, 215
Guildford (Surrey):
  Clarke, John, 175
  Cooke, Robert jnr, 194
  Fawkes, John, 293
Guisborough (Yorks.):
  Carrick, Mark, 147
  Clarke, Morley, 175
Guiting (Glos.): Crump, William, 216

H

Hackney (London):
  Canton, James, 144
  Fersey, Francis, 298
  Fletcher, James, 304
Hadleigh (Suffolk): Clarke, Joseph, 175
Haggeston (London): Conley, John, 191
Halesworth (Suffolk):
  Clapham, Richard, 172
  Cook, Daniel, 192
  Freeman, Charles, 320
Halifax (Yorks.):
  Camotta, Richard, 142
  Chambers, George, 154
  Chambers, William, 154
  Cordingley, David, 199
  Crowder, William, 215
  Crowther, Hannah, 215
  Crowther, William & Hannah, 215
  Fearnley, John, 294
Halstead (Essex): Cooper, Thomas, 197
Hammersmith (London):
  Carter, Timothy, 148
  Froy, William, 323
Hampstead (London):
  Farrington, John, 291
  Fawcett, Jos., 292
Hampstead Marshall (Berks.): Cox, Francis, 204
Hanley (Staffs.):
  Cliff, James, 178
  Fenton, George, 296
Harleston (Norfolk): Fletcher, Samuel, 305
Hartland (Devon): Cory, Thomas, 200
Harwich (Essex): Crickmar, Robert, 209
Haslingden (Lancs.): Clare, William, 172
Hastings (Sussex):
  Carly, James, 145
  Cox, James, 204
Hatherleigh (Devon): Chudley, John, 171
Haymarket (London):
  Cure, George, 219
  Faulding, R., 292
  Fenton, William, 296
  Fradin, Abraham, 315
  France, —, 315
  France & Paten, 317
Hebden Bridge (Yorks.):
  Clegg, George, 177
  Cockcroft, John, 185
Heighington (Co. Durham): French, Michael, 322
Helmsley (Yorks.): Frank, William, 318
Helmsley Gate (Yorks.): Cooper,

Thomas, 197
Henley-on-Thames (Oxon.):
  Cooper, John & Son, 196
  Cooper, William, 198
Hereford:
  Cooke, Thomas, 194
  Corbett, Thomas, 199
  Flanegan, John H., 303
  Fuller, Thomas, 325
Hertford:
  Cary, John, 149
  Clark, John, 174
Hexham (Northumb.):
  Charlton, John, 159
  Craft, William, 207
High Wycombe (Bucks.):
  Cannon, Charles, 143
  Cannon, George, 143
  Cannon, John, 144
  Cannon, Joseph, 144
  Cannon, Mary, 144
  Cannor, Charles, 144
  Carr, Ann, 146
  Carrs, Henry, 147
  Chadley, James, 153
  Chilton, Thomas, 163
  Clark, Charles, 173
  Clark, George, 173
  Clark, Joseph, 174
  Clark, Thomas, 174
  Clark, William, 174
  Clarke, James, 175
  Collins, James, 189
  Collins, Joseph, 189
  Collins, William, 189
  Coltman, George, 190
  Compton, William, 191
  Cooper, James, 196
  Cooper, John, 196
  Cooper, Thomas, 197
  Cooper, William, 197
  Couchman, William, 201
  Cox, James, 204
  Cox, Joseph, 204
  Cross, James, 213
  Cross, Richard, 214
  Cutler, Richard, 222
  Fehrenback, Henry, 294
  Fehrenback, Joseph, 294
  Foote, Richard, 308
  Ford, Henry, 309
  Ford, Richard, 309
  Ford, Samuel, 309
  Fountain, Daniel, 312
  Fowler, Joseph, 313
  Francis, Joseph, 317
  Fuller, William, 325
Hitchin (Herts.): Cooper, James, 196
Holbeach (Lincs.): Capp, James, 144
Holborn (London):
  Clancy, John, 172
  Clapcott, Henry, 172
  Clarkson, John, 194
  Clayford, J., 177

Coffee, George, 186
Collett, James, 188
Collett, John, 188
Cook, J., 192
Cooke, Thomas, 194
Copini, Gatini, 198
Cowdry, Samuel, 203
Cranford, William, 207
Crawford, William, 208
Cribb, Robert, 209
Croft, William, 211
Crohan, Edward, 211
Crowdy, Richard, 215
Curry, John, 220
Farmer, Richard, 290
Faulkner, M. & J., 292
Field, John, 299
Finch, James, 300
Fincher, S., 300
Firmin & Sutton, 301
Fisher, Peter, 302
Fitzgerrald, James, 303
Fontaine, George David, 308
Fret(t)well, Allen, 322
Fuller & Levet, 325
Fusedale, Thomas & John, 326
Holderness (Yorks.): Fish, George, 301
Holme (Yorks.): Cater, David & Son, 151
Holt (Norfolk):
  Carr, James, 146
  Fuller, James, 325
Honiton (Devon):
  Flood, James, 306
  Ford, James, 309
Hopetoun House (West Lothian): Cullen, James, 218
Hopton (Suffolk): Fish, Peter, 301
Hornby Hall (Lancs.): Channon, John, 156
Horsham (Sussex): Cooper, Henry, 196
Horsleydown (London): Fowler, William, 313
Houghton-le-Spring (Co. Durham): Clennell, George, 178
Houndsditch (London):
  Cohen, Alexander, 186
  Constable, John, 191
  Cordelle, Thomas, 199
  Fisher, Joseph, 302
Howden (Yorks.): Fletcher, John, 304
Hoxton (London):
  Clarkson, Thomas, 176
  Colsey, William, 190
  Fairful, Thomas, 288
  Farmer, Benjamin, 289
  Fassett, Elias de Gruchy, 292
  Field, J., 299
Huddersfield (Yorks.):
  Carter, David & Sons, 147
  Cresswell, Henry, 208
  Fawthorp, Richard, 293

Flockton, John, 306
Foster, Edward, 311
Hull (Yorks.):
  Calam, Richard, 141
  Campion, Thomas, 143
  Campsall, John, 143
  Carhill, George & Joseph, 145
  Carlill, George & Joseph, 145
  Carlill, Thomas & George, 145
  Carnley, John, 146
  Carrall, Richard jnr, 147
  Carter, Joseph, 148
  Castle, Samuel, 150
  Catley, James, 151
  Champman & Son, 154
  Chapman, Edward, 157
  Chapman, George & John, 157
  Charleton, John, 159
  Charlton, William, 159
  Chester, John jnr, 161
  Church, Thomas, 171
  Clare, John, 172
  Clark, John, 173
  Clark, Peter, 174
  Clark, William, 174
  Clark, William jnr, 174
  Clay, Samuel, 177
  Clay, William Hopper, 177
  Clough, Ralph Burnell, 180
  Coates, Edward, 181
  Coates, Henry, 181
  Cobb, Thomas, 184
  Cockhill, John, 185
  Codlin, Thomas, 186
  Codlin, William, 186
  Codlin & Hick, 186
  Collinson, Leonard, 190
  Collison, Sarah, 190
  Collison, William, 157
  Collison, William Gilbank, 190
  Conkerton, Alexander, 191
  Cook, John, 192
  Cooper, George, 196
  Cooper, James Winter, 196
  Cooper, Richard, 197
  Corroll, Richard, 200
  Cottam, William, 200
  Coupland, Thomas, 202
  Coupland, William, 202
  Court, Philip, 202
  Cowham & Clark, 203
  Crackles, John, 206
  Crackles, Richard, 206
  Crackles, Richard Slack, 206
  Crackles, Robert, 206
  Craven, George, 208
  Craven, Joseph, 208
  Craven, William, 208
  Cross, George, 213
  Crowder, William, 215
  Cutsforth, Thomas, 222
  Farrar, Richard, 290
  Farrow, Benjamin, 292
  Farrow, Daniel, 292

Faulkner, Jeremiah, 292
Feetam, John, 294
Feet(h)am, Thomas, 294
Fergusson, Duncan, 296
Finlay, John, 300
Fisher, King, 302
Fletcher, Mrs Ann, 304
Fletcher, John, 304
Fletcher, Roun(d)cival, 305
Fletcher, William, 305
Fleuriot, William & Russell, James, 305
Ford, James, 309
Foster, Edmund, 311
Foster, Edward, 311
Foster, James & Edward, 311
Foster, John, 311
Foster, Robert, 312
Foster, William, 312
Fox, Edward, 313
Fox, James, 313
Foy, Mary, 315
Foy, William, 315
Fram, Samuel, 315
Francis, Thomas, 318
Free, Thomas, 320
French, Robert, 322
Fry, William, 323
Fullerton, Francis, 325
Hungerford (Berks.): Coxhead, William, 206
Huntingdon:
  Cawley, William Bale, 152
  Fox, George, 313
  Fox, John, 314
Hythe (Kent):
  Finnis, George, 300
  Finnis, Robert, 300
  Finnis & Ronalds, 300
  Flashman & Horne, 303

I

Ipswich (Suffolk):
  Calver, William, 142
  Cartwright, —, 149
  Catt, Benjamin, 151
  Chamberlain, T., 154
  Chaplin, William, 157
  Chapman, —, 157
  Chapman, Edward, 157
  Chenery, Benjamin, 161
  Chilver, Robert, 163
  Coe, Anthony Stephen, 186
  Collier, George, 188
  Collins, James, 189
  Cooper, Francis, 195
  Fokard, William, 307
Islington (London):
  Chester, Joseph, 161
  Chopping, Mat., 170
  Clark, John, 174

Cole, William, 187
Comfort, John, 191
Fall, Jonathan, 288
Forfar, John, 310
Ixworth (Suffolk): Canter, William, 144

J

Jarrow (Co. Durham): Cameron, George, 142

K

Keighley (Yorks.):
  Carter, Anthony, 147
  Corlass, John, 199
  Craven, John, 208
  Feather, John, 294
Kendal (Westmld): Coward, William, 203
Kennington (London):
  Clark, John, 173
  Colston, Daniel Edward, 190
  Conway, C., 192
  Finnis, William, 300
  Frankland, James, 318
Kensington (London): Collin(s), William, 189
Keswick (Cumb.):
  Clark, James, 173
  Cockbain, Joseph, 185
Kettering (Northants.): Clipsham, William, 179
Kidderminster (Worcs.): Fellows, Edward, 295
King's Cross (London): Colton, William, 190
King's Lynn (Norfolk):
  Carr, William, 147
  Carse, Samuel, 147
  Chadwick, Benjamin, 153
  Chadwick, John, 153
  Coates, Daniel, 181
  Cooke, Henry, 193
  Cooper, Osborn, 197
  Cooper, Thomas, 197
  Crawson, William, 208
  Crisp, Thomas, 210
  Crowson, Elizabeth, 215
  Crowson, John, 215
  Crowson, William, 215
  Crusoe, Charles, 216
  Crusoe, Robinson, 217
  Custance, 222
  Farthing, John, 292
  Ford, John, 309
Kingston-upon-Thames (Surrey):
  Chandler, John, 154
  Clarkson, Knight & Pratt, 176
  Fidoe, Thomas, 298
  Fricker, Charles, 322

Fricker, James, 322
Kington (Herefs.): Crump, Benjamin, 216
Kirkby Stephen (Westmld):
    Close, William, 179
    Fawcett, John, 292
Kirkbymoorside (Yorks.):
    Clark, John, 173
    Clark(e), Cornelius, 173
Knaresborough (Yorks.):
    Cawood, Benjamin, 152
    Fawcett, George, 292
Knightsbridge (London):
    Cooper, S., 197
    Fletcher, Elizabeth, 304

L

Lakenham (Norwich):
    Culyer, Thomas, 219
    Culyer, William, 219
Lambeth (London):
    Carpenter, Samuel, 146
    Caston, Thomas, 151
    Chester, E., 161
    Conway, Henry, 192
    Cosser, Andrew, 200
    Crichton, Joseph, 209
    Finnis, Henry, 300
    Forman, Archibald, 310
    Foster, Edmund, 311
    Fowler, Richard, 313
    Fry, Samuel, 323
    Fussell, John, 326
Lancaster:
    Calvert, Nathaniel, 142
    Calvert, William, 142
    Canway, John, 144
    Cape, John, 144
    Capstack, James, 144
    Capstick, Thomas, 144
    Carr, John, 146
    Carter, Robert, 148
    Carter, Wright John, 148
    Casson, Thomas, 150
    Caton, John, 151
    Caudby, —, 151
    Chambers, James, 154
    Clark, Arthur, 173
    Clarke, Anthony, 174
    Clarkson, Robert, 176
    Clemmy, William, 178
    Cook, William, 193
    Cooke, J., 193
    Cooper, C., 195
    Cooper, Edward, 195
    Cooper, Edward jnr, 195
    Cooper, John, 196
    Cooper, Robert, 197
    Cooper, Samuel, 197
    Cooper, Thomas, 197
    Cooper, William, 197

Cotton, William, 201
Coulstone, Richard, 202
Coupland, Richard, 202
Cowper, Thomas, 310
Craskel, John, 208
Croft, Joseph, 210
Croft, Nicholas, 210
Crookall, John, 212
Crookham, John, 212
Crowdson, John, 215
Cumpsty, Thomas, 219
Cumpsty, William, 219
Curry, —, 220
Farmer, —, 289
Fawcett, Christopher, 292
Fayrer, Edmund, 293
Fayrer, James, 293
Fayrer, John, 293
Fayrer, William, 293
Fearenside, John, 293
Fearnley, Peter, 294
Fell, John, 294
Fell, Robert, 295
Fell, Thomas, 295
Ferguson, William James, 297
Fisher, John, 302
Fisher, Robert, 302
Fisher, Thomas, 302
Ford, John, 309
Forrest, William, 310
Forton, Thomas, 311
Foster, John, 311
Fox, John, 314
France, John, 316
Francis, R., 318
French, J., 321
Fryer, Thomas, 323
Lane End (Staffs.):
    Clewlow, William, 178
    Cope, Edward, 198
    Cope, William, 198
Leamington (Warks.):
    Cartwright, —, 149
    Cookes, William, 195
    Cooks & Sons, 195
    Fitzhugh, Samuel, 303
Ledbury (Herefs.):
    Cox, Philip, 204
    Crump, William, 216
Leeds (Yorks.):
    Calvert, William, 142
    Carlton, Samuel, 145
    Carrack, John, 147
    Carter, William, 148
    Chapman, Thomas, 158
    Chorlton, James, 170
    Clark, John, 173
    Clayton, John, 177
    Cock, William, 185
    Constantine, William & Co., 192
    Cook, John, 192
    Coupland, Robert, 202
    Craister, William, 207
    Craven, John, 208

Craven & Smith, 208
Craven & Worswick, 208
Croft, Isaac, 210
Croft, Samuel & Son, 211
Crosby, John, 212
Crowther, Ely, 215
Curtis, John, 221
Curwin, John, 221
Farrar, Abraham, 290
Farrar, Christopher, 290
Farrar, Simeon, 290
Fawcett, William, 292
Fearnside, Henry, 294
Fearnside & Morton, 294
Feetham, Elizabeth, 294
Feetham, Mark, 294
Feetham, Mary, 294
Fell, Thomas, 295
Fenton, Thomas, 296
Ferguson, John, 297
Fish, John, 301
Flesher, Benjamin, 304
Fletcher, Thomas, 305
Forsyth, James, 310
Foster, William, 312
Fothergill, Christopher, 312
Fothergill, Frederick & John, 312
Fothergill, John H., 312
Fox, James, 313
Foy, Thomas, 315
Fozard, John, 315
Frank, John, 318
Fretwell, Peter, 322
Fryer, Richard, 323
Leek (Staffs.):
    Clewlow, William, 178
    Ferniough, James, 297
    Furnihough, James, 326
Leicester:
    Carr, John, 146
    Caulton, Edward, 151
    Caulton, John, 151
    Caulton, Richard, 151
    Chawner, William, 160
    Clark, John, 174
    Clarke, John, 175
    Clarke, Michael, 175
    Clements, George, 178
    Clements, John jnr, 178
    Clements, John snr, 178
    Clements, Joseph, 178
    Cooke, Richard, 194
    Cooke, Robert, 194
    Cook(e), Robert & Thomas, 194
    Cooke, Thomas, 194
    Copley, Samuel, 199
    Fewkes, Joseph, 298
    Fewkes, William, 298
    Findley, William, 300
    Firmage, W., 301
    Foden, Henry, 306
    Ford, Humphrey, 309
    Fosbrook(e), John, 311
    Foulds, Francis, 312

Leicester Fields (London): Fenlyson, James, 295

Lewes (Sussex):
Carter, Henry, 147
Chassereau, —, 160
Cheale, Charles, 160
Chilton, John, 163
Curtis, James, 221
Farnes, Nicholas, 290
Fuller, Thomas, 325

Lewisham (London):
Cole, James, 187
Cotman, Robert Sargent, 200

Lichfield (Staffs.):
Chatterton, Richard, 160
Collins, William, 189

Limehouse (London): Cleugh, George, 178

Lincoln:
Carrington, Benjamin, 147
Chalk, Thomas, 153
Clapham, Edward, 172
Cooke, George, 193
Curtis, William, 221
Curtois, Charles, 221
Curtois, Mary, 221
Curtois, William, 221
Fisher, Francis, 301

Lincoln's Inn Fields (London):
Collins, Isaac, 189
Coulson, Ralph, 201
Courtnay, J., 202
Crace, John & Sons, 206
Cramp, Thomas, 207
Freelove, William, 320

Little Bolton (Lancs.):
Charnley, Richard, 160
Foster, George, 311
Fryer, Ralph, 323

Little Brickhill (Bucks.): Chapman, Thomas, 158

Little Britain (London):
Cronk, John, 211
Farley, John, 289
Flather, E., 303

Liverpool:
Cadow, Matthew, 140
Cafrani, Lewis, 140
Cain, Henry, 140
Calken, Thomas, 141
Calvert, William, 142
Campbell, Samuel, 143
Cannell, Hugh, 143
Cape, Thomas, 144
Caprani, John B., 144
Caprani, Lewis, 144
Caprani & Sanderson, 144
Capstick, Thomas, 144
Carkman, Robert, 145
Carkman, Thomas, 145
Carter, John, 148
Carter, Robert, 148
Cartwright, John, 149
Cartwright, Joseph, 149

Cary, Robert, 149
Casartelli, Lewis, 149
Cash, Charles, 149
Cashen, Charles jnr, 150
Cashen, Charles snr, 150
Cashen, Christopher, 150
Cashen, David, 150
Cashen, Edward, 150
Cashen, Ellen, 150
Cashen, Henry, 150
Cashen, James, 150
Cashen, Philip, 150
Cashen, Thomas, 150
Cashen, William jnr, 150
Cashen, William snr, 150
Castell, Peter, 150
Cataneo, Evangelista, 151
Cattaneo & Co., E., 151
Catterall, John, 151
Catterall, William, 151
Cattrall, John, 151
Cattrall, William, 151
Caunce, William, 151
Cavey, James, 152
Cawthorne, William, 152
Chadwick, Joseph, 153
Chadwick, Richard, 153
Chantrell, Jane, 157
Charles, Charles, 159
Charles, Edward, 159
Charles, George, 159
Charleton, John, 159
Charnock, John, 160
Charnock, Thomas, 160
Charter, Charles, 160
Charters, John, 160
Chatham, Charles, 160
Chatham, Thomas, 160
Chester, Robert, 161
Chesters, James, 161
Chesters, John snr and jnr, 161
Chesters, William, 161
Chesworth, George, 162
Chesworth, William, 162
Chew, John, 162
Chew, William, 162
Chrichley, Hugh, 170
Christian, John Houghton, 171
Christian, Thomas, 171
Christmas, William, 171
Chubbard, Samuel, 171
Clansey, Michael, 172
Clare, John, 172
Clarke, Daniel, 174
Clarke, John, 175
Clarke, Thomas, 175
Clarke, William, 175
Clarkson, Mary, 176
Clarkson, Thomas, 176
Clarkson, William, 176
Cleator, George, 177
Clegg, James, 177
Clementia, Samuel, 178
Clements, James, 178

Clemesha, Samuel, 178
Clough, Jemima, 180
Clugston, James, 180
Cockney, Mary, 185
Codling, George, 186
Coghlan, John, 186
Coghlan, T., 186
Collett, John, 188
Colley, John, 188
Collier, Thomas, 188
Colling, Edward, 188
Colling, William K., 188
Colling & Hargreaves, 188
Collingwood, Robert, 189
Collins, Pendlebury, 189
Connell, William, 191
Connor, Daniel, 191
Cook, Robinson, 192
Cook, Thomas, 193
Cooke, Thomas, 194
Cookson, John, 195
Coopland, Richard, 198
Cope, Thomas, 198
Copeland, Richard jnr, 198
Copeland, Richard snr, 198
Copeland, Robert, 198
Copeland, William, 198
Coppell, James, 199
Coppell, John, 199
Coppell, Richard, 199
Corcorine, Philip, 199
Corkhill, Thomas, 199
Corless, James, 199
Corless, John, 199
Corless, Joseph, 199
Corless, Roger, 199
Corlett, Edward, 200
Corlett & Owen, 200
Corley, Roger, 200
Corran, Henry, 200
Corran, John, 200
Corrin, Robert, 200
Corrin, Robert jnr, 200
Cottrell, Richard, 201
Coultart, Francis, 202
Coventry, Edward jnr, 203
Coventry, Thomas, 203
Cowley, —, 203
Cowx, John, 203
Cowx, Thomas, 203
Cox, Thomas, 205
Cox, Thomas Jupeth, 205
Creer, Gilbert B., 208
Creighton, Adam, 208
Crellin, John, 208
Critchley, Hugh, 210
Critchley, John, 210
Critchley, Thomas, 210
Croft, John, 210
Croft, Joseph, 210
Croft, Robert, 210
Croft, Simon, 211
Croft, William, 211
Crompton, John, 211

Crook, William, 212
Crosby, Robert, 212
Croskell, Thomas, 212
Cross, Adam, 213
Cross, Nicholas, 213
Cross, Simon, 214
Cross, Thomas, 214
Crouchley, Henry, 214
Crumpton, —, 216
Crye, Robert, 217
Cuddy, Joseph, 217
Culligan, Mary, 219
Cumming, John, 219
Cummings & Barrow, 219
Cummins, William, 219
Curran, Robert, 220
Currie, Samuel, 220
Curry, Joseph, 220
Curtis, Benjamin, 221
Cushen, William, 221
Cutler, Samuel, 222
Fairclough, Henry, 287
Fairclough, Robert, 287
Fairclough, William, 287
Fairhurst, Robert, 288
Falciola & Co., Benjamin, 288
Fallows, John, 288
Fallows, Joseph, 288
Farmer, Thomas, 290
Farrell, Thomas, 290
Farrimond, Thomas, 291
Farrington, William, 291
Faulkner, Hannah, 292
Fawcet, Peter, 292
Fawcett, James, 292
Fayrer, John, 293
Feen, William, 294
Fell, William, 295
Felton, Mary, 295
Felton, Patience, 295
Fennesy, Richard, 296
Ferguson, Adam James, 296
Ferguson, James Adam, 297
Ferguson, Thomas, 297
Fewller, Samuel, 298
Fisher, John, 302
Fisher, Robert, 302
Fisher, Thomas, 302
Fisher, William, 302
Fishwick, Edward, 302
Fleetwood, Richard, 159, 303
Fleming, John, 304
Flemming, Lancelot, 304
Fletcher, Ellen, 304
Fletcher, Henry, 304
Fletcher, Peter, 305
Fletcher, Samuel, 305
Fletcher & Hollingsworth, 305
Fodden, William, 306
Fogg, John, 307
Fogg, Samuel, 307
Fold, James, 307
Fold, John, 307
Folds, James jnr, 307

Folds, John, 307
Folds, John jnr, 307
Folds, William, 307
Foley, William, 307
Ford, John, 309
Forde, John, 309
Forrester, John, 310
Forsyth, Margaret, 310
Forsyth, Samuel, 310
Forsyth, William, 310
Foster, Benjamin, 311
Foster, James, 288, 311
Foster, Joseph, 311
Foster, Samuel, 311
Foster, Thomas, 312
Foster & Co., 312
Foulkes, John, 312
Fowler, Benjamin, 312
Fowler, Samuel, 313
Francis, Maria, 318
Frankland & Co., 318
Fraser, William, 319
Frazer, John, 319
Furnas, Thomas, 326
Furness, Thomas, 326
Furr, Thomas, 326
London Wall (London): Fox, Charles, 313
Long Acre (London):
Chesworth, William, 162
Clarke, Elizabeth, 174
Clarke, John, 175
Clarke, William, 175
Clater, John, 176
Cleere, George, 177
Comery, James, 191
Cramp & Tolputt, 207
Fearn, John, 293
Felliot, Nicholas, 295
Ferraby, George, 297
Fischer, William, 301
Fish, John, 301
Fox, Benjamin, 313
Fox, Hepworth & Raynes, 315
Long Ditton (Surrey): Chisholm, Charles, 169
Long Melford (Suffolk):
Chaplin, James, 157
Churchyard, John, 172
Longford Castle (Wilts.): Chipchase, Robert & Henry, 163
Longtown (Cumb.): Currie, William, 220
Loughborough (Leics.):
Clarke, Joseph, 175
Farmer, Richard, 290
Louth (Lincs.):
Copeland, James, 198
Coulam, Henry, 201
Coulam, Richard & Henry, 201
Coulam, William, 201
Coupland, James, 202
Crampton, James, 207
Fell, George, 294

Forth, William, 311
Foster, Richard, 312
Foster, Robert, 312
Foster, William, 312
Ludgate (London): Cowper, Simon, 203
Ludlow (Salop): Felton, Joseph, 295
Luton (Beds.): Foster, Thomas, 312
Lymington (Hants.):
Footner, James, 308
Footner, R., 308
Furner, William, 326
Lytham (Lancs.):
Cookson, Richard, 195
Fox, William, 314

M

Madeley (Salop): Currer, Thomas, 220
Maidenhead (Berks.): Cooper, John, 196
Maidstone (Kent):
Cadwell, William, 140
Carter, Thomas, 148
Carter & Morris, 149
Chittenden, George, 170
Collens, George, 188
Couchman, Richard, 201
Crispe, John, 210
Maldon (Essex):
Choat, George, 170
Cotte, James, 200
Cottee, William, 201
Malton (Yorks.): Flint, William, 306
Manchester:
Cadman, John, 140
Cadman, Rebecca, 140
Caminada, Francis, 142
Capprani, Antonio, 144
Carter, Thomas, 148
Cartwright, Elizabeth, 149
Cartwright, Jane, 149
Cartwright, Thomas, 149
Caunce, John, 151
Cave, Henry, 152
Cazzanigha, F. & Co., 152
Chadwick, William Henry, 153
Chantler, John, 157
Chapelow, Thomas, 157
Churchill, John, 171
Clarke, William, 175
Clegg, Andrew, 177
Cockrell, Edward, 185
Collinson, William, 190
Conlan & Nicholson, 191
Cooke, Joseph, 194
Cooke, Samuel, 194
Corbet(t), William, 199
Cotterell, Samuel & Co., 201
Cowperthwaite, William, 203
Craw, Thomas, 208
Cresswell, John, 209

Critchley, George, 210
Critchlow, Esther, 210
Critchlow, George, 210
Critchlow, Henry, 210
Critchlow, John, 210
Crompton, Ellis, 211
Crossley, John Mather, 214
Crossley, William, 214
Croxton, George, 215
Fallows, James, 288
Fallows, John, 288
Farrand, Roger, 290
Farrow, Henry, 292
Faulkner, Thomas, 292
Fawcett, John, 292
Fearnley, Matthew, 294
Fell, John, 294
Few, Edward, 298
Fildes, James, 299
Flood, Patrick, 306
Fluke, Isaac, 306
Follows, John, 308
Forrest, James, 310
Foulkes, Edward, 312
Foulkes & Darnton, 312
Fox & Grundy, 315
Franklin, Jacob A., 319
Froggart, Abraham, 322
Fullerton, William, 325
Mansfield (Notts.): Cash, William,
150
Margate (Kent):
Carraway, —, 147
Finnis, Jeremiah, 300
Market Drayton (Salop):
Clews, James, 178
Critchley, Cornelius, 210
Crutchley, Cornelius, 217
France, Stephen, 316
Market Harborough (Leics.): Cook,
Thomas, 193
Marlborough (Wilts.): Cully, David,
219
Marlow (Bucks.):
Crowder, James, 215
Fletcher, Charles, 304
Marske (Yorks.): Cole, John, 187
Marybow (London): Fairn, Robert,
288
Marylebone (London):
Catesby, Frederick, 151
Champ, George, 154
Collin, George, 188
Collins, Robert, 189
Cook, J., 192
Cooke, George, 193
Cooke, Joseph, 194
Cuffians, John, 217
Cummins, Peter, 219
Cummins, Philip, 219
Cummins, R., 219
Cushing, T. jnr, 222
Cussans, John, 222
Fisher, James, 302

Fox, William jnr, 314
Fraser, John, 319
French, C., 321
Maryport (Cumb.): Charles, Walter,
159
Masham (Yorks.):
Fisher, John, 302
Fryer, George, 323
Mayfair (London):
Clare, John, 172
Coleman, William, 187
Flock, Richard, 306
Melton Mowbray (Leics.): Callow,
Martin, 141
Middleham (Yorks.): Clarkson, John,
176
Middlesbrough (Yorks.): Chapman,
George, 158
Midhurst (Sussex): Clarke, Henry,
174
Mile End (London): Court, David
snr, 202
Milnthorpe (Westmld): Cornthwaite,
George, 200
Milton (Kent): Foster, William, 312
Milverton (Som.): Cossway, George,
200
Mitton (Lancs.):
Chippindale, Edmund, 169
Chippindale, Mark, 169
Moorfields (London):
Campbell, Robert, 143
Camper-Harris, James, 143
Carto, David, 149
Chitty, John, 170
Clark, Thomas, 174
Clarkson, William, 176
Clinch, Thomas, 179
Cloak, Jacob, 179
Cloak, Thomas, 179
Cole, Jonathan, 187
Cooke, Joshua, 194
Craggs, John, 207
Crosby, Thomas, 212
Cummings, James, 219
Flamston, Richard, 303
Flamston, Thomas, 303
Freeman, Rob, 321
Moorgate (London): Collyer, —, 190
Morpeth (Northumb.):
Charlton, John, 159
Cornfoot, John, 200
Mortlake (Surrey): Cook, John, 192

N

Nantwich (Cheshire):
Chesters, Thomas, 161
Clewes, Jacob, 178
Cliff, George, 178
Cliff, J. Needham, 178
Cliff, Joseph, 178
Cliff, Washington, 178

Cooke, Charles, 193
Cooke, Joseph, 194
Corkwell, William, 199
Farnworth, Samuell, 290
Fenna, John, 295
Fenna, Mrs Mary, 295
Freeman, Edmund, 320
Needham Market (Suffolk):
Colchester, Benjamin Russel, 186
New Woodstock (Oxon.): Churchill,
John, 171
Newark (Notts.):
Caistor, Thomas, 140
Cole, William, 187
Coleman, Francis, 187
Colton, Richard, 190
Cosins, William, 200
Crosley, James, 213
Cross, George, 213
Crow, Edward, 214
Crow, William, 215
Cruse, Catherine, 216
Cruse, William, 216
Curtis, Joseph Digby, 221
Cuthey, Samuel, 222
Newbury (Berks.):
Farmer, Richard, 290
Finch, Gray, 300
Finch, Stephen, 300
Newby (Yorks.): Coupland, Charles,
202
Newcastle:
Calbreath, Robert, 141, 160
Cannaway, Walter, 143
Carmichael, John, 145
Carnaby, John, 146
Carnaby, Ralph, 146
Carnaby, Robert, 146
Carnaby, William, 146
Carr, George C., 146
Carter, William, 148
Chapman, John, 158
Charlton, Thomas, 159
Charnley, William, 160
Chorley, John, 170
Chubb, William, 171
Churnside, Thomas, 172
Clark, George, 173
Clark, William, 174
Coates, Edward, 181
Coatsforth, John, 181
Coatsworth, Hugh, 181
Coatsworth, John, 181
Coatsworth, Robert, 181
Cook, Walter, 193
Corner, William & Son, 200
Cotesforth, Hugh, 200
Cotesforth, John, 200
Cottesforth, Robert, 200
Coulson, Thomas, 201
Cowan, David, 203
Cowen, David, 203
Craig, Andrew, 207
Craig, John, 207

Crool, David, 212
Crosby, Thomas, 212
Crow, James, 214
Currie & Gibson, 220
Curry, Joseph, 220
Curry, Robert, 221
Cuthbertson, Daniel, 222
Cuthbertson, J.W., 222
Farrier, George, 291
Farrier, Robert, 291
Farrington, Richard snr and jnr, 291
Faulkner, Charles, 292
Fearnley, John, 293
Fell, Joseph, 294
Ferguson, Robert, 297
Fife, George, 299
Fitzwalter, Thomas, 303
Foggo, William, 307
Foreman, Francis, 309
Foreman, Peter, 309
Foreman, William, 309
Forester, John Bruce, 310
Forster, Arthur, 310
Foster, John Bruce, 311
Fraser, Robert, 319
Furnass, Joseph, 326
Newcastle-under-Lyme (Staffs.):
  Cartwright, —, 149
  Cockersole, Sampson, 185
  Cooper, William, 198
  Fox, William, 315
Newent (Glos.): Farley, Richard, 289
Newington (London):
  Cooper, John, 196
  Flowers, Henry, 306
  French, Thomas, 322
Newington Butts (London): Fox, Robert, 314
Newington Causeway (London):
  Cavel, George, 152
  Clayton, William, 177
Newmarket (Suffolk):
  Chapman, Charles, 157
  Chapman, John, 158
  Frost, George, 323
Newport (Isle of Wight):
  Cheverton, John, 162
  Crook, Charles, 212
  Crook, Robert, 212
Newport Pagnell (Bucks.): Capon, William, 144
Newport (Salop):
  Cobb, Samuel jnr, 184
  Commell, George, 191
  Cooper, Thomas, 197
  Corbett, John, 199
Newton Abbot (Devon):
  Crews, C., 209
  Cruse, William, 216
North Shields (Northumb.):
  Calder, Robert, 141
  Fairweather, George, 288
  Foster, George, 311

Fowler, John, 312
North Walsham (Norfolk):
  Crawston, William, 208
Northallerton (Yorks.):
  Chapman, George, 158
  Chapman, James, 158
  Flower, Matthew, 306
Northampton:
  Campbell, George, 142
  Campion, Thomas, 143
  Clark, Josiah, 174
  Clayson, William, 177
  Coulson, Thomas, 202
  Cox, Edward, 204
  Cox, William, 205
  Cross, Charles, 213
  Fox, Benjamin, 313
  Fox, Francis, 313
  Fox, George, 313
  Fox, Thomas, 314
Northwich (Cheshire): Fowles, Jonathan, 313
Norwich:
  Camms, James, 142
  Canham, William, 143
  Cann, James, 143
  Cann, John, 143
  Canns, James, 144
  Carter, James, 148
  Castoll, John Soames, 151
  Chamberlain, Charles, 153
  Chamberlain, William, 154
  Chapman, Charles, 157
  Chapman, John, 158
  Chapman, William, 159
  Christmas, Erasmus, 171
  Church, Christopher, 171
  Church, Robert, 171
  Clapham, John, 172
  Clapham, Samuel, 172
  Clapham, William, 172
  Clarke, Francis, 174
  Clarke, Robert, 175
  Clarke, Thomas, 175
  Claxton, Thomas, 176
  Clayton, Theophilus, 177
  Clements, John, 178
  Coates, William jnr, 181
  Cock, James, 185
  Cocks, John, 186
  Coe, John, 186
  Colby, James, 186
  Coleby, James, 187
  Colombine, Paul, 190
  Cook, Gregory, 192
  Cooke, Isaac, 193
  Cooper, Thomas, 197
  Cork, Joseph, 199
  Cox, James Valentine, 204
  Cox, John, 204
  Crane, Edward, 207
  Craske, James, 208
  Crow, John, 214
  Cubit, Thomas, 217

Cubitt, Richard, 217
Culler, Thomas, 219
Culley, John, 219
Cullington, Robert, 219
Currey, William, 220
Curtis, Augustine snr and jnr, 221
Curtis, Henry, 221
Curtis & Drake, 221
Cushing, Charles, 221
Cushing, John William, 221
Cushing, Robert Harley, 221
Cushing, Samuel snr and jnr, 221
Custance, William, 222
Cutler, Thomas, 222
Fabb, Charles, 287
Faulke, James, 292
Feldgate, Andrew, 294
Fenn, Robert, 295
Fiddeman, Robert, 298
Fish, Thomas, 301
Fitter, B.P., 303
Fletcher, William, 305
Flint, Charles, 305
Flood, John jnr, 306
Flood, John snr, 306
Freeman, Edward, 320
Freeman, James, 320
Freeman, Jeremiah, 320–1
Freeman, John, 321
Freeman, William, 321
Frint, Charles, 322
Frost, James, 323
Frost, Thomas, 323
Nottingham:
  Caistor, Thomas, 140
  Caistor, William, 140
  Calar, William, 141
  Carroll, Andrew, 147
  Caulton, Edward, 151
  Chiswell, Jock, 170
  Chiswell, John, 170
  Clarke, John jnr, 175
  Clarke, Robert, 175
  Collinson, John, 190
  Collinson, William, 141
  Cooper, Henry, 196
  Cooper, John, 196, 197
  Cooper, Samuel, 197
  Cope, James, 198
  Cordon, J., 199
  Crosland, Mess(?), 213
  Cross, William, 214
  Cullen, James, 218
  Cullen, John, 218
  Cullen, Samuel, 218
  Cullen, Thomas, 218
  Falkner, William, 288
  Fancote, James, 288
  Fancourt & Pratt, 288
  Farrands, John, 290
  Fiora, J., 301
  Fisher, Hannah, 301
  Fitzwalter, Francis, 303
  Fitzwalter, Fraser, 303

Fitzwalter, Joseph, 303
Fitzwalter, T., 303
Fitzwalter, Thomas & Francis, 303
Fitzwalter, Thomas jnr, 303
Fitzwalter, Thomas snr, 303
Fitzwalters, —, 303
Flamstone, Thomas, 303
Fleuritt, Benjamin, 305
Foster, John, 311

O

Oakland (Rutland): Cave, James, 152
Old Bethlem (London): Chapman,
 Thomas, 158
Old Ford (Middlx.): Coventry, John,
 203
Old Malton Gate (Yorks.): Flewker,
 Rob., 305
Oldbury (Glos.): Chapman, —, 157
Oldham (Lancs.):
 Chapman, John, 158
 Chapman, Thomas, 158
Ormskirk (Lancs.):
 Clarkson, George, 176
 Corrington, William, 200
 Fletcher, John, 304
 Forshaw, Nathaniel, 310
Oswestry (Salop): Farmer, John, 289
Otley (Yorks.):
 Carter, Joseph, 148
 Chippendale, Benjamin, 164
 Chippendale, John, 164
 Chippindale, William, 169
 Cundall, William, 219
 Curtis, Joseph, 221
 Fieldus, Peter, 299
Oundle (Northants.): Corbett,
 William, 199
Oxford:
 Callcott, William, 141
 Chadwell, —, 153
 Chettee, William, 162
 Clackson, William, 172
 Clarke, James, 175
 Clive, Mr, 179
 Collier, Brooks, 188
 Cooke, William, 194
 Cooling, William, 195
 Cowderay, William, 203
 Cox, John, 204
 Coxeter, William, 205
 Fleshman, Henry, 304
 Folker, William, 308
 Franklin, Jeremiah, 319
 Freeman, —, 320
 Frogley, Arthur, 322

P

Paddington (London):
 Chrystall, D., 171
 Freeman, W., 321

Painswick (Glos.): Cook, Henry, 192
Penrith (Cumb.):
 Cartner, Isaac, 149
 Cockin, John, 185
 Cockin, William, 185
Pentonville (London):
 Crump, Edward, 216
 Fitt, James, 303
Penzance (Cornwall): Crocker, John,
 210
Pershore (Warks.): Clarke, Samuel,
 175
Peterborough (Northants.):
 Cole, James, 187
 Foot, John, 308
Petty France (London):
 Charles, Michael, 159
 Fipps, John, 301
Petworth (Sussex):
 Chrippis, Thomas, 170
 Coote, R., 198
Piccadilly (London):
 Carter, Mr, 147
 Cawston, James, 152
 Chevers, Philip, 162
 Chivers, Philip, 170
 Cooper, George, 195
 Crozier, John, 215
 Fifield, William, 299
 Ford, George, 309
Pickering (Yorks.): Crosier, John, 212
Pimlico (London):
 Cambridge, John, 142
 Chandler, Edward, 154
 Fleming, Matthias, 304
 Furness, Martin, 326
Plymouth (Devon):
 Came, J., 142
 Carver, Richard, 149
 Catear, Jewell, 151
 Cater, J., 151
 Chaffe, Stephen, 153
 Chambers, Henry, 154
 Chambers, Thomas, 154
 Claron, —, 176
 Clements, John, 178
 Cock, J., 185
 Cock, Wiltshire, 185
 Collings, William, 188
 Cooper, Mrs, 195
 Crew, Arthur, 209
 Culverwell, Charles, 219
 Fey, William, 298
 Fice, William, 298
 Fielding, O., 299
 Fleming, Thomas, 304
 Foy, A., 315
 Foy, Henry, 315
Plymouth Dock (Devon): Cowan,
 Alexander, 203
Pocklington (Yorks.): Collinson,
 David, 189
Pontefract (Yorks.):
 Carr, Thomas, 147

Foster, Thomas, 312
Fretwell, Allen, 322
Poole (Dorset):
 Cathery, Desbrough, 151
 Cawley, Edward & Joseph, 152
 Cawley, James, 152
 Cookman, Henry, 195
Poplar (London): Carter, John, 148
Portsmouth (Hants.):
 Castle, Thomas, 150
 Churchill, George, 171
 Closson, Joseph, 180
 Crook, James, 212
 Fairman, Francis, 288
 Fielder, Richard, 299
 Fleming, E., 304
 Fleming, William, 304
 Fletcher, William, 305
 Foster, Nicholas William, 311
 Fowler, Joseph, 313
Portsmouth Common (Hants.),
 Closson, Josiah, 180
Preston (Lancs.):
 Campbell, Edward, 142
 Carter, Andrew & John, 147
 Carter, James, 147
 Carus, Edward, 149
 Charnley, Jane, 159
 Charnley, Richard, 159
 Clarke, Joseph, 175
 Cooper, William, 198
 Corry, William, 200
 Critchley, Hugh, 210
 Croft, Joseph, 210
 Cubbin, William, 217
 Fisher, Evan, 301
 Fisher, W. & H., 302
 Forrest, William, 310
 Foster, John, 311
 Frankland, Joseph, 318
 Freckleton, Henry, 320
Princes Risborough (Bucks.): Crook,
 Joseph, 212

R

Raistrick (Yorks.): Fox, Joseph, 314
Ramsey (Hunts.):
 Colshaw, Thomas, 190
 Coulsher, Thomas, 201
Ramsgate (Kent):
 Cull, James, 218
 Cull, Robert, 218
 Cull, Thomas, 218
 Friend & Vinton, 322
Ratcliffe (London):
 Carby, William, 144
 Collier, James, 188
Reading (Berks.):
 Cole, Edward, 187
 Cooper, Thomas, 197
 Cutter, William Biggs, 223
 Ford, John, 309

Ford, Samuel, 309
Reigate (Surrey): Curtis, John, 221
Retford (Notts.): Fotheringham,
  William, 312
Richmond (Surrey):
  Cain, James, 140
  Careless, Henry, 145
  Carter, Samuel, 148
  Chiles, Edward & Gumbrett, John,
  162
  Clubb, John, 180
Richmond (Yorks.): Freetum,
  William, 321
Ringmer (Sussex): Cosham, William,
  200
Ringwood (Hants.):
  Cooper, Samuel, 197
  Cranston, George, 207
  Cranston, John, 208
  Cranston, John jnr, 207
  Cranston, John snr, 207
Ripon (Yorks.):
  Cant, William, 144
  Clark, George, 173
  Cockfield, George, 185
  Cundale, Thomas, 219
  Forth, George, 311
  Forth, George jnr, 311
  Foxton, Dixon, 315
  Foxton, James, 315
  Foxton, John Dixon, 315
Rochdale (Lancs.): Fletcher, Kay, 305
Rochester (Kent):
  Chickley, Richard, 162
  Corral, Charles Prow, 200
  Critchley, Richard, 210
  Cutbush, Edward, 222
  Franklin, Thomas, 319
Rochford (Essex): Fairchild, James,
  287
Romford (Essex):
  Clube, Ann, 180
  Club(s), John, 180
  Collier, Stephen, 188
Romsey (Hants.): Chaunder,
  Thomas, 160
Rossendale (Lancs.):
  Clare, Elizabeth, 172
  Cockrill, Mark, 185
Rotherham (Yorks.):
  Coe, David, 186
  Frame, John, 315
  France, Joseph, 316
Rotherhithe (London):
  Clover, Edward, 180
  Crane, Jeremiah, 207
  Faldo, George jnr, 288
  Fox, Henry, 313
  Franklin, J., 318
Royston (Herts.): Cakebread,
  William, 141
Rugeley (Staffs.):
  Cheshire, Thomas, 161
  Cross, T., 214

Rye (Sussex):
  Croskey, John, 212
  Crosskey, William, 214

S

Saffron Hill (London):
  Carbery, Christopher, 144
  Chapman, John, 158
Saffron Walden (Essex): Cardinal,
  Roger, 145
St Albans (Herts.):
  Cosier, Henry, 200
  Ferrari, Bernard, 297
  Fitch, James, 302
St Bride's (London):
  Clackson, William, 172
  Crump, Daniel, 216
  Field, Robert, 299
St Catherine's (London): Carbinall,
  William, 144
St Clement Danes (London):
  Collishaw, Charles, 190
St Columb (Cornwall): Cayzer,
  James, 152
St George's in the East (London):
  Carter, Samuel, 148
  Clyatt, Henry, 180
  Collins, Thomas, 189
  Cook, Jeremiah, 192
  Farmer, Henry, 289
  Field, William, 299
  Finnemore, James, 300
  Fleming, Richard, 304
  Fores, John, 310
  Furranie, Jacob, 326
St George's Fields (London): Frembly,
  John, 321
St Giles's (London):
  Field, Thomas, 299
  Cook, William, 193
St Giles in the Fields (London):
  Clements, William, 178
  Facon, William, 287
St Giles without Cripplegate
  (London):
  Combee, Peter, 191
St Helens (Lancs.):
  Callon, James, 141
  Clayton, William, 177
St Ives (Hunts.):
  Cope, Henry, 198
  Fitzjohn, Daniel, 303
  Fox, John, 314
St James's (London):
  Campfield, Richmond, 143
  Campfield, Robert, 143
St Leonards (Sussex): Carey, John,
  145
St Luke's (London):
  Clements, William, 178
  Cook, J., 192
  Fisher, King, 302

St Martin-in-the-Fields (London):
  Cerne, John, 152
  Child, Michael, 162
  Clare, Francis, 172
  Fallet(t), Nicholas, 288
  Fox, Francis, 313
  Fox, William, 314
  Fulwood, Charles, 325
St Michael le Quern (London): Clark,
  James, 173
St Neots (Hunts.):
  Franklin, James, 319
  French, Flanders, 321
Salford (Lancs.):
  Coates, George, 181
  Collier, Joseph, 188
  Constantine, William, 192
  Consterdine, William, 192
  Crompton, Robert, 211
  Fensom, George, 296
Salisbury (Wilts.):
  Callowey, R., 142
  Chater, Thomas, 160
  Chinn, Frederick, 163
  Cookman, Giles, 195
  Costar, Henry, 200
  Crouch, George, 214
Salterton (Devon): Cowd, Joseph, 203
Saltram (Devon): Campbell, Robert,
  143
Sandbach (Cheshire): Colclough,
  James, 186
Sandon Hall (Staffs.): Cable, —, 140
Sandwich (Kent):
  Crosoer, Francis, 213
  Famariss, Frederick, 288
  Famariss, Robert, 288
  Franks, —, 319
Sarnesfield Court (Herefs.):
  Calldicolt, 141
Sawbridgeworth (Herts.): Fairway,
  Charles, 288
Scarborough (Yorks.): Ford, William,
  309
Sedgley (Staffs.): Fereday, Thomas
  jnr, 296
Selby (Yorks.):
  Cromack, John, 211
  Cryer, John, 217
Seven Dials (London):
  Canning, Joseph, 143
  Conway, Charles, 192
  Coward, John, 203
  Cressy, George, 209
  Cressy, Sarah, 209
  Crump, Ely, 216
  Flinn, Henry, 305
  Foxhall, Mar., 315
Sevenoaks (Kent): Cooper, J., 196
Shaftesbury (Dorset): Child, I., 162
Shap (Westmld): Castley, William,
  151
Sheerness (Kent): Carter, Thomas,
  148

Sheffield (Yorks.):
Champion, John, 154
Clark, William, 174
Cluley, —, 180
Cocking, Robert, 185
Cocking, William, 185
Cocking, William & Robert, 185
Coldwell, Benjamin, 186
Cooper, Henry, 196
Cooper, Stephen, 197
Cowen, Thomas, 203
Cowparthwaite, William, 203
Crawshaw, Charles, 208
Croft, James, 210
Croft, Joseph, 210
Cropland, Richard, 212
Crosland, Richard, 213
Crossland, Richard, 214
Cuckson, Francis, 217
Fairest, Jeremiah, 288
Fairest, Joseph, 288
Fairest, Mary, 288
Farrist, Jeremiah, 292
Fletcher, John, 304
Foote, Samuel, 308
Forster, George & Thomas, 310
Fowler, Samuel, 313
Fowler, William, 313
Fox, James & Charles, 313
Fox, Joshua, 314
Fox, William, 314
Sherborne (Dorset): Cox, Thomas, 205
Shifnal (Salop): Fenn, William, 295
Shoreditch (London):
Carter, William, 148
Clark, James & Thomas, Philip, 174
Clark, Thomas, 174
Clemmans, James & Son, 178
Comte, Henry, 191
Copini, Gatini, 198
Cotterell, Richard, 201
Farrer, John, 291
Fassett, —, 292
Fisher, John, 302
Frankland, Henry, 318
Franklin, James, 319
French, John, 321
Shoreham (Sussex): Chandler, John, 154
Shrewsbury (Salop):
Careswell, John, 145
Cawthorne, William, 152
Cheshire, John, 161
Cocks, John, 186
Cooper, James, 196
Cooper & Son, 198
Cowthron, William, 203
Cross, James, 213
Fogden, John, 306
France, Richard, 316
France, Richard jnr, 316
Sible Hedingham (Essex): Firman, Robert, 301

Sidmouth (Devon):
Churchill, John, 171
Farrant, Richard, 290
Sittingbourne (Kent): Catchpool, John, 151
Skipton (Yorks.): Coates, John, 181
Sleaford (Lincs.):
Clipsham, John, 179
Cook, Jos, 192
Cropper, James, 212
Smarden (Kent): Fleet, Richard, 303
Smithfield (London):
Carberry, Christopher & Cubett, Benjamin, 144
Cook, Edward, 192
Crow, Augustin, 214
Ferguson, Barnaby, 296
Fiske, Robert, 302
Flather, James, 303
Fletcher, James, 304
Flintoff, William, 306
Float, Thomas, 306
Snettisham (Norfolk): Chapman, George, 158
Snow Hill (London): Cooper, Joseph, 197
Snowfields (London): Cumine, Francis, 219
Snowhill (London): Fallshaw, John F., 288
Soho (London):
Cairncross, William, 140
Chalmers, Charles, 153
Champion, John, 154
Chapman, Thomas, 158
Cheater, Sara, 160
Cheater, William, 160
Chissholm, John, 170
Chowne, John, 170
Clark, Robert, 174
Cleets, J., 177
Cluit, William, 180
Cobley, J., 185
Cock, William, 185
Collinson, George, 189
Collison, George, 190
Cook, Harriet, 192
Cook, Henry, 192
Cook, William, 193
Cooke, Edward, 193
Cooper, George, 196
Corney, William & Hodson, Richard, 200
Cragg, James, 207
Craigall, Francis, 207
Crichton, David, 209
Crichton, William, 209
Criswick, J. jnr, 210
Crompton, John, 211
Crystall, Alexander, 217
Cullen, James, 218
Currie, Archibald, 220
Curtis, James, 221
Farrer, John, 291

Farr(i)er, John, 290
Faulkener, James, 292
Fawley & Ward, 293
Fenny, John, 296
Ficke, Peter, 298
Field, Thomas, 299
Fielder, Thomas, 299
Fisher, T., 302
Fitch, J., 302
Flashman, Joseph, 303
Fletcher, —, 304
Flint, Henry, 305
Flintof(f)t, James, 306
Flintoft, John, 306
Foord, George, 308
Foster, Francis, 311
France, Robert, 316
Fredric, George, 320
Somerstown (London):
Fowler, Giles, 312
Fowler, James, 312
South Molton (Devon): Fouracres, John, 312
South Shields (Co. Durham): Frizell, George, 322
Southampton (Hants.):
Callen, Charles Coombes, 141
Callen, John, 141
Carp, Plenty, 146
Carpenter, William, 146
Carr, Andrew Henry, 146
Carr, George, 146
Chambers, Samuel, 153
Chaplin, William, 157
Chapman, James, 158
Clark, James, 173
Clawson, Joshua, 176
Coates, Daniel, 181
Coles, Robert, 188
Colson, William, 190
Coombes, Stephen, 195
Cornish, Charles, 200
Cornish, Samuel, 200
Cornish & Monday, 200
Finlayson, John, 300
Foster, Nicholas William, 311
Foster, William, 312
Franklin, Thomas, 319
Southwark (London):
Calow, John, 142
Cark, John, 145
Carle, Charles, 145
Chaddock, Charles, 153
Chantler, Joseph, 157
Chapman, William, 159
Charnley, Alexander, 159
Clapham, George, 172
Clark, John, 173
Clarke, W.D., 175
Cockerell, G.W., 185
Cockerell & Clarke, 185
Coe, Charles, 186
Collins, —, 189
Collins, T., 189

Cook, Jeremiah, 192
Cook, John, 192
Cooknall, John, 195
Cooper, John, 197
Copley, William, 199
Corbett, Alexander, 199
Cotton, William, 201
Coventry, John, 203
Crabb, B., 206
Crabb, T.R., 206
Crabb, Thomas, 206
Culverwell, Robert, 219
Fagin, Robert, 287
Falck, Joakim, 288
Farrance, Thomas, 290
Farrand, Matthew, 290
Fentham, William, 296
Fernyhough, James, 297
Finnis & Co., 300
Fisher, Joseph, 302
Fores, Thomas, 310
Foster, James, 311
Fox, John, 314
Freeman, James, 320
Freeman, Jonah, 321
Spalding (Lincs.): Chapman, J., 158
Spilsby (Lincs.):
Clipsham, William, 179
Coupland, William, 202
Flint, Charles, 305
Spitalfields (London):
Carter, Edward, 147
Clare, James, 172
Clark, Thomas, 174
Clements, Robert, 178
Conigrave, James, 191
Crafter, Richard, 207
Crispin, William, 210
Crookbain, Henry, 212
Felton, Michael, 295
Fowler, Benjamin, 312
Frankland, Joseph, 318
Spofforth (Yorks.): Crosby, John, 212
Stafford:
Carter, Thomas, 148
Chapman, John, 158
Collier, Francis, 188
Crutchley, Henry, 217
Follows, Thomas, 308
Staines (Middlx): Clarke, Elizabeth, 174
Staithes (Yorks.): Chapman, John, 158
Stamford (Lincs.):
Clapton, William, 172
Cook, John, 192
Cordell, Thomas, 199
Crofts, William, 211
Fairchild, Charles, 287
Fairchild, John, 287
Fearson, Elizabeth, 294
Fipping, Benjamin, 301
Stannington (Yorks.): Fairest, Joseph, 288

Stapleton (Glos.):
Cater, Andrew, 151
Cater, John Wyatt, 151
Stockport (Cheshire): Fidler, Richard, 298
Stockton-on-Tees (Co. Durham):
Charlton, John, 159
Clark, W., 174
Conn, P., 191
Cooper, Richard, 197
Corner, William, 200
Forster, W., 310
Stoke (Staffs.): Ferryhouse, William, 298
Stokesley (Yorks.): Coates, John, 181
Stoneleigh Abbey (Warks.): Frost, Daniel, 323
Strand (London):
Claus, William, 176
Clearson, James, 177
Clearson, Samuel, 177
Cobb, Thomas, 184
Collins & Clearson, 189
Coombes, J.J., 195
Cording, J. & W., 199
Cordy, William, 199
Cramp, James, 207
Crompton, Thomas, 211
Cust, George & Cox, John, 222
Farlam, Jonathan, 289
Farquharson, James, 290
Farquharson, William, 290
Fauset, Nathaniel, 292
Fentham, Thomas, 296
Field, H.W., 298
Fletcher, Jeremiah, 304
Flight, B., 305
Flight, Benjamin & William, 305
Flight & Kelly, 305
Fortune, Timothy, 311
Froom, William, 322
Furness, Martin, 326
Stratford (London):
Cox, John, 204
Cunningham, Vincent, 219
Stratford-upon-Avon (Warks.):
Cooper, George, 195
Frangton, George, 318
Freeman, Thomas, 321
Stratton (Cornwall): Fish, Joseph, 301
Stratton St Mary (Norfolk): Field, Robert, 299
Stroud (Glos.): Franklin, William, 319
Sunderland (Co. Durham):
Carr, Thomas, 146
Chater, William, 160
Crawford, John, 208
Crow, Robert, 215
Fenwick & Pringle, 296
Ferrimond, Joseph, 298
Foreman, Henry, 309
Friend, Thomas, 322
Sustead (Norfolk): Cozens, James, 206

Sutton Coldfield (Warks.): Carr, 146
Swaffham (Norfolk):
Coates & Girdley, 181
Coward, Michael Godman, 203
Fuller, John, 325
Swalwell (Co. Durham): Forster, John, 310

T

Tamworth (Staffs.):
Cotton, Samuel, 201
Freer, John, 321
Taunton (Som.):
Channon, Thomas, 157
Cocking, Joseph, 185
Fickus, Thomas, 298
Teignmouth (Devon):
Carder, Thomas, 144
Coleridge, James, 188
Temple Bar (London): Claney, Daniel, 172
Tendring (Essex): Finer, William, 300
Tenterden (Kent):
Collins, William, 189
Fleet, Jos., 303
Tetbury (Glos.):
Cox, James, 204
Crew, Milburn, 209
Fowles, Charles, 313
Fowles, Samuel, 313
Fowles, Thomas, 313
Tewkesbury (Glos.):
Chapman, Francis, 157
Chapman, John, 158
Compton, Richard, 191
Cull, James, 218
Freer, John, 321
Thaxted (Essex):
Cocke, George, 185
Cole, William, 187
Cooke, George, 193
Thetford (Norfolk): Faux, Grey F., 292
Thirsk (Yorks.): Coulson, Joseph, 201
Thorne (Yorks.):
Crosland, Andrew, 213
Crowcroft, John, 215
Firth, John, 301
Thorpe Arch (Yorks.): Chippendale, A., 164
Thrapston (Northants.): Charles, Edward, 159
Tichfield (Hants.): Cushen, Edward, 221
Tickhill (Yorks.): Faris, Joseph, 289
Tilehurst (Berks.): Farley, James, 289
Tipton (Staffs.): Cox, Thomas, 205
Tiverton (Devon):
Chaplin, John, 157
Fowler, George, 312
Fowler, Thomas, 313

Todmorden (Yorks.):
Constantine, Benjamin, 192
Firth, John, 301
Tonbridge (Kent):
Corke, William, 199
Cox, Zachariah, 205
Finch, Stephen, 300
Totnes (Devon):
Croydon, Elizabeth, 215
Croydon, William N., 215
Tottenham (London):
Christie, J., 171
Farrand, Matthew, 290
Tower Hill (London): Cooke,
Thomas, 194
Truro (Cornwall):
Carkeet, Nathaniel, 145
Clemence, Thomas, 178
Clyma, Catherine, 180
Francis, Jacob, 317
Tunbridge Wells (Kent):
Clinch, John, 179
Fenner, William, 295
Foley, William, 307
Friend, James, 322
Fry, John, 323
Fry, Mary, 323
Twyford (Berks.): Colbourne, James,
186

U

Ulverston (Lancs.):
Case, Matthew, 149
Fell, James, 294
Fell, Jane, 294
Fell, Thomas, 295
Fell, William, 295
Upper Slaughter (Glos.): Collett,
Samuel, 188
Uppingham (Rutland):
Cant, James, 144
Cant, Robert James, 144
Upton-on-Severn (Worcs.): Farmer,
William, 290
Uttoxeter (Staffs.):
Calvert, Rupert, 142
Charles, William, 159
Chatfield, Thomas, 160
Chatfield, Thomas & Joseph, 160
Cross, Ralph, 213
Uxbridge (Middlx.): Fassnidge,
James, 292

W

Wakefield (Yorks.):
Camplin, William, 143
Collet, R., 188
Fawcett & Walker, 293
Walcot (Som.):
Cheppett, Elias, 161
Colborne, Benjamin, 186

Walham Green (London): Foulger,
Lock, 312
Walket (Glos.): Cook, Isaac, 192
Wallingford (Oxon.): Field, John, 299
Walsall (Staffs.): Crump, Richard, 216
Walworth (London):
Carly, Cornelius, 145
Clowes, Joseph, 180
Francis, Stephen, 318
Wandsworth (London): Choles,
Joseph, 170
Wapping (London):
Carrivon, Mr, 147
Cotter, William, 201
Fairfax, Benjamin, 288
Flower, James, 306
Wareham (Dorset):
Card, C.H., 144
Card, Edward, 144
Warminster (Wilts.):
Churchill, John, 172
Cox, William, 205
Cutler, William, 222
Warrington (Lancs.):
Copple, Richard, 199
Cunningham, John & James, 219
Fairhurst, Elizabeth, 288
Fairhurst, John, 288
Warwick:
Cookes, William, 195
Fairfax, William, 288
Watford (Herts.): Cape(l), James, 144
Watlington (Oxon.): Coles, William,
188
Weaverham (Cheshire): French, J., 321
Wednesfield (Staffs.): Foster, John,
311
Wellington (Som.):
Conway, Phillip, 192
Cossway, Philip, 200
Wells (Norfolk): Fox, Samuel, 314
Wells (Som.):
Chippett, John, 169
Curtis, Cornelius, 221
Wem (Salop):
Foulkes, Richard, 312
Francis, Thomas, 318
Wendover (Bucks.):
Cole(s), James, 187
Coxford, William, 206
Weobley (Herefs.): Carver, Thomas,
149
West Ardsley (Yorks.):
Fozzard, Jonathan, 315
Fozzard, William, 315
West Bromwich (Staffs.):
Fisher, Benjamin, 301
Flint, Edmund, 305
West Hampton: Coleburn, Isaac, 187
West Wycombe (Bucks.):
Collins, Samuel, 189
Fryer, Jonathan, 323
Westminster (London):
Camory, James, 142

Campfield, Richard, 143
Carpenter, Andrew, 146
Carter, George, 147
Carter, John, 148
Case, Peregrine, 149
Chandler, John, 154
Chappell, Thomas, 159
Charley, Josiah, 159
Charnock, Robert, 160
Cheere, Sir Henry, 160
Clarke, Joseph, 175
Claxton, William, 176
Clayton, Theophilus, 177
Clementson, Thomas, 178
Clow, Alexander, 180
Cole, John, 187
Collins, George, 189
Collins, Samuel, 189
Cooknall, John, 195
Cooper, Thomas, 197
Cope, Joseph, 198
Corden, John, 199
Cotton, Joseph, 201
Coultart, Richard, 202
Courrant, Peter, 202
Couzins, George, 203
Cox, Edward, 204
Crake, John, 207
Crawford, George, 208
Crawford, James, 208
Creyghton, Matthew, 209
Crump, James, 216
Cummins, Andrew, 219
Cure, George, 219
Farmb(o)rough, William, 289
Farnham, Owen, 289
Feild, Abraham, 294
Field, Charles, 298
Finch, John, 300
Firth, Gabriel, 301
Fitchet(t), William, 303
Flintham, Robert, 306
Folker, S.S., 308
Franklin, John, 319
Frith, Gabriel, 322
Fusedale, John, 326
Wetherby (Yorks.): Forrest, Jeremiah,
310
Weymouth (Dorset):
Chalker, George, 153
Clark, Morris, 174
Clark, Richard, 174
Commins, Richard, 191
Corp, William, 200
Fooks, Charles B., 308
Whickham (Co. Durham): Collins,
George, 189
Whitby (Yorks.):
Cavallier, William, 152
Cowley, J., 203
Cudbart, John, 217
Frankland, William, 318
Whitchurch (Salop):
Churton, William, 172

Foulkes, Richard, 312
Whitechapel (London):
    Case, Richard, 149
    Cassell, J.H., 150
    Chaffin, Charles, 153
    Chiffen, William, 162
    Cohen, Jacob, 186
    Collinson, Enoch, 189
    Compte, Henry, 191
    Cotterell, Richard, 201
    Fane, William, 289
    Fiddeman, James, 298
    Forster, John, 310
    Fowler, —, 312
Whitefriars (London): Cookman, —, 195
Whitehaven (Cumb.):
    Clemenson, Joseph, 178
    Connell, James, 191
    Copeland, Joseph, 198
    Cragg & Maxwell, 207
    Crawford, George, 208
    Crossthwaite, Jonathan, 214
    Fearon, John, 294
    Fearson, John, 294
    Fisher, Henry, 301
    Fisher, John, 302
    Fleck, Henry, 303
Wigan (Lancs.): Chadwick, Joseph, 153
Wigton (Cumb.): Casson, John, 150
Willenhall (Staffs.):
    Clark, Phineas, 174
    Foster, John, 311
Wimborne (Dorset): Flook, John, 306
Winchester (Hants.):
    Cales, Charles, 141
    Coles, Charles, 188
    Crabb, John, 206
    Fowler, Joseph, 313
Windsor (Berks.):
    Campbell, Robert, 143
    Colter, Thomas, 190
    Fuller, John, 325
Winterton (Lincs.): Fowler, William, 313
Wisbech (Cambs.):
    Cave, George, 152
    Clarke, Massey, 175
    Claxton, Samuel, 176
    Curtis, John, 221
    Curtis, Thomas, 221
    Flanner, James, 303
Witham (Essex):
    Coote, John, 198
    Cott(e), Benjamin, 200
    Cott(e), John & Co., 200
    Cottee, Joseph, 201
    Cracknell, George, 206
Wiveliscombe (Som.):
    Chadwell, Robert, 153
    Frost, Sam., 323
Wokingham (Berks.):
    Chambers, Richard, 154
    Collins, Francis, 189

Wolverhampton (Staffs.):
    Checketts, John, 160
    Child(e) & Walker, 162
    Clarke, Thomas, 175
    Cooper, Francis, 195
    Critchley, John, 210
    Crockett, William, 210
    Crutchley, John, 217
    Crutchley, Sarah, 217
    Fieldhouse, Richard, 299
Woodbridge (Suffolk):
    Chaplain, Robert, 157
    Cross, Edmund, 213
    Fisher, John, 302
    Fisher, William, 302
    Fisk, Samuel, 302
    Flaxman, William, 303
Woolwich (London):
    Carter, John, 148
    Furlong, John, 326
Worcester:
    Calder, John, 141
    Cave, William, 152
    Chandler, George Loudon, 154
    Cole, William, 187
    Collins, Finch, 216
    Cook, Vincent, 193
    Cooke, Samuel, 194
    Corbett, Edward, 199
    Cottrell, Richard, 201
    Cowell, Daniel, 203
    Cowell, William, 203
    Cox, Thomas, 205
    Crump, Charles Collins, 216
    Crump, Ely, 216
    Crump, James, 216
    Crump, John jnr, 216
    Crump, John snr, 216
    Crump, John III, 216
    Crump, Richard, 216
    Crump, Robert, 216
    Crump, William, 216
    Crump & Timmings, 216
    Curtis, William, 221
    Fides, Benjamin, 298
    Field, Nicholas, 299
    Fildes, Benjamin, 299
    Fincher, William, 300
    Fluke, Abraham, 306
    Fluke, Isaac, 306
    Freame, —, 319
    Freame, Charles, 319
    Freame, T., 319
Workington (Cumb.):
    Carter, Joseph, 148
    Christian, John, 171
    Crakeplace, Henry, 207
    Farlam, Isaac, 289
    Farlam, Joseph, 289
    Fisher, Jacob, 301
    Fisher, John, 302
Wrotham (Kent): Clements, George, 178
Wye (Kent): Fuss, George, 326

Wymondham (Norfolk):
    Canham, Peter, 143
    Chaplin, William, 157
    Coleman, James, 187
    Foulsham, William, 312

Y

Yeovil (Som.):
    Cole, W., 187
    Coles, Francis, 188
    Cornish, Thomas, 200
    Critchell, John, 210
York:
    Calvert, Thomas, 142
    Carlton, John, 145
    Carlton, Sarah & Co., 145
    Carpenter, John, 146
    Carter, Richard, 148
    Catton, William, 292
    Charlton, Sarah & Co., 159
    Clapham, Charles, 172
    Clarke, Joab, 175
    Cluderay, John, 180
    Coates, William, 181
    Cobb, William, 185
    Cockin, —, 185
    Colbeck, John, 186
    Colbeck, William, 186
    Consilt, John, 191
    Copeland, Charles, 198
    Coward, Henry, 203
    Craggs, Thomas, 207
    Cross, William, 291
    Cundall, William, 219
    Fairbank, John, 287
    Fairfoot, William, 288
    Faner, Robert, 289
    Farnsworth, Maurice, 290
    Farrer, Richard, 291
    Farrow, Richard, 292
    Fawbert, William, 292
    Fawdington, William, 293
    Fearby, Charles, 293
    Fearby, Thomas, 293
    Fearnley, Charles Bewstead, 293
    Fearn(s)ley, Thomas, 294
    Fenteman, Michael, 296
    Ferrand, Thomas, 297
    Field, Henry, 299
    Firbank, Christopher, 301
    Firbank, John, 301
    Firth, James, 301
    Fisher, Thomas, 302
    Fisher, William, 302
    Flemming, James, 304
    Forster, Thomas, 310
    Fountain, Nathaniel, 312
    Fowler, John, 312
    Foy, Henry, 315
    Freer, Matthias, 321
    Fryer, Michael, 323
    Fryer, Ralph Page, 323
    Fryer, Robert, 323